# The Parish of St. Paul's

## A VIEW FROM THE BACK PEW

*Harry B Barrett*

*by*
*Harry B. Barrett*

© 2006 by Patterson's Creek Press
Harry B. Barrett, Box 29, Port Dover, Ontario N0A 1N0.

ALL RIGHTS RESERVED

No part of this publication may be reproduced, stored in a retreival system or transmitted in any form or by any means - electronic, mechanical, photocopying, recording or otherwise - without prior written permisssion of Patterson's Creek Press.

Library and Archives Canada Cataloguing in Publication

Barrett, Harry B., 1922-
    The parish of St. Paul's : a view from the back pew / Harry B. Barrett.

ISBN 0-9686080-3-5

    1. St. Paul's Anglican Church (Port Dover, Ont.)--History. I. Title.

BX5617.P57S25 2006    283'.71336    C2006-902040-X

PRINTED IN CANADA

AYLMER EXPRESS LTD.
Fine Print Division

# TABLE OF CONTENTS

Preface ............................................... vii

Foreword ............................................... x

Acknowledgements ..................................... xii

CHAPTER ONE
    Beginnings of the Church of England in Canada ......... 1
CHAPTER TWO
    The Church and Settlement in the Long Point Country ...20
CHAPTER THREE
    Other Early Denominations ..................... 36
CHAPTER FOUR
    St. John's Anglican Church, Woodhouse ............. 46
CHAPTER FIVE
    St. Paul's Church, Port Dover ................... 93
CHAPTER SIX
    Early Pew Renters and Incumbents ............... 114
CHAPTER SEVEN
    Rev. M. S. Baldwin comes to St. Paul's ............ 155
CHAPTER EIGHT
    The Reverend Dr. William Tibbetts [1867-1875] ...... 165
CHAPTER NINE
    The Church of England & Free Masonry ........... 174
CHAPTER TEN
    St. Paul's Church – 1875-1900 .................. 204
CHAPTER ELEVEN
    Reverend M.M. Goldberg's Term ................ 238
CHAPTER TWELVE
    St. Paul's Church – 1900-1911 .................. 254
CHAPTER THIRTEEN
    Incumbency of H.J. Johnson ................... 271
CHAPTER FOURTEEN
    The Early Years of Canon Cornish ............... 324
CHAPTER FIFTEEN
    Canon Cornish - The War and Beyond ............ 408
CHAPTER SIXTEEN
    Reverend Herbert James Ernest Webb – 1952-1960 ....439
CHAPTER SEVENTEEN
    Reverend Alan Gardiner's Incumbency – 1960-1965 ....444

CHAPTER EIGHTEEN
   Reverend Donald Gray – 1965-1968 . . . . . . . . . . . . . . .453
CHAPTER NINETEEN
   Reverend Douglas Steele Henry – 1968-1983 . . . . . . . . .465
CHAPTER TWENTY
   Reverend Canon Keith Brett – 1984-1995 . . . . . . . . . . .485
CHAPTER TWENTY-ONE
   Reverend Robert Doerr – 1996-2003 . . . . . . . . . . . . . .494

# APPENDIX

1. St. Paul's Memorials
2. Highlights - St. Paul's Church Registers.
    July 21st, 1889 to Dec. 30th, 1911
    Jan. 1st, 1912 to July 6th, 1924
    July 7th, 1924 to Dec. 30th, 1937
    Jan 1st, 1938 to July 17th, 1949
    July 18th, 1949 to Dec. 30th, 1957
    Jan 1st, 1958 to Mar 20th, 1966
    Mar 21st, 1966 to Feb 22nd, 1975
    Mar 1st, 1975 to Dec 20th, 2004
3. Wardens - 1856 to 2005
4. Miscellaneous Reports, Bills & Accounts -1863 to 1901
5. Warden's 1863 Report
6. Membership of St. Paul's - 1878.
7. History of the Women's Auxiliary - Hilda Butler.
8. Quilt names - 1914 quilt.
9. Membership of St. Paul's - 1922
10. An Agreement to Pay
11. A. Y. P. A. membership in 1930's
12. Membership of St. Paul's in 1976.
13. St. Paul's Club Presidents & Chancel Guild Presidents
14. Quilt Names - 2002 quilt

## DEDICATION

To the memory of all those parishioners of St. Paul's Church,
Port Dover who have worshipped here these many years.
To Norah Marjorie Barrett, Sister Nonah,
of the Sisters of St. John the Devine.
And more particularly to my Grandfathers & Namesakes,
W. H. "Harry" Barrett and Harry Hawkins Clarke.

*All we can do is nothing worth,*
*unless God blesses the deed.*
*Vainly we hope for the harvest-tide,*
*till God gives life to the seed.*

A. C. Ainger, 1894.
Hymn 271.

# PREFACE

Since 1950 when Canon Cornish began discussions with my parents, and others, about the one hundredth anniversary of the laying of the cornerstone of St. Paul's Church, Port Dover, I have been interested in my church's history. Our family have had close ties to the church from the time it was built, up to the present. Later, acting as "the gopher" between my mother and the good Canon, as they exchanged letters, documents and general information, my interest intensified.

When Canon Cornish published "The First One Hundred Years" and challenged others to dig deeper into the history of the parish, with the admonition that "an enlarged edition may be printed, richer by far than the present. May we waken memories worth recording!" I began a file on church happenings.

On returning from a winter in Florida in March of the year 2000 I was mildly surprised to be accosted by Hilda Butler at the door of the church with "Well! How are you coming along with our history?"

"What history, Hilda?" was my reply.

"The history of St. Paul's," she retorted, "Hasn't Joy Field spoken to you about that?"

Joy, as the official Church Historian, later confirmed that she would like me to update Canon Cornish's research for the past 50 years, for our 150th Anniversary, ideally in June, 2002.

I set to work.

On my return from Florida the following spring I was relieved to read in the Church Bulletin that Mrs. Burbidge was writing the church history at the request of the Select Vestry. I was off the hook! Rob Doerr seemed very relieved at my reaction, too, for I had been requesting Registers, documents and other church records which often proved difficult, or even impossible, to unearth.

I had never thought of making any charges for my efforts, nor had I talked to the Wardens or any members of the Board of Management regarding the project. It became obvious that my involvement had been brought before the Board, however, when Rob rather hesitantly gave me a letter addressed to Mrs. Joy Field, with a copy to me. It too, has become a part of our history and is therefore included here:

---

**ST. PAUL'S ANGLICAN PARISH,**
BOX 33, PORT DOVER, ONTARIO,
N0A 1N0

January 22nd, 2001

Mrs. Joy Field,
30 Sunninghill Dr.,
Port Dover, Ontario.
N0A 1N6

Dear Joy,
    In your recent conversation with Archie Morris you commented that you had Harry B. Barrett working on the church history for our 150th anniversary.
    Since the only person that has been authorized by the Board of Management to produce such as history is Kay Burbidge, we felt we should write to you to point out three important matters for you to bear in mind:

1. No expenses incurred in the research, compilation, publication or promotion of any history of the parish, by you or any other party, will be paid by this parish unless permission is granted, in advance of any such expenses being incurred, by the Board of Management of this parish.

2. This parish will not recognize, or be bound by, any agreement or contract entered into, by you or any other party, concerning the research, compilation, publication or promotion of any history of the parish, unless permission is granted by the Board of Management of the details of any such agreement or contract in advance of its being entered into.

3. The parish's name or picture may not be used to promote or raise funds for any history of the parish unless permission is granted by the Board of Management, in advance of any such promotional or fund-raising activity.

Trusting this makes clear our position on this matter,
The Wardens of St. Paul's Anglican Parish.

Sylvia Bruley    Archie Morris    Herb Rogers    Jim Lomas

copies to: Harry B. Barrett & Rev. R. Doerr

---

    Joy was very upset by this, which I perceived as an unfortunate breakdown in communication between the Church Board and their very competent and diligent Historian. Joy had assembled, in the meantime, an awesome collection of papers, documents, minute books and photos relating to St. Paul's in a file cabinet, acquired and set aside specifically, for that very purpose.
    Our 150th Anniversary of the laying of the cornerstone was celebrated appropriately. A highlight was the delightful and very professional, illustrated History of St. Paul's by Katherine E. Burbidge. This was made available to all. The Parish could now

relax, and rest on its laurels for another fifty years.

In May of 2003 I suffered my third heart attack in a year and a half. I was told to go home and in effect "do nothing." This is the sort of direction we all wish for, at one time or another, in our lives. When I attempted to put it into effect, however, there were almost instant drawbacks. I was driving my family over the edge, and I was bored. I was eventually allowed to put in some time at my computer [for me, just a typewriter, that does not require white-out] and so the admonition of Canon Cornish came to the fore again in my mind.

I already had a good start and a wealth of family letters, diaries and memorabilia relating to St. Paul's. More importantly, to me, much of that material gave an insight into how many of the members of the parish went about their daily business and, through them, gave a unique view of the life of the whole community of Port Dover - Woodhouse. This was the Parish of St. Paul's. Now over two years later we will soon celebrate one hundred and fifty years since the first service was held in St. Paul's church. My life and memory, though faulty, extends well over half of that period of time.

The "icing on the cake" as we say, came when my long-time friend, the Right Reverend Clarence Mitchell, who I and the whole parish lean on in times of stress, as simply Clarence, agreed to give credibility and worth to my effort by penning the Foreword which follows.

My mother's admonition to all comers, to "Sit Down! You'll live longer" came to mind. I have taken her advise and now present the results. My aim is to present a complimentary copy to each family registered as members of the congregation of St. Paul's Church at no cost to them or to the Wardens. I hope that errors, though entirely my responsibility, are few. Your enjoyment of the end result will be ample reward to me for what has grown into a "labour of love". May my wandering diatribe open a deluge of further memories worth recording and may someone see merit in recognising and recording them, before they are lost to us for all time.

Harry B. Barrett.<br>October 25, 2005

# FOREWORD

In 2002, St. Paul's Anglican Church in Port Dover, Ontario, observed the 150th Anniversary of the parish establishment. Subsequently, Harry B. Barrett, a local resident of Port Dover and member of St. Paul's, was persuaded to put pen to paper, (or, fingers to the keyboard of a word processor), and produce a parish history. Since Harry B. is a well known local author, this task was easily undertaken.

For my part, I have been honoured by Harry B. in asking me to write a foreword to this history. St. Paul's Church has been very important in my life beginning in my teen-age years. It was really my introduction to Church. Together with Canon David J. Cornish, the rector of St. Paul's at that time, ( circa 1940 ), and my becoming a member of the Choir, my early spirituality was beginning to form. That formation is still going on, sixty-five years later.

There are more important reasons for recommending/commending this story of St. Paul's. Churches and some towns belong together. It seems to me they are reflected in the lives of one another. That is not at all strange but natural. The values reflected in the members of a church are those in a general way, that are the values of the town. Both are, at least in small town Southern Ontario, beneficiaries of the Judeo-Christian tradition. This may change in the future as we become more and more a part of the "Global Village". For the moment, the above is true.

By reading the story of St. Paul's and by noting those persons who were active in the story, one can gain an insight into both church and community.

The author in this instance, has given facts as expressed in both persons and events. He has also in numerous cases, enhanced his story with anecdotal material. I find this method very appealing, and I trust you will also. I am reminded of one particular History Professor in college days who did the same thing in his lectures. I enjoyed the method then, and still do today.

Another feature that I found both impressive and helpful is the Author's attention to the story of the Anglican Church beyond Port Dover. The narrative traces the story from Anglicanism's earliest days in Canada. We are given (without a lot of detail which is not required in this case), the necessary information to get us from the Dioceses of Nova Scotia through Quebec, Montreal, Toronto and Huron which is our present Diocese. Similarly, we are given some data about our "Mother Church" of St. John's, Woodhouse from whence we were born. Brief mention is made of the other Anglican neighbours comprising the Deanery of Norfolk.

Finally, keep in mind that although much of the story is told under the tenures of the various Ministries, the important persons of this or any other Church history, are the men and women and families who are the Church! Without them there is no history of St. Paul's.

Thank you St. Paul's for giving me the nourishment of worship, teaching and fellowship in my early years as well as providing my spiritual home in my retirement years. And, thank you Harry B. for telling our Parish story.

Your friend in Christ

*Clarence Mitchell*

Clarence Mitchell
Right Reverend Clarence Mitchell

*Clarence checks me out*

# ACKNOWLEDGEMENTS

May I first acknowledge the affliction of most members of the Barrett clan since their arrival from Ireland in 1830, which is the tendency of some in each generation to keep, or should I say horde, things. This has given me a wealth of letters, diaries and documents to draw on in the writing of this rambling record. I am deeply indebted to my parents and grandparents, and my great aunts, Auntie Wese and Auntie Alice, for their guidance and concern in teaching me to recognise right from wrong and for my spiritual upbringing. They all worked diligently over the years ensuring my regular attendance, as a youngster, in Sunday School and Church.

I am deeply indebted to the work of St. Paul's historians, Joy Field and before her Georgia Morris Painter and her resource, the Port Dover Maple Leaf. I wish to acknowledge too, the friendly assistance of Sandra Manuel, church secretary, for her help in so many ways to ferret out material in the church office and make it available to me as required.

The archives of the Eva Brook Donly Museum and the assistance and interest of its enthusiastic Curator, Bill Yeager, has proven invaluable to my search for information over the years. Through the Museum, the writings of Port Dover's Master Historian, Dr. Bannister, as well as William Z. Nixon, Monroe Landon, Bruce Pierce and many others whose work is recorded there, have been most appreciated. Having known them all since the 1930's when my own interest in local history first surfaced, makes their contributions even more meaningful to me now.

Since the arrival of Canon Cornish in the Parish of St. Paul's, in 1921, which incidentally coincided quite closely with my own arrival there, in 1922, I have personally known and prospered from the guidance of the Rectors of St. Paul's church to the present time. This has given me insights into the workings of the Parish, I would otherwise not have had.

Serving at various times as Sunday school student, teacher and superintendent as well as in the affairs of St. Paul's Church itself, as choir boy, rector's warden, and member of the Select

Vestry plus lay delegate to Synod, has added immeasurably to my understanding of how it all works, and at time does not.

To my sisters Dorothy Burfoot and Emily Molewyk, both active members of St. Paul's, and Alice Browne, a member of St. John's, I am indebted for anecdotes and constructive criticism. My late cousins and lifetime friends, David Yerex and Tobe Snowden, as well as Pat Yerex and his sister Jacqueline Clarke, have made meaningful contributions to the text that follows. Many more including the Reverend Malcolm Muth, Harry Smith, Archie Morris, Kay Burbidge, Bob Ryerse, Bob Smythe, Betty Murton, and Anne Wynia have aided me in its production in many different ways.

In addition to this I have a huge store of old photographs and portraits of family and their friends over the years, but there is one serious drawback to their use. Everyone knew who they were at the time of their being taken, so no one saw any need to identify them. This oversight means that a large percentage of them are completely unknown to any one in the family living to-day. I am also indebted to Ian Bell for allowing me the use of the photo archives of the Port Dover Harbour Museum for many pictures and still others came from the archives of St. Paul's church itself. As always I am indebted to the artistic skills of my daughter Elizabeth for the line drawings she has provided.

All errors that remain on publication are solely my responsibility, but they are fewer than might have been due to the expertise and proof reading skills of Right Reverend Clarence Mitchell who also brought credibility to the whole venture by agreeing to provide the Foreword.

Invaluable as well has been the expert guidance and advice of Michelle Barrett and Karen Hueston plus the layout and printing skills of the very professional staff of the fine print division of Aylmer Express Ltd.

Finally I am beholden to my wife Joan, for her unfailing support and constructive criticism as the work progressed or at times failed to. Also, for her timely provision of hot and cold beverages, at times alcoholic, to revive my flagging spirits. She suffered many hours as a "computer widow" for the cause.

Harry B. Barrett<br>
October 25, 2005.

George Stuart Pelly

# 𝔗𝔥𝔢 𝔄𝔫𝔤𝔩𝔦𝔠𝔞𝔫 𝔈𝔥𝔲𝔯𝔠𝔥 𝔬𝔣 ℭ𝔞𝔫𝔞𝔡𝔞

### St. Paul's
### Port Dover, Ontario

CHAPTER ONE

# Beginnings of the Church of England in Canada

The first Christian service to take place in the "Long Point Country" was celebrated in October, 1669 on the banks of present day Black Creek, approximately a mile from its juncture with Patterson Creek [now Lynn River] at Colman's Point. Of interest to us is the fact that it took place over 186 years before the first service was held in the newly opened St. Paul's Anglican Church, Port Dover in February 1856.

Those early Sulpician celebrants, Father Dollier and Deacon Galinee, built a snug log cabin and an altar at the mouth of a spring-fed stream flowing into Black Creek. In this forested valley, with seven French companions, they prepared to spend the winter of 1669 - 70. Galinee describes their quarters as being located in "this earthly paradise of Canada." He describes the open woods and meadows, watered by streams teeming with fish and beaver as most attractive. Fruits, nuts and grapes are present in abundance and game is everywhere in the nearby forests.

Again from Galinee's journal: "Prayer was offered with tranquillity in the midst of this solitude, where we saw no stranger for three months." At the end of that time they were visited by Iroquois hunting parties, who proved friendly, and were intrigued by their snug log cabin and its secluded location.

We are reminded today of this visit of the first white men to the Norfolk area by the large commemorative cross overlooking Port Dover harbour. It was erected by the Ontario Historical Society and dedicated by their President, Dr. Coyne in 1922. It was originally placed on the bluffs of Brant hill as close as possible to

## 2 The Parish of St. Paul's

*Cross erected in 1922 to commemorate the visit of Sulpicians in 1769 - 1770*

the site of the original wooden cross placed there on Passion Sunday, 1670. In doing so the Frenchmen claimed the whole area for the King of France. As the bank eroded, and access could only be gained by crossing private property, it was moved to its present location at the end of Brown Street on Brant hill.

In 1928 a stone cairn was erected at the wintering site and a sturdy iron fence was built to enclose an earthen mound, all that remains of the original cabin and altar. Finally the beautiful stained glass window, located in St. Paul's and dedicated to the Barwell family, illustrating the conversion of the apostle Paul, has a panel depicting the Sulpician altar of 1669.

As it was an early custom with British seamen to hold religious services aboard ship, it is very likely that Church of England services were held in Nova Scotian waters during their many expeditions to that part of Canada. However, no record of such services seems to exist. The first priest of the Church of England to officially set foot on Canadian soil was a chaplain to the Royal Navy, in the person of the Reverend John Harrison. His first service, as chaplain to Commander Martin, was held to celebrate the taking of the French fort at Port Royal, now Annapolis, on Tuesday, October 10, 1710. Reverend Harrison took the service of thanksgiving for their successful capture of the fortress, and Reverend Samuel Hesker, chaplain to Colonel Reading's marines, preached the sermon. Harrison is said to have travelled in that same year, throughout Nova Scotia, which at that time included present day Prince Edward Island and New Brunswick. From 1728 to 1739 Reverend Richard Watts, chaplain to the forces, taught some fifty children in a school at Annapolis.

Upon the founding of the sea port of Halifax on June 21, 1749, the first Anglican service was held in the open air. Two clergymen, William Tutty and William Anwyl, were present in the newly designated city, having been sent out with 2,476 discharged soldiers and others in that same year by the Lords of Trade and Plantations. The Governor's drawing room was used for public worship thereafter, until the opening of St. Paul's. Plans had been made for the erection of the impressive wooden St. Paul's church, below the Citadel on Signal Hill, and it was opened for public worship in 1750, by command of King George III. The pine and oak from which it was framed and decorated was imported to the site from Boston, Massachusetts. The cost was £1,000 and it could accommodate a congregation of 900 souls. The first service was held in the as yet uncompleted structure on September 2, 1750. St. John's, Lunenburg, N. S., was founded in 1753.

*Wintering Site of Dollier & Galinee*

I was intrigued to find that at the time I was researching this fact, the September 2003 issue of the Anglican Journal under a photo of the Primate, Archbishop Michael Peers, in St. John's, Lunenburg to celebrate their 250th anniversary, told the congregation that very few Canadian churches are old enough to celebrate a 250th anniversary and, he joked, it is even rarer still to find one so old still under construction. St. John's, founded in 1753, is being restored after a disastrous fire in 2001.

From missionary reports at the time, it would appear that the colony was sorely in need of the influences of religion. They described "the lower sort" of the new settlers as "a set of abandoned wretches, so deeply sunk into almost all kinds of immorality as to scarce retain a shadow of religion." This seems to be a harsh indictment, but it was obviously the view of some at that particular period.

Government policy was to provide clergy of the Church of England, to minister to the spiritual and moral needs of the population and schoolmasters to educate their children. To achieve this it was planned to set apart in each township a plot for a church, as well as 400 acres for the minister, and 200 acres for the schoolmaster. The minister was allowed a salary of £70, the teacher £15. In 1750 Halifax had a population of some six thousand souls, of which half, or three thousand, claimed allegiance to the Church of England. Roughly two thousand of the remainder were described as "dissenters of all sorts," and the remaining one thousand were Irish Roman Catholics and Jews.

Actually St. Paul's Halifax, was not completely finished until 1755 and the first meeting of the vestry took place on October 10 of that year. Until 1798 the church had no source of heat save foot warmers in the form of either iron boxes filled with burning charcoal, or wooden ones containing hot bricks. Lord William Campbell supplied two new stoves in 1773 but when finally installed five years later they smoked so badly they could not be used. Two common stoves, borrowed from the garrison in 1798, eventually supplied reliable heat some forty-eight years after the church was first used for services. It is the oldest Anglican church still in use in the whole of Canada. I was both impressed and awed by its antiquity and simple grandeur, upon attending services at various times, while serving in the Royal Canadian Navy, during World War II.

In 1783, following the expulsion of eighteen thousand United Empire Loyalists to Nova Scotia, the work of the church was greatly enhanced. Similar progress was made throughout the Province, particularly in Annapolis, Lunenburg, Windsor, Cape Breton and Prince Edward Island. Slowly churches were established as priests and schoolmasters were appointed to serve the needs of the new communities.

The first Bishop of Nova Scotia, the Right Reverend Charles Inglis was appointed in 1787. His diocese covered, in effect, the whole of British North America. During his tenancy the Church of England grew and prospered. In 1793 he was relieved of responsibility for much of the diocese by the appointment of Dr. Jacob Mountain as Bishop of Quebec. Bishop Inglis travelled extensively throughout the settlements during his tenancy. Following twenty-nine years of dedicated service he died in 1816 and was buried under the chancel of St. Pauls, Halifax.

On July 1, 1769 Reverend Thomas Wood arrived in the harbour of Saint John, New Brunswick, where on the following Sunday he conducted divine service, preaching to an English congregation in the morning. During the afternoon he preached to a large gathering of Indians in their own language, and in the evening he held a service in French, which was attended by many of the French inhabitants of the area. Later at a service in Gagetown he baptised twins, Mary and Joseph Kenderick, who had been born in an open canoe, on the river, far from any habitation, a short time before his arrival.

The influence of the church continued to grow in the Province with the building of Trinity Church, Saint John. The first service, under the Reverend John Beardsley, was conducted in 1783. Bishop Inglis, a distinguished Loyalist in his own right, laid the corner stone of the church in 1788. The clock and chime of bells were given in memory of the Loyalists, and the communion plate was sent in 1790 by the Archbishop of Canterbury.

The royal coat of arms which is proudly displayed on the west wall of Trinity, was taken by British troops, during the evacuation in 1776, from the State House in Boston, where it had been displayed for many years in the Council Chamber. From thence it found its way to New York and by ship to Halifax, and in 1785 found its final resting place in Trinity Church, Saint John. This story was told to me by one of the wardens of Trinity, when Hellen and I attended services there from October 1943 to April 1944. I was serving at the time, as a Leading Seaman, radar, aboard the Fairmile, Q 072 on patrol in the Bay of Fundy.

Trinity Church, Saint John, is considered to be one of the most beautiful and graceful structures in Canada, standing as a monument to the large numbers of displaced Loyalists who settled in that city and along the banks of the Saint John river. It was a welcome haven to us, newly married, and setting out, in wartime, on a new and different sea for both of us, the sea of matrimony.

Until the conquest in 1759 there had not been one English resident in what is now known as the Provinces of Quebec and Ontario. The first settlers were camp followers, who came in the wake of the armies. General Murray referred to them as the most immoral class of men he ever knew. The majority settled in Quebec City, Three Rivers, Sorel and Montreal. They were soon followed by a better class of men, however.

The first Anglican clergymen to be recognised in both Lower and Upper Canada, sailed up the St. Lawrence river in June of 1759, following the conquest, on the Plains of Abraham, by General Wolfe in that same year. They came with the Navy and their first services were held in the fleet, in Levis and on the Island of Orleans. Among them were John Lloyd, Robert McPherson, Richard Kendall, Ralph Walsh, Michael Houdin, John Ogilvie and John Brooke.

The Reverend Michael Houdin had formerly served as a Roman Catholic priest and Superior of the Recollet Convent in Canada. In 1747 he had been duly received into the Church of England, where his knowledge of the country and the French inhabitants proved invaluable to the English in a smooth transition of power. He remained in Canada until 1761. Dr. John Brooke was the first clergyman to officiate in Quebec. He held regular services in 1760, and helped establish the first school for the children of both soldiers and civilians. Dr. John Ogilvie, chaplain to the army of General Amherst and its Mohawk allies, had been present at the capture of Fort Niagara and accompanied them to Quebec. Here he was commissioned by Amherst to take charge, as incumbent, of the congregation at Montreal, while remaining chaplain to the troops.

The promotion of the Church of England in Quebec by appointing French Roman Catholic priests did not always prove the answer to the problem. Many of those who had converted to the Church of England had done so for all the wrong reasons. In 1787 Bishop Inglis visited the western part of his vast diocese, in part due to perceived discontent in many Quebec parishes. During his pastoral visit he was not impressed with the conditions that existed in many of them. On his return to Halifax he set about to correct them, and many improvements were made. The British government was also lobbied to divide the jurisdiction of Bishop Inglis into more manageable units.

A recently arrived Anglican priest, the Reverend Philip Toosey intrigued me, not so much for his contributions to the advancement of the Church as for his contributions to the advancement of Agriculture, in Canada. He was the son of Reverend John Toosey, rector of Hesselt, Suffolk. He attended Trinity Hall, Cambridge in 1762, becoming ordained a priest in 1769 and rector of Stoneham, Suffolk the same year. He retained this living throughout his life.

In 1785 Toosey with his family immigrated to Quebec, where the stipend of £200 paid to the incumbent of the parish of Sorel, Quebec, by the British government, was transferred to him, the Reverend Philip Toosey. As Philip Toosey had no definite ecclesiastical appointment, and received no encouragement from the Rector of Quebec to remain in Sorel he stayed for only one year.

Forty-five years later my great, great grandfather, Hugh Massy Barrett, was forced to leave his home near Clonmel, in Ireland. On his arrival in Canada he purchased a farm in the parish of Sorel.

The following year, 1786, Reverend Toosey travelled to Detroit. Here working among the Indians, he baptised several Indian children. Reverend Toosey was intrigued by the fertile soils and the climate in the Detroit area and petitioned The Society for the Propagation of the Gospel to give him a permanent position there. They refused.

Disappointed, he returned to Quebec where he attracted the attention of the Governor General, Lord Dorchester and Bishop Inglis as well. As a result he was licensed in 1789 to assist Reverend David-Francois De Montmollin, Rector of Quebec, with English services in the lower province. Aware of the petition to the government by Bishop Inglis to appoint a Bishop of Quebec, Toosey returned to England, in 1792, for the express purpose of applying for that post. His efforts resulted in failure however, as in 1793 the government appointed Dr. Jacob Mountain, Bishop of Quebec. The Reverend Philip Toosey returned to Canada in 1794 and was appointed Ecclesiastical Commissary for Lower Canada by Bishop Mountain. From 1796 until his death in 1797 he was also Curate of Christ Church, Montreal.

In 1769, while Rector of Stoneham, Suffolk, Reverend Philip Toosey operated a prosperous 70 acre farm. He was described at the time by Arthur Young, a noted Agriculturalist and writer on that subject, as "a very accurate and ingenious cultivator." Upon his arrival in Lower Canada Philip Toosey acquired a large tract of land some eighteen miles from Montreal. The Estate he subsequently carved out of the wilderness in this place could only be reached by water at that time.

Reverend Toosey had maintained contact with Arthur Young in England and in 1791 was able to write to him and report that he had "erected a very complete barn, lofty enough to give shade all around it for fifty cows or oxen, stables for twelve horses, and flanked by sheep houses and hog sties." Shortly before his death it was reported that he had "a neat, boarded little mansion" complete with a farm yard and barn "the largest in Canada, exactly in the English style."

Reverend Philip Toosey, over the years had erected log houses for English settlers that he brought out to assist him in clearing and settling the land. In 1789 he became one of the founders, and a director, of The Quebec Agricultural Society. From the several letters written to Arthur Young, many of which were included in Young's "Annal of Agriculture," Squire-Parson Philip Toosey is proven to be not only an able writer, but also a practical, intelligent farmer and promoter of settlement.

Bishop Mountain, as Bishop of Quebec, was responsible for both Upper and Lower Canada. At that time there were only six clergy in Quebec and three in Ontario, five of whom were missionaries of the Society for the Propagation of the Gospel. The other four were paid by the government. He set about his new duties vigorously, as both the Eastern Townships of Quebec and Upper Canada were on the verge of experiencing explosive growth by United Empire loyalists and other English-speaking settlers. Bishop Mountain visited his vast diocese every three years, to encourage the clergy, visit every mission, encourage the building of churches and schools, and confirm the young.

At the urging of Bishop Mountain, and through the bounty of King George III, the cathedral at Quebec city was erected in 1804. He proposed a plan for superior education in the whole country, and obtained a royal charter for McGill College. He also instigated the proper training of a native ministry. Bishop Mountain made an intensive tour of his diocese, a distance of three thousand miles, eight times, being pronounced one of the greatest preachers of the age. He died on June 18, 1825.

As the Eastern Townships began to attract settlement at the turn of the century there was a need for the services of the Church of England. This need was filled by a very gifted man in the person of the Honourable and Reverend Charles James Stewart, fifth son of the Earl of Galloway. In 1820 having taken the post of visiting missionary, he visited settlements throughout Upper Canada from Ottawa, through Indian settlements on the Grand River, the Long Point Country, the Talbot settlement and on to Amherstburg.

Reverend Dr. Stewart succeeded Dr. Jacob Mountain as Bishop in 1825. By this time the population of Upper Canada had reached 164,000. The promotion of the Church of England, dependent on outside help, was suffering from a hopeless lack of both money and men. Although Dr. Stewart established the Stewart Mission Fund, Canadian Churchmen were slow to adopt methods of self-support. This was due in part to the fact that in the established church in Britain, stipends for priests were covered by the government, or missionary Societies, as were salaries for recognised schoolmasters, who were, for the most part, trained by the Church of England.

Upper Canada, or Canada West as present day Ontario was known, had services held in the chapel of Fort Niagara after its capture by General Amherst in 1759. These ceased when Reverend John Ogilvie, as their chaplain, left with the troops for Montreal.

At the outbreak of the American Revolution in 1775 the Indians were forced to leave their traditional hunting grounds in New York State for Canada. The majority under Joseph Brant, the renowned Mohawk chief, settled in Niagara. By 1784 they had moved to their grant of land along the Grand River and the following year erected Her Majesty's Chapel of the Mohawks near present day Brantford. It was the first Protestant church, if not the first church of any denomination, to be built in Upper Canada after the Conquest. Upon completion it was dedicated by the Reverend John Stuart, former missionary of the Mohawk Valley. The Chapel was consecrated by the second Anglican Bishop of Quebec, the Right Reverend Charles James Stewart, in 1830.

The entrance to the chapel originally faced the nearby Grand River. The Chapel bell, caste in England in 1786, was the first in Upper Canada. The coat-of-arms, one of the finest in Canada, was carved from a single piece of wood and presented by George III. The Chapel of the Mohawks is the only Indian Royal Chapel in the world.

The history of this Mohawk church dates much further back, however, to the conflict between England and France for control of the North American continent. In 1710 a group of sachems of the Five Nations from the State of New York, accompanied by Colonel Peter Schuyler and Colonel Francis Nicholson, sailed for England where they attended the Court of Queen Anne. Their petition to the Queen asked that a fort and chapel be built at the junction of Schuharie creek and the Mohawk river, a place later known as Fort Hunter, in the Mohawk valley. As a result of their petition the Queen Anne Chapel and Rectory were built. The communion silver and a Bible together with other items were presented by the Queen, in 1712. The Bible and silver were buried for ten years during the American Revolution.

Meanwhile Lieutenant-General John Graves Simcoe, who had gained recognition as a brave officer and brilliant strategist with the Queen's Rangers during the Revolutionary War, was exhausted and seriously ill by October 17, 1781, when Cornwallis surrendered. Simcoe had escaped to New York with a party of Loyalists and was invalided home to England on parole. His active military career was ended.

Simcoe recuperated on the family estate in Wolford Lodge, in Devon. On December 30th, 1782 he married Elizabeth Posthuma Gwillim, whose father had been aide-de-camp to General Wolfe. He settled in to the life of a country squire, moving between his home and London where he was often required to give advice on military matters. He was elected briefly to Parliament. On passage of the Canada Act in 1791, it is probable that Simcoe's appointment as Lieutenant Governor of Upper Canada followed.

On July 26, 1792 Lieutenant-Governor Simcoe arrived at his headquarters at Niagara. He had ample time to plan his strategies while making his way to Niagara and wasted no time in establishing his authority once all the hurdles had been cleared. Simcoe though he had an excellent military training and mind, was no politician, let alone a statesman. His vision of government was one in which church and state should go hand-in-hand to the understanding and satisfaction of everyone. His model was that of Britain where an established clergy was essential and as in the old country, so in Upper Canada, the morality of the people should be guided by the Church of England.

Further evidence of Governor Simcoe's influence on the clauses written into the Canada Act, while he was still in Britain, appear in the establishment without question of the clergy reserves. These lands were to be set aside in each county as it was surveyed, to support the established church. Simcoe even envisaged hereditary titles being granted to members of the legislative council. Responsible government and religious freedom was assured in Governor Simcoe's mind, provided the leaders rule was obeyed without question, and the principles of the Church of England were accepted, as they were in Britain. Even the performance of marriages were to be the exclusive right of the Church of England under the clauses of the Canada Act. Though the majority of the Loyalists were adherents of the Anglican faith, there were many other factions, as well as some Loyalists among the settlers who were not, and many felt strongly about it. To the Governor these inhabitants were written off, or ignored, as "dissenters."

By 1783 some ten thousand United Empire Loyalists had found refuge in Upper Canada. The following year in June the Reverend James Stuart set out from Montreal to visit the settlements on the St. Lawrence and along the shores of the Lakes. By June 18th, 1784, he had reached Niagara, where he preached to the garrison on the following Sunday morning. That afternoon he held a service with the Indians present. In July of 1785 the Reverend Stuart made his permanent home in Kingston, from whence he regularly visited the neighbouring townships, preaching often in the homes of the settlers.

In 1787 the Reverend John Langhorne took charge of the Bay of Quinte district and within five years he had opened eight places of worship. By 1792 the Reverend Robert Addison was in residence in Niagara. By 1794 it was reported that St. George's, Kingston was completed 'with a pulpit, desk, communion table, pews, a cupola and bells.' There were by now six clergymen in Lower Canada and three clergymen in the Upper Province.

By 1793 Governor Simcoe had established fortifications at York, and he moved there in July. He was anxious as well to establish a university, though he thought the possibility of establishing one to be some time in the future. Some two years at least after Simcoe left the country a young and ambitious Scot had been told that a head master was needed in York and he was told in Britain he had a good chance at the post. The person in question was John Strachan, born in Aberdeen, Scotland. He was the youngest son of a quarryman and had been raised a staunch Presbyterian. Primarily through his own efforts, as a teacher and tutor, he obtained a good education. There was little opportunity at the time for meaningful employment in Scotland, and partly on the strength of the establishment of a university in York he immigrated to Canada. Following a long and tedious voyage Strachan arrived in Kingston on December 31st, 1799. The job he envisaged was mythical, it did not seem to exist, but he soon had gained employment with a well to do and prominent loyalist, Richard Cartwright. It had been Cartwright among others who had begun enquiries in St. Andrews about the possibility of their sending a qualified man to organise a University in York.

By 1803, John Strachan was ordained as a clergyman in the Church of England. This ambitious and personable young Scot met many influential people involved in colonial affairs, while working in both Kingston and Cornwall. By 1812 Strachan had been appointed rector of St. James Church, York and the Headmaster of the York Grammar School. Recognised as a respected leader Strachan became a member of the Executive Council of Upper Canada in 1818. John Strachan was a strong supporter of maintaining close ties between the State and the Church of England and soon became a prominent member of the increasingly criticised Family Compact. Many of this close-knit Tory group of the most powerful in the government of the colony had been students of Strachan himself, and willingly supported his ideals.

A hard cover book in the Verschoyle Phillip Cronyn Huron Archives entitled "The John Strachan Letter Book, 1812 – 1834." gives some interesting insights into the character of John Strachan the man. The following letter, to my mind, showed an ingratiating, as well as petty side to his nature. It intrigued me and is self explanatory.

> "Monday Morning, April 29th, 1816.
> Dr. Strachan presents this humble duty to His Excellency, the Lieutenant-Governor.
> He intended yesterday to apologise to his Excellency for omitting two prayers in the Service owing to the stupidity of the Sexton, who in cleaning the Church, swept them away. The Dr. not perceiving the loss till the moment of using them, as they are always kept in the part of the Prayer Book to which they belong, became a little agitated, otherwise he could have repeated the more essential one, had he noticed the accident in time. The Company he met at the Government House prevented him from stating these particulars to his Excellency yesterday, but he felt uneasy at the delay.

The Dr. will guard against such an accident in the future and flatters himself that this explanation will prove satisfactory."

As would be expected Strachan and the Family Compact had many critics and soon he was at loggerheads with Norfolk's own Egerton Ryerson, who had become a prominent Methodist preacher and educator in his own right. Their opposing views on both education and government coupled with the increasing dissatisfaction with the government's often high-handed policies, culminated in the ill-starred rebellion of 1837 led by William Lyon McKenzie. Although this uprising eventually destroyed the Family Compact and much of Strachan's political influence he remained one of Ontario's most prominent Churchmen.

In 1839 the diocese of Quebec was divided and John Strachan was appointed Bishop of the newly established See of Toronto. This new diocese of Toronto gave Bishop Strachan jurisdiction over the whole of Upper Canada.

Although now in his sixties Strachan travelled by foot, waggon and canoe throughout his large diocese visiting as many churches as possible annually. On a local note we know that in 1846 he visited several Haldimand churches. On June 15th he consecrated the church of St. John the Evangelist, in South Cayuga. The following day he consecrated Christ Church, Port Maitland and on June 17th St. Paul's Church, Dunnville. Strachan also preached at Nanticoke where he found: " a small church, framed of upright lumber, to be in an unfinished state." John Mencke and Will Wood were Lay Readers at that time. In the early days the Anglicans of Haldimand County had been served by a hard working circuit rider, Cudmore Hill [1790 - 1870] who lived on the Grand River at York. Services were often held in McGaw's school, now known as the Wilson Pugsley MacDonald Memorial Museum.

In 1860, now eighty-three years of age, John Strachan returned to Nanticoke to consecrate the Anglican Church there and the newly built Anglican Church in the village of Jarvis. In 1886 the present Christ Church, Nanticoke was built. The old original church to the east of it was brick-sided and serves to this day as the Parish Hall and Sunday School.

In the early 1800's Colonel Talbot had engaged Colonel Mahlon Burwell, a land surveyor to survey the extensive lands granted to Talbot by Governor Simcoe, on condition that he establish loyal settlers on the said lands. This was done and Burwell was granted a large tract of land for his services at the mouth of Big Otter Creek, in the township of Bayham. Here Burwell wasted little time in developing a port that to this day bears his name. Realising that a Church of England was essential to the proper development of his growing settlement, Colonel Burwell set aside a plot of land for this purpose and at his own expense began to build Trinity Church.

The first Church of England service in Port Burwell took place on Sunday, February 2nd, 1836, being conducted by the Reverend Thomas Greene, a travelling missionary. Met by Mahlon's brother, John Burwell, Reverend Greene was cordially received and soon a large and attentive congregation, mostly of English and Irish descent, were accommodated in a room of the local tavern. Reverend Greene went on to Vienna that same evening where he preached to almost one hundred people. He recommended that a minister be appointed to Burwell's church, which was almost completed, and that he serve the community of Vienna as well.

On April 12, 1836, Colonel Mahlon Burwell wrote to Archdeacon John Strachan in Toronto;

> "My church in Port Burwell is now in a state to preach in. You promised me that you would be the first to preach in it, and I must keep you to your word. .... Can you meet me in Port Burwell on the 21st of May. Preach on the 22nd, and let me drive you to St. Thomas for the Talbot anniversary on the 23rd." He further stated that; " The Church has already cost me a good deal, but I shall put myself to considerable more expense to complete it to my mind. Between ourselves, I intend to do that which I am not aware of any other person in the Province having done. I intend making a deed for the church and about

five acres of land adjoining it on which is a beautiful spring brook, and a site for a parsonage house, and I will seek no remuneration."

On May 22nd, 1836, Reverend John Strachan was true to his promise and did indeed preach the first service in the large and impressive frame Trinity Church, Port Burwell, that Sunday. Reverend Greene, reports that in November, 1837: "Colonel Burwell had the church plastered throughout and had set apart a neat and comfortable house for the residence of a rector; and from his own property has endowed the church very liberally with lands." Colonel Burwell had indeed endowed the church with "glebes and lands" which were then sold and the proceeds invested in a permanent endowment. The indenture made in Toronto in 1840 reads as follows;

> "Whereas the said Mahlon Burwell exclusively, at his own cost, hath erected a church and rectory on his freehold estate at Port Burwell, and owing to the apparent apathy of late years evinced on the part of the Imperial Government, in not supporting the established church of the United Kingdom of Great Britain and Ireland in this province, hath determined to convey the said church and rectory and grounds on which they are situated, to be known as Port Burwell Rectory.

> And whereas the said Mahlon Burwell is in the humble hope that his own sins, negligence and ignorance's may be forgiven through the merits of our Lord Jesus Christ, and in the prayer and blessings of God may rest upon his posterity.... that the said Mahlon Burwell and his heirs forever, being members of the established church, shall possess and enjoy the right to nominate and present the rector, when a vacancy shall occur... and is to possess and occupy as a pew a part of the northeast corner of the church measuring eight feet by twelve feet on the ground floor."

At the second vestry meeting in October of 1843 the installation of two cast iron stoves was approved. They performed their purpose so well that a later incumbent, Reverend Murton Shore was said to have remarked that he dreaded the heat of winter far more than the heat of summer. The church bell, made by Maneeli, of Troy, New York, was installed in 1856, having been brought into the harbour by schooner. Many of the early pioneers of the district are buried in the church yard cemetery. Many others were the victims of an epidemic that raged through the village in 1878.

No changes occurred in Trinity church, Port Burwell, until 1909 when the church was re-shingled and re-decorated. The windows were re-glazed and new seats were installed. Many were upset at the passing of the old enclosed and latched pews. The church remains as a fine example of framed simple early Gothic Revival Architecture.

Meanwhile the extension of the church was spreading rapidly throughout the province. Almost all the larger towns of Ontario were supplied with clergymen and churches. In 1843 King's College was opened as a Church of England university in the town of Coburg, having begun as a divinity school under the Reverend A. N. Bethune. In 1852 Trinity College, Toronto was established. In 1851 the laity met for the first time in conference with the clergy and in 1857 a synod was held by the authority of an act of parliament. In 1854 the clergy reserves were finally secularised, ending a long and bitter struggle.

In 1857 the See of Huron was established. The Reverend Benjamin Cronyn, who had been appointed to London in 1832, was appointed the first Bishop of the Diocese of Huron in the first episcopal election held in Canada. At that time the diocese consisted of 43 clergymen, 46 parishes and missions, and 59 churches. Within fifty years the clergy serving the Diocese of Huron were, for the most part, men born in this country and educated in Huron College.

In 1861 the diocese of Toronto was further divided by the formation of the See of Ontario in the eastern part of the province. By 1873 the vast and barren lands lying to the east of Georgian Bay and north of Lake Huron and Lake Superior were set apart as the missionary diocese of Algoma. At the formation of this diocese there were no roads or railways, no See-house, parsonage or endowments to serve it. It boasted nine small frame churches, seven clergymen and a population of a few hundred souls.

In 1875 the six counties of Lincoln, Welland, Haldimand, Wentworth, Halton and Wellington were formed into the Diocese of Niagara, under the Right Reverend T. B. Fuller. There were 40,000 members of the Church of England, in a total population of 250,000, in the diocese at that time. It held 46 parishes and 50 ordained clergymen. In 1896 the diocese of Ontario was again divided to establish the see of Ottawa.

Before leaving the early history of the Church of England in Canada, mention should be made of the work of Wilfred Thomas Grenfell in Newfoundland and Labrador. Born February 28th, 1865 in the coastal town of Parkgate, England, Grenfell was an adventurous, often impetuous boy who loved the outdoors and the sea. In 1883 he entered the London Hospital Medical School, where he was greatly influenced by the American evangelist, Dwight L. Moody.

Upon graduation as a doctor, he joined the National Mission to Deep Sea Fishermen, who provided medical and missionary services to Fishermen of the North Sea. In 1892 Grenfell travelled to Newfoundland on a Mission ship to investigate conditions in the Labrador fishery. He was appalled at the poverty he discovered and the following year returned with two doctors and two nurses. With government help he established the first hospital at Battle Harbour on the Labrador coast. In 1896 he started a Fishermen's Co-operative at Red Bay, to help the fishermen become more independent. During the winter of 1898 Wilfred Grenfell supervised the construction of a new hospital in St. Anthony, in north-eastern Newfoundland.

In 1900 Dr. Grenfell chose St. Anthony as headquarters for the Grenfell Mission. They also acquired their first hospital ship, the Strathcona I. The following year he established a co-operative lumber mill at Rodickton. In 1905 he started an orphanage at St. Anthony and Andrew Carnegie donated a travelling Library. By 1907 Wilfred Grenfell was knighted and the Grenfell Association of America, and Grenfell Association of New England were formed. About this time he met Anne Elizabeth Caldwell

MacClanahan. They were married on November 8th, 1909, and she became completely involved in the work of her husband. They built a home, Grenfell House, in a secluded part of St. Anthony, where they raised three children. Upon their moving to Vermont it became part of the Grenfell complex, serving as a residence for mission workers.

In 1912, the International Grenfell Association was formed, taking complete control of the Mission's North American operations. By 1914, under Grenfell as Superintendent, it administered four hospitals and six nursing stations. More than 6,000 patients a year were receiving treatment. By 1927 a new and modern hospital was opened in St. Anthony.

When Lady Grenfell died in 1938 Dr. Grenfell was heart-broken. He made one final trip to Labrador and Newfoundland after his wife's death, where he was welcomed as a hero, before returning to his Vermont home, worn out. He died there on October 9th, 1940. His ashes, with those of his wife, are buried on Tea House Hill, St. Anthony.

CHAPTER TWO

# The Church and Settlement in the Long Point Country

Once established in Navy Hall at Niagara, Governor Simcoe wasted no time in making a careful survey of all that needed to be done, and, in acquainting himself with the vast territory he was expected to govern. An early interest in Agriculture saw the council, on October 21st, 1792, order the establishment of an annual six day fair, to be held at Newark beginning on the second Monday of October. It is interesting to note that this minute was passed on a Sunday, as were many other, often trivial, matters. Did Simcoe and his Council believe in the adage "The better the day, the better the deed?"

On February 4th, 1793, Governor Simcoe set out in sleighs with six of his officers to tour his western domain. His aide-de-camp was a young Lieutenant Thomas Talbot, who on this tour found the ideal area in which he decided to settle. He was to later negotiate the acquisition of the lands we speak of today as the Talbot settlement.

They first visited Chief Joseph Brant and his followers, at their settlement on the Grand, where they attended a Church of England service on Sunday, February 10th, 1793 in the Chapel of the Mohawks. They set out on foot for the west that same day, guided by Brant himself accompanied by twelve of his Mohawk braves.

For the first time Governor Simcoe saw the Long Point Country, and was quick to recognise its potential for settlement and defence from the invasion he feared from American forces. Turkey Point was seen as a major location for a town site, military fort and naval depot, being strategically located directly across from the American's potential base at Presque Isle. They travelled on to inspect the fortifications at Detroit and on February 23rd, they began their return journey.

On March 2nd, they reached a fork on the Thames River, where Simcoe envisaged the capital of the Province being established. This location was to eventually become the City of London. Suffering through severe cold and incessant snow storms, they arrived back at Navy Hall on Sunday, March 10th, 1793. Simcoe immediately began the construction of a military road from Burlington Bay to the site selected for the capital at the forks of the Thames River. He named it Dundas street after the Secretary of State for the Colonies, the Right Honourable Henry Dundas. He also began the construction of a military road to Georgian Bay, which he named Yonge street after the English Secretary of State for war, Sir George Yonge.

During the summer of 1795, Governor Simcoe again travelled west to visit the Long Point area. Here he specified the site, on the bluffs above the Turkey Point marshes, where the town of Charlotteville would be established.[named by Simcoe in honour of Queen Charlotte.] A town plan was made and included a large four acre lot for the establishment of an Anglican church as well as a location within the same plan for a Church of England rectory. A barracks was specified overlooking Lake Erie and below that site a pier and naval depot were to be built for the use of war ships and gun boats. It would seem the future of the Church of England, in the Long Point Country was assured.

Governor Simcoe's ambitious plans for the defence of the Province were met with a very cool reception by Lord Dorchester, Governor General of Canada, who felt that, following the signing of Jay's Treaty, increased fortifications and a large number of troops were unnecessary in Upper Canada. Governor Simcoe's Long Point plan received very little support, and very little happened there. One entrepreneur, Job Lodor, [also spelled Loder] did build a tavern at the town site about 1800, and later a modest fort was built near the entrance to the present-day golf course. Governor Simcoe's plan for a naval establishment never materialised, however. Job Lodor, a native of Sussex, New Jersey, was an experienced millwright and builder, who saw potential for the village plan and whose tavern was well patronised.

The first Court of Quarter Sessions for London District were held on April 8th, 1800, in the first, and only, two storey home and licenced tavern in the district. This had been built by Lieutenant James Monroe in 1796 on Lot 14, in the fifth concession of Charlotteville Township. Fort Monroe as it came to be known was the first "hotel" in Norfolk as well as the location of the first store. Colonel Samuel Ryerse had been commissioned to set the judicial system for the London District in motion. He and his associate justices met regularly thereafter and dealt with the granting of tavern licences, (the first being to James Monroe) appointments, fixing of statute labour, as well as convictions and fines for offences against the Court. These seemed for the most part to be for profane language, selling liquor without a license, Sabbath-breaking and assault and battery.

At the winter term in January, 1801, upon the appointment of Grand Jurors, Daniel Freeman and Jabez Culver, Senior, prayed before the Court for licenses to perform marriages. Not being of the Church of England, they were both refused. The Court had previously approved the construction of a set of moveable stocks and whipping post. This had been carried out. They had also made a contract with Levi Comber for the building of a Court House at Charlottevilla, Turkey Point, at a cost of £312 10s. 0p. This had not yet materialised.

As a result of Comber's reneging on his contract for a Court House it was agreed that a small district jail should be built at once. This was to be a temporary measure. James Monroe was instructed to have it built and to act as jailer, for which he could take one hundred dollars per annum. He must also continue to provide a good room in his house for the holding of the Court of Quarter Sessions.

The said jail was to consist of two rooms, one for debtors, the other for criminals. It would be twenty-five feet by fourteen feet and of log construction. Conrad Zittle was to be allowed ten shillings a day, New York currency, to superintend the project and work on the building. During its short life as a jail this building would imprison Moses Rice, an early tavern keeper, for a total of two hours, for contempt of court upon his being fined two shillings for swearing.

At the spring term, 1801, Mordecai Sayles was convicted and fined £10 for taking more than one-twelfth as toll for grinding and bolting [of wheat] at his mill. At the fall term David Palmer was fined two shillings for swearing and Albert Berdan was fined £5, Halifax currency, for assault and battery. [It is interesting to note the various currencies that were in use in the settlement at the time and being used for the levy of fines by the Court.] The summer session of 1802 was the last session of the Court to be held in the tavern of James Monroe.

In 1803 Job Lodor's tavern in Charlottevilla, Turkey Point, was made the judicial headquarters for all of the London District, until a proper court-house could be built. On December 10th, 1803, Job Lodor contracted to build a court-house and jail at Turkey Point for £250. He was also appointed jailer for a salary of £25 a year. The jail was soon built of logs but Lodor built the court-house, on a grander scale, of frame construction.

Job Lodor went on to build many of the early mills in the Long Point Country, including the Finch mill at Newport, later named Fisher's Glen, and Gustin's mill at Vittoria. Still later he purchased and expanded the flour mill in Waterford. He built a saw mill and established a store there as well. Israel Wood Powell, who was destined to later lay out the village of Port Dover, was a clerk at this time in Lodor's Waterford store.

> The first sign of an interest in establishing a permanent place of worship for the Church of England came with the calling of a meeting of the members of the "Protestant Episcopal Church of England," for the County of Norfolk, in the District of London and Province of Upper Canada, at Job Lodor's tavern. The date was Monday, January 3rd, 1803.
> From those settlers who attended the meeting, Mr. John Backhouse, builder of the 1798 flour mill north of Port Rowan, was chosen chairman. Three trustees were next chosen to represent the Church in the persons of Jonathan Williams, William Hutchinson and Isaac

Gilbert. Stephen Bartow was elected Clerk of the meeting.

Following discussion of the problems facing the adherents of the Church of England it was resolved that two subscriptions be drawn, one for the support of an Episcopal clergyman, and the other for the building of a rectory. This was done accordingly and presented to the members for signing.

It was further resolved that this meeting adjourn, to meet again at this place on Saturday the 22nd day of January, Instant.

                    Signed: Stephen Bartow, Clerk.

*******************

Saturday, January 22nd, 1803. The members of the Episcopal Church of England Committee met on January 22nd, 1803 according to adjournment. John Backhouse, Esquire in the Chair.

It was moved by Mr. Jonathan Williams that: the Parsonage House (when built) shall be a joint Property of the three Townships of Woodhouse, Charlotteville and Walsingham, and in which of the said Townships the Parsonage House may be built, that Township shall be answerable to the other two Townships and pay the valuation of their shares of said House at the separation.

It was moved by Mr. Henry Van Allen that: it be resolved in which of the said Townships the Parsonage House shall be built. It was resolved that the Parsonage House be built in the Township of Charlotteville.

It was moved by Mr. Hutchinson that: Samuel Ryerse, John Backhouse and Jonathan Williams, Esquire, be, and are hereby authorised to enquire in what manner a Glebe Lot may be obtained from Government, and also to enquire in what manner a clergyman may be established according to the customs of the Church of England.

It was next voted and agreed that forty pounds be offered as a support to a clergyman for the said three Townships,

and that such support be paid in Produce of this Country. Adjournment was moved, to meet again at this place on Easter Monday for the purpose of electing Trustees to represent the said Church.
Signed : Stephen Bartow, Clerk.

*******************

Easter Monday, April 11th, 1803. The members of the Episcopal Church of England Committee met according to adjournment on Easter Monday, the 11th day of April, 1803. Jonathan Williams, Esquire in the Chair.

On the motion of Henry Van Allen it was resolved that: Jonathan Williams, William Hutchinson and Isaac Gilbert be, and are hereby appointed, Trustees to represent the said Church and Stephen Bartow, Clerk [for] the present year.

The meeting adjourned to meet on Easter Monday next, unless called by special authority.
Signed : Stephen Bartow, Clerk.

*******************

Easter Monday, April 2nd, 1804. The members of the Episcopal Church of England Committee met according to adjournment the 2nd day of April, 1804. William Hutchinson Esquire in the Chair.

By motion of Mr. Isaac Gilbert: that Lot Tisdale should be appointed Clerk of the said meeting instead of Stephen Bartow, [who] resigned, and accordingly was agreed upon.

They then proceeded to the choice of two Church Wardens, when Isaac Gilbert and Joseph Ryerson were unanimously appointed.

[It was] then resolved that seven men should be appointed as a Vestry to represent the said Church and accordingly Samuel Ryerse, Esquire, Jonathan Williams, Esquire, Stephen Bartow, Ephraim Tisdale, Israel Wood, Henry Van Allen, John Backhouse were unanimously appointed as a Vestry.

By motion of Mr. Chairman that all the proceedings of the former meetings should stand and was agreed too.[sic]

By motion of Samuel Ryerse, Esquire that four men should be appointed to secure the money that was subscribed for the Church Clergyman when he arrives and accordingly John Backhouse, Samuel Ryerse, Esquire, Thomas Welch, Esquire, and Joseph Ryerson, Esquire were appointed for that purpose.

By motion of Samuel Ryerse, Esquire that the Church Wardens and Vestry shall collect the subscription and pay it into the hands of John Backhouse, Samuel Ryerse, Thomas Welch and Joseph Ryerson for the use of the Church Clergyman when he arrives.

Adjourned to meet on Easter Monday next unless called by special authority.

Lot Tisdale, Clerk.

*******************

It is perhaps no coincidence that on the evening of January 3rd, 1803, in the public house or tavern of Job Lodor, in Charlotte Villa, [sic] overlooking Turkey Point, seven Master Masons met to lay the foundations of Masonry in the Long Point Settlement. Some of those same men who had that day gathered in that same place as members of the Protestant Episcopal Church of England to organise the established church, were already Master Masons in British Lodges of Ancient Free & Accepted Masons. At that first meeting a formal application was made to the Grand Lodge of England for a warrant to establish a new lodge. This was granted and later in that same year, 1803, Union Lodge, No. 22, was established. Among its first officers were William Hutchinson, Worshipful Master, Benjamin Caryl, Senior Warden and Job Loder, Junior Warden. The local Mason's efforts had borne fruit

Lancashire in England and later from Yorkshire. He left his native shire in 1793 to spend two years in New York, followed by three years in New Jersey. John Backhouse first appeared in 1798, in the Long Point Country, where he took up Lots 16 & 17 in the first concession of Walsingham. He is said to have brought with him cattle, horses and sheep, as well as waggons loaded with implements and supplies. Even a pack of hounds, whose baying announced their progress along the forest trail, was part of his retinue. Here he built the now famous Backhouse mill. It is touted as the longest operating mill for the production of flour in the whole of Ontario, having shut down in 1955. Not long after their arrival his wife Margaret Longbottom died and he returned to Lancashire to marry a dairymaid, Jane White, he fondly remembered. She proved to be an industrious helpmate and maker of excellent cheese.

John Backhouse was among the first seventeen Justices of the Peace appointed for the London District in 1800. The following year he became an Associate Justice for the District of Walsingham. The District Court of Requests were convened in his own home. In June 1809 he was sworn in as High Constable for the District of London. During the War of 1812 Squire Backhouse was gazetted a Major in the First Norfolk militia. Upon Jane's death he married Hanna Haines. By his first wife he had four sons and three daughters. By his second wife he had one son and two daughters. He had no children by his third wife.

Trustee **Captain William Hutchinson** was originally a resident of New Jersey where he engaged in several military assignments for the British during the Revolutionary War. He served as a scout and had many thrilling adventures before being forced to leave, as a widower, for Saint John, New Brunswick. He remarried there and with his new family came in 1798 to settle near the Hazen tract in Walsingham. As a Justice of the Peace he served in the Quarter Sessions at Turkey Point. In 1804 he was appointed Associate Justice for the Court of Request for Walsingham He had also served as Judge of the Courts and in March, 1809 was elected Chairman of the Court succeeding Thomas Walsh, [or Welch] Esquire. Remembered as one of the jolliest of the pioneers, Hutchinson had a host of friends in the settlement. He had a family of five sons and three daughters.

Trustee **Captain Jonathan Williams** of Long Island, New York traced his ancestry back to Wales from whence they had emigrated in colonial times. He had married Maria Titus of Long Island and at the outbreak of the Revolutionary War was twenty-four years of age. Serving as a Captain in a Loyalist contingent of the British Army throughout, he was wounded and at the close of the war found his way to Long Point at the close of the century. He settled on Lot 7, concession 1, of Woodhouse, which he purchased from Albert Berdan. He was appointed Coroner for the London District in March, 1804. By 1812 when war broke out the Williams family, complete with seven children, had one of the finest two-storey homes in the Township. This, with all they owned, including many family treasures brought from their old home in Long Island, was burned to the ground by McArthur's raiders. Captain Williams died in 1832, on the old homestead, in his eighty-first year.

Trustee **Isaac Gilbert** was born in England about 1743. He came to New Jersey with his family soon afterwards, but little is known of the family in the American colony. Isaac enlisted as an officer in the British Navy at the outbreak of war and at the end of it he settled in New Brunswick. Leaving there in 1800 they came up the Lake in small boats to Port Ryerse, soon to become fast friends of the Ryerse and Ryerson families. Although entitled to land as Loyalists, they arrived too late for such an award. Isaac and his family settled on Lot 4, broken front, of Woodhouse, where they built a cabin on the banks of Hay creek.

**Stephen Bartow** was active in early meetings but no record of his activities or occupation have been found.

Vestryman **Colonel Samuel Ryerse** was the grandson of Joris Ryerson who in 1707 received the survey of 5,500 acres of virgin land, purchased from the Indians in the New Jersey Territory. Upon his death a portion of this land was divided between his sons, Joris Jr. and Lucas. Lucas built a comfortable Dutch-style home on his inheritance where he raised twelve children, among them Samuel and Joseph. By 1776, twenty-four year old Samuel, who had supported the Patriot's defence of American rights would not agree to their separation from the British tradition of law and order. For taking this stand he was imprisoned but made his escape.

He and his brother Joseph wasted little time in joining, as early recruits from Saddle River Township, the 4th New Jersey Loyalist Volunteers.

Samuel before the Revolutionary War was known to all, as a well educated, prosperous businessman of Bergen County. Samuel and his wife were respected leaders in Colonial Society. They were staunch United Empire Loyalists, as were most of the leading families, as well as the more prosperous farmers and tradesmen in the older settlements. With the outbreak of hostilities volunteers were recruited in New York and New Jersey under General Howe. When a brigade of five battalions was authorised, under Cortlandt Skinner, to be known as the New Jersey Loyalists, Samuel and Joseph were among the first to qualify as officers.

Through some clerical error, on their being registered, Samuel Ryerson became Samuel Ryerse. It was not noticed until he came to draw his pay, by which time the army refused to change it. If he wished to exist in the army records, he must become Samuel Ryerse. This he did. Upon the defeat of the British, Samuel and his family fled to New Brunswick, in 1783. Here in 1794 he was persuaded by Governor Simcoe to come into Upper Canada. He set out with his family at once for Long Point, building a log cabin at the mouth of a clear stream, which became known as Young Creek. Later Samuel built a mill on the creek, and the settlement which developed became known as the village of Clarence. On the building of a harbour, it took the name of Port Ryerse. For his loyalty to the crown, and status as a Colonel, Samuel Ryerse was granted 3,000 acres in the Townships of Charlotteville and Woodhouse.

With his background and experience it was only natural that Samuel Ryerse would be looked to for leadership in the developing settlement. In March, 1800, Colonel Ryerse received an official packet of documents naming him with sixteen others as Commissioners of the Peace for the London District. Commissions for other officials were enclosed and on April 2nd, 1800 Samuel administered the oath of office to them at James Monroe's tavern. Immediately following this Colonel Ryerse took the Chair to set up the procedures for the holding of the Court of Quarter Sessions of the Peace. Samuel Ryerse, by this act, became Norfolk's first Judge. At the first Court a week later his brother, Joseph Ryerson was appointed Norfolk's first Sheriff. He was succeeded in 1805 by John Bostwick. Samuel Ryerse had been named First Lieutenant of the County of Norfolk as early as 1798. He was therefore addressed as Colonel and commanded the Norfolk Militia. Colonel Samuel Ryerse died in 1812, to be buried in what later became the churchyard of Memorial Anglican Church, Port Ryerse.

Church Warden **Colonel Joseph Ryerson**, younger brother of Samuel, was born in Bergen County, New Jersey in 1761. He served as a Lieutenant in the Prince of Wales New Jersey regiment. On one occasion, while reconnoitring enemy positions, a high-ranking officer rode within a few feet of his hiding place. Noting his fine mount Joseph considered shooting him on the spot, but his sense of fair play overruled the impulse. On the officer's return he again allowed him to pass unharmed. He was to learn later that the man whose life he had spared was none other than the enemy Commander, George Washington.

On the defeat of the Loyalists, Joseph fled with the others to the Maritimes. Joseph had married Mehetabel Stickney in New Jersey and in 1799 they left the Maritimes for Long Point. His allotment of 1,200 acres was in Lots 23 and 24 of Charlotteville Township. On the completion of a proper survey he was found to have been short changed and as compensation Joseph was granted that island of Long Point known to this day as Ryerson's Island. On his arrival in Upper Canada Joseph was thirty-nine years of age and his wife was thirty-three.

Joseph Ryerson was appointed the first Sheriff of Norfolk as well as the First Treasurer of the new County. During the War of 1812 he was very active as the Colonel of the 1st Norfolk Battalion of Militia. He later commanded both Battalions until at least 1828. He was the father of six famous sons, none of whom held to the Anglican faith of their father, and three daughters. Of the six sons only one remained a farmer, the other five all became Methodist preachers. Joseph often referred to the five as his "good-for-nothing boys" who, when sent to work on the farm, would be found in a fence corner, or under a shade tree, reading a book. Joseph Ryerson died on August 9th, 1854, in his 94th year.

Vestryman **Captain Ephraim Tisdale** was the son of Captain Ephraim Tisdale of Boston who owned a deep-sea sailing vessel, and traded very successfully into the West Indies. In the early days of the Revolutionary War Captain Ephraim Tisdale Senior, served the Government in the distribution of army supplies. He fought for King George as the war progressed, and, on the defeat of the British, his position became untenable. The extensive Tisdale Estates were confiscated and as a result, the family were forced to leave the country for New Brunswick, where lands designated for U. E. Loyalists, were granted to them, between Parr, as the harbour of St. John was then known, and Fredericton. They set to with a will to improve their lot and were soon on the road to prosperity again. Captain Tisdale resumed his old calling as a sea-captain in command of the schooner "Polly."

The Tisdale family roots date back to an old Welsh family, who, when Sir John Tisdale rose to prominence and the peerage, moved to the County of Lancaster, England. A descendant came to America much later and settled on land granted to them in the old Massachusetts Colony. Prior to the outbreak of war, Captain Ephraim Tisdale Senior's father was a prosperous, and influential business man who conducted a thriving business from the busy shipyard he owned near Boston. Captain Ephraim Tisdale's son, named Ephraim too, began his life at sea as a cabin-boy aboard his father's vessel a few years before the war. He too, was a Captain of his own vessel prior to coming to Upper Canada.

Clerk **Lot Tisdale** was the first son of Ephraim, Senior, to come to the Long Point Country, taking up land along the Lake in 1798. He wrote glowing accounts of the area to the family in New Brunswick, with the result that Ephraim Junior and his family, his widowed sister, Hannah, her three children and his brother William all came up in small boats to Long Point.

On arrival Ephraim settled on lot 18, concession broken front, Charlotteville, on the lake shore, and began farming. In June, 1803, he was appointed High Constable for the District of London. Ephraim Tisdale Senior, on being flooded out on his farm in New Brunswick sold his holdings and followed his sons to the Long Point Country in 1808, taking up land near Vittoria. He died, age seventy-five, in 1815.

Vestryman **Israel Wood** was twenty-nine years of age when the Colonies declared their independence. With his father, Caleb

Wood and wife Mary Vail, they fled to New Brunswick with the other Loyalists who were driven from their homes. Caleb, who had two sons, Israel and Caleb, and three daughters, died there in 1794, aged seventy-one years. His wife died eight years later. Our churchman, Israel, settled in New Brunswick with his wife Ruth Goold, where his children were born. In 1798 when about fifty years of age, Israel, his wife, and their six sons and three daughters, came to Upper Canada, where he drew land near Port Ryerse on the lake front. Israel, who was revered by his neighbours, died in 1815, aged seventy years. His wife lived on to 1829, dying in her eighty-first year.

Vestryman **Henry Van Allen** was of Dutch ancestry, being born on Long Island. He and his wife Winifred Rapelje came to Long Point shortly after their marriage in 1895. They lived "near Patterson's Creek" having purchased 85 acres from William Francis in the south-east corner of Lot 10, Con. 1. Woodhouse, in the hamlet of Dover, on February 16th, 1801. In February of 1806 Henry was recommended by Samuel Ryerse as Captain of the Grenadier Company of Militia.

Colonel Henry Van Allen and his nephew, Daniel Ross Van Allen, moved to Chatham as early as 1833 where they were engaged in ship building and also owned a sawmill from 1859 to 1897. The Dover property was sold to Israel Wood Powell by his executors.

**Thomas Welch** [spelled Walsh after arrival in Upper Canada] was descended from one of the ancient families of Wales. The Welches came into Ireland, in the 12th century, with Strongbow and soon became a family of importance in Kilkenny county. In 1740 Francis Welch came to America and was employed in Philadelphia where he married the daughter of his Quaker employer. He later was engaged in shipping, during which time he and his vessel were captured by the French. He managed to escape to England.

Francis's son, Thomas, had also volunteered in the war against the French. On the cessation of hostilities he gained a good education and became a land surveyor, as well as a deputy sheriff in Pennsylvania. Refusing the rank of Colonel in the American rebel army put Thomas in a precarious position for a time. He finally reached safety and joined the British as an officer in a regiment of the Maryland Loyalists. During the following three years of conflict, while stationed in Florida, Thomas became a Spanish prisoner of war.

Thomas Welch became one of many United Empire Loyalist refugees in New Brunswick, upon the defeat of the British, where he was kept busy surveying lands for the tremendous influx of Loyalists. On the death of his first wife Thomas returned to Maryland to marry and to try to regain possession of his property there.

In 1793, having failed to negotiate the return of his holdings, Thomas, his wife and two sons, nine year old Francis Leigh and the younger Aquila M. came to Upper Canada to settle on Lot 12, Concession 5, Charlotteville. Here he was immediately engaged to survey parts of the Counties of Lincoln and Norfolk. In 1796 Thomas Walsh was appointed Registrar of Deeds for Norfolk, which at that time included the Townships of Walpole and Rainham. The first recorded election to take place in Norfolk was held at Avery's Mills, Waterford and Thomas Walsh was the first Returning Officer. On the formation of the London District in 1800, Thomas was appointed Clerk of the Peace, Registrar of the Surrogate Court, and Deputy Secretary for the issuing of Land Patents. In 1810 he became Judge of the District and Surrogate Courts.

Thomas Walsh's son, Francis Leigh Walsh, took charge of the County Registry office in 1810, having been appointed Deputy Registrar, under his father, in 1808. He continued in this position until his death in 1884, an amazing seventy-six years of outstanding service. It is said that when eighty years old he wrote the Episcopal Creed, the Lord's Prayer, "God save the Queen" his name and the date, all on a surface the size of a dime. This was done without the aid of a magnifying glass. Upon examination with a magnifying glass it proved to be in a clear and legible script. Francis Leigh Walsh married Elsie, daughter of Noah Fairchild, by whom he had five sons and six daughters.

Promoted by such an illustrious gathering of supporters, as those named above, of the Church of England, the establishment of a church and appointment of a qualified priest seemed imminent, but it was not to be. There is no record of any further meetings of the 1803 committee, and little is recorded of the progress of the Church of England beyond the occasional visits of men such as the Reverend James Charles Stewart, Reverend C. J. Usher, of the Chapel of the Mohawks and Reverend Robert Addison, of Niagara. These men travelled to the District to perform baptisms and marriages and hold services in the homes of those faithful to the Anglican communion.

The Reverend Robert Addison came to Canada as a missionary, from Westmoreland, England, in 1792. He became a military chaplain and Rector of St. Mark's church, Niagara. He was Chaplain to Parliament as well, and his personal library is said to have contained 1000 volumes. There is on record a visit of Reverend Addison to the hamlet of Dover on September 6th, 1807, when he baptised 12 persons, including children of Henry Van Allan, Abraham Rapelji, Jonathon Williams, Thomas Bowlby and Henry Bostwick.

On November 5th, 1815 Reverend Robert Addison was in the Vittoria area where he baptised Hetty Stickney, Joseph Ryerson, and John & George Luke Bostwick, children of John and Mary Bostwick. The sponsors were Joseph Ryerson Sr. and James Mitchell, the District Schoolmaster. The following day he baptised Mary Ann, John A. & Sally Bowlby, all children of Abraham and Mary Axford, of the Gore of Woodhouse. Their sponsors were Henry Bostwick, Jonathon Williams, John Backhouse and Daniel Freeman. By 1815, occasional services were being held in the Courthouse in Vittoria. The large body of Church of England adherents in the settlement were still being very poorly served.

CHAPTER THREE

# *Other Early Denominations*

**The Presbyterians.**
One of the earliest permanent preachers, to come into the Long Point Country, was the Reverend Jabez Culver. In the early days of colonisation of the Americas, three Culver brothers emigrated from England to Connecticut. We know of Culvers, grandparents of Jabez, who are buried in a Culver burying ground in New Jersey, near Schooley's Mountain. The father of Jabez is known to be buried in a family plot near Chester, in Morris County, N. J. Jabez moved to Sussex County, N. J. where he acquired a large estate and, in fact, Culver Lake and Culver's Gap are said to be named after him. Jabez went on to become a Presbyterian Minister, ordained in 1760.

Upon the outbreak of the Revolutionary war Jabez Culver's sympathies were with the British. If he were to retain his property, however, discretion dictated that he disguise that fact. As a result he joined General Washington's Army as his Chaplain for the duration of hostilities. He then returned to his home, but found living under the new regime increasingly difficult. When Governor Simcoe was reported to be in Upper Canada, Jabez Culver travelled on horseback to Newark, to negotiate terms of settlement, should he and his family decide to take up land in the new territory. Governor Simcoe, seeing him as a highly desirable type of settler, offered large tracts of land to Jabez Culver and all family members who were willing to settle there.

Jabez Culver returned to New Jersey to discuss with his family the agreement he had made with Governor Simcoe. In 1794, at the advanced age of sixty-four, he and eight of his thirteen children, which included several families, set out for the Long Point Settlement. Jabez Culver erected the first log house to be built in what became Windham Township on Lot 1, Concession 5. He also, as a Presbyterian minister was the first ordained preacher to settle in the Long Point Country. His home became the first to serve as a regular place of worship in the new settlement.

Jabez Culver wasted no time in putting his special talents to use, travelling widely to take the gospel to all who were willing to listen. He travelled on foot or horseback, and eventually built for himself a rough sulky-like conveyance to carry him from one clearing to another, as he made his rounds. His faithful mare wore a large cow-bell round her neck, which enabled her to be found on the termination of a meeting. It also served to alert his followers of the arrival of the Reverend gentleman in their midst. Old Windham, and the Presbyterian Congregation in Simcoe are the oldest of those founded by the Reverend Jabez Culver, as he and other pastors travelled the countryside, establishing other churches throughout the settlement.

**The Baptists.**

The man who did more than any other, in the beginning of settlement in the Long Point country, to promote the Baptist cause, was a British soldier, Titus Finch. Titus Finch came to America with his regiment to fight for King George in the war of American Independence. While crossing he and a married comrade were afflicted with a fever, from which his comrade failed to recover. His lonely widow turned her attention to nursing her husband's friend, Titus, back to health and in the process they fell in love and married. Always of a very religious turn of mind, Titus invoked the blessing of divine providence before each engagement of his regiment. On discharge at the end of the war in Halifax, Titus sought employment in a back settlement where the majority of the settlers were Baptists. He became very involved with them to the point where they advised him to turn his whole attention to preaching the Gospel. He was ordained soon after and devoted his life's work from then on to the ministry.

By 1798 Titus Finch had found his way to Long Point and settled on the banks of Young creek, where he had been granted six hundred acres. Part of this grant was on Lot 19, Concession 4, of Charlotteville, where he built a snug log cabin. The first Baptist congregation met in the home of Oliver Mabee, east of Vittoria, in 1803. By 1804 Titus Finch shared the distinction of having built the first Baptist church, with one built in Beamsville that same year, in all of Upper Canada. Titus asked little, and received very little, for his ministrations to his faithful little flock. He proved to be a zealous and indefatigable worker, however, and twice set off on missionary tours into the surrounding countryside in search of adherents to the Baptist doctrine. For twenty-five years he preached in Vittoria, being lovingly referred to as Elder Finch by his followers. Over the ensuing years he and his flock were responsible for the formation of other churches in the area. Elder Titus Finch died in 1821, in his seventy-ninth year.

**The Methodists.**

Foremost among the Methodist pioneers to settle in the Long Point country was James Matthews, who settled on Lot 3, in the Gore of Woodhouse. Little is known of his ancestry save that he was of English and Scottish descent. His wife's people were Dutch. He came first to Lyon's Creek, in the Niagara District, where he took up his grant of land, having served as a cavalryman in the Revolutionary war. Friends, including Joseph Ryerson, persuaded him, however, to exchange that block of land for land he acquired in Woodhouse Township. It was here that he established a meeting place for the first Methodist society in the area.

A Methodist preaching point is said to have been established in Woodhouse as early as 1795, and circuit riders occasionally visited there. Tradition has it that the first Wesleyan Methodist Church was formed here by 1800, meeting in the schoolhouse in Lot 2, Woodhouse Gore, next to James Matthews home. The first local preacher was Elder Daniel Freeman, whose daughter holds the unenviable record of being the first burial in the community.

It should be of interest to Anglicans to realise that John Wesley, who founded this new Protestant Society in England, known as Methodists, was a Church of England priest and remained so all of his life. He never intended that this "Society" which he and his brother Charles founded within the established church should ever be more than just that, - another Church of England Society. His original purpose was to bring new life and more informality, into the very formal ritual of the Anglican church of his day.

Born in 1703 John Wesley and his brother Charles were both educated at Oxford, studying at Christ Church. While there Charles organised a Holy Club, made up of young men who sought spiritual growth and John soon became very involved in its growing popularity. They were soon being referred to as "Methodists" a name which appealed to John Wesley, and he adopted it to describe the popular movement. By 1739 his Methodist societies were spreading rapidly and spontaneously throughout England and Ireland. John Wesley travelled constantly preaching the tenets of his new society. Soon he experienced opposition and even persecution for his theories. In the late 1700's the Church of England refused to accept Wesley's efforts and ideas of reform. As a result the separate Methodist Church was established. John's brother Charles Wesley, became known as the Poet of Methodism, and is often referred to as England's greatest hymn writer. A more eloquent preacher than John, Charles is credited with writing over six thousand hymns.

By 1784 the Methodists were recognised as the Methodist Episcopal Church in both the United States and Canada. Their organised effort and doctrine of free will appealed to the hardy, individualistic pioneers as an alternative to the Church of England which they saw as being arbitrarily imposed upon them. With the influx of settlers into Upper Canada after the Revolutionary war the country was starving for religious leadership and support. Although the majority of the Loyalists supported the Church of England, if there was not a concerted effort to provide for their desire for qualified clergy and places of worship, they found solace and a sympathetic alternative in the Methodist movement.

The authorities also accepted those settlers of the Methodist faith as members of the Church of England. Many other Anglicans among the burgeoning population were drawn to the lively revival and camp meetings of the early Methodists and others, which on occasion carried on for several days. The companionship and evan-

much more rapidly than the efforts of some of the same pioneer members of the Church of England to establish a church, having assembled there on the same day.

A substantial brick Courthouse was built in the newly designated District Capital, the thriving village of Vittoria, in 1815. This proved the death knell to Charlotte Villa. [Charlotteville] The new Vittoria building not only housed the Courts of the London District, but also came into use as a school, a Community gathering place and a place of worship. It also housed the Lodge room of Union Lodge, # 22. A. F. & A. M. The building served these several purposes admirably for the next ten years until it was destroyed by fire, and the District Capital, as a result, was transferred to the growing town of London on the forks of the Thames, in 1825. Neither Vittoria, nor Union Lodge, A.F. & A.M. survived this unfortunate turn of events. With the loss of their records, charter, furniture and jewels, as well as their meeting place, the members of the Settlement's first Masonic Lodge went elsewhere as well. One of the few tangible reminders of that far off time is the Judge's chair, rescued from the burning Courthouse, which to this day serves as the Master's Chair in Vittoria Lodge # 359, A.F. & A.M., Vittoria.

Although no further minutes of meetings of the members of the Episcopal Church of England have been found, one would assume from the minutes recorded to this date, April 1804, that the building of a Church and the arrival of a Rector for said Church was imminent. This, however, did not prove to be the case. We are left with the nagging question. Why not? It is said that a one hundred acre tract of glebe land was secured in Turkey Point but this land was never improved or occupied for the benefit of the Church of England. This was no doubt due to the fact that the "Town of Charlottevilla" was never fully improved or occupied either, fading quietly into oblivion.

The members recorded in the above minutes were all staunch supporters of the Church of England, their King and their new found fertile lands in the Long Point Country. What do we know of the background of these stalwart United Empire Loyalist pioneers?

The first Chairman, **Major John Backhouse**, came from an old and distinguished Quaker family first recorded as being from

*William Pope*

gelical preaching, thus provided to the otherwise lonely existence of the pioneer families resulted in many conversions.

We are indebted to the rather cynical comments of a young, well-to-do Englishman, the hunter-artist William Pope for an insight into how these often impromptu gatherings were conducted. The leaders in many cases were ill-trained in religious thought, but what they lacked in education on doctrine they more than made up for in fervour and religious zeal. On June 22nd, 1834, Pope recorded one of his infrequent church attendances:

> "Fine day. Went to church at St. Thomas - service performed in a truly miserable manner - I think worse than I ever heard it in my life."

By 1843 William Pope had mellowed a bit in his outlook on life in Long Point Country. He had also returned to England for an inheritance and to marry Martha Mills. His longing for the life he had enjoyed in Canada West brought him back, however and he settled down on a farm east of Port Rowan. His religious affiliation was to the Church of England, but his cynicism in such matters remained as can be seen from a meeting he and Martha attended in the hamlet of St. Williams on February 10th, 1843.

> "Went this evening to a Missionary Meeting about two miles from here at the Town Line, where is a small village and Chapel; at the latter the meeting was held. When we first arrived they were in the midst of a Hymn which done – Mr. I. Hutchinson was chosen chairman of the meeting and proceeded forthwith with the first resolution which having read - followed with a few remarks upon its import etc, the business of the meeting – in the midst of which he alluded to a person who being drunk mistook a large stump in the road for a ghost – which short anecdote I could not see very applicable to the subject before us. Having sat down, a Mr. Somebody rose and seconded the motion with a pretty long speech of which the description of his own individual feelings took up a large share. Next followed the second motion brought forward by a Missionary of some 12 or 13 years standing in the North-West amongst the Hudson Bay traders. He told some rather marvellous stories about the Indians – their murderous propensities and canabalism [sic] – especially when the man dying, his widow was left with five children, which the Indians of a neighbouring camp successively demanded and ate up. Also after a battle, the conquerors picking out the fattest of the prisoners – cutting open his breast and quaffing off draughts of blood from the cavity – and cutting off chunks of flesh from the slain and eating them.
> This resolution being duly passed, a converted Indian next held forth – commencing with a short Hymn, then went on to show that his race once held possession of the whole surrounding country where now the white man lays claim to, how they killed the Beaver and the Otter

and caught fish, but now the white man ploughing up his field turns up the arrow head and the stone hatchet – the relics of the red man; – after some remarks upon the state of wretchedness and moral darkness of his tribes, he proceeded to relate some anecdotes, one of which was of an old Indian who wished that his throat was a mile in length so that he could be able to swallow and store more whiskey [or fire-water as they term it] – Another was of an old Chief and his tribe having met to worship a large image which they had elected as their God and which they set upon a stump – this Missionary and the Indian coming up at the time when they were playing their mad pranks around their wooden idol upon the stump – held a talk with the Chief and succeeded in converting him – whereupon the old Chief harangued his young men and women – told them their errors – upset the old wooden image from the stump with a blow of his war club, collected the contents of the various medicine bags – including snakes and bull-frog skins to the amount of twenty-five, placed them by the image, set them afire, lighting the old image that he had worshipped then for the space of forty years and during the whole time they had never 'made his heart glad' – and that if they were any of them real Gods they might save themselves by flight – later being burnt up – but said he 'they were all burnt up'. After some few more remarks he concluded with an appeal to the audience for aid in the cause of civilisation and Christianity.

After another hour and by far the best speech of the evening from another Missionary & Preacher who finished his speech by a short anecdote in which he said that a person going to a similar meeting with two and a half Dollars in his pocket – gave one of those; – but in going home, when two miles away from the place of meeting, he bethought to himself that he ought to have given the other also, and he actually turned back – found the collector in the act of making up the accounts – gave him the other half, and then went home with a clear conscience. Now said he – alluding to the wind and rain beating against the casements, 'I hope none of you will have to return some two miles through the storm to give the other half Dollar' – At last two persons came round with hats to make a collection – some who had nothing with them having their names put down for a subscription. One anecdote of the Missionary's was the following – an Indian having two wives – one of them died – the body he carried away some little distance and threw it carelessly upon the ground where he left it – some time afterwards coming by he saw that the wolves and the beasts had been preying upon her – whereupon he set up traps, baiting them with pieces of the body – caught the 'varmints' and sold their skins to the fur traders. Concluded about ten o'clock – when the rain luckily cleared off, we had a dry ride home."

A year later, in early September, 1844, William Pope and his wife Martha attended a much more elaborate Camp Meeting, held in the town of Simcoe. They with others from Port Rowan and area attended. His account of it from his diary follows;

"Mrs Kilmaster, Mrs. Pope, W. Wilkins & Self went to a Camp Meeting which was held near Simco [sic] about eighteen miles from hence. – stopped at Vittoria where we had some dinner at Mr. Hewitt's – arrived at Simco [sic] in the evening – the meeting was held upon a piece of ground belonging to Mr. Culver near his Sawmill – Shanties built of boards were placed in the form of a square – a pulpit for preaching being placed centrically [sic] – benches for the hearers in the midst – a small place Railed off at one corner for the 'Prayers and Mourners' to perform their antics in and four fire stands one at each corner to give light in the Night-time; – when we first arrived there was nothing going forward – but shortly a Horn sounded to call the meeting to-gether; — when a hymn being first sung two or three preachers in succession delivered extensive discussions with an accompaniment of gesticulations – 'hurling anathemas' at the heads of all disbelievers and sending the souls of sinners 'to everlasting perdition' looking particularly hard at the female part of the congregation when uttering any word in sentence of damnation from whom they evidently trusted to gain the strictest attention, and perhaps from whom they hoped to get the most Dollars; – but I should not slander the worthy and revered men – who delight in terming their fellow-worms 'My dear Brothers and Sisters". At length having finished their lecturing in the Pulpit or front of a penny show-box which it greatly resembled – an invitation was given to all such as felt disposed to go into the place fenced off [about 20 ft. square] which was called the 'alter' [sic] or 'prayer circle' – which invitation being duly accepted by several males – females a short exhortation was first given by one of the preachers – in which he admonished the surrounding congregation to observe due silence and attention to what was about to be performed however discordant and confused their religious exercises might appear to those outside the 'Circle'; this being finished, Preacher and brothers and sisters soon commenced howling, praying, bawling, and ranting to the very utmost that their voices and lungs would allow – kneeling and sprawling upon the ground – and making such a hideous uproar that it was scarcely possible to hear a person speak; – this hullabaloo was kept up for the space of an hour or so, and in fact 'till they all appeared totally exhausted – when at length the congregation was thanked for their orderly behaviour and the meeting dispersed somewhere about two o'clock. Afterwards the Preachers renewed their praying and exhorting in the tents and shanties – keeping it up for nearly the rest of the night. We went to Simco [sic] where after trying three taverns we managed to get one bed for the ladies – contenting ourselves with some Buffalo skins upon the floor; – rose next morning soon after day-break – breakfasted for which the charge was one quarter Dollar each; – went to the Campground –

stood till noon – when I should suppose there were 1500 to 2000 people assembled – being Sunday. We bade adieu to the dear Brothers & Sisters and departed to-ward home where we arrived about dark, in the evening – stopping at Mr. Hewitt's by the way...'

Meanwhile Upper Canada had been welcoming a heady religious mixture of settlers for some time now, as smaller groups of New England Congregationalists, Roman Catholics, Irish Protestants, Lutherans, Quakers, Tunkers, Moravians, as well as many with no religious beliefs were added to the mix.

George Stuart Pelly

## Chapter Four

# St. John's Anglican Church, Woodhouse
### The Mother Church

With the demise of Governor Simcoe's proposed village of Charlotteville, so also ended the ambitious plans of the Church of England supporters to build an Anglican church on that site. The final blow came with the burning of Job Lodor's tavern, in 1814, and the resultant move of the Courts to the growing village of Vittoria, as the new centre of the London District. With the building, in 1815, of an impressive brick Courthouse and jail on high ground in the village centre, the Anglican supporters, along with many other groups, met there until their own church building could be built. Meanwhile plans went forward among the residents of the Townships of Walsingham, Charlotteville and Woodhouse, for the building of an Anglican church on a knoll south of the growing village. Money and timbers for this long dreamed of project was raised and the materials delivered to the site. For reasons that remain unclear to us today, the project collapsed and hopes of their own place of worship again faded. Disappointed by this lack of progress many would-be parishioners joined other denominations.

Through the Society for the Propagation of Christian Knowledge, the Reverend Charles Stewart had been attempting, since 1822, to bring the message of the Church of England to the more western parts of Canada West. His work was primarily in the area of The Forks, now London. In 1825 he reported that the church in the Township of Woodhouse was nearing completion, but he added in his report that; *"the part of the country in which it is situated, commonly called The Long Point Settlement is populous, but* in no part of the province are the people so far removed from any of our missionaries and so destitute of the worship and ordinances of our Church."

It was primarily under the guidance of this travelling missionary, Reverend Charles Stewart, that St. John's, Woodhouse came into being. In 1825 he was appointed the second Bishop of Quebec. Five years later on visiting the area he asked the Reverend Francis Evans to enter into the church register several baptisms that he had performed here between 1820 and 1825. The said register is still in St. John's, Woodhouse with the names inscribed in it over the signature of Reverend Charles Stewart.

First William Hough and then Robert Lugger, missionaries to the Mohawks, gave occasional services to the Long Point area and in 1828 the Reverend George Archbold visited Woodhouse to report that the Salmon family had started a Sunday School.

There had been a goodly number of supporters of the Church of England in the eastern half of Charlotteville, and in Woodhouse Township, and with the collapse of the plan for an Anglican church in Vittoria, the Culvers, Bowlbys and others living south of the village of Birdtown [later Simcoe] began to agitate for a Church to be built that was central to the two major villages at that time. For some time prior to 1820 a log structure on the side road, now St. John's Road, on land that now accommodates the cemetery, had served as a place of worship for local Anglicans. In 1821 a modest log building was built to

*St. John's Church, a frame building replacing the original log church which burned*

replace it and now served as a church on what was at that time, John Misner's farm. On June 7th, 1823 Misner deeded sufficient land for a church and burying ground to Jacob Potts and Aaron Culver, church wardens, on the north east corner of present day Highway 24 and the St. John's road, County road 3. They paid him five pounds.

About a year later the log church was lost in a fire. With the land secured, no time was wasted in building a new and much larger frame church, complete with an impressive multi-storeyed belfry and steeple. This impressive structure was named St John's, by its enthusiastic congregation. Still the parish had no permanent Priest. Finally in 1828 the Church of England in the Long Point Settlement came into its own, with the appointment of the Reverend Francis Evans as the first Priest of St. John's Church, Woodhouse.

**Reverend Francis Evans** was born in 1801, in Robinstown, Westmeath, Ireland, and educated in Trinity College, Dublin. At age 24 he married Maria Sophia Lewis, daughter of the Reverend Thomas Fry Lewis of Somersetshire, England. On his arrival in Canada, in 1824 he was posted to Three Rivers, Quebec, as Curate under the Reverend R. Q. Short. He was ordained as a priest in 1827 by the Reverend Charles Stewart, who only the year before had been consecrated Bishop of Quebec. In 1828 the Reverend Francis Evans was posted to Woodhouse Township, Canada West.

Both the Reverend Evans and his wife were very well educated people, who brought a sense of

*Rev. Francis Evans*

good taste, intelligent conversation and refinement to their new post. They also, in time, brought a family of twelve children to the frame rectory provided for them. The stipend of £40 in local produce, barely met the needs of this large and active family and to supplement his meagre income, Reverend Evans established a Boarding and Grammar school in the rectory. In 1836 Sir John Colborne, Lieutenant Governor, set up his famous Rectories in the Province. One of these was the Township of Woodhouse and Francis Evans, as a result, advanced to the status of Rector. This edict attached all glebe farms in the Township to St. John's Church, with revenue from them going to the church. Canon Cornish points out that these farms were sold eventually and the capital realised was invested by the Synod.

Reverend Francis Evans proved to be a very efficient and effective educator. When the County Grammar school was established in Simcoe he was placed in charge of its operation and management. He served the congregation of St. John's faithfully for thirty years on an annual salary of £40, paid primarily in produce. He obviously launched into his religious duties with vigour for in an 1830 report to his Bishop, Right Reverend Charles Stewart, he states that he is holding services eight miles to the north in Windham, as well as Waterford and five miles south-west in Vittoria. In addition through the week he regularly holds services in Simcoe and Dover.

On September 23rd, 1842 Dr. Strachan visited St. John's and comments from his report "A Journal of Visitation to the Western part of his Diocese by the Lord Bishop of Toronto" as follows; "Thursday September 22, 1942: We proceeded on our way toward Woodhouse twenty-five miles, to Sovereign's Inn, where we were glad to halt for the night. Here we met the Reverend Francis Evans, Rector of Woodhouse, who had, with the kindest intentions, come thus far, twelve miles, to escort me to his hospitable home, but having already travelled nearly fifty miles, in a very rough wagon, and through bad roads, and having also performed a great deal of duty, I felt too much fatigued to proceed further so late at night, it being then past 10 p.m. Mr. Evans, however, being well acquainted with the road and anxious to make further preparations for my reception on the following morning, returned home by the light of the moon, which was just rising."

"Friday, September 23rd, 1842: The church at Woodhouse was built many years ago, when the population was very thin, ...... It is therefore quite in the country, and is, unfortunately, at a distance from several villages, which have since its erection grown up in the vicinity. The locality of the church is now felt to be a great inconvenience; the county town, Simcoe, for instance, is nearly two miles distant, and at this spot one must of necessity soon be erected; while several other villages in the neighbourhood are in a similar situation.

The congregation of Woodhouse was very respectable, and more numerous, indeed, than could have been expected, as many were absent at the assizes, which were then being held in the County Town. Twenty-two persons were confirmed, seven of whom had come, through very bad roads, seventeen or eighteen miles. Among the candidates for confirmation it was very pleasing to see the children of several immigrants who had recently arrived and retained all the feelings of attachment to the church of their native land.

Upon the conclusion of the service, we returned to the parsonage, where we were hospitably entertained by the rector and his accomplished partner, Mrs. Evans. We resumed our journey and drove to Brantford, a distance of twenty-six miles, where we arrived about eight o'clock, p.m."

An account of a confirmation service at the Mohawk Chapel on September 24th, follows, and then brief accounts of services in Paris, Burford, Galt, Guelph, Dundas and Ancaster.

The work of the Reverend Francis Evans over this time in the County was directly responsible for the establishment of fourteen Anglican churches in this area. His children all did well and grew up to be respectable adults with interesting, productive careers. Three of his four sons became clergymen, and a daughter married one. Toward the end of his career he returned to Ireland in an attempt to regain his failing health, but it was to no avail. He died at his brother's home, within a week of his arrival, on September 5th, 1858. Reverend Francis Evans was buried at Castle Pollard, Ireland.

*St. John's Church, the third building, dedicated Dec. 14th, 1913*

**The Reverend Elliott Grasett, B. A.** [1859 –1879] followed the Reverend Francis Evans, as rector of St. John's. He had been born in Gibralter where his father, Major Henry J. Grasett, was the Gibralter Hospital's army surgeon in 1826. He received his education in Canada. He called himself Rector of Woodhouse and Incumbent of Trinity Church, Simcoe. During his twenty years at St. John's, fire struck for the second time in 1874, completely destroying the wooden structure. The following year it was rebuilt of much more durable brick. Reverend Grasett's ministry came to an abrupt end on his sudden death on August 10th, 1879. He was assisting Bishop Helmuth at a Confirmation service in neighbouring St. Paul's, Port Dover, when he was taken ill very suddenly, and removed to the vestry. On being later transferred to the rectory he passed away at 10.00 p.m. the same evening.

**The Reverend William Berthome Evans** [1879 –1884] was the third Rector of St. John's, Woodhouse, and the son of Reverend Francis Evans. He served the two parishes of Woodhouse and Simcoe. During his five year term, however, they became separate parishes and St. John's became a three-point charge. Reverend Evans thus was made responsible for the parishes of Waterford and Port Ryerse in addition to St. John's parish. He died in office in 1884.

His family was represented in the community until recently, as his eldest daughter, Marion Frances Evans, married Frances Henry Kent. Their son Reg Kent and his wife Edith were staunch workers in St. John's for many years. Another daughter, Maud Drayton Evans, married Frank L. Bowlby, whose daughter Maud was for many years in charge of the Anglican mission in Chapleau, Ontario. Another stalwart of the parish was Sarah Williams Covernton, wife of James Covernton, of Dryden farms, who served St. John's as organist for thirty years.

**The Reverend William Davis** [1884 – 1890] a native of Ireland, succeeds Reverend William Evans., retiring in 1890 after serving the parish for six years.

**The Reverend Canon W. A. Young** [1890 – 1908] became Rector for the next eighteen years. He took up residence in Simcoe, as the rectory a mile south of the church was sold. After reclaiming the abandoned place of worship in Waterford, Canon Young established a new church in the village. In 1900 he encouraged church members of St. John's to clean up and further beautify the old and historic cemetery grounds and church yard, surrounding the church. A special fund was established to look after maintenance on an ongoing basis. Extensive renovations were carried out as well, during Canon Young's tenure.

He had a keen interest in gardening and was instrumental in the founding of the Simcoe Horticultural Society, serving as their first President. Henry Johnson, the historian, was the first Secretary. While Rector of St. John's Canon Young became an Archdeacon, and was appointed Secretary Treasurer of the Diocese of Huron.

**Mr. Hardy** [1908] a student minister, conducted services at St, John's, upon Archdeacon Young leaving to take up residence in London, from April through August, when a permanent appointment was made.

**The Reverend James Ward** [1908 – 1929] a resident of Waterford brought great enthusiasm to his new charge. He reopened Memorial Church, Port Ryerse, after nineteen years of inactivity, and St. John's became a three-point charge as Trinity Church, Waterford and Memorial Church were added to his responsibilities. In 1917 Waterford was made a separate parish.

*Sketch of St. John's Church, rebuilt in 1913, by Elizabeth Barrett, 1978*

James Riley points out in "If These Doors Could Speak" that the Reverend Frank Anderson, Waterford's first incumbent went on to become a Professor of New Testament Greek and Church History at Huron College in London.

On June 12th, 1912, tragedy struck the community when Wallace Baker's hired hand retired to the Baker barn for a relaxing pipe. A spark from the pipe set hay on fire and aided by the very dry weather and a strong breeze it was soon out of control. Although neighbours rallied round there was little they could do to save the barn and several outbuildings. They could only concentrate on preventing the house from being burned to the ground as well. In all the excitement no-one realised that the south-westerly wind was blowing sparks across the road to where St. John's church lay directly in their path. Sparks, carried in the black pall of smoke, had ignited the shingles on the church, before it was, belatedly, discovered that the church was on fire. With neither water nor ladders available to the horrified neighbours, nothing could be done to save the structure. Many, at considerable risk to their own safety, did enter the burning building to save church files, communion silver, the altar cross, the pulpit and most of the pews but the church was completely gutted. Within eighteen months St. John's was completely rebuilt, as the congregation held their services in the Woodhouse United Church, a mile south along the highway.

On December 14th, 1913, Reverend Lewis Evans, Dean of Montreal, and another son of Reverend Francis Evans, took the service of dedication of the rebuilt church. On July 19th, 1914, Right Reverend David Williams, Bishop of Huron, consecrated the new St. John's Church. In 1916 a new rectory was built to the north of the church and Reverend James Ward moved into it a year later. On September 2nd, 1917, 120 parishioners attended a commemorative service for one of their own, Ernest Quanbury, killed while fighting in France.

When the debt for the rectory was retired, the congregation were invited to the John Baker residence to burn the mortgage. Apparently not comfortable being debt-free and noting the crowded conditions in the homes where they met, Mrs. Henry Selby suggested it was time St. John's had a proper Parish hall. The cheese factory at Rockford was for sale and the church bought it. Members of the congregation set about dismantling it and with their teams and waggons it was loaded and brought to the site to be assembled again near the north boundary of the property and behind the rectory in 1924.

On August 8th, 1924 the Right Reverend David Williams, Bishop of Huron, and other guest clergy took

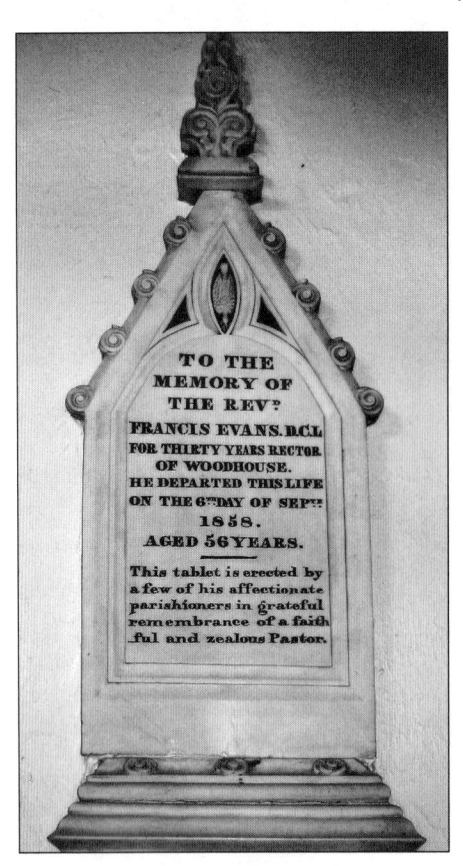

*Memorial tablet to Rev. Francis Evans*

*Chancel & Altar of St. John's Church, Woodhouse*

part in a special service to celebrate the centennial of the founding of St. John's, as well as the grand opening of their new Parish Hall. About this same time the grounds were much improved with the planting of trees and shrubs and additional land was acquired from John Wilson, their farmer neighbour. In 1929 Reverend James Ward retired and moved to Toronto.

**The Reverend T. B. Holland** [1930 –1941] who had worked extensively with First Nations People in Moose Factory, and came to St. John's from Chesley, became the eighth rector of the parish. He came at the height of the Great Depression and soon had the love and respect of the congregation for his frequent visits to all, in their homes. He became particularly active in promoting the Sunday School and in forming an AYPA., as well as leadership courses in Bible Study.

Electric lights were installed about this time. On May 5th, 1935, a special Jubilee Service was held for King George the Fifth. Barely eight months later on January 26th, 1936 an official memorial service was held following the death of King George the Fifth.

**The Reverend William Crarey** [1941 – 1946] a native of Yorkshire, England arrived from an Arctic parish near Dawson City. He explained his rather awkward, rolling gait, from having to walk for miles on the railway ties, while visiting members of his scattered congregation in the far North. I was intrigued by the fact he counted Robert Service as a friend, and had as neighbours the Bertons and their young son, Pierre Burton, so soon to make a name for himself as an historian. Reverend Crarey served St. John's during the war years. On October 9th, 1943, he officiated at my marriage as an able seaman, RCNVR, to Helen Mary Bowlby Browne of that parish, in the attractive and historic old church, surrounded by plaques and memories of the ancestors of both of us. Our soloist during the ceremony was a young man with a deep and appealing voice, Clarence Mitchell. An obelisk in the churchyard of St. John's marks the last resting place of my Irish Great Grandparents, Hugh Massy & Caroline Butler Barrett, and two of their sons, Hugh Quintin and Thomas Hubert.

**The Reverend E. L. Vivian** [1946 – 1954] a native of Basingstoke, England followed. He had served in the Canadian Army Ambulance Service during W. W. II. Attractive new entrance doors were installed and dedicated during the Reverend Vivian's tenure, a gift of Hellen's great aunt Erie Bowlby. In February, 1952, a saddened congregation attended a Memorial Service for King George VI. Reverend E. L. Vivian died in 1957.

**The Reverend W. B. Wigmore** [1954 – 1956] freshly graduated from Huron College, was a breath of fresh air to the parish, in his positive approach to his duties as a young parish priest. The choir were asked to don new robes, sewn by the Ladies' Guild, as other enthusiastic parishioners held work bees to renovate and paint the basement for the accommodation of the revitalised choir. Mrs. Wigmore attracted more than fifty children to her summer vacation Bible School. An attractive stained-glass window, gift of the Baker family, was installed and dedicated by Right Reverend David Luxton, Bishop of Huron. In 1956 the Reverend Mr. Wigmore was appointed to Christ Church, in London.

**The Reverend David Milne** [1956 – 1961] came to St. John's directly from England, and his powerful voice was welcomed in both the pulpit and by the choir. Through his efforts a Cub Scout group was sponsored by the parish, and annual bazaars and strawberry teas became a popular part of parish activities. Summer vacation Bible Schools continued to thrive. In 1961 Katie Bullock, who had been St. John's faithful organist for many years, retired, to be replaced, to this day, by the equally popular Anne Judd. In the same year Reverend David Milne was transferred to Rosedale Church, Windsor.

**The Reverend James M. Donaldson** [1961 – 1969] came to St. John's from Brantford. On leaving school Reverend Donaldson took employment with the Canadian Imperial Bank of Commerce, only to enroll later in St. John's College, Winnipeg, where he obtained a degree in theology. Serving first in several parishes of the far North Reverend Donaldson finally transferred to Huron Diocese, coming to St. John's via a posting to Brantford in 1956. He gained a reputation as a quiet, gentle, but effective priest, with a great sense of humour. Through him the youth of the parish became much more involved, as assistants, in the services.

**The Reverend Frank Tomkinson** [1969 – 1974] was a Welshman, who is fondly remembered by his Church Board for his annual feast of prime roast beef and Yorkshire pudding. Discussions of the need of an extension to the Church during Reverend Tomkinson's tenure, were discussed but finally vetoed by the congregation.

**The Reverend Robert Bennett** [1974 – 1975] was given responsibility for the parish of St. John's while serving as Curate to the Rector of Trinity Church, Simcoe. He was soon ordained a priest at Trinity, later to be made a Canon, and still later he became Archdeacon of Brant and still later a Suffragan Bishop of Huron.

**The Reverend Richard Anions** [1975 – 1980] coming from Southampton, proved to be a friendly, outgoing priest, who rapidly gained the confidence and respect of this rural parish. His circle of friends widened significantly when he was named Chaplain of the Hugh Allan Branch, No. 158, Royal Canadian Legion, Port Dover. He also became the Rural Dean for Norfolk County. In 1979 a Chapter of the Brotherhood of Anglican Churchmen was established. The still popular annual Corn Suppers were begun during Reverend Anions tenure and fans were installed in the Church. Leslie Quanbury, long time Warden and Cemetery Superintendent, as well as Church Treasurer for the past eighteen years, retired from these duties on Reverend Anion's watch.

**The Reverend Douglas Fuller** [1980 – 1985] seems to have exchanged his parish in Listowel with Reverend Anions from St. John's. He also followed him in the post of Chaplain, of the Hugh Allan Branch, No158, Royal Canadian Legion, Port Dover. Reverend Fuller had an uncanny knack of embarrassing me, during his sermons, when I attended service at St. John's, by posing direct questions to me from the pulpit. We shared our experiences in the Navy during war time, and this seemed to give him the right, in his mind at least, to single me out over anyone else in the congregation. He was a rather strange man in many ways, but likeable. He attempted to introduce the Contemporary Form of Services, as well, which certainly did not appeal to me.

In 1982, long-time friend of our family and faithful worker for the good of the parish, Mrs. Reg Kent, known to all throughout the County of Norfolk, simply as Edith, died. The following year, in 1983, another of St. John's stalwart defenders and supporters, Leslie Quanbury died.

**The Reverend John Hofland** [1985 – 1989] a native of the Netherlands arrived, complete with his traditional wooden shoes. First ordained in Saskatoon, Reverend Hofland served in the far North, where but for his faithful dog, who awakened him when his house burned to the ground, he might not have survived the conflagration. In 1986 Reverend Richard Anions returned to assist, as guest preacher, in celebrating the 165th Anniversary of the founding of St. John's, Mother Church to all other Anglican churches of the District. Reverend Hofland introduced the very controversial Book of Alternate Services, and also re-established a parish Sunday School which had fallen by the wayside. With the moving of the abandoned Rowan Mills church, Jireh, to Turkey Point for summertime services, it became the responsibility of the rector of St. John's. Thus St. John's became a four-point parish which included Christ Church, Vittoria, Memorial Church, Port Ryerse, St. Andrew's by the Sea, Turkey Point, as well as old St. John's, Woodhouse. Reverend John Hofland retired to Strathroy.

**The Reverend Celia Howard** [1990 – 1992] was the first female rector to serve St. John's, coming as a Deacon. She was ordained while serving this parish, and living in Port Dover with her family. The new electric organ was dedicated during her tenure in memory of Misses Helen, Alice and Victoria Ward, who as daughters of the Reverend James Ward, lived nearby.

**The Reverend John Course** [1992 – 2002] had retired from the ministry to Delhi, but agreed to come to St. John's, as priest, on an interim basis. Memorial Church, Port Ryerse, after a one hundred year association with St. John's became a separate parish. Reverend Course was responsible for new signs for the front of the Church and with his Warden, Everett Lampman, designed, built and installed new leaded-glass windows for the porch. The year long 175th Anniversary Celebrations were launched with a special Harvest Festival Service, with Right Reverend Jack Peck, Bishop of St. Clair, officiating. Archbishop Michael Peers also visited the parish.

### CHURCHES FOUNDED BY REVEREND FRANCIS EVANS, RECTOR OF WOODHOUSE, INCLUDE:

**Christ Church, Vittoria,**

Christ Church was built on the site of the brick Courthouse, built in 1815 and burned in 1825, in 1844. On June 17th, 1844 the cornerstone was well and truly laid, with full masonic honours, with Colonel Rapelje, the Reverend George Salmon, the

*Christ Church, Vittoria*

Reverend Francis Evans and the Reverend J. C. Usher, of Brantford officiating. The church stands today on Lamport Street, in the centre of the village, on a lot 110 feet by 165 feet and set back 106 feet from the street line. It measures 55 feet by 30 feet externally.

Christ Church, Vittoria is reported, in the book by Marian MacRae and Anthony Adamson entitled "Hallowed Walls," as one of the handsomest of the timber churches left standing in Ontario.

They point out that it is built in the Georgian tradition, and displays a number of Regency characteristics. The church is clad with flush-boarding, bevelled on each matching edge, and grooved to give the impression of having the vertical joints of ashlar masonry. The corners were built with much heavier planks to give the impression of stone quoins. When first painted and still wet the whole exterior surface was dashed with fine sand to enhance the appearance of being built of stone. The entrance at the base of the square bell tower, at a later date had two small vestries built on either side of the tower. These one story additions were finished with quoins similar to those on the main building.

There are fine examples of early cabinet work displayed in the altar table, altar rail and the Regency style pulpit, with its flat fil-

*Altar, Christ Church*

*Choir Loft, Christ Church*

lets. The pews which originally had doors enclosing them, are also simply panelled. It is thought that the imitation graining of the pews, to simulate oaken seats, was a much later addition.

When growing up in St. Paul's, Port Dover and particularly, when I was a member of the Junior Choir, I looked forward to the services taken by Canon Cornish in Christ Church, Vittoria, as a bit of an adventure. The whole building had an aura of age that bordered on the spooky in my young mind. The congregation was not large, but being greeted warmly by the Harry Gundry and the Harry Lawrence families, who were long-standing friends of our family, was something to look forward to. As these supporters of Christ Church grew older, the church went into a decline and services became fewer and finally ceased.

On October 1st, 1975 Christ Church, Vittoria was detached from St John's, Port Rowan, where it had been attached some years before, and was attached to St. John's, Woodhouse and Memorial Church, Port Ryerse. It was noted as being closed in 1976, but regular services had been discontinued many years before that.

In March of 1977 I attended as a member, a meeting of the Executive Committee to Synod, for St. Paul's. This proved to be a very impressive committee with Bishop Ragg, Bishop Robinson and Bishop Parke-Taylor, plus 8 Venerable members, 8 Canons and 10 other clergy plus 21 lay persons of the Diocese.

Shortly after my arrival, Reverend Harvey Parker, of Trinity Church, Simcoe, approached me to second a motion he wished to put before the Executive Committee regarding the restoration of Christ Church, Vittoria. He had no time to explain it fully, but assured me he had the consent of a committee of local parishioners for his proposal and as I was the only one on hand from the area at that point, he asked my help in bringing it forward. I agreed, although I had yet to see the motion in its entirety.

At the time Harvey's motion came before the Executive Committee, he read an extensive preamble, some of which made me wonder just what I had, rather hastily, put my name to in the interest of the historic old Vittoria church. The motion itself was even more of a shock to me, for its first point asked that the church be deconsecrated, a detail Harvey had failed to point out to me. The second point asked formal recognition of a seven person committee, to act on behalf of the church. Third, that this committee be empowered to advertise for future uses that might be made of the church. Fourth, they were requesting a grant of $500.00 to expedite the same. There was little discussion.

As it came home to me that the proposal meant that almost any secular use could be made of the old church if this motion passed, I spoke to the motion and objected to the building being deconsecrated. I explained that I wholeheartedly approved of designation by the Ontario Heritage Foundation, and the restoration of the building through this organisation. This had been a part of Reverend Parker's preamble. I also suggested that failing this, the interest from moneys held from bequests to Christ Church over the years, could go a long way toward restoration, and keep the church as an active church property. Needless to say I had "upset Harvey's apple cart" and he fixed me with a most hostile glare during the whole of my presentation, nor did he speak to me for some time thereafter. There was now lively discussion, and Harvey assured those present that the "parishioners of Christ Church" were well aware of his intentions in the motions before us. They were approved.

On May 4th, 1977, an advertisement having been placed in several appropriate papers, the Committee looking into the fate of Christ Church met to discuss the result. Members of the Committee present were Chris Lee, Rector's warden of Trinity, Reverend Harvey Parker, of Trinity, Catherine Smale, of Trinity and a Director of the Ontario Heritage Foundation, and Ruth Loughton of Vittoria, who attended St. John's, Woodhouse. Absent were Reverend Richard Anions, rector of St. John's and Christ Church. James Tyrrell, Lawyer and past Rector's warden of Trinity and Harry Gundry, of Christ Church, Vittoria. Also in attendance were fifteen local Anglicans of Vittoria.

If nothing else the activities of the original Committee had fired the zeal of the local, and hitherto rather inactive, parishioners of Vittoria. They proved quite vociferously angry over the advertisement, which they obviously had been unaware of previously. They, in no way, would sanction their beloved church being deconsecrated. They would like a minimum of ten services to be held annually in Christ Church. They also were sceptical and completely opposed to the proposal that the church be designated under the Ontario Heritage Foundation, declaring that the grandiose scheme of insulation of the building, installation of washrooms and an upgraded heating system were completely unnecessary frills. The meeting adjourned after the following resolution was passed by those present. It read as follows, that: "The Bishop instruct the Rector, Richard Anions, to call a Vestry Meeting of interested Anglicans to appoint Wardens, A Board of

*Joan Barrett attends Harvest Home Service, in Christ Church, Sept. 25th, 2005*

Management and to establish regular services of worship in Christ Church, Vittoria."

On October 12th, 1977, Chris Lee chaired a meeting and reported on it as follows: The parishioners present discussed with Bishop Ragg the services to be held. Doug Trafford would provide an estimate of the cost of repairs. Cath Smale would approach the Ontario Heritage Foundation regarding help and under what terms they might be provided. Harry Gundry agreed to contact potential members of the congregation. Christ Church remained in the Diocesan family of ancient Anglican places of worship.

In the year 2005 the fate of Christ Church is once again in a precarious position. The endowments are barely providing enough to cover upkeep of some $1,500.00 annually. Insurance costs keep increasing, whereas income from interest on endowments has decreased in recent years. Trustees Everett Lampman, Doug and Grace Trafford continue to ensure that at least two services are held each year making the church a "chapel of ease." This designation ensures that the property's tax-free status is ensured. As Doug Trafford points out, however "We are not getting any younger." There is no new blood in evidence in the parish, at this point in time, to ensure the survival of this unique gem in the diocesan crown.

*Interior of Christ Church, Vittoria, on Sept 25th, 2005*

The Norfolk Heritage Committee have recently shown concern for the survival of the 161- year-old Regency-Gothic building. As Chairman Jim Wies points out; "It's rare that the Regency style found its way into church architecture and even rarer that this style found its way into Canada. Architecturally, it's one of the most significant church buildings in Ontario, if not Canada." As Ross Bateman, Heritage Committee member, states; "We'll be looking at fund raising." Then "as long as there are trustees for the church, it has a future."

**Trinity Anglican Church, Simcoe.**

As Simcoe grew in population, the adherents of the Church of England grew impatient for a church of their own within the town. In 1848 a site was chosen on the south-east corner of Colborne and Court Streets. From the sale of clergy reserve lands, subscriptions and donations, enough money was raised to build a rectangular brick building. A square tower was erected on the corner of the building at the north end and by 1850 the building was complete and ready for services. This served the congregation well for the next ten years under the guidance of the Reverend Francis

*Trinity Church, Simcoe*

Evans, of St. John's. Reverend John Gemley became the first permanent Rector of Trinity, following the death of Canon Everett Grasett. Trinity church was established as a separate parish on it's own at that time.

By 1860 the congregation had increased to the point where more accommodation was needed and so a new chancel and two transepts were added to the south end of the resultant nave. The contractors appear to have been Messrs. Thompson and Smith. Catherine Smale, a Simcoe architect with her husband Bud after W.W. II, became very interested in the architectural history of Trinity and tried to ascertain the name of the architect for the 1860 additions. She questioned it having been Thomas Gundry, born in England in 1830, who trained as an architect and engineer in that country. He arrived in Canada about 1853 and the following year is reported to have commenced a survey of Simcoe. He was living in Simcoe at the time, but there is no hard evidence that, although he might have been involved, that he was Trinity's architect. Cath also investigated the possibility of the work being performed by the firm of Fuller and Jones, but without any great success. Regardless of who drew the plans, many were dissatisfied

*Chancel of Trinity Church, Simcoe*

with the result of this addition and finally a new design was put forward with the result that in 1882 the original building was dismantled. This was replaced by a new nave with a Gothic form of Architecture. The church took on its present beautiful cruciform shape at that time.

In the beginning, lighting in the church was by candles and coal-oil lamps. These had to be regularly trimmed, the lamp chimneys cleaned, and their reservoirs topped up with kerosene. Later an acetylene or carbide generator was installed in the basement and the church was lighted by carbide lamps. Before the turn of the 20th century the town installed an artificial gas plant which functioned until the change to natural gas in the early 1900's. Several lamp standards were installed on alternate ends of some of the pews down the central aisle. Fitted with brass sleeves, these were quite ornamental in appearance. Colonel Douglas Stalker laments the fact that these showy fixtures disappeared following the installation of electric lighting. He blames the hastening of their removal to the fact that the late Walter Bradfield, on sitting down under one of these fixtures following the singing of the processional hymn, had the top of the fixture fall off and strike him, painfully, on the top of the head. Mr. Bradfield subsequently became a staunch advocate for the removal of the ornamental standards, post haste.

The impressive vaulted style of the church coupled with the distinctive bell tower in the north-east corner of the nave, immediately catches the eye of anyone coming down Colborne street. A large furnace in the north end of the basement heated both the church and basement Sunday School for many years. The chimney for the furnace was cleverly concealed behind the bell tower and a large circular register in the centre aisle, a short distance inside the narthex, effectively heated the whole church. For many years before the turn of the century, Trinity's bell served not only the church but the citizens of the town as well, as the town bell. A rope hung down the outside of the tower allowing any citizen who noticed a fire in the town to give the alarm to the Fire Department by pulling lustily on the church bell rope. As in all churches a separate bell rope allowed for the tolling of the bell at funerals, one stroke for each year of age of the deceased.

Colonel Stalker also reminds us that most early churches that possessed a pipe organ had to rely on air to coax music from the array of large pipes that were a part of it. In Trinity's case the air was supplied by a large bellows, operated by hand for many years by a stalwart bellows pumper, named Frank. The organ manual was eventually placed at the west side of the chancel not far from Franks station at the large bellows handle. Sometimes on hot Sunday mornings Frank would doze off during the sermon with the result that on its termination there would be no air for the pipe organ. On these occasions an additional duty, for the organist, was to slip out quickly to give Frank a good swift kick. Frank would then spring to life and pump vigorously to build sufficient air pressure to permit the playing of the recessional hymn.

With the installation of a waterworks system in Simcoe in 1907, a water-motor was installed in the church basement alongside the organ bellows. Soon these water motors were installed in the other churches in the town, to the point where the operator at the pumping station had to ensure that there was a full standpipe prior to services on Sunday morning. The pumps, being rather temperamental would often refuse to perform if there was not a full head of water pressure available. With the coming of hydro-electric power in 1915 a much more reliable source of air for the organ pipes was made available. Organ pumpers, though out of work, were assured finally of peaceful slumber throughout the sermon and beyond, if they were so inclined.

The Parish hall was built in 1914 on land acquired directly south of the church. The house on the property was moved westerly and attached to the rear of the hall, thus providing a residence for the verger. The new Hall was financed primarily by donations and was erected to the memory of Canon Richard Hicks, a much beloved rector of the parish. A stage was built at the east end of the hall and a balcony erected at the opposite end. The hall soon became a popular meeting place for many groups and organisations. The stage and balcony were eventually removed and the hall was returned to the form it bears today.

The Trinity church complex has no less than three cornerstones. The 1882 construction is recognised by a stone at the north-east corner of the nave. A cornerstone at the north-east corner of the Parish Hall designates it as the Canon Hicks Memorial Parish Hall. The third cornerstone is placed at the south-east corner of the chancel to commemorate, in 1948, the one hundredth anniversary of the building of Trinity Church, at which time the chancel was extended in a southerly direction and the beautiful Memorial Chapel added to the west of the chancel. The Canon Mixer room was added at this time as well.

On the completion of Trinity Church, Simcoe, it was added to the charge of the Mother Church, St. John's, and thus the Reverend Francis Evans became the first rector. Reverend Francis Evans died in 1858 and the beautiful memorial window above the altar in Trinity Anglican Church is an on-going reminder and memorial to the tremendous work carried out in the Rectory of Woodhouse and County of Norfolk by the Reverend Francis Evans, our first resident clergyman.

**Trinity Anglican Church, Waterford.**

The present Trinity Church stands on what began as a burial ground for the village of Waterford. Prior to 1818 a nucleus of an Anglican congregation existed in the village but it was served intermittently by travelling missionaries as they passed through the district. The land for the church was donated by Jacob Lodor, who we first hear of as owning the tavern at Turkey Point where in 1803 the first attempt was made to establish an Anglican presence in the Long Point Country. At the time of Lodor's donation of the one acre plot, which he gave jointly to the Anglicans and the Presbyterians of the community, he was the owner of a general store in Waterford.

Jacob Lodor's wife was an invalid, confined to her bedroom above the store, while the rest of their living quarters were in the back of the store. One very hot, humid day at noon hour Jacob feeling sorry for his bed-ridden wife, gathered her in his arms and brought her down to the dining room to enjoy her noon meal and the company of her family. During their meal, the room grew dark as a severe thunderstorm developed. As a vivid flash of lightning crackled over their heads an immediate deafening thunderclap was heard. Within minutes a customer appeared from the store looking very dishevelled, with burns to his face and hands. He reported

*Trinity Anglican Church, Waterford*

that the store had been struck and that several barrels of gunpowder had taken a direct hit. The force of the resultant explosion had completely demolished Mrs. Lodor's bedroom and blown the roof entirely clear of the building. As a thank offering for the deliverance of his wife from an untimely death a grateful Job Lodor donated the acre of land jointly for the Anglican and Presbyterian adherents of the community. It was first used by them as a burial ground.

Eventually the recipients of this generous donation of land built a small frame church. It is not known how long joint services continued in this first edifice, nor what the fate of it was, but it could not have served for any great length of time. The Lodor plot then returned to being a burial ground, and its significance as a church site was forgotten.

In 1852 Leonard Sovereign reserved an acre of land at the head of the 7th Concession road which he deeded to the Rt. Rev. Dr. John Strachan, Bishop of Toronto, for an Anglican church. The Brantford Courier of September 4th, 1852 reports – "The laying of the corner stone of the new Episcopal Church, Waterford, took place on Tuesday last under most propitious circumstances. The Rev. M. Boomer, B. A., of Galt kindly read the prayers, the Rev. Frank Evans, Rector of Woodhouse, took the Lessons, and, as was announced, Rev. W. Betteridge of Woodstock, preached an appropriate sermon." Mrs. W. Matthews then layed the corner stone, following which Rev. Mr. Stinson and all those present "repaired to Mr. W. Matthews' where a rich collation was laid out."

The church built in 1852 was apparently of shoddy construction and a severe storm demolished it in 1867. The lot was subsequently sold. To accommodate their immediate needs Trinity Church purchased a brick building, on Lot 21 of West street, from the Free Baptists. The congregation was small and services seem to have declined. In 1868 land was acquired at 23 Church street, and the congregation began saving for a new building. It is known that the Rev. Samuel Harris was the incumbent from 1862 to 1875. Rev. John A. Ball served from 1882 to 1884 followed by Rev. E. Softley from 1884 to 1886.

No record of regular services follow, although the rector of Woodhouse, Rev. W. Davis took occasional services until his death in 1890. In 1893 Ven. Archdeacon W. A. Young, Rector of Woodhouse, began regular services which he continued until his retirement in 1908. The congregation relocated a number of times in other locations in the village before returning to their present location in 1909.

For many, many years the church had been ignorant of its claim to the cemetery lot donated nearly a century before by Job Lodor. When they eventually found out about it action was taken culminating in an Act of the Provincial Legislature granting the acre to the Rector and Wardens as a site for a Church of England. Wishing to be assured of clear title, the matter was referred to the Pastor and Trustees of the Presbyterian Church in Simcoe. Rev. W. J. Day, Frank Reid, G. J. McKiee and J. B. Jackson, on being informed of their dilemma, graciously recommended that the Presbytery assign all rights and title to the said land to the Rector and Wardens of Trinity Church, Waterford. A large number of the graves had been relocated in Greenwood Cemetery, when it was established in 1872. The remaining graves were moved prior to the building of the present church.

Progress was slow but chiefly due to the efforts of Dr. Fred S. Snyder, Dr. William McGuire, Arthur Cowdry, J. Mitchell, and Arthur Bowlby the present church was built, in 1909, on the one acre lot on the north-east corner of Main and Temperance streets.

The cost was eleven thousand dollars, which included the installation of a pipe organ.

Eight years later on Tuesday, September 4th, 1917 headlines in the Brantford Courier read: "Trinity Church, Waterford, Consecrated Last Sunday." The church, finally debt free, was dedicated by Rt. Rev. David Williams, Bishop of Huron. He was assisted by The Venerable Archdeacon W. A. Young and Rev. James Ward. The congregation celebrated being finally debt-free with a congregational supper in the town hall.

The Gothic style of the church was designed after an Anglican church in England, leading to its being touted as "the Cathedral of Western Ontario." It was constructed of coarse cement block, with the arched interior being of oak and plaster. Everything was new and of most modern design. It can accommodate a congregation of two hundred. The basement accommodates a meeting hall and a kitchen. A Rectory was added later.

A chronological list of Early Rectors to have served the Waterford parish to the time of Reverend David G. Rees follows. Reverend Rees in 1960 published "A History of Trinity Church, Waterford." This rare and delightfully written little history was kindly loaned to me by Mrs. Douglas Murton. It is to Betty Murton, a daughter of William Hammond of Woodhouse, that I am indebted for much of the above information.

| | |
|---|---|
| Prior to 1818 Itinerant Missionaries | 1821-1852 Occasional services by Rev. F. Evans. |
| 1862-1875 Rev. Samuel Harris | 1882-1884 Rev. John Ball |
| 1884-1886 Rev. E. Softley | 1886-1890 Occasional services by Rev. W. Davis |
| 1893-1908 Ven. Archdeacon Young. | 1908-1917 Rev. James Ward |
| 1917-1920 Rev. F. Anderson | 1920-1929 Rev. F. G. Rickard |
| 1929-1930 Rev. M. A. Hunt | 1931-1934 Rev. T. B. Howard |
| 1934-1942 Rev. T. H. Inns | 1942-1943 Rev. Ll. C. Edwards-Graham |
| 1943-1944 Rev. J. C. Coles | 1944-1949 Rev. F. W. Davis |
| 1949-1954 Rev. Alan Gardiner | 1954-1957 Rev. V. K. Blake |
| 1958- Rev. D. G. Ll. Rees | |

## St. John's Anglican Church, Port Rowan.

Like other Anglican communities in Norfolk County, the Port Rowan area was served from early times by itinerant priests.

*Rev. William Wood, first Rector of St. John's, Port Rowan*

As Long Point was a naval base for the British during the War of 1812, it is reported that Anglicans of Port Rowan were present to supply the spiritual needs of the naval ratings aboard the British ships. Port Rowan's first permanent rector was Reverend William Wood. He was the son of Reverend John Wood of Swanwick, Derbyshire, England, who came to Canada in 1834. In 1855 William was sent to Port Rowan, as a Catechist, to establish a permanent parish. He held his first service in a rectangular brick courthouse on Easter Sunday, 1855 and the following Sunday a Sunday School of thirty-four pupils was begun. Services continued to be held there until 1858.

In 1858 a small frame church was built on the front road leading to Port Royal on the west side of the village. William Wood was ordained that same year by the Right Reverend Dr. Cronyn and made a fully qualified priest in 1859. The new church was opened in December of 1858. The Select Vestry met for the first time in April of 1859. Dr. Phelan and William Stephenson were the first church wardens. On Wednesday, April 29th, 1862 the Bishop consecrated St. John's, Port Rowan and confirmed the first class of fourteen candidates. In 1863 the congregation installed a new bell in the church tower.

On July 1st, 1864 the Reverend H. I. Evans was appointed to assist Reverend William Wood and continued for one year, to July 1st, 1865. In July of 1866, the Reverend Daniel Dease took charge of St. John's and William Wood withdrew to the church in St. Williams, due to ill health. In 1877 St. John's, Port Rowan was ren-

74 *The Parish of St. Paul's*

ovated and in 1879 the Reverend William Wood resigned as Rector. The Reverend J. Coy was appointed as his replacement but withdrew soon afterwards. From August 16th, 1878 to July 26th, 1879, Reverend R. S. Asbury appears to have been officially in

*St. John's Church, Port Rowan*

*Interior of St. John's, Port Rowan*

*Memorial Window, St. John's, Port Rowan*

charge. He was succeeded as Rector by Reverend E. Stewart-Jones.

Under Reverend Stewart-Jones St. John's flourished. The exterior of the original frame church was covered by a brick veneer and the interior was beautifully renovated throughout with tongue-and-groove sweet chestnut. During this period the parishioners met for services in the Masonic Hall on Main street. St. John's was re-opened for services in 1883. In 1884 Reverend E. Stewart-Jones left for Niagara, to be replaced by his brother, Captain Bailey Jones, who was succeeded in turn, by Reverend Mr. Freeman, in July, 1885.

In February, 1886 Reverend J. A. Ball took charge until October, 1887 when he was replaced by Reverend William Stout. The Reverend Stout resigned in 1889. The Reverend R. W. Johnstone was appointed to St. John's on February 8th, 1890 and remained until his resignation at Easter of 1893. In June of 1893 Reverend Arthur Shore was appointed and served for nine years until 1903. The Reverend C. W. Sanders followed as rector from June 1903 to June of 1905. Reverend Horace Bray took charge in 1905 until February of 1911, when he left to take charge in Hespeler.

**Jireh Anglican Church, Rowan Mills.**

From a family history by Margaret Isobel Frazer, a grand daughter of Butler Hutchinson and wife of Mr. Wales Candee Brewster, of Arlington, Virginia, we learn that:

"William Hutchinson and his son Alexander and their families took up land about 1798, four miles north-west of Port Rowan, west of Big Creek. [at Rowan Mills] Alex was killed in the War of 1812 and his son Butler Hutchinson inherited the farm, known as "Rose Hill Farm."

"Butler Hutchinson, his wife and nine girls developed Rose Hill into a very beautiful place. There was a large circular driveway bordered with trees and flowering shrubs, leading to an inner lawn bordered with gardens of every flower imaginable. There were over ninety varieties of roses – climbing, pillar, bush and moss roses of every shade. There were also many different species of lilacs, lilies, ferns etc., and flowering fruit trees as well as a towering grove of pine trees."

This section of the township was growing fast and the families wanted a church nearer than Port Rowan. The Reverend William Wood of St. John's, Port Rowan, began holding services in the schoolhouse in Rowan Mills, on Big Creek in the early 1860's. This school was on the corner of the farm established by William Hutchinson, now owned by Butler Hutchinson. Margaret Brewster's account continues: "One Saturday morning [in 1869] the little schoolhouse burned to the ground. The Rector, Reverend William Wood, started out as usual to drive from Port Rowan for morning services. He met a farmer driving into town. 'It is no use your going out, Mr. Wood, the schoolhouse burned down.' The Rector thought this over for a minute; then said, 'Never mind about the schoolhouse. You just follow me. The Lord will provide.'

Other farmers, who had started in to town, turned and joined the procession. When he came to Grandfather Hutchinson's place, he gave a cheery command and all the teams turned in the long driveway. They decided to hold the service on the lawn. Mother, just a young girl then, pushed the piano over to the parlour door that opened onto the porch, and the young singers stood out on the porch to lead in the hymns.

Mr. Wood told them the story of Abraham and his readiness

to sacrifice his only son and his boundless faith in God. 'God's promise to Abraham is as real today as it was then, Oh Jehovah Jireh, the Lord will provide, if we, like Abraham, are willing to make sacrifices. What will you give to help God's Kingdom in this Community?'

Butler Hutchinson immediately offered the land and timber to build a Church, and others offered to help with supplies and labour and the church, named "Jireh", was built. All the Hutchinson girls helped to beautify the little church. Some embroidered stoles, hangings, and altar clothes, some bought leather lectern books. One daughter left her portion of land to Jireh, another left a memorial window."

"The two who worked most for its success were Amelia Breadon and Lorenza Morton. Amelia played the organ for many years, taught in the Sunday School, encouraged good singing and reading among the country boys and girls and worked hard to supply them with books and pictures. They could not afford palms, but Amelia used pussy-willows for the children for a Palm Sunday procession. She taught them to weave garlands for Christmas decorations, using wild fruits and berries for colour. In the summer the church was always fragrant with roses from Rose Hill. We, as children, carried up baskets of them every Saturday and arranged them for the service.

Lorenza Morton inherited Rose Hill Farm as her share of the Estate and it was there that the Sunday School picnics were held - a joyous occasion. She gave generously of her time and money to keep Jireh Church active as a community centre for God's work. Bishop Baldwin always stayed at Rose Hill. I remember hearing him say as he looked around the flower-bordered lawn, 'This, to me, is Paradise!'

When Mrs. Morton died, a farmer bought Rose Hill Farm. He tore up the roses, cut down the trees, ploughed under the hundreds of bulbs and planted a field of rye. That is the story of so many of the fine old homes established by our pioneer ancestors, who loved beauty and who wanted to keep their churches and other cultural activities alive in their community."

Rowan Mills was the terminus of the wooden railroad of the firm of DeBlackiere and Farmer, which carried the big pine out of the Venison creek valley and area, to their mill in Rowan Mills, or, in the case of some eighty foot logs, dumped them into Big Creek to be floated to the Inner Bay and rafted, to be towed by tugs to a saw mill in the Buffalo area, at Tonawanda, New York , for sawing into eighty-foot timbers, many of them for export to Britain. Still others were rafted and towed all the way to Montreal for use as spars and masts by the ship building industry, or for transport overseas.

Mr. DeBlackiere and Mr. Hutchinson supplied the materials and labour to build the attractive frame church, which opened for services on the donated lot from "Rose Hill Farm," in 1870. The interior of the church was lined with tongue-and-groove sweet chestnut. On October 14th, 1870, a few short months after its construction, the church was dedicated. The incumbent's text at the opening of the new church was taken from Genesis, Chapter 22, Verse 14 : "Jehovah Jireh! The Lord will Provide." The name Jireh for the church came from the same text. For the next sixty plus years Jireh was attended by the Hutchinson, Chamberlain, Lounsbury, Poole, Rokeby, Townsend and Trickett families.

A final note [about 1960] is added by another Grand daughter of Butler Hutchinson, Mrs. W. Edgar Bates, whose mother was the youngest of the daughters, Amelia Breadon.

*Jireh Church, Rowan Mills, now St. Andrews-by-the-Lake, Turkey Point*

"When I drove out to see it [Jireh Church] a few years ago, I was so unhappy to see the neglect and utter desolation of the whole neighbourhood. Many of the Hutchinson's, who built and worked for Jireh, are buried in St. John's, Woodhouse, so it is not inappropriate for Jireh to be moved to Turkey Point, not far from our "beloved dead." Jireh's east window was put in by Ruth Hutchinson Starr, one of Grandfather's nine girls. Ruth was the widow of Reverend Reginald Starr, D. D. There is a memorial to him in the Cathedral in London, where they are buried, and a pulpit to his memory in the Brantford church, where he was Rector years ago. He later served in several parishes in New York. After his death his wife gave the memorial Medical bay — altar, windows and rose-window — at the cathedral Church of St. John the Divine, in New York City."

**St. Andrews-by-the-Lake, Turkey Point.**

In 1946 the forlorn little Jireh church, of the once thriving hamlet of Rowan mills, which is now only a memory, stood abandoned west of the place the Concession road crosses Big Creek, at what is now known to locals as "three bridges." For the previous twenty years the Reverend T. B. Holland, of St. John's, Woodhouse, and Reverend D. J. Cornish, of St. Paul's, Port Dover had taken summer services at Turkey Point, during the summer months. Their "church" was a simple platform built on the beach with benches placed in front for their congregation. There was no shelter from the elements, the often noisy revellers nearby, or from the voracious mosquitoes.

Canon Cornish, with the encouragement of Bishop Luxton, was instrumental in having the Jireh church moved to Turkey Point. The collections, totalling $50.00, from the Turkey Point services helped to finance the moving of the Jireh church in 1947, by Harry Gamble of Port Dover, to its present location just west of the new road into the beach strip. Unfortunately during the move the bell-tower and bell fell off. There is still a bit of mystery as to why the bell was not recovered from the wreckage and replaced on the church in its new location. Now known as St. Andrews-by-the-Lake, the picturesque little church caters to all denominations who wish to attend of a Sunday, near the little stream flowing to the Lake from the Turkey Point marsh.

Moneys left by the Reverend Andrew Jamieson, a missionary of Walpole Island, in Lake St. Clair, helped to cover the expenses of purchasing the lot and cottage, $2,200. and the adjoining empty lot,$600. to provide a location for the church. Other expenses included the cost of moving, $1,000. Building a foundation, $1,800. as well as painting, repair, and purchase of used seating, which added another $1,057. To the total expenditure.

Twenty-one years later, to the delight of Canon Cornish now 92 years of age, the Jireh church bell was recovered and pealed out its welcome to all for a service of dedication to its return home. Canon Cornish was present to help officiate as Rt. Rev. George N. Luxton, Bishop of Huron, dedicated the bell, comfortably ensconced in its impressive new bell tower at St. Andrews-by-the-Lake.

## St. Williams Anglican Church, St. Williams.

The third charge, under the Reverend William Wood, of Port Rowan, was the tiny parish of St. Williams, a mile north of the early settlement of Cope's Landing, on the north shore of the Inner Bay of Long Point. An English gentleman, William Nevett, deserves much of the credit for the founding of the St. Williams Anglican Church in 1866, built on a plot of land donated to the parish by the Reverend William Wood.

William Nevett, son of William & Elizabeth

*St. Williams Church*

*Rev. Tony Boumeester makes the author welcome to the Anglican Church, St. Williams*

Nevett, was born on October 20th, 1821. He grew up in "Westgate", Louth, Lincolnshire, where he received a good education before joining the East Indiaman Clipper ship "Larkin" as Midshipman. In 1849 William Nevett immigrated to Canada, where he married Elsie McCall, of Vittoria. Being independently wealthy William was able to indulge in his many interests, including horticulture, biology, meteorology and photography. His home soon became a show piece with its spacious lawns and attractive flower-beds. Soon his influence was felt throughout the village as he planted trees and flowers along St. William's streets.

With an excellent microscope he studied specimens of snakes, amphibians, insects and plants that he collected. A talking crow, Jim, entertained his visitors and family for many years with its witty comments and antics. He also made daily observations of the weather, noting wind direction and speed, barometric pressure and temperature variations with minimum-maximum thermometers. One of these was wired to ring a bell if either frost or fire were to occur. He was also an accomplished amateur photographer.

William Nevett played an active role in the establishment of the Anglican church and his influence is to be seen in its pleasing

*Royal Coat of Arms over entrance to the nave of church, said to have been presented by the Duke of Wellington, while a guest at the Long Point Company*

English-style architecture. Inside the church are two tablets displaying the Royal Coat-of-Arms. These are copies of identical tablets to be found in the Anglican church in Louth, England, Nevett's boyhood home.

By 1865-66, through the leadership of Reverend Wood and William Nevitt, the Anglicans of St. Williams, had mustered the determination and the finances to build the attractive frame church, lined in its interior with the warm tongue-and-groove sweet chestnut, that until the 1930's grew so abundantly in the Carolinian forests of Norfolk County. Rev. William Wood, due to ill health, had semi-retired to St. Williams in 1866 and was able to give his undivided attention to the construction of the new church.

The church was opened on December 30th, 1866. By 1870 regular services were being conducted by Reverend William Wood, and the day following the dedication of the new Jireh church, on October 15th, 1870, St Williams Anglican Church was also dedicated. By 1896 seventeen families made up the congregation, among them Walter & Alice McCall, Bruce & Beatrice McCall, John & Sarah Brock, William & Elsie Nevett, Frank & Clara Mason, John & Helen Fielding, Alfred & Nettie Walters, Whitney & Helen Smith, Charles & Minnie Woodward, Warren & Elvira MacDonald, Jane Ann Woodward and Ann Fenton.

## Port Ryerse Memorial Church

With the erection of St. John's church, Woodhouse, in 1827 the good people living between Port Dover and Vittoria finally had a permanent place of worship. By 1862, however, many of the Anglicans of Port Ryerse responded enthusiastically to the efforts of Major Edward Powers Ryerse to establish weekly open air services in his yard near the little burial ground to the south of his prestigious home overlooking the creek and harbour. These services were taken by Reverend Maurice Scollard Baldwin, newly appointed rector of St' Paul's Church, Port Dover.

As time passed the location of these services was moved under the apple trees to the west of where the church now stands. As the site proved favourable a desk was provided for the preacher and planks set on blocks of wood were set out for the comfort of the little congregation. As the weather was not always cooperative the location for the services was soon moved to a large room in the home of Charles Shellburg. The Reverend R. V. Rogers of Christ Church, Vittoria, was taking the services by this time.

*Carl Ryerse & Dr. Bannister at the dedicationof the Lieut. Col. Samuel Ryerse plaque in the Memorial Church churchyard, Port Ryerse*

When Walter Holmwood was appointed Harbour Master of Port Ryerse, in 1865, he and his wife as staunch supporters of the Church of England, encouraged the thinking of many others that it was time to build a permanent place of worship in the village. By 1869 a building committee consisting of Reverend R. V. Rogers, E. P. Ryerse, Walter Holmwood and H. Leaney was formed to raise funds to build a church as a memorial to the founder of the settlement, Colonel Samuel Ryerse, whose grave was but a few feet west of the proposed location for the church. They wasted no time in issuing the following proclamation:

"It is proposed to erect a Church in connection with the Diocese of Huron for members of the Protestant Episcopal Church. Port Ryerse promises to be a place of importance although now consisting of a population of 200, a majority of whom are either members of, or friendly to, and attendants on the ministry of the Reverend R. V. Rogers. Believing the present to be a very favourable opportunity, which, if not embraced might never return, the Committee earnestly and respectfully entreat the aid of friends in general, and especially the descendants of the late Colonel Samuel Ryerse."

The response was most gratifying as many pledged to pay specific amounts to the fund on or before November 1st, 1869. Edward P. Ryerse pledged $200.00 toward a burial ground reserve, plus $25.00. Holmwood and Leaney pledged $50.00 & $20.00 respectively, and some twenty other supporters pledged lesser amounts. William Pope's brother, Horatio Pope, made a donation of $100.00. The church was built in 1869 - 70. One of the builders was John R. Gunton of Vittoria, who walked every day from his home to the site and each evening walked home again. It was customary in those days to begin work on any such project at daybreak, prepare your meals on site, and lay down your tools and return home when you could no longer see to work. Memorial Church was consecrated in October, 1870.

The following statement indicates that Memorial Church was built to honour the pioneers of the settlement: " who first braved

*Sketch of Memorial Church, Port Ryerse, by Elizabeth Barrett, 1973*

the loneliness, privations and perils of the unknown wilderness of Upper Canada, to create new homes in a strange land for themselves and their children, who cleared forests, blazed the roads, bridged the fords, drained the swamps, introduced British institutions, laws and ordered liberty; and men and women alike, sacrificed and endured, that their inheritors might enjoy in peace and comfort the fruits of their toil and in grateful recognition of the debt to wise leaders and trusted councillors of original pioneers at or near Port Ryerse."

The following names with their accomplishments are a part of the above memorial tablet:

"***Samuel Ryerse, U. E. L.****, a captain in the New Jersey Volunteers, who settled here in 1794, And became Lieutenant of the County of Norfolk, organiser of the administration of London District, first Lieutenant-Colonel of Norfolk Militia, first judge of the district, buried here in 1812.*

***Joseph Ryerson, U. E. L.****, brother of Samuel Ryerse was also an officer in the Revolutionary War. He was first sheriff and a Lieutenant-Colonel of Norfolk Militia in the war of 1812-14. Also his sons, George, William, John. Edgerton and Edway who became pioneer*

Methodist preachers. Edgerton is renowned as the founder of the public school system of Upper Canada as well. His second eldest, Samuel, stayed at home on the farm.

**Robert Nichol**. A native of Scotland was a Lieutenant-Colonel of the 2nd Regiment of the Norfolk Militia. An M.P.P. for the County of Norfolk, and Quarter-Master General of Militia for Upper Canada throughout the war of 1812-14.

**Thomas Welch, U. E. L.**, was the first Registrar of Norfolk from 1797 to 1810. He was named first Clerk of the Peace and Registrar of the Surrogate Court of London District in 1800. He was District Judge in 1810.

**Francis Leigh Welch**, son of Thomas, was Registrar of Deeds for Norfolk County from 1810 until 1884.

**Donald McCall**, a native of Argyleshire, fought as a soldier under Wolfe at the taking of Louisburg in 1758 and at the fall of Quebec in 1759. He was also a member of the expedition that in 1761 took over the French forts of the Upper Lakes. During a skirmish which took his patrol inland to the present-day Walsh area, he saw what he considered an ideal location for his home. In 1796, some 35 years later, he returned as a U. E. L. to claim it and build a snug cabin on Young Creek, south of Walsh, in Charlotteville Township."

This lengthy inscription on the tablet which was dedicated in 1926, in Memorial Church continues: "*who by their service in peace and war, aided conspicuously in fostering and transmitting in this region the spirit of loyal devotion to Canada and the Empire. This tablet is dedicated October 1926 by a grateful posterity.*"

The faith of the building committee in the growth of the village was more than justified as it had become an important shipping centre. In fact it could claim the best natural harbour on the north shore and improvements to the harbour had only then begun. Several new warehouses were built, harbour improvements and better wharves were constructed, and the first harbour Master, in the person of William Mercer Wilson had been appointed. A thriving ship-building industry was also in operation with David Foster building schooners on the beach west of the harbour. It was estimated that in 1871 seven and a half million board feet of lumber was shipped from the Port as well as a tremendous tonnage of grain, as the long lines of farm waggons would attest in the fall of the year. No-one could foresee the depletion of the seemingly endless forest cover in Norfolk, nor the coming of the Canada Southern Railroad in 1873, at that time. This spelled the gradual decline of the shipping industry over the next twenty years with the resultant decline in importance of the Port and its' inhabitants.

I am indebted to Colonel Douglas Stalker, whose father Robert Stalker operated the Blacksmith's shop in Port Ryerse for many years, for two stories that relate indirectly to churches. The blacksmith's brother had studied in the U. S. of A. to become a Doctor and before graduation he had to provide himself with a human skeleton for demonstration. To buy one ready-made, so to speak, was an expensive proposition. He managed to acquire a cadaver from an Erie graverobber quite reasonably, however. Telegraphing to his brother to have a large kettle of water boiling on the forge fire, he arrived just after dusk in a small sail boat with a bulky, canvas-covered object trussed up securely, as in a sailor's hammock.

This rather bulky package was quietly and swiftly transferred to the Blacksmith's shop where a large hog-scalding kettle of water was boiling merrily. The shop to all appearances was closed. The corpse was quickly unwrapped and lowered carefully into the kettle. The brothers had only to keep a brisk fire burning until the bones of the unfortunate victim emerged glistening white and devoid of all flesh. The conspirators relaxed to visit and catch up on each others activities while the large, boiling hog-scalding kettle did its work.

Suddenly their visit was interrupted by loud hammering on the shop doors. The visitor was a farmer who had been imbibing late at the local tavern. He had seen the glow of the fire in the shop and decided he could save a trip to the port the next day if Mr. Stalker would give him the ploughshares he had left for re-tipping, that night. As he was persistent in his demands, Robert Stalker finally opened the door wide enough to hand out the shares to his customer.

Not satisfied with that reception, the farmer lurched inside, and seeing the boiling kettle on the forge demanded to know just what they were cooking. Dissatisfied with the smithy's rather evasive reply he suddenly grabbed a long hook and plunged it into the grey, frothing brew. Hooking into something solid he pulled it to the surface. This action exposed a human skull that seemed to leer from over the edge of the blackened kettle at the unsuspecting farmer. He passed out cold on the dirt floor of the shop.

The brothers quickly gathered up their inebriated visitor, layed him out in his waggon with the plough shares beside him, and drove to the nearby hotel. Here they located a friend who was willing to drive their customer- "who had suddenly taken ill, from too much whisky" - home.

Returning to the shop they continued their grisly vigil until the bones emerged in the early morning hours completely devoid of all flesh. Unfortunately they were anything but white, being a dull grey in colour and in places quite black. They decided the only answer to the problem was to bleach them in the coming summer's sun for two or three months. Armed with two large sacks of the bones and an extension ladder they climbed to the top of the hill behind the shop where the white outline of the Anglican Memorial church, built some ten years before, gleamed in the

*The congregation in Port Ryerse worshiped under the skull & cross-bones, by Elizabeth Barrett Milner*

moonlight. The bones were carefully layed out on the enclosed belfry roof. As my story-teller concluded, the good people of Port Ryerse, quite unwittingly, worshipped under the skull and crossbones throughout that long, hot summer.

The second tale also involved the unsavoury practice of grave robbing. Two rather uncouth characters arrived in the village one evening to put their team and open democrat into the drive shed of the Port Ryerse hotel. They wasted no time in entering the tavern to refresh themselves after a rather strenuous evening's work. It was a cold evening and one refreshing drink of whisky led to another. Meanwhile two adventurous boys of the village, seeing the travellers, who were unknown to them, enter the tavern decided to investigate the lumpy cargo in the back of their democrat. Upon raising the heavy tarpaulin that covered it they discovered to their surprise that it hid a large corpse. Immediately they devised a plan and after carefully removing and hiding the body they crawled in under the tarp.

They had only a short time to wait before the two strangers appeared flourishing a bottle to sustain them for the balance of their cold journey. Soon they were heading north out of the village at a brisk trot and taking regular turns at sampling the contents of the bottle they shared. One of them feeling no pain and in a lame excuse at a joke, turned toward the back of the rig and raising the whisky bottle offered their passenger a drink. As the tarp suddenly rose toward him a pale hand emerged to grasp the bottle and a hollow voice allowed that: "I sure could use a stiff drink right now!"

It was reported later by the stowaways that they had to move quickly to get the horses under control as the owners of the democrat could not get out of it fast enough. As they turned the rig back toward the village, the boys had a glimpse of the grave robbers disappearing in opposite directions into the cover of the darkness of the night, on each side of the road.

Grave robbing was much more common than we would like to imagine in the nineteenth century. Medical knowledge was evolving rapidly and serious young medical students required a steady supply of cadavers for both demonstration and practice. Very few of the general public understood this need, and everyone regarded dissection as ghoulish and sickening. As a consequence of this a lively trade in grave robbing had developed in the Long Point Country and elsewhere.

The congregation of Memorial Church had dwindled so badly by the latter part of the 1890's that the church was closed. Regular services were resumed in July of 1909, by Reverend James Ward, rector of St. John's, Woodhouse. He covered the two point charge for the next twenty years. This was continued by the Reverend T. B. Holland. [1930 - 1941] Among historic mementoes preserved in the church to this day are the original large key to the front door, cut by hand by the father of Robert Stalker, both of whom served the area as blacksmiths. Their shop stood below the church to the west for many years. Also retained are six beautiful antique brass chandeliers, each carrying two coal-oil lamps. The original solid walnut alter was re-discovered and lovingly restored, to be re-dedicated in 1956, by Bishop Luxton. Mr. Leslie Adams, a long-time warden of Memorial church, made a replica of the original prayer desk to go with the original pulpit.

In July of 1939 a gala Garden Party was held in the grounds and gardens of Mr. Arthur Lea and Dr. Alan Jackson. It proved most successful in raising funds for the much needed renovations of the old church. A highlight of the afternoon was the raffling of a painting of the historic church by Miss Helen Straith which had been donated by her. The winner was Mrs. Robert Gunton whose great grandfather donated the land upon which the church stands, and whose forebearers are buried in the church yard. The sum of almost $200.00 raised by the garden party made it possible to put a new roof on the church and do other needed repairs.

A marble plaque in the church honours Arthur C. Lea, who donated land to restore the original churchyard to the parish. Among the first burials in the adjoining churchyard are those of the Port's founder, Samuel Ryerse and his wife. On first viewing the stream and fertile banks of the future site of the hamlet, from the Lake, Samuel Ryerse is said to have exclaimed that; "Here I wish to live and die." A Provincial historic site plaque to the north of the church, describes his achievements and a lichen-covered, simple stone behind it, bears testimony to his wish having been granted. Also buried in the little churchyard are Major Edward Powers Ryerse and his wife, Martha. Nearby a flat stone serves as a memorial to three unknown British soldiers, who died while serving at Fort Norfolk, above the beaches and marsh of Turkey Point.

Long after the burial grounds were closed the body of Theodore Brown was laid to rest here. Theodore, a negro slave, had accompanied his owner from Buffalo to Niagara many years before, where he met and was persuaded to seek his freedom from slavery by Major E. P. Ryerse. A powerful man and an accomplished boxer, Brown maintained law and order, among the seamen and stevedores, on the docks of Port Ryerse for his new employer, Major Ryerse. He had been granted a plot of land by Ryerse opposite the church, but it had not been registered at the time and he lost it. Upon his death sympathetic residents of the hamlet ensured his proper burial in the Anglican churchyard. His son Albert, a well-loved and accomplished blacksmith, of Simcoe, will be remembered by many local residents.

About 1970 a member of the congregation of Memorial church, Mrs. David Goodlet, wrote under the title "Times Change! But the Church Goes On." the following poignant account:

> "The grey, rundown church perched atop the hill, stood as a lonely sentinel, staring down on the forsaken village of Port Ryerse. The years pass quickly. One hundred years ago this little church was the hub of a thriving community. The village boasted five hotels, sawmills, smithy and general store: a bustling port where farmers came from miles around to ship their grain via the great lakes.
> Times changed. The port closed, activities ceased, buildings collapsed, only the store remained open every summer to serve the people who holidayed at their cottages nestled among the hills and along the sandy beaches. Every summer the port came alive and the little church was opened for Sunday service. But there was never enough money to carry out needed repairs. Money was barely sufficient to repair windows broken by errant boys for which the idle church was a perfect target. It was not

uncommon to hear the church bell rung in the middle of the night, by teenagers looking for amusement.

Times change once more. Returning veterans found a housing shortage in their home town of Simcoe, so one by one the cottages were purchased and made into winterised homes. The idea caught on and many families now liven up the Port during the winter and the general store remains open. The Church has once again become the centre of the community. The residents of different denominations, but with one purpose in mind, rallied. There was a painting bee, a repairing bee and a house-cleaning bee. A Sunday School was formed and each family shouldered their responsibilities in order to keep the church going. Because of their interest, other people who in the past had worshipped at the little church in Port Ryerse, came forward and made it possible for Memorial Church to become one of the most beautiful churches in Huron Diocese.

The setting now on a moonlight night shows a shining white church and steeple keeping watch over a small community, where the twinkling lights show that families have once again found haven in Port Ryerse. Memorial Church has been adorned with loving hands, reminding one of a gracious old lady who has fulfilled her struggling duties toward her Lord and is now serenely welcoming people into her quiet sanctuary where there is tangible evidence of what can be accomplished through steadfast faith and perseverence."

# Chapter Five

# St. Paul's Church, Port Dover

**INSCRIPTION**
This corner-stone of
St. Paul's Church, Port Dover
was laid by Maria Sophia,
Wife of the Reverend Francis Evans,
First Rector of Woodhouse, and Rural Dean
of the Brock and Talbot Districts;
June 21st, Anno Domini 1852
in the sixteenth year of the reign
of her gracious Majesty Queen Victoria,
The Right Honourable the Earl of Elgin and Kincardine
being Governor General of British North America,
The Honourable and Right Reverend
John Strachan, L.L.D.
Being Bishop of the Diocese of Toronto
and the Reverend Francis Evans
Incumbent

Thomas Waters, John A. Bowlby, Frederick Haycock,
and James McCoy, Esqs., Building Committee.

With the dedication and laying of the Cornerstone, as shown by the above Inscription, the long awaited building, to be known as St. Paul's Anglican Church, Port Dover, seemed assured.

But first let us attempt to understand the circumstances which led up to this momentous event, in the lives of those adherents of the Church of England, resident in Port Dover and the immediate area.

Prior to this, in the early hamlet of Dover, an occasional service by a Missionary of the Church of England was known to have been held in one of the homes in the area. One of these missionaries was the Reverend Robert Addison, who on September 6th, 1807 is known to have baptised twelve persons "near Patterson's creek." Among them were John Rapelje Van Allan, son of Henry & Winifred Van Allan; Henry Van Allan Rapelje and Hellen Rapelje, children of Abraham & Sarah Rapelje; Henry Bostwick Williams, son of Johnothon Williams; Richard Woolson Bowlby, son of Thomas & Sarah Bowlby and Henry Williams Bostwick, son of Henry & Mary Bostwick.

The Reverend Robert Addison came from Westmoreland in England as a missionary in 1792. He became a Military Chaplain and rector of St. Marks church, Niagara, as well as Chaplain to Parliament. His extensive library for the time, of over one thousand volumes is still to be found in the Rectory. He carried out several visits to the Long Point Country, holding services and carrying out baptisms, and other special services.

Henry Van Allan, of Dutch ancestry, was born on Long Island where he married Winnifred Rapelje in 1795 and soon after came to the Long Point Country. He purchased 85 acres in the southeast corner of Lot 10, Con. 1, of Woodhouse from William Francis on February 16th, 1801. In 1806 he was recommended by Samuel Ryerse as a Captain of the Grenadier Company. On February 1817 it is recorded that Henry & Winnifred's daughter, Winnifred Van Allan, was baptised in Dover, by Reverend Robert Addison. Col. Henry Van Allan and a nephew, Daniel Ross Van Allan, were in Chatham as early as 1833 and by 1859 operated a sawmill and were engaged in shipbuilding.

The name Rapelje reminds us that Abraham A. Rapelje, who was born at Newtown, Long Island, on May 15th, 1772, had married Sarah Wycoff, of Flatlands, L. I. They came to Canada, settling in Dover, on July 4th, 1800. He was appointed Captain of an infantry company by Samuel Ryerse in 1806. He fought for his country in the war of 1812 - 14, his home in Dover being destroyed by fire by Campbell's raiders. Abraham and Sarah later built a home on Lot19, Con. 3 of Charlotteville, near Vittoria. In 1818 Abraham Rapelje was appointed Sheriff of the London District, succeeding John Bostwick. He served ably as Sheriff for the next thirty years and saw active service during the rebellion of 1837. Abraham Rapelje also served as Colonel of the 1st Regiment of Norfolk Militia. His wife Sarah died November 12th, 1841 aged 65 years. On February 26th, 1852 Col. Rapelje's house burned to the ground. On January 31st, 1859 Colonel Rapelje died in his 87th year.

Captain Daniel Rapelje left Newtown, Long Island, for Upper Canada in 1802, to found the village of St. Thomas in 1810. He, too, was active in the War of 1812. He gave land for St. Thomas churchyard in 1821, and was buried there in 1828, aged 54 years.

After the burning of the Mills and homesteads of Dover on that infamous day of May 15th, 1814, the little community, hitherto so vibrant, collapsed. A squatter named Patterson, who had a cabin at the mouth of the creek, had given his name to the stream that meandered back into the township of Woodhouse and through present day Simcoe into Windham township, where it is still known as Patterson's creek. Two hundred acres of land west of the creek and south of the first concession road had been established in 1794, by Peter Walker as his farm, on parts of Lots 11 & 12 in the front Concession of Woodhouse township. His home, a sturdy log cabin, hidden by clap-board, is said to exist to this day on McNab street. In recent memory it was the cosy home of a faithful parishioner, Winifred Diver Howell.

Peter Walker cleared land near the creek and set out an orchard of apple trees. In 1806 Lieutenant Peter Walker was made a Captain of Norfolk Militia by Samuel Ryerse, Lieutenant of the County, and given command of a Company of Militiamen living in the townships of Rainham and Walpole.

Peter Walker sold the north-west part of Lot 11 to Daniel McQueen in 1813. In 1818 he sold part of the south-east part to William Steel and another part of that parcel was willed to Ann Margaret Walker. I n 1834 Peter Walker sold his remaining holdings to Ephraim, Samuel and Moses Birdsell. They in turn sold to Moses Nickerson and Israel Wood Powell, who were planning to develop the village of Port Dover.

I am not sure of the date of Peter Walker's death but Miss Buckwell is credited with this story of his inability to remain properly buried. When they commenced to build the Buckwell house on Clinton street, near the present Erie Beach hotel, the workmen uncovered the mortal remains of Peter Walker. They were re-buried with due ceremony but later inadvertently dug up again when a drain was being installed in the area. Again they were re-buried, only to be unearthed for a third time later, when workmen were cutting through a street. Where his restless remains were interred finally is open to question, as far as I am aware.

For some time nothing happened in the way of re-building on the site of the hamlet of Dover.

By 1829 two schools appear to have been in operation in the area, however. A lady who had come from the West Indies, Mrs. Lawhead, was teaching in a small frame building on Brant Hill. Her students graduated when they could add, subtract, divide and multiply, recite the multiplication table from memory, write a fair round hand with a quill pen, and read appropriate passages from the New Testament.

A two-room frame school was built about 1829 near the present head of Main Street as well. This sturdy oak post and beam building, as well as serving as a school, often was used for religious services, at times conducted by a passing Anglican missionary, as

*The home of Dr. Craigie, Prospect St., Port Dover*

well as "saddle-bag preachers" of other denominations. Still later Bishop John Strachan, in his travels of inspection throughout his diocese of Toronto would travel through this area. My first memory of this original school, as a boy, was as the home, at the head of main street, of Mr. Alva J. " Rosy " Jones, whose wife was a much-beloved teacher in the public school at that time. Though considerably modified since it served as a school the building still stands at 1011 Main Street.

Long after the burning of Dover, as homes were built and the town site laid out by Israel Wood Powell in 1835, the Presbyterians, under Dr. Craigie, built the "Auld Kirk" as their place of worship on McNab street. His home was the large two storey brick manse built on the east side of Prospect street. The Reverend Mr. Robinson lived there much later before building a new Presbyterian manse, which is now the Dover Cliffs Nursing Home on St. George street. In the 1930's the Craigie house was the home of Mr. Charles "Charlie" Martin, MPP a younger brother of John S. Martin. He and brother Harry owned and operated Martin's Music store in Simcoe, owned until recently by Robert "Bob" Castles.

The Presbyterians very graciously offered the "Auld Kirk" to the Anglicans of the village for services which were held at intervals, prior to their having their own place of worship. The majority of these services would have been held by the Reverend Francis Evans, incumbent at St. John's, Woodhouse. The services were held here more regularly, but most often on a week day, and as time permitted. Other denominations as well were permitted to use the Auld Kirk at that time.

As pointed out earlier, the Reverend Francis Evans worked diligently to establish churches in the Long Point Country, and St. Paul's, Port Dover is thought to be the fourth such church that he founded from his position as priest of the Mother Church, St. John's, and Rector of the Township of Woodhouse. The faithful of the Port Dover area had been planning and saving under Reverend Evans guidance, for the establishment of their own place of worship for some time.

Under the sanction and recommendation of the Rector of Woodhouse, funds originating in England were tapped by him " for

*Originally the "Auld Kirk" of the Presbyterians, McNab Street*

the accomplishment of a benevolent purpose to aid in the erection of a church in the rising town of Port Dover, in the County of Norfolk, Canada West." This unexpected source of help came in the form of what must have been the original pyramid scheme, instigated by supporters in many parishes in England.

Through their parish churches each member of a committee formed in the parish, was asked to donate sixpence and in turn ask twelve friends to do the same, while also acting as Receivers. Each Receiver then in turn donates sixpence and asked twelve of their friends to act as Collectors. Each Collector donates sixpence and requests the donation of a sixpence, [twelve and a half cents] from each of twelve friends as Donors. [12 x 6p = $1.50 ] Thus $1.50 is raised by each Collector in the scheme. The twelve Collectors turn their total collected [12 x 12 = 144 six penny bits or $18.00] over to their Receiver. Each Receiver now turns in the $18.00 to the original member of the parish committee, which by now totals [$18.00 x 12 = $216.00] This amount, multiplied by the number of members, for example five on the original committee, [ 5 x $216.00 = $1,080.00] would be a considerable sum of money. Yet no one individual had been taxed beyond one small piece of silver, a sixpence. Although such a scheme would be declared illegal today, it proved a real boost to St. Paul's fund raising effort, since a portion of the collection made in England in 1852, was designated for our new, and struggling parish.

Mr. George Hotchkiss, writing an article entitled "Port Dover, 1851 to 1861" in the Maple Leaf several years later gives a glimpse of other efforts locally at fund raising. He credits the following ladies of the congregation for organising a Fair in Simcoe. Mrs. Alfred Buckwell and her daughters, who would become Mrs. Skey and Mrs. Nelles respectively; Mrs. Thomas Waters and her daughter "Gussie", who later married George Van Etten; Mrs. Andrew Lees and her daughter who later married Berkley Powell; Mrs. Henry Wheeler and young daughters, Charlotte and Frances or Fanny and Miss Shaw, a maiden lady, living on Clinton Street, back of the Royal Exchange Hotel, now the Norfolk House.

The culmination of these ladies efforts was realised just four days prior to the dedication of the Cornerstone and took place at the Courthouse in Simcoe on June 17th, 1852 in the form of a Fair which raised £140 for the cause. On the day of the laying of the Cornerstone the assembled parishioners, after the service, repaired to a room over the Powell brothers store where items, left from the Fair the week before, were offered and realised a further £30. The ladies were ecstatic, as were the congregation, with the resounding success of their combined efforts.

They had just enjoyed a powerful sermon, as well, by the Reverend M. Boomer, Rector of the Anglican church in Galt, who took as his text the first Epistle of Peter, Chapter II, verses 4 & 5. The reference being to Christ, as the chief corner stone of Christianity.

> "To whom coming, as unto a living stone, disallowed indeed of men, but chosen of God, and precious, Ye also as living stones, are built up a spiritual house, an holy priesthood, to offer up spiritual sacrifices, acceptable to God by Jesus Christ."

Canon Cornish failed to identify the location of the cornerstone in his history, and today nobody seems to know where the exact location of it is. It is thought by some that it is located in the east wall to the left of the large chancel window. It would seem much more likely that it was placed on the St. George Street side of the church and if this is true it has been completely covered by the addition of the Vestry. This took place after the lightning strike which did so much damage in 1862.

The plot of ground upon which St. Paul's was built had been generously donated by the late Israel Wood Powell, as part of his plan for the new village. The deed to the property is recorded as having been issued by Israel W. Powell to John, Lord Bishop of Toronto on May 25th, 1847.

*Israel Wood Powell, founder of Port Dover and donor of site of St. Paul's, 1843*

As the enthusiastic Worshippers left the service of dedication of the cornerstone, held just a block north in the Methodist Church, which had been loaned for the occasion, I expect their hopes were high that in a year or less they would be able to worship in their very own church. Little did they know their church would be three years and eight months in the building.

The laying of the cornerstone on Monday June 21st, 1852 by Mrs. Evans, the rector's lady is reported thus in the Maple Leaf: *"The proposed church at Port Dover will be indebted to the exercises of a very wide-spread liberality, as contributions [for the most part in small sums] have ben obtained from distant friends in many parts of Canada, in England, and in the United States. For all of these, as the congregation stood around the spot, upon which, with his blessing, a temple of God's Holy Name will be reared; the earnest prayers of the assembled worshippers was lifted up."*

What do we know, over one hundred and fifty years later, of

the four men who accepted the responsibility of seeing the construction of St. Paul's to its completion? They were :

**Thomas Waters,** [1812 –1892] who was born in Surrey, England. He married Georgianna Spence Stephens at Christ Church Cathedral in Hamilton. She was the daughter of the Reverend B. B. Stephens, Chaplain to His Majesty's Forces stationed in Montreal. Thomas Waters was a partner in the firm of Lee and Waters, merchants and lumber shippers of the town as well as a partner in the Buckwell and Waters distillery. Thomas also was a land owner holding title to eighty acres in Woodhouse and two hundred acres in Walsingham Townships. When he accepted a position on the Building Committee he was 39 years of age, his wife Georgianna was 28, and their children were Elizabeth A., 10; Henry H., 9; Erie, 7; Mary, 5 and Drifield aged 3 years.

**John A. Bowlby** [1808 –1881] was the fifth son of Squire Thomas Bowlby. He was married to Rachel Ann Birdsall. They lived, and farmed, on the original homestead, taken up in 1797, by his father, Thomas. Thomas Bowlby and his family had left Brickton, in the Annapolis valley, Nova Scotia, where his father Richard Bowlby had taken up land after their flight as Loyalists from the American Revolution. Thomas Bowlby was the only one, of the twelve Nova Scotia families, that had commissioned William Francis to find them land in the Long Point Country, who actually came into Canada West. When Thomas arrived here in 1797 he was granted 400 acres in Lot 4, Concession 1 & 2, of Woodhouse, where he built his home. In 1800 he bought the triangle of land enclosed by present-day Mill road on the north,

*Home of John Bowlby, on Crown grant of 1797 to Thomas Bowlby, Woodhouse*

Black creek to the east and Patterson's creek to the west, to add to his holdings.

Thomas Bowlby had married Sarah Axford, daughter of a wealthy New Jersey planter, and they had a son, Axford, before being forced to leave their New Jersey home for Nova Scotia. After their arrival in Woodhouse they had five more sons and a daughter. As a United Empire Loyalist, Thomas was appointed one of the pioneer magistrates of Woodhouse. He was thereby authorised to perform many of the early marriage ceremonies in the district prior to the arrival of the Reverend Francis Evans. Thomas Bowlby was an active Free Mason, and served with distinction in the War of 1812. His son John Bowlby was a well established farmer on the home farm at the time of his joining the building committee for the new Anglican church in Port Dover.

**Frederick H. Haycock** [1829 – 1879] who was the Customs Officer, or Collector of Customs in Port Dover in the 1850's, prior to William Higman's tenure. He died on October 26th, 1879, aged 59 years, 3 months.

**James Cowain Prince of Orange McCoy** [1815— 1882] a son of James and Jane McCoy was born in County Down in Ireland about 1815. He was only five years old when he came to Canada with his parents and siblings in 1820. By June of 1842 they had taken possession of the west half of Lot 9, Concession 1 in Woodhouse Township as a grant from the Crown. In March of

*Salt-box home of James Corwain Prince of Orange McCoy just prior to demolition*

1830 the first grant of that land was made from the Crown to Benjamin Mead. It would appear that he could not meet the requirements of the grant and it reverted to the Crown again.

The old, rather neglected salt-box style house to the west of the present day IGA Mall was their home. The farm ran south right through to the Lake shore. Also of note is the fact that James C. P. of O. McCoy's sister, Maria, married David McFall Field in 1827 and they settled on a two hundred and fifty acre farm east of Nanticoke, where the Fields prospered. Their farm was purchased from descendants as part of the parcel of land required for the construction of the Nanticoke Power Station. Another sister, Anne Jane McCoy, married Colin McNeilledge, Port Dover's first Postmaster and Manager of the flour mill that replaced the one burned in Dover in May of 1814.

James C. P. of O. McCoy and his parents are buried in the cemetery of St. John's, Woodhouse. Graydon Field, a great, great grandson of James McCoy, and his wife Joy not only supplied me with the above information but have played an important role in the well being of St Paul's through Joy's work as organist and historian for many years and Graydon's activities in the BAC and church affairs generally.

On May 26th, 2005 the desolate, old and abandoned McCoy house was being stripped of its siding and being curious I investigated. Yet another Port Dover sub-division is planned for the farm of James McCoy. The men were friendly and anxious to learn the history of the house as it is being taken apart carefully for re-assembly near Kingston. Each beam, stud and joist was being numbered for that purpose. They had found a pair of square-toed leather shoes, the soles attached by tiny maple pegs, in the outer wall of the house. They told me that placing an old shoe in the partition was a common practise in building a new house, to bring the owners good luck. The Curator of the Bata Shoe Museum informed them that a shoe of this type would have been made between 1840 and 1860. This would indicate that the house was built by James McCoy, possibly soon after their purchase of the property. In 1922 Ann Maria McCoy sold the farm to Thomas Hammond. It was later owned by John Aaron McBride.

Little is recorded of the progress of the church following the

*McCoy home demolition for careful reconstruction elsewhere*

dedication of the cornerstone. It is suggested that funding delayed the construction and it is recorded that one of the workmen suffered a severe injury, which also delayed the work considerably. The bricks for its construction were fired in kilns of the brickyard located along Patterson's Creek where the T. A. Ivey Inc. greenhouses stood, many years after the formation of Silver Lake in 1861. It is now the location of the Port Dover Lion's Club Silver Lake Park. It is obvious that several kilns of inferior brick were used in the construction as noted by their light colouration and tendency to spauld.

    It is of interest to note that the Presbyterians built their brick church, at their present location on St. George street, in 1853, and in the same year the Wesleyan Methodists built a frame church. The Universalist church was built two years later in 1855. The Baptists also had a place of worship in Port Dover. This seeming flurry of religious fervour also saw the establishment in 1853 of a Union Sunday School. The large teaching staff that were active in this "all denomination" Sunday School was made up of Episcopalians, Presbyterians, Methodists, Universalists and Baptists. School was held for that first year in the Methodist church.

For most of the period from 1854 to 1861 this Union Sunday School met every Sunday in what was known as the Massecar Building, on the north-east corner of Market and St. Andrews Street. This corner was later to accommodate the Thomas L. Gillies Lumber Yard. Today it is a vacant lot. By 1861 it was agreed that each denomination should take responsibility and organise their own Sunday School.

For the next fifteen years the Parish of St. Paul's held their Sunday School classes in the Scofield block, built a few years earlier by Norman B. Scofield on Main street. In fact a great deal of change had been taking place in the developing village since Israel Wood Powell, late of the Colborne settlement north of Simcoe, had planned the village's streets and harbour. Aided by his brothers-in-law, Nickerson and Boss, Powell acquired what had originally been granted to Peter Walker by the Crown in 1794. Israel Powell built a comfortable and impressive brick home on the promontory to the north and overlooking the mouth of the river. The river, at the time of Powell's arrival, was blocked to all shipping by an extensive sand bar that extended across the river mouth.

Under the impetus of Powell's plans the development of a proper harbour became of major importance to the community if the economical export of their logs, lumber, grain and livestock was to be accomplished. Soon a group of far-sighted business men had raised funds for the dredging of the entrance to the Lynn river and the establishment of a harbour. With government aid, pilings, a sturdy dock and break wall were built. By 1844 a lighthouse was in operation on the end of the new pier and Mr. Fyfield was appointed the first lighthouse keeper. The Government was still very concerned about the possibility of attack from the United States and as a result commissioned the survey of a road from Port Dover to Hamilton in 1838.

By 1844 the plank road to Hamilton had been completed by the Government, which had also taken over the new harbour. All this activity had provided welcome employment for the burgeoning town-site, which in turn was drawing business to the area. Now having the finest harbour on the north shore of Lake Erie and roads to major markets, schooners soon crowded the pier and docks

*Andrew Thompson, an early developer of Port Dover*

along either side of the river, as warehouses sprang up along its banks.

A man who was to play a prominent part in the development of the new town was Andrew Thompson, of Dunnville, where he was said to have been the first Post Master. He came to Port Dover in 1844, buying the site of the Dover Flour & Grist Mill burned by the Americans in 1814. He built the impressive home on the west side of the creek, next the McQueen dam. By the winter of 1849 he financed the building of the first steamboat built here, to be used in the increasingly popular Grand River trade. Captain D. McSwain had the contract for her construction. In 1861 Andrew Thompson built the Norfolk Knitting Mill, including the dam which formed Silver Lake and provided power for the Mill. The mill was burned in 1885 but rebuilt. He is best known today as the builder of Ruthven, in Cayuga.

By the time St. Paul's Building Committee was struck and began their work their were eight warehouses in the harbour, each filled with grain for export and the area around the pier and lower main street was piled high with lumber and good pine and hardwood logs for export to American and British markets. Schooners were being built in the neighbourhood of Peter Lawson's tannery and even on the beach to supply the ever increasing demand for more and more shipping.

Israel Wood Powell had built what was no doubt the first store on the south-west corner of Main and Market streets. In 1856 this original frame building was destroyed by fire, to be quickly replaced by an impressive three-storey brick building that accommodated three modern stores. The Riddell brothers, from Scotland, had built a large frame store on the north-east corner of Main and Market streets, which later became known as "The Fair" operated at the turn of the century by Truesdale and Bond. A brick building further north on Main Street was occupied by Howell and Wilson who carried on a grocery business. This later housed the telegraph offices and post office, with Mr. Tibbetts as Postmaster.

By 1856 yet another firm was established as a general store in the village, known as Scovell and Scofield, also spelled Schofield. Their exact location as well as any background on Mr. Scovell is not known to me. Mr. Scovell was thought to be Mr. Scofield's

*The Erie House, an early Port Dover hotel*

*Main St. view showing "The Fair," built by Riddell Bros.*

brother-in-law however. Mr. Norman B. Scofield was born in St. Armand, Quebec and no doubt saw Port Dover as place where an ambitious merchant might make a good living. By 1859 Scovell and Scofield had chosen the lot directly south of the existing block of the Powell Brothers and had let the contract for the construction of a modern brick building, to Brian Varey, grandfather to Harry and C. C. "Tip" Varey. Tip's son Brian Varey, on returning from serving in the Navy during World War II, joined with his father in the business which he retired from in the mid 1990's. This was Varey's haberdashery in the centre store of the Powell block which his father had bought from my great uncle, Hubert Barrett, in 1909.

*Mr. Truesdale, of Truesdale & Bond, later owners of "The Fair"*

Mr. Brian Varey came well recommended to Mr. Scofield having built the brick Union School three years earlier on Main Street. This school replaced the grammar school that had been established in the Powell block, as well as the common school, which occupied a frame building on Nelson street, east of the present day Mac's Milk store. This school for many years after its closure, was the home of the Leaney's who supplied the town with ice, cut from Silver Lake.

Aware of the ever present threat of fire Scovell & Scofield were determined to build a fire-proof substantial brick three-storey building. This impressive building became known as the Scofield Block. From Customs records we learn that in July of 1859 the schooner "Lerwick" delivered sculpted iron columns, cast by Edyd Bingham, Buffalo, N. Y. for the front of the Scofield building. Their name can still be found on the base of each column. The Lerwick later delivered 900 feet of flagstone from Cleveland for the project. It is assumed this was to be used for sidewalk in front of their store. The outer walls, as well as the walls that divided the three separate units of the building, were of solid brick construction, 23 inches thick. The ceilings of each storey were 15, 13 and 12 feet in height respectively. The doors in the brick partitions were of iron. The semi-circular attic window, with its iron shutter can be seen to this day on the south wall of the building. In August the barque "Mary Jane" delivered 4,572 slate shingles from Buffalo. All of these precautions against fire were justified when the building survived the burning of the adjoining Powell block, by then known as the Meade House in the Beaupre Block, in 1900.

*Mr. Ferguson, manager of Scofield & Co.*

By 1865 Scovell's name is no longer associated with the business. In 1871 Scofield and Company were on the brink of bankruptcy but survived it. In 1867 my great grandfather Henry Healing Clark , keeper of the Long Point lighthouse died, leaving his family destitute. The children were farmed out and my grandfather Harry Hawkins Clark was taken in by Mr. Ferguson, Manager of the Norman B. Scofield store. In time he replaced Mr. Ferguson as manager and successfully carried out those duties until 1883 when he left Port Dover, to go on his own.

He found his way into the north country where he managed and later owned the general store in Haliburton owned by the late Jack Anderson and his wife Bessie Bemister Anderson. When Mrs. Anderson's niece Fanny Bemister came from Beaverton to visit she fell in love with Harry Clark. The feelings were mutual and she changed her name to Clarke, on condition, apparently, that the "e" be added.

*Old Sovereign home on Prospect St. in 1916*

Mr. Norman B. Scofield, who provided a Sunday School room for the children of St. Paul's Church in his building until the parish could build their own, left many descendants. His daughter Lucy married Ward Sovereign who was born on January 6th, 1858 on the Sovereign farm between the south end of Prospect street and the Cockshutt road. The house, demolished in the 1970's, was reached by a short lane directly across from the drive to the present Dr. Thompson house. It was said to have housed the fugitive William Lyon McKenzie for a night when he was on the run following the aborted 1837 rebellion. Much later the Sovereign family traded properties with the Bowlby family, who lived on the west side of Prospect Street opposite the Sovereign farm. Bowlby street still exists, though unused, running from the Cockshutt road at the base of the hill, north to the home built by Lewis Bowlby, and presently owned by Paul Morris.

Ward and Lucy Sovereign were married in 1882. He was a business man who later travelled as a salesman for a wholesale house across western Canada. He became their Sales Manager in Edmonton, Alberta for a time. Returning to Port Dover, they lived on Prospect Hill in the house now owned by Dr. Thompson, where Ward grew some 15 acres of tomatoes on their land south and west of the house. Ward served on town council and became both Assessor and Tax Collector for Port Dover. For several years he was

Secretary of the very active Port Dover and Woodhouse Horticultural Society. Ward Sovereign and my grandfather Harry Barrett were cousins through a common relationship to the Langs. Ward Sovereign died in 1928, aged 71 years.

Their daughter Adah Sovereign was busy during W W I knitting mitts and balaclavas for servicemen overseas. My grandmother's youngest brother, George S. Pelly from Otter Lake, Spallumcheen, in the Okanagan Valley of British Columbia, having received one of her parcels while in France, wrote to thank her for it.

As he and my Uncle Frank Barrett had grown up together at Otter Lake, after my Grandmother died, Uncle George decided to kill two birds with one stone, as it were, and visit Port Dover on his way back to Otter Lake, after the war. He stayed at the farm with his brother-in-law, Harry, and hunted up his lady benefactor, Adah Sovereign. He never did make it home.

He and Adah were married and lived in the Sovereign house. Uncle George loved children, though they never had children of their own, and we kids all loved him dearly. He was for many years a teacher and Superintendent of the St. Paul's Sunday School. He also drew the design of the church which has for many years graced the weekly church bulletin. He was always the life of the party at Halloween and at Christmas, or any other family gathering that came along.

Mary Scofield married F. W. Denton who for some time managed the Scofield store. Alice Maud Scofield married my Uncle Hubert Baldwin Barrett, third son of Toby, who operated a haber-

*Mr. F. W. Denton, later manager of Scofield & Co. He married Mary Scofield*

dashery in the centre store of the Powell Block He sold the business in 1909 to Tip Varey and later became Customs officer for Port Dover. They had a son Quintin, who on returning from overseas operated a booth and the Tibbett's bathhouses on the beach. I still have men's and women's bathing suits, found in the Bridge street barn and stencilled with "B & T, size 40" for example. Quintin married Gladys Farrar and established a fishing and hunting camp on the Lake of the Woods, thirty miles out of Fort Frances.

*Alice Maude Scofield, who married Hubert B. Barrett*

Huby and Maud's daughter Lila, who was loved by everyone, and a great swimmer went into nursing in Toronto where she contracted Tuberculosis at 21 years of age. She never recovered. Her sister Winnifred, married Cecil Yerex who had come to Port Dover to work on the Fishery Patrol vessel, Vigilant. He later became a pattern-maker and expert carpenter. Their children, David, Hilton, Jacqueline, Pat and Andrew, all spent many happy hours at our farm on the Cockshutt road. David, Jacqueline and Pat having recently returned to Port Dover, we again spend happy times together reminiscing about our youthful escapades.

Chauncey Scofield married Bessie Innes. One of their sons was drowned in Silver lake in 1888 and two years later another son, Norman, while skating on Silver lake with three companions broke through the ice and was also drowned. Yet another son, Harry Scofield, lived out his life in Port Dover. He was manager of the knitting mill which today houses the Veterinary Clinic of Dr. Brenda Jones.

Harry's son Gilman married Helen Caley whose father Thomas G. Caley bought the Scofield store and stock in 1929 and installed electricity in the building. The second storey of the store had always been apartments but the third story had remained unfinished. During WW II the demand for housing in Port Dover by servicemen became so acute that Mrs. Caley converted the third floor into four very comfortable apartments. She continued to operate the store after Mr. Caley died suddenly in 1955.

Harry Scofield's youngest son, Clayton, was interested in electronics. Soon after the outbreak of WW II, when a course was offered, by the Royal Canadian Navy, in Radio operation and maintenance, under the Dominion-Provincial War Training Programme, Clayton, David Yerex and I all signed up for it at Westdale Collegiate in Hamilton, in September of 1941. David was mustered out on medical grounds to later join the Army. Clayton and I went on to serve in the Royal Canadian Navy Volunteer Reserve.

By the time my Great Aunts, Alice and Louise or "Wese" were growing up, the widow of an Army officer lived in the Israel Wood Powell house and operated a school for young ladies of the Port, which they attended. In our memory Powell's home was incorporated into what was known as the Orchard Beach Hotel by Morley Buck. It was a prestigious and popular summer hotel for many years, though no remnant of it remains to-day, it having been demolished in 1953.

CHAPTER SIX

# Early Pew Renters & Incumbents

While searching for a package of letters recently, I happened on an old customs register. I was most surprised and pleased to find, tucked inside its back cover, a hard cover book that recorded the pew rent paid by parishioners of St. Paul's, Port Dover, for the period beginning February 1856 to 1859. This must have gone unnoticed in the cache of large, leather-bound customs registers that my Great Grandfather, T. B. Barrett, had stored here at Riverbank when he was employed by the Customs Service from 1853 to 1892. On the death of his daughter, my Great Aunt, Mrs. H. R. Parke, my father and I discovered some fifteen of these in the manger of a horse stall in the barn. We assume that on the death in 1910 of T. B. Barrett, affectionately known to the family as Fa, they were put in the barn as no-one could bring themselves to throwing them out entirely. The majority of these interesting records of activities in the harbour, dating from 1846 to the 1880's, I have turned over to Ian Bell, Curator of the Port Dover Harbour Museum.

The register of heads of households paying pew rents in the newly opened St. Paul's Church records twenty-six (26) families who were assessed and paid rents in the early months of 1856. The earliest is dated February 8th, 1856. **Captain Alexander McNeilledge** notes in his diary two days earlier, on February 6th, that he and his wife had gone to Dover," there being a sale of pews of the new English Church." Although listed in the 1851 census for Woodhouse as a sixty-one year old Presbyterian, the Captain rented pew #17 for seven months on February 8th, for £1 9s 6p. There are an additional twelve (12) families recorded from 1857 or

*Captain Alexander McNeilledge*

later in the register. All the 1856 payments are made in pounds, shillings and pence. The majority, though not all, for the following years are in even dollars. The going rate for a year after 1856 appears to be $14.00. Few pay a full year at a time, however. Some parishioners also are recorded as paying an amount toward the Rector's stipend. Some entries are made of rentals for 1860 as being carried forward to the new ledger. To date no new ledger has been located. Many of the pews rented were box pews, with straight-backed seats all round the square, entrance being gained by a narrow door with a latch.

The church was finally completed for the sum of $3,000.00 and upon completion was free of debt. The impressive shingled

*Original appearance of interior of St. Paul's*

steeple was soon recognised as an important navigational aid to the many schooners trading in and out of the busy port. The new church, to be known as St. Paul's Church, Port Dover, was officially opened on February 10th, 1856.

### Reverend R. S. Birch [Burch] - 1856 - 1858.

Captain McNeilledge notes on February 10th, 1856 that the new English Church was opened with a large and respectable attendance. We assume that the Reverend Francis Evans took the first service as again from the Captain's diary a month later, for March 11th, we learn that Mrs.[Nancy] Wheeler, wife of Henry Wheeler, an American Lumber merchant in Port Dover, with her daughter Charlotte, age 17 and brother James, brought the young minister for the Episcopal church in Dover, the Reverend Mr. Birch, to town. Little is known of his incumbency, but from an entry in the Captain's diary we gather it was not without problems of some sort. He notes on the arrival of his successor, Reverend Johnstone Vicars, in November 1858 that he "thinks he will be a good man as things have not gone altogether right since the consecration of the Church". It is known that he eventually left the church altogether and took up the law as a profession.

It is noted that Rev. Birch wore a cassock during services and made use of the 1662 edition of the Book of Common Prayer. His wife was a Wilson from Simcoe, and they lived in Port Dover for at least eight years. He seems to have been Rector from March 11th, 1856 until as late as November of 1858. . Captain Alex McNeilledge hints in a diary entry that all was not as the congregation might have wished since the consecration of St. Paul's and during the incumbency of Rev. Mr. Birch. Little else seems to be known of him, or have been recorded about his ministry.

From my Auntie Alice's diary of January, 1893, when she, her husband Hal Parke and her brother Harry were returning to their new home in Vernon, B. C. after their marriage in St. Paul's, we glean this bit of information. They are travelling the north shore of Lake Superior on the train. It is Sunday morning and she reports: "We have had quite a Sunday concert - hymns of all kinds from church to Salvation Army. The little woman opposite is a Methodist & I never yet saw a Methodist who couldn't sing. I have discovered that the man with the glass eye is a son of the Clergyman who christened me! Mr. Birch. He was born in Port Dover and lived there until he was eight or nine years old. .... His mother was one of the Simcoe Wilsons. He is a cousin of Bob Wilson's. It is so strange how one meets familiar names - I can't say faces - for that eye is unlike anything I ever saw before, and his mind and manners seem equally original and unconventional." .....later; "Harry has just been asking Mr. Birch if he had read Bret Harte, and I hear him reply 'I have read everything except red hair.'"

They run into a blizzard crossing the prairies; "the worst weather they say since the C. P. R. was built. It is 40 degrees below." Their train is the only one still running between Vancouver and Ottawa and they expect to be days late. Wednesday night they have reached Tilley, 21 hours late. Mr. Birch has a severe cold and feeling sorry for him, Aunty reports; "I sacrificed some of my black currant jam to make a drink for Mr. Birch's cold. He said it made him think of his Mother."

We learn from the McNeilledge diary entry of July 18th, 1855 that a bazaar was held to raise money for a bell for the new church. There must have been other successful fund raisers for on July 5th, 1856 it is recorded that the schooner Mayflower delivered a bell from Buffalo, consigned to Reverend Mr. Burch. Captain McNeilledge reports it weighed 501 lbs. On July 13th, 1856, the new bell was rung for the first time. It is noted , with a note of smugness, that our bell predated the Town bell by a full year.

A meeting was held on September 3rd, 1856 to consider acquiring a town bell A special bell tower of

*Town bell tower*

heavy timber frame construction was built in the park for the express purpose of housing the bell. The 808 lb. bell was installed in the recently completed tower in April of 1857. This Town bell was said to have been imported by George Hotchkiss, another American lumber buyer, and he reports it weighed more than twice the weight of the Anglican bell at 1060 lbs. Don Buscombe records that Mr. George Hotchkiss presented the bell as a memorial to his mother Mrs. Mary St. John. As George's wedding to Miss St. John, on August 14th, 1856, is thought to be the first wedding performed in the newly opened St. Paul's Anglican church, it would seem that the presentation by George Hotchkiss, should be as a memorial to his mother-in-law, Mrs Mary St. John. On the 17th of August the bell was tolled for the first time for Mr. Hill's funeral.

The customs register, reports that on July 9th, 1856 the schooner Fame delivered one church bell consigned to A. Walsh. [Was this another church bell?] In September the schooner Mayflower delivered one town bell, weighing 808 lbs. consigned to Walker Powell. It would appear that this bell was the one that was placed in the newly constructed bell tower, said to be located on Main street, in the centre of Powell Park. The Anglican church bell was already installed and ringing by the time the town bell was being delivered, by the Mayflower.

It was reported that an exhibition of tight-rope walking was performed on September 23rd, 1865. The "rope" being strung from the top of the bell tower [in Powell Park] to Powell's block, across Main street. On May 28th, 1868 a meeting of local townspeople was held in the old schoolhouse, to consider the building of a Town Hall. On February 24th, 1869 the British Canadian reported that a By-law was to be submitted by Council, to the ratepayers of Woodhouse, on March 19th, to raise $1,630.00 for the building of a Town Hall. The March 24th, 1869 issue of the British Canadian reported that the By-law had carried by a majority of 44 votes. On March 25th, 1869 the Council of the Township of Woodhouse, which also included the hamlet of Port Dover, appropriated $1,600.00 for the erection of a Town Hall, in Port Dover.

On April 28th, 1869 it was reported that Council had appointed Messrs. Austin, Sharpe, England and Ryerse a committee to procure a site, plans and specifications for a new Town Hall.

The Town Hall was built in Powell Park about where the Band Shell stands to-day.

For over thirty years the town bell had served the community well from its tower in the centre of the town. An exterior rope was available to any citizen should an alarm need to be raised in case of fire or other disaster or for the enthusiastic celebration of occasions of note. A specified Bell Ringer was also employed by Council on a year round basis. In November 1890 it is reported that Master William Austin was made Bell Ringer at $50.00 per year.

A ground swell of opinion for a proper town clock had been building and the August 16th, 1889 issue of the Maple Leaf reported a concert was being held to raise funds for a town clock. An argument was made that the Council was paying $50.00 a year for a bell ringer, whereas for one payment of $200.00 a reliable clock could be purchased which would regularly strike the hours and half hours on the town bell. On March 5th, 1890 another successful concert in aid of the town clock fund was held. A recital by E. Pauline Johnson, the Indian poetess, in February 1894 was highly

*First Town Hall in Powell Park*

*Main Street, showing ruins of the Mead House*

praised and netted $47.43 for the clock fund. Fund raising continued and by March, 1900 the fund in the bank totalled $286.60.

The wooden, original Powell Block had been completely destroyed by fire in 1856 and was rebuilt as a fine three storey brick building which accommodated three stores on the ground floor. Lodgings and the Lodge rooms of Erie Masonic Lodge, No. 149. A. F & A. M. from its founding in 1861 were accommodated on the second floor. In 1889 it was purchased by Mr. Beaupre and renovated as a hotel, known as "The Meade House". It stood on the South-west corner of Main and Market streets. Erie Lodge was forced to find new quarters in the Caley block. The Mead House burned on the night of February 2nd, 1900 and had been an eyesore to the town ever since. The Council finally bought the site for a new Town Hall.

On March 7th, 1902 tenders were called to add twenty feet to the Town Hall and to prepare a tower for the clock. On April 15th, 1904 a meeting of Port Dover Town Council was called, at which it was resolved to submit a By-law, which would bind the village for a sum of $8,000.00 to build up [re-build] the Powell Block.

The corner-stone for the new Town Hall was layed in 1904. Three stores were accommodated, by the building, on the ground floor. The second floor held a three hundred seat theatre, complete with balcony, as well as council chambers, a band room and other offices. A tower was built into the north-east corner to hold a clock.

The Maple Leaf reported on May 4th, 1906 that the tower for the town clock was being raised about ten feet. About this time

*New Town Hall with original clock tower*

*Looking north on Main Street, showing extended clock tower & clock*

Architect Clarence Barrett, who is said to have provided the design and specifications for the new Town Hall, was paid $25.00 to design the clock tower. This must have been for the extension of the tower by ten feet over the original design he had submitted and which by this time had been built. "The Howard Clock Company of Boston, U. S. A. has been contracted to install a clock of four faces for a cost of $740.00. This clock will strike the hours and half hours on the town bell, with a forty pound hammer". In the July 27th, 1906 issue of the Maple Leaf it is reported that the clock is installed. The clock fund which has been building for the past fifteen years has reached nearly $600.00. The Howard Clock Company had reduced the price by $25.00, making the final cost for the clock and its mechanisms $715.00. This impressive Main Street building is now home to the Lighthouse Festival Theatre.

The two storey wooden bell tower which had accommodated the town bell, was demolished in 1903, by Garfield Porritt and Jesse Thompson. Mr. Porritt claimed it stood on the Harding lot on the north-west corner of St. George and Market streets, across from St. Paul's church. This seems very unlikely, however, as that was the home of Chart Woolley, long time reeve of Port Dover.

## THE FOUNDING MEMBERS OF ST. PAUL'S
### AS RECORDED IN THE FIRST PEW RENT BOOK.

Listing the founders of St. Paul's in alphabetical order I will attempt to record what is known about them to-day.

**Ozias Ansley** [1828 – 1901] It is noted that he rented pew #14 to January 20th, 1857, by deducting from account in full – £1 13s 6p. The last entry for 1860 -By amount of account rendered and not before credited – $16.26. Carried to new ledger – $7.76. He was a tinsmith, dealing in stoves, tin, copper and sheet metal wares. He obviously does work for the church as his bill is deducted from the outstanding pew rent. Ozias Ansley married Clara Hortense Langs, a sister of Emily Langs Barrett, and daughter of Jacob Langs and Phoebe Sovereign Langs, of Round Plains.

**John A. Bowlsby** [Bowlby] is shown as renting Pew #5, for which he is billed and paid by cash – £2 16s 3p in 1856. In 1857 - billed and paid cash – £3 10s 0p. In 1858 - billed and paid cash – $14.00. In 1859 - billed and paid cash to Thomas Waters – $14.00.

Ozias Ansley

Clara Hortense Langs, wife of Ozias Ansley

As he was a member of the Building committee his background is recorded in more detail there.

**Alfred Buckwell** [1813 – 1881] is recorded in 1856 as paying; cash in full to March24th, 1857 – £3 18s 01/2p. In 1857 - three payments of cash to Easter 1858 – £3 10s 0p. In 1858 - two payments of cash to April 1859 – $14.00. In 1859 - stipend to Haycock – $10.00, balance – $30.00 = $40.00, pew rent, 2 pmts. to Easter 1860 – $14.00. To balance carried to new ledger – $27.00. In 1851 census Alfred Buckwell is listed as a merchant, 38 years old, with wife Louisa Waters, [1816 – 1909] 36 years of age, and native of Hailsham, Sussex.

They emigrated as a married couple from England, in 1835, and first settled in Brantford. In 1844 the family moved to Port Dover as Alfred and his brother-in-law, Thomas Waters, had under a partnership of Buckwell and Waters obtained a distillery licence in 1841. Alfred took a contract to supply plank for the Port Dover to Hamilton plank road, in 1843 - '44. Alfred Buckwell was a merchant in Port Dover and agent for the British American Fire and Life Insurance Company. By 1865 he has a thriving wholesale -

retail company, with Mr. Skey as partner, dealing in Drugs, Groceries, Wines, Liquors as well as Books and Stationery located in the Powell Block on Main Street. His home was on the site of the present day Erie Beach Hotel.

**Quinten [Quintin] Barrett** rented pew #18 and in 1856 is recorded thus ; From Feb. 8th – 3s 6p. + 2 x 6 months @ 15s, pd. – £3 3s 6p. In 1857 - 1 year rent ending Easter 1858 – £1 10s 0p. In 1858 - balance due brought down – $9.00 – Bad. There is no further entry and Jaffray Harvey is listed as paying part rent of the pew, broken time, by cash – $5.50. As Quintin Barrett lived in Vittoria he may have begun attending services in Christ Church there.

*Quintin Barrett*

Quintin was a son of Hugh Massy Barrett. He was born in Ireland in 1815. As a 22 year old at the time of the rebellion of 1837, he joined the militia in the Lower Province. On the militia being disbanded he came to Vittoria, where he established a store in the village. He married, Winifred, the daughter of Sheriff Abraham A. Rapelje. Quintin later worked as a lumber agent in the Port Rowan area. He died September 20th, 1860. Winifred married Col. Charles Perley, February 21st, 1866.

**Theobald Butler Barrett** [1817 – 1910] rented pew #24 for which he paid by cash, being the assessment for each year through to 1860. In 1858 he made a contribution to the stipend fund of $5.00. A staunch supporter, and Lay Reader, of the Church of England throughout his life, Toby was born in Banagher, Tipperary, Ireland in 1817. He was twelve years old when his parents, Hugh Massy & Caroline Butler Barrett emigrated from Ireland to a farm outside Sorel, Quebec or Lower Canada as it was then known.

As a twenty year old, working on the farm, he joined the militia with his older brothers, William and Quintin, upon the out-

*Hugh Massy & Caroline Butler Barrett with grand daughter Caroline of Port Royal*

break of the rebellion of 1837. On being disbanded the three boys left the rest of their family to go their separate ways. William, who had been stationed in the hotel at Huntingdon, Quebec, married Amanda Fitch, the hotel keeper's daughter and remained to run the hotel for the rest of his life. Quintin, as noted, moved to Vittoria. Toby joined the Bertierville police force as a constable.

Some time later the Bertierville force was absorbed, with the village, into Greater Montreal and Toby lost his position as constable. Armed with a glowing recommendation from his Chief of Police, Toby joined his brother in Vittoria, Canada West, about 1845. With his experience as a policeman he soon was appointed Deputy Sheriff for the county of Norfolk, under Sheriff Abraham A. Rapelje. The fact the Sheriff's daughter was his sister-in-law no doubt had some bearing on his good fortune. The fact he was six feet, four inches tall, with a powerful build and an easy going manner, made his job easier, I am sure. He was soon both well known and well liked in the community.

*Theobald Butler Barrett*

Both Quintin and Toby were no strangers to the rector and congregation of St. John's Church, Woodhouse, and as they became better known in the county, they wrote home to Sorel of the opportunities available in the Upper Province. Two of their younger brothers, Joseph and Henry, joined them and one gets the impression they were the life of the party in the local taverns, and at the many dances held in the homes and halls of the growing settlement. The two brothers were soon escorting the McInnes sisters of Vittoria, but then news of the discovery of Gold in California spread through the community like wild-fire. By the summer of 1849 Joseph and Henry were on the Merced River, California, prospecting for gold.

Toby had become interested in Free Masonry and in 1850 joined St. John's Lodge, #500 in Simcoe, Canada West. William Mercer Wilson was the Lodge's Worshipful Master at that time. Theobald Butler Barrett was received and initiated into St. John's Lodge, #500 on January 24th, 1850 and raised to the third degree on March 21st, of that same year. Degrees were granted at that time under the jurisdiction of the United Grand Lodge of Ancient, Free and accepted Masons of England. The Earl of Zetland being the Grand Master. The Grand Secretary, William S. White, did not sign and affix the seal of the Grand Lodge of England, in London, to Toby's certificate until July 22nd, 1851. The certificate would still have to be returned to St. John's Lodge, in Simcoe, before being formally presented to Brother Barrett by the Worshipful Master.

Israel Wood Powell's son, also of that name, having returned from McGill University, Montreal, where he had earned a medical degree as well as having been introduced to the mysteries of

*The Allan house, east of the Norfolk Hotel, rented in 1850 by T.B. and Emily Barrett, while their house was being built*

Masonry, set about forming a Masonic Lodge in Port Dover. He was aided and abetted in this by members of the original St. John's Lodge, which had been reorganised as Norfolk Lodge # 10, in Simcoe, when William Mercer Wilson had formed the Canadian Grand Lodge in 1855. Wilson was the founding Grand Master of this Grand Lodge of Canada, in the Province of Ontario, thus bringing control of Masonic matters in Canada, from the English and Scottish Grand Lodges to a Canadian jurisdiction.

With the formation in 1861 of Erie Lodge, #149, by Worshipful Master Israel Wood Powell under the Grand Lodge of Canada, in the Province of Ontario, Port Dover had its own Lodge. Brother Michael Haycock became the first Senior Warden, and Brother T. B. Barrett the first Junior Warden. Upon Worshipful Master Powell's sudden departure for what was thought to be Australia nine months later, Brother T. B. Barrett was elected the Worshipful Master of Erie Lodge before its' first year of existence was complete. Powell on reaching Vancouver Island decided to settle there and within a year he had founded the first masonic Lodge in British Columbia and was on his way to becoming one of that Province's more famous sons.

Meanwhile T. B. "Toby" Barrett's love for, and allegiance to, Erie Lodge throughout his lifetime could only be matched by his love for, and the allegiance he held for the Church of England, as represented by St. Paul's Church, Port Dover. He was a proud charter member of both. This same love and respect for both Institutions has carried down through his descendants unabated, in each succeeding generation. His great, great grandson and namesake, Theobald Butler Barrett III, being a Past Master of Erie Lodge, # 149, A.F. & A.M., Port Dover.

*Emily Langs, wife of T. B. Barrett*

In March 1850, Toby married Emily Langs, [1827 – 1902] of Windham township and they built a salt-box style home, on three lots fronting on the river to the east and backing on two lots fronting on St. Patrick street to the west. They rented the Allan house, newly built east of the Norfolk Hotel, until the late summer when their new home was completed. They are listed in the 1851 census as T. B. Barrett, gentleman, Irish, age 34 years; Emily, Canadian, age 24 years, their only daughter at that time being Phoebe Caroline, age 1 year.

In 1853 Toby entered the Canadian Customs Service as a Landing Waiter. In 1869 he succeeded William Higman as Customs Collector, a post he held until superannuation in 1892.

**Joseph Bell** [1809 – 1886] is entered as having paid pew rent from March, 1856 to March 24th, 1857, in cash in full, amounting to £2. There are no further entries, nor is the pew number recorded. Joseph Bell was born in County Fermanagh, Ireland and during his lifetime had travelled to Australia, California and the West Indies. He came to Port Dover in 1835 and on May 13th, 1839 it is recorded that Israel Wood Powell, President of the Harbour Company, called a Director's meeting at the Inn of Joseph Bell.

My Auntie Alice told me that Mr. Bell came to Port Dover after having prospected for gold in western Canada, with considerable success. On crossing the prairies on horseback carrying a small fortune in gold nuggets, he was aware of a fellow traveller riding a few miles behind him. When he realised, near nightfall, that the stranger was matching his pace to that of Joseph Bell himself, he became suspicious and when he camped and the stranger did not come on along the trail to join him he became even more uneasy as to the man's intent. Ignoring the stranger, he hobbled his horse and built a small fire for his evening meal. As dusk turned to night he crawled into his bed roll, first carefully placing the loaded pistol he carried under his pillow.

Feigning sleep, but keeping a wary eye on his back-trail, Bell did not have long to wait. As he watched, the stranger could be seen stealthily approaching his campsite. When within a few feet of his camp the intruder drew a heavy colt from its holster, but as he aimed it at Bell's head, Bell drew his own gun and fired. In the light of his own gun's flash Bell saw the man pitch forward, to drop within inches of his own head. Assuring himself that the thief was indeed dead, Bell turned in again, until daybreak.

Following breakfast, Bell saddled his horse and rode back to the intruder's camp where he found a pouch of gold nuggets in his saddle-bags as great, or greater, than his own. Finding no identification, Bell saddled the stranger's horse, tying the extra bed roll and supplies to what now served as an additional pack animal. Bell then returned to his own camp to bury his would-be killer, break camp, and continue his journey a much richer man than when he had stopped the night before.

With the proceeds from his gold Joseph Bell was able to build the prestigious Dominion Hotel, in Port Dover, in 1875. The building still stands on the north-west corner of Main & Market street. He was found dead in his hotel Saturday, September 10th, 1886.

**G. N. Buck** is almost the last entry in the Pew Register, as renting pew # 29 in 1857, at the back of the church. He paid one years fee of $8.00 to Easter of 1858. For the next two years he paid only $4.00 per year by cash. The rate may have been reduced because his pew was at the back of the church, or did he only rent half of the pew. The register does not make this clear. In 1860 he paid $4.00 by cash, but for one half year only, to October 1860.

**Dr. Culver** and **Walker Powell** shared a pew between them for pew #6 and each party paid promptly. In 1859 the Culver share was paid by Mrs. Culver to 1860 at $7.00. They also paid that year toward the stipend for the rector, the sum of $20.00 each. [Walker Powell was a son of Israel Wood Powell, became Adjutant-General of Canadian Militia. His brother Berkley Powell built the fine home on Main Street, now known as "The Port of Call."]

**Dr. Caughill's** name does not appear in the register until an 1858 entry for pew #21. – To 1/4 years rent to half back seat to Easter 1859 – $2.00. To stipend contribution – $12.00. In 1859 – To one year rent to Easter 1860, half seat – $4.00. This is followed by the entry for March 24th, [1859?] – By "cleared account and Bad."

**Miss Carpenter** was billed in 1859 for pew rent for half the year to December for $3.00 on pew #28. She paid $1.50 to Easter, when the pew was given up and let to Mrs. Clarke.

**William Dixon** listed as the Butcher, as opposed to William Dixon the farmer, rented pew #20 for the full five years of the Register, paying half-yearly. In the 1851 census a William Dixon is noted as being an Englishman, forty-eight years of age and an Innkeeper. Had he by age fifty-three become a butcher? The census goes on to point out that his wife Jane is 45, son Charles, born in Canada is 22, Mary 16, Thomas 14, Ann 13, Harriet 12, John 6, Jane 5, and George is 3 years of age.

**William Dixon** the Farmer rented pew #2 paying cash each year and entered always in pounds, payed half yearly. In 1859 he is billed on April 25th – To 1 year pew rent to Easter 1860 – £14 0s 0p. On May 14th, 1859 he paid £7 and again on November 6th, 1859 he paid £7. This seems a very high rental charge, but one wonders if it is all intended to be in dollars, not in pounds as recorded.

**F. W. Ellis** rented pew # 16 which he paid up from February 8th, 1856 to March 24th 1857 as billed at £1 13s 6p. W. H. Newell is billed for pew #16 from 1857 onward. He contributed to the stipend in 1858 – $10.00. In the 1851 census F. W Ellis is listed as a Canadian, a foundry man, and 33 years of age.

**Mrs. Ellis** is recorded as renting pew #31 and payments are recorded as being settled from September 10th, 1856 to March 24th, 1857. Is she now the widow of F. W. Ellis? Her account for 1857 notes that she now rents only half of pew #31. In each year she settles her account by charging for duties around the church, such as washing surplices regularly and cleaning the church. On April 8th, 1860, it is recorded that Mrs. Ellis is owed $26.00 for services as Sexton etc. for the previous year, and on that date a balance of $10.50 is paid to her.

**Captain William Fyfield** On the last page [page 38] of the pew rent register Capt. Fyfield's name is recorded and is followed by Sexton.

| In 1856, | July 10th | To cash paid Revd. Mr. Birch your subscription to Church bell | $ 1.50. |
| In 1858, | July 4th & 15th | to cash $4.00 & $6.00, Dec 17th, $2.00. | $12.00. |
| In 1859, | Feb. 11th | to cash $2.00, to cash from Richard Stephens $3.50 | $ 5.50. |
|  | Mar 11th & 17th | $1.00 & $2,00, Apr. 1st & 23rd, 2x $2.00 | $ 7.00. |
|  | Apr. 30th $0.50, July 19th to cash $1.00 |  | $ 1.50. |
|  |  |  | $27.50. |
| Contra | April 24th, | By amount one years Salary | $26.00. |

In the 1851 census William Fyfield is entered as Lighthouse keeper of the Port Dover lighthouse, born in England, aged 55 years. Sarah, wife of William Fyfield, is recorded as having died September 2nd, 1834, aged 39 years, and buried in Doan's Hollow cemetery. On December 7th, 1861, Captain McNeilledge records that "Old Mr. Fyfield died this morning. He's been ill this some time. He has been tending the light house at Port Dover since first built in October 1845." & on December 8th, 1861, "I went to Dover to see when Mr. Fyfield was to be buried. – I went to the funerele [sic] in the afternoon. He was interred at Dones [sic] burying grounds. Revt. G. Salmon attended, a respectable turnout. The vessels in the harbour had their colours half-mast, he being an old seafaring man." No stone has ever been located for William Fyfield in the Doan cemetery.

The 1851 census also notes an Ellen Fyfield from Ireland, aged 30. Was she a daughter, or any relation to William? Richard Fyfield is also recorded as a sailor, English, a Methodist age 31. His wife Maria is Canadian, Methodist, age 42, with a son Richard, 4 years of age.

**NOTE:** The Doan's Hollow Cemetery is one of the oldest burying grounds in the County, part of it having been given by Captain William Park for a public burial site in 1798. A unique feature of the cemetery is the iron roadside fence with its interesting "witches' gate." W. E. Cantelon has left us a painting of the unusual white oak tombstone made by a pioneer German carpenter to be placed as a head "stone"over his grave upon his death. It is now fastened to a tree at the rear of the cemetery. Many of those early pioneers interred in the Doan's Hollow cemetery were parishioners of St' John's Church, Woodhouse.

**Samuel Gamble** rented one half of pew #15 in 1858 for $7.00. In 1859 the other half is recorded as rented by W. Dixon, who paid $3.00. Gamble made a $5.00 stipend contribution. Samuel Gamble was known to be an Insurance agent in Port Dover at this time.

**Mrs. Hall** - no further record has been found.

**Jaffrey Harvey** rented pew #16 when Quintin Barrett gave it up in 1858 paying part of pew broken time for cash at $5.50. In 1859 – this entry appears – Feb. by cash borrowed - [toward stipend?] - $40.00. Also, pew rent $7.00, four debit entries to August for stipend - $38.00.

**J. A. Haviland** - no record found of this name.

**Messrs. J. F. Haycock & Co.** This account for pew #3 was billed and paid in 1856 £4 9s 2pence ha'penny. Each year thereafter to 1860 they were billed and paid $14.00 as pew rent. In 1858 & 1860 they were billed for and paid $36.00 as contribution to stipend. Final 1860 entry is of $9.00 carried to new ledger. **W. A. Haycock.** The following entry on pg. 15 of the pew rent book is found; In 1859 – By order on Vickars [contribution to stipend] – $40.00. Next entry is cash, $5.00, cash for J. F. H[aycock] for S. B. Hill, [?] $5.00 equals $10.00. Balance to new ledger - $10.00.

Frederick H. Haycock was the Collector of Custom for many years in Port Dover, being replaced about 1859 by William Higman. The death of F. H. Haycock, at his home in Brantford, aged 59 years, 3 months, is recorded on October 26th, 1879. William Higman died, aged 80 years on February 2nd, 1869. He was replaced as Collector of Customs by his assistant, T. B. Barrett.

**Mrs. Honan** is shown as renting pew #25, but no details are recorded.

**G. W. Hotchkiss**, rented pew # 2. There are a number of entries recording payments of rent at odd periods over the five years, and of different amounts. In 1858 a $6.00 contribution was made to the stipend. Mr. Hotchkiss was the author of an article in the Maple Leaf entitled "Port Dover, 1851 to 1861" which provided invaluable insight into the state of the parish at that time. He came to Port Dover in 1851 being employed by Israel W. Powell and later by his brother-in-law Henry Wheeler. By 1856 he is recorded as a Lumber merchant.

In 1860 the family sold everything and moved to the United States. Some time later this "tongue-in-cheek" advertisement appeared in the Post Office in South Evanston:

"Cutter for Sale - $25.00. Will trade for a brick house on a corner lot, a 2:06 3/4 trotting horse, groceries, dry goods or a good-

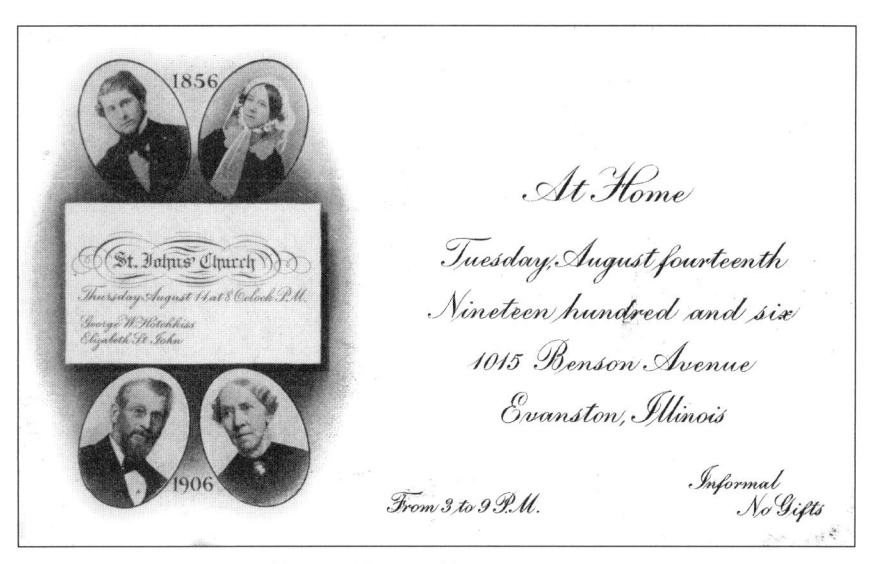

*George & Elizabeth Hotchkiss Golden Wedding Announcement*

looking servant girl, blond with black eyes preferred. The same (cutter, not girl) may be seen at my house; George W. Hotchkiss, #241 Benson Ave,"

A December 26th, 1890 issue of the Maple Leaf noted that G. W. Hotchkiss was the President of the "Lumber Trade Journal Company."

**George Husted** seems to have rented pew #19 from 1857 onward, when he made a $6.00 payment to Rev. R. S. Birch [Burch] in full. In 1859 he paid $4.00 of the bill for $6.00 billed as of May 31st, by cash. The next entry being May 31st, 1859 by order [of Reverend Johnstone] Vickars, $5.00. Balance on new ledger $3.00.

**Mrs. Howard** rented pew #25 being billed in 1856 to pew rent £1 10s 7pence, ha'penny, of which she paid 16s 10 pence ha'penny. In 1857 – Feb. 3rd by cash W. Jenkins 13s 9p. In 1858 – April 5th, paid $5.00. In 1859 – Jan 3rd & April 25th paid $2.50 each time. Pd to S. Gamble, see C. B. [?] apl. [application] 1860 paid $5.00.

**William Inman** rented pew #13 in 1856 and paid in full. In August 1857 billed for pew #34 and paid $14.00. In 1858 – April by cash in full $14.00. In 1859 – pew rent is billed at $7.00 for ½ seat and paid, plus $5.00 to stipend. The other half of the seat is billed to S. Gamble, but he paid nothing in that year. In the 1851 census William Inman is recorded as a clerk, English, 21 years of age. William Inman was book keeper at the Woollen Mills of Mr. Jonathon Ellis.

On February 20th, 1860, Captain McNeilledge reports the death of Clara Van Norman, aged 24 years, wife of William Inman. February 22nd, 1860 he continues "Alexander and I went in the buggy to Mrs. Inmens funerul [sic] at Dover. Large and respectable attendance, beautiful carving of an anchor, with S.[amuel] Gardner's signature. On the base of her tombstone is carved; "She left a loving husband, two children dear, to mourn her loss."

**Andrew Jamieson** rented half of pew #31 in 1856 & 1857 paying 13s 6p & $4.00 respectively. In 1858 the entry is made thus – rent of ½ pew ending Easter 1859 - $4.00. Repudiated. The 1851 census shows the following; Andrew Jamieson, farmer, born in Scotland, age 28 years of age; Isabella, 50 years of age; Peter, sailor,

20; Robert, labourer, 15; James, 13; Charles, 10; James, 1; Listed as well are Jane [Jamieson], born in Scotland, age 22, and C. of E. who is married to J. Andrews, a joiner, born in Scotland, aged 24 and member of the K of S.

**Andrew Lees** rented half of pew #11 and is noted as renting the parsonage house. The first entry is in 1858 when pew rent of $14.00 plus house rent of $21.00 equalled $35.00 paid. In 1859, pew rent is $14.00 plus cash overpaid in Matthews order $5.00, to cash for house rent $30.00 equalled $49.00. In 1860 – a 1/4 year rent on parsonage is $35.00 & on Feb. 8th a further payment of $35.00 is made for a total of $70.00 paid. On April 9th, [1860?] this entry is made – ($40.00 pmt. To Thomas. Waters) By balance forward – #30.00 - Carried to new ledger.

Andrew Lees was born in Berwickshire, Scotland in 1809. He graduated as a Civil Engineer in Edinburgh, and came to Canada to enter into the lumber and timber business. He became a partner of Thomas Waters, married Maria McCoy, and lived in the house, at the head of Main Street across from the McCoy farm, that was owned by Ansley Evans, of the Dove Stock farm, when I was growing up. Andrew Lees was involved as an Engineer in many important projects, including the lighthouses of Long Point. Andrew is listed in the 1851 census as being 42 years of age and Presbyterian. His wife Maria, born in Ireland, is C. of E., aged 34 years. Their family consisted at that time of Jane, Canadian, Presbyterian, age 14; Barbara, 12; William, 10; Andrew Jr., C. of E.3.

I have been unable to locate the "Parsonage House" or ascertain why it was rented to Mr. Lees. A daughter Elizabeth, or Bessie, married Harry W. Ansley. Andrew Lees died September 8th, 1873 aged 64 years. His wife, Maria McCoy Lees, died August 4th, 1881 aged 83 years. Their son Andrew Lees Jr., a promising young Barrister married Mary, a daughter of Andrew Thompson in 1870. He died October 18th, 1874 aged 25 years. His widow, Mary, married Crosbie Morgan in 1890.

Clifford H. A. Lees, a son of Andrew Jr., developed a Cider Mill run by horse-power in 1891, and soon after bought a large ice house between the factory and the tannery which he converted to an Evaporator. By October of 1892 the Evaporator was in operation, employing nine hands to keep it working.

**Edward Matthews** is first listed in 1858 as paying pew rent to Easter of 1859 - $7.00 plus stipend payment of $6.00. In 1859 he is billed pew rent to 1860 of $14.00. In May - by order on Lees he pays $20.00 and on December 31st, by cash for balance - $7.00. The pew number is not recorded.

James Prince of Orange McCoy shared pew #7 equally with Benjamin Williams and in each year from 1856 to 1859 when billed they paid the fee equally and on time. The 1851 census lists James McCoy as a farmer, born in Ireland aged 31 years; Jane McCoy born in Ireland, aged 73. He was one of the members of the Building Committee, where more is recorded about him.

**John McQuade** [also McWade] rented pew #27. In 1856 – to pew rent billed 23s 9p. Credit six weeks services as Sexton @ 2/6 [2shillings, six pence.] equals 15s. In 1857 – 1 year pew rent to Easter 1858 – £1 5s 0p. – Repudiated. The 1851 census lists John McWade as a labourer, aged 30 years; Margaret, aged 24 years; Anne, 5; George, 1.

**Alexander McNeilledge**, as mentioned earlier, rented pew #17 from February 1856 to 1860, and paid his dues promptly. In 1851 he is recorded as a farmer, a Scottish Presbyterian, aged 61 years. His wife Mary Ann [Thumb] of Philadelphia, 54 years of age; Alex Jr. of Philidelphia, 29 years of age; Aletta, Canadian, 28 years of age. Mary Ann is recorded as being of the Church of England.

Captain Alexander McNeilledge was born in Greenock, Scotland on November 8th, 1791. He went to sea with his father Daniel on May 2nd, 1800 aboard the Pandora, bound for St. John's, Newfoundland. He sailed the world in Clipper ships, working his way to Master of his own vessel. In 1830 he retired from his deep sea life to join his brother Colin, operator of the new flour and grist mill, in Dover in June of that year. He worked with Colin from 1830 to 1835 as book-keeper. Though he purchased a farm on the St. John's road, he was never meant to be a farmer.

He regularly used his ship's quadrant to shoot the sun and set the town clock. Ship's Captains welcomed him aboard their schooners and he often advised them on ways of getting more speed and better service from their vessels. Captain McNeilledge produced a Lake Pilot for the north shore of Lake Erie which was welcomed by all those sailing the Great Lakes as the first reliable guide to the courses and hazards when navigating Lake Erie's north shore. Sketches made for friends of vessels, named for family members, are prized possessions in many Woodhouse homes and local museums today. He died August 20th, 1874 in his 82nd year.

**Henry Morgan** rented pew #30. The entry in the pew rent book reads; In 1857 – April to rent pew #30 ending April 1857 – $4.00. Aug 8th, to rent pew ending Easter 1858 – $8.00 equals $12.00. In 1858 – April to one years pew rent $8.00. To stipend - $12.00. In 1859 – April 24th, one years pew rent to Easter, 1860 - $8.00; May 16th, By cash on a/c - stipend $6.00. Nov. 6th, by balance to Thomas Waters – $10.00.

Henry Morgan, born in Ireland, in 1803, was a ship's captain. On July 10th, 1841, McSwain, shipbuilder of Port Dover, launched the schooner Margaret Morgan. A part owner was H. Ross & Co. of Simcoe but as Henry Morgan's wife, also born in Ireland, was Margaret Benner Newell, 1812 – 1900, one wonders if Henry Morgan, as the Captain, was also part owner of the schooner, naming it after his wife.

Henry was also a noted Meteorologist, having equipment located on the roof of the old Town Hall. Every day he walked from his home on Prospect Hill to take observations from the Town Hall roof. After his death the work passed to L. G. Morgan, and in 1919 it passed to Crosbie Morgan. For over 75 years the local meteorological service was in the capable hands of the Morgan family. Morgan Ave. a short street running west from Second Ave. was named in their memory. Their four children were Llewellan G., Crosby, Florence and Semina.

Llewellyn G. Morgan took over publishing the Maple leaf from E. D. Passmore on September 14th, 1883. The Maple Leaf offices were in the lower level of the impressive Town Hall in Powell Park at this time. His first issue was Vol. IX, No. 6. He made many improvements in the paper. He was a Public School teacher and after obtaining a B. A. taught High School until forced to give up due to deafness. He was Editor of the Maple Leaf for 38 years. Llewellyn Morgan was burned to death in his home on January 18th, 1920. Crosbie Morgan, a Fenian raids veteran, died on August 28th, 1931 in his 87th year.

**Charles Mudford** rented pew 26. In 1856 he paid cash to

William. Inman – £1 5s 1/2p. The next entry is 1858 – 1 year pew rent from Easter 1857 – Bad.

**Reverend J. G. Mulholland** is entered in the same column, following Joseph Bell's account, which was not paid for by him after March 24th, 1857. The following entries appear after the name of Reverend Mulholland. He seems to have acted as Rector, at least on a part time basis, prior to the arrival of Reverend Johnstone Vicars, as well as during his incumbency. Although Mr. Burch is recorded as the first Rector, from 1856 to 1858, after St. Paul's was completed. We know very little about him even as to when he left the parish. Reverend J. G. Mulholland seems to have been engaged for $4.00 per Sunday, beginning perhaps as early as April of 1858. It would seem, therefore, that Mr. Burch remained as rector of St. Paul's until the spring of 1858. From the entries in the pew rent register it would appear that the services of the Reverend Mulholland were required for a minimum of thirty-four Sundays in 1858 and until the arrival of Reverend Johnstone Vicars on November 21st, 1858, from Mount Pleasant. The record as it appears in the pew rent register follows :

| | | |
|---|---|---|
| In 1858 | - July 23rd, to cash on account $20.00. Expenses to Synod | $ 4.00 |
| | - Nov. 14th, to cash on Salary $20.00. By expenses to Synod | $ 4.00 |
| | - By duty in Church, 34 Sundays @ $4.00 [8 months] | $136.00 |
| | - By horse hire, $4.00, claimed & not allowed by congregation | $ 0.00 |
| | | |
| In 1859 | - Jan 26th to Salary $40.00. May 16th to order Woolenough | |
| | - $20.00. To cash paid Mail $20.00. Nov. 5th, to balance of Woolnough's order $20.00 = $144.00. By balance forward | $140.00 |
| | - November Balance forward, carried down $4.00. | |
| | - This leaves $8.30 still claimed by him on horse hire. | |
| | - [Was Woolnough an ordained priest? He seems to have been paid for services taken prior to Rev. Mr. Vicars arrival.] | |

**Reverend G. Mulholland** is noted as being Principal of the Norfolk Grammar School in 1857. He was succeeded by J. J. Wadsworth in 1869. He is also listed as Principal of Maple Lodge Academy for Young Ladies and Boys under 9 years of age in 1865. He died in San Antonio, Texas on June 17th, 1895.

**Robert Nicholl Esquire.** is the first name recorded in the register, as renting pew #1. He is billed in installments from February 8th, 1856 and on Sept 24th, - to amount due as rendered – (Settled) — £5 11s 7pence ha'penny. In 1857 – April 23rd - By check on the Bank of Upper Canada, Toronto - £5. The next entry is; April 23rd, - By relinquished balance - 11s 71/2p equals - £5 11s 71/2p.

**W. H. Newell** rented pew #16 from August 1857 to 1860 paying as billed plus a $10.00 contribution to the stipend.

*Walker Powell*

**Walker Powell** shared pew #6 with Dr. Culver from 1856 to 1860. In 1859 they both paid $20.00 as a stipend contribution.

**James Riddell** was entered in the register as sharing pew #11 with Andrew Lees. He appears to have paid half the billing in 1856 but then Riddell's name was crossed out. [Did he join the congregation of the Presbyterian church, perhaps?]

James Riddell was born in Roxboroughshire, Scotland, in 1820. He emigrated to Canada in 1840 and settled in Port Dover in 1844 where he served as Post Master for ten tears. He also served as a Justice of the Peace for twenty years. He was appointed Captain of the Volunteers during the Russian War, in 1854. In 1860 he was named to the post of Passport Agent for the Canadian Government. In 1871 James Riddell became an Inspector on the Inter-colonial Railway, being stationed in Cedar Hill, where he also served the community as Post Master.

While in Port Dover he succeeded Hammond & Knight as a Forwarder & Commission Merchant and for several years operated a highly successful and extensive business as a General Merchant. Married to Catherine Morgan who bore him three daughters; Mrs. Jerome Platt, Mrs. R. M. Bundy and Miss Edith Riddell and four sons; John M. of Montreal; James D. of Stratford; Allan M. of San Francisco and Lorne, of Toronto.

James Riddell died on May 14th, 1896 aged 75 years. His wife Catherine died at the home of her daughter, Mrs. Jerome Platt, in Horseheads, New York on January 29th, 1899 aged 71 years.

*Catherine "Kate" Morgan, wife of James Riddell*

**Captain John Shaw** rented pew #9 for 1856 and 1857 but there was no further record. He is listed in the 1851 census as a Scottish mariner, aged 30 years; also Captain Alex Shaw, mariner age 33 years; and Mary Shaw, aged 40 years.

Captains Alex and John Shaw were born in Scotland, sons of Alexander McKenzie Shaw, Aide-de-camp to General McKay at Corunna. He was in charge of the burial detachment for the Army at the funeral of Admiral Lord Nelson. They lived originally in a house on Broad Street, when it extended from Brant Hill along the east side of Black creek marsh to a bridge crossing to Colman's Point and on to the bank of Patterson's creek near the Holmes distillery. With the coming of the Hamilton and North-Western Railway, from Jarvis, Broad street was taken over for the railway roadbed and the homes along it were demolished. Two short blocks on top of Brant Hill and a right-of-way to Highway 6, served by a wooden stair, are all that remains of Broad street to-day.

**Dr. Charles Seager** rented pew #8 from 1856 to 1860, paying as billed. The 1851 census records that he was born in England, aged 39 years; Mary, his wife was 29 years of age. Their children were Charles, 8; Francis, Canadian, 6; and Edwin E., Canadian, 2. They lived in the cottage on the south-west corner of St. Andrew's and Nelson St. East. Their grandson, Charles Seager, became Bishop of Huron.

*Home of Dr. Charles Seager, s.-w. Corner of Nelson & St. Andrews Streets*

**Richard Stephens** rented pew #23 from 1856 to 1860 paying in installments throughout. Richard "Dickie" Stephens was an Architect, Civil Engineer and Solicitor of Patents, who designed an addition to St. Paul's after the devastating lightning strike that is recorded elsewhere. He also laid out the Port Dover Cemetery and is credited with planting the now mature Sweet Gum trees, which until Brian McClung discovered the secret of their propagation, were the only known specimens to be found growing in southern Ontario. In 1867 Captain McNeilledge notes that Dickie Stephens conducted a Drawing School in Port Dover. His residence was at the upper end of Silver lake.

**John Salt** rented pew #28 in 1857 paying half yearly. Mrs. Hall is listed as collector in 1859 for half yearly payments of $3.00 on Jan.14th, and July 14th, to 1860.

John Alphery Salt was born in Sorel, Quebec on July 19th, 1829. He came to Haldimand County when 16 years of age and two years later he moved to Port Dover, where he became a schooner builder. On November 18th, 1856 he married Agnes Smith and they had seven offspring. Agnes died in 1884 aged 43 years and John married Esther Exelby on December 24th, 1884. Esther died on February 13th, 1930. John lived with his only surviving daughter, Agnes, in a solid brick house on the north-east corner of St. George and McNab street until his death on September 7th, 1928 aged 99 years. I remember him vaguely as I often visited with his daughter Miss Agnes Salt, until her death in April, 1947 aged 75. John Salt was a descendant of Sir Titus Salt, Bart, who was knighted for important discoveries he made in textiles.

**John Stevenson** rented pew # 13 from 1857 to Easter of 1859 when F. W. Ellis picked up the rental of pew #13.

**John Train** rented pew #15 from 1856 until May 24th, 1858 when he made a final pmt.

**Reverend Johnson Vicars** who followed Reverend Birch, moved to Port Dover on November 21st, 1858. He was listed in the book, with more detail as he takes his place as Rector.

**Solomon Walker** and Dr. N. O. Walker were listed originally as renting pews #19 & #28. In 1857 pew #1 was rented to Easter 1858. On August 1st, 1858 the $7.00 balance owing was repudiated. In 1859 **Miss Carpenter** was billed $3.00 for a half year to December. It was paid until Easter- $1.50 when the pew was given up and let to Mrs. Clarke. In the 1851 census Solomon Walker is listed as a 47 year old Canadian farmer. His wife Sarah, 43; Their children are Henry, labourer, 22; Nathaniel, student, 20; David, labourer, 18; Solomon, labourer, 15; Sarah, 13; and Celia, 5.

**Dr, Nathaniel Osborne Walker** was a grandson of Henry Walker, who came into the Long Point Country in 1793. He petitioned for land at Long Point in July of 1796. Henry married Mary Austin, daughter of Solomon Austin. Their second son Solomon Walker, 1805 - 1881, married Sarah Osborne, 1812 - 1888, and they farmed in the County. Sarah and Solomon gave birth to Robert Walker on April 12th, 1824. Robert graduated from McGill in Montreal as a Medical Doctor and returned to practise in Norfolk. Dr. Robert was found dead in his buggy on October 8th, 1875 at St. John's. He was in his 51st year.

Their second son, N. O. Walker, was born in 1833 and he too obtained a medical degree, but from the University of Toronto. He practised medicine for the first three years in Vittoria. He then moved to Port Dover, where he practised for many years. Dr. N. O. Walker married Mary Cross Burt of Toronto and they had four sons and three daughters. Of their sons, Fred went to Los Angeles, George to Idaho, Philip to Edmonton, Alberta and Paul to Peterborough, Ontario. The daughters married to become Mrs.

*Memorial tablet to Thomas Waters & Georgianna Spence Stephens Waters*

Tyrrell, of Toronto, Mrs Henry Walker of Enderby, B. C. and Alice Victoria, born in 1864, married Joseph Frederick Smythe to live on his attractive farm in Doan's Hollow, west of the cemetery on the Lynn river.

Interested in politics, Dr. Walker ran against A. Walsh in 1863 but was defeated. He ran again for a seat in the House of Commons in 1867 against Peter Lawson, but was again defeated. He joined the Central Medical Staff during the North-west Rebellion, for which he received a handsome silver medal for services rendered. Dr. Walker retired in 1911 and died in 1915.

**Thomas Waters** rented pew #10 from February 8th, 1856 to 1860. He made two contributions to the stipend of $10.00 each, paying them to C. Haycock. The 1851 census lists Thomas Waters as a farmer born in Surrey, England, aged 38 years; his wife Georgiana a Canadian aged 27 years; their children, Elizabeth A., 9; Henry H., 8; Erie, 6; Mary, 4; Drifield, 2

Thomas Waters was the first name listed in recording the members of the Building Committee. Do we interpret that as meaning he was the Chairman? See more about him there.

**Henry Y. Wheeler** rented pew #4 in 1856, but on May 12th, 1857 the account was transferred to G. W. Hotchkiss. The 1852 census records Henry Wheeler as an American lumber merchant, 35years of age. Nancy H. aged 32 years; Children were Charlotte, 12; Frances A., 9; Mary W., 4; Henry W., 2. From Captain McNeilledge's diary we learn that Mrs. Wheeler, her daughter, [Charlotte] and her brother James, brought Mr. Burch [also spelled Birch] the young minister for the Episcopal Church at Dover.

**Charles Williams** rented pew #21 from March 8th, 1856 for one year. In 1851 Charles Williams is recorded as being a 49 year old Canadian farmer. His wife Ann, 48, is Irish. They have 2 daughters, Sarah, 18 and Margaret, 14.

*******************************

We are reminded at this time that the Reverend Francis Evans, first rector of St. John's, and the priest credited with founding fourteen other Anglican churches in the parish of Woodhouse, after thirty years of outstanding service, had become ill. In 1858, due to his failing health, and on the advice of his doctor, Reverend Evans took a leave of absence and returned to his brother's home in Ireland. He had been back home barely a week, when on September 5th, 1858 he passed away. His widow returned to Canada to spend her remaining years in Toronto.

Noted in the McNeilledge diary is the arrival of Rev. Birch's successor, Reverend Johnstone Vicars, in November 1858. He goes on to say that he *"thinks he will be a good man as things have not gone altogether right since the consecration of the church."* **Reverend Johnstone Vicars, 1858 - 1860** moved his family from Mount Pleasant to Port Dover as the new Rector of St. Paul's on November 21st, 1858. On January 17th, 1859, he officiated at the funeral service in St. Paul's of the Reverend James Evans.

It was at this time that Mrs. Gerald O'Reilly, of Hamilton presented the Wardens with the alabaster baptismal font that had been in the Cathedral in Hamilton. A copy of a letter of thanks now in the Archives of the O'Reilly Family in Canada, at Ballinlough House, Co. Mayo, Ireland, follows;

Port Dover, March 4th, 1859.
To Mrs. Gerald O'Reilly, Hamilton.
C/o. Gerald O'Reilly, Esquire, Hamilton, Ontario.
Madam;
On behalf of the congregation of St. Paul's Church of this place, I beg to assure you of our thanks for the handsome present of a Baptismal Font to St. Paul's.
I remain,
Yours respectfully,
(Signed)   William Inman, Church Warden.

In the summer of 1859 Reverend Mr. Vicars became ill to the point where he could not take the services on Sundays, nor carry out his normal duties. The Reverend George Salmon, Jr. took charge in his absence. Though no records for this period have been found, one would assume that Lawrence Skey and Toby Barrett, who were both qualified Lay readers, would have stepped in to assist with the services. It is recorded that the Reverend Johnstone Vicars preached his last sermon in St. Paul's on April 29th, 1860.

This copy of a letter addressed to Reverend Johnston Vicars from Dr. Charles Seager may be of interest to some of my readers. It goes on at great length and in very convoluted language and seems to involve a petty disagreement over a charge for medical services. It is very difficult to interpret and I do not vouch for a correct interpretation of many of the words, on my part.

Port Dover, May 18th, 1860.
To the Rev'd Johnsten Vicars, late Member of the Royal College of Surgeons, London.
Licentiate of the Apothecaries Company In. - Ingersoll.
Rev'd Sir.
I was at a distance from home when yours of the 8th, inst. arrived here, which circumstance probably obtained for the point at issue a more speedy arrangement than might otherwise have taken place; Mrs. Seager having hastily settled it in my absence; for I should not have held the paltry sum of six dollars, the ballance [sic] over costs, of much importance. - You say, why I should have

been in such extraordinary haste to send you a summons you could not understand; My reply is my reasons were two-fold - In the first place, you, must be aware that had I not done so I would have gone to your present place of residence to have effected it; and in the next, what else could I have done after the very decided & uncouth verbal message you sent to my oft repeated written requests before you left. – But my principal object in writing, is to reply to your remarks respecting the cause of my attendance upon yourself; & I do say in regard to that part, that I cannot, for a moment, form such an unfavourable opinion of Dr. Covernton as your communication would lead me to entertain; nor do I believe, that he would, for his own purposes, wish to reduce me to the situation of an underling ; and, further I totally repudiate such a dishonourable closure with him. But, on the contrary, he called upon me in his usual courteous manner & asked me to meet him in your case on equal & friendly terms; & I cannot think he had any other conclusion in his own mind; for I have always received at his hands the most friendly consideration, & that honourable courtesy owed from one member of the Profession to another, which I assure you I do, and always shall, duly appreciate. – You must also know that your own Son followed me from place to place to request me to meet Dr. Covernton in consultation (such were the exact words, of which I have evidence to prove, had it been necessary ) at your house, on the day following that on which he called upon me. Indeed for what other purpose could I have been sought. Again, you sent directly yourself by different member of your own family, and at various times, to request my attention long after the time above referenced to. — I do indeed, with some degree of submission, admit that the finance part of my attendance upon you was constrained, and as such, on my part, neither very creditable nor desirable; which was the cause of my intimating to Mrs. Vicars, that (notwithstanding that, & you may suffer, it was never entirely off my mind) I was willing to visit you at any time you might require it, as I thought your Life then in rather a critical state; the complaint being to some extent masked; and so many fatal cases of the same having occurred about that time from the same cause; but certainly I never insinuated that it would be gratuitous, nor did I suppose you even expected that to be the case, sent in such unpleasant circumstances; and had you placed yourself in my position I doubt not you would have felt as I did. I do not wish to say much for my own share in your ultimate restoration to health, at the same time, I do believe that I did contribute (altho' you intimate not to your final recovery) at all events, to ward off perhaps what might have proved fatal consequences, which you yourself cannot be altogether unmindful of. – With respect to that part of your note in which you wish to prove your practice of the Medical Profession as exemplified in my own case, I must say that you are remarkably unfortunate in the choice of example. That Mrs. Seager in a momentary situation produced by some rather disagreeable effects of an Anodye, did send for you, altho' contrary to my expressed wish, is perfectly correct, but she did the same once before and in remarkably similar circumstances by your prediction, Mrs. Birtch, for I do believe she thought I was dying. She did not think at the time of your medical capabilities; nor do I recollect your even prescribing for me, medically or otherwise, and I am quite sure I never took a dose of medicine of your prescribing. I am aware that Dr. Covernton, happening to be in the neighbourhood, did make me a visit once, a day or two previous to that on which Mrs. Seager sent for you, whilst I was suffering from the effects of buoysissilus [?] & at the same time he mentioned you. But I was so much better then than I had been that with the exception of the Anodye above alluded to (which was of my own prescribing) I had no occasion to take, nor indeed have I ever had occasion to take any medicine of Dr. Covernton's prescribing. — In fact I looked upon your visits as entirely pastoral; which the circumstances of your bringing me Tracts, will render sufficiently obvious.

On taking a review of all things, it is somewhat surprising, & I do not wonder at your assuming great credit for such an unwanted act; that you did not try the paltry and dishonourable expedient referenced to in your note. Truly it was very considerate of you not to make a set-off for services which had to be paid for another way; but then, how you care to, with your broad sense of Medical Ethics, be so paltry & dishonourable, as you commit to charge a brother Medical man for any service at all is truly astounding. —

Your extreme liberality in allowing fifty cents a visit including prescriptions & illustrations (together with costs, while you left me to pay myself) must be regarded as really munificent, & calculated to raise the professional integrity (of which you claim to be a party to a very elevated & prosperous condition, all of which I hope will be only appreciated by the Profession at large.)—

I cannot conclude without making a few remarks with one deference to your Holy Orders, or your multiferous occupations, which however anomalous & universal they may appear I sincerely hope may have the effect of conducting you to the highest pinnacle of one another of the Trofiferous, [?] for there is nothing like having two strings to your bow; but then, you must not be altogether unmindful of that unfortunate old saying "between two Shoals, etc." — I know the Monks & Priests in other times were in the habit of visiting & relieving the sick, but that they received payment for each separately is very equivocal, their [?] (religious) and medical services being blessed. One of the Apostles too was a Physician, but it does not appear that he received pay for his ecclesiastical ministrations, & others might have done the same & vice versa. —

I wish you success in your endeavours to resuscitate the custom, which has now been obsolete, & I cannot help

thinking it wise that it is so, for the ancient adage that "a lack of ale traded is apt to be good ale none" [?] is I think a very true one. — As you have been at the trouble of sending a copy of yours to Mrs. Matthews, I cannot do better than follow such a worthy example.---
I remain Sir, Your ob'l Servant
(Signed)   Chas. Seager.

The **Reverend George Salmon** was no stranger to Woodhouse, being the son of Colonel George Salmon, who came to Canada West from Gloucester, England in 1810. He played an important part in the War of 1812, and in affairs in the district. The Salmon family had already started a Sunday School some time before the arrival of the Reverend Francis Evans. The Reverend George Salmon played an important role in the building of the first church at St. John's in 1821. After taking Holy Orders Reverend George Salmon served as curate to Bishop Mountain in Montreal. For much of his life he was involved with the Canadian Missionary Society. He took part in services in St. John's, Woodhouse, when visiting the area, and was available to assist with services in St. Paul's when Reverend Vicars became ill.

*Rev. George Salmon*

The **Reverend William Evans**, son of St. Paul's founder the Reverend Francis Evans, was appointed Rector of St. Paul's later in 1860, following the forced retirement due to illness of Reverend Johnstone Vicars. During his incumbency on July 23rd, 1861, disaster hit in the form of a devastating lightning strike which shattered windows and damaged walls of the church. Several pews were badly damaged as well. The Melodion was completely destroyed. Samuel Gamble, a parishioner, who was also the insurance agent for the $400.00 insurance policy carried by the Wardens, was badly injured while helping in making repairs afterwards.

At this time the vestry and organ chamber were built on the north-west corner of the existing church building. As Kay Burbidge suggests in her excellent history, celebrating the founding of the church 150 years ago, it is most likely that the cornerstone was hidden from view for all time upon that being done. It is logical to assume that the cornerstone would be laid on the St. George Street side of the new church, in 1852 and that it has therefore been hidden from view for well over 140 years.

No written record of the appointment of Mr. Richard "Dickie" Stephens, a local engineer, to draw up plans and specifications for the addition of a Vestry and the making of repairs to the building have as yet been found. We do know, however, that detailed plans for such an addition were made by Engineer Stephens. Richard Stephens was also a faithful charter member of the congregation.

A few years ago I asked to borrow a large leather-bound volume from its caretaker, Mr. Earle Awde. This had been found abandoned in the home of Richard Stephens to the east of the river, at the head of Silver Lake, on Mill Road. Mr. Stephens, who had lived there for years, had been called away very suddenly to California and never returned. Frank Awde, Earle's father, moved into the abandoned residence, living there for the next twelve years.

This heavy book obviously had been the original record book for engineering plans and specifications for projects undertaken by Sandford Fleming, Engineer, later Sir Sandford Fleming, who brought us daylight saving time, and designed our first Canadian postage stamp. The first pages contain drawings of bridges proposed for the Mirimachee river in New Brunswick. Detailed drawings of inventions by Fleming, and perhaps Stephens as well, are also included.

One assumes that Richard Stephens worked with, or for, Sandford Fleming, and inherited the projects book, as several of his projects are also recorded, with meticulously detailed drawings on

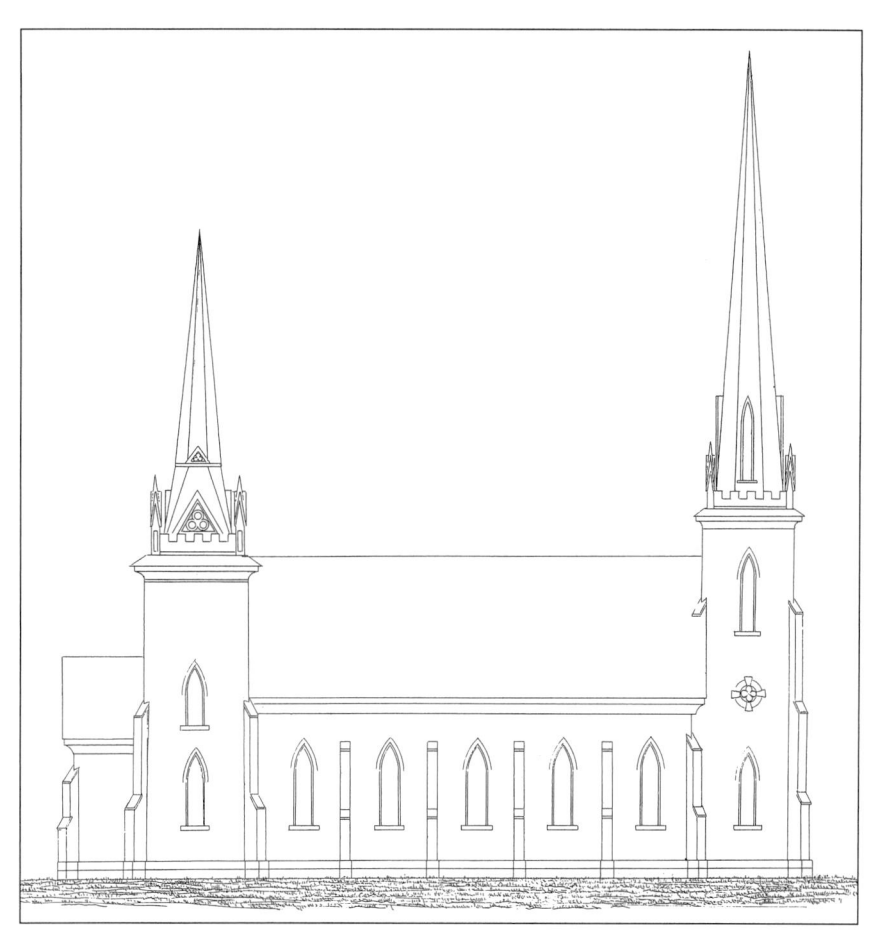

*Elaborate plans for addition & repair to St. Paul's after lightning strike.*

later pages of this historic volume. Detailed notes of his work and expenses in outlining the feasibility of building a channel, schooner basin and harbour to serve the village of Port Royal are included. He spent several days in taking soundings and in boring into the bottom of the cat-tail- choked Walsingham Marsh to plan this interesting project, which never did materialise. A design, floor plans and instructions for the building of the Rectory for Christ Church, Nanticoke was another of Stephen's projects, illustrated in the book.

Of particular interest to members of St. Paul's, Port Dover, are the detailed drawings of a proposed addition to the north end of the church. These grandiose plans included two lesser towers and

*Another elevation of Engineer "Dickie" Stephens plans for St. Paul's*

steeples as a part of the new Vestry and enlarged organ space, as illustrated. Though certainly impressive, the Select Vestry and congregation obviously did not elect to build such an addition at that time. I am sure the extra cost of such a venture was the major deciding factor in their decision against it. A much less impressive addition was finally accepted and built and has served the congregation well to this day. Although there is no date on any of the renditions, we can be almost positive that they were done in response to the damage done by the lightning strike in July of 1861.

From the Church Archives comes an interesting document entitled :

## Report of Expenditures on St. Paul's Church – 1861
Arising from damage by lightning.

A numbered list of the tradesmen and firms who were paid for services rendered in the renovations that followed the devastating lightning strike is written out as follows;

| | | | |
|---|---|---|---|
| Osias Ansley a/c | $49.34 | Robert Riddell | 5.05 |
| Chas. R. Robinson | 3.33 | – Beckstrom | 4.00 |
| John Holland | 20.00 | John O. Robertson | 16.20 |
| William Wallace | 2.00 | – McGra[w] | 2.00 |
| William Law | 28.12 1/2 | William Dixon | 19.00 |
| F. M. Ball | 8.25 | Robert Law | 33.00 |
| H. Hussey | 18.00 | N. O. Walker | 5.62 1/2 |
| P. Edsale | 1.50 | Bricklayers | 29.00 |
| Martin Smith | 4.50 | John Lamican | 4.50 |
| A. Pursell | 6.00 | C. B. Gustin | 22.53 |
| C. Robinson | 10.79 | J. F. Haycock | 4.29 |
| Samuel Gamble | 17.50 | Jaffray Harvey | 5.90 |
| John Holland | 32.50 | N. O. Walker | 1.50 |
| H. Hussey | 15.25 | J. Slocum | 5.25 |
| Paid for cleaning Church | 4.00 | Robert Riddell | 0.84 |
| Silas Jennings | 2.50 | Brush | 0.25 |
| – Powell | 1.85 | [Harry] Ansley | 6.00 |
| | | Total = | $390.37. |

On the back of this sheet are a great many calculations in pencil. Then this in brown ink
400.00 – Cash drawn
390.37 – Expended   Balance $9.63 on hand, pd. to A. Law for Jaffray Harvey.

---

Little else is known of the incumbency of the Reverend William Evans save that he presided over the traumatic period for the parish following the lightning strike. He seems to have lead his congregation well in handling this experience, and repairs proved satisfactory. No undue strain seems to have been put upon the congregation in the financing of the project. A new organ was installed and was to accompany the choir for many years into the future. It did require the services of a young man however to pump the bellows which supplied the air required to activate the pipes. If the pumper was derelict in his duties the sound produced by the organist left much to be desired.

CHAPTER SEVEN

# Reverend M.S. Baldwin Comes to St. Paul's

Maurice Scollard Baldwin, born in Toronto in 1837, came from an educated, well-to-do Irish family who had emigrated to Canada early in the nineteenth century. He had an uncle who was an Admiral in the British Navy and on his mother's side of the family, his grandfather was a General in the British Army. The Honourable Robert Baldwin, an Upper Canada reformer and statesman, was a cousin, who served for years as the President of the Upper Canada Bible Society. Maurice as a boy was not strong and for several years had to rely on crutches to get around. He loved his no nonsense mother dearly and obviously had a very happy childhood. On the day he gave up his crutches his brothers assisted him in a funeral procession to the bottom of the garden where they solemnly buried them for all time. His brother Edmund was destined to become the much loved Canon of St. James Cathedral. Arthur was to become the Reverend Arthur Baldwin, popular rector of All Saints', Toronto. Morgan Baldwin grew up to become the Harbour master of Toronto harbour.

Maurice Baldwin's father died at a young age leaving his mother to raise four boys on her own. The family were obviously financially independent, however, and Maurice received an excellent education, attending the newly established Upper Canada College, which in 1852 had been founded as a Church of England College by Bishop Strachan. He next enrolled in Trinity College, University of Toronto. He received his B. A. In 1859 and went on to win an M. A. in 1862.

Diocesan records indicate that Maurice Scollard Baldwin was

made a deacon in St. Paul's Cathedral, in London, in 1860. In 1861 he was ordained a priest by Bishop Cronyn, of the Diocese of Huron. He was serving as the Assistant Curate of old St. Thomas church, in St. Thomas, Ontario, from 1860 to 1862. Here he met and married the charming sister of the late Judge Ermatinger of that city.

Shortly after their marriage the Reverend Maurice Baldwin, on February 9th, 1862, was appointed to St. Paul's, Port Dover. The happy young couple were very well liked and accepted at once into their new parish. A lasting friendship was soon established with my great grandfather's family, and on the birth of their sixth child and third son on January 29th, 1867, his parents named him Hubert Baldwin Barrett, in deference to their one time rector and friend. From a 1902 article in the Maple Leaf we learn that the Baldwin's moved into a house on Main Street, once owned by the late William Walker. Their happiness was short-lived however, as Reverend Baldwin lost both his wife and their first-born child here.

I have in my possession a letter from Reverend Baldwin which I am unable to place in context with his supposed movements. Is he between leaving Port Dover & taking his charge in St. Luke's, Montreal? Here is the letter and I leave the reader to decide. The envelope long ago fell prey to a family stamp collector, so no year is noted. Punctuation is a very haphazard thing, as you will see. Paragraphs are non-existent.

Berlin, November 24th, [no year]

Dear Barrett.

I received your kind and I must say heart-rending letter for it goes to my soul to think of you being in want of the bread of life – Now my dear brother you do not know all that I have gone through of late being so unsettled and of a truth I had made up my mind to start for Dover long before this, but I have had to [do] the duty at this Berlin as the incumbent has been away and is indeed wholly unable to do any duty as he has had quite a severe attack of inflammation of the lungs – I have therefore been doing duty here and it has been arranged that I am to do so, during his absence. I write, my dear friend to say that

I am only looking for an opportunity to run down and see you all and preach for you – You see it is hard to manage it when there is no-one to do duty here while I am away, however I hope to be able to arrange it very soon when I will go down if spared. I had made up my mind to go before this as you know but have been prevented by having to fill this pulpit. I hope therefore in a couple of Sundays more to be with you as I do from my heart long to see you all. Do not therefore forget me for if spared you will see me there before long. My dear friend I hope all is well with you as regards the interests of the undying soul. In my feeble prayers I mention perpetually your name and most earnestly do I hope that you and your dear wife will both fight on in good warfare until the great crowning day comes and then you will both find it was good to have born on this earth the cross, to have labored and toiled hard for great then will be found to be the reward. And now expect me soon. Give my kindest regards to your wife Dr. Walker (I was going to commence an enumeration but think it is best to say) Mr. Higman Harvey and all the kind friends –

Yours in Christian Love<br>Maurice S. Baldwin

P. S. I am told a letter was sent to Dover for me – You will oblige me by having it re-mailed.

Upon leaving Port Dover Reverend Maurice Baldwin moved to Montreal, where he was appointed to the parish of St. Luke. They were inveterate letter writers and I include this example as much for the language as the content. It also illustrates the punctuation common to that period in time, or, rather the lack of it. He kept in contact with his friend and lay reader as this letter, one of many, to T. B. Barrett will attest:

Montreal, Feb. 8th, 1866.

My beloved friend;
Time rolls rapidly away. It is now the fifth month since I left Port Dover and yet I have not started, but the fact is

dear Barrett I do not find St. Luke's, Montreal like Dover with respect to getting away - in fact it is almost impossible without causing great confusion to get away for any time at all - There are so many things to be done, so many duties that cannot be neglected that you are like a bull in a net – I had most fondly hoped ere this to be in Upper Canada but the Bishop of Montreal has appointed me to one of those miserable deputations with which you all in the west are so well acquainted. I am to leave, God willing, on Monday the 19th going into the Eastern Townships and will be engaged about two weeks, I am also under engagement to give a lecture in Montreal on the 12th of March so that it will be impossible for me to leave for the West Prior to that date – I received your most kind and welcome letter - but my dear friend and brother you do not say one word about the inner life – You know I always like to hear in my letters from you something about that which concerns me most – I hope – most deeply do I hope my beloved brother that it is "well with you, well with the wife and well with all in your house" O My dear friend live near to Jesus – near to Him – now is your salvation nearer than when you believed. Do bend daily at a Throne of Grace for strength and assistance in each hour of need – The race cannot now be long - but the prize will be exceeding great - Be steadfast - be faithful for a little while longer and then will come the rest – the Kingdom and the glory – O My dear friend I could throw my arms about you for very love and to urge you to live nearer to Jesus, nearer to Jesus. Give my very kindest love to your excellent wife, and tell her I hope that you and she will go hand in hand together leading the little ones to a purer and a better world – O My dear brother what is there worth living for but Jesus – let this then be all our desire to know nothing but Christ and Him crucified –

Remember me please to the Higmans and tell them I will write all being well soon to them – Please give my kindest regards to Dr. Walker and tell him I will write to him,

D V, this week – Remember also your servant to the Morgans and Tom Clark, dear fellow. How I would like to see him. I cannot tell you how exceedingly kind the people all are here to me from the Bishop on his throne down to the humblest of the people – but all the kindness I receive does not obliterate from my heart the **indelible** marks made upon it by my beloved friend T B Barrett.

        Your Most affectionate friend.
        Maurice S. Baldwin.

Once established in St. Luke's the Reverend Baldwin's reputation grew as a powerful orator but a very caring, unassuming and modest man. Here he met and married a Miss Day. He and his family returned to Port Dover for a visit in May of 1866 with all his many friends in the parish.

In 1872 he was made dean and rector of Christ Church Cathedral, Montreal. He had always possessed the Irish gift for flamboyant oratory, and his reputation as a dynamic preacher soon blossomed to an incredible degree. Soon he was the most talked about and notable clergyman in the Province and beyond, yet he remained an unassuming and modest man, committed to his message and to the needs of his parishioners. He was a most sincere and caring individual beloved by all.

Perhaps the Reverend Dyson Hague gives us the best impression of Canon Baldwin at this time in this excerpt from his treatise on "Bishop Baldwin. One of Canada's Greatest Preachers and Noblest Church Leaders." I quote : "*A sea of upturned faces turned with an expectant hush as they discerned in the middle of the long chancel aisle the figure of Montreal's greatest preacher, moving with slow and set steps toward the pulpit. Canon Baldwin was then a man of medium size, and his rather plain, clean-shaven face was inscribed with a seraphic earnestness. He preached throughout his sermon with singular energy. His words burst out with tremendous force. His mouth worked like an engine. It seemed at times as if he were battling with some unseen antagonist between the pillars, and there was a curious intensity of accentuation, which to the very end of his life was the marked characteristic of his speaking. He beat out each word with a hammer of emphasis, and put an incisive accent not only on each word, but on every syllable and almost on every letter of every syllable; and yet, though he propelled the sentence with such an intensity of seriousness, there was, amidst all the rush of emotion and crack of intonation, a cadence, a musical interest, an attractive variety in his delivery, that held one fascinated to the very climax."*

Canon Baldwin was not only a great preacher, idolised by his congregation, but an accomplished administrator and worker at the parochial level. He was President of the Bible Society and a leading spirit in the Y. M. C. A. as well as the House of Refuge, the Hospital and almost all other benevolent institutions in the City.

It came as a tremendous shock to the citizens of Montreal, when in 1883 it was announced that Canon Baldwin had been elected Bishop of the diocese of Huron. "What will our church do without him?" was the cry. Accepting the call as the will of God, the popular Canon told his people in the Cathedral that he would have to leave them. Few men had a finer send off than the one accorded their beloved Canon Maurice S. Baldwin. It is reported that "the Jewish Rabbi, the leading editor, the foremost merchant prince, headed an innumerable body in their tribute of satisfaction at his elevation to the Episcopate, and their regret at their irreparable loss." Just prior to Christmas the following letter arrived in T.B. Barrett's mail:

> The Deanery, Montreal, Dec. 21st, 1883.
> 
> Dear Mr. Barrett
> 
> It is with feelings of heartfelt gratitude I acknowledge your warm congratulations upon my elevation to the Bishopric of Huron.
> 
> At this time more than ever do I need the earnest prayers of God's faithful people that "grace sufficient" may be given me to fulfil the arduous and responsible duties pertaining to this high office.
> 
> Again thanking you for your kind and sympathetic letter.
> 
> Believe me, Yours most Sincerely,
> Maurice S. Huron.

At his inaugural, Bishop Baldwin said : I desire to state as forcibly as I can the elements of ministerial success.

**First** : We need a ministry that believes in Jesus Christ ....... One not afraid to step out on the deep blue of God's promise, and trust where the whole world derides.

**Secondly** : We need a ministry baptised with the Holy Ghost and with fire ....... What the church needs most; ..... is the personal power of the Holy Ghost. A preacher without the Holy Ghost is like a professor giving his students a lecture on botany at midnight. ... stoop down and feel these flowers, you will perceive how exquisite is their structure, how various their growth. Botany cannot be studied at midnight. Christ cannot be preached at midnight either, without the Holy Ghost.

*Bishop Maurice Scollard Baldwin*

**Thirdly** : We need a ministry courageous and outspoken for the Truth...... Especially to the younger clergy would I say: Fear not, and though a thousand brilliant men affirm they have disproved some point of Revelation, believe them not. They are blind leaders of the blind.... Let us stand as Protestants for the Scriptural and Evangelical teaching as set forth in the 39 Articles of the Church of England, and sealed with the blood of martyred Bishops.

**Fourthly** : We need a ministry understanding the relative position of the Church to the world. The fierce demand of the world is that we should conform to its pleasures and its aims; the precept of Christ that we should come out and be separated from it..........

**Fifthly** : We need a ministry thoroughly alive to the great necessity of missionary activity. Everywhere as with the impulse of a new life, we see the Church awakening to do her long-forgotten work in the great harvest fields of the world. .........

This was the inspiring message given by the newly named Bishop of Huron as his primary charge to his clergy and laity alike. For the next twenty-one years, from 1883 to 1904, Bishop Baldwin was the indefatigable and revered head of his Diocese of Huron.

Bishop Baldwin launched into his new duties with his usual fervency and zeal despite the tremendous change from the life of a great cathedral preacher to that of Bishop of a Diocese with its many mundane problems, endless visitations and deputations of often disgruntled parishioners. The travel involved over the extensive territory of the diocese alone; by buggy, wagon and railway train must have been a heavy burden, on top of the endless problems of the struggling parishes.

An 1886 letter to T. B. Barrett from the Bishop raises more questions than answers as to what had actually transpired in the Bishop's visits to Port Dover. It was as follows under the Bishop of Huron's letterhead :

London, March 27th, 1886.

My dear friend

How can I thank you as I ought for all the kindness I received from you and your dear family. I think it was a great mercy that I was with you and not with strangers as then my sufferings would have been far greater. God willing I propose going down again next week but I think I must pitch a tent in the square for I really feel ashamed to go to anyone's house after all the trouble I caused in my last visit.

I have been much occupied since I saw you and have in fact been on the trot more or less all the time. I am anxious to make good my former promise and therefore anxious to start once more. Please give my kindest regards to Mrs. Barrett and your daughters and with my best love to yourself, believe me ever to be,

Yours in the blessed Word
Maurice S. Huron

On his arrival in London, Bishop Baldwin found that his predecessor Bishop Helmuth had set in motion plans for a new cathedral in London for the Diocese. After a detailed study of this plan Bishop Baldwin chose to keep St. Paul's as the Cathedral. Among other priorities, due to his notorious love of children, he promoted Sunday Schools. Quoting from an address once to Sunday School teachers he fervently stated : "I know of no time so opportune as youth for the acceptance of Christ, and no place so fitting as the Sunday School. This fair earth was developed into loveliness when it was yet young."

He became an advocate for both domestic and foreign missions. He promoted the temperance cause. He also encouraged the formation of Woman's Auxiliaries, a movement that was begun during his tenure. Due to his fund raising and accounting skills Huron was the first Anglican Diocese in Canada to guarantee minimum stipends for her clergy. Serving as President of Huron College, Bishop Baldwin attended the First Lambeth Conference, in 1888, in England.

The Bishop took a lively interest in every thing going on around him, having a special interest in chemistry and astronomy. His sermons were lavishly illustrated by examples taken from both the historic and scientific world. He also published at this time two evangelistic works, titled "A Break in the Ocean Cable" and "A Life in a Look" We in St. Paul's should feel great pride in the fact that our pulpit is dedicated to the memory of this amazing man, whose first parish in his own right, as a newly ordained priest, was ours. Bishop Baldwin died at the See House in London in 1904.

Returning to the fortunes of St. Paul's, there seems to be no record to date of the man who followed the Reverend Maurice Scollard Baldwin, save his name. On May 10th, 1863 the **Reverend Samuel Harris** [1863 - 1865] held his first service and was listed as the incumbent of St. Paul's. Although he held service for the next eighteen months nothing seems to be known of him. In researching the history of Waterford the Reverend Samuel Harris was listed as the incumbent there from 1862 to 1875. Did he just fill in for the ensuing eighteen months while St. Paul's was without a regular Rector?

On November 5th, 1865 the **Reverend John Irwin** [1865 - 1866] replaced Reverend Samuel Harris as Rector of St. Paul's. Canon Cornish informs us that on July 7th, 1867, just one week after Port Dover celebrated confederation, Reverend Irwin became ill and left the parish for good on July 14th, 1867. The Reverend Irwin later became rector of the Anglican church in Jarvis. One has to wonder at the nature of his illness, and if it may have been self-inflicted. Kay Burbidge notes that; "Mention of the fact that in April, 1872, [the Reverend John Irwin] gave a lecture on temperance in the Port Dover Town Hall is followed by the cryptic comment that 'he's quite a reformed man.'"

For the next four months at least services were carried out by lay readers and others, including Thomas Waters. Though not mentioned, I expect that Lawrence Skey and Toby Barrett, qualified lay readers, played a role in the services of the church for that period, as well.

## Chapter Eight

# The Reverend Dr. William Tibbetts [1867-1875]

From "Ministers I Remember" by my great aunt, Alice Butler Barrett Parke, we are told that the **Reverend Dr. William Tibbetts** [1816 - 1889] a very scholarly man - with many letters after his name, took charge in St. Paul's on October 27th, 1867. William Tibbetts was a son of William Tibbetts, a hatter, and his wife Elizabeth Gray of Edinburgh, Scotland. He was the middle one of seven children. William was educated in the famous George Herriot Hospital, Edinburgh, placing first of three hundred boys for three consecutive years. Following graduation he spent three years in the Royal Navy as a mathematical instructor. He then returned to the University of Edinburgh to obtain his Master of Arts degree following that he went on to study medicine. He graduated in due course with an M. D. winning the gold medal for standing first in a class of two hundred students.

William married Laura Richardson, widow of Dr. William Cheyne, who

*Rev. Dr. William Tibbetts*

brought to the union a daughter, Mary G Cheyne. By 1846 he was living on the Portugese Island of Madeira, as a British Naval Surgeon. Of the eight years spent in Madeira William spent only one in general practice. This came about when the ship they had taken for either Mexico, or as others maintain for South Africa, became wrecked on the Island. William Tibbetts spoke fluent Portugese, Spanish, German, French and Italian and had a good knowledge of several other European languages. He was a classical scholar and an accomplished musician on several instruments. William while working at Funchal became a member of the Royal College of Surgeons of Lisbon, Portugal. He is also thought to have acted as the British Consul on the Island.

Laura Matilda, born in Marseille on June 25th, 1815, was the daughter of an English family involved in shipping out of Marseille, France. She was one of a large family. While married to Dr. Cheyne Laura lived in several locations in Mexico. An accomplished linguist she was very much at home with these Spanish speaking people. Laura and William, while living in Madeira, had several children, four of whom died there in infancy.

In 1854 the Tibbetts left Madeira for Covington, Kentucky across the Ohio river from Cincinnati where Laura's sister lived with her husband, a river boat Captain. Their youngest son, John Camnitz, was born here the following year. William practised medicine here and during the Civil War was a surgeon and in charge of the Covington Military Hospital. Here he ministered to the spiritual as well as the bodily welfare and the medical needs of Union and Confederate soldiers alike. While in Covington William joined the Masonic order as a craft mason and member of the Royal Arch.

William had had a long and lasting interest in theology and in 1863 he was admitted to Holy Orders as an Episcopal Deacon by Bishop Smith of Kentucky. Two years later he gave up his medical career to become involved in the work of the church on a full time basis. He was assigned to the Diocese of Ohio. While resident in Cincinnati in 1865 he extended his masonic interests to become a Knight Templar within the order.

In 1866 the Tibbetts family moved to Point Edward, near Sarnia, in Canada, where William became a Deacon in the

Anglican Church of Canada. Shortly after his arrival he was ordained a priest by Bishop Cronyn of Huron Diocese and served as assistant at St. George's Church in Sarnia. William's first church following his ordination was St. Paul's, where he and his family took up residency during Canada's recognition as a Dominion on July 1st, 1867. William and Laura Matilda were both about fifty-one years of age on their arrival in Port Dover and they brought with them their children Isabella Murray, age 21, James Irving, age 19, William Francis, age 15, and John Camnitz, age 12. Laura's younger unmarried sisters, Eliza and Henrietta, also came to Port Dover to live with the Tibbetts at this time.

Quoting from Auntie Alice's "Ministers I Remember", she points out that following the Reverend John Irwin "Dr. Tibbetts was perhaps not too well suited to be the Parish Priest of a small country church. He simply would not visit though he received courteously and charmingly those of his congregation who visited him. However his witty and sprightly wife undertook these duties for him, and "was soon known and loved by young and old – by all sorts and conditions of men, women and children."

Reverend Dr. William Tibbetts affiliated with Erie Lodge # 149, A. F. & A. M. where he was welcomed wholeheartedly and served most ably as Lodge Chaplain. On July 6th, 1870, during Dr. Tibbetts incumbency at St. Paul's, Memorial Church, Port Ryerse was dedicated. When Bishop Cronyn of Huron Diocese died in September of 1871, Dr. Tibbetts attended the service of consecration of his successor Bishop Helmuth in August. A shock came to the whole Anglican community in Norfolk when the frame church of St. John's, Woodhouse was burned to the ground in November, 1874.

Reverend Dr. William Tibbetts served as Rector of St. Paul's for eight years. As his health had deteriorated to the point that he could not carry out his duties as he felt he should, he moved to Simcoe in 1875, to serve Trinity Church as their assistant. In the period from 1876 to 1979 he moved to the Goderich area, serving as assistant in Holmesville, Summerville and Sterling. Finally, in 1879, due to his poor health over several years Reverend Tibbetts was superannuated and returned to Port Dover to live with his son, William Francis Tibbetts. Laura's sisters, Eliza and Henrietta Robertson, also continued to live with the extended family in Port

Dover. Here the Reverend Dr. Tibbetts, being always of a modest and retiring disposition, spent his declining years surrounded by his beloved library and family.

Laura Matilda died on February 8th, 1885 at seventy years of age. She was pre-deceased by her sister Henrietta and Eliza died on September 26th, 1894, aged seventy-six. The Reverend William Tibbetts died on February 4th, 1889, at seventy-three years of age. He was eulogised as "one of the most learned and scholarly priests in the Diocese of Huron" and touted as a "scholarly and sound churchman" by his colleagues in the clergy.

Of their several children, William Francis was the only one to settle close to his parents final home. On their arrival in Port Dover in 1867 they came to a thriving community surrounded by productive farms and lands still producing quality timber of all kinds. The harbour area was a busy one with a prosperous schooner and steamship trade. Exports consisted of grain, particularly malting barley, timber and livestock. Imports were heavy in all sorts of goods as the Lake was at that time the main "highway" for most trade in the area between manufacturing centres on both the Canadian and American sides of the lake. Fishing was also becoming an important industry. The bathing beach was also being discovered and with the coming of the railway in a few short years, Port Dover was soon to become famous as a summer holiday resort.

On completing his schooling in Port Dover William Francis apprenticed as a Pharmacist to John McBride, the local Druggist and owner of the present rectory. On July 1st, 1877, at twenty-five years of age, William Francis married Charlotte Emily Ansley, the daughter of Ozias Ansley. Ozias was Reeve of the town, and with his sons involved in many business ventures in town. Charlotte's mother was Clara Hortense Langs, sister of Emily Langs Barrett, and daughter of Jacob Langs, a well-to-do farmer of Windham township.

The newly-weds moved to Woodstock where William Francis started a pharmacy business. Here their first son Hugh Ansley Tibbetts was born on May 15th, 1878. They had returned to Port Dover shortly before his father had retired and moved back in with them in Port Dover. William Francis came back to form a partnership with his brother-in-law, Harry W. Ansley, in Ansley and

Tibbetts Drug Store. In 1880 William Francis succeeded his father-in-law Ozias Ansley as Reeve of Port Dover. On September 1st, 1882 their second son, Edward Leigh Richardson "Dick" Tibbetts was born.

William Francis, always interested in sailing had joined the Port Dover Yacht Club on his return to Port Dover. Through this connection, in the fall of 1883, William Francis and Harry Ansley had the honour of taking Queen Victoria's son, then Prince of Wales, to the Long Point Company cottages in their steamer , the

*William Francis Tibbetts*

"James Buckley." The Prince, destined to become King George V and his party, had a most successful two day hunt over the Long Point marshes before returning to Port Dover, to continue his tour of Canada.

On April 1st, 1886, William Francis's loyalty to the Conservative party bore fruit when he was appointed Postmaster by the Dominion government of Prime Minister Sir John A. Macdonald. He was thirty-four years of age at the time and he held the position until his death, forty-four years later. Upon receiving the appointment he and Harry Ansley wasted no time in fitting out a store in the Ansley block on Main Street as the new Post Office.

On February 4th, 1889 William Francis's third and last son, Alan Newell was born. Having served as Councillor, School Board member and Reeve of the town William Francis was quite well off. In 1890 he built his own sailing yacht "Trixie". In 1892 he competed for the Fair Cup, just offered as a trophy for a six mile race off the harbour. Trixie came in first ahead of five competitors, but lost on a handicap which gave the win to Fred Leaney's yacht

"Foam". In August 1893, against four other boats, "Topsy" captained by A. J. Dell proved to be the winner. During the next three years, twice on handicap over six other yachts, William Francis as skipper of "Trixie" won and was awarded the trophy permanently. In 1902 William Francis sold his yacht "Trixie" and her new owners converted the vessel to steam power.

William Francis had purchased river front property, cleaned out the coal chutes and made a mooring for the yacht "Trixie". By 1893 in partnership with Harry Ansley and Captain Battersby he purchased the bankrupt stock of Grant & Hoover of Aylmer, reopening the store under W. R. Reid as manager. In 1897 he was trustee for the Port Dover Electric Light & Power Company, which had a contract with the village. Despite William Francis sitting on Council, their contract was cancelled. Meanwhile the government inspectors report on the Post Office was declared "eminently satisfactory." By the end of the century he was also Secretary of the Ontario Financial Company, another of his wide-ranging interests.

In 1896 the Ansley store featured the first bicycles, or "wheels", to be sold in the area. It was William Francis and his eighteen year old son Hugh Ansley, who bought the first ones

*Typical Sailing Yacht of the time*

[called Cleveland Wheels] in town. In 1897 William Francis took a holiday trip to St. Catherines, Niagara Falls and back on his wheel. That same year Hugh A. articled to Tisdale, Tisdale and Reid in Simcoe and "wheeled" from home and back each day. He completed his degree at Osgoode Hall in 1901. Hugh A. moved to Rainy River in 1904, married Florence Irene Davis of Vancouver in 1906, and they finally settled in Fort Frances in 1909. He remained there until his death in 1936.

In 1900, second son Dick, joined the Canadian Bank of Commerce in Port Perry. He later worked in Toronto and for a short time in 1914 in Fort Frances. Dick joined up during World War I and when he returned to Canada at the cessation of hostilities he brought an English war bride home, Martha Caroline Stammers. As a youngster I was impressed with her strange accent and her friendly, jolly manner. They returned to Port Dover and in 1919 moved in with his parents. Dick worked at first in the insurance business moving on to other enterprises during his business career.

The third son, Alan Newell Tibbetts, married Zeitha Barwell of Port Dover on June 27th, 1925, and moved to Fort Frances, where his brother Hugh Ansley had become established, in the early 1920's. Here he went into the hotel business among other ventures. He later became a government license inspector. He died there in 1952.

In 1901 Charlotte Emily Tibbett's father Ozias Ansley died. In 1904 her mother Clara Hortense Langs Ansley also passed away. As a memorial to her parents Charlotte Emily presented an alms basin to St. Paul's Church.

*Ozias Ansley*

By 1912, William Francis and Charlotte Emily were the only residents of the St. George street house and they rented it, moving out to establish themselves in an apartment above the Post Office. All went well until March 5th, 1920, when the whole Post Office block, including the apartments were completely destroyed by fire. The Tibbetts lost everything as did Dick and Martha who had moved in on his returning from overseas. The building as well as housing the Post Office was also home to the J. G. "Pat" Patterson Drug Store, the store of Walker Evans and the Telephone Exchange. The Post Office and telephone Exchange, being vital to the life of the village were re-located elsewhere at once. By May a frame building was erected at the north-east corner of Main and Chapman street as temporary housing for the Post Office.

To assist financially with the Post Office construction at this time the Tibbetts Brothers bathing change houses on the beach were sold. Quintin Barrett, son of Hubert Baldwin Barrett, who had recently returned from W. W. I managed them under the name Barrett & Tibbetts, thus continuing their operation. Quintin also operated a booth with games of chance and souvenirs for the entertainment of the visiting public.

> [on moving to Riverbank, original home of T. B. Barrett at 11 Bridge street, in 1970, I found several men's wool bathing suits, and even more, faded blue women's bathing suits, circa 1920. The ladies suits covered the upper body completely with short sleeves, and pant legs, as well as modest skirts. The whole suit was trimmed with narrow white bands. Each suit had the initials B & T – Barrett & Tibbetts – painted on the chest followed by the suit size, ex. 40, 44 etc. I have donated samples of each to the Port Dover Harbour Museum and to the Eva Brook Donly Museum, in Simcoe.]

Charlotte Emily Ansley Tibbetts died on September 3rd, 1921, having been married for forty-four years. William Francis carried on as Postmaster and in real estate transactions prompted primarily by the fire. He bought "The Fair" building, which had been operated by Truesdale & Bond, on the north-east corner of

Main and Market streets, planning to move it to the site of the burnt out Post Office. This plan did not materialise and the building was finally moved to the north side of McNab street, where it was turned into a double house by J. H. Brock and Co. The move also incurred a bill from Council for "broken crossings" caused by the move. Following the moving of The Fair, and the destruction of an adjoining old house, the Royal bank was built on the site.

In August of 1922 the Post Office moved into the new brick Tibbett's Block constructed by A. C. Stewart and Sons on Main Street. William Francis, as well as Dick and Martha moved into the second floor apartment and Dick established his insurance office in the temporary Post office that had been built at Chapman and Main streets.

William Francis died on January 31st, 1930 and was buried from his church of almost sixty years, St. Paul's, and with full masonic rites as a Past master of Erie Lodge, A. F. & A. M. He had been Port Dover's Postmaster for forty-four years, and a leading member of civic and business life in the village. Pallbearers were the Honourable John S. Martin, Conservative MPP and Minister of Agriculture; W. H. "Harry" Barrett; his wife's cousin and sometimes business partner; J. G. Patterson, who owned the Drug Store established by William's father; James R. Waddle, a prominent farmer, living on Lot 9, Con. 3, Woodhouse; Dr. Albert H. Cook, whose home and office stood on the site of the present Dover Dairy Bar; and Captain P. C. Robinson, who had come to Port Dover to command the fishery patrol vessel "Vigilant".

Reverend David J. Cornish, Rector of St. Paul's, paid William Francis Tibbetts a glowing tribute at his funeral service and an eloquent eulogy was given by his friend and Lodge Brother, Captain Robinson. His sons Hugh, Dick and Alan dedicated a large stained glass window in St. Paul's to the Glory of God, and in loving memory of their parents. It depicts Mary washing the feet of Christ, while in the background Martha sets a table for a meal. Through an arched window can be seen the bare hills and the blue sky of the Holy Land. Designed and constructed by Lyons Limited of Toronto this memorial window was dedicated on Sunday, September 28th, 1930.

CHAPTER NINE

# The Church of England and Free Masonry

The first masonic gathering in old Norfolk was held on the shores of Lake Erie in Brother Job Lodor's tavern, in Charlotteville, atop the Turkey Point hill. A group of settlers had called a meeting to establish a Church of England in the new hamlet on land set aside for that purpose. Among them were seven Master Masons who on that same day, January 3rd, 1803, agreed that they would organise a Lodge and petition the Grand Lodge of Upper Canada for a warrant. The establishment of a Masonic Lodge proved much more successful than did the establishment of a Church of England in the burgeoning Long Point Settlement.

Before the meeting adjourned they elected the following temporary officers. Worshipful Master, Bro. Joseph Ryerson; Senior Warden Bro. Titus Williams; Junior Warden, Bro. William Hutchinson; and Secretary, Bro. Thomas Welch. Colonel Ryerson, like many other early members of the craft, had been made a member of the order in a military lodge, while living in the United States.

The next meeting on record was again held at Bro. Lodor's tavern on December 27th, 1803. A formal application for a warrant was made to the Provincial Grand Lodge of Niagara, which had been formed at Niagara in 1792. It held allegiance to the Grand Lodge of England. Those present also subscribed forty-two dollars for the expenses incurred in obtaining a warrant and for the purchase of jewels. The following names were put forward as officers if a warrant was granted. Worshipful Master, Bro. William Hutchinson; Senior Warden, Bro. Benjamin Caryl; Junior Warden, Bro. Job Lodor; Secretary, Bro. Thomas Welch; Treasurer, Bro.

John Heath. The Warrant was approved and issued in January 1804 and regular meetings of Union Lodge No. 22 were held, at the full of the moon, from that time forward. Members came from throughout the London District on horseback and by wagon over the rough trails to Job Lodor's Tavern.

The War of 1812-14 created a severe setback to the lodge as members were called away on military duty. Masonic tradition relates to the harassment of the district by General McArthur, who on attempting to burn Gustin's mill in Vittoria, was entreated by Bro. Thomas Bowlby, a member of the Church of England as well, to spare the mill as it supported a large Masonic community in the area. McArthur, himself a Mason, granted the appeal.

A similar incident took place when the American raiders attacked Waterford and fired the grist mill owned by Bro. Morris Sovereign. Three times it was set ablaze and three time Sovereign extinguished the fire. Enraged by this action Sovereign was seized by the American raiders and taken to a convenient tree nearby. As the hangman slipped the noose over his neck, Sovereign gave the masonic sign of distress to their commanding officer, General McArthur, and his life was spared. The Mill however was not.

By 1820 the village of Charlotteville was abandoned and the seat of government moved to the growing hamlet of Vittoria. Lodge No.22 moved there as well to take up permanent quarters in the new courthouse that was built to serve the London District. The local school was housed in the same building. In November of 1825, as a result of the schoolmaster leaving an open fire in the schoolroom, the building was completely destroyed and the charter, minutes, furniture and jewels of Union Lodge No. 22 were destroyed with it. The Lodge never recovered and its members transferred to Lodge No. 26 in Townsend township. They met regularly at Bro. Arthur Murphy's tavern, some three miles north of Waterford. Later the lodge moved about the district to accommodate its widely scattered membership. In 1822, Lodge No 26, became Lodge No. 14 on the Provincial register. In 1832 the Lodge had its English registration number changed from 767 to 500. In 1839 the Lodge took up permanent quarters in the newly built Norfolk House in Simcoe. In 1840, an Anglican, William Mercer Wilson was initiated into the lodge.

In 1851 a warrant of confirmation, issued by the United Grand Lodge of England, named the lodge St. John's Lodge No. 500. Three years later, at the same time as St. Paul's Church, Port Dover was being completed, the brethren determined to change the Lodge name to Norfolk Lodge. There was also a movement to free the Lodges from British rule and in 1855, William Mercer Wilson, as Master of Norfolk Lodge, took a leading role. A convention in Hamilton organised itself into the Grand Lodge of Canada, electing William Mercer Wilson as First Grand Master. Wilson, who served eleven years as Master of Norfolk lodge, was destined to serve the Grand Lodge of Canada for ten years as Grand Master.

In 1872 Norfolk Lodge, now numbered 10 on the register of Grand lodge, moved into its present quarters in the block on Peel street, which had just been completed by Dr. John Wilson. William Mercer Wilson had been called to the Grand East for a third term in the same year. He served as Grand Master until his death on January 16th, 1875. His funeral service was conducted by the Grand Lodge, A.F. & A.M. with burial in the St John's Church cemetery. Over one thousand masons from all parts of the Province were in attendance and it was touted as the most impressive Masonic function ever witnessed in Canada.

Some 45 years later another very prominent Mason and Anglican, in the person of Worshipful Brother John Strickler Martin, of Port Dover, was instrumental in having Mercer Wilson's modest tombstone replaced by a monument more fitting to his illustrious career. Each year since 1920, on the last Sunday in June, a pilgrimage is held to the last resting place of our First Grand Master, William Mercer Wilson. This is held under the auspices of his Lodge, Norfolk No. 10 and consists of a service in St. John's Anglican Church, with a sermon by an outstanding Masonic leader. The brethren then assemble at the grave site where further tributes are offered.

**The Formation of Erie Lodge No. 149, Port Dover**

Israel Wood Powell laid out and founded the town of Port Dover, later building a substantial brick home on St. George Street, south, overlooking the lake. This was incorporated into the prestigious Orchard Beach Hotel much later by Mr. Morley Buck. The Powell family had their origin in Wales, where for over three hundred years they controlled a five thousand acre estate on the outskirts of Aberystwith, within the valley of Nantes. Their stately Georgian mansion, known as Nanteos, surrounded by magnificent lawns, gardens and stables, overlooks the Bay of Cardigan. In the hallway of this beautiful and grand old home is the family crest on a huge oak panel. Below it can be traced the descendants of the original founder of the family, showing the South African branch; the Australian branch and the Canadian branch. Near the bottom of the Canadian line is inscribed the name of our town's founder, Israel Wood Powell.

This historic home is filled with family portraits, silver, furniture and other heirlooms, but the greatest treasure of all is the "Nanteos Grail", believed to be Christ's cup, "The Holy Grail." For centuries the Powell's have been the stewards and protectors of this mysterious cup. From an article that appeared in Time magazine, September 3rd, 1956, we learn that:

> "The most precious part of the Nanteos estate is a crumbled, blackened wooden cup, held together by wire, which, according to one legend, is the Holy Grail itself, from which Christ drank at the last supper and in which Joseph of Aramathea caught some of his blood. Other tradition has it that the Holy cup of Nanteos is not the Grail but a vessel later made from the wood of the cross. During Henry the VIII's reign, when monasteries were abolished in England, the relic was smuggled to various monks' hideouts, until they were able to take refuge with the Powell family, founders of Nanteos. Whatever its origin the cup is a Holy relic of Christendom."

The last male heir of Nanteos was Athelston Powell who died in 1930. His only son and heir, Lieutenant George Pryse Powell, was killed in France on November 5th, 1918. The son of Walker Powell of Port Dover, and grandson of Israel, C. B. Powell was invited to take ownership of Nanteos and the Welsh estates. He was a federal member of parliament in Ottawa and a Civil Engineer, founder of the Ottawa Country club, at the time. He declined the offer. Nanteos is now under the control of the National Trust.

Returning to the progenitor of the Canadian branch of the family we learn that Sir Thomas Powell of Nanteos was one of the four judges in the trial of the seven Bishops in 1688. He and one other ruled in the Bishop's favour, at great personal risk, against the illegal edict of King James II. The Bishops were liberated as a result.

Sir Thomas' son, Thomas Richard Powell was an independent thinker and a Quaker who sailed with a tutor for New York state in 1695. His grandson William D. Powell, a judge in New York state, was forced to flee with his family, when the States sought their independence. Leaving all they possessed behind, the family fled, as United Empire Loyalists, for the safety of New Brunswick. They arrived in the late 1890's to found the town of Richebucto, N. B.

William D. Powell's son, Abraham, married Ruth Wood and with her brother Israel Wood the two families came to the Long Point Country prior to 1800. Abraham settled on Buckwheat Street, in Windham township. He farmed and operated a small store there on what came to be known as Powell's Plains. His third son, Israel Wood Powell, was born in 1801. Israel apprenticed to Job Lodor as clerk in his store in Waterford. He later married Melinda Boss and established his own store in Colborne village, north of Simcoe.

In 1835 Israel Wood Powell bought the original Walker farm, west of Patterson's creek, from his brother-in-law, Moses Nickerson. He then laid out the plan for a town site, which is present day Port Dover. On the site of our present Lighthouse Festival Theatre and clock tower, he built a substantial store. This burned in 1856 to be immediately replaced by a brick building.

Captain Israel W. Powell commanded a militia company during the 1837-38 rebellion. From 1841 through 1848 he was a member of the Legislative Assembly for Norfolk. When the first district council was convened on February 8th, 1842, Israel W. Powell was its first Warden. Upon the formation of the first Municipal Council for Norfolk on January 28th, 1850, he served as the first Deputy Reeve for Woodhouse Township, which included Port Dover. He was also a Justice of the Peace.

Israel Wood Powell and Moses Nickerson were partners in a shipping business, Powell & Nickerson. They began harbour improvements in 1842 by dredging the sandbar at the mouth of the creek with horses and scrapers. They next established permanent piers and docks. With the aid of friends like Sir Alan McNab and John A. MacDonald, Israel W. Powell brought about the building of the plank road from Port Dover to Hamilton in 1844. Israel Wood Powell died in 1852.

**Israel Wood Powell the II.**

Israel Wood Powell the II was born in Colborne on April 27th, 1836. He attended school in Colborne and Port Dover. Upon the death of his father, Israel, at age 17, apprenticed to Dr. Charleston Covernton of Simcoe to study anatomy and physiology. In 1856 he enrolled in medical school in McGill University, Montreal. In 1858 he was raised to the sublime degree of a Master mason in Elgin Lodge No. 348, A.F. & A.M. Montreal, under the Grand Register of Scotland.

At twenty-four Israel W. Powell II, in the spring of 1860, graduated with an M. D. and returned to Port Dover to set up his medical practice. He no sooner arrived than he began contacting local masonic brethren regarding the establishment of a Masonic Lodge in Port Dover. His efforts bore fruit when on May 20th, 1861, Grand Lodge convened in Port Dover under Most Worshipful Bro. William Mercer Wilson. From among the thirty-five brethren assembled that

*Dr. Israel Wood Powell, M. D.*

evening, in rooms above one of the stores of the Powell block, the founding officers, of the newly constituted Erie Lodge No. 149, were duly installed by the Grand Master.

The newly constituted lodge boasted twenty-eight charter members. They were launched under the able guidance of Worshipful Brother Israel Wood Powell as Worshipful Master; Bro. Michael Haycock as Senior Warden and Bro. Theobald Butler Barrett as Junior Warden. All three of these brethren belonged to the Parish of St. Paul's. Bro. Barrett had been initiated on January 24th, 1850 in St. John's Lodge, No. 500, in Simcoe which at the time Erie Lodge was formed, in 1861, had become Norfolk Lodge, No. 10, A.F. & A.M., Simcoe.

When only ten months into their inaugural year Worshipful Brother Powell called an emergent meeting of the Lodge on March 18th, 1862, to announce that he was leaving Port Dover for New Zealand. He then proceeded to install the newly elected officers. Bro. T. B. Barrett was installed as the second Master of the Lodge and Wor. Bro. Powell was presented with his Past Master's jewel and wished the very best in his new venture. He left via Montreal and Panama for Victoria on Vancouver Island. Arriving in May of 1862 he was soon caught up in the excitement of the discovery of gold in the Caribou, and his plans to emigrate to New Zealand were forgotten.

He opened offices in the Anglo-American Hotel at Yates and Broad streets in what was destined to become the city of Victoria. Powell was described at that time as "a young man, 5' 10" in height, of slight build, with a medium dark complexion. He is a good speaker, devoted to sports and a good horseman. He is a member of the Church of England."

Powell brought impressive credentials with him as a member of the College of Physicians and Surgeons of Lower Canada and a licentiate of the Medical Board of Upper Canada. He also carried a letter of introduction from his father's old friend, The Honourable John A. Macdonald. He soon found that there were many masons in the territory who missed the Scottish ritual common to California and Washington state. Being himself familiar with it from his home Lodge in Montreal, he cheerfully joined with others to petition for a charter for a new lodge to be named

Vancouver Lodge and numbered #421 on the Grand Register of Scotland.

In less than ten months from vacating the oriental chair of King Solomon, in Erie Lodge No. 149, A.F. & A.M. Port Dover, Wor. Bro. Powell was installed on December 27th, 1862 as the founding Wor. Master of Vancouver Lodge No. 421, A.F. & A.M. in Victoria, British Columbia. This is an accomplishment that I doubt has ever been duplicated.

In 1867, a significant year for Canada, Israel Wood Powell was appointed the Provincial Grand Master of British Columbia under the Scottish jurisdiction. When the Scottish and English Grand Lodges agreed to the formation of a Grand Lodge of British Columbia in 1871 Powell was elected the first Grand Master and held that office for the next three years. The two old lodges were renamed as one at this time, as Vancouver and Quadra No. 2. A.F. & A.M.

*Most Wor. Bro. Israel Wood Powell. First Grand Master, Gr. Lodge of British Columbia*

Dr. Powell's practice grew rapidly. He took the lead in organising the first local militia, the Victoria Volunteer Rifles, in which he served as Volunteer Surgeon. He served the volunteer Fire Brigade in the same capacity. He organised and served as first President of the British Columbia Medical Association. In 1863 he won a seat in the Colonial House of Assembly. He lobbied hard for a free port and harbour improvements, a pilotage system, better postal laws and a system of free education.

On January 25th, 1865 Dr. Powell married the beautiful and talented Miss Jane Branks. Nine children were born to their union in the impressive home "Oakdene" that he built on Vancouver

Street. In 1921 "Oakdene" became the residence of the Anglican Bishop of British Columbia.

In 1866 the Island was annexed to the Colony of British Columbia. Even before this Dr. Powell and another Canadian, Amor De Cormos, were fighting a losing battle to have the Pacific Colonies made a part of Confederation. Powell lost his seat in the Legislature in 1867 as a result. They both ran again in 1868 and were both defeated.

Powell's brother, Walker Powell, was in Ottawa at this time as Assistant Adjutant General of Militia. Between contact with him and his friend the Honourable John A. Macdonald, Powell was better informed than anyone else of the political climate in both Ottawa and British Columbia. As a result his efforts finally bore fruit when the Colony's terms for union were accepted by Ottawa in 1870. Dr. Powell was jubilant.

Sir John A. Macdonald offered Powell the post of first Lieutenant Governor of British Columbia, but he refused the honour, with thanks. A seat in the Senate was offered and Powell declined that honour, as well. The following year he accepted the offer by the Dominion Government of the post of Superintendent of Indian Affairs for the Province. He launched vigorously into his new duties, visiting all the tribes on the Island and recommending military posts to control warring tribes, as well as better medical and educational services. He next visited even the most remote Indian settlements of the Province to view their problems first hand, travelling by canoe, gunboat, on horseback or on foot.

In 1881, when visiting the coastal settlements, aboard H. M. S. Rocket, her commander Lt. Cmdr. Orlebar, named Powell Lake and Powell River in his honour. Today the thriving city of Powell River lies at the mouth of the river that bears his name. Dr. Powell served the department for seventeen busy years and was proud of the fact he had established seventeen Indian schools in that time. One for each year of his tenure.

The Powell's, with their daughter, travelled to Britain and Europe in 1889, in part due to Dr. Powell's failing health. On his return he became very interested in Agriculture and its promotion in the Province. He never lost his enthusiasm for better medical and educational services, either and in 1886 he was named the first

President of the Medical Council. His efforts in education helped in the establishment in 1890 of the University of British Columbia. Dr. Powell served as the first Chancellor.

On January 25th, 1915, friends thronged into "Oakdene" to celebrate the Powell's Golden Wedding Anniversary. Congratulations poured in from far and wide. Just one month later on February 25th, 1915, Dr. Powell passed away in his sleep. Services were held from the Masonic Temple and St. John's Anglican Church.

Historian B. A. McKelvie states, of this famous, one time resident of Port Dover, that; *"Truly few men have left such a splendid record of unselfish devotion and achievement for the public good than has Lieutenant Colonel Israel Wood Powell, M. D., C. M."*

*******************************

Meanwhile the Powell name was still prominent in the affairs of Erie Lodge. Israel Powell's youngest brother, Berkley Powell, was the first application considered by the newly formed lodge and he was accepted and initiated at the second communication of the lodge. He operated the Powell business for many years, living in the fine home he built on Main street, known today as the "Port of Call." Berkley Powell was installed as Worshipful Master in 1866 and remained Master for the ensuing three years. The last of the Powell family to live in Port Dover, Berkley Powell died on July 19th, 1872. The eldest son of the Powell Family, Walker Powell, was initiated into Erie Lodge in September of 1861. He went on to become Adjutant-General of Canadian Militia in Ottawa.

Before the year was out, another parishioner of St. Paul's, Ozias Ansley, who operated a hardware and tin-smithing business on the north-west corner of Park and St. Andrews streets, was initiated. His son, Harry W. Ansley, was a life-long member of the lodge serving as Master in 1881-82. Bro. O. Clayton Ansley gave the alter and kneeler in the Lodge room in memory of his grandfather and father, Ozias and Harry respectively.

On February 26th, 1866, the applications of two prominent Anglicans in Port Dover were received and duly admitted to the lodge. They were Thomas Douglas Buckwell and Frederick Skey, business partners in the Powell block, dealing in wholesale and retail drugs, wines, liquors, groceries and books etc. Fred Buckwell's home stood in the centre of what is today the Erie Beach Hotel - Arbor complex. Frederick Skey built the charming home, recently restored on the north-west corner of Chapman and St. Andrew streets.

Isaac Hoover, of Selkirk, was an Anglican and early applicant for membership, as were J. V. and Silas Hoover. The latter two served as masters of Erie lodge in 1870-71 and 1873 respectively Later Abraham Hoover, a warden of St. Paul's, who operated the Hoover Fishery in Nanticoke, moved to Port Dover and joined the Lodge. His son Alton Hoover served as master of Erie lodge in 1947.

In 1900, on November 24th, a double tragedy rocked the town when two prominent citizens and masons, Horatio Holden and C. D. Warren, were reported drowned off Long Point. They, with Hubert Barrett, a fellow mason, had been taken to the Anderson property by the Angler, a fishing tug, for a week of duck hunting. A strong east wind made launching their skiffs very difficult. The two victims had started in with the first boat, while Huby had loaded all their gear and supplies in the second skiff and headed for the shore. He could not see his companions, but as the waves were high he suspected nothing until he safely beached his boat. The other skiff and its occupants were nowhere to be seen. As Huby searched frantically along the shore, no sign of his companions was to be found. The tug, unaware of their loss had quickly backed into deeper water and returned to Port Dover. It was thought that the articulating oars, which Mr. Holden was using for the first time, may have been the main cause of the skiff foundering and its occupants being drowned.

Anglican Charles W. Barwell affiliated with the Lodge, to later become Master in 1913 and 1914. He also served his lodge as Treasurer until 1932, when Ian Menzies Macauley assumed those duties. Wor. Bro. Barwell was a business-promoter, who, with William F. Tibbetts, financed the first gas well in town in Elm Park. It was a high producing well over a long period of time.

As noted elsewhere Theobald Butler Barrett came to the Long Point Settlement in 1845. He was a charter member of Erie

Lodge and its second Master. He served in 1865 as secretary of the Lodge and for several years as Secretary-treasurer of the Province-wide Masonic Benevolent Society. For forty years he was Secretary of the Upper Canada Bible Society.

On July 7th, 1864 William Henry "Harry" Barrett, eldest son of Theobald, was born at "Riverbank." In 1887 he joined his bachelor uncle, Henry Barrett, on his ranch in the Spallumcheen District, of British Columbia. Here he farmed, and married Rebecca Julia Pelly, who bore him three sons; namely Theobald Butler II, Richard Pelly, and Francis or Frank Barrett. My Grandmother, Rebecca Julia, known as Winonah, meaning first born by the Indians, died when Frank was born and Harry and his two eldest sons returned to "Riverbank" Port Dover, in 1899.

In 1904 Harry Barrett was initiated into Erie Lodge, No.149. In 1906 he graduated as a Doctor of Veterinary Medicine and on May 16th, 1906 married Hattie James. In 1930 Harry was installed as Wor. Master of Erie lodge. He had the unenviable duty of presiding over the Masonic funeral arrangements of his long-time friend and neighbour, the Most Worshipful, the Honourable John Strickler Martin, on May 16th, 1931, when he was buried from St. Paul's. In 1934 Wor. Bro. Barrett was appointed Grand Organist to Grand Lodge. Harry's brothers, Frank, Clarence and Hubert Barrett were all masons as well.

*Erie Lodge Brethren, Hubert, Clarence, Harry & Frank Barrett*

Harry Barrett's three sons were all initiated as third degree masons in Erie Lodge and went on to join the Chapter. In 1911 Toby left school in 2nd form to move to the farm on Mill road and work with his father. On October 16th, 1920 Toby married Marjorie Hazel Clarke, in her home town of Haliburton, Ontario. As St. George's Anglican church had recently burned down, they were married at her father's picturesque old home on Highland Street. This house was built in 1882 by Alexander Niven the first land surveyor in the Haliburton area of Victoria County. Her father Harry Hawkins Clarke, was at the time a Past Master and Secretary of North Star Masonic Lodge, Haliburton. His home which was in the very heart of the village was demolished on the 24th of August, 2005 to make way for a bistro & grill. On September 15th, 2005 I received two 3 inch machine cut square nails as a souvenir of the old family home, thoughtfully provided to me by the Haliburton Museum Curator, Stephen Hill.

Toby was initiated into Erie Lodge on February 21st, 1927. He served as Wor. Master in 1935. He and a friend, the well known lawyer and mason, McGaw McDonald, joined the local militia in October 1939 and with the rank of Lieutenant, R.C.A., Toby was posted to Brandon and later Vancouver Island, as Adjutant, in the training camps. In 1945, at the end of hostilities, he was elected Conservative member of Parliament for Norfolk, in Ottawa.

In 1949-51 I drove my father to meetings of the Lodges of Wilson District, first to announce his candidacy and the following year, to attend official and special visits to the said Lodges, on his being elected as the District Deputy Grand Master for Wilson District.

I, Harry Bemister Barrett, as the only local male member of my generation was born on St. George Street, Port Dover, in May of 1922. I grew up on the Woodhouse family farm and in October of 1939 joined the Canadian Militia, R. C. A., where weekly drills were held in the Simcoe Armouries. After 2 summer camps at Niagara-on-the-Lake and being eighteen, I joined the Royal Canadian Navy, in 1941. Discharged as a Lieutenant in October of 1945 I enrolled in the Ontario Agricultural College in Guelph. I was initiated into Erie Lodge No. 149, A.F. & A.M., on October 29th, 1945.

Ninety-nine years after my Great Grandfather was installed as Junior Warden of Erie Lodge, I was installed in the chair of King Solomon as Master of the Lodge, by my father. Again I visited the lodges of Wilson District in my capacity as Worshipful Master of Erie lodge, and had the pleasure of inviting them to attend our celebration of the fact we had been in existence for one hundred years. I was also in the company of Wor. Bro. Harold Smith, another member of the Parish of St. Paul's, who was a candidate for District Deputy Grand Master and was elected to that office in 1961, as part of Erie Lodge's Centennial celebrations.

*District Deputy Grand Master T. B. Barrett*

Wor. Bro. Archie Morris, a past Warden of St. Paul's church and for several years Sunday School Superintendent, was the Worshipful Master of the Lodge during our Centennial. For some time before this I served under the Chairmanship of Erie's long time Chaplain, Canon D. J. Cornish, in the preparation of the history of Erie Lodge, No. 149. For the past several years I have served my Lodge as official historian.

On January 8th, 1965 my son, Theobald Butler "Toby" III, represented the fifth generation of the Barrett clan to be initiated into Erie lodge. He served the lodge as Worshipful Master in 1990. Ours is now the only family which has had a continuous connection with Erie Lodge to this day. In June of 1995 Toby III was elected Conservative Member of the Provincial Legislature for the riding of Haldimand-Norfolk-Brant and at the time of writing he still holds that office.

\*\*\*\*\*\*\*\*\*\*\*\*\*\*\*\*\*\*\*\*\*\*\*\*\*\*\*\*\*\*\*\*\*

Another family to hold a long connection with Erie Lodge down through the years, was the Varey family. Two Varey brothers came here from Ireland, to become well-known builders in Port Dover, early in the century. They built a large addition to the Methodist church in Port Dover, to which they were affiliated. In April, 1871 Brian Varey, age fifty, was initiated into Erie Lodge and by 1876 he was installed as Master of the Lodge. His son, Josiah Varey, age twenty-eight, was initiated in 1873. Joseph J. Varey, his brother age twenty-seven, was initiated in 1874 serving as Master of the Lodge in 1891. From 1895 to 1907 Joseph served the Lodge as Secretary.

Clifford Caley Varey, known to all as "Tip" took charge of a haberdashery in the new Town Hall block after the turn of the century in 1909, having bought out Hubert Barrett's establishment. He was initiated into Erie Lodge in 1915. His son Brian M. Varey, a member of St. Paul's, though serving in the Royal Canadian Navy, was installed as Worshipful Master of Erie Lodge in 1944. Brian became the Secretary of the lodge in 1951, serving his lodge in that capacity for over thirty years.

He was the genial proprietor of the clothing business operated by his father in the same location until his retirement in the mid 1990's. At age 93 Brian is the last remaining charter member of the Port Dover Lion's Club, an Honourary Member of the Port Dover Fire Brigade and senior living member of Erie Lodge.

Brian Varey passed to the Grand Lodge above in February 24, 2005.

### Erie Lodge No. 149, A.F. & A.M. Boasts a Grand Master

Another adherent of the Church of England, a devout member of St. Paul's Church, Port Dover and our most prestigious, best loved member of Erie Lodge, No. 149, A.F. & A.M., was the Most Worshipful, the Honourable John Strickler Martin.

John S. Martin was born, on October 11th, 1875, on the family farm in the township of Walpole, in Haldimand County. He was the first of seven children born to George Martin and his wife, Clara Strickler Martin, of United Empire Loyalist stock. John

Martin's great grandfather, a devout church worker, deeded the land for St. John's Anglican Church, Cheapside, where the Martin family lived. George Martin was a successful dealer in pianos and organs.

All the Martin children were musical, and accomplished pianists, who often demonstrated their father's pianos at many prestigious events. In 1897 both John and his brother Charles Martin played for the Dominion Piano Company in their pavilion at the Canadian National Exhibition, Toronto. Two brothers of John S. Martin, Charles and Harry became expert piano tuners under the tutelage of Heintzman & Company. Their sisters were equally well qualified and became teachers of music.

In September of 1902, George Martin sold his prosperous Cheapside farm and purchased the Knox Church Manse on Prospect Hill, in Port Dover. He died there in his 59th year, in 1905. John S. and Charles rented, from the O. F. Falls Estate, the store at the north-west corner of Peel and Norfolk Streets, Simcoe, where they continued the piano business. Brother Harry soon joined them, and later became the proprietor of the business.

John S. Martin had enrolled in the University of Toronto in 1893, where he won his Arts degree in 1897. That fall he enrolled in the Hamilton Normal School, to return to Port Dover as a teacher of Moderns & Classics in the Continuation School. He was assistant principal to W. R. Liddy. Roy Hammond a Woodhouse neighbour of ours and a student under John S. described him thus: "he had a soft voice, was well liked, but was a poor disciplinarian."

In 1904, after two years of no initiations, Erie Lodge sprang to life again with the initiation of members of St. Paul's parish, John S. and Charles Martin and their good friend and neighbour W. H. "Harry" Barrett. Harry's cousin, Roy S. Scott, and the incumbent of St. Paul's from 1900 to 1907, Reverend Robert Herbert were also initiated. Other prominent residents included W. J. Slocomb, W. J. Thompson, Norman Holden [H. M. Customs], Francis Henry Stringer [public school teacher], Charlton D. Woolley [destined to become mayor], George Thompson [undertaker], and John C. King, who twenty-six years later became the Lodge Secretary, serving for thirty-one years from 1930 to 1950.

In the same year Charles W. Barwell affiliated with Erie Lodge, to become Wor. Master for 1913 and 1914. Bruce C. Dell, son of Alpheus Dell a thirty year member, was initiated as well. For years Dell's bakery operated on the south-west corner of Main and Chapman streets.

In 1905, John S. Martin resigned as a teacher, to follow his love of poultry, indicated at age 10 when a clutch of eggs and a setting hen were found hidden under his bed. He gained the nickname later of "Hen Coop John." John S. visited the Pan American Exhibition in 1901, and for the first time in his life, he could study the best of all the breeds of poultry at one time. In 1906 he was appointed lecturer in Poultry at the Ontario Agricultural College, Guelph.

In October, 1908, John S. Martin bought the beautiful brick home across the street from his parents, from the Estate of Eleanor Battersby, overlooking Silver Lake, for $2,480.00. On September 18th, 1909, at the home of Mr. and Mrs. J. Arthur Cope, Arlington, Mass. John S. Martin was married to Miss Lillian Else, Mrs. Cope's sister, and they returned to their new home in Port Dover. He was being pressed for room for his expanding poultry operation and in 1914, bought the property of Mr. James Bannister, across the street from his home, where he built twenty colony houses for his range birds.

The White Wyandotte, soon named "the Bird of Curves," became John S. Martin's passion and soon he was winning all prizes in their class, as well as best of breed, in major competitions. One hen that layed 241 eggs in its first year, he named Dorcas, and she became the foundation for his heavy-laying strain of Wyandottes. He was soon selling stock all over the world. By 1914 he was shipping some 7,000 hatching eggs world wide. In August, 1915, Winnifred Barrett recorded in her diary: *"We all went over to the Chicken Farm this morning and Gladys [Farrar Barrett, her brother Quintin's wife] took a picture of the $1,000.00 rooster."*

I remember as a youngster going with my Grandfather to the Main street grocery store of Harry Marlatt. They got into a great discussion one morning, about the phenomenal reputation John S. Martin had brought to the White Wyandotte breed, now known and admired world-wide as "The Bird of Curves." Mr Marlatt's final comment was: "Harry, John S. would have done the very same thing for an unknown breed, if he had chosen Crows!" They were a truly beautiful bird and I never ceased to admire the many fine Wyandotte roosters, with their harems of a dozen hens, as they strutted and crowed from their individual pens across the road from the farm.

John S. Martin was elected Reeve of Port Dover in 1921 by a handsome majority. Though he served for under two years, he stirred things up for the better, at both the local and County level. Port Dover's waterworks were begun during his tenure and at his instigation.

John S. developed his own feed formulas and marketed them through the Regal Poultry Feed Company. John S. Martin was President and Charles G. Ivey, General Manager. In 1922 they erected a four storey mill on the south-east side of the railway crossing and Mill road. On the stuccoed side of the building was painted in large white letters, on a blue background, "John S. Martin's, 'Just as he feeds it,' Poultry Feed." John S. was now issuing catalogues in English and in Spanish, for his South American customers, promoting his Regal Dorcas, White Wyandottes.

In July 1920, John S. Martin bought the beautiful old home of Mrs. Arthur Battersby, opposite the juncture of Mill Road and Prospect Hill, owned today by Scott Malcolm. Built in 1867 for Arthur Battersby, an Irish tea merchant, it was of the Gothic Revival style, and with rolling lawns and large oak and walnut trees on the bank , from which it overlooked Silver Lake, it was a most impressive residence. His previous home to the south became offices for his poultry business.

On July 9th, 1923 John S. Martin resigned as Reeve to run as a Provincial Conservative, representing South Norfolk. He won, to become Minister of Agriculture in the Howard Ferguson Government. On his return to Port Dover after taking the "Oath of Office" a huge demonstration was staged in his honour. Thousands from all parts of the Province came to pay tribute, making it the biggest such gathering in anyone's memory for the Port. In the 1926 election his majority doubled. In 1929, despite being ill and unable to campaign, he was again elected, being touted as "a thru and thru Conservative, but an all round dirt farmer." He had put his own special and positive stamp on Ontario agriculture.

By 1925 Port Dover was becoming the Poultry Capital of Ontario. Mr. Penhall, another parishioner of St. Paul's, won ten Record of Performance Certificates, as egg layers, for his Dover White Leghorns, at the Ontario Egg Laying Contest in Ottawa. J. Hambleton "Ham" Thompson, of Parfaite Poultry Farms, located where the IGA and Mergl subdivision are now, had entered hens, as had his brother and partner, Bert, in the R.O.P. competition, as well. A Parfaite hen carried off the top performance, over 400 birds entered, with a record of 257, 2 oz. eggs laid. She and her owner, Ham Thompson, were the talk of the Province at the 1925 Royal Winter Fair, vying in popularity with the large, attractive exhibit of the Regal Milling Company, Ltd. Port Dover. Port Dover was really on the poultry map of Canada.

In 1926, Archie Milne of Markham, purchased the mill property and marketed breakfast cereals, under the name "Sunera." As a 4H'er I planted two acres of Egyptian Amber wheat, under contract to Archie Milne, in 1937, which he claimed had properties that would protect the consumer of Sunera, made from it, from cancer. We never found out if it were true or not, for in April, 1938 the building was completely destroyed by a spectacular fire. Archie's dreams went up with it, in the same smoke, and I grew no more Egyptian Amber wheat.

John S. Martin's successes as a Poultryman were parallelled by his advancement in Masonry. He was initiated into Freemasonry on December12th, 1904. On the day of St. John the Evangelist, December 27th, 1911, he was installed as Worshipful Master of his Lodge. On May 12th, 1911, fifty years after the forming of the Lodge, the largest gathering of brethren ever to attend the lodge, gathered at a special communication of Grand Lodge to dedicate the new and fully refurbished Lodge rooms over the Caley block. A number of presentations followed. One of note was a beautiful gavel made from the wood of a table owned by the first Grand Master, William Mercer Wilson. This was presented by Brother Dr. McIntosh, of Simcoe. He had earlier presented the Lodge with a bust of the Grand Master, crafted by the sculptor, Samuel Gardiner, whose beautifully rendered tombstones can be seen in many local cemeteries.

On July 21st, 1920, John S. Martin was elected District Deputy Grand Master of Wilson District. He took his new duties very seriously as he travelled throughout his district. He noted, on celebrating the life of Mercer Wilson, Past Grand Master, at the June gathering in St. John's Church and the grave side, that the stone marking his grave was a disgrace to masonry. He reported to Grand Lodge that: *"It is neither level nor plumb, and is most ordinary in appearance. Has the time not come for a suitable stone, properly inscribed, to be erected to preserve this ancient landmark?"*

On June 16th, 1922, a special communication of Grand Lodge met at St. John's Anglican cemetery, where R. W. Bro. Martin unveiled an imposing monument to the memory of the first Grand Master. The Grand Master M. W. Bro. William Ponton was present and said in part: *"The massive granite, the appropriate inscription, the exquisite beauty of the surroundings, the large concourse of masons present, the whole character of the function, left nothing to be desired."*

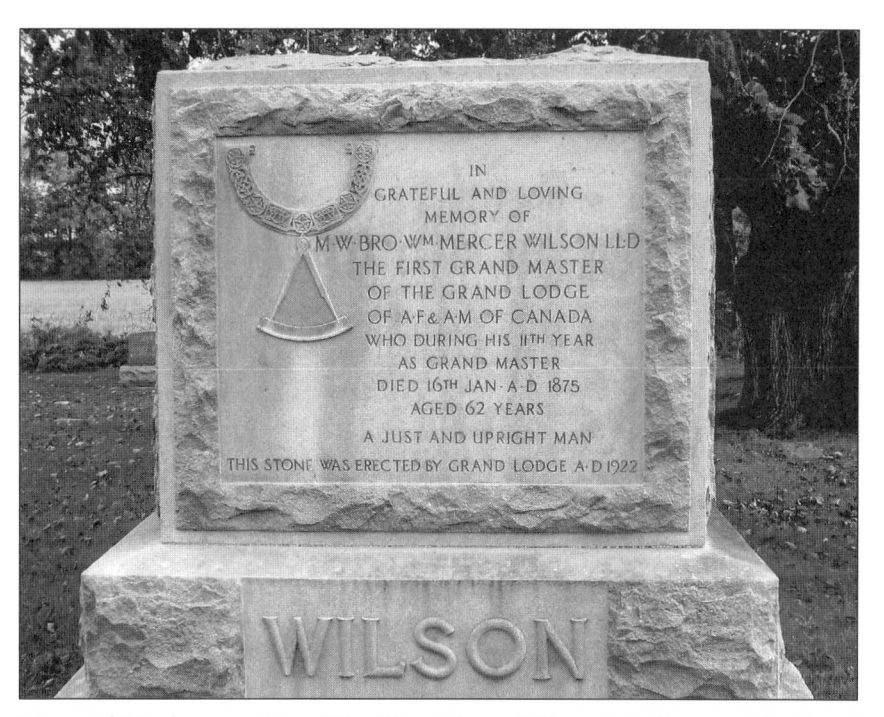

*Memorial Headstone to Most Wor. Wm. Mercer Wilson, L.L.D. erected by Grand Lodge*

John S. Martin had been elected to the Board of General Purposes of Grand Lodge, where he contributed more than his share for the good of Masonry. He had become widely known in Masonic circles and had made friends wherever he went. In 1925 he was elected Deputy Grand Master. John Martin said his primary reason for accepting this high office was; *"because he felt the need existed for a greater unity between rural and urban people. Nowhere was that unity found to exist as it does in Masonry and he hoped that it would be developed to an even greater degree in the future."*

In 1928 Grand Lodge convened for its 73rd Annual Communication in Memorial Hall, built to the memory of those students and graduates who fought in the First World War, on the campus of the Ontario Agricultural College, Guelph. It was here that the Honourable John Strickler Martin was elected the 33rd Grand Master of the Grand Lodge A.F. & A.M. of Canada in the Province of Ontario. I t was a most appropriate location as it was here John S. Martin had been a lecturer and later as Minister of Agriculture had done so much to advance the influence and prestige of the Ontario Agricultural College.

A highlight of John S. Martin's first year in office was the unique ceremony at St. John's Church, Woodhouse, on Sunday June 24th, 1928. He and almost all of his Grand Lodge officers, as well as over twenty-five hundred masons from far and wide assembled to pay tribute to the memory of William Mercer Wilson. Following the laying of a wreath by M. W. Bro. Martin and a glowing tribute paid to our first Grand Master, the huge assembly

*Grand Master John Strickler Martin, of the Grand Lodge of Canada, in the Province of Ontario*

were invited to the home of the Grand Master, where refreshments were served. The minutes of Erie Lodge record that:
"*About fifteen hundred people from all Ontario accepted John S. and Mrs. Martin's invitation to afternoon tea. Prospect Hill was 'eaten out'.*" This was quite literally true, for their generous hosts had not anticipated the throng that descended upon them. They could only regret that the larder was empty before the end of the line was reached..

Two very, very busy years of travel, receptions and attendance to the detail of his office as well as his duties as Minister of Agriculture took a heavy toll on John S. Martin's health. He became physically exhausted. On June 13th, 1929, the Honourable Dr. Forbes Godfrey, Minister of Health, visited John S. at his home and gave him a thorough examination. "It's just a matter of rest, he has been overworked and must take it easy," the good doctor declared.

Seeking to improve their quarters and at the same time honour the exalted position of their own member and Grand Master, members of Erie lodge began thinking of building their own Masonic Temple. A meeting was held at which Erie Temple Limited was formed and Most Wor. Bro. John S. Martin made the first contribution of $2,000.00. This was matched by W. H. Barrett. Another parishioner of St. Paul's, W. Morley Buck gave $500.00 toward the project. In one afternoon it had been well launched. Shares were sold among the brethren and soon added to the funds for a building. On August 26th, 1929 purchase of the lot on the south-west corner of Nelson and Main Streets was finalised, the contract to build the Temple having been already awarded to Bro. George W. Nunn.

Letters patent, incorporating Erie Temple Limited, were issued on September 4th, 1929, naming C. W. Barwell, President; John C King, the town clerk, Secretary; with the following Directors, William Morley Buck, Orchard Beach Hotel Proprietor; Dr. Albert H. Cook, Physician; and Clark P. Freeman, Royal Bank Manager. The building was already begun and completed as scheduled November 20th, 1929. Many faithful brethren assisted by their purchase of shares, while the following brethren added their particular building skills during the construction of Erie's Masonic

Temple. Bro. George Nunn as contractor was ably assisted by master carpenters, Wor. Bro. Peter Brock, Wor. Bro. Ernest Hind, Bro. Wilfred Place, Bro. Cecil C. Yerex, and Bro. Wm Duff. The brickwork came under the operative, as well as speculative, skills of Bro. George Phillips and all electrical work was carried out by Bro. Aaron McKnight.

On December 16th, 1929, seventy-five members and thirty-one visitors assembled in the new temple for the first time. The Worshipful Master W. McGaw Macdonald opened the lodge and raised it to the third degree at which time Right Worshipful Brother James R. Waddle installed Bro. Ernest Hind as the new Worshipful Master. His officers for the ensuing year were as follows: Sr. Warden, W. H. Barrett; Jr. Warden, Dr. Howard McLachlan; Chaplain, Very Worshipful Bro. Reverend David J. Cornish; Sr. Deacon Bro. Sam H. Morris; Jr. Deacon Bro. T. B. Barrett; Sr Steward, Bro. Wm A. Ferguson; Jr. Steward, Bro. Dr. I. P. Asseltine.

Grand Master John S. Martin was present and gave the final charge relating to the ideals of a speculative mason. He then, with a few congratulatory remarks, presented the Past Master's jewel to

*Lodge Room of Erie Lodge, No. 149, A. F. & A. M.*

Wor. Bro. W. McGaw Macdonald. The fourth degree followed in the basement banquet hall.

John Strickler Martin died at his home on May 13th, 1931 in his 56th year. Typical of the newspaper headlines that announced his death to the nation were: "*Ontario Mourns the Loss of Much-beloved Son.*" "*He Served his Fellow Men.*" Tributes poured in from far and wide. "*Mr. Martin will be mourned not only by his former colleagues and fellow members of the Legislature regardless of party position, but by all the people of the province amongst whom he was so widely known and highly regarded.*" and this "*Ontario never had a Minister who devoted himself so earnestly and so sincerely to the improvement of agricultural conditions in the province. - If ever a man was a sacrifice to public service it was Mr. Martin.*"

The Masonic preparations for the funeral were the responsibility of his good friend and neighbour, W. H. "Harry" Barrett, as Master of Erie Lodge. Eighty-four members registered on the opening of the Lodge, and over three hundred visiting brethren signed as well. Many more were present at the home, the church and the cemetery, who could not get into the Lodge rooms. Active pall bearers were W. H. Barrett, Frank M. Bond, John C. King, Dr. Stevens, W. J. Thompson, James Vokes, S. J. Waddell and James R. Waddle. Honourary pall bearers included four members of cabinet and four personal friends.

Canon Cody and Bishop Williams of Huron took part in the Masonic service in Erie Temple, which was followed by a walk of the throng of Masons present to St. Paul's Church, where only a small part of the huge crowd of mourners could find accommodation inside. Quoting from my father's diary following the church service:

> "It got very black as we were forming up again in the cemetery and just as the bearers were walking from the hearse to the grave the rain came down by the bucket-full and continued while the service was in progress. A good many top hats and frock coats got a good soaking for the rain fell more on the great men who were clustered around the grave than it did on the rest of us, who sought shelter under the trees. It helped to abbreviate

the ceremony and very shortly the largest funeral service that ever assembled near here, was dispersed.

Jack Martin was known and respected, even loved, from one end of Ontario to the other, by high and low alike and it would be hard to say that the crowd was not drawn as much out of respect as curiosity. His popularity was easily accounted for as he was so friendly, so interested in everybody, but that did not account for his great success, which must have been due to some remarkable qualities not so apparent and hard to define. It seems tragic that he should pass out at the age of fifty-five; but he lived a large life while he was here.

*****************************

Tragedy struck the Martin family again in the early years of W.W. II. The only male heir, named John Strickler after his famous uncle and son of Charles Martin, was a medical student who was meant to inherit his uncle's estate. At the outbreak of war John S. Martin Jr. joined the Royal Canadian Air Force and following

*Memorial Headstone to Most Wor. Bro. John S. Martin in Port Dover Cemetery*

training as air crew was posted to Britain. On a raid over Germany his bomber was struck, forcing the crew to parachute out of the crippled plane. John S. Martin was reported missing and his exact fate was never known. His parents later attended the dedication of the Memorial to the 20,000 youth of the British Empire and Commonwealth whose graves are unknown. This monument is at Runnymeade, Magna Carta Island, on the Thames River, in England.

Another outstanding Mason and Lay Reader in St. Paul's was Dr. Embury Andrew Williamson, who had opened an office in the rear of the original Crown Bank building on the north-west corner of Main and Chapman Streets. In October 1939, he affiliated with Erie Lodge. With a quick, attentive mind and a love of the masonic ritual, Dr. Andy progressed rapidly in his masonic knowledge to become Wor. Master in 1948. He received his 33 degree in Halifax, Nova Scotia, in 1959. The whole of Wilson District expected that Wor. Bro. Williamson would serve as District Deputy Grand Master during Erie Lodge's Centennial year, but it was not to be. While attending a medical convention in Detroit during Easter of 1960, he suffered a massive heart attack from which he never recovered. The whole community was deeply saddened by the passing of this most promising General Practitioner, Churchman and active Mason in our midst.

The post of District Deputy Grand Master. was won by Wor. Bro. Harold W. Smith, who served as Worshipful Master of Erie Lodge in 1953 and who most ably represented the Lodge during our Centennial year in 1961. He was ably supported during his year by Wor. Bro. Elmer Lewis as District Chaplain, Wor. Bro. H. J. H. Barrett, Masonic Education for the District and Wor. Bro. Harold Scruton as District Secretary.

Over the years many masonic brethren, belonging to the Parish of St. Paul's Church, Port Dover, have served as members and officers of Erie Lodge No. 149, A. F. & A. M. Several have already been featured in the preceding account. Those known members of St. Paul's Parish to serve as Worshipful Master of the Lodge are noted with a double asterisk [**] in the following list of Masters since the inception of Erie Lodge # 149, A. F. & A. M.:

| | | | |
|---|---|---|---|
| 1861 | Israel Wood Powell** | 1862-3 | Theobald Butler Barrett** |
| 1864-5 | Peter Lawson | 1866-69 | Berkley Powell** |
| 1870-1 | J. V. Hoover** | 1872 | J. W. Stewart |
| 1873 | Silas Hoover** | 1874-5 | H. H. Sovereign** |
| 1876-8 | Brian Varey | 1879-80 | A. F. Turnbull |
| 1881-2 | Harry W. Ansley** | 1883-4 | Rev. W. F. Tibbetts** |
| 1885-6 | Brian Varey | 1887-8 | William Duncan |
| 1889-0 | R. M. Taylor | 1891 | Josiah Varey |
| 1892-3 | J. A. Innes** | 1894-5 | H. Fawcett |
| 1896 | A. C. Matthews | 1897-8 | J. Alex Innes** |
| 1899-0 | Silas L. Butler | 1901-2 | James R. Waddle |
| 1903 | Frank M. Bond - appointed Grand Steward in 1906. | | |
| 1904-5 | James R. Waddle - elected D.D.G.M., Wilson District for 1905. | | |
| 1906-7 | John R. Davis** | 1908-9 | R. J. Miller |
| 1910 | William Fasken | 1911 | John Strickler Martin** |
| 1912-3 | W. J. Thompson** | 1914 | Charles W. Barwell** - Grand Steward, 1927 |
| 1915 | F. H. Stringer** | 1916 | John C. King |
| 1917 | Guy Teeple | 1918 | R. O. A. Hobbes** |
| 1919 | J. Gordon Patterson - appointed Grand Steward, 1921. | | |
| 1920 | Dr. Albert H. Cook** | 1921 | Landon B. Ivey** |
| 1922 | Milton Woodger | 1923 | C. P. Freeman** |
| 1924 | Lea Marshall** | 1925 | Leigh Corbett** |
| 1926 | Reverend David J. Cornish** appointed assistant Grand Chaplain, 1927. | | |
| 1927 | William J. Wamsley** | 1928 | Joseph Lamb |
| 1929 | W. McGaw Macdonald - elected D.D.G.M. of Wilson District, 1932 | | |
| 1930 | Ernest Hind - appointed to Board of General Purposes, 1934 | | |
| 1931 | William Henry Barrett** - appointed Grand Organist, 1934 | | |
| 1932 | Howard T. McLachlan | | |
| 1933 | Sam H. Morris** - appointed Grand Steward, 1933 | | |
| 1934 | Cameron Thorburn** | | |
| 1935 | Theobald B. Barrett** - elected D.D.G.M. of Wilson District, 1950 | | |
| 1936 | William A Ferguson | 1937 | Dr. I. P. Asseltine |
| 1938 | William E. Cruise - appointed Grand Steward, 1951. | | |
| 1939 | Edward M. Jacques | 1940 | Peter M. Brock |
| 1941 | Ora Charlton | 1942 | George R. Martin** |
| 1943 | Fred M. Given | 1944 | Brian M. Varey** - Grand Steward, 1976 |

| | | | |
|---|---|---|---|
| 1945 | Hubert J. H. Barrett** | 1946 | Harold R. Scruton |
| | | | - Grand Steward, 1961 |
| 1947 | Alton E. Hoover** | 1948 | Andrew E. Williamson** |
| 1949 | Thomas G. Caley | 1950 | Willard Butler |
| 1951 | Ray H. Ivey** | 1952 | J. Chris Quanbury |
| 1953 | W. Harold Smith** - elected D.D.G.M. of Wilson District, 1960 | | |
| 1954 | Elmer Lewis - appointed Grand Steward | | |
| 1955 | Albert Blake** | 1956 | H. Vernon Ryerse** |
| 1957 | Jack B. Quanbury | 1958 | Bruce R. Reid** |
| 1959 | Andrew C. Lowe** | 1960 | Harry B. Barrett** |
| | | | - Erie Lodge Historian. |
| 1961 | F. G. Archie Morris** | 1962 | Parker M. Leney |
| 1963 | Harold S. Miller | 1964 | Robert L. Hazen |
| 1965 | William C. McNeilly** | 1966 | Walter C. Long** |
| 1967 | Allan W. Smith | 1968 | Leonard Murrell** |
| | | | - Grand Stewrd, 1981 |
| 1869 | A. Donald Simpson | 1970 | Gordon A Reid |
| 1971 | Charles L. Heaman** | 1972 | Edward J. Holland |
| 1973 | Thomas Fallis | 1974 | Paul V. Lewis |
| | | | - elected D.D.G.M. 1980 |
| 1975 | Kenneth A. Simpson | 1976 | Albert A. Sauve |
| 1977 | Thomas Fallis | 1978 | William A. Smith |
| 1979 | Paul S. Cober | 1980 | J. Willard Challand |
| 1981 | Gary S. Emmons | 1982 | Charles Grant |
| 1983 | Cornelius Groen | 1984 | Alex A. Pow |
| 1985 | Thomas A. Pow | 1986 | Henk Serbee |
| 1987 | Hamilton Jackson | 1988 | Norris Lennox |
| 1989 | Walter Farr | 1990 | T. B. "Toby" Barrett** |
| 1991 | James Drummond | 1992 | John Dan O'Neill |
| 1993 | John Slade | 1994 | Cornelius Groen |
| 1995 | Dennis Koluk | 1996 | Lee Buffin |
| 1997 | Ronald Collis | 1998 | Alain St. Jacques |
| | | | - D.D.G.M. in 2003 - 4. |
| 1999 | Thomas Pow | 2000 | James Maki |
| 2001 | Mark Hagen | 2002 | Aubrey Cox |
| 2003 | William Jukes Jr. | 2004 | David Berta |
| 2005 | Leslie J. Lasko | | |

In 1994 Very Worshipful Brother Brian Varey was honoured by his Lodge when Very Wor. Bro. Elmer Lewis presented him with a lapel pin for sixty years service as member of Erie Lodge, this was followed by the presentation by Wor. Bro. Harold Miller of a lapel pin to V. Wor. Bro. Varey for fifty years service as a Past Master of Erie Lodge. It was also noted during the congratulations of the Brethren that Very Worshipful Brother Varey had served a total of thirty-five years, from 1950 to 1985, as Secretary of his Lodge.

Upon the formation of the Lodge in 1861 their quarters were established on the second floor of the Powell Block. In 1889, when the building was purchased by Mr. Beaupre, the Lodge rooms were moved to the Caley Block further up Main Street. Mr. Beaupre renovated the building turning the centre store, which had been occupied by Mr. Denton, into a lobby, office, bar, sample room, for the use of travelling salesmen, and stairway for his hotel. The front was removed and a handsome front entrance was built supported by iron columns. On the second floor was a dining room that seated from 48 to 60 guests, as well as a kitchen, parlour and several bedrooms. The third floor was devoted entirely to bedrooms.

The roof being flat and easily accessible, presented a charming view for miles in all directions. There was a verandah in the rear and a large balcony was erected on Market street, where the main entrance was located . The Hotel was completed by July of 1890 and ready for guests. Mr. Robert Meade took charge as proprietor of the hotel which was named "The Meade House". From the Maple Leaf we learn that; "the summer of 1890 was a busy one with cots and shakedowns being brought in to accommodate the flood of visitors arriving by train from inland towns, such as Brantford and Woodstock".

Again quoting the Maple Leaf of February 2nd, 1900 - "Last Saturday morning about half-past three our peaceful residents were rudely awakened from their slumbers by the ringing of the fire bell and the scream of the Knitting Mill whistle. The scene of the disaster found one of our finest business blocks completely engulfed in flames, which spread [so] rapidly that it was found impossible almost for anyone to enter either Mr. A.W. Lawrie's store, The Mead House or H. W. Ansley's.

"About all Mr. Lawrie saved was his dog and the books from

his safe. Mr. Ansley saved a couple of showcases near the door, some wall paper and white lead. He made an ineffectual attempt to apprise the Simcoe Fire Brigade of our danger, but the flames drove him out. Mr. James Acker, lessee of the Meade House with his family, and the boarders and guests had to flee for their lives, losing about everything they had. The mercury was hovering round about zero F. and the wind blowing very fresh".

Erie Lodge had settled in to their new quarters in the Caley Block when the building of the Meade House forced them from their original home. In 1921 the Lodge rooms were again moved to the second floor of the McQueen Block, further south along Main Street.

In 1929, to honour Erie Lodge member, Past Master, Past District Deputy Grand Master and finally Grand Master John S. Martin, the members built and opened their own Masonic Temple on the south-west corner of Main and Nelson Streets, to commemorate their illustrious Brother's term as Grand Master of the Grand Lodge of Canada in the Province of Ontario.

CHAPTER TEN

# St. Paul's Church – 1875-1900

Upon Reverend Dr. Tibbetts moving to Simcoe, **Reverend John Frederick Renaud** was appointed to St. Paul's. Quoting from "Ministers I Remember" when Dr. Tibbetts left :

"a young man succeeded him, Mr. Fredric Renaud fresh from college, full of enthusiasm, and love for his work. He was unmarried and his mother came to keep his house and help him in the church work. She was a very clever woman – it was whispered that she often wrote his sermons, and she certainly was untiring in her efforts to aid him. He was always doing unexpected things. I remember once he preached a forceable sermon urging more generous giving to missionaries, and then he forgot to have the collection taken up! He was well liked and everyone regretted it when he left to go to a larger church."

Mr. Renaud's mother was an ardent worker among the young people of the church. Her influence on her charges is credited by some with developing Mrs. Alice Parke and her sister, Miss Emily Louisa "Wese" Barrett, into the wonderful church visitors that they became. It was during Mr. Renaud's tenure that the Sunday School was built about 1876-77. Sunday School sessions that were exclusive to the Anglican children began in 1861. The classes were first held in the Scofield residence above their store on Main street. Later the students met in the church.

In 1876 Mr. Joseph Bell, owner of the Dominion Hotel sold Lot 30, north of the church Lot 33, and at right angles to it, to " The incumbent [ the Reverend John Frederick Renaud] and Church Wardens of St. Paul's Church, for the sum of two hundred dollars." The Sunday School & Parish Hall, a plain rectangular brick building was built on this lot soon after it was acquired by the Parish.

At this time Miss Emily Louisa [Wese] Barrett began as a teacher of the beginners or primary class in the new Sunday School. She was to maintain an almost perfect attendance as the primary school teacher for the next fifty-two or more years.

Wese's eldest sister, Phoebe Caroline Barrett, had served as Organist of St. Paul's from 1868 to 1875. On October 7th, 1875, she married James Scott and was about to move out of the parish. A special celebration was held in the Parish Hall on the evening of October 5th, 1875 to wish her well. During the evening a very ornate gold mantle clock was presented to Miss Barrett by, I assume, one of the Wardens. His presentation speech has been preserved and was as follows:

> Dear Miss Barrett,
> I have been requested by your many friends connected with St. Paul's congregation to present to you in their name, with this token of their grateful and appreciative acknowledgement of your long and gratuitous services in conducting the music of our church and I am certain you have always felt it no common privilege to be enabled to do this for your Master's sake, and to lay the gifts, He Himself has bestowed, upon His altar.
> To the congregation at large, the benefit of having an able, willing and punctual leader, always ready, always, always at the post has been grate,(sic) and they trust you will accept this memorial as an expression of their thanks.
> About to take up the onerous duties of a housekeeper the presentation of a timekeeper may not be inappropriate, although it may often echo the dictates of conscience unlike that inward guide it is no silent monitor but

minute by minute lets the voice be heard proclaiming how time flies and audibly reminding us to redeem the time at intervals enforcing its admonitions by striking argument.

In your new home we doubt not an honourable place will be accorded this memorial, just as we believe a warm place in your affections will ever be given to those who have so harmoniously aided you in this labour of love.

Allow me to conclude by wishing you every true happiness so that when time shall be no more a blissful eternity may open upon you.

Reverend John F. Renaud was a convert from Roman Catholicism. He was very conscientious as to the keeping of accurate church records, and the reliable records of St. Paul's date from his tenure.

From the British Canadian we learn that the Reverend John Frederick Renaud was married to Harriet Sophie Covernton on January 10th, 1877. The wedding took place at Trinity Anglican Church, Simcoe, with Reverend Edward Sullivan D. D., Rector of Chicago, and brother-in-law of the bridegroom officiating. He was assisted by Reverend Canon Grassett, incumbent of Trinity, and Reverend W. B. Curran, of Galt. His bride, Harriet Sophie, was the eldest daughter of James Covernton of "Dryden Farm," Charlotteville.

Though the records from 1875 to 1878 have

*Lawrence Skey, Lay Reader & Sunday School Superintendent of St. Paul's*

apparently been lost, the first recorded baptism on January 7th, 1878 is that of Reverend Renaud's son, Edward Claude Hamilton Renaud. Reverend Mr. Renaud spent the summer of 1878 in Europe, and his place was taken by a young **Fred DuVernet**, then a divinity student in Toronto; years afterwards he became Bishop of Caledonia, in British Columbia.

Upon returning from his extended stay in Europe it would appear that Reverend Renaud became seriously ill, to the point where he could not perform his duties regularly as Rector of St. Paul's and of his other charge at Centennial Church, Port Ryerse. On these occasions the services were taken by Lawrence Skey or Theobald B. Barrett, who were both qualified Lay readers for the Church of England.

In a letter, dated March 2nd, 1879, written by Emily Barrett, wife of Theobald, to her sister Mrs. C. H. Moodie, of High Park, Massachusetts is the following:

> "This is Sunday evening and I am quite alone, something very unusual but I will tell you how it is that the rest are all away. Toby has gone to Port Ryerse to read the Church services and a sermon for our clergyman Mr. Renaud, who is not at all well. He is but just recovering from a very severe illness. Toby read for him here in our Church to-day, and he has now taken with him Louisa, Harry, Hubert and Clarence, also Luly Skey. Alice and Katie Skey have gone to the Presbyterian Church here."

The Reverend John Frederick Renaud left Port Dover in 1879, following a tenure of some four years to take up duties in Seaforth. He preached his last sermon in St. Paul's on November 2nd, 1879.

### Vestry Meeting, October 20th, 1879.

A Vestey Meeting of the congregation of St. Paul's Church, Port Dover held in the Church on October 20th, 1879.

It was moved and seconded that Arthur Battersby Esquire take the Chair and that Robert Hellyer act as Secretary of said meeting.

Moved by Mr. Morgan, Seconded by T. Barrett – That Mr. Lawrence Skey be appointed Delegate for the purpose of conferring with the Bishop as to the appointment of the successor to the Rev. F. Renaud, of St. Paul's Church, Port Dover.   Carried.

Moved by T. B. Barrett, Seconded by Mr. Reid — That the Delegate Mr. Skey be instructed to ascertain if an arrangement can be made giving St. Paul's Church two services every Sunday and if not what other arrangement can be made and to report to a Vestry to be called for that purpose.   Carried.

Moved by T. Barrett, Seconded by Mr. Reid — That this Vestry now adjourn until the return of the Delegate, when the Vestry will be convened to receive his report.   Carried.

At that time the **Reverend William Berthome Evans** [1879 – 1880] was appointed Rector of St. John's, Woodhouse, and the churches at Port Dover and Port Ryerse were included in his Parish. As St. John's had no rectory he rented the large, two story brick house on Prospect street in Port Dover that had been built by Lewis Bowlby. It had been formerly known as the Prospect Hill Seminary for young ladies, who lived in the house and were taught by his sister, Miss Hellen Bowlby.

Referring to "Ministers I Remember" by Auntie Alice we learn that the house, though large, was fully occupied: "He [Rev. Evans] had to have help and always had a curate. Mr. Turnbull, Mr Seaborne and Mr. Ball were here for short periods of time. Mr. Evans house was a happy, merry one. It was a large household too, for besides Mr. & Mrs. Evans, six children and a curate, there was always a governess and generally one or more guests. Mr.

*Lewis Bowlby*

*Home of Lewis Bowlby, Prospect Street, later rectory to Rev. William Berthome Evans*

Evans loved fun and entered into the pleasures of his children and their young friends, – but he was truly good – devoted to his God and his church. When a parsonage was built at St. John's the family moved there."

The Reverend William Evans was a son of Francis Evans, first rector of St. John's, Woodhouse. He was well liked and accepted into the life of the village of Port Dover as were the young curates who assisted him. Mr. Turnbull, in particular, became a friend of the Barrett clan. He was quite artistic and while here he sketched Port Dover as it appeared from the Bowlby home above Silver Lake or The Pond as most locals referred to it. The needle-like spire of St. Paul's is easily recognised in the drawing. This was presented by him to one of my aunts and is now in my possession. Mr. Cornish notes that the Reverend Evans last baptismal entry, which may have been his last official service in St. Paul's before moving to the new rectory in St. John's, was recorded on December 6th, 1880.

The replacement for Reverend William Evans, appointed by the Bishop, was the **Reverend Marmaduke Martin Dillon. [1880 – 1884]** Reverend Dillon was born in England in 1820. As an officer in the 89th Regiment, of the British Army, he was posted and served in the West Indies. He was first licensed as a missionary in Antigua. In 1854, aged 38 years, Mr. Dillon came to Canada and was accepted by Bishop Strachan into the ministry here. Mrs.

Burbidge reports that Mr. Dillon "operated the Free Mission School in an abandoned artillery barracks in London, Ontario. Synod records stated that 'at its zenith 203 to 450 children attended the mission, where they could receive communion and sit anywhere in St. Paul's [Cathedral]."

Turning to Auntie Alice's memoir we are told that : "Mr. Renaud and Mr. Evans had been so popular that it was hard for the people to be satisfied with someone so entirely different. Mr. Dillon had been an officer in the British Army before he entered the church and had travelled to the far corners of the earth. His wife was an invalid, and rarely went out anywhere – but she loved to have young people about her. Perhaps Mr. Dillon was a little autocratic, I do not know, – but I know some members of the congregation opposed him consistently and finally made him realise that they wished his resignation. He was disappointed and disheartened. I think really they broke his heart – but he never had to look for another church, (as) he fell ill and just quietly slipped away to Heaven. I was young and bitterly resentful of the way he had been treated as I admired him so much. – Even yet I don't like to think of it."

*Home of the Harding family, 1881 Rectory to St. Paul's, and home of Charlton Woolley*

My aunt as an impressionable teenager was obviously a friend and admirer of both Mr. and Mrs. Dillon, who were highly thought of by her whole family. This was not the opinion held of his ministry by a majority of the congregation, however. From Mrs. Burbidge's recent research it would appear that Auntie Alice's account of Mr. Dillon's final days are not quite correct, or at least incomplete. Kay reports that Reverend Mr. Dillon preached in 1885 at a service in St. Paul's, London, to which 700 ex-slaves had paraded. Ill health however forced him to return to England to recuperate. He later returned to Canada and served, at least for a time at Port Stanley and at Port Dover. A son of Reverend Dillon married a sister of Crosby Morgan of Port Dover.

*Harry Harding, Lizzie Harding & Fanny Harding*

As of the 1st of May, 1881 the Wardens, "of St. Paul's Episcopal Church," Harry W. Ansley and William F. Tibbetts leased from Edward J. Low village lots 18 & 19 on the west side of St. George Street, for a term of 1 year. The lease was for eighty-four dollars per annum to be paid in quarterly payments. Mr. Low agreed to repair the barn on the property for use as a stable. Was this leased to supply a rectory for the Reverend Mr. Dillon?

This property was and is on the north-west corner of Market & St. George Streets directly across from the church. It was the home of the Harding family prior to this time. Harry Harding was ranching in the Okanagan valley at the same time Harry Barrett was living on Mountain Meadow ranch in the same area, from 1885 to 1899. Two of Harry Harding's sisters were also in British Columbia teaching at that time. They had all grown up in Port

Dover and visited and worked together while living in the Spallumcheen District of the Okanagan, near Armstrong, B. C.

On October 5th, 1883 the whole town was agog when a very special guest of the Long Point Company arrived at the station to take passage to the "Cottages" of the Company for some duck hunting. Their guest was none other than the son of Queen Victoria, Prince George, Prince of Wales, destined eventually to become King George V. A host of prominent gentlemen accompanied the Prince as he disembarked from the rail car and moved to the wharf where the steam yacht "James Buckley", owned by two good Anglicans, Messrs. Harry Ansley & William F. Tibbetts, was awaiting his arrival. While baggage was being loaded, the Prince appeared on deck to graciously meet and greet some of the assembled crowd.

Returning in mid-week the Prince expressed his great pleasure with his visit to the prestigious hunting club, where it was learned that he had bagged 50 ducks on his first day in the marsh and on the second day 84 birds. As the train left the station he accommodated the large crowd who had assembled for glimpse of him by appearing on the rear platform of the last car, to acknowledge the cheers and waving handkerchiefs.

*Grange or Wiggins Community Hall, Lot 13, Con. 5, Woodhouse*

During the incumbency of Mr. Dillon Anglican services for which he was responsible, were established in the Grange Hall on the Cockshutt Road. The Hall stood in the north-west corner of lot 13, Concession 5, Woodhouse. The Grange movement was an early form of farm co-operative which by buying farm staples like binder twine, farm implements, sugar and livestock salt in bulk, or in rail-car lots, made the price, at cost, to the farmer much less. The movement began in the United States and spread into Canada. Soon a social wing of the Grange developed and Halls were sponsored by the movement. As Mr. Henry Misner, owner of the farm on Lot 13, Concession 5, Woodhouse, was a proponent and held office in the local Grange, he may have donated the land [one full acre] on which the Grange Hall, or Wiggan's Hall as it was to become known, was built.

This hall served the local community until about 1940, when it was demolished and replaced by a new Hall. These two Halls served for religious meetings, receptions, dances, and political gatherings, as well as a local polling station at election time. It was guaranteed to produce interesting and often violent arguments, both inside and outside the hall, at nomination meetings for township and county council candidates, when I was growing up. Even fist fights were not unheard of at that time, and were something we youngsters looked forward to with excited anticipation.

As Wiggan's School, S.S. # 13, Woodhouse, was directly across the road, the hall and school were the site for several years of the rural school fairs, where students from Woodhouse could display vegetables, grain and livestock in competition, and the girls could vie with each other for prizes in sewing, and other home making arts. I showed poultry and a sheep, usually a ram or market lamb, each year of my public school life, as well as fruit and vegetables and the occasional bird house. Most of the other boys from our own and neighbouring schools, competed in the poultry, colt and calf classes and the grain, fruit and vegetable classes.

The school today is in disrepair and the weathered old board and batten Grange Hall and its 1940's replacement are no more. Perhaps as early as the 1880's a school fair was held in Port Dover, first at the fair grounds, where the Composite School is now situated and later at the Public School on Main street. My first experience at showing a ram lamb, poultry, vegetables and a wooden window stick was at this site.

**The Reverend John Robert Newell [1884 – 1898]** was appointed to St. Paul's on August 2nd, 1884. For an opinion by one who knew him, I again quote my Great Aunt :

"The Reverend John Newell now took charge, and the critics now had something fresh to consider. At first the new man was not popular, but perhaps the conscience of the fault-finders pricked a little and made them more tolerant, so they put up with what they did not like, and after years of quiet work Mr. Newell endeared himself to most of his people and was regretted when he decided it was time for a change, in 1898."

Although Aunty Alice told me that her father T. B. Barrett served St. Paul's as a Lay Reader almost from the time the church was built, his position may not have been completely official. If he had the knowledge and desire to do so, that may have been all that the incumbent priest of the time required. It was noted earlier by his wife, Emily, that he had served in this capacity during the illness of Reverend John Frederick Renaud and no doubt he had done so on many other occasions.

The following letter from his old friend Maurice Scollard Baldwin, now Bishop of Huron, indicates that T. B. Barrett was finally granted "License and Authority to perform the duties of Lay

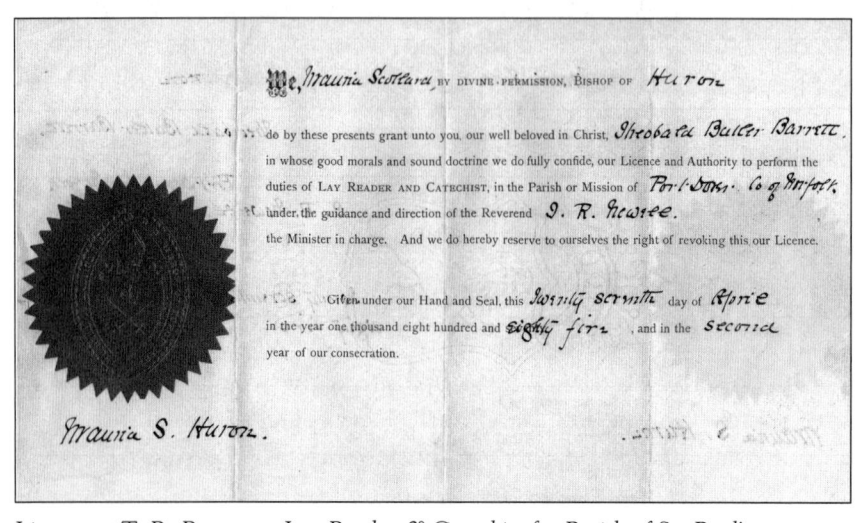

*Licence to T. B. Barrett as Lay Reader & Catechist for Parish of St. Paul's*

Reader and Catechist in the Parish or Mission of Port Dover." Under separate cover a parchment thus inscribed was received, complete with the official red seal of office, stating that it was "The seal of Maurice S. Baldwin, D. D. Bishop of Huron – 1883." It was signed on "this twenty seventh day of April in the year one thousand eight hundred and eighty five, and in the second year of our consecration."

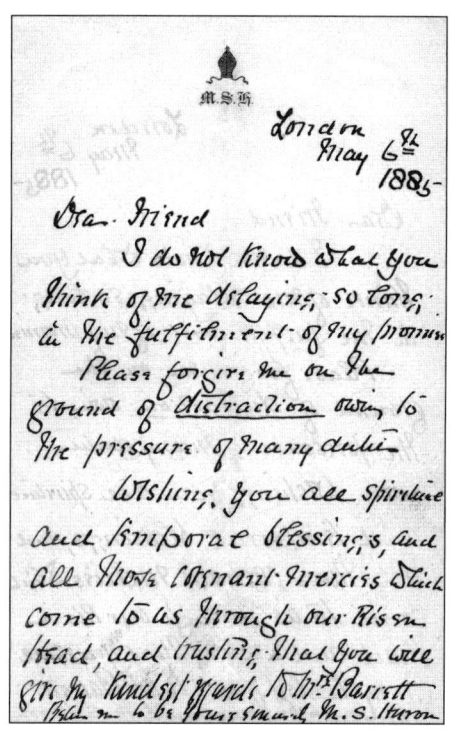

*Bishop Baldwin's letter to T. B. Barrett re his appointment as Lay Reader*

London, May 6th, 1885.
Dear Friend
I do not know what you think of me delaying, so long, in the fulfilment of my promise.
Please forgive me on the ground of distraction owing to the pressure of many duties.
Wishing you all spiritual and temporal blessings and all those covenant mercies which come to us through our Risen Head, and trusting that you will give my kindest regards to Mrs. Barrett.
                Believe me to be yours sincerely,
              ( Signed ) M. S. Huron.

On March 5th, 1886 a special meeting was called in the Sunday School to bring to a head a long-time desire on the part of many parishioners to supply a church drive-shed to accommodate those who used a horse and buggy to attend services. It was reported that a portion of the requisite sum had already been promised and the Church Wardens had taken the matter in hand. The meeting expressed the view that immediate steps be taken to supply this long wanted convenience in the hope it can be erected at once.

On July 9th, 1886 the Maple Leaf reported that; "The driving shed in connection with St. Paul's Church here is progressing favourably. The frame was to be put up yesterday. It is 64 feet long and 20 feet wide. As the structure is for the benefit of the farming community, it is hoped they will contribute handsomely to its immediate completion. This shed has long been wanted ... It will prove a boon to many."

On July 30th, 1886 a notice in the local paper reported that; "Next Sunday the Free Masons of Port Dover and others from a distance will attend in full regalia, a special service in St. Paul's Church at 3:00 pm. Seats will be free and all are cordially invited. Members of the Lodge and visiting brethren will please assemble in the Lodge Room at 2:30.

On the same date the Maple Leaf reported as follows "From the Synod Journal just issued, we find that in the 13 counties composing the Diocese of Huron, only 20 congregations out of 254 exceeded St. Paul's, Port Dover, in contributing to Missions, etc., during the past year. The following are the contributions from this County:

| Trinity, | Simcoe | $ 167.74 |
| St. Paul's, | Port Dover | $ 130.01 |
| St. John's, | Woodhouse | $ 78.33 |
| St. John's, | Port Rowan | $ 45.18 |
| Christ Church, | Vittoria | $ 35.61 |
| Jireh, | Rowan Mills | $ 30.69 |
| St. Williams, | St. Williams | $ 19.77 |
| St Alban's, | Delhi | $ 19.77 |
| Christ Church, | Lyndoch | $ 14.03 |
| Courtland | | $ 10.25 |
| Grange Hall, | Wiggan's | $ 7.69 |
| Trinity, | Waterford | $ 5.09 |
| Langton | | $ .31 |

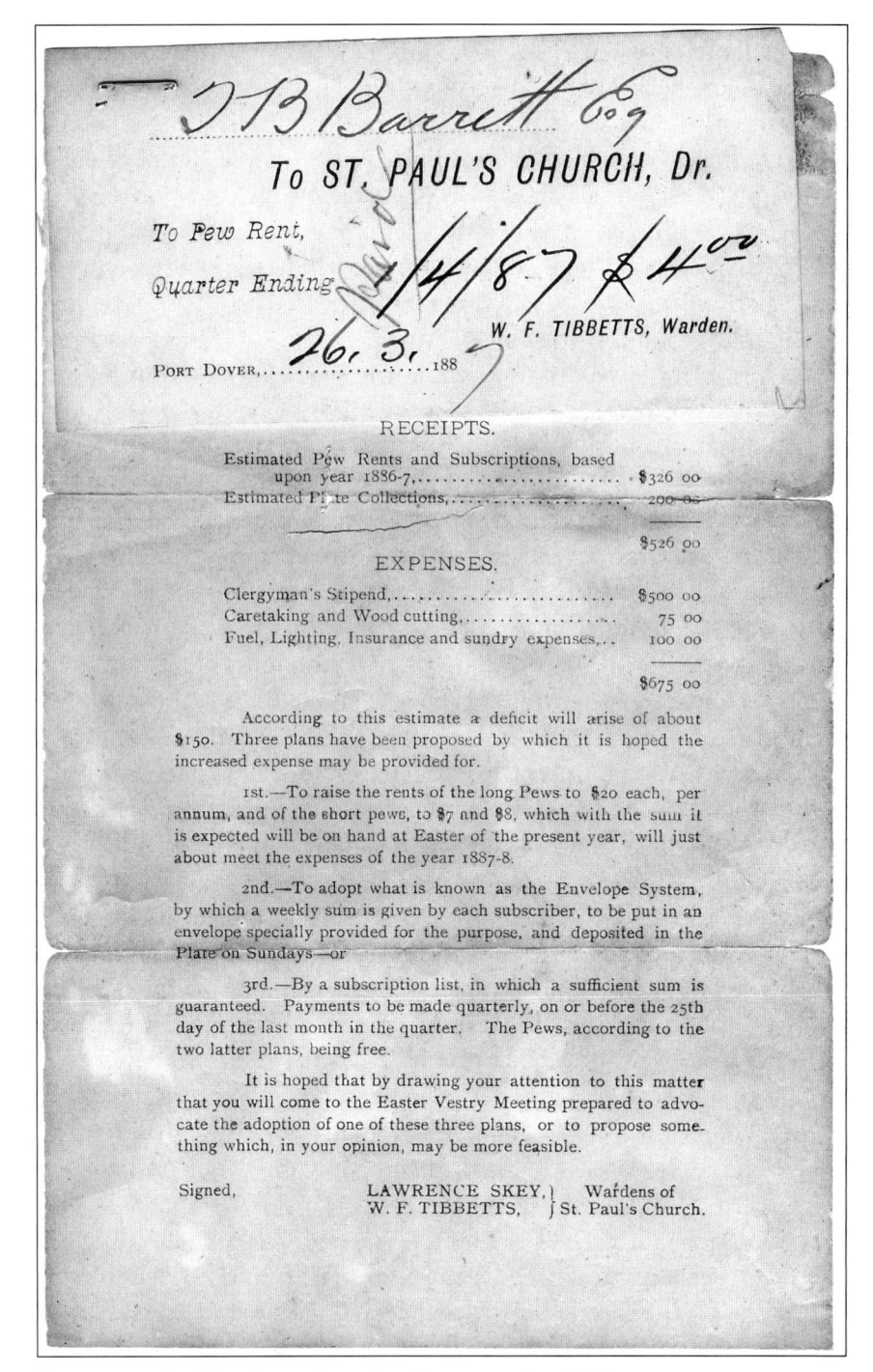

```
            J B Barrett    6.9
         To ST. PAUL'S CHURCH, Dr.
To Pew Rent,
Quarter Ending      1/4/87   $4.00
                         W. F. TIBBETTS, Warden.
Port Dover,  26, 3,  188
```

## RECEIPTS.

Estimated Pew Rents and Subscriptions, based
   upon year 1886-7,........................... $326 00
Estimated Plate Collections,....................... 200 00
                                                                  $526 00

## EXPENSES.

Clergyman's Stipend,.......................... $500 00
Caretaking and Wood cutting,.................. 75 00
Fuel, Lighting, Insurance and sundry expenses,... 100 00
                                                                  $675 00

        According to this estimate a deficit will arise of about $150. Three plans have been proposed by which it is hoped the increased expense may be provided for.

        1st.—To raise the rents of the long Pews to $20 each, per annum, and of the short pews, to $7 and $8, which with the sum it is expected will be on hand at Easter of the present year, will just about meet the expenses of the year 1887-8.

        2nd.—To adopt what is known as the Envelope System, by which a weekly sum is given by each subscriber, to be put in an envelope specially provided for the purpose, and deposited in the Plate on Sundays—or

        3rd.—By a subscription list, in which a sufficient sum is guaranteed. Payments to be made quarterly, on or before the 25th day of the last month in the quarter. The Pews, according to the two latter plans, being free.

        It is hoped that by drawing your attention to this matter that you will come to the Easter Vestry Meeting prepared to advocate the adoption of one of these three plans, or to propose something which, in your opinion, may be more feasible.

Signed,       LAWRENCE SKEY,   Wardens of
               W. F. TIBBETTS,    St. Paul's Church.

*Pew rent receipt & estimate of receipts & expenses for 1887 year*

In January of 1887, Christ Church, Vittoria, was added to the Port Dover charge and the services regularly held at the Grange Hall on the Cockshutt Road were discontinued. Memorial Church, Port Ryerse had been a Port Dover charge since its dedication in 1870 and it also was dropped.

In early January of 1889 considerable excitement was created and a good deal of damage was done in the harbour by a severe winter storm which caused the lake level to rise over five feet flooding the Grand trunk railway tracks at the foot of Main street. The Grand trunk which also owned the harbour had been put on notice that the rings and hooks in the wharf to which vessels tied up were not strong enough to hold should any undue strain be placed upon them. The advice of the vesselmen had been ignored, however, which now would be responsible for considerable damage to both vessels and warehouses in the harbour.

The "Dauntless," the "Eliza Ann" and the "George Dow" were all tied to the outer wharf and as the storm increased in violence during the night the two Allan Bros. schooners tore their rings from the timbers of the wharf and being jammed together were carried up the creek. They crashed into the Grand Trunk Railway warehouse, tearing most of the end out of it as well as carrying away a large section of the roof of the building. One vessel lost her topmast and the jib booms of both were carried away along with other damage to both of them.

The "George Dow" also broke loose due to the inadequate rings and hooks to which she was tied and was carried even further up the creek where she demolished the boathouse of Mr. Crosbie Morgan, tore a large hole in his warehouse and destroyed its large door. The Dow went on to partially destroy Mr. Morgan's coal wharf allowing large quantities of lumber, posts and shingles to be dumped into the creek where the current rapidly carried them away. The high water also flooded Mr. Morgan's office and caused a good deal of other damage at the harbour front.

On April 26th, 1889 during the Annual Vestry Meeting of St. Paul's a letter was presented by the Wardens from the Executors of the Estate of the late Mr. & Mrs. Jaffray Harvey. It stated that by Mr. Jaffray Harvey's will, [who died on November 25th, 1873, aged 62 years], the sum of $900.00 had been left to St. Paul's Church for

*Jaffray Harvey house on Prospect Hill, Port Dover, as drawn by Hellen Bowlby*

the purpose of procuring a suitable Parsonage. Further it was stated that by the will of Mrs. Catherine Harvey, [who died in October 1888, aged 88 years], an additional $300.00 was left to St. Paul's for the same purpose. The monies would be handed over to the Wardens as soon as they were prepared to comply with the conditions attached to its receipt.

The Harveys are buried in St. John's cemetery. Very little is known of them though they were thought to be friends of the Battersbys and they lived in, and may have built, the attractive brick house, which at that time was directly south of the Battersby home on Prospect street, overlooking Silver Lake. It was destined to become John S. Martin's office much later, when his poultry enterprises prospered.

On April 26th, 1889 the Maple Leaf carried the following news item: "Last Friday night, it being an excessively wild, dark night, as Reverend Mr. Newell was returning home after conducting the services in Trinity Church, Simcoe; his horse fell over the edge of a very deep culvert in front of Mr. H. H. Groff's residence, carrying everything with him and landing the buggy across the sidewalk."

"Strange to say the only damage done was a slight one to the buggy. Considering the dangerous nature of the spot, it is miraculous that the reverend gentleman was not seriously hurt. The horse made no effort to extricate himself. Mr Groff and a hotel porter appeared promptly with a lantern, and everything was soon all right again. Mr. Groff kindly tendered the hospitalities of his home to Mr. Newell, who accepted them and returned next morning."

In the spring of 1889 another concern of the Wardens was brought forward when a special Vestry Meeting was called for early May, in the Sunday School to decide on much needed repairs to the tower and steeple of the Church. The meeting agreed that the Wardens should carry out the repairs to the brick work of the tower at once and that a scaffold be erected to the top of the steeple.

Messrs. Ozias Ansley and R. Law were named a committee to examine the steeple and report on the advisability of repairing the tin work, now up and painting it well with some weather proof paint, or, remove the old metal and re-tin the steeple throughout. It was estimated the total job would probably cost $100.00. The Ladies Aid Society had already generously offered to foot the bill. The reporter concluded with the question: "How long would our different Churches last if it wasn't for the Ladies Aid?"

The expected construction of the costly scaffolding on St. Paul's tower and steeple did not take place and from the Maple Leaf of June 7th 1889, we learn why.

"Quite an admiring crowd gathered round the steeple of St. Paul's Church last Monday morning to admire the agile movements of Captain John Battersby, who took the contract of repairing and repainting the steeple.

One of the chief expenses connected with repairing the steeple was the building of a scaffold to the top; deemed necessary by some of the workmen. The Captain thought this a needless expense and undertook the job himself. He climbed up the inside of the steeple, the top of which is 95 feet from the ground, as far as possible, cut a hole, climbed out, tied a stout rope around the steeple and swung himself up and down as the nature of the work demanded. When the tin work is repaired it will be painted.

Many admiring remarks were made as to the method of procedure. One man said he wouldn't take a gift of the Church and go up there that way. Another would promptly decline the whole

*St. Paul's viewed from Main Street. Note Faulkner Livery sign in lower left corner*

town as a fair consideration for such a risk, but the Captain seemed to enjoy it."

In April of 1890 an entry in the Maple Leaf reminds us that the high and somewhat unique wooden fence which enclosed the grounds of St. Paul's was by edict of the Select Vestry to be removed in an effort to improve the appearance of the Church. The fence, built to protect the grounds from wandering livestock, had served its purpose and was no longer thought to be needed. It consisted of squared posts, ten feet tall, with four inch square bars set into them on an angle. It had proved a very effective fence over the years. It was also noted that Messrs. Skey and Tibbetts were re-elected Wardens.

In case you might think Port Dover's popularity as a tourist town is a recent phenomenon, we need only note a July 18th, 1890 article in the Maple Leaf: "Last Sunday St. Paul's Church was crowded to the doors. The usual congregation being supplemented by the large number of summer residents whom we have the pleasure of yearly welcoming to our village. On October 12th, 1890 a terse entry appeared in the register; "Organist [Mrs. Dillon] overslept herself. No music." In December W. F. Tibbetts bought the coal chutes of the Grand Trunk Railway and removed them which much improved the appearance of that part of the river.

December 10th, 1890 saw the beginning of an organisation

that to this day quietly meets to carry out an important role in the outreach of St. Paul's Church. On this day **St. Paul's Port Dover Branch of the Women's Auxiliary to the Missionary Society of the Church of England in Canada** received their charter. Their motto being: *"The Love of Christ Constraineth Us."*

From Canon Cornish's history we learn that Mrs. Tilley, of London, assisted in organising the St. Paul's Branch and was in attendance to present the charter to their founding President, Mrs. J. R. Newell, wife of the Rector. Miss Edith P. Battersby was first Vice-President. Miss Alice Maud Scofield and Miss Emily Louisa Barrett, secretaries and Mrs. E. J. Low, treasurer. Twenty-one ladies of the parish made up the charter membership. This was only the second Women's Auxiliary Branch to be organised in the Diocese of Huron. Canon Cornish goes on to say;

> "The policy adopted at that time, of carrying on their work through the free-will offerings of the members, has never been changed. It has truly been — as the W. A. Prayer so beautifully puts it — "a service of faithful women". Every Tuesday throughout the years has been W. A. Day – the first Tuesday of the month – for study and prayer, 'to aid and encourage missionaries', the remaining Tuesdays to be used for sewing, quilting or knitting. There are no records to be found of the early work of the organisation, but every year for a number of years recently, an Indian girl has been provided with clothes, and always quilts, quilts and more quilts. If those ancient W. A. quilting frames could talk, what a tale they would unfold! Always too, came the great day when the bale was packed, its fat sides bulging with warmth and comfort for the boys and girls of the Indian Schools. Not even the letter of appreciation from the missionary could equal the satisfaction of that yearly event.

At the April, 1891 Vestry Meeting of St. Paul's the Wardens presented their annual financial report showing the finances of the Church to be in a very favourable condition. After all claims had been settled there was a balance of $100.00. The collection plate

*Miss Edith P. Battersby*

income for the year amounted to over $455.00. This optimistic balance combined with the bequests [for the purpose of acquiring a Parsonage] of Mr. & Mrs. Jaffray Harvey led to the formation of a committee of Messrs. Lawrence Skey, William Tibbetts and Crosby Morgan to look for a suitable house to serve the parish as a Parsonage. If a satisfactory residence could be located the committee were empowered to purchase the same. The only other business of note was the lowering of the pew rents by about 20%.

On the morning of the second Sunday in June, 1891 news reached the community of the death of Prime Minister Sir John A. MacDonald. It was reported that Reverend Newell preached an excellent sermon around the life and times of this colourful, well known Canadian at the evening service. It was thought the closing hymn "Days and Moments Quickly Flying" was a most appropriate choice on Reverend Newell's part.

The register notes on June 21st, 1891 - Incumbent [in charge of service] at St. John's, Woodhouse, Theobald B. Barrett, Lay Reader, officiated [at St. Paul's]. On July 5th Reverend Lawrence Skey read prayers. On July 7th, Maurice S. Huron confirmed 16 at 8:30 a.m. and later 12 in Vittoria. On October 4th & 11th, Lawrence Skey, Lay Reader, [father of Reverend Lawrence Skey, of Toronto] officiated at morning services as the incumbent was away in Detroit for vacation and repair.[?]

On August 12th, 1892 the Maple Leaf reported on a Regatta, held by the local yacht club, in which several members of St. Paul's were involved. Captain Battersby had offered a silken pennant as prize, and a large crowd of spectators watched from the park and along the shore. The race commenced at 2.30 around three buoys and was six miles in length. Competing were "Foam," owned by Fred Leaney; "Gypsy," owned by Captain Norquay; "Marion," owned by Captain Battersby; "Topsy," owned by A. J. Dell and "Trixy," owned by W. F. Tibbetts. "Trixie came in first but because of handicaps set by the Club Mr. Fred Leaney's "Foam" was declared winner of the prize.

The following August of 1893 the local yachtsmen competed for "The Fair" cup in a five mile race off the harbour. About a thousand spectators turned out in near perfect weather as the following yachts left harbour to compete; "Alafarata," owned by E. J. Low; "Foam" owned by Fred Leaney; "Marion," owned by Captain Battersby; "Topsy," owned by A. J. Dell and "Trixie," owned by W. F. Tibbetts. "Topsy" was handled admirably by Mr. Dell to pass the judge's boat ahead of all others and Mr. Grant, generous donor of the cup came down from Brantford to present it.

The April 14th, 1893 issue of the Maple Leaf quoted some interesting statistics from the Dominion Census giving the strengths at that time, of the various religious denominations in Port Dover.

| Episcopalians | 420 |
| Methodists | 316 |
| Presbyterians | 262 |
| Baptists | 107 |
| Roman Catholics | 36 |
| Salvation Army | 29 |
| Universalists | 12 |
| Other Denominations | 10 |
| Not Specified | 17 |

A special meeting of the Select Vestry was called on a Monday evening in May of 1893, to decide if possible on the purchase of a Parsonage. A motion was made to purchase the brick cottage of Mr. Whittaker Dixon. There was considerable discussion, but no resolution to the problem was made before adjournment, and no time for a later meeting was announced. The Whittaker Dixon house on the [north-west] corner of Chapman and First Avenue was later occupied by Mr. Dixon's daughter, Mrs

Braven. In October of 1893, Lawrence Skey, Lay reader, took charge for two Sundays as the incumbent was in Chicago. No sermon was preached. On November 19th, the new furnace was used for the first time.

On January 20th, 1894 125 attended the funeral of Mr. Arthur Battersby. February 4th, marked the last service at which Mrs. Dillon acted as the church organist. On March 11th, the register recorded that Reverend Newell's child was very ill and Mr. Lawrence Skey took charge of the evening service. The boy, Arthur Lawrence Newell, died later that week and on Saturday March 17th, 220 parishioners attended the funeral in St. Paul's at which Reverend R. Hicks, Reverend R. Gardner and Reverend A. Garden assisted.

On May 25th, 1894, a special meeting of the Vestry was called due to the considerable expense incurred by repairs to the furnace and other unanticipated repairs made to the Church. Ways and means had to be found for paying off this debt. The solution was arrived at they hoped, when the incumbent, Reverend Newell, was requested to appoint a committee of two ladies of the congregation to take up a subscription to cover the debt. If this should prove to be insufficient, a collection would be taken up in the Church to procure the balance owing.

On May 20th, 1894 260 Masons attended a 3:00 p.m. special service sponsored by Erie Lodge, A.F. & A.M. On July 1st, St. Paul's recorded an attendance at matins of 315 worshippers, including the 13th Battery of the Norfolk Militia who marched to the Church under the command of Captain Ross. Though no explanation is given, there was no choir in attendance on July 22nd, when 200 attended matins and 275 evensong. Lawrence Skey, Lay Reader, read prayers for both services. The following Sunday the Reverend J. C. Farthing took the morning service and with him were the vested choir of New St. Paul's, Woodstock. On December 2nd, 1894 the parishioners of St. Paul's worshipped in the glow of electric lights for the first time.

**The Girl's Branch of the Women's Auxiliary** was organised in 1894. Miss Edith Battersby was their Superintendent, assisted by Miss E. Louise Barrett and Miss Wheeler. They began with twenty-two members. They proved a very active and useful adjunct to the senior W. A. until their demise, for lack of a leader, in 1922. Their first officers were Lilly Fawcett, Kathleen Low, Lilly Faulkner, Rachel Quanbury, Mary Fawcett and May Martin. They met in the Sunday School every Tuesday evening, the last Tuesday of the month being a business meeting. The entrance fee was five cents, with one cent a month being required thereafter. In 1896 this was increased to five cents a month.

An early expenditure was the use of sixty cents, cash on hand, to buy factory goods, from the Penman Knitting Mill powered by water from Silver Lake, with which to make clothing. A minute book entry of May 1894 indicated they would use the money from the Mission boxes to buy nails for Mr. Wright's new church.

Reverend A. H. Wright had taken services in St. Paul's at this time to tell of the work in Saskatchewan where he served as a Missionary. He also lectured here on his missionary work for the Saskatchewan Diocese. On March 28th, 1895 Reverend A. H. Wright addressed the G.B.W.A., saying how pleased he was to meet his friends who had been working for his people. He told the girls that the Bishop had only recently dedicated his new church, St. Stephen's Church, at Fort a la Corne. St Paul's Church had sent [supplied to] St. Stephen's their communion table, the communion vessels and planned to give them their chancel window. In addition Misses Edith Battersby, Ethel Phipps and Tiny Ansley each had painted a text in the Cree language for Reverend Mr. Wright.

A minute book beginning January 1895 is in the Archives of St. Paul's. The membership, five years later, is no doubt little changed from the original. Mrs. Newell is now Honourary President, Miss Battersby is President, Vice-Presidents are Mrs. Low & Miss Barrett, Treasurer is Miss Fanny Harding, Recording Secretary is Miss Maud Scofield & Cor. Secretary is Mrs. L. Skey. Members include Mrs. Hamilton, Mrs. Parke, Mrs. Martin, Mrs. Faulkner, Mrs. Harding, Miss Buckwell, Mrs. C. Morgan, Mrs. Williams, Mrs. C. Battersby, Mrs. A. Laurie, Mrs. Quanbury, Miss N. Harding, Miss Annie Harding, Miss McCoy, & Miss Wilson.

Meanwhile competition is keen for "The Fair" yachting cup and in August 1894 on the appointed day the following yachts started. "Alafaretta," [note change of spelling] owned by E. J. Low; "Foam," now owned by B. Dixon; "Marion," owned by Captain

Battersby; an un-named yacht owned by Leslie Battersby; "Moxie," owned by John Horn and "Trixie," owned by W. F. Tibbetts. "Trixie" soon took the lead and seemed to hold it with ease to make Mr. Tibbetts the proud owner of the cup for the ensuing year.

On the appointed day for the Regatta, in 1895, there were very strong winds with white caps breaking over the east pier, which prevented some of the smaller yachts from competing, although the local yacht fleet numbers eleven craft by this time. Mr. E. Tisdale had planned to enter his fine new boat but with a handicap of 28 minutes on a six mile course, he declined. A large crowd of spectators had assembled, with the Woodstock and Simcoe contingents alone numbering over two thousand. The following yachtsmen entered being the Moon brothers, Captain Battersby, Leslie Battersby, W. F. Tibbetts and Captain George Allan. They were required to sail twice round the three buoys marking a three mile distance.

The Moon Brothers were making a valiant effort to win and very well might have, had they not lost their top mast when well into the race. Captain Allan's "Meringo" completed the course in

*Schooner Erie Stewart and Sloop Viking lie below Brant Hill in the creek*

1:48:15 hrs. to be followed by W. F. Tibbett's "Trixie" in 1:56:15. As the Meringo had a fifteen minute handicap, however, the race was won for the second time by W. F. Tibbetts, with a seven minute margin. Captain Battersby's "Marion" had a time of 2:11:10.

The Maple Leaf of September 11th, 1896 reports; "The fifth and last contest for "The Fair" cup was the last that will ever be sailed here. At the boom of the gun one of the best starts ever seen on the Great Lakes took place. The "Irene" crossed first, immediately followed by the "Gypsy." Then came "Foam", "Trixie" and "Meringo" followed by the "Edith." At the completion of the first round the "Edith" withdrew, owing to her foremast becoming unstepped and punching a hole through her planking." Next the "Irene" withdrew. The "Gypsy", "Meringo" and "Trixie" crossed the finish line in that order, but with little time between them. On their corrected time W. F. Tibbetts with "Trixie" won the cup for the third time and it now is permanently his property.

In 1896 the Girl's Branch of the W.A. agreed to send an amount annually to Lion's Head, also, to a lady missionary in Japan, and to the north-west and to Kanyangeah Reserve. In April their delegate to the W. A. Annual gave her report. Miss Daisy Misner gave a gift of 3 pounds of factory goods.

Both the W. A. and the girl's branch maintained contact with the famous missionary for the Yukon, Bishop Bompas and his wife, who had visited the ladies of the Auxiliary at about this time. Mrs. Bompas had congratulated them on their efforts for the Canadian Missions. Canon Cornish tells us that the local ladies, being impressed by the Bishop's lady, wished to give her a small token of their appreciation for her visit. Wishing it to be a practical gift an attempt was made to find out what she would particularly like. She at first indicated that they should not give her anything, but on being pressed she did allow that a small tea tray would prove to be very useful in her home. In explanation of her request she explained that "The Bishop brings me my tea every morning and as we do not own a tray, he has to use a shingle for the purpose."

Missionaries made frequent visits to St. Paul's as the church register confirms, in part because Miss Edith Battersby corresponded with many of them regularly. When home on furlough many of them would accept her invitation to spend a few days in Port

Dover as her guest. It was also due to Miss Battersby's efforts that the Deanery Women's Auxiliary was formed in 1898, being the second one formed in the Diocese. Members of St. Paul's W. A. have held office in the organisation and have served as active Deanery workers over the years.

Two letters in my family files, one dated 1903, the other 1909, from the Yukon attest to the fact that the W.A. and members of the congregation of St. Paul's still maintained contact with Bishop & Mrs. Bompas and their Yukon missions:

> Caribou Crossing, Yukon Territory,
> January 3rd, 1903.

My Dear Miss Barrett

Your kind letter was a great surprise and pleasure to me. Thank you so much for remembering me and for all your kind thoughts and wishes for me at the Holy tide. Thank you also for your kind little Christmas gift. You do not know how much I value it. I hesitated a little as to how to spend it, but it did decide to creep into the little leather bag where I keep my nest egg for the Caribou Church; so **there** it is, and you have added another brick to St. Saviour's, Caribou.

I am thankful indeed for your sake, as well as my own, that Christmas is over. I feel for you so very much and know the strain on your heart strings that such seasons bring, but you will be brave and strong as your mother would have you be; – cherish her memory as a sacred deposit, to be guarded and kept as an incentive to all good and noble deeds — How can we honour the memory of our departed better than by treading in their footsteps and trying in all things to do as they would have us do? —

My Christmas has also been shadowed by the memory of my dear sister who left us so suddenly last July – Her two dear girls are alone in Montreal – It is sad work for them as they are left with small means and have to earn their own living. But "God tempers the wind to the shorn lamb" and God helps them on day by day and gives them grace and courage – I have no Church services this Christmas. I miss them sadly – The Bishop is detained at Forty Mile, and we have too few hands on our Mission staff to afford a man, even a Deacon for Caribou.

Let us hope for better times and learn by these times of privation of spiritual blessing to value them more highly when we have them – I must apologise for my blots and smudged paper –

I have a small kitten who objects to my writing letters and insists on walking over them as I write – She fancies herself a sheet of blotting paper and only answers my remonstrances with a prolonged purrr....rr.

    Sincerely and lovingly yrs.
    C. S. Bompas

P. S. Kindly tell Miss Battersby when you see her, that I have received her letter and beautiful text– I hope to write in a few days.

The other letter is addressed to T. B. Barrett from the Yukon in 1909.

    Moosehide, Dawson, Yukon Territory.
    November 8th, 1909.

My Dear Sir;

With very great pleasure I have received a letter from Mrs. Bompas, enclosing your kind gift to the Bompas Memorial Church. Please accept our warmest thanks for your kindness to the Indians and for this expression of your kind interest in our Memorial Church.

We had a very happy Sunday yesterday. In the morning we had a good congregation of Indians to whom I preached from 2 Timothy ii. verse 1. "Therefore my son, be strong in the faith that is in Christ Jesus." In the afternoon we held Sunday School, and read Wilkinson's Catechism – At seven in the evening we had a very happy and blessed communion service, when sixteen of our number assembled around the Lord's Table.

Though the church is not yet quite finished we are able to use it, and I can thankfully say what a great blessing it is to have a convenient and suitable Building in which to worship our Heavenly Father. He indeed is very good to us though we do not deserve the least of his mercies.

> With many thanks and best wishes.
> Yours sincerely,
> Benjamin Totty
> Missionary of the Gospel

Two hundred attended the wedding on January 8th, 1895 of Jasper F. Lynch and Miss Tinita Millman. L. E. Skey assisted with the service.

On March 17th, 1895 300 attend the funeral in St. Paul's of James W. Scott. His wife, Phoebe Caroline Barrett, the eldest daughter of T. B. Barrett, died in 1884, aged 33 years, leaving two sons and two daughters. She had served as organist of St. Paul's Church for some time prior to her marriage. Their sons, Walter, 8 and Roy, 5 on their mother's death, came to their grandfather's home at Riverbank, Port Dover, where they were brought up by their Aunty Wese. Their daughters, Mildred, 3 and Carrie Louise remained in their home in Toronto with an aunt, Miss Scott.

In five years time two more young boys in the persons of my father and his brother, Richard Pelly Barrett, would join the household at Riverbank, upon the death of their mother, Rebecca Julia "Nonah" Pelly Barrett in the Spallumcheen of British Columbia. [Nonah was an abbreviation of "Winonah" a name given her by the local Indians, meaning - first born.]

*Miss Nita Millman at the time of her marriage to Jasper Lynch*

*Roy Scott*  *Walter Scott*

On May 19th, 1895 a terse entry appears in the register; "Choir on Strike!" There is no indication of what led to this state of affairs or what might have caused such drastic action. By June 16th, a reassuring entry appears but with no explanation; "New Choir to the fore!"

The Government Fisheries Patrol vessel "Petrel" came into port in May of 1896. On Sunday May 19th, Captain Dunn and the ship's crew of 16 men attended Divine Service at the morning service of St. Paul's Church. On June 28th, Bishop Maurice [Scollard Baldwin] Huron is recorded as attending the morning service. No confirmation candidates were recorded, however. In August Reverend C. A. Seager, Curate of St. Thomas Church, Toronto, took the evening service, as the incumbent was on holiday. [This was Charles Allen Seager, whose grandfather Dr. Charles Seager, lived in Port Dover, in the attractive cottage on the south-west corner of Nelson and St. Andrews streets. Reverend Seager served as the fifth Bishop of Huron from 1931 until his death on September 9th, 1948.]

On May 27th, 1897 it is recorded that only 20 attended Matins, there was no evensong and no collection is recorded for the day. Lawrence Skey, Lay Reader, took the service as the incumbent (had) a "kink" in his throat. On June 20th, though no explanation is given, 300 attended evensong which was held at 4:21 p.m.

On the first Friday in July of 1897 we learn that the pupils of St. Paul's Church Sunday School held their annual picnic at "Orchard Beach" with a large attendance of both pupils and congregation. The Register showed 114 pupils at the time with seven teachers on staff under Superintendent Lawrence Skey. Miss Louisa "Aunty Wese" Barrett taught the infant class of 50 youngsters.

On August 29th, Reverend F. C. Piper was in charge of both services.

*Louisa "Wese", Harry, Toby & Dick Barrett*

*Louisa "Wese" Barrett, Sunday School Teacher of Primary Room*

*Charlton "Chart" Woolley*

No attendance was noted but in the remarks column is this entry: "PROHIBITION: Woolley was roaring at the Pavilion!" It is not indicated whether he was "roaring" for or against!

An invitation was extended to T. B. Barrett, Lay Worker in St. Paul's Church, to attend a Conference in London beginning Wednesday, October 27th, 1897. It is thought that he, though 80 years of age, attended. The invitation was found in his papers.

**Huron Anglican Lay Workers' and Sunday School Conference. And Diocesan Re-union**
[excerpts from the invitation follow]

The Seventh Annual Conference and Re-union will be held in London, 27th to 29th, of October,1897. It also marks the fortieth year of the separate existence of the Diocese. The clergy of the See City and their congregations...... with their usual generous and hospitable spirit, extend a cordial offer of entertainment to all comers. The railway companies will grant reduced rates ....

The Right Reverend Bishop of Huron will preside at all Sessions.

**Wednesday, October 27th,**
Conference will organise at 2:30 p.m. in Bishop Cronyn Hall. At 7:30 there will be divine service in St. Paul's Cathedral.

**Thursday, October 28th,**
Holy Communion in St. Paul's Cathedral & Memorial Church, respectively, at 9:00 a.m.
At the same hour a meeting of women will be held, at which Miss Jeannette Osler will read a paper on "The Usefulness of a Good Church Woman at Home."
Conference sessions from 11:30 - 1:00, 2:30 - 6:00 and 8:00 to 10:00.

**Friday, October 29th,**
Morning Prayer in the cathedral at 9:00. Conference sessions from 10:00 - 12:30, 2:30 - 6:00
At 8:00 a closing public meeting, in Bishop Cronyn Hall.

Speakers included the Bishop of Toronto; the Bishop of Niagara; His Honour, Judge McDonald of Brockville, "The Call to Service." Hon. S. H. Blake Q.C. "The Bible Class." Rev. A. H. Baldwin, M.A., Toronto. "Parish Work" Miss Cross, Head Deaconess, Deaconess' House, Toronto. "Deaconess Work." Rural

Dean McKenzie, Brantford. "Parochial Lay Help." James Morgan Esq., M.A. Barrie. "Sunday Schools, their shortcomings and great opportunities." General Trowbridge, Detroit. "The Laity in Church Extension." Mrs. Grace E. Denison, Toronto. "Necessity of Spiritual Teaching in Sunday Schools." N.W. Hoyles, Esq., Q.C., Toronto. "Missionary Work in the Canadian Church." It is hoped that Dean Carmichael, just returned from Europe, may add his valued contribution.

We appeal to you and all your friends in the Diocese to make this meeting widely known.......especially urge its importance on the younger members of the church......where consideration of expenses stands in the way.........[it] may be removed by local subscription.

A. H. Dymond, Chairman of Lay Workers' Execurive.<br>Jno. Downie, Chairman of Diocesan S. S. Committee.<br>*********************

Richard "Dickie" Stephens, a charter member of the congregation and a well qualified Engineer, had been concerned about the stability of the Church spire for some time. In November of 1897 he reported to the Wardens his misgivings following a thorough inspection of the bricks at the top of the tower and of the pine frame-work which made up the base of the steeple. He felt the base of the spire, in the way it was constructed, and being of pine, was unsafe when the full force of westerly gales were taken into consideration. Apparently nothing was done in response to Engineer Stephens warning at that time.

On February 9th, 1898 Reverend J.J. [was this John Frederick, incumbent - 1875 — 1879?] Renaud was the speaker for the Wednesday evening Annual Missionary Meeting. On February 13th, the collection was designated to "The widows and orphans". On February 23rd, Reverend Newell held an Ash Wednesday service but there was no address or collection. Reverend F.C. Piper officiated for the next six Wednesday services.

On June 19th, it is noted that F.W. Denton's child was baptised. "The Mother stood alone" being added. Beginning on August 14th, 1898 while Reverend Newell was on holidays the following priests took turns at holding the services; Reverend W. A.

Young, Reverend Horace E. Bray, Reverend Richard Hicks and Reverend Fred C. Piper.

September 29th, 1898 the register records that it was: "Thursday Evening Harvest Home: Reverend Edward A. Irving, Dundas, Preacher, assisted by Reverend E. H. Maloney, of Nanticoke and Reverend Arthur Francis, of Cayugah(sic). The Church was beautifully decorated." [The Church was so beautifully decorated that someone photographed the result. We can note in this picture the original flat arch leading into the chancel, the chestnut ceiling, the box pews, the plain painted walls and plain glass windows. The original coal oil lamps with chimneys and glass shades still hang within the chancel. The newly installed large, bare carbon-arc electric bulbs can also be seen throughout the body of the Church.]

From our Archives the following letter under the seal of the Bishop is of interest.

*St. Paul's decorated for Harvest Home, Sept. 29th, 1898*

The Bishop's Room, Bishop Cronyn Hall.
London, Ont. Oct. 19th, 1898.

Messrs Lawrence Skey          Church Wardens, St. Paul's Church
W. F. Tibbetts                Port Dover.

Dear Gentlemen;
    The Bishop has requested me to say that he has much pleasure in informing you that he has appointed the Rev. M. M. Goldberg, late of Markdale, to the incumbency of the Parish of Port Dover and Vittoria and trusts that under his ministration your Parish will thrive and prosper.
                Yours truly,
                (Signed) E. Maingault.

    On October 30th, 1898 Reverend John Robert Newell preached as Rector of St. Paul's for the last time. 102 attended Matins, with 47 communicants and 300 attended evensong. The Reverend T. A. Fawcett read prayers. Total collection for the day was $6.38.

# Chapter Eleven

# Reverend M.M. Goldberg's Term

The Reverend Mordecai Meyer Golberg [1898 – 1900] was appointed to replace Reverend Newell. Reverend Goldberg had been born a Russian Jew, but had converted to Christianity. From the beginning he did not fit in to the community. The congregation found him to be very eccentric in his behaviour and he soon gained a reputation for "stirring up trouble".

On November 6th, 1898 Reverend M. M. Goldberg first officiated as Rector of St. Paul's. The register records a drop in attendance, but the winter was a cold one, with high winds and bad roads reported. On February 12th, 1899 it was too cold to preach a sermon. Reverend Fred Piper, Reverend D. Waters, Reverend J. R. Newell and others officiated on various Sundays throughout the year.

In 1899 Mr. Charles H. Corton, Peoples Warden of St. Paul's, began keeping a personal account of progress in the church, or lack of it. He notes each Sunday's collection and on the remainder of the page comments on other matters. Some highlights are included;

March 4th, 1899 - A committee appointed by the Vestry to make an offer of $1,000.00 down to Mrs. B. Fuller for her brick house and 5 lots, about 4 ½ acres of ground. I addressed a letter to Mrs. Fuller for the Committee: C. H. Corton, J. R. Davis, W. F. Tibbetts & Lawrence Skey. $40.00 cash on hand from W. A. for repairs. Not used.

May 7th, 1899 - Miss Copway only Soprano in the Choir. Service satisfactory. Mr. Goldberg was thought to be going to refer

*Patrol vessel Petrel entering Port Dover harbour*

to his precious Resignation but did not say anything and Wardens hopes [sic] the trouble may blow over. Collection: Envelopes and Plate for both services – $9.92.

May 21st, 1899 - Wood fire in Furnace, congregation small. Mr. Barrett called 2 of 5 and said he could not come to Church & could not continue his Contributions. So long as Mr. Goldberg remained he would go to St. John's and the Presbyterian Church here. Cliff Lee also does not come.

May 28th, 1899 - Rev. Maloney [Nanticoke] preached two very creditable & interesting services. Fair congregations, weather very fine. Miss Copway not in Choir and it is said she has resigned. Cliff Lee and also Mr. Barrett came to services. Collection; Env. $6.71. Plate $3.22. Total - $9.93.

Sunday, June 4th, 1899 - Congregations rather small. Methodists and others in evening congregation. Choir in evening neglected only by Mr. & Mrs. Lawson & Miss Battersby. Miss Nash left Choir after psalms. Members of Congregation absent; Smith, Lee, Harris, Barrett, Denton & wife, & others. Sermons fair. "Jewish."

June 23rd, 1899 - Thos. Fawcett gave notice that at the end of the month he would give up the Position of Caretaker as he is moving away. Mr. Mason read the Lessons am & pm. Rev. Goldberg in fair good form. Mr. Laurie has left the Choir. I am informed he sat in church in pm.

July 2nd, 1899 - Some of Crew of [Fishery Patrol Vessel] "Petrel" attended am & pm. I attended to the Church and rang the Bell at 10.30. Have not engaged a man yet. Total collection — $17.06.

July 16th, 1899 - Opening of new Methodist Church. Our congregation made up of Presbyterians and our own people. Rev. N. Nigh preached – Mr. Newall [sic] read the service.

July 30th, 1899 - No Gentlemen in the Choir morning or evening. Only myself & Roy Scott in the evening. No Sidesmen, Mr. Davis & myself acted.

August 6th, 1899 - Mostly visitors. Choir fair, Messrs Roy & Walter Scott & Mr. C. [Clarence] Barrett. Mr. Mason read the services. Mr. Goldberg preached good sermons. Collection - $15.93.

August 13th, 1899. - Mr. Mason assisted & officiated at Vittoria. Mr. Goldberg arranged for Woodstock Boys surpliced Choir in evening. Rev. Mr. Skey preached, church crowded. Had to get seats from the Sunday School. Mr. Smith ushered. Collection in total - $17.83.

August 20th, 1899 - low attendance due to heat. Mr. Goldberg has an attack of Asthma of the Throat. Messrs [Roy & Walter] Scott, Organist & Tenor. I assisted in the Choir. Collection - $10.13.

August 27th, 1899 - I helped in Choir in am. Messrs Scotts & T. Barretts, Miss Battersby & Davis in the evening. Mr. Goldberg requested that Miss Ansley, who was looking up hymns, not to turn

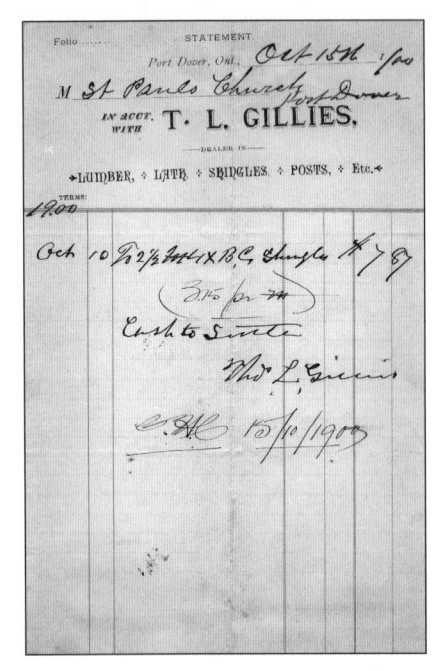

*Thomas L. Gillies account for shingles*

over the leaves as he wanted to preach.— "Sensationally, too Bad." — Collection $7.82.

September 3rd, 1899 - Mr. Goldberg has a bad cough interfering with his discourse. Mr. Thompson commenced as Caretaker at same salary. $3.25 summer, $4.25 winter months.

September 17th, 1899 - Mr. Goldberg's cough still remains bad. Rev. Mr. Spencer of Jarvis drove down with Mr. Bourne and [was] in congregation. We spent evening with Mr. Laurie seeing their new piano, a Heintzman Transposing. Lovely moonlight night.

October 1st, 1899 - Church cold. Furnace ordered from Buck, Brantford. Price $105.00. To put it up - $10.00. Harvest Festival announced for 22nd, inst. Collection - $5.81.

October 8th, 1899 - I made arrangements with Mr. Goldberg to hold services in the Sunday School but on Sunday morning he refused to have service there. In Consequence a large number of the Congregation went to other churches. No organist, no Choir etc. Mr. Goldberg handed me the collection outside - $8.40. As it is Diocesan Missions Sunday and collection so small he wishes it held for next Sunday's amount. Evening service held in Sunday School with 40 out. Mr. [John S.] Martin played the hymns only at the organ. Furnace did not come Wednesday last as promised.

October 15th, 1899 - New Furnace installed, weather warm. Mr. Goldberg announced meeting to discuss a letter from the Bishop re exchange of ministers.

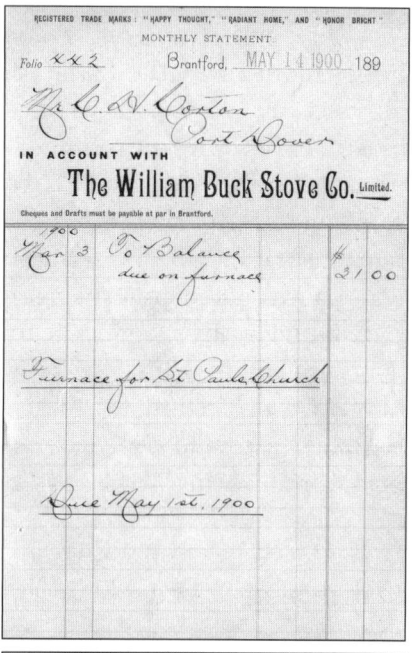

*Final payment on new furnace to Buck's of Brantford*

October 22nd, 1899 - Thanksgiving. Raining. Church tastefully decorated by the Ladies. Congregation small. Collections in aid of Furnace - $24.50. Weather rather indecent, Church very hot as Mr. Thompson put too much coal in.

November 5th, 1899 - Holy Communion. Good congregation, largely Methodists. Furnace smoked due to north wind & burning wood. Special sermon on Guy Fox & National Anthem. Mr. Laurie acted as usher or sidesman, others not acting. Mr. Goldberg coughed a great deal. Choir not full.

November 12th, 1899 - Church warm, lighted by coal-oil lamps - no electric lights. Choir of 5 sopranos, 2 altos, & 2 bass. Sermons good. No week day service on a/c of Recital in Town Hall. [sponsored by the Wardens of St. Paul's for Furnace Fund.]

November 15th, 1899 - Wednesday Evening Recital by Webb-Hodsdon Entertainment. Mr Calton reports a great success both financially and otherwise. It took in $51.60 gross, less $27.35 expenses, for a profit of $24.25. Several firms and parishioners loaned props, flags and furniture. The Hall was free and John S. Martin loaned a piano upon which he played two solos during the evening performance.

December 3rd, 1899 - First snow of season. Electric lights went out and lamps had to be lighted after service had started. Church fairly warm, congregation fair. Collection - $ 9.96.

December 17th, 1899 - Rev. Spencer of Jarvis took services. No service in Presbyterian Church. Good congregation, Rev. Spencer stayed with Mrs. Low. Collection $9.60.

December 24th, 1899 - Church decorated by Misses

*Thomas L. Gillies, Lumber Merchant*

Harding and others. Choir augmented by Harry Battersby, Walter & Roy Scott, Harry & Clarence Barrett. Congregation as usual. Coll. $7.96.

January 21st, 1900 - Church cellar flooded yesterday but OK to-day. Message at 3.00 pm that Mother died. Go to Toronto in am. Dined at Mrs. Skey's, Tea at Davis's. Lights went out during service caused by Boys tampering with them. [The notebook entries end here.]

**Note by Canon Cornish on June 13th, 1952.** —— This record and other papers, some of which follow, kept by Mr. Corton, were kept in the vault of the store in which he was a partner [with Cy. Butler] - now held by Mr. Thos. Caley. They were handed to me on the death of the surviving partner. They were removed from the vault when the store was sold in 1927. Why did the record end in January?

On January 14th, 1900 the outbreak of war in South Africa is noted. There is a collection for Sunday School prises (sic) and collections for the Patriotic Fund. On Good Friday, April 13th, with 60 in attendance, the collection of $3.71 is designated as is usual each year, for the Jews. On April 29th, 1900 Reverend Mordecai Goldberg served his last Sunday as Rector of St. Paul's Church.

The Wardens, Mr. Calton & Mr. Davis had obviously been searching for a replacement for Rev. Goldberg, but as these letters will attest with little encouragement.

Chesley, Ont. March 26th, 1900.

Mr. C. H. Calton and J. R. Davis,
Wardens, St. Paul's Church, Port Dover.

Dear Sirs;
In reply to your letter of the 22nd, inst. We did not know that an exchange between Rev. M. M. Goldberg and Rev. J. C. McCracken was being considered. We received no word of it from Rev. J. C. McCracken. However, We cannot consider an exchange. If it is Rev. McCracken's desire to leave us we will offer no opposi-

tion to his going if it is to his interest or be beneficial to him in any way though we would be very sorry to lose him.

But as for an exchange we cannot consider it at all as the majority of the members of the Church here are against the proposition. And we would have to consult Grace Church, Sullivan, which is part of this Parish.

>Very Sincerely Yours,
>(Signed)   George Tolchard
>            Ben Cass   Wardens.
>Holy Trinity Church.

\*\*\*\*\*\*\*\*\*\*\*\*\*\*\*\*

### A List of Subscriptions
towards paying [Rev.] Mr. Goldberg's expenses in moving his furniture etc.

| | | | |
|---|---|---|---|
| Mr. Skey | $5.00 | Mr. Battersby | $5.00 |
| Mr. Low | 1.00 | Edward Harris | 5.00 |
| C. H. Corton | 1.00 | John R. Davis | 1.00 |
| Mrs. Morgan | 1.00 | A. W. Lawrie | 1.00 |
| L. G. Morgan | 2.00 | N. McInnes | 1.00 |
| H. W. Ansley | 2.00 | T. B. Barrett | 1.50 |
| W. Harding | 1.00 | Dr. Walker | 4.00 |
| W. Thompson | .50 | | |

Received payment of $32.00, on May 2nd, 1900.    (Signed) C. H. Corton.

>The Bishop's Room, Bishop Cronyn Hall
>May 15th, 1900.

To Messrs J. R. Davis, C. H. Corton. Wardens of St. Paul's Church, Port Dover.

Dear Gentlemen;

I quite agree with you that the Rev. M. M. Goldberg had no right to leave his post before the time specified. As regards the appointment of a new man, I am Sorry to hear you say that the Rev. A. N. Duthie would not suit. I know him to be a most estimable man, and an excep-

tionally good preacher. However, I shall not press this name but I think you are making a mistake. I now send you the name of the Rev. J. C. McCracken of Chesley who is quite young, and energetic. I would also mention the name of the Rev. E. Lee of Hespeler and the Rev. W. J. Reilly of Chatsworth. Do you need a supply for Sunday. Trusting, God will guide you to a right judgement in this matter. Yours Sincerely.
    (Signed)  Maurice S. Huron.

\*\*\*\*\*\*\*\*\*\*\*\*\*\*\*\*

       The Rectory,
       Simcoe, May 19th, 1900
My Dear Sirs;
In reply to yours of May 14th, would say it is a somewhat delicate matter to give advice under such circumstances both as to the parish and to the clergymen concerned and also from the fact that I have no official authority in the case. I can assure you I would only wish to see the best possible appointment but I could not in any way permit my name to be used as interfering with His Lordship's authority. So that anything I say will be only to help you in your selection of those whom the Bishop may permit you to consider.

Of those named I would consider either Rev. J. C. McCracken or Rev. W. J. Reilly an excellent appointment. If I might also suggest you might ask His Lordship through the Vestry or officially if he would allow the name of Rev. A. Shore, of Port Rowan to be placed on the list to be presented to the Vestry, if you thought well. I do not know whether he would wish to change but I do know that he is a most excellent man and would I am sure do well among you. I would ask you not to use this letter publicly in any way as it is only my desire to help you in the private capacity of one who has the kindest feelings toward many members of the parish. You will understand I could not enter into a general discussion of

the qualifications of the men mentioned and it is only my desire to serve you that has led me to interfere in any way with regard to the appointment. Trusting everything will turn out to the best welfare and satisfaction of all.
                              Believe me,
C. H. Corton & J. R. Davis      Very Faithfully Yours,
Wardens, St. Paul's, Port Dover.(Signed) Richard Hicks.

*********************

Simcoe, 21st, May, 1900.

Messrs. Calton & Davis, Church Wardens,
St. Paul's Church, Port Dover.

Gentlemen
Your favour of the 17th, reached me on Saturday - I think –   I am very willing to give you my best advice in the matter you do foolishly approach me on – but before doing so I wish to say that in my judgement a better arrangement in all respects is possible  – I think Port Dover should revert to its legal position as a part of the Parish of Woodhouse – in that case it would be under the general oversight of the Rector of Woodhouse but would be served — ordinarily by a resident Curate. – this would give the Parish many advantages which it cannot now possess & would at once solve the financial difficulty which will it is probable be with you continually — having stated this however I shall not press the matter nor take any further steps other than may be necessary to preserve my own rights and those of my successor —
In regard to the names suggested - I know all the gentlemen though not intimately - the Revd. Mr. Duthie is an elderly man a gentleman and a scholar - Mr. McCracken I know less of than the others and can say nothing against or for him - he is young – the Rev. Mr. Lee has had three parishes already in three or four years – I think – and is not very strong I believe though I know he was

acceptable at Princeton – the Rev. Mr. Reily is a hard working clergyman of middle age and I understand has been successful in the parishes he has served – of course this must be regarded as confidential - if there are any other gentlemen whose names occur to you I shall be ready to give you my best opinion on them – Trusting you may be guided aright herein –

       I am yours very sincerely,
     (Signed)  W. A. Young.

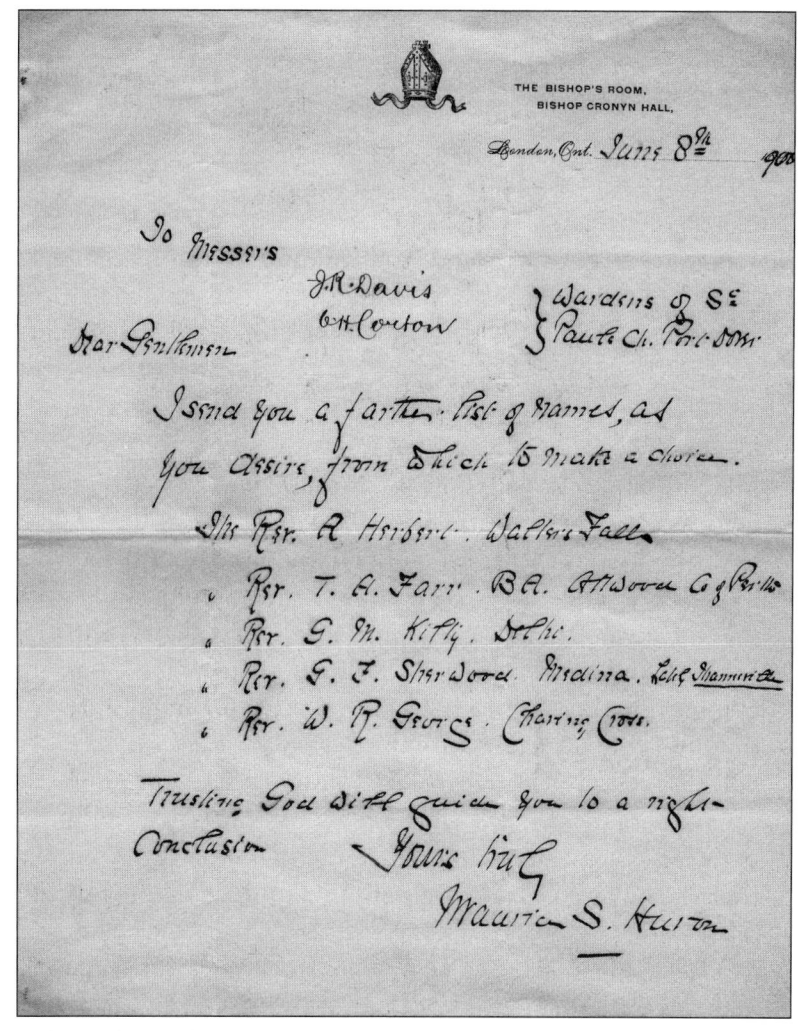

*Bishop Baldwin's list of candidates for Rector, June 8th, 1900*

The Bishop's Room, Bishop Cronyn Hall
London, Ont.,   June 8th, 1900.

To Messers  J. R. Davis      Wardens of St. Paul's
            C. H. Corton     Church, Port Dover.

Dear Gentlemen;

I send you a farther list of names, as you desire, from which to make a choice.

| | |
|---|---|
| The Rev. A. Herbert. | Walter's Falls. |
| " Rev. T. A. Farr. BA | A. M. Wood   Co. of Perth |
| " Rev. G. M. Kilty | Delhi. |
| " Rev. G. F. Sherwood | Medina, Lately Shannon Lake |
| " Rev. W. R. George | Charing Cross |

Trusting God will guide you to a right conclusion.

        Yours truly
        (Signed)   Maurice S. Huron.

\*\*\*\*\*\*\*\*\*\*\*\*\*\*\*\*

        Simcoe, Ont.   June 25th, 1900.

Dear Mr. Corton;

Mr. Thompson of your congregation saw me yesterday in reference to taking service for you next Sunday and I told him I would write and let you know without delay – I therefore write now to say that I find it impossible – You are aware that I take Waterford as well as St. John's & there is absolutely no way of supplying my place if I am absent – and as I am about to be away in England for three months at least I could not leave my parish without Service – I sincerely hope you may soon have a minister amongst you and that when he comes you & he both may be mutually helpful since only in this way can there be any reasonable hope that you can get along happily ——

        I am yours very sincerely
        (Signed)   W. A. Young.

\*\*\*\*\*\*\*\*\*\*\*\*\*\*\*\*

Reverend M. M. Goldberg did not remain as the incumbent for more than about a year and a half. For the next year or longer the parish was served by a series of student priests. There seems to have been no records survive to give us names or other information as to the fate of the church during this period of obvious upheaval. My aunts have left some indication of their feelings, at least, about this difficult period in the life of the congregation. This is indicated by a long letter from Reverend John Newell, in answer to a letter which my Auntie Wese [Emily Louisa Barrett] had written to him, expressing interest in joining the Plymouth Brethren, she was so upset with the direction Reverend Goldberg was taking in his services in St. Paul's.

\*\*\*\*\*\*\*\*\*\*\*\*\*\*\*\*

Rev. J. R. Newell.
## CHRIST CHURCH RECTORY
Diocese of Huron
Markdale, Ont., Oct. 13th, 1899.

*My Dear Miss Barrett, –*

*Your letter came to hand in due time, and I assure you it gave me very much pain. Of course I regard your avowal of regard for Plymouth Brethren doctrine as an outcome of your present unhappy relations with the Rector of St. Paul's. Since you cannot attend church and worship "with a glad mind", it is natural that the thought should occur to you that anywhere the two or three may assemble together and worship as acceptably as in "the great congregation".*

*I am not a Plymouth Brother as you well know, and I believe absolutely in an Apostolic Church : but if I were as you are, I should perhaps feel very much as you feel. The man Goldberg would be an insufferable barrier in the road to heaven if I had to get there by his agency, mediation or ministry. The one chief element of my indifference for Port Dover in July was caused by Goldberg's admirers. The Morgans ( Crosbie excepted ) seemed to have lost all interest in me and mine and to have fallen into a violent fit of admiration for G's "very open counte-*

nance" ( as Mrs. M. expressed it .) I thought at the time that our little pug, Jum, was gifted too with an open countenance when he felt somewhat warm.

But, after all, G— will not remain forever. The Bishop is to be with me for a whole day and night, Nov. 8th. If my words can do any thing for you, why, I intend to talk. But, my dear Miss Barrett, Dover has got a hard name. It is reported that I was starved out; and I declare it was true. There again some of the people there are always wanting a " a cheap man ". That was a common expression in my time. Mrs. Harry Ansley told my wife once that " a cheap man" was the necessary article for Pt. Dover. Then Mr. Skey has told the Executive Committee at London that a young man alone can be supported in Dover.

The shoddy article has been asked for so often and so long that, I am told, the Bishop would have great difficulty in filling the vacancy if Goldberg were removed, so fearful are the clergy of having anything to do with the parish. A prominent member of the Executive Committee gave me these views. That cry for a "cheap man" must cease. Can you realize how it used to make my hope for the parish wither? Never again will Dover have a clergyman who with all his heart will love his parish as I loved you the people of my first charge : and never again can I love another congregation as I loved that first congregation.

And I knew well, as I waved a last good-bye, on the evening of Oct. 31st as the train steamed out and we were being borne away at last, that no other clergyman would patiently endure the little slights and sometimes unkindly words which I frequently had to endure for the good of the parish in general. There are some of the people of St. Paul's who are very hard to endure. I speak of an experience of 14 years.

I don't admire G[oldberg] one little bit; but still there is no doubt the fault is not all with him. I tell you honestly that after a year without an insult being offered to me here, I could not live over again the years I spent in Dover and preserve my meekness as I did, generally, from 1884 to 1898. I tell these things to you because you are, above all others, the one who never in word or in deed gave me the least idea that anything but goodness of heart was meant for me. And while you and I are not perfect, we still believe that when a new pastor is appointed to St. Paul's, there should be less crankiness shown him and more real co-operation and, if need be, forbearance.

October 19th, —— This letter will "get there" sometime. I have been very busy doing nothing most of the days since I last " took my pen in hand ". Rev. Mr. Roy was here and left yesterday. Two weeks and a half ago he came to collect money for the Diocesan debt. He collected about $600.00 in this parish. Farthing got $14.00 in Dover two years ago. Roy is going down to takle [sic] you all. Then the money will jingle.

Until that name of sin (or other causer of sin) be removed, I cannot advise you in Church matters. The one thing, however, which I must warn you against with all the energy I have is **Schism**. You cannot cut yourself off from the Church without committing that great sin which is so rampant to-day and which is fast bringing in those "damnable heresies" of which St. Peter spoke. But I feel assured that when the hinderer is removed, you will naturally take your old place in the Church, perhaps purified and made better by the struggles now being experienced.

I could wish that your Father would attend St. John's. In July he went to the Methodist Church for Communion. To my mind it was an awful sin. People who don't know better may regard such a communion valid; but the Church's estimate is that it is not a commemoration of Christ's death, but a commemoration of the Lord's Supper — not the Supper itself. The Church's Eucharist is the real Supper – every other Eucharist is but an invitation more or less like the original, but not the original.

Your Father knows that the Church takes this high ground ; and it grieved me when he who so often at my hands had received the real communion went to receive a counterfeit communion. I know you may dissent from some of these ideas ; but the best people disagree on certain points. I for my part believe in my Church because she is a Church. I don't believe in Dissent because no man can institute a Church. "The Witness and Keeper of Holy Writ" must be of the same origin as Holy Writ. As well might an uninspired man write a new Bible as institute a new Church.

Therefore stand by the old Church. Every new church is simply an institution. Inspiration such as moved men to write the Scriptures and institute the Church is not in the world to-day, nor has it been since the First Century. Calvin, Luther, Wesley and others were uninspired men. They were not Apostles filled with infallible wisdom. Therefore they wrote no Scriptures, nor did they institute a Church. They made Conventiales.

Away down in your heart you know that my arguments are correct, but out of charity you want to give others "a chance". Well, let others stand or fall to their Muster. We have a Church whose interests it is ours to guard, and it is no uncharitableness on our part to let the world know exactly what we believe. For ourselves we cannot believe in Methodism or Presbyterianism. If others believe in Churches many, well and good – it is their privilege. And so my dear friend, be true to that Church which bears upon it the stamp of Divinity. It is "disguised and rejected by men", but in that it is like Him who through his chosen few founded it.

I believe the nearer we come to Christ's idea of the Church the nearer Christ will come to us. And it is because of Spiritual Communion that I want the proper channel of Grace, and I want to be sure that it is not a make-believe. If Satan can transfigure himself into an Angel of light and deceive us, can he not transform a human institution into the likeness of a Church and palm off on us the dangerous deceit? It is "the spiritual wickedness in high places" which alarms me and causes me "to prove all things". I cannot accept a Church or a Bible newer than the First Century.

Well, this is a crusty old sermon. You will think it is one of Mr. G's. I will end right here. Don't think me cross. I am not a bit that way; but I become "terribly" in earnest when I touch on **the Church**.

I hope this may find you all well. And, my dear friend, if you find not much comfort in this letter, tell me the truth of the matter. In any case, let me be some help to you, if I can be such, until "this tyranny be overpast".

Kindest regards to Mr. & Mrs. Barrett.

I pray for you every day; and I know that prayer is being offered up for me, for I have had evidences of it in experiences which I have had. "The Grace of our Lord Jesus Christ, and the love of God, and the fellowship of the Holy Ghost be with us all ever more. Amen."

Faithfully Yours,<br>
[signed] J. R. Newell.

*****************

In spite of problems the congregation were having in obtaining a priest, they were working hard at paying off the cost of their Rectory. Again from St. Paul's Archives we present.

September 11th, 1900.
## ST. PAUL'S CHURCH RECTORY FUND

To the Members and Friends of St. Paul's Church. Your Wardens having been instructed by the Vestry to complete the purchase of a Rectory think the present time opportune to increase the Harvey Fund in order to reduce the debt as much as possible. We therefore respectfully ask your kind and liberal contributions to be applied in reducing the Mortgage to be given on the Rectory.

Yours Faithfully,

(Signed)   J. R. Davis & C. H. Corton, Wardens.

| | | | |
|---|---|---|---|
| Mrs. A. Battersby | $50.00 | Mr. C. C. Low | $50.00 |
| M. Hodge | $ 2.00 | E. J. Low | $10.00 |
| Lawrence Skey | $10.00 | E. P. Battersby | $10.00 |
| Miss E. Battersby | $ 5.00 | Mrs. Phipps | $ 5.00 |
| Wm. F. Tibbetts | $ 5.00 | Mrs. Fyfield | $ 5.00 |
| T. B. Barrett | $ 5.00 | F. N. Denton | $ 3.00 |
| L. G. Morgan | $ 5.00 | | |

*****************

CHAPTER TWELVE

# St. Paul's Church – 1900-1911

On July 1st, 1900, **Reverend Robert Herbert [1900 – 1907]** was appointed to the parish of St. Paul's. He was born on a farm just west of the village of Warwick, west of Sarnia, Ont. He came to us as a graduate of Huron College. D Company, of the 13th Regiment of the Norfolk Militia, attended the first service taken by Reverend Herbert, on Dominion Day. On September 20th, Reverend Richard Hicks took charge of the evening service, reporting that there was a counter attraction at the Methodist Thanksgiving services. 150 attended. On October 18th, he reported on an evening service for Huron College, which 52 attended and $1.92 was collected. It was assumed that many more would have attended, but the Norfolk County Fair proved a more powerful draw.

Some insights into life in Port Dover at the turn of the century can be gleaned from entries in Mrs. Hubert Barrett's diary which she [my great aunt Maude Scofield] began on October 17th, 1900. "The diary of a married woman will no doubt prove a very prosaic affair, resolving into receipts and remedies and such motley affairs, but it is begun." A rather prosaic but interesting account of a typical day in her life follows; "I arose at 7:00 a.m., got baby a bottle of milk, built the fire, got breakfast, dressed the children, made the beds, washed dishes, went to the butcher shop and up to see Mother as Hubert and Clin. [Warren] were making a summary of affairs in the store."

The reference to the store was the haberdashery that Uncle Hubert operated on Main Street. The diary continues; " 'Peace,

*Hubert & Maude Barrett*

perfect peace, our future all unknown.'— I think they will decide today whether Clin. or Harry [Barrett] will take over the stock so that much will be settled. Hubert has gone down home to help get Grandpa Barrett up for first since his accident a week ago." [He had fallen off a ladder while picking pears and broken his hip, at age 83. Hubert sold the store to Clifford C. Varey in 1909 and he, followed by his son Brian Varey, operated it until the mid 1900's.

Saturday, October 20th, 1900; "Went to a lecture on South Africa by Dr. Ryerson. Enjoyed it but not as much as Andrew Thompson's." Sunday, Oct. 21st. "Up late. Missed church. Harry, Hubert and I and the four children drove to Forey's for hickory nuts for Alice. Got maple leaves for Mother. Hubert sat with his father, while Harry went to church." On Wednesday Hubert told Maude he was bringing Mr. Sproat, for dinner so she "hurried my work, went to grocery for a chicken, can of peas, bunch of celery and canned peaches from the cellar. I got a cake and a pint of oysters from Jimmie's [Leaney] making quite a presentable lunch for such short notice. In p.m. I went to Mrs. Morgan's funeral. A peaceful ending to a useful and happy life." On Sunday 24th, she noted that "Mr. Herbert preached Mrs. Morgan's funeral sermon and spoke so nicely of her."

Aunt Maude's response to the next death to occur in the parish was quite different as she records events in her journal, beginning on October 31st, 1900. "Harry came at 11.00 p.m. to have Hubert stay all night down home. [Bridge Street] We were asleep. He was wanted to stay at Dr. Battersby's as Edith was dying. A terrible shock as I was talking to her in the Post Office on

Monday. Such a young, bright life, everything to live for. So terribly sad. I went down this afternoon and they said she was quite unconscious."

Thursday, November 1st, 1900. "Quintin and I walked to meet Hubert and saw the black symbol of death floating from the Battersby's door. Tied with white ribbon on account of her youth. Poor Edith, so bright, so pretty, so talented. Truly 'They whom the gods love, die young!' Hubert and Mr. Sproat hunting so I stayed in the store from 11.00 a.m. to 3.00 p.m. I wrote to Simcoe for flowers. Poor Mrs. Battersby and the Dr. too."

Friday, Nov. 2nd. "Harry telephoned Roy, [Scott, in Toronto] to ask if he, Walter, [Scott] Clarence [Barrett] and Hugh Tibbetts could be bearers. They were all here tonight."

Saturday, Nov. 3rd. "Went to Battersby's to see Edith. She looked at rest, lips parted as if smiling. Dressed in white organdy muslin bridesmaid dress for Miss McKillian's wedding. One white rose on her breast and sprays of Lilies of the Valley in her hand. The coffin covered with beautiful flowers and the room full. Miss Battersby and Alice Clark and Mrs. Battersby were there. I went to Mothers and at 2.00 p.m. to the funeral, locking the store. Mr. Hicks and Mr. Herbert both there. It was unutterably sad. They sang two of her favourite hymns; "Saviour Breathe an Evening Blessing" and "I am a Stranger here." The Dr. bowed his head on the rail and cried and people all through the church were sobbing and weeping. At the end of the service the sun shone on the coffin, to me like God's benediction. Hubert drove to the cemetery and I opened the store. Walter came for a nice talk, then Roy Sovereign, Mary [Scofield, her sister-in-law] and Adah [Sovereign]."

Sunday, Nov. 4th, "Mr. Herbert's text for Edith's funeral sermon was 'God is not the God of the Dead, but of the Living,' drawing therefrom most comforting thoughts for the many aching hearts of his congregation. Last Sunday she sang with her own inimitable sweetness, Holy! Holy! Holy! Today she is chanting Holy! Holy! Holy! with the innumerable white-robed throng before the throne of the Lamb. A beautiful thought that, that talent which she possessed, her beautiful voice should be still hers in

Heaven and with its earthly restrictions gone, should be purified and perfected in the service of the Master."

On November 3rd, 1900, the church register recorded that two hundred mourners attended the funeral of Miss Edith Battersby, a long-time supporter of St. Paul's. [Her home became the present Rectory.] The Reverend R. Hicks assisted at the service.

On Monday Aunt Maude reports a very busy day in the store. Miss May Nash had sent flowers to Harry [who was courting her at the time] to be placed at Miss Battersby's grave-side, and that evening in the store Maude, Harry and Mrs. Laurie had a long talk about Edith. She reports two days later on Election Day – "Little excitement or interest. Mrs. Herbert was to organise a Society for Parish Work tonight, but there was nobody there."

On November 18th Aunt Maude records her very happy birthday celebrations and "lots of good wishes." Then on Friday, Nov. 23rd, begins her recording of a tragedy that deeply affected everyone in the whole community of Port Dover and the parish of St. Paul's in particular. She pointed out that on Friday, Nov. 23rd, Hubert had not been able to get to Long Point to hunt due to weather so bad that Jim Low, of the tug "Jim & Tom", would not leave port. She records; "When getting meat, Clin [Clinton Warren] told me if they were at the pier at 7.00 a.m. tomorrow the Captain of "The Bell" would take them. I was in the store to let Hubert get ready. I will miss him, but it is his one pleasure and I do not like to raise objections. I hope it may do him some good. I think he will miss us, too. Tonight he said he was homesick already."

Saturday, Nov. 24th, "Harry rattled us up about 6.00 a.m. and went down to see them get off all right. I stayed at the store until Harry came up from dinner. On coming home Mr. Stringer said; 'Well! is this report true?' He was addressing me. 'What report?' I asked. He retorted; 'Why that Clin Warren and Mr. Holden are drowned.' My heart gave one bound. 'Well, but Hubert went in the boat with them.' He said 'Yes, but he is all right.' Everyone confirmed the story."

"It seems Hubert had got in Clin's skiff as Clin wanted him to load it, he and Mr. Holden having been sea sick. Hubert took nearly everything in his skiff and started somewhat in advance. The sea was high, but [they] did not anticipate any danger. The men on the tug were watching, but chiefly [they watched] Hubert with the heavy load, when they saw the other boat [skiff] capsize, and then two figures clinging to it. Then one [was seen to] drop off, and then [they] lost sight of the skiff.

The bar kept them [the tug] from going closer, but they felt Hubert could not have missed them until he got to shore. He then threw out his load and started [back] out and then stood up, using one oar as if on shallow ground. He then went back to shore, ran up and down the beach, then ran steadily toward the lighthouse. They [the fishermen in the tug "Bell"] waited some time then went to their nets and got in about 5.00 p.m. Harry was in the store and was just shaking with nervousness and so was I. I went home at 7.00 p.m. Mother got tea, but I could not eat anything."

Sunday, Nov. 25th, "Could not sleep and woke tired. Thinking, thinking of Hubert. What a terrible day and night it must have been. I see him pacing the beach, hoping to find the bodies and yet the terrible feeling of dread that at any moment he may come upon them. I wish I could be with him. I went down to Barrett's as Harry planned to go over on the tug but it could not go because of high winds. I went to church to thank God for his great mercy to me. Mr. Herbert's text; 'It is appointed unto man once to die.' "

Monday, Nov. 26th, "Another anxious day of suspense. Too stormy for a tug, but Mr. Miller and Mr. Ross plan to drive to the Point by way of Port Rowan. It is terrible, terrible." The following day broke clear and cloudless and the tug left for the tip of Long Point, returning at 5.00 p.m. "The suspense was almost unbearable. I was alone in the store. Norman [Schofield, Maude's brother] and Mary came in, then Hubert. He kissed me but our hearts were too full for words. They found Mr. Holden's body but not Clin's or the skiff. – Hubert later went to the Holden's having been in to see Mrs. Warren."

The diary next records Hubert's account of what happened after he set out in the skiff, with their supplies, from the tug "Bell." "He said after he had started out, he thought he heard a cry but could not tell. He stood up and saw the other skiff coming but it may be possible it was the upturned boat with one of them clinging to it, but he does not know. He shipped a couple of seas and had all he could do to manage his own boat. On reaching shore he could not see their boat so threw the stuff out, emptied the water and started back. He saw Mr. Holden's hat, then Clin's cap and bag of bedding. He rowed around, broke a thole pin and had to paddle back to shore. He ran first to Clemens shanty, finding him not home he ran for the Lighthouse, back to the beach, and then to Newkirk's.[the lighthouse keeper] He ran thirteen miles and is quite lame. They did not find Mr. Holden's body until Tuesday."

The tragedy hung over everyone like a cloud for some time. Huby could not sleep, and kept reliving the whole experience. It was learned that the one skiff was equipped with articulating oars, which allowed the rower to face in the direction the boat was travelling as he rowed. Mr. Holden was not used to them and they may have contributed to their skiff's upset. Mr. Bell and Maude, his wife, came to the store and talked at length about the venture, which was good for Huby. The following night she and Harry visited Reverend Mr. Herbert, finding Mrs. Herbert sick in bed. He and Miss Hughes entertained them for some time, however, talking about dogs. Though she found they [the Herberts] had little in the way of furnishings, the colours of the drawing room harmonised nicely and were in very good taste.

A day or two later, a visit to the Jacques, who had a new baby prompted the following diary entry. "I love little, new babies. They are such innocent bits of humanity, yet when one thinks of all they must go through, if they live! Suffering sorrow no human life is free of, one feels like gathering them up and flying away with them. It resembles little Charlie around the mouth and nose. Wese and I went to Bible Class. Lesson on Jonah. I was glad as I have often wanted that book explained to me. Days go by like a dream or as Hubert once wrote to me 'like a shadow over the heart.' I feel lonely for Hubert's old self. He sits thinking, thinking often an hour at a time. I try not to talk of the accident when he is upset, but so many come into the store with questions."

A week later Aunt Maude left the baby, Winifred, with her mother and went to Auxiliary, where she consented to take on the job of treasurer. "May God help me do the work faithfully and well.

Wese and I had a talk. Her mind is full of the most beautiful thoughts. I always feel better having been with her. She was speaking of Clinton Warren and thinking of the verse, 'With what measure ye mete, it shall be meted to you again.' Certainly his was an unselfish life."

Tuesday, December 18th, 1900. The entry for this day brings home to us the constant threat of diseases and other hazards, of which the population had so little knowledge or control, one hundred years ago. So many mothers died at childbirth and, even if they and their newborn survived, the chances of the baby reaching a healthy adulthood were fraught with many hazards as the diary now discloses;

"Just a year today since we came to this little home and in spite of all, the happiest year of my life. [However,] I feel like the Israelites at Passover. On one side little Charlie Jacques, a few months younger than Quintin, suddenly died of diphtheria. On the other side little Ethel Slocomb, a playmate of Quintin's, was talking to me at 6.00 p.m. one evening in July. Hubert told me at 7.00 p.m. she had gone over to Joe Howell's [the Blacksmith, who lived next his shop on Main Street, north of the Norfolk Hotel] and drowned in the cistern, on their verandah. And now this last terrible accident when Mr. Holden and Clin perished and my darling came back safe to me. Oh God! What would I have done if he too had gone."

Diary entries record the fact that Mrs. Lou Laurie has been terminally ill, but seems to will a postponement of her death until Mr. Laurie returns from a business trip. "Dr. Taylor gives her only a few days. Life is most uncertain and full of suffering and sor-

*Mrs. Lou Laurie*

*Peter Lawson, owner of the Tannery & an M. P.*

row, yet how intensely we all cling to it. She is just about my age." Her husband arrived home the same night the town had turned out for a most amusing and highly successful High School Concert.

The next day's entry: "Poor Lou Laurie died at noon but did speak to Mr. Laurie as she had hoped she could, She has had a sad, lonely life since her mother died." She was buried the next day, Hubert being one of the bearers. A highlight leading up to Christmas was the Golden Wedding celebrations, at her mother's, Mrs. Norman Scofield, for Mr. & Mrs. Adam Lawson on Christmas eve. Maude reported that all went pleasantly, with fifty in attendance. She danced a few times but was tired, They got to bed at 2.30 a.m.

The final page describes the activities of all the family, Christmas Day, at the Barrett home on Bridge street, with a detailed description of the gifts she received from everyone. "The children were delighted with their toys. I received some very nice presents, too. A sofa cushion, from grandma; Vaseline jar, from Wese; primrose in flower from the children; painting, from Clarence; fancy match scratches, from Louise; [Scott] embroidered doily, from May; one of Carlyle's books, from Walter and Roy; [Scott] knitted lace arrangement for a pudding dish, from Alice; Lovely silver berry spoon, from Frank & Hattie; [Barrett, New York]. I left the children with Mother to attend church and communion. We had a lovely dinner and after the children went to sleep had a few games of whist."

We are also reminded that the automobile has made an appearance in Port Dover, and has obviously had a mixed reception. "Harry went to a meeting about the 'anti- mobiles' as Mr.

Lawson calls them." This admission follows; "I am afraid this diary, instead of being prosaic as I first thought, will be a fearful record of calamities."

The formal use of Mr. and Mrs. in reference to people well known in the diary reminds me of the confirmation of this by my Auntie Alice, when I lived with her at Bridge Street, while attending Continuation School on Main Street. She told me the business men of the town were always very formal with each other in their dealings, one with another. For example, even though her father and Peter Lawson, who owned the nearby shoe factory and tannery and lived in the house west of the present lumber yard, had known each other for over fifty years they still greeted each other regularly with "Good Morning, Mr. Lawson," and in response "Good Morning, Mr. Barrett," when they met.

For over forty years, Fa, as my Great-grandfather was known, was Secretary-Treasurer of the Upper Canada Bible Society. On the occasion of a visit by a member of the Society, Fa invited him into his home for a cup of tea. While preparing it he casually mentioned that it was 'Green Tea' he was about to serve his guest. The response was "Why Mr. Barrett, do you not know, that is a slow poison!" To which Fa, now in his eighties, responded lustily, "Faith and it is. I have been drinking it all my life."

On Saturday, February 2nd, 1901 a special Memorial Service was held for Queen Victoria. On April 10th, 1901, Bishop Maurice S. [Baldwin] Huron confirmed 25 candidates. An advertisement appeared in the local paper on May 30th, 1902 as follows. Wanted: General Servant wanted, Apply Mrs. Herbert, The Rectory, Port Dover.

An interesting letter [at least to me] was found in the church archives from "J. R. Hamilton, M. D. Office & Residence, Corner of St. George & Chapman Streets. Hours - 1 to 3 P.M., 8 to 10P. M.

Port Dover, Ont. Feby. 4th, 1901.

My Dear Corton;
I would ask you to kindly look carefully through the documents I sent you, in reference to the Rectory, as I am very forgetful and cannot see where I mislaid some

papers that [are] pertaining to the Rectory.

You will kindly rectify [an] error in your statement, as I am now looking over all my papers having a commotion with moving here. I am sorry I could not attend to it sooner.

I hope Mrs. Corton and Miss Weaver are quite well. Remember me to Mr. Davis.

Very truly Yours, (Signed) J. R. H.

Note by C. H. C.

A mistake of a dollar was made abstracting $2.75 from $2.60.

Aunt Maude's diary begins again on September, 23rd, 1901 and she puts some of her inner thoughts and misgivings in print; "Thinking I should like to start a diary again. Life uneventful since January last. It is said that 'Happy people have no history,' and I certainly am happy. Since coming from Toronto I lack ambition, but it seems this incessant striving to keep up an appearance more or less beyond your real position in life is wearying and very exhausting, and most of the women look it. Glad my lot is not cast in the city but do wish I could improve myself more than I have.

There are so many things in which I feel that I am shiftless, unsystematic, careless. I wonder if a good determination to conquer my besetting sin – procrastination – would be of any avail. I keep thinking of Ezekiel ( 11,19 ) 'And I will give them one heart, and I will put a new spirit within you.' Alas we lack faith and need to pray like the sorrowing father; 'Lord I believe! Help thou my unbelief.' "

As their daughter Winifred needed a daily bit of fresh air, Huby would proudly wheel her in her buggy to the Post Office and back, as he went for the mail. As many of the matrons of the town would be there as well it was not long before they asked to see the new baby. Huby put them off with the excuse that she had a bit of a cold that day and as it was drizzling rain he hesitated to unbundle her. However if it was nice the next day he would be coming for the mail at eleven o'clock and would be glad to show her off at that time.

Next morning sharp at eleven the news had spread, and a goodly crowd of ladies were gathered at the Post Office as Huby promptly at eleven wheeled the covered buggy up the sidewalk for his mail. As the ladies gathered round the buggy in expectation, Huby, always the showman, grasped the cover and whipped it off with a flourish to disclose, not baby Win, but the ugly face of a huge catfish, complete with embroidered bonnet and scarlet cape, nestled in the bottom of the buggy. Quite unabashed by the loud expressions of horror and disgust from the rather flustered audience, Huby covered his "baby" again, picked up the mail and sauntered off gaily down the street to the store.

Thursday, September 26th, 1901. "Hubert went hunting with Russell and Ernie Skey. I went to the church to decorate for Harvest Home. Few there, little accomplished." Next day – "Took till 4.00 p.m. preparing bushel of crab apples for jelly." On the 28th. "Finished jelly and went to the church till six. It looks very pretty. I wanted grapes for the altar railing but used barberry instead. Sunday, Sept. 28th, "Took Winifred to church to try her. She kept up such an incessant chatter, Adah took her home. Will wait till she gets more sense. We went to Barrett's to tea. Went to church at night."

Friday, October 3rd, 1901. Aunt Maude was very impressed by a lecture given by Mr. H. H. Groff of Simcoe on his trip and exhibit at the Pan American show. "He described flowers, with special reference to his hobby, the 'gladioli.' He took 16 of 18 prizes, including gold medal and silver vase. He gave a brief description of the buildings and their colouring and mottoes : 'Speak to the Earth and it will teach thee.' – 'He who fails bravely, does not fail, but is also himself a conqueror.' – 'He who shuns the heat and dust of the conflict shall not rest under the cool shade of the olive.' He spoke earnestly of the benefit of work and how it was the secret of all success. One hundred years ago those grounds were covered by the trail of the Mohawk. What may the next hundred accomplish."

From September 27th, to October 11th, 1903, Lay services were held, mornings only, in the Sunday School as the Church was closed for repairs. The total cost of repairs was $583.11. October 30th, 1904, the Reverend Henry Murton Shore officiated for a Memorial Service for the late Bishop Maurice Scollard Baldwin, who served St. Paul's as rector from 1862 – 63. November 20th, 1904, the 10th anniversary of the re-opening of the church was celebrated. This must have been following the installation of electricity in St. Paul's.

In May of 1906 Reverend Herbert took an extended holiday in the Old Country. Fifteen services were taken by Reverend Henry M. Shore from May 27th to August 26th. Mr. C. S. Mason, Lay Reader, officiated at 4 more and Reverends W. Harvey Moore, Horace Brey, P. L. Spencer, J. K. Golden, and Robert H. Ferguson covered for the balance until Reverend Herbert's return to duties on September 2nd, 1906. On October 28th, 1906 the parish celebrated the Diocesan Jubilee. On January 27th, 1907 115 attended matins and 123 attended evensong for the last Sunday that Reverend Robert Herbert officiated as Rector of St. Paul's.

[The Reverend C. S. Mason had studied Architecture, as a classmate of Clarence Barrett. He later went into the ministry and spent the balance of his working life as Chaplain to the inmates of the Don Jail. He retired to Port Dover, where he indulged his boyhood hobby as a stamp collector. He was among the first collectors in Canada to issue catalogues of stamps for sale, from his collections, and is thought to have made handsome profits from this practice.]

Reverend Herbert later served as a Chaplain during the first World War and upon demobilisation became Rector in Preston. Here he retired to have only a few short years before his death.

Services were taken on February 3rd, 1907 by Reverend S. S. Hardy, followed by Reverends T. J. Hamilton, Henry M. Shore, W. B. Hawkins, and for the month of March by Reverend W. R. Westly. On April 7th, 95 of the congregation attended matins, and 75 took Communion at services conducted by Reverend T. H. Cotton. 67 attended evensong. On the following Sundays Reverends W. B. Hawkins, Charles F. Washburn, and G. Benson Cox officiated in the absence of a rector.

On May 5th, 1907, **Reverend Cyril George Browne [1907 – 1910]** took charge of the parish. He was an Englishman who had found his way to the Barbados, in the West Indies. It was here that he studied theology and was ordained a priest. The large, two-storey building on the north-west corner of St. George and Chapman Streets had been acquired by Mr. Harry Ansley as a rectory and the Reverend Mr. and Mrs. Browne took up residence

*Rev. & Mrs. Browne at the Rectory on n-w corner of Chapman & St. George Streets*

*The Peter Lawson home - much altered and as we see it today*

there. [this building was purchased in 1937 to become the Odd Fellows Hall. It is presently made up of private apartments.]

Mr. Henry Misner, among the oldest members of the parish today, [2005] remembers, and thought very highly of the Reverend Mr. Browne. He also remembers the large home of Mr. Lawson, across from the Royal Canadian Legion, serving as the Rectory at

*The Tuxis Boys - back row - Hazen Waddle, John Spain, Norman Denton, Toby Barrett, Alex Spain. - 2nd row - Edgar Thompson, Rev. Cyril Browne, Rector. Quintin Barrett, Murray Dillon. Front - Walter Warren, George Slocomb*

about that time. Henry told me he started Sunday School at age three, in Miss E. L. Barrett's class.

The Reverend Cyril Browne was a great worker and exerted a considerable positive influence among the boys of the congregation. My father remembered him fondly and often spoke of the good times they enjoyed under his guidance.

The Reverend Cyril Browne made an entry as to the weather each Sunday in the Church Register after noting the attendance and amount of the collection, etc. Example: Lovely day; very hot; wet; snowing hard, or damp, dull & raining. On July 28th, 1907 a special appeal was made for heat, light and repairs to both the rectory and the Sunday School.

On October 12th, 1907 Arthur Clarence Barrett died at Riverbank. He was the youngest son of T. B. Barrett, born on May 7th, 1869. Clarence received a Degree in Architecture and is credited with designing the Port Dover Town Hall and Theatre. He had joined an Architectural firm in Regina, Saskatchewan where he had a part in the building of several of their important Government Buildings among others in that City. In the fall of 1907 he became ill and rather than go into hospital there he came home. He died of diphtheria shortly after his arrival home at Riverbank. Always well liked and full of fun, he left many good paintings of the Port Dover area as well as a photograph album with comments and floral illustrations in oils. Reverend John Newell wrote a letter of condolence to Clarence's father from his parish in Wallaceburg, Ontario.

> Wallaceburg, October 15th, 1907.
>
> My Dear Mr. Barrett,
>
> When I received yesterday evening, the notice from Erie Lodge to attend the funeral of Clarence, I just cried like a child. I could not help it. It was the first intimation I had of his death. Dear Clarence was a member of my first or second confirmation class. Never have I had such gentlemanly boys to deal with as I had at Dover, and Clarence was one of the best. I can remember nothing but that which is good of him.
>
> My dear old friend, you and Miss Barrett are being left desolate indeed. But it is God's doing; and because it is His, we know that it is right. Many treasures of yours have been laid up in heaven, where moth and rust corrupt not; and where your treasures are, there your heart is. In a little while you will be in person where your treasures are, and see face to face.
>
> Thank God for the hope set before us in the Gospel. It binds up the broken-hearted and gives medicine to heal their sickness. God be merciful to you and bless you, my dearest old friend. I am one of the mourners to-day. I am dropping tear for tear. But God's will be done.
>
> With kindest regards to Miss Barrett and all the members of your family, I am,
>
> > My dear Mr. Barrett,
> > Your sincere friend,
> > (Signed) J. R. Newell.

*Illustrated photo of St. Paul's by Clarence Barrett*

On December 15th, 1907, attendance at St. Paul's was 102 and 104 respectively, Collection was $3.10 and it was noted - Good deal of snow, fine day with good sleighing. On December 31st, 75 parishioners attended a Watch Night service at 11:15 p.m. Fine night.

On Sunday, January 17th, 1909 a special collection for the Foreign Missions netted $101.70. On April 25th, 1909 the Odd Fellows attend Evensong, 261 in attendance. Collection $10.87. Wet in the morning, then fine.

From Port Dover Maple Leaf, of March 19th, 1909, we learn that: Port Dover's "first" Rifle Company attended church in a body.

We are also informed that, in fact, this same Rifle Company was the first military volunteer corps of Norfolk County, having been organised early in 1857. On May 24th, 1857, the Company also paraded and marched to St. Paul's Church and attended service. The report goes on to say that this was the occasion of the Queen's birthday and the weather was fine. The Company looked well in their new uniforms.

On May 23rd, 1909 Reverend S. Gould preached at matins and Charles H. P. Owen at evensong. I assume they were missionaries as the offertory of $16.92 was directed to the M. S. C. C. for the benefit of Palestine and the Blackfoot Indians. October 17th, 1909 was Children's Day with the $27.33 collected going to the Sunday School.

On February 27th, 1910 a terse message in the Register notes; "Morning service suspended, no evensong." One can only assume that Reverend Browne was taken seriously ill as the following Sunday, March 6th, through to August 14th, 1910, Frank O. Vain, a student, officiated for most of the services. Others assisting or officiating during this period were Reverends Cyril Browne, Richard Hicks, Brian Howard, George Forneret, H. G. Leaske, Cameron Waller, E. Frank Salmon, Horace E. Brey, W. C. Robarts, G. M. Cox, Stanley H. Bree, Percy N. Harding and Lawrence E. Skey. By August 21st, 1910 Reverend Browne was officiating and signing the Register as Rector again, but he often needed help.

He remained the incumbent until November 27th, 1910 when he signed the Register for the last time. He reported a fine day. The Reverend W. C. Robarts officiated at the majority of services from then through January 1st, 1911. Reverend Stanley H. Bree then took charge for the period from January 8th to February 12th, 1910 when Reverend Percy N. Harding was in charge of the services. The Reverend Cyril Browne and his wife left the parish of St. Paul's to move to Young's Point, near Peterborough, in the Diocese of Toronto.

## Chapter Thirteen

# *Incumbency of H.J. Johnson*

On February 19th, 1911 the **Reverend Herbert John Johnson [1911 — 1921]** officiated for the first time at St. Paul's, Port Dover, with an attendance of 101, 55 of those being communicants, at matins, 88 attended evensong. The Reverend H. J. Johnson was a native of Stratford, Ontario. He studied both Arts and Theology in Trinity College, University of Toronto, graduating with first class honours in both disciplines. He later travelled to England where he enrolled in a post-graduate programme in Lichfield college, graduating with an M. A. On his return to Canada he became rector of the Nova Scotia parish of Parsboro, an area made famous by the interesting fossils that appear along the Fundy shore, as the cliffs in the area erode over time. It was here that he met and married Miss Bessie Upsham.

My father, T. B. (Tobe or Toby) Barrett had toyed with keeping a diary, and began in earnest in 1910, which was to be his last year in school. From these diaries I have learned a great deal about life around Port Dover, and his relationship to St. Paul's Church. A few excerpts will give some feel for a fourteen year old boy's impressions and activities in 1910.

On January 9th, 1910 he reports that he saw the new teacher for the first time. He is obviously not impressed: "She is not at all pretty, mouth on her about a foot wide, very young." January 10th "Went to school all day. Man killed up in Done's [sic] Hollow by the train. Had his brains knocked out on a gate post when train threw him 20 feet. Never hurt the horse. Went with Dad to see a sick horse at Art Ryerse's, after school."

January 11th, 1910 "Went to school all day. Teacher had on the dirtiest blouse I ever saw on a woman. Proved herself a Papist by saying that Bloody Mary was a really good woman. She left out in the history about the persecution of the Protestants." On Saturday he, Dick and Quint shot the puck around on the creek below the house on Bridge Street. Later they dug caves in the snow banks. Quint shot a "Cock-of-the-North" [Pileated Woodpecker] which Huby says is very rare. On Sunday they went to Sunday School but not to Church as he was allowed to drive his father to Port Ryerse with Dr. Coleman [Jarvis veterinary and taxidermist] to attend a sick horse. The horse was worse. Monday evening "Dick and I went to the Methodist Church to some crazy thing."

Later in the month he reports "Teacher's blouse getting dirty again under the arms. She left out more in history about Mary, Queen of Scots, and other things pertaining to the religion of the Elizabethan Period. I went to Brotherhood [a church boy's club, begun by Rev. Browne] to-night and found the only members present were Egg Thompson, Ferdy Wiser, Quint, Rev. C. G. D. Browne and myself.

January 31st, 1910, Toby got up at six to accompany his father and Aunty Alice to Jarvis, where she was catching the train to Toronto to hear the Meddlesome [Mendelssohn] Choir Concert. Stayed with Dr. Coleman until the train came. That afternoon Dad took Enah [Toby's step-mother Hattie, who the boys called Enah, a Cree name for mother-in-law or step-mother] to post a letter, driving his favourite mare Josephine, or Joe for short. As they rounded the corner at Tommy Gillies's [lumber yard at the foot of Powell Park] a trace dropped. "This scared Joe and she lugged Dad over the dash board, ran all over town and then came home." That night at 1:00 "I was awakened by Dick putting his dinner in the wash basin. I told Dad who stayed with him all night."

On February 8th, Toby, Enah and his father "went down Mud Street [Broadway or the Rainham road] to a concert and drove into the fence, thinking it was the gate, and broke the cross-bar and whipple-tree on the cutter. We heard several dialogues and speeches from the preacher. The chief reciters being Lornie Slocomb & Red Kinsular, musick [sic] from the orchestra with Mrs. & Dave McNeilly, and songs from Mrs. Billy Faloon which were very wonderful." They borrowed Kinsular's cutter to get home. February 9th, Ash Wednesday, In the evening "went to church and stayed behind the organ with Joe [Thompson, the pumper?] where I enjoyed myself immensely."

Had a Latin match at school. I went down on first question as did most of the boys. It came out a tie between Sadie Davis and Edna Sidway. On Saturday February 12th, 1910 Toby went to the rink where "I was one of the few spectators to a match between Mud street and Dover. 5 to 1 in favour of Dover. Fatty Turner let in one just to encourage the fellows a little. They put Fat off for two minutes for going out of his goal. (Poor fellow got cold)." On Sunday, February 13th, "I went to Sunday School, but not to Church. I took a picture of the big old tree [ a Sycamore on northeast corner of Nelson and St. George Streets] in front of Mrs. [Ed] Bagley's. Home to stay with Fa. "

Sunday February 27th, 1910. "I went to Sunday School and Mrs. Browne taught us and told us all about the lovely English lanes, that were not in Canada. I wish I had gone to church as Mr. Browne fainted and they all got out early. I stayed home and milked the cow, while Dad and Enah went to the Methodist service. Dr. Jolly came down to see Fa." the following Sunday Toby recorded that on going to church "there was a new preacher, a queer cuss." On Sunday, March 8th, "when Mr. Browne got up to give the sermon, as I thought he said he was not well and would have to close the church, I was about to give him a clap."

Another Lease by the Wardens of St. Paul's has appeared in the church archives. It is dated May 1st, 1910. The property leased is described as being composed of the northerly feet of Lot 19 in Block 40, according to registered map number 22B. It is leased from John Allan, who is entitled to half the apples on the premises, and either party if they break the lease shall pay compensation of $15.00. Another clause states that "no thoroughfare for trains or traffac [sic] is to be allowed, except for use of the tenant. This refers to a lane on the northerly side of the property. If the Wardens were to buy or build a Rectory they shall have the right to sub-let the premises for the unexpired portion of the lease.

This lot is located north of St. Paul's on St. George Street, being two lots south of the corner lot [No. 17] on the south-east

*The house leased in 1910 by the Wardens to serve as a Rectory*

corner of Chapman & St. George Streets. The Wardens leased this property, as they require a rectory for the incumbent. Rev. Mr. Browne had lived in what later became the I.O.O.F. Hall on the north-west corner of Chapman & St. George Streets.

Tuesday May 10th, 1910 from the diary; "Nothing has happened of much consequence lately, The King died on the 6th, at midnight and Aunty [Alice from Fort Saskatchewan] came home yesterday. Dad, Enah and I came home from Port Rowan to-day. We drove Joe and Ginger up yesterday on a double-seated rig of Faulkner's. [a Port Dover livery stable] Aunt Ida [Hugh Massy Barrett's wife] is pretty sick. The flags all through the country are flying at half-mast." He goes on to report a wonderful spring, very little mud on the roads, in fact they were dusty all through March and April, which was most unusual. Halley's Comet was "kicking around somewhere in the heavens and some of the wise people think it is affecting our weather."

Theobald Butler Barrett, affectionately known to his family as Fa, had taken out an agency with the Norwich Union Insurance Company on being forced to retire from Her Majesty's Customs Service, following his seventy-fifth birthday in 1892. He was in high dudgeon over the official notification of his superannuation from the Customs Department. He would continue to service his insurance customers for another eighteen years, to the day of his death.

My father told me that on December 27th, 1910 Fa drove in the back lane from St. Patrick Street about four o'clock, having just renewed a policy with one of his customers. To Toby's surprise Fa asked him if he would mind putting his horse away for him and feeding her after giving her the usual rub-down. Fa took particular pride in always looking after his own horse, but on this occasion he admitted to feeling a bit tired and Toby was more than willing to look after his grandfather's horse for him. When he had bedded the horse for the night and returned to the house, Fa was asleep on a sofa in the kitchen.

Later that evening as supper was ready in the dining room, Toby was sent to waken his grandfather for his evening meal. On calling him without getting a reaction, he went to the sofa and shook him gently by the shoulder. Fa still did not respond. He had quietly slipped away in his sleep. Needless to say everyone was very upset by this sudden turn of events, but for Fa, active to within an hour of his death, in his 93rd year, no-one really could ask for a more peaceful way to go to meet his Maker.

The greatest shock would be borne by Aunty Wese, who had been the family member to stay home and raise the boys of her sister Phoebe Scott, on her death in 1884, and the boys of her brother Harry on the death of his wife, Rebecca Julia "Nonah", in 1898. She also had run the household for her parents as they became older. Her mother, Emily, had passed away in 1902. Early in the new year Aunty Wese

*Theobald Butler Barrett, known to family as "Fa"*

received a letter of condolence from her long time friend, and earlier Rector, Reverend John Newell, from his parish church in Oldcastle, Ontario.

Oldcastle, January 2nd, 1911.

Dear Miss Barrett.

You need no letter nor other mode of intelligence to inform you of my profound sorrow regarding your father's death. You know how I loved him, the dear, kindhearted man. Twice in my New Year sermons I mentioned him as the dearest parishioner I ever had.

We feel sure that it is well with him. Your dear mother, and Bishop Baldwin, and other dear friends are his companions in that better world, where God wipes away all tears.

It is we ( for I say we, for I am a mourner) whose condition deserves commiseration. We have been bereaved of as genial a companion as ever scattered sunshine on the wayside.

Still you, my dear friend, above all others will feel the great loss which has befallen you. But you know whom you have believed and are persuaded that He is able to keep that which you have committed to Him. "Cast thy burden upon the Lord, and He shall sustain thee." Only a little while and these severed ties shall be reunited never to be broken again.

*A few more years shall roll, A few more seasons wane,*
*And we shall be with those that rest, Till Christ shall come again.*
It is not worth the while to mourn over earthly trouble. Soon, very soon, we shall be with those "whom we have loved long since, and lost awhile." God bless you, dear Miss Barrett, and may you more and more realize the comforting words:

"I am with thee, and I will keep thee in all places whither thou goest."

With kindest regards to all the family,

Sincerely Yours,
(Signed) J. R. Newell.

The Maple Leaf of May 19th, 1911 carried the following notice:

——— To All Whom It May Concern. ———

The members of St. Paul's Church, Port Dover, propose to erect a Memorial Pulpit in the Church, as tangible evidence of their love and esteem for the late Bishop Baldwin, whose first charge was this parish. Scattered far and wide are those who reverence his memory as that of an earnest and faithful clergyman and a saintly Bishop. As it has been decided to do this by the aid of purely voluntary contributions, will all who desire to assist kindly send their donations to Miss Ida Davis, Treasurer of St. Paul's Women's Guild. Pulpit Committee of the Guild: Miss Barrett, Miss Battersby, Miss Phipps, Mrs. Tibbetts, and Reverend H. J. Johnson, M.A., Rector of St. Paul's.

The spring of 1911 was an exciting time for the W. H. Barrett family for they were finally able to finance the purchase of the William's place, Lot 12, Concession 2, on the north-west corner of the Cockshutt Road and what is to-day known as Mill Road. It was called a 120 acre farm, with 80 acres of arable or working land and the balance gully pasture and woodland. The house and buildings were in disrepair due to neglect and lack of funds by the previous owner. A recent survey indicates the farm contains just over 132 acres. [as if you were interested.]

"Cnochfiernah", meaning Fairy Mound, Lot 12 Con. 2. Woodhouse - The Farm.

Toby was greatly excited as he was permitted to leave school in second form at age 15 to help his father, Harry, who as a practising Veterinary-Surgeon would often be called away from the work of the farm to attend a neighbour's sick horse or other farm livestock.

Toby's diary took on a whole new emphasis as he used the balance of the pages of his hard-cover Chemistry and Biology notebooks to record the happenings of each day on the farm. Without these records most of the trivia, along with some noteworthy lost information regarding St. Paul's Church, would, no doubt, be unavailable to us.

*Graduation photo of W. H. "Harry" Barrett. Dr. of Veterinary Medicine*

It begins on May 24th, 1911 with; "We moved enough stuff over last Saturday May 20th, to get along. Bill Oakes is preparing ground for corn. I got up at six o'clock, being led to believe by Dad I would have to fetch the cows from back the lane. After breakfast Bill took Belle and Harry, the big black horse we borrowed from Harry Ansley, to plow for corn. Dad and I took Josephine [a favourite driving mare, usually referred to as Joe, or Josie] and Ginger out, to lead to town to get Faulkner's [the livery stable on Main Street, where the store "Peggy's Cove" is now] wagon, to get oats at Flemings. At the gate we met Bill Donald with a horse with sore shoulders, which he requested Dad to lance, after telling him the whole story of how they got sore and everything that happened between that time and this.

Accordingly, Dad tied Joe up to the fence and after informing Mr. Donald he was going to stop practising and receiving full protestations against that point, he commenced examining the horse's shoulder." Toby goes on to tell in detail that Joe got loose and while chasing her she gave the ailing horse "a biff in the slats." They went to Flemings, bagged up the oats, later returned to lance the shoulder of Bill Donald's horse, fix blisters on a horse that Walker Wells had brought in, caught the chickens at "Riverbank" to move to the farm and finally got the wagon at Faulkners. "In the afternoon we put in the pump and had a long visit, 2 hrs or so, from Billy Barlow, who had taken a holiday and got lonesome." This gives an idea of the kind of information that filled some 40 hardcover Student's MSS Books in the ensuing years.

Sunday May 28th, "Went to Sunday School with Dad behind Belle, and after church drove home with Dad and Enah." Toby was responsible for the library in the Sunday School, recording loans and returns to students and parishioners and keeping the material used in the S. S. filed properly. Enah as organist attended all services, as well as choir practice sessions. His father missed countless services for Sunday, being a day of rest, was the day when many farmers called him to treat their ailing livestock.

We learn that on Tuesday, June 6th, 1911 "Enah went to a [Women's] Auxiliary tea-shine in Waterford this morning with a load driven by Johnny Walker [who later built the Gem movie theatre, and was a stalwart member of the St. Paul's choir] and hauled by Faulkner's Arabs. She got back after nine o'clock, earlier than she expected. We could hear Mrs. Skey and Miss Wheeler yelling way down at Mrs. Battersby's corner."

Sunday, June 11th, 1911, "I went to Sunday School and found a lot of books waiting for me. Miss Battersby was just going to start on them, thinking I had jumped my job." The family spent the afternoon at the Harvey Shand's enjoying a musical time [I own the H. Shand farm, Dad having purchased it at my request, while I was overseas, from Charlie Shand in 1943]. In the evening, after tea at Huby's, Toby walked Enah and Ada [Sovereign] up to church, and then went up the beach with Murray Dillon. He also reports on a group of friends who were on the lake in the "Cygnet," who on their return accidentally hit the "Vigilant," breaking their tiller and badly crushing the hand of Mrs. Roy Silverthorne.

Sunday, June 18th, 1911, "I walked down to Sunday School and was not late, which broke the record for the first time since we have been on the farm. Dick was not up in time to go. He, Enah

*The Patrol vessel Vigilant steams into Port Dover harbour*

and Roy [Scott] came to church. ..... Saw the launch 'Miriam' come in from the Erie Yacht Club. Joe [Thompson] was out in the "Pilot" and Mid [Thompson] in the "Cygnet." Hardly enough wind to get in. .... Found out McBain's old barn burned, down by Bob Leitch's place."

"Went to church this evening alone, and went behind the organ with Wiser, who wanted to get off early. [Wiser was the friend, who was officially hired to pump the organ. Toby often filled in for him.] Mr. Johnson and Murray [Dillon] went up to Port Ryerse in the former's gasoline launch and broke down. Haymaker [owned a repair garage where the coin laundry is now] towed them in. I guess Mr. Johnson had to preach on an empty stomach. Hot day, but nice breeze. After church went up to old Walker's strawberry patch with Egg Thompson and Rank [Coville Rankin.] It was too dark to find the berries well."

The following Sunday Toby went to S. S. but his father was called over to the Vyse farm to treat a colt. He worked on the colt all day with little chance of saving it. Punk Wiser, the organ pumper, told Toby that he had the summer job of gate keeper for Buck's Park and so convinced Toby to take his job of bell ringer and organ pumper at the church. He and Enah went to evensong, where Toby pumped for Wiser who had to go and see his girl, with Fatty Turner. They had a special, longer service for the Coronation, [Edward VII] and on coming out it was pouring rain.

Auntie Maude, the Hobbes, Mr. Morgan, an able seaman from the "Vigilant" and Toby all huddled in the porch for some time waiting for it to let up.

The June 25th, 1911 issue of the Maple Leaf informed its readership that: "Beginning on Thursday July 4th, and continuing every Thursday during July and August, 'Afternoon Tea' from 4:00 to 5:00, will be served in St. Paul's Church School Room, by members of the Women's Guild. Members of the Women's Exchange will also offer 'Garden and Home Products' for sale, or receive orders for the same."

On Sunday July 9th, Toby carried out his church duties and after dinner got stationary from Miss Battersby on which he listed all the books in the S. S. Library. He was late arriving for the evensong, but as he crossed Main Street the bell began to toll. On entering he found Fatty Turner with the rope. He said that some of the girls started to ring the bell but got the wrong rope. Toby pumped the organ while his cousin Quintin left with Fatty. On Sunday, July 9th, Toby went to S.S. taking a pint of cream to Miss Phipps on the way. He was asked to return Reverend Mr. Johnson's dog, as it had spent the night with her. Enah played the accompaniment for Miss Hunt's solo. Harry treated all his and Huby's family to dinner at Henderson's Hotel after church [the Commercial.] On July 19th, Dick attended the Sunday School picnic at one o'clock, Toby went at five.

On July 30th, 1911 Reverend E. G. Dimond preached the sermon. Toby nearly turned the church bell over and accused Wiser of greasing it too much. He reported that a Miss Hunt sang a solo, but unlike Miss Hunt, the usual soloist, who was older and an alto, this Miss Hunt was a soprano. A fund was begun to put a new roof on the Church. The collection raised $30.03 that day.

Sunday August 27th, quoting the diary "Mr. Johnson was on the job this morning again. He christened a couple of kids before service. They were kicking up an awful row when I went in to ring the first bell for church. I came home for dinner. Mrs. and Miss Woodson, Miss Robinson and Paul Lee were all here. Dick is staying with Allan and going to the Toronto Exhibition in the morning." On Thursday, August 31st, Harry gave Toby a plowing lesson, and mid-afternoon: "I took Enah and Lila down town. Enah stayed

*A Sunday on the Farm -Standing - Hubert, Frank & Harry Barrett. - Seated - Wese, Tim, Lila, Alice and Hattie*

at the church practising with Miss Drayton till six o'clock. We brought Kathleen Millman home to stay for a few days."

Thursday, September 7th, Harry and Toby were up before five o'clock to get chores done and catch the train for the Exhibition grounds, arriving about eleven o'clock. "The Widespread [this was a furniture factory, that originally manufactured manure spreaders, located on the site of Lawson's Tannery, at the corner of Bridge and Lynn Streets] had a very fine exhibit of crates, chests and wardrobes. A large number of cattle on show. The trains were very crowded and everybody talking about Reciprocity. Few seemed for it and they did not seem very sure whether they ought to be or not. Home about half past nine nearly frozen."

Thursday September 21st, "This afternoon Dad, Enah and I went down town. Dad went to the schoolhouse to vote, while Enah got the books out of our pew in church. They are fixing the church all different inside. About half the population of Dover was Drunk to-day. I suppose because the bars are all supposed to be closed. There have been two or three election fights and a lot of money

Incumbency of H.J. Johnson 283

bet...... Surprised to hear Charlton elected by 181 majority and only two polls to hear from......Went to the Hall later and heard encouraging reports for the Tories. There were three Grits on the platform reading the lists as Dick [Toby's brother] brought them from the telegraph Office. Although they tried to smile, their faces grew blacker every minute as the majority for the Tories rose. .....home at 9:30 to be told Dad had gone to look at Welch's cow which had choked on an apple. When they tried to push it down with a broom stick, it [the broom stick] broke off in her throat. Dad had a deuce of a time with her."

Friday, September 22nd, 1911. "HOORAY FOR BORDEN. Dick came home with the Globe and tidings that Borden had 43 seat majority. The Liberals were skunked owing to Reciprocity. Most of the Cabinet was defeated. Canada is Saved From Yankeedom."

Sunday, September 24th, "No Sunday School to-day as they have church there now, while the church is being fixed up." They got a telegram at the farm that afternoon from Grandfather Pelly, that Frank [Toby's and Dick's youngest brother] was coming from Otter Lake, where they were all born in the Spallumcheen District of the Okanagan Valley, to live in Port Dover. Their mother,

*Peter Lawson's Tannery*

Rebecca Julia "Nonah" Pelly Barrett, died after Frank was born and he was raised by their Grandmother Pelly.

As his grandmother had just died, Frank now twelve years old, was coming home to Port Dover. He was accompanied by Mr. Willie Taylor, a Presbyterian minister in the Okanagan, who was originally from Port Dover. His brother, Dean Taylor, was a dentist in the Okanagan. Frank had gone to Dean for some dental work. Dean recognised Frank as a Port Dover Barrett and when he heard he was returning to Port Dover he took him to Sicamous to meet his brother Willie, who was coming east to get married. Frank said Dean, who was homesick for Dover, told him he would really like it better there than in the west.

By September 24th, 1911 the work on the roof of St. Paul's, as well as other repairs and upgrading, had begun. Services were held in the Sunday School while this was being done. From my father's diary we get a further insight into this exciting period in the life of our church. He reports that on Sunday, October 1st, 1911 it was "raining so hard all morning only Enah and Roy went to church. Dad drove them down. We read, slept and starved until four o'clock when we had dinner. ...... Quint went down to church [evensong] with us boys. It was in the town hall and they had it decorated for Harvest Home. Frank and I got reserved seats. Dick went under the gallery with Jim Lowe. We came home nearly right after."

Sunday, October 8th, 1911. "All hands went to church. Dick and I walked down with Miss Battersby's kittens, Dad, Enah and Frank drove [with Mexico, their pony, on the buggy]. They had church in the Sunday School and had a cracking good house but poor entertainment and accommodation. Jim Blakie, Frank Wiser, Katie Spain's husband [Powell, from down the lake shore] and I were crowded into the back seat. Charlie Martin and Miss McCoy had the seat ahead."

"We went in and saw the church and it looks pretty fancy. They are painting a high pattern around the wall as high as high wainscotting would be and trimming around the windows. There are little round pictures around the walls. ---- [in the evening] Dad, Enah and I walked down to church. Nothing much doing except

*Interior of St. Paul's Church after decoration - note gas lights*

for Mr. Hobbes [Manager of the Royal bank] who spent most of his time trying to keep the preacher's dog out."

Sunday, October 29th, 1911 "They were going to have church in the Town Hall again, but George Steele did not light the furnace, the cellar door was locked, so they got frozen out and had to adjourn to the Sunday School where it was just as hot as the other was cold. ..... I walked down to church after tea with Roy. We went to Huby's where most of the Lawrence Skey family were assembled. The Reverend Larry had been up preaching to-day and [now] with Quint and Warren were arranging for a hunt to-morrow, as it was Thanksgiving day.

November 5th, 1911. "The church was re-opened this morning and looked fine. The Bishop was to have been there but could not come so he sent his man, [Archdeacon W. A. Young presided over the re-opening of the Church.] He dedicated the three memorial pieces that had been put in. The Pulpit, in memoriam of Bishop Baldwin. The brass desk [lectern] to Mr. Skey and the Prayer Desk to Fa. [Toby's grandfather and namesake, Theobald Butler Barrett.] We went up to the church with Aunty [Wese] at three o'clock for a Children's Day Service. Aunty went over to Miss Battersby's for tea. I went up to church after tea but was late so went behind the organ, where I found Wiser and Fatty Turner.

*Skey lectern, baptismal font and flags in 2005*

They said Dad had come down with Enah, but had to go off to kill Holden's old mare."

Harry's diary has the following entries for the Re-opening. "We all walked down to church. They had the re-opening, not a very large congregation. [102 at early communion, 80 at the eleven o'clock dedication service, 104 at evensong] ..... Went to church in the evening but George Holden caught me to go up and kill his old mare, so I did not hear the service of induction. Canon Young preached both morning and evening." As well as the re-dedication of the church, and the dedication of the Memorials, it was the occasion of the official induction of Reverend Herbert J. Johnson as Rector of St. Paul's.

The Reverend Johnson was obviously artistically inclined, as he had not only designed the beautiful wall adornments now stencilled on the walls of the church, but he had also designed the Communion Table, the Choir pews, the Prayer desks, Lectern and Font. He oversaw production of the wall decorations, which were done by a young and accomplished, Scottish artist, sent from Toronto by Thornton and Smith. As the job required several weeks to complete the artist took lodgings and most of his meals in the Commercial Hotel.

Inevitably, his name became linked with a very attractive chambermaid at the hotel, and some of the ladies of the church professed to be scandalised by the quite unfounded, albeit malicious, rumours that were soon circulating about the unsuspecting couple. The artist worked on diligently, apparently quite oblivious to the rumours of his improper behaviour. My father, who never believed the insinuations made in the first place, was highly amused, on the re-opening of the church, to discover that the Heavenly Host above the Communion Table included an angel with a striking likeness to the hotel chambermaid. Her beauty stood out amongst the other angels. The artist had quietly gained his revenge over the gossip of some of the pious matrons of the congregation.

An indication of the artists skill was apparent many years later, when I became a choir boy. Sitting in the Choir pew I had plenty of time to study at close range, the angels above the Communion Table and Memorial window. I was always drawn to one among them, who stood out above all others. She also looked uncannily like an attractive young woman in the choir at that time. It struck me so forcefully that I finally mentioned this fact to Dad. He chortled and replied; "Well, so she should, her mother was the artist's model at the time it was rendered in 1911." He then told me the background story.

Canon Cornish also saw more than what, to most observers, met the eye in the original rendering of the Heavenly Host

*Original border around the windows*

*Chancel with original angel choir*

in St. Paul's. In his history, "The First Hundred Years," he points out that regardless of the compass direction of the chancel of an Anglican Church, it is always referred to as if pointing to the East, the remaining walls being North, South and West in relation to the Chancel. In his description of the ornamentation of our church he comments; "Having slowly progressed toward the East, we see the Heavenly Host above the Holy table.

Perhaps the artist only meant to represent a church choir offering its high and glorious worship, for, with a touch of realism he sets two dark faces in profile at the bottom to represent demons. Reverend Mr. Johnson is said to have maintained that the demons bore a striking resemblance to some of the scandalised ladies of the congregation, which if so, was a further revenge on the part of the artist. The artist in 1950, [when the church interior was redecorated] not knowing the interpretation, altered the original by making them like unto angels." Unfortunately, due to the devastating fire of November 20th, 1965, present members of the parish have no reminder of these stories, from which to draw their own conclusions.

My father gave the view of a fifteen year old, of the wall decorations during the time they were being rendered but in the two official histories of St. Paul's since that time we are given much more enlightened insight as to their symbolism and interpretation, primarily by Canon Cornish, with additions by Mrs. Burbidge from other learned sources. I can add little and therefore can do no better than to draw on their research and accounts. Canon Cornish takes us back to the beginning of Christianity and the frequent use of symbols to convey a message. I quote;

> "In ancient times two factors forced the use of symbols; one was space economy. Ancient texts leave no space between words and abbreviate whenever possible. The second reason was fear; when to be identified as a Christian or caught with Christian writings might mean death, symbols were used for safety."

High on the north wall of the Nave are four medallions which represent to us the human Jesus. Directly opposite, on the south wall, are complementary medallions representing the divine Christ.

## On the North Wall

*Six-sided star*

**Double triangles,** superimposed over each other as a six-sided star, represent God and man, each in his three-fold nature; Father, Son and Holy Spirit, and for mankind, body, mind and spirit. It illustrates the Incarnation. – Jesus said; "I and my Father are one."

**On the South Wall, and directly opposite**

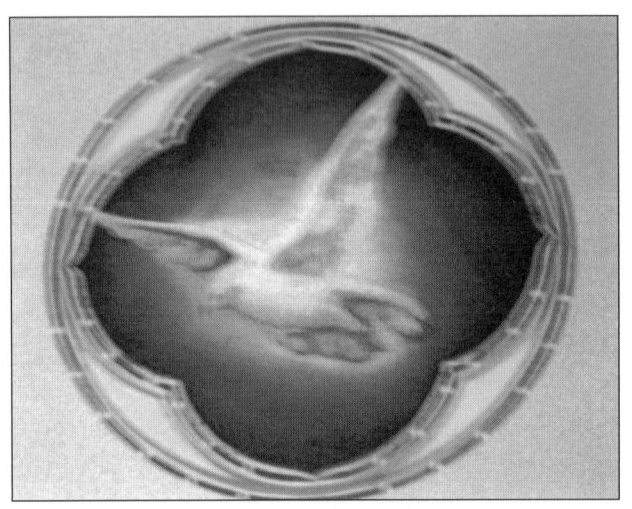

*Dove in flight*

The **Dove in flight** symbolises the descent of the Holy Spirit, as it had descended upon Jesus at his baptism.

*Entwined letters I.H.S.*

The **Entwined Letters I.H.S.** has more than one interpretation. One being that it became the Christian symbol for Jesus as these are the Greek letters which begin His name. Others interpret the letters as standing for the Latin "in hoc signo" meaning "in this sign." The sign in this case is seen as standing for Christ. Still others maintain that they represent the Latin phrase "in Hominem Salvator" meaning "(Jesus) the Saviour of Men." Whatever the interpretation may be, this is a very easily recognised Christian symbol.

*The Greek letters Chi Rho*

The **Greek letters Chi Rho** are on the south wall again, opposite the above medallion. Chi and Rho are the first two letters of the Greek name Christos. In the wall medallion of ours they resemble the capital letter "P" with crossed bars on the lower part of the P like an awkward "X." This Chi Rho symbol was adopted as the logo to identify the Anglican Young People's Association, or A. Y. P. A.

The **Pelican (?) Feeding its Young** from a wound in its breast, with its own blood, was believed by the ancients to symbolise Jesus shedding his own blood for the sins of the whole world. Canon Cornish further suggests that the blood of the bird may represent the mystic wine of the Eucharist, when the priest chants to each communicant "This is my blood of the New Testament, which is

*Pelican [?] and young*

shed for you." [It has puzzled me, since a youngster, that the large white bird in our medallion has the bill of a Swan, which is not at all like the capacious, pouch-like bill of the Pelican.]

*Agnes Dei - Lamb of God*

The **Agnes Dei, Latin for the Lamb of God**, is found in the medallion opposite the Bird. The staff and banner draped around the Lamb carries the title. Everyone is familiar with the Agnes Dei, an ancient chant, sung in English during the Communion Service as follows:

> *O Lamb of God that taketh away the sins of the world,*
> *Have mercy upon us.*
> *O Lamb of God that taketh away the sins of the world,*
> *Have mercy upon us.*
> *O Lamb of God that taketh away the sins of the world,*
> *Grant us Thy peace.*

*Anchor of Hope*

Finally on the north wall is an anchor lying on the bottom, its cable fouled and broken. The anchor the symbol of Hope, with the broken cable wrapped or tangled around its stock, represents the shipwrecked, lost and broken life still clinging to the anchor of hope. Christ, our anchor in life, gives us hope in eventual salvation. We are instructed in our service of prayer to "Come unto me all ye that travail and are heavy laden." The anchor holds a unique significance in our parish where so many make their living from the fishery, and we are reminded of this annually by the blessing of the nets and the safety of all "that go down to the sea in ships" in our special Fishermen's Service.

Opposite the anchor is the cross, the symbol of triumph, with a halo-like circle behind it symbolising the crown, reminding us of Christ's admonition to "Fear not, for I am with you."

*The Cross & Crown*

Although they are now hidden by the pipes of the new organ, installed at the rear of the Church above the entrance from the narthex, symbols of a much more local significance still remain in medallions on either side of a golden cross above the entrance. Quoting from Canon Cornish we are told that:

"Service over, the worshipper turns to the door in the centre of the west wall. Over the door is a cross with a background of gold. High on the left, in medallion form, is one of our Lake Erie fishing tugs and on the right a landscape with a flowering rose bush. They are all of a piece! The worshipper takes up the cross of daily living, backed by the spirit of God in all His works and ways. Here is a local touch, as in 'The wonders of the Sea,' or of the land, lies the way of so many of our people, fishing in the miracle Lake Erie or growing roses, literally, for the Dominion."

When the new organ was installed in the church after the fire, my brother-in-law, Stephan Molewyk, was adamant that the pipes should not be placed at the opposite end of the building from the Organist and the Choir. Unfortunately he was over-ruled and to my mind the congregation has lost out on two counts because of it. Firstly, the choir sounds slightly out of sync with the distant sounding of the organ pipes, which often drown out the voices of the choir for the congregation. Secondly, we have lost the attractive medallions signifying the two predominate industries in our com-

*The Border Design*

munity; fishing and agriculture, specifically represented by a modern steel-hulled fish tug and by the town's major industry, Ivey's Roses, respectively. You might argue of course that their demise was prophetic, for Ivey's Inc., at one time the largest Rose Growers in Canada, are no more and the Port Dover fishing fleet is a mere shadow of its former self.

Canon Cornish takes the interpretation of the medallions that were added later to the west wall a bit further. Originally the wall was a blank. With the Select Vestry's approval of the addition of the two medallions he suggests that it illustrates a change in theological thought. From the blank wall, representing a lost and worthless world, we have taken a new tack in our thinking and feel that we work in a productive, supportive environment. He then quotes from Isaiah: "The whole earth is full of His Glory."

From the time I was old enough to appreciate anything, I used to sit in church and wonder at the intricate and colourful design of the border, or dado, on three walls of the nave. My father at the time of its installation likened it to a high wainscotting. I had no idea of its symbolism or meaning to knowledgeable Anglicans, but it intrigued me immensely. As Canon Cornish succinctly points out: "In richness of tone and symbol it can scarcely be excelled!" He goes on to say:

"Here you find the Holy Trinity in a variety of emblems, the Cross and Crown in dominant form, the pomegranate, symbol of plenty [In Masonic ritual we are reminded that: "the pomegranate, from the exuberance of its seeds, denotes plenty."] and long sweeping curves indicating the passing of time, the ebb and flow of the generations. The most conspicuous feature is the long blue ribbon of human contemplations running the whole length of the lovely pattern. Blue indicates that it is human and the thought of man flows on through time, dominating all things until it reaches its limitation and then disappears under the shield of faith only to emerge and pursue the endless but rewarding quest. The Shield of Faith has a touch of gold but also a clouded side — on this as on other features, the worshipper may make his own interpretation." Rt. Reverend Clarence Mitchell points out that the shading on the shields and the cross in the cross and crown was lost when the church was re-painted for the 100th Anniversary in 1952. It was at this time that the "Fake stone" was painted around the windows and arches of the Church.

Mrs. Burbidge adds from the research of Shirley Presland the idea that: "the band of blue ribbon suggests serenity and peace. The vine-like branches which serve to bind everything together remind us that Christ said, "I am the vine and you are the branches." A narrow border was painted where the wall meets each window to outline the tall, narrow windows in the body of the church. This was replaced by the simulated stone in 1952.

On December 3rd, 1911 Bishop David (Williams) Huron was able to visit the newly opened and beautifully decorated St. Paul's. He confirmed 11 candidates at that time. Toby complains it was a very long service. The following Thursday Aunty and Enah went to Bible

*Archbishop David Williams of Huron*

Class and Harry joined Enah after tea for choir practice. Dick and Toby went to see a Magic Lantern show in the Town Hall but were not impressed.

On December 17th, the register notes that Mr. William Tibbetts, Lay Reader, officiated for both matins and evensong as he did again on December 24th, 1911. Toby gives us a good deal more detail in his interpretation of events. "Mr. Johnson is off at Barrie where they have him up for some scrape he got into last summer, or so I hear, but it is without doubt stretched." A lay Reader from Nanticoke was arranged for, but it was thought he got stuck in the Walpole clay as he never showed up. Toby adds: "Cousin Willie [Tibbetts] did the deed and he cut it very short."

On Wednesday, December 20th, 1911 Toby reports: "We shot two pigs and had them all gutted and scraped by noon. Blaikie and Alfred Ryerse came over and the former brightened the scene by a few pig-sticking anecdotes and other yarns. Did chores, sawed wood and blew up a [pig] bladder which we kicked around. I went to choir practice with Enah.... pumped the organ until they quit about ten o'clock. On the 23rd, after chores were done everybody went to town. The boys bought Christmas presents and then went to the Sunday School where Aunty was making wreaths and decorations. They helped put them up in the church.

Christmas Day: "Dad did all the chores and cut enough wood to last all day. We went to church at eleven. Aunty and I called for Cousin Clare [Langs] who came over for the day. Huby's family came to dinner at three at which I increased my waist measure to nearly bust measure on the turkey, plum pudding, mince pie and homemade candy. We were all lead to believe there would be no presents this year, as we are hard up, but I did not notice any difference."

Sunday January 21st, 1912. Dad drove us three boys down to Sunday School. Homer Martin looks after the Church now. Moved the piano into the dining room as it is too cold to play it in the parlour. The following Sunday Toby reports Homer did not have the church fired up very well and everybody nearly suffocated with gas. February 15th, All the Ryerse bunch and Miss Blaikie came over to go down to the Parish hall with Enah and Frank to a lecture by a Chinese Missionary. Dad hooked up the team and took them down in the bob sleighs. Reports follow this same vein for the whole of 1912.

Friday March 1st, 1912 everyone turned out for the farewell address and presentation to Mr. Liddy, retiring High School Principal. On Monday Frank had only 3 mistakes in spelling. Dick "had the new teacher, Dr. O'Connor and when Mr. Liddy started to make a farewell speech but couldn't fetch it and broke down and had to leave, Dick said Corby wept all morning and seemed very much affected, the girls too, but he guessed a lot of them were putting it on."

On Sunday Dad and Enah were late for church and their seats were taken in the choir, so they had to sit behind the organ. Toby reports "Dad vowed he would never go in the choir again, but he has vowed that about a dozen times before." On March 17th, "Dad as usual was in the choir again. He and Aunty went to see Miss Battersby while I pumped the organ for Enah and Mrs. Hobbes to practice a duet. Toby and Dick have joined the Port Dover Band and Walt. Steele sent them home with instructions and a horn and a clarinet respectively. Aunty sold the back lot on St. Patrick Street to Mr. Barwell. He is drilling there for gas."

*"The Stump" by Clarence Barrett*

Toby records the fact Mrs. Waddle and Miss Harding came in "begging for the church tea in the town hall." Dick was in town selling tickets. He sold enough to get Toby, his Dad and Enah in free, when it was held a few days later. Toby found the food good but the programme too long. Quint joined the crew of the patrol vessel Vigilant that night, being a Thursday. Huby did not want him to start on a Friday. [sailors consider it bad luck. Alan Law would not start a threshing job on Friday for the same reason.] Mrs. Moon reported that vandals got in the town hall after the St. Paul's tea and dumped coffee all over the piano, " messed the hall up, and committed a lot of depredation."

In April Toby reports that George Johnson, a relative of the rector assisted, on Good Friday. On May 19th, "There was a strange preacher, a student Mr. [David M.] Rose. On May 24th, all helped move the kitchen stove to the summer kitchen, and then Toby went for the first swim of the season at "The Stump." [this was a big willow stump that was just at the surface of the Pond, and from which all the boys in town learned to swim, more often than not, in the nude.]

On July 1st, 1912 Toby goes to town to see the American Navy training ship "Wolverine," which was in harbour. He is more impressed by the steamer "The City of Dover." He writes "John Gordon, is owner, proprietor, captain, chief cook and bottle-washer. She runs by side paddle wheels propelled by hand." [someone was pulling his leg]

July 4th, 1912. "Enah and I drove up to the Smythe Garden Party about six. We were too early, being under impression you pay at the gate and get your supper. You were supposed to have had your tea, then buy your refreshments and stuff at the booths plastered all over the place. We missed paying, being early and they gave us a little supper, so I never put up a red cent. I had a slow time as I hardly knew anybody. Listened to Simcoe band. Louise [Scott, Toby's cousin] and I went over to the old grave yard [Doan's Hollow cemetery] I believe there are some epitaphs worth reading, but it was too dark and dismal. Came home about eleven, road very dark, ghosts and fire-flies were much in evidence. Louise went up to Bowlby's."

Saturday October 19th, 1912 "I drove Auntie to Miss

Battersby's to decorate the church for Children's Day. I drove slowly so as not to get the nice clean buggy all splashed up. I just about killed myself trying to smoke Dad's pipe and blow smoke through my nose. Frank and I tied the old cow bell to Dad's nightshirt. Heard later (not from Dad) that it scared the wits out of him."

Saturday, November 9th, "Picked apples, 2 crates of Seek-no-furthers, an orange crate of Canada Reds and then some Russets and Tolman Sweets. Frank and the Ryerse's came by hunting. When they got over the fence Colin spilt some powder out of his powder horn. Then the crazy jay touched a match to it. When he came up he was black as a nigger, and all the hair under his cap was singed off. He washed his face at the pump and found it was burned, and hurt pretty badly. He came in and got some powder and coal-oil on it."

Wednesday, November 20th, 1912 "John Wess McBride, his son and Harvey Shand came by. They had been duck hunting at Long Point. We visited John Shand this evening. Mr. & Mrs. Harvey Shand came over and we spent a lively evening. Harvey entertained us with some classy fiddling. They brought out tea and cake at midnight which I bet a cookie was for the Presbyterian tea and bazaar to-morrow night. We finished it right down to the pattern on the plate.

On November 23rd, Toby drove Aunty to the Poor House to take some tobacco to Captain "Fagan" Shaw. They arrived in Simcoe later than expected and the road out to the Poor House was "a holy fright." Auntie's efforts to make anyone hear at the Visitor's Entrance were in vain, so she went to the kitchen door where they could hear a "grafaphone"[sic] playing. "Her knock was answered by a hideous old female who was just crazy enough to work and who said she would find Mary." Mary was the Matron, who told us Fagan had been sick for three months. Aunty went to see him but they could not rouse him. They said he didn't suffer.

On Sunday November 24th, 1912, Toby spent his last day as librarian as Dick was taking charge of the job from him. He came home to saddle Joe and go to Smythe's at Doan's Hollow for dinner. He and Pud [George Smythe] went riding back in the woods. On his return home, a colt they had named The Artful Dodger had jumped the bars of his stall and Toby had quite a chase getting him

*Outdoor rink where Canning Factory later stood. Note Wool Shed, Penman's Knitting Mill behind it and Silk-knit building on right*

back in. The next night they all went to see a Magic Lantern show at A.Y.P.A.

These diary entries, I hope, convey some idea of the life of a typical [?] farm family in rural Ontario at this time. In attempting this history of our church, St. Paul's, Port Dover, I have been more interested in the lives and times of the parishioners, than in the more sterile recounting of prominent members, priests and organisations of the Parish and the dates during which they were active.

Jan. 1st, 1914 "I began the year very badly by allowing the sun to get up before me. ---- Enah and Auntie Maud went over to Mrs. Johnson's Reception tonight, where Winnie was tending door. Mrs. Johnson had sent word over yesterday to have Huby go over in the morning as she wanted a man to be her first caller on New year's Day." [Auntie Alice always hoped for a tall dark-haired man to be first over the threshold on New Years, as it brought good luck for the rest of the year.]

Louise Scott wrote to Enah, April 28th, inviting her to come to Toronto to hear the new organ in St. Paul's Cathedral, where Louise was a choir member. It had been touted as the best organ in North America, and they had hired the best-payed organist in the world to play it. After some protest on Enah's part, that she could not get away, Cousin Clare came to fill in. Enah returned on the train the following night, ecstatic about the organ recital and having had a great time "to the city."

Sunday, July 5th, 1914 "Enah and I managed to get to church this morning." — "Enah had to play the organ as Topsy [Walker] who had applied for the job, and who has been practising, came this morning without her hat and had to go back to the Methodist choir for to-day, where they've eliminated their roofs. The family spent the afternoon in slumber or in literary pursuits."

Life went on in much the same way until the World War broke out. July 30th, 1914 "According to today's reports nothing short of a miracle can prevent a general war in Europe. Austria has declared war with Serbia and Belgrade is taken. Russia is mobilising an enormous army to support Serbia and Germany. Britain and France are all beginning to squirm."

By April 1915 the first heavy casualties are reported in the fighting in Europe. In May the world is shocked by the news of the torpedoing of the Lusitania, in the Irish Sea, with a loss of 1500 lives. By the end of the year Col. A. C. Pratt is recruiting for the 133rd Regiment, which is expected to go overseas.

On Sunday, December 26th, the choir of St. Paul's church wore new surplices for the first time, or as Whit Dixon reported they appeared in the choir loft in their new "shrouds." [money to pay for the surplices was raised in part by selling names, to be

*The 133rd drill on the Gillies lot, under Lieutenant Lloyd Hammond*

*The home of Miss Battersby became the Rectory about 1915*

stitched onto a new quilt, for ten cents a name. There were 48 squares in the finished product and many of them sported eight or more names. This was done by a group of quilters called only "The Willing Workers."]

The quilt in question was recently [2005] brought out of hiding and framed, to be hung on the north wall of the Sunday School for all to see, behind a plexiglass screen, made by Harry Pos.

On Friday, the last day of the year, the girls of the church sponsored a dance in the town hall to raise funds for the Red Cross. There was a big turn-out. At 11.30 p.m. many of the dancers went to St. Paul's for a service to pray for victory for the allies. It had been a very black year for the world.

Monday Jan. 10th, 1916 - "Glad. Law and Marj. Clarke had a Dicken's Evening at the A.Y.P.A. to-night. Dad and Enah sang "What are the Wild Waves Saying." Cousin Willie, Jack Martin and Aunty Maude also took parts. Dad had to be Chairman." Later that month, Zenus MacPherson came to the farm with a petition to ask the Government to enact a bill for total Prohibition. Everyone signed but Toby had wished they had more background information on the bill first.

In early February Miss Minnie Misner left for Egypt, to serve as a Red Cross nurse. Humy Innes and Bill George enlisted for overseas. Later still Ed. Moon and Jonas Green were recruited by

*Reunion of Mr. William Henry Smith, July 1st, 1916*

the 133rd., although there was a good deal of dissension between Col. Pratt, his officers and the rank and file. On July 1st the whole of the population of Port Dover were outraged with Col. Pratt for refusing to give leave to any of the past students of Mr. W. H. Smith, who were serving in the 133rd regiment, at the Armouries in Simcoe. It was the occasion of a huge Reunion for Mr. Smith, long-time Principal of the Port Dover school, and students from the past fifty years had come from near and far to help him celebrate. John S. "Jack" Martin, who had been on staff at one time, acted as Chairman for the event.

Next day, Sunday, Enah and the family were at the church early so Zeitha Barwell could practice the solo she was to sing. Zeitha never showed up, however, and neither did most of the choir. Harry Moon was so upset he resigned as the Choir leader because of it. There was a tremendous thunder storm, that raged throughout the service with very heavy hail. Next day all were talking of the big drive that had begun on the Western Front in Europe. Many prisoners and eleven villages have been captured. On Sept. 16th, 1916 prohibition went into effect at 7:00 p.m. The "City of Dover" was launched with a big crowd on hand, on Sept. 30th. They then had to pump a good deal of water into the hull to clear the bridge, when she was moved down stream. She made her maiden voyage to Erie, with passengers, on July 4th, 1917.

On the first Sunday in August Enah, Harry and the baby attended the morning service in the Presbyterian church, that Enah might hear their newly installed organ. She found it a bit disappointing. On Sunday September 9th, 1917 Harry finished up chores and then despite it being Sunday he shocked up the remaining sheaves of oats, prompting Auntie Alice to comment that he had shocked more than the oats.

The diary notes that the country is now into the fourth year of the war and though the allies are gaining ground the Germans are far from being demoralised. They have plenty of resources in food and manpower, despite losses of over three million men to date, there are nine million in uniform with some four hundred thousand coming of military age annually. Toby notes that "now that the U. S. has come down off her lofty seat of super-civilisation where she was 'too proud to fight' as Wilson commented, and stoops to the barbarous position of a belligerent."

"It is very inspiring to hear the Yankees talk of how they are 'wielding the sword of liberty and democracy' to annihilate a war-mad tyrant whose atrocious deeds of barbarism have shocked their refined natures and provoked their holy wrath. It is a little hard for

*Passenger Vessel, "City of Dover"*

me to understand just why the sword of liberty and democracy was allowed to hang rusting in Uncle Sam's chimney-corner for two and a half years before his refined nature was shocked or his holy wrath provoked etc." There are regular prayers in St. Paul's for the safety of those fighting overseas and for a speedy victory that they may come home. "Jack [John S.] Martin has started teaching Sunday School again."

There had been problems with low natural gas pressure all fall and on Sunday, November 25th, 1917 a notice on the door of St. Paul's announced that there would be no service due to lack of gas. Toby attended the Catholick [sic] service and the rest the Presbyterian. An evening service was held in the Sunday School, "Cousin Willie" gave a very nice address and took charge as Mr. Johnson was in Stratford. The following Sunday Toby was the only one from the farm to get in for matins and after dinner spent the afternoon in courting Marjorie Clarke. They attended evensong and found the church packed, with extra seats brought from the Sunday School, as the Bishop preached and conducted confirmation of twenty-two candidates, five of whom were from Christ Church, Vittoria.

Christmas day service was met with a very small attendance of both choir and congregation, and the church was undecorated. This was attributed in part to the fact that Harry Moon seemed to have dropped out of the choir and church life due to some election remarks made from the pulpit, by Mr. Johnson, the day before the election.

A huge crowd turned out at the town hall New Year's evening of 1918 for a dance sponsored by the

*Lila & Winifred Barrett with Chummy*

I.O.D.E. Toby, Enah, Win, Dick and Dessa Dyer all arrived to find a very impatient crowd waiting for the arrival of the orchestra. Finally, an hour late, a "young duck" from Simcoe came in and sat down at the piano. A few couples danced the one-step to his playing but the majority were becoming very angry and saying so, in no uncertain terms. Art Ryerse found Dr. Cook, who had locked himself in the Council chambers behind the wicket, and demanded that they have proper square-dance music or their money back. Those in charge managed to find some fiddlers and a caller and eventually everyone got their fill of the old-time dances. The party broke up about 2:30 a.m.

By the summer Tim was attending Sunday School and very much enjoying Auntie Wese's junior class. He regaled everyone with his interpretation of the story of the Burning Bush, and Moses standing on Holy Ground. "This man saw a burning bush and a voice came out of it saying take off your boots, because the ground all around here is full of holes, and you will get your feet muddy." As Tim usually took off his own boots whenever he went back to the gully, to keep them from getting muddy, he figured Moses must have done it for the same reason. That same Sunday Toby had met Professor Andrews, who had come to take the morning service. On his arrival he found no choir, nor an organist, but undaunted he held matins and played the organ himself. Toby and his Aunts invited him down to "Riverbank" for dinner after the service. Enah played the organ that night for evensong.

About this same time Dick who was home on leave from the army, had a telegram from Col. Syer offering him a place in a tank battalion going either overseas, or to Siberia. He was very excited at this prospect, as Quintin had already gone overseas as a machine gunner. As it turned out they both ended up in Siberia and would not return to Port Dover until well after the termination of hostilities.

On Oct. 6th, 1918 there was a good turn-out at church, the service being taken by Cousin Willie. Enah played the organ and Zeitha Barwell sang a very pretty solo. That afternoon Toby and Marj. Clarke drove up toward Vittoria for chestnuts. They visited with their friend, Gladys Law in the evening. The next day Toby had help to dig his plots of different varieties of potatoes which he had grown for the Experimental Union, sponsored by the Ontario Agricultural College. To their surprise, the old Ontario seed yielded better than the Green Mountain and some other new varieties. Toby had belonged to this organisation for some time, testing grain and root crop varieties, in an effort to improve on existing stock.

On Oct. 9th, Toby left early for Hamilton where he had been told to report for another medical examination for the Army. After a multitude of questions and tests of his bad knee, in particular, he was upgraded from an E to B2 and given a certificate. He stayed with the Herrings as it was too late to get a train back to Port Dover. Mr. Herring took him to the officers mess in the Armouries and then to a matinee of "The Bells." That evening they attended the Shakespearean play "Julius Caesar," which Toby thoroughly enjoyed.

Due to the outbreak of the "Flu" church service and Sunday School were cancelled from Oct. 20th to Nov. 10th, 1918. On Thursday, Nov. 7th, an aeroplane flew over town, followed by the distant sound of whistles blowing in the direction of Simcoe, and they kept it up for some time. The noon paper reported that the Germans had approached Foch in the French lines under a white flag of truce. In no time the whistles began blowing in Dover and the fire bell was being rung as it was reported that the German delegation had signed an armistice.

That night the whole town was out on the streets. All the kids were out with tin cans and horns making a merry row. The older fellows gathered all the rubbish from behind the stores in town to pile it on the main street in front of the flag pole, where it was lighted to produce a monster bon-fire. Some young fellows produced a barrel, full of tarred pound nets, and set fire to it. Speeches followed from John S. Martin and others, with prayers by Mr. Robertson and singing by the assembled crowd. "Then Cousin Willie got humourous, the kids banged their tin cans, we all gave three cheers, sang God Save the King, then there were more speeches, more singing, more cheers, more noise and everybody just felt good. Every now and then some kid would start ringing the fire bell or Harry Moon would fire his shotgun. All the time cars were tearing up and down the street honking and cutting up as many dido's as a car is capable of."

"When the nine o'clock car came in we found the rumour was denied. Everyone feels that if the fighting isn't over yet it soon will be, and we can have another celebration, when the real thing comes. In spite of all the jollification there were some sad hearts as Ina Nunn and Charlie Long joined the list of those who had succumbed to the flu."

On Sunday Nov. 10th, all hands attended church, which has re-opened. After evensong Miss Martin and Marj. inform Toby that he and Jack Martin are to canvass Prospect hill residents for Victory Bond subscriptions. The Sunday School instigated this effort, to be put in an endowment fund for Esquimaux Missions and to get a shield with maple leaves on it, on which to inscribe all the names of boys from the Sunday School who have been killed at the front. Every Sunday School in the country that buys a Victory Bond will get one. Harry W. Ansley had donated the price of one bond and they now want to get at least one more.

On Nov. 11th, Toby did his canvass, getting a dollar each from the Quanbury's and Carl Colman. All the rest promised something, save Jack Pickford who is peeved at all the preachers for talking politics and prohibition in church. Later Toby took apples to the station, to be shipped to Roy Scott, and found the town decorated with flags. Jack Martin and others gave their employees a half holiday, then the town fathers declared a half holiday to celebrate "the dawn of peace."

*Port Dover Brass Band on parade*

Frank went to Pickfords to thresh and Harry was ploughing, but Toby took Enah and the baby to town at 3:00 p.m. and put Joe in Auntie's barn at "Riverbank." He went up town to join the band in the big impromptu parade. "Everybody in town was in it. Carl Colman had the band's big drum and Harry Moon, Ed. Bagley, Jack Walker and Art Lawson with their horns and several kids with bugles and snare drums. After the parade they settled in the park for a lot of speeches from the band stand where all the preachers, town fathers and returned soldiers were collected. " They told me to come down again to-night, so I polished up my E flat bass horn on getting home, and returned."

"With our horns, drums and tin cans we raised a great hulla-baloo, prancing around Main Street, blowing "Hail! Hail! The Gang's All Here!" – the only thing we could play – until my lungs were sore. Harry Moon and Billie Gordon had a dummy made to represent the Kaiser, we rode him around on a rail, before soaking him in coal-oil and setting him alight. He was finally dumped in the big bonfire in front of the Town Hall. Everybody was out singing, cheering and raising Cain in general. About as much racket as if there had been lots of booze, instead of none."

The following Sunday St. Paul's held regular Thanksgiving services as well as a special thanksgiving for peace, and the following Thursday evening and the next Sunday special services were devoted to celebrating the end of the War, at long last.

On Thursday, January 30th, 1919 Toby, Frank and Enah went to the Sunday School to hear a lecture by a missionary, Miss Wade, on her life in China. It proved very interesting and they continued to discuss it with her as she came back to "Riverbank" to spend the night with Auntie Wese. On February 6th, Toby and Enah attended a presentation for all local men returned from overseas. Reverend Mr. Johnson had helped organise it and he called out the names as R. M. Taylor handed out the five dollar gold pieces each man received. Ed. Moon and Ed. Taylor gave short speeches of appreciation.

Two days later the whole town was saddened by the death of three little boys, two West brothers and Johnnie Miller, who had drowned trying to save the others. They had gone through the ice on the Lake. Ed. Moon and Capt. Macauley, who got them out of the water, made every effort to revive them, but their efforts were in vain.

Tuesday, Feb. 18th, 1919 a letter was received from Dick recounting his trip across the Pacific to Vladivostock through typhoons which caused the loss of one of the ship's propellers. There was an outbreak of typhus in the City, but, as he could not speak the language anyway, there was little incentive to go into the city. They had a picture show, which ran infrequently as it required so much power the street cars all stopped when it was started. The flags in Port Dover were at half-mast in memory of Sir Wilfred Laurier, whose death had just been reported.

On Tuesday, May 6th, 1919 George Pelly arrived on the morning train. That evening they all attended a Memorial Service at St. Paul's, where the Reverend Jenkins, an ex-chaplain, from Brantford, assisted Mr. Johnson in the dedication of the new altar. It was unveiled in memory of all those who had lost their lives in the recent war against Germany.

Through the efforts of the local Women's Institutes a memorial had been proposed, and Rev. H. J. Johnson and Hubert Barrett were instrumental in putting it into effect. The official dedication ceremony was planned for two o'clock on Friday, May 9th, 1919. Toby had polished up his horn and joined the Port Dover Brass Band in time to march up Main Street from the Town Hall to the Schoolhouse, while playing rousing Sousa marches. The Girl Guides, followed by all the school children fell in behind them. On arrival, more marches and hymns were played by the band, interspersed with speeches and prayers, by dignitaries and the ministers of the several churches.

Reeve R. M. Taylor then explained the reasons for planting a memorial grove of fifty Elms on either side of Main Street. John S. Martin complimented the Women's Institutes for their part in the proceedings, pointing out that the soil of Dover was very good for trees. Mr. Robertson concluded with a prayer, followed by the school children singing "Oh! Canada" and "The Maple Leaf Forever." Mr. Neff, the County Agricultural Representative, supervised the planting of the first tree. Mrs. Bell, as President of the W.I., actually planted the first tree with due ceremony. The Band then struck up a lively march and led the whole crowd off down

*Reeve R. M. Taylor*

Main Street to the Town Hall again. Mr. Johnson and Huby were left all alone to plant the remaining forty-nine trees.

The following Sunday Toby was late getting to Sunday School and found Olive Ryerse marking the attendance book for him, as Miss Martin was sick and did not come in. He sat with George Pelly and Frank in church and all three went to "Riverbank" for dinner. Later Toby and Marjorie Clarke took the Sunday School collection up to Miss Mae Martin, who looked quite unwell. They then visited with Miss McQueen [public school teacher] for the remainder of the afternoon. George Pelly and Frank had gone to visit Adah Sovereign.

There was a great dinner party at the farm after church on May 18th, 1919 as Enah brought George Pelly and Adah Sovereign home after church, and Toby had picked up Marjorie Clarke. All complained of it being so late as Mr. Johnson had preached an inordinately long sermon on the subject of having his salary raised. It would seem it may have had the opposite effect in the parish, to that which was intended.

The talk of the town was the bitter Winnipeg strike which had isolated the City from the rest of the country. Another source of great excitement was the news of the aviator Hawker's attempt to fly the Atlantic with his pilot Grieve, in a little Sopworth Biplane. Confused reports by telegraph and the newspapers ranged from their safe landing in Ireland to their having been lost off the Irish coast, or in mid-Atlantic. It seemed the latter report was closest to the truth. Hawker, an Australian, was competing for a $50,000 prize offered by the London Times. News of his leaving

Newfoundland, sparked several other attempts to cross. All failed, but two U. S. Navy seaplanes did reach the Azores.

On Friday, May 23rd, 1919 Toby polished up his horn to attend a school sports day. As the band assembled at one o'clock in the afternoon to march to the school, it began to rain and the students all came down to the park, where the Band entertained them from the band shell. As the rain continued and a crape on George Thompson's door alerted the dignitaries to the fact old Mrs. Hambleton had died, they folded their umbrellas and retired to the Town Hall. Here Reverend Mr. Johnson, the Reeve, Principal W. H. Smith, teachers and other dignitaries took charge. The Band played, there were several speeches relating to Victoria Day, and Inspector H. Frank Cook explained the formation of the Union Jack.

Following this Cousin Clare, representing the Independent Order Daughter's of the Empire, or I.O.D.E. presented the school, through Mr. Johnson, with a flag, neatly folded. Reverend Johnson brought the proceeding to a close with some appropriate prayers. Reeve R. M. Taylor declared Monday, May 25th, would be celebrated as a holiday. Mr. Watson announced to the kids that it did not apply to the school, only to the townsfolk, and they better be in attendance at school. Mr. Taylor took umbrage at that remark and made it very plain to Mr. Watson that he, with everyone else, would have to observe his proclamation. This prompted loud and prolonged cheers from the students.

The town was saddened next day to learn that five year old William Zealand had drowned in the pond, Silver Lake, just below their house.

*Quintin Barrett finally returns home from serving in Siberia*

He and Billie Mills little girl had been playing on a new boat house landing when they fell in. It was thought William was either hurt in the fall, or, too frightened to save himself, whereas the little girl clung to a piling until rescued.

The School celebrated the unexpected holiday with a great Sports day, that had been frustrated by Friday's rain. Enah learned at a tea at Mrs. Battersby's that Quintin was among those to land on a troopship in Halifax. A letter from Dick indicated that he expected to be on the "Empress of Russia" due any day now in Vancouver. There was great cause for celebration. Quint finally arrived June 6th, 1919 but Dick was delayed until June 28th.

The whole parish was invited to a Church Strawberry Social, or Garden Party at the Smythe's in Doan's Hollow Friday afternoon, June 20th. There was a great turnout. Toby joined the Band, in the Town Hall band rooms, at 7:30 p.m. and they attended en masse. Everyone had a great time, getting all the strawberries and ice cream they could eat. Over $220.00 was raised, as well. A special treat, in the form of 21/2 per cent beer, had been ordered for

*Port Dover Brass Band relaxes at Fisher's Glen - Front row - F. H. Stringer, Harry Dyer, Chris Quanbury, Roy Dell, Murray Simpson, seated, Mid Thompson, "Doc" Lemon, Ed. Steele, Harry Blake, Walter Steele. Back row - Ed. Moon, George Slocomb, Charlie Bridgewater, Carl Colman, Ed. Bagley, Lea Corbett, Harry Moon, Tobe Barrett. Among those with drum - Eddie Bond, Brian Varey, Cliff Long*

the soft drink booth. This caused such a scandal among the pious folk present, however, that it was hastily hidden behind a sofa in the house. It was quietly provided to the Band boys later, who wondered what they had done to deserve such a fate, as it was warm, flat and quite un-drinkable.

Toby left with Bill Barwell and Rev. Johnson at dark, but got only as far as the cemetery, when a car stuck in the mud blocked their way. While they waited a couple of kids told them there were human bones on the side of the road nearby. They went looking and while Rev. Mr. Johnson lit matches, Toby groped in the grass, until sure enough he discovered a human skull. On hearing the story next day, Harry insisted that they drive out to see it and they ended up bringing the skull home with them. The Band were kept busy attending Strawberry Socials.

To celebrate July 1st, 1919 the Band played on the "City of Dover" on the Lake and on their return they played all evening in Buck's Orchard beach Park. Pete Holmes opened his new Casino and Quint, who had partnered with Allan and Dick Tibbetts in the expanded bath houses on the beach, had a very good day. He also operated his half finished refreshment booth, and though the ice cream he ordered never arrived, he did well from soft drinks and cigarettes. There was the usual sports competitions, a Callithumpian parade and something new, a baby show in the bandstand.

Frank and Toby went down to Sunday School as usual on Sunday, October 19th, but did not have regular lessons as it was Children's Day and the pupils were readied to go to matins as the choir for the day. They filled the chancel and sang well. Rev. Ralph Mason preached a sermon directed at the youngsters and "they never wiggled all through it." Nancy Dyer sang a solo to Enah's accompaniment on the organ.

On October 30th, 1919 Harry spent the whole day and evening figuring and filling out the complicated income tax forms. It rained all day which suited his mood very well. The next day Frank attended a Halloween Party, put on by the Women's Institute, in the Town Hall. Toby's pullets just began to lay eggs. Everyone attended both services at St. Paul's as usual on November 9th. Zeitha Barwell came over to the farm to practise with Enah as she was to sing at a programme in the Town Hall next day, when the Prince's flag was to be presented to the municipality for winning their objective in the money raised for the Victory Loan.

Toby was at the Exhibition in Toronto on November 11th helping Mr. Neff, the Ag. Rep. with a Horticultural exhibit for Norfolk and staying with his cousin Roy Scott. He noted that everyone was to stop work at eleven o'clock for two minutes, throughout the whole Empire, at the request of the King. They complied at the Exhibition grounds and then everyone joined in singing "God Save the King." That night he and Neff were part of a Reunion celebration of a local Battalion and later took in an open air dance on University Avenue.

On going in to church on Nov. 24th, 1919 it was learned that the roundhouse had burned down destroying two engines that were housed in it. The following Sunday, besides the benefit of the service, everyone caught up on the extensive damage done by a near cyclone the previous night, which destroyed windmills and blew down trees and unstable buildings. A new building Kolbe's were building and the big drying kiln at the brickyard were destroyed.

John Walker and others of the choir are canvassing the parish for funds to buy a new organ for the church. Sunday, December,

*Engine 906 on the Turntable in front of the Roundhouse*

21st Harry and Enah spent two hours in the afternoon at choir practice. Then after tea Enah and John Walker drove to Hagersville to hear an organ in the Methodist church. The last day of the year was spent drawing ice from the pond to fill the ice house and whooping it up at a Women's Institute sponsored dance in the Town Hall. They got home at 2:00 a.m.

On Sunday, January 18th, 1920 as the congregation of St. Paul's was assembling for matins the fire bell rang, and on going outside the firemen could be seen getting the engines out of the old jail. A crowd followed to L. G. Morgan's house where the smoke was billowing out of the windows. Apparently Mr. Morgan had upset a coal-oil stove in his room, and being so crippled could do nothing to put it out or escape the fire. He was horribly burned and beyond help by the time Val Leaney reached him and brought his body out of the burning house. He had called Miss Morgan but she could do nothing due to the suffocating smoke. Miss Newell was almost suffocated as well and was only semi-conscious. There was no service held in St. Pauls as a result of the tragedy.

Sunday, February 8th, 1920 found both Mr. Robertson and Mr. Johnson sick and as a result everyone attended the Presbyterian service. John S. Martin and a student took charge to harangue those present, at great length, about the Forward Movement. That evening a Union service of the two parishes was held in St. Paul's church, where Cousin Willie Tibbetts took charge and gave a nice address. This was followed by Mr. Bose, the same Presbyterian student, who spoke again, at great length, to an overflow congregation about the Forward Movement. All this was leading up to a major financial drive for the movement, which it was hoped would provide food and clothing for those starving in Europe, and to those in heathen lands that find themselves in similar circumstances.

Mr. Johnson was still ill in bed on Wednesday, the 18th, 1920 but it did not prevent Charlie Innes and Nellie Barber from getting him out of bed to marry them. They had intended to have Reverend Mr. Ward, of St. John's, do the deed but it had been too stormy to get there safely, yet they were determined to be married at once. Miss Newell, who had told Auntie Wese about it, saw them arrive at the Rectory in Isaac Johnson's old covered bus and thought it was the hearse, which had caused her considerable concern.

Jack Martin expressed pleasure with the progress of the Forward Movement campaign and told Toby the Bishop was pleased with Norfolk's effort, which made them the first in the Diocese to reach their target. Jack and the Bishop were very displeased with Reverend Johnson, however, who he learned had been offered two other parishes and had refused to accept either of them.

About 3:00 a.m. on Friday, March 5th, 1920 a fire, that began in a shed back of Patterson's Drug Store, completely destroyed the Post Office block. Dick and Molly Tibbetts lost everything, as did Cousin Loll, they being fortunate to escape with their lives. Dick attempted to open the Post Office safe to save any thing of value but was driven back by the heat and smoke. A temporary P. O. was opened in Harold Sloan's old ice cream parlour and The Drug Store is moving into the little building of Colman's, south of the Commercial Hotel block.

Although some of the sheeting had blown off the steeple at St. Paul's the previous fall, many were unprepared for the announcement by Mr. Johnson that it was thought to be unsafe and a meeting was being held to consider taking it down. Col. Smith and Jack Martin seemed to agree. Roy Scott, Toby and Jack Walker climbed up to inspect it and felt that with some minor repair it could be as good as new. They argued that it would not only destroy the beauty of the church, but would remove the most outstanding and picturesque feature of the town itself.

Roy put up such a strong argument for retaining the steeple at the meeting on Monday evening, March 29th, that Mr. Barwell, Hubert Barrett and Cousin Willie Tibbetts were named to a committee to have Bill Rankin, Perce Ryerse and Jack Spain check the old steeple, and advise them on the best course of action. This they did Tuesday morning and came to the conclusion that it was not necessary to demolish it, as many at the meeting had argued in favour of doing, immediately.

Monday, April 5th, 1920 Toby attended a meeting of the Select Vestry to act as Secretary at Reverend Johnson's request. He returned to the Rectory to copy the minutes into the record book afterwards. Mrs Johnson treated Toby to crackers, cheese and wine that were left from the afternoon party in the Rectory following the wedding of Perce Dunkin and Miss Bagley. It was Perce's wine they were making merry with and to this Mr. Johnson added a cigar for Toby's enjoyment. He was so late he spent the night with Auntie Alice, at Riverbank.

Some members of the congregation are working at funding for the church steeple. Toby and Frank got lists of potential donors from Mr. Freeman and in the next few days Toby got promises of $5.00 from several. After attending the regular meeting of the Tuxis Boys on May 20th, he finished his canvass list collecting a promised grand total of $46.00. On Sunday, May 23rd Mr. Johnson dedicated the memorial font presented by Miss Buckwell in memory of her parents, Alfred and Louisa Waters Buckwell and their family. This is the font used today. It replaced a small alabaster font, the gift in 1859 of Mr. O'Reilly, who brought five of them from Ireland, giving a slightly larger one to Memorial Church, Port Ryerse. The one in St. Paul's had first been used in Christ Church Cathedral, in Hamilton.

It was about this time that Rebecca Scott, whose parents, Roy and Vernon were visiting at Riverbank, attended St. Paul's Sunday School for the first time. On her return her great Aunts were both surprised and amused by her report of the morning lessons. She told them that they sang a hymn about "The Mother's of Sailors, who brought their children to see Jesus, but the 'derned' disciples turned their backs (on the children) and sent them to the Park." The hymn begins with "When Mother's of Salem their children brought to Jesus, the stern disciples turned them back and bade them depart."

On Sunday, June 27th, 1920 Toby spent some time educating his brother Frank as to how he should look after the Sunday School library. He could no longer take care of it, as Marjorie Clarke had convinced Toby to take over her S. S. class, when she returned home to Haliburton at the end of the month. Toby's correspondent's course in commercial art, was beginning to pay off, as well, and he was being asked to make up advertising signs for many businesses in town. He was painting new signs on the bath houses for Quint and his new partner in the business, Joe Thompson.

Mrs. Battersby held her sale, which attracted a huge crowd, on the afternoon of Thursday, August 12th, 1920. John S. Martin had bought her beautiful property, overlooking Silver Lake and Goosey Island. The family continue to attend Church twice each Sunday as well as Sunday School. Enah relieved Mrs. Andrews as organist on many occasions. On Sunday, September 26th everyone in the family turned out for a well attended service to celebrate Harvest

*The Captain Battersby house with hanging dormers added by John S. Martin. Present owner Scott Malcolm debates how to replace them with original windows*

*Silver Lake & Goosey Island*

Home. The church was beautifully decorated. Mr. Ward, of St. John's, preached a good sermon at evensong.

Toby and Auntie Alice left by train for Haliburton where he and Marjorie Clarke were married on October 16th, 1920. They returned to settle into the Zealand cottage on Prospect Hill for the coming winter. On November 16th Marjorie's trunk of possessions arrived by train from Haliburton, and they were truly settled in. Auntie Alice was the first to call and "break bread" with them.

They both settled in as teachers in the Sunday School, Marj. taking Mrs. Smith's class and Toby teaching the Tuxis boys. On November, 19th, 1920 they used complimentary tickets of Enah's, to attend Wilson Pugsley MacDonald's musical farce, in the Town Hall, entitled "In Sunny France." It was of special interest to Port Dover folk, as the playwright/poet's grandparents, the Pugsleys, lived [in the house south of the present Beer store] on St. Andrew's St. and the cast of fifty players were drawn from local talent. It was enjoyed immensely by all those present, especially the dances by several little girls.

On Sunday, January 2nd, 1921 Toby provided a little different emphasis for his Sunday School class. They all assembled at 2.00 p.m. at the farm, since named "Cnochfierna," meaning Fairy Mound for an oval mound in the gully. The group, "one with a bottle of cider sticking from his hip pocket in a most un-Sunday School-like manner," hiked cross country to the Lake. They crossed Black creek at the wintering site of the Sulpician missionaries, and on to the shore. A bit further down they crossed into George Hammond's bush, where they picked a good deal of Wintergreen. From there they headed up the

*Toby Barrett & Marjorie Clarke are married in Haliburton village*

Plank Road to the Dog's Nest, where they struck west on the 2nd concession road back to the farm. The boys then headed for their respective homes, wet and muddy, and as happy as "mudlarks," having enjoyed a great adventure in the great outdoors.

On the 16th, Mrs. Johnson invited Toby and Marjorie to dinner at the Rectory. A she had to prepare it first, they ate at three o'clock. Because of so many cases of Smallpox in the parish, Mr. Johnson's normal afternoon service in Vittoria was cancelled, and the church was closed. Toby is working at making an illuminated scroll for Reverend Mr. Johnson. He was also playing in a local orchestra for dances and at a Hockey Concert on the 31st of January.

The Concert began with demonstration dances by little girls. Then Marie Mitchell, aged eight, played the violin very well. Mary Crone, Agnes Sterling and Lila Barrett gave readings. Zeitha Barwell, Charlie Nunn and a Mr. Hodgkins all sang several songs. A boxing contest followed between Charlie Warren and Captain Robinson, who could not contain his mirth at Charlie's efforts in the ring. After the Captain's second had shaken the rocks out of Charlie's gloves, Charlie was at a disadvantage against Capt. Robinson's prowess with the gloves. He proved quite adept at leaping at the Captain's face, then ducking between his legs, however. He was eventually floored and Skinner Manning counted him out.

Frank Lemons' orchestra, which played for dances all winter, was made up of Cam McBride, violin; Mrs. Frank Lemons, pianist; Karl Lemon, second coronet; Frank Lemons, solo coronet; Charlie Blake, clarinet; Jim Ryerse, and Toby alto & bass horn. Respectively. There were always great meals, including oyster suppers, provided at these affairs and they usually carried on into the wee small hours of the morning.

Sunday, February 13th, 1921 Mr. Johnson reminded the congregation that it was the tenth anniversary of his coming to St. Paul's church and this parish. He reviewed the work of the church in the past ten years, attempting to show the progress made had been very satisfactory. He then announced his acceptance of the parish of Parkhill. He did not know when he would be moving. That afternoon Toby and Frank took the Tuxis boys, his Sunday School class, on another long hike up Black Creek. When they returned to the farm Zeitha Barwell and Frank Lemons were practising their roles in the play "H.M.S. Pinafore." Harry had the part of Dick Deadeye and Harry Moon was Captain Corcoran.

There seems to have been considerable friction over Mr. Johnson's ministry among various members of the congregation. Toby was rather upset by it and commented after the [Women's] Guild put on a farewell tea for the Johnson's on Wednesday, April 6th, 1921 that; "They are a bunch of hypocrites, all right." The following day he helped, with several others of the parish, to load the Johnson's belongings in readiness for moving out of the Rectory. They were staying with the Harding's until after the Sunday, April 10th services, which would be Reverend Johnson's last official duties to the parish.

A very successful Father and Son banquet was held in the St. Paul's Sunday School on Thursday night, April 14th, 1921. John S. Martin and Jack King were very much involved. There was an excellent meal followed by several speeches and "other nonsense." Jack Martin had been urging Toby to take over the job of Clerk of the Select Vestry and he had been arguing that the management of the Sunday School, and the book keeping there, was all that he could handle.

Jack Martin kept insisting as Mr. Barwell was definitely giving the job up and he wanted to get the affairs of the church on a more business basis. He even offered to pay $50.00 annually, which Toby refused, agreeing finally that if Marj. would keep the books he might attempt the secretarial part of the Job. On approaching Marjorie on the subject, he got a flat refusal, however. She said she would tell Jack herself as well as make a few suggestions about some of the men who were doing nothing in the church. The next day as Marjorie went past the Martin's, Jack ran out to plead with her to agree to take it on, she consented.

# Chapter Fourteen

# The Early Years of Canon Cornish

**The Reverend David John Cornish, 1921 - 1952.** Canon Cornish was born near Streetsville, graduating from Huron College in 1906. He was ordained a Deacon and became curate to the Venerable Archdeacon A. C. Hill at Trinity Church, St. Thomas, that same year. On December 31st, 1907 he married Helen Agnes Stuart and served for the next four years in the parish of Granton. A ten year incumbency followed, in October 1911, when he moved to Christ Church, in Forest, Ontario. In August of 1921 he and his family moved to Port Dover.

The Sunday after Reverend Johnson's departure, on April 17th, 1921, John S. Martin as Warden, arranged for the Bishop's secretary, Mr. Doherty to take the service. As Marjorie Barrett had met him at the Lake Couchiching Conference she piloted him to the Martin's for his dinner.

The following Sunday, Mr. Doherty again took the service, and Mr. Barwell, who, as Warden, had been looking after the church's affairs, gave all the church books and the collection, to be counted, to Marjorie Barrett, after she, hesitantly, had agreed to take on the task of keeping them. After spending all afternoon and evening at it, she had the receipts and expenses squared away and every thing balanced to her satisfaction.

At this same time John Walker, a stalwart choir member, had undertaken a personal campaign to increase the financial well-being of the church and was proving to be very successful at it. Meanwhile, the only other major subject of heated debate among the parishioners, locally, was the vote for the non-importation of

Ida Ruth Backhouse, wife of Hugh Massey Barrett II

Hugh Massey Barrett, who died at his farm north of Port Rowan in 1902

Liquor into Ontario. This was won by a 150 vote majority in Port Dover, and by 100,000 votes province-wide, causing jubilation among all those in the temperance movement.

On April 20th, Dick Barrett, who had been moved to Montreal from Saskatchewan by the Royal bank, surprised everyone by arriving home in the middle of the night, to stay at Riverbank.

Early the next morning, Aunt Ida, who had been living at Riverbank since the loss of her husband, Hugh Massey Barrett of Port Rowan in 1902, died unexpectedly. Reverend Mr. Ward of St. John's came down with the Bowlby's for a service at the house at 9:00 a.m. on Friday, and as the roads were too muddy to use automobiles, Faulkner's team and double carriage was used to transport the body to Port Rowan for burial. They were gone all day, returning at 10:30 p.m.

Everyone in town seemed even more involved with practices for the play "H.M.S. Pinafore" as opening night drew ever closer. The dress rehearsal did not go well, in part because Doc Lemons

> The Captain 'e says to
> Dick 'e says
> I'm a sober man and true
> And the tar that can make
>    me crack a smile
> Is a better man than you
>
> Old Dick 'e gives 'im a
>    ugly leer
> And 'e rolls 'is quid awhile
> Then as he spit 'e won
>    the bet
> For 'e made the Captain
>    smile.
>
> This wager was won by
> Dick Deadeye fore-mast-jack
> from Capt. Corcoran aboard
>    H.M.S. PINAFORE.
> MAY 3rd 1921

*The "HMS Pinafore" wager won by Harry Barrett, alias Jack Jackstraw*

arrived half drunk, and could neither sing nor remember his lines. However, the following two nights, they brought the house down, with stellar performances. It was a full house of enthusiastic townsfolk on both nights.

I have a framed H.M.S. Pinafore cap tally with a dime sewed on it, stating that Dick Deadeye [Harry Barrett] had won his bet of one dime that he could make Captain Corcoran [Harry Moon] laugh. He achieved this by interrupting his dialogue with the Captain long enough to remove an imaginary cud of tobacco from his mouth, walk to the ship's gunwale, then toss it overboard. These plays, put on in the Town Hall under Mrs. Ethel Steele's direction, were the highlight of the long winters of bad roads, often impassable due to snow drifts or bottomless mud, and boredom.

In July of 1921, the Chatauqua came to Port Dover for the first time and entertained with plays, music and lectures for most of a week. There was still no regular priest at St. Paul's, but the Reverend Anderson from London took the majority of the services. Enah, also was pressed into service regularly as organist as Mrs. Andrews, the regular organist was often unwell. By September she had given up and Enah was now the full time organist again. Many people were visiting John S. Martin's home, especially on Sundays, to see the herd of fallow deer he has established on the hill below his newly acquired home [the Battersby house] on Prospect Street.

On Sunday, August 7th, 1921 Reverend David J. Cornish, who had arrived in town late the night before, took his first service in St. Paul's. There was a very large congregation at both matins and evensong and he made a very good first impression on those present.

On Sunday, October 16th, 1921 the church was beautifully decorated for Harvest Home. Doc and Mrs. Lemons sang a duet. Mr. Cornish had circulated a letter inviting the recipients to attend the thanksgiving service, and to consider making a special donation toward putting hydro in the Church and Sunday School. Many parishioners did not get the letter, though several of the Methodist congregation did. The response was very good, however.

Next day Toby and Marjorie begged the day off to celebrate their first anniversary. Taking Josey, a picnic lunch and their old courting buggy, they drove up around Spooky Hollow and Normandale, looking for sweet chestnuts. They had a grand outing and brought home a washtub full of plump and delicious nuts.

The following Saturday evening the Tuxis boys, with Toby as their mentor, were entertained to supper by Marjorie. Lila Barrett came to help prepare the food. Mr. Cornish spoke to the group and his friend John Dunn played for them. It proved a very enjoyable evening. The next day was Children's Day so the pupils met at the Sunday School and went in a body to the church, where the choir was made up of children only. Nancy Dyer sang a solo. Two boys took up collection. Mr. Cornish baptised Bill Wamsley's baby as well. This was John Landon "Buck" Wamsley and the first of many baptisms to be performed over the years by Canon Cornish in St. Paul's. The Mason's attended evensong in a body, marching to the service from the Lodge Hall.

On Tuesday night a reception was held for Reverend Mr. & Mrs. Cornish in the Parish Hall, which was full to overflowing. Mr W. "Cousin Willie" Tibbetts was chairman. He, Mr. Barwell, Jack Martin, Dr. Cook, Col. Smith, W. J. Thompson and Sam Morris all made very flattering speeches. Mr Cornish responded, although he appeared ill at ease over it all. Coffee and cake followed. The Lemons sang a few appropriate songs, as had been planned, to bring the celebrations to a close. Mr. Farnsworth, a substitute customs official in town at the time, insisted on singing a few songs of his own, which had not been planned, nor would they have been, if those in charge had heard him first.

On November 8th, 1921 Toby reports: "Old Dover looks like old Miss New Rich, with a new set of jewels, as she is gorgeously illuminated with the Hydro Electric, which was turned on this afternoon. It is hard to judge just how grand they are, as the snow makes the night quite bright anyway. They are placed high up on the poles and make the few gas lamps, we were once so proud of, and which are now nearly all out of commission, look like puny candles, in comparison. Aunty Alice considers it a shameful waste of gas when it is so scarce." He also comments on the drastic drop in prices for farm stock and produce, but allows that it is still far better than being out of a job in the City. The depression that followed the World War is beginning to make itself felt in the community.

Mr. Cornish appealed to the congregation for their prayers that the Washington Conference on the Limitation of Armaments should produce positive results. He is hopeful something wonderful will come of it. Others are much more sceptical. He also reported in his sermon one morning, that no priest should stay in one parish for longer than five years. One has to wonder when, in the next five years, he changed his mind with regard to that theory.

Now that Mr. Cornish is the incumbent, the Thursday night Bible Classes have taken on a much more interesting tone, with healthy differences of religious opinion being expressed among the participants. Other church organisations are thriving and Mr. Cornish is being accepted by his parishioners quickly, due in part to his regular visits to their homes, his calm, unflappable nature, and his genuine interest in their well-being. He is soon accepted, as well, by the community at large as he does not restrict his concerns to his parishioners only, but to anyone in the town who is known to be in trouble. The feature speaker at the Father & Son Banquet that year, in the Methodist Sunday School, was Captain Tom Best of the Y.M.C.A.

On Thursday, December 29th, 1921 the second phase of the Memorial Row of elm trees project, dedicated to those local servicemen who had lost their lives during the war, was officially recognised. This consisted of the unveiling of two sets of Memorial gates placed on either side of Main Street. The first set, consisting of two sturdy stone pillars about eight feet apart and joined by a wrought iron fence, were matched by a similar pair on the other side of the street. They were built opposite the school at the southern entrance. A second set of gates were built to the north of the first where St. Andrews Street joined Main Street. Between the two were the memorial elm trees planted on either side of the street in May of 1919. This section of the street was officially named Memorial Avenue.

    This impressive Memorial was made possible by the continuing efforts of the Port Dover Women's Institute who had raised the unbelievable sum of $751.00 to make it possible. As with the dedication of the trees themselves the Port Dover Band led a procession from the Town Hall up Main Street to the first set of gates. Behind them came the local veterans under command of Colonel A. C. Pratt followed by a Company of Norfolk Rifles under the command of Colonel A. A. Winter. Members of the Women's Institute were next, followed by the school children guided by Mr. Joseph Lamb and Mr. T. N. Kaufman. The Warden of Norfolk, who was also Reeve, Robert M. Taylor, retired Port Dover druggist, was Chairman for the ceremony. This was led off by pieces including "Oh God our hope in ages past" played by the Band, prayers and the unveiling of the bronze plaque by Colonel Pratt. Speeches by several dignitaries and songs by the school children followed. "Last Post" was sounded by bugler Charles Bridgewater. The final benediction was pronounced by Reverend D. J. Cornish of St. Paul's Anglican church.

    Plans for the Memorial Pillars had been donated by builder Murray M. Dillon, while others donated their labour to build them. Even then, as now, their were negative thinking persons in the town, who vandalised this community effort a month prior to the dedication. Both Council and the Institute posted $25.00 rewards for the apprehension of the guilty parties. Ten years later a plaque naming those who had made the supreme sacrifice was affixed to the gates.

    On Remembrance Day, November 11th, 1949 the Port Dover Legion, led by their colour party, marched up Main Street, where a second plaque was dedicated by Reverend Mr. Cornish, at the Memorial Gates, to the boys of Port Dover and Woodhouse, who had given their lives for our freedom in W. W. II.

In the early 1960's two things happened to virtually destroy this impressive memorial. The Dutch Elm disease had taken its toll of the now stately trees on either side of Main Street. Then plans to widen the street to four lanes necessitated the removal of the Gates. Upon their demolition the stones were recycled into the Memorial Cairn in Powell Park, while the bronze plaques were installed on the cairn's western face.

From January through March of 1922 Mr. Cornish missed several services due to a bout with Rheumatic Fever. William Tibbetts, Lay Reader, and others officiated at that time.

On April 4th, 1922 the funeral of Miss Clare (Clara) Langs, a well known resident of the town, was held from the church. Miss Langs, born August 5th, 1850 was the daughter of Ezekiel Foster Langs, born February 14th, 1818, and Maria Holmes. Her father Ezekiel was the second of eleven children born to Jacob and Phoebe Sovereign Langs, on a Windham township farm, near Round Plains. Miss Langs, a registered nurse, had been for many years a nurse and governess to a wealthy family in Seattle, Washington. Upon retirement she moved back to this area, living on McNab Street, Port Dover with her sister, Phoebe Louise Langs. When our parents took us to visit "Cousin Phoebe" who by then was a very reserved, rather frail old lady, we were a bit fearful, and somewhat in awe of her. She died on October 20th, 1936.

The fifth son of Jacob was John W. Langs, who married Charlotte Ansley of Port Dover. Their daughter Charlotte Malenda Langs, born in 1849, married J. H. Herring of Hamilton. Their son, John Henry Herring Jr., married Eugenia Beatty, and moved to New Bedford, Mass. He was the donor of the new organ in St. Paul's, in 1923, to the memory of Miss Clare Langs.

*Miss Clare Langs*

*The Early Years of Canon Cornish 331*

Another to be closely linked with St. Paul's, Port Dover was Jacob's seventh child Emily Langs who married my Great Grandfather T. B. Barrett, in 1850. Their descendants have had close ties to St Paul's through each generation to the present day.

The eighth child of Jacob and Phoebe Langs was Clara Hortense Langs, born on November 5th, 1829. She married a prominent resident of Port Dover in the person of Ozias Ansley, who owned a metal and tin-smithing business at the foot of Powell Park, on the north-west corner of St. Andrews and Park Streets. Their son, Harry Wilmot Ansley, married Beatrice Lees and became a prominent businessman of the town. Their daughter, Charlotte Emily Ansley, married William E. Tibbetts, and they and the descendants of both families figure prominently in the life of Port Dover and the parish of St. Paul's.

*Charlotte Malenda Langs, wife of J. H. Herring & her son John Henry, donor of the organ*

In the early hours of May 29th, 1922 at the home of midwife Mrs. Law, at 425 St. George Street, your scribe of this rambling account made his noisy appearance on the scene. In keeping with the latest theories of the day, for the mothers of new-born infants, he and his mother were kept to their upstairs room for a full two

*Beatrice Lees, wife of Harry Wilmot Ansley*

weeks before being allowed to return to life on our recently acquired twenty-five acre farm, a part of Lot 12, Concession 3 of Woodhouse township, on the Cockshutt Road.

Here, I am told, my first crib was the partially open, second drawer of a sturdy old dresser. I was on my way to a childhood of carefree, and happy experiences, roaming the fields and woods or playing for hours on end along the creek or in the barn, where cattle, sheep and horses became my pets and an integral part of every day life in the country.

*Clare Langs as a young lady*

*Woodstock Pipe Organ invoice for St. Paul's Pipe Organ*

The donation of the new organ to St. Paul's in Miss Clare Langs memory necessitated the holding of five Sunday services, commencing on December 10th, 1922, in the Town Hall, while the organ, with its many impressive golden pipes, was being installed. The Christmas service was held in the Presbyterian Church. On January 14th, 1923 the parishioners were able to return to a reopened St. Paul's. On January 21st, 1923, Bishop David Williams, of Huron diocese, officially dedicated the new organ, presented by J. Henry Herring of New Bedford, Massachusetts, in memory of Miss Clare Langs.

*Marjorie Barrett, holding Alice Louisa "Gay" following her baptism. Toby, Dorrie Clarke, Rev. David Cornish, Louisa "Auntie Wese", Mrs. Lawrence Skey, Harry B. in cart*

On February 14th, 1923 funeral services were held for Captain Leslie Battersby. Lenten services were cancelled, however, due to the extreme cold. On May 31st, Reverend H. J. Johnson officiated for the baptism of my cousins, David Yerex and Clayton Scofield. On June 1st, 1923 the wedding of Sam H. Morris and Frances Slocombe took place. On August 14th, 1924 Knox Presbyterian Church celebrated their 75th anniversary. Doris Marie Kitchen was baptised in St. Paul's.

On June 27th, 1925 the wedding of two very popular members of the congregation took place when Allan Tibbetts married Zeitha Barwell. On July 5th, Dorothy Mary Barrett was baptised. Also in July of 1925 the shingles on the Sunday School were replaced chiefly by volunteers, and the old shingles were gathered up by two of the work force, Toby and Frank Barrett, for use at their farms for kindling.

334  *The Parish of St. Paul's*

In 1925 Reverend F. A. Robinson, a well known evangelist, spent the whole summer at St. Paul's. One August Sunday with the help of the great evangelist of the day, Reverend Hill, a very high powered programme was presented to the congregation. The Port Dover Band was looking forward to a special excursion to Erie, Pa. on the ferry "Colonial" on September 7th, 1925. This never took place, however, as the Colonial burned to the waterline on September 1st at Crystal Beach. Miss Battersby died that same evening.

Mr. Cornish noted on October 11th, 1925 that Radios were becoming very popular and common in the community. It seemed significant as well that fewer people were attending both matins and evensong, apparently thinking one service on a Sunday was sufficient for their religious well being.

On Monday November 2nd, 1925 the Port Dover Band members all turned out to receive $17.00 each as their share of the season's proceeds. They then proceeded to the home of Mr. Ed. Bagley to serenade him on his retirement from the Band after fifty years of

*Ed. Bagley, Mary Bagley, Toby Barrett, Frank Barrett, Alice Parke, Marjorie with Gay, Irene Pickford, Winnifred Barrett Yerex, Louisa Barrett, Harry B. & David Yerex*

continuous service. He said he retired, not because he wanted to, but because he felt he was no longer doing justice to the horn. Harry Moon presented him with a gold-headed cane suitably engraved. Mr. William Henry Smith, revered Principal of the Port

*Auntie Wese in nursery with Gay on her first birthday, Nov. 20th, 1924*

*Cecil & Winifred Yerex, with son David*

*Family at "Riverbank" - Alice Parke, Toby, Frank, & Quintin Barrett, Hattie Barrett holding David Yerex, Winifred Yerex, Louisa "Wese" Barrett, kneeling W. H. "Harry" Barrett holding Harry B. Barrett*

*Port Dover Brass Band on steps of old Town Hall in Powell Park - included in group is Bruce Dell, Harry Moon, Matt. Truesdale, Francis Henry Stringer, Bob Rankin, Ed. Steele & Ed. Bagley*

Dover School, who had become a member of the Band sixty years before, came over and regaled the members with the history of Port Dover's Band from the early days. He told them it was formed in 1860, about the same time as the town bought the town bell which still records the hour from the clock tower. He told them of the world renowned clarinetist, Charlie Petit, who received his initial training from one of the early Port Dover Band Leaders. He noted that in the early days the membership was primarily made up from workers in the several flourishing enterprises in the town.

For some time the ladies in the Shand's School area had been concerned that due to often impassable roads, young families and farm chores, they were unable to attend church and Sunday school on a regular basis. Miss Clara Campbell, teacher at Shand's, Flossie Shand and Marjorie Barrett met on Thursday evening, January 6th, 1926 to organise a Sunday school in the Schoolhouse. On Sunday January 16th, at three o'clock the opening of the first meeting was advertised locally and Toby, who was school caretaker, had a good fire going to warm the place up. It proved a disappointment as only six people came and my sister and myself were the only children.

On succeeding Sundays the number coming out for instruction gradually grew, but it was very slow progress. Janet, Max and Charles Monroe were the most faithful in attendance. Reverend Mr. Cornish came out on a few occasions to try and breathe life into the pseudo-Sunday School without a great deal of success. The venture lasted for a couple of years and finally fizzled out.

One Sunday morning in the spring of 1926 Mr. Cornish preached on Prohibition and the evils of alcohol. On discussing the subject after the service with my grandfather, Mr. Cornish claimed that he never saw any evidence of drunkenness down at the Summer Garden, attributing this to the beneficial effects of prohibition.

My father at this point joined in the discussion and said he remembered the old Pavilion dances, in the wild and wicked days of the open bar, where there was always an orderly crowd of merry-makers. Furthermore Mr. Buck, the proprietor, did not find it necessary at that time to have a "burly man of brawn" at the door to prevent drunks from entering, whereas Ben Ivey now had Mr. Cronk on duty, for that very purpose, and he nightly earned his keep.

*Terrace Inn or Palace of Pleasure on NE corner of St. George & Walker Streets, Port Dover*

As further evidence to disprove Mr. Cornish's claim, Toby told him Quint had seen only the night before, Captain Milton Jones of the M.V. Elsie Doris, the fishery patrol vessel, "pickled to the ears." Although normally as sober as the next man, Captain Jones had fallen in with a young fellow whose father had served with him years before on the "Vigilant." In Quint's version of the evening this fellow had a whole suitcase of various liquors and Captain Jones had felt duty bound to sample them all. It was further pointed out that none of the local bootleggers seemed to be complaining of a lack of clientele, either.

Although most roads had not improved that much automobiles were becoming more frequent on them. Ben Ivey had acquired the ultimate in motor cars when he bought a Stutz automobile. Morley Buck also had a high-priced vehicle. Johnnie Walker was the agent for the Nash automobile and was selling a few of them. My uncle Dick purchased a deluxe, four door model, super six Nash from him for three thousand dollars.

George Cruickshanks, of Simcoe, was pressuring Dad to buy a Chandler at $1,550. with little success. My grandfather, claiming he shuddered with apprehension every time he saw us in the buggy with a week's groceries, empty egg crates, and those of our feet that would pack in, — the rest dangling over the edge of our old rattletrap buggy, — told Dad he considered a motor car in our case to be a dire necessity. He was also willing to help financially on condition that my Mother was the driver. His argument being that when Dad headed home in the buggy and frequently fell asleep, old Queen got him home safely, but in the case of a dumb motor car no such guarantee of safety existed.

Once the word was out car agents appeared from all directions. Dad had promised Johnnie Walker he would not buy without looking at the Nash, however. The upshot of all this was the delivery, for about $1,500.00, of a reasonably priced Nash, light six, four door sedan. A big sales feature was the fact it had solid disc wheels, not wooden spokes, and four wheel brakes. A month or so after acquiring it a red metal triangle was affixed to the back bumper, with the words four wheel brakes, proudly inscribed on the three sides of the triangle.

Mother was then given several lessons by Johnnie in the pasture field in front of the house while the rest of us hung on the gate cheering her on. The way it leaped the dead furrows, it must have been a very sturdy automobile. Although the state of the roads was still a limiting factor, in the winter or in wet weather, we were now able to attend church and Sunday school on a much more regular schedule.

On Sunday, November 7th, 1926, I was required, quite reluctantly on my part, to walk down to church with my parents. Imagine my glee on finding there would be no service as Mr. Cornish had strained his back lifting a stove and was unable to hold a service. Instead, Dad and I with Cecil and David Yerex, walked up the beach and back. It was a beautiful fall day. On our return we stopped to visit with Dave Waddle, where David and I were enthralled by his old fashioned music box.

Friday, July 1st, 1927 marked sixty years of Confederation and Canada's Jubilee. Port Dover went overboard and in debt for the occasion, celebrating for all of four days. The 91st Highland Regiment of Hamilton were in attendance and added greatly to the prestige and colour of the celebrations. Bob McPherson, the town's celebrated piper, with his own band of pipers, combined with the pipe band and bugle band of the Highlanders, gave the local Brass Band a tremendous boost during the ongoing festivities. The annual parade on Friday was a highlight with floats representing all the provinces of the Dominion. That evening the Highlanders put on a spectacular ceremony of "The Trooping of the Colours" before a large and enthusiastic audience, on the school grounds.

Saturday the celebrations continued unabated, and on Sunday morning at 10:00 a.m. the local band took turns with the pipe band and bugle band, in playing, as they marched up Main Street to the Memorial Gates. Here a brief service and laying of wreaths took place. From there the bands formed and marched up to the McQueen cemetery above the mill in old Dover. Here the Highlanders played their lament, followed by the last post in memory of old Alexander McQueen, who had served in the 75th Fraser's Regiment under General Wolfe, reputedly at both the taking of Louisburg and the defeat of Montcalm at Quebec.

The band played in the bandstand in the park that afternoon, and when the Highlanders returned to Hamilton later, they

*Band head for the Bandshell during celebrations on July 1st, 1927, Canada's Jubilee*

accompanied them to the station, playing "Auld Lang Syne" and "Bonnie Dundee." The Officer Commanding and the old Pipe Major thanked them profusely and bid them a fond farewell. The Pipe Major was said to have been the Queen's piper at Balmoral Castle, and the only piper in the British Army to hold a commissioned rank as a Lieutenant. Sid Beaumont said he had heard him and his pipers playing in the front lines in France during the first World War, an experience never to be forgotten. That evening Reverend Mr. Cornish took a prominent part, representing St. Paul's, in a combined church service in Powell Park.

Monday July 4th, 1927 the band was on hand again to celebrate American Day, as there were a great many American visitors in the harbour. There were to be yacht races and base ball games between Canadians and Americans. Dickie Edmonds, the revenue officer from Simcoe, spoiled the fun in this regard, however, by searching all the American boats for liquor. Highly incensed by this treatment, the Americans all pulled out for home, doing nothing for the intended "hands across the border" theme of the day. This left a bad taste in everyone's mouth in more ways than one. The Canadians were furious with Dickie, who had no authority for his high-handed behaviour in the first place. The Dominion Day celebrations ended with a Street Carnival that night.

I was now attending church quite regularly, sitting either with my Grandfather or with Aunty Alice. They both sat in the very front pew, he on the left and she on the right, in what had become known to all as the Barrett Pew. This often got me in hot water, for if my cousin David Yerex joined us we rarely behaved appropriately. Aunty, on any sign of restlessness, would immediately sit between us, to diligently monitor our behaviour. We, therefore, preferred to sit with my grandfather, who let us get away with much more. This postponed the dressing down we invariably got later.

The family from the time of St. Paul's being opened had a reputation for regular church attendance at both the morning and evening services. From the 1860s to the time of the children leaving home, the Barrett pew was filled by the growing family. Their father made sure that even Hubert and Clarence, who were usually up to something, behaved themselves.

One minor annoyance to them both was the lady who always sat directly behind them, and was forever picking lint, hair and other bits from their clothing. The boys hatched a plan. The next Sunday the lady in question could not resist the sight of a bit of white thread on Hubert's shoulder. Deftly retrieving the offending bit of thread she discovered, to her horror, that it had no end. Threading a needle, the boys had pushed it through the shoulder of Hubert's jacket, removed the needle and put the spool, to which it was still attached, in his jacket pocket. Needless to say the annoyance of "lint-picking" ceased.

Family stories of the boys endless pranks amuse their descendants to the present day. On one occasion, armed with a loaded shot gun, they crept up under the window where their father was enjoying a quiet snooze. At the loud report of the firearm, Fa leapt from his chair, shouting his strongest curse whenever he was upset; "Jupiter Almon, boys! Do you want to scare your poor mother to death?"

On another occasion, having been up creek and shot a groundhog, they pried a molar from the jaw of a cow's skull, and returned home with their trophies. While Hubert bound his jaw with a bloodied bandage, Clarence dipped the tooth in more of the blood of the woodchuck. They then appeared before their father, Clarence implying that Hubert had had the tooth he held out to him extracted from his jaw. Looking at it in amazement Fa exclaimed; "Jupiter Almon, boy! I can scarce believe my eyes, you best lie down and rest."

Now that I was being introduced to regular Sunday School and the instruction of Aunty Wese in the Junior's Room, and as I moved into more senior classes, I was often allowed to go across the road and into Uncle Hubert's back yard, with my cousin David, until picked up there after church. On presenting ourselves to Uncle Hubert, or Gramps as we all called him, he would invariably ask us what we had learned in Sunday School. Our answers often being vague or evasive he would undertake to give his spin on the bible stories we told him we had learned. His interpretation was always much more interesting, colourful and exciting than that presented to us by our dedicated Sunday School teachers.

*Hubert Baldwin Barrett*

His stories of the disciples, or as he called them the boys, and their behaviour with that red-head, Jezebel, on a Saturday night in Jerusalem, held us spellbound. Whole new insights into life at the time of Christ were opened up to us, as we heard his version of Christ walking on the water or fishing with Peter during storms on the sea of Galilee. Gramps also quizzed us on various texts and verses in the Bible and their meaning. When asked our favourite verse we were stumped, upon which he told us his was; "Peter said; I go a-fishing."

Often he would accost us with a riddle. What was the colour of Zebidee's white Horse? or, Who was the father of Zebidee's children? The answer to the latter might not be as certain as we found it, in this day and age. Then, "Harry B., what was the slipperiest day in Jerusalem?" The answer to the latter riddle involved Absolum and his donkey.

Two other family riddles, that have come down through our family, and perhaps only have meaning to us, were first introduced to David and myself by Gramps.

"Why is a Raven like a writing desk?" Answer: once we were stumped, "Nobody knows."

"Why is a brick like an elephant?" Answer: "Because it can't climb a tree." I could go on.

I once overheard my father and Canon Cornish discussing Uncle Hubert. Canon Cornish's parting remark was; "Hubert Barrett has a greater knowledge of the Bible than any man I ever met. He does not always use that knowledge in the best context, however."

Christmas Day, 1927, began at five-thirty a.m. in our household, when I, aged five, and my two younger sisters awoke to check out Santa's contribution to the festive season. As the Diary reports "confusion reigned supreme." It goes on with "We managed to get through breakfast and by way of experiment we all got ready and went to church. We stuck it out through Communion service but it was a terrible ordeal, and I think it will be some time before we try taking all three again."

"Miss "Allie" Buckwell asked Marj. if it was her young one making all that racket in church and opined that she should have

*Ward Sovereign, Toby Barrett holding Alice L."Gay", Lucy Scofield Sovereign, Marjorie Barrett holding Dorothy Mary, Harry B. Barrett & Adah Sovereign Pelly*

*Adah Pelly, Dorothy Mary, Cat & Alice L. "Gay" Barrett in hammock*

been gagged. Poor Jack Riddle who was in the same seat with us endured the agony up till the sermon and then 'folded his tent like the arab, etc.' Most of the congregation were very tolerant and said they behaved pretty well, which was rankly false. Harry B. was pretty good but the other two were like a pair of electric chipmunks. Marj. took Gay up and left her in the front seat with the rest of the family when she went up to Communion, but in the midst of a prayer she escaped and came clumping down the aisle to where we were, making as much racket as an armoured elephant."

On Wednesday, March 28th, 1928 the whole town was concerned as one of the Kolbe tugs, the Altawondron, with Captain Johnnie Matthews and crew of four, had been stuck in the ice off Long Point, after going to lift their nets last Friday. Prayers were said for their safety in St. Paul's at both matins and evensong. Two of the crew did get ashore over the ice for provisions from Port Rowan. In the last two days, however, they had been driven some nine miles south-west of the Point and though several tugs had gone out to free them, they had been unable to reach them. It is now feared that they will be running out of provisions and fuel.

On Thursday Henry Misner had attempted to break through the ice with the tug "Jean F." and an aeroplane from Camp Borden had flown over them, dropping food and fuel. That evening the tug "Racey" returned to port bringing crew members, Harry Phillips and McLeod and announced that the rest of the "Altawandron" crew were safe. Captain Matthews and Murphy had reached the "Jean F." over the ice hummocks, but the "Jean F." was now stuck tight and her rudder was jammed against her propeller by the ice floes. A Swede, the remaining crew member of the "Altawondron," had been taken into Port Stanley by a tug from there.

The weather remained very stormy with strong east winds. On Saturday Shelley Cook, Lighthouse Keeper of the east end light, telephoned that he could just make out the "Altawondron" sitting high on the ice flows, but saw no sign of the "Jean F." The fishermen however felt she was reasonably safe. An icebreaker from Ashtabula was on her way to try and free them. That afternoon an army plane flew over town, dropping a message that the "Jean F." was still fast in the ice but the icebreaker was making headway toward her and the men were all safe. A map accompanied the message showing their location to now be about thirty miles southwest of the tip of the Point.

Prayers for the safety of the fishermen were offered in all the churches on Sunday April 1st, 1928. As if in answer to them the American Icebreaker came into harbour about noon, with the Jean F. in tow, and the crews of both tugs on board. There was great rejoicing as the tired but very relieved victims of the ordeal set foot

*Fishing Fleet in Port Dover harbour*

on terra firma again. "The Icebreaker" left soon after to recover the still stranded "Altawondron." The ongoing saga had been front page news in all the newspapers for over a week by this time.

On Saturday, May 26th, 1928, the whole family turned out at St. Paul's to see my Uncle Frank and Irene Pickford married. A neat sign, "Happy though Married", was wired to the front bumper as they drove off. Next day, after church, many attended the funeral of Bill Laings. Tobe drove Fred Colman, Jack King, Sam Morris and Dave Waddle to the cemetery. Following the grave-side service they all trooped over to see the foundations of the new Mausoleum being built by A. C. Stewart.

In mid-August an air ship flew directly over the farm and on over Port Dover. It was a Goodyear Rubber Company balloon, and the first one anyone locally had ever seen. It created a great deal of excitement as it silently drifted out over the lake, bound from Toronto for Akron, Ohio.

On August 30th, 1928 the Port Dover Brass Band competed for the first time at the Canadian National Exhibition, most of them travelling there, in the back of a large stake truck. Fortunately they had a large tarpaulin, for as they went through Caledonia the heavens opened, and but for the tarp, would have soaked all hands to the skin. Others drove themselves and their families or friends in their own autos. Chick Weatherspoon who had Ernie Knight, the band leader, with him almost came to grief when his old pick-up caught fire. In a panic Ernie jumped out of it before it had even come to a full stop. Fortunately they found a pail in the ditch, which also had a foot of water in it. A half pail of water thrown under the hood doused the fire and they were on their way again. Ernie, expecting to either be arrested or wrecked before reaching the Exhibition grounds, vowed he would never travel with Chick again, however.

They drew sixth place among the several bands competing in their class. When their turn came it was felt they made a bad start and after finishing several members felt they had done badly and their chances of a prize were nil. Walkerton, Beeton and Petrolia played after Dover and then the winners were announced. The Dover boys could not believe their ears when it was announced that Petrolia was first, Port Dover second and Goderich third.

They were all with Ernie when he was presented with their prize of $200.00, and those who still were doubtful of their actually doing so well, had their doubts dispelled.

The Anglican Young People's Association, A.Y.P.A., had been started in St. Paul's Parish, perhaps as early as 1926. My parents attended a meeting in the Parish hall on November 5th, 1929 and having enjoyed the meeting joined the organisation. A list of members from its inception to the outbreak of war is included in the Appendix. On Tuesday, December 3rd, 1929, Jack Fenton, a young Engineer, graduate of Trinity College, Dublin, and recently arrived from Ireland sponsored by my grandfather, gave a very interesting, illustrated lecture on his native land using slides he acquired from the central Sunday School Supply Centre in Toronto. He was employed by A. C. Stewart in designing the new east pier in the harbour.

The A.Y.P.A. was a very active organisation within the Church during the 1930's. Many talented members met weekly in the Sunday School or in members homes for a wide variety of programmes. They competed with plays, debates and similar activities with their fellow Anglican members from Simcoe, Waterford, St. John's, St. Williams and Port Rowan. They were also active in a Deanery, or Local Council Organisation of Young People as well. They adopted a Sunday School each year and collected presents and useful articles for the children in often remote or poorly served communities.

Their meetings opened with the singing of a hymn, followed by prayers, often led by Reverend D.J. Cornish, who was very much involved as their mentor and guide. An evening of skits, new and interesting games, cards, singing, speakers on topical subjects, etc. followed. Movies, Books, and plays were reviewed. For example; Harry Waddle spoke on "The World Fair", Oscar Sutor on "Coin Collecting", Knud Rasmussen on "Bull Fighting in Spain", having witnessed one as a 15 year old in 1925. One evening a serious discussion was held on "Ways to Improve Port Dover." More Factories and a Gymnasium were recommended. Meetings ended with a social hour, refreshments, a hymn and Benediction.

An unusual incident occurred on Sunday, January 12th, 1930 and enlivened the beginning of the new year for the congregation of St. Paul's. It was reported as follows; "The service proved entertaining if it wasn't very instructive. Jonas [Ryerse] occupied the prayer desk arrayed in a surplice and led in several prayers. The choir, Mr. Cornish and Jonas all right turned to say the creed, which, seemed rather amusing, after the unholy row caused some years ago when Molly [Tibbetts] and Mrs. Gibbons, having done it all their lives, [they were war brides] turned toward the Communion table in an unostentatious manner. They were asked at that time by Mr. Cornish, at the behest of some cranks in the congregation, to desist."

"Mr. Cornish also mildly rebuked the congregation for not turning out to the Vestry Meeting and [for] showing such a lack of interest in the financial welfare of the church. They are about $300.00 odd in the hole, principally due to the fact that they pay the organist $3.00 a Sunday and Jack Walker, as Choirmaster, $60.00 a year. As a final thrill the McQueen girl sang a solo which contained several blood-curdling war whoops, and in the midst of which she stopped, turned to the organist, and coolly asked her to start a certain section over again as she had got on the wrong track."

The month of February, 1930 was devoted to celebrating the seventy-fifth anniversary of the opening of St. Paul's church in 1855. On Monday, February 10th a special church supper was held in the Parish Hall and in spite of very stormy weather and snow-blocked roads it was very well attended. Those present enjoyed an interesting programme of entertainment and history of the Parish. The Bishop was in attendance on Sunday, the 16th, to take part in a special celebration service to commemorate the occasion. The A.Y.P.A. held a very successful Pancake Supper in the Parish hall the evening of March 4th, and many of those attending went on to a Heather Club concert in the Presbyterian Church afterwards.

On Sunday, April 6th, 1930 Tobe and Marjorie, left the kids with Bessie Andrews, a live-in girl, freshly arrived from, her term for her birthplace, "The back parts of Donegal," in Ireland. They drove down to a special evening service which was in charge of the A.Y.P.A. "Jonas [Ryerse] read the prayers, Billy Cornish the psalms. Young Fulkrod read the first lesson, Jack Fenton read the second. Tim [Barrett] and the other Fulkrod kid took up the collection."

As January, 1931 drew to a close everyone got a bad scare when Crosbie Morgan was found unconscious on the floor of his home, overcome by fumes from his gas stove. He finally recovered, however. Captain Johnnie Allan, who had been very low for some time, died and was buried on January 28th. Reverend Perkins, who had charge of the service, "thundered long and vehemently." I was very upset to learn that Mr. Tote Smith, who had a small store between Miss Giles and the Royal Bank, had died.

He was a spritely little man, whose store was full of clocks. To go in on the hour was bedlam to some, but, to me a delight, as several clocks began chiming pleasantly, while others clanged and tolled the hour, in a wide variety of sounds and notes. David and I stood enthralled in front of his cuckoo clocks, to watch the bird pop out, to "cuckoo" loudly. Dad reported of the funeral: "The church was packed, which was to be expected, as he was a friend to everyone. He will be greatly missed in Dover and I hate to think of his old sociable store being modernised."

As few roads were even gravelled properly, getting around in wet spring and fall weather was hazardous for automobiles. Few trips were made to town under these conditions, without having to fix a flat tire, another ever present hazard, or having to get a team of horses to pull you out of the ditch or an unexpected mud-hole. When too muddy for the car, we often reverted to Queen and the buggy, my sister Gay and myself, sitting on a wooden bench against the dash-board. We actually looked forward to these returns to pre-Nash days, when this was the way we normally went to church, or to town on Saturday nights to shop. The only minor hazard for us was our proximity to the intermittent exhaust from the "one-horse-power engine," old Queen, ever present only inches in front of us. When snow drifts became too deep, the cutters and bob-sleighs were often the only means of getting around. They had the added advantage of being able to leave the road entirely for the fields, if conditions were bad enough to prevent the use of the road.

In early February it was reported that Mr. Hair, whose family has farmed east of Renton for generations, had died at eighty-six years of age. "He died in the room he was born in. Nor is his an isolated case by any means. Jack Shand, for instance, is the fifth generation of Shands to have occupied that farm. Willie Sidway, Alex

England and Willie Nixon are all third generation, at least, and there are many old men in the locality and I suppose all over eastern Canada, working the farms that their Grandfathers, Great Grandfathers or some more remote ancestor cleared. Therein lies one of the reasons for the conservative (not politically speaking) attitude of the countryman compared to the general energetic restlessness of the urbanite. Another fine day."

March 14th, 1931 was a banner day for those who had signed up for electric power. At noon it was turned on from the new power line installed along the Cockshutt road. The first surge blew several fuses and shattered some light bulbs, as Stub Osborne, the electrician from Simcoe, had inadvertently hooked us up to the 220 volt line instead of the 110 volt source. For me this amazing advance over coal oil lamps and blackened lamp chimneys, that were forever in need of either filling or cleaning, respectively, was an unbelievable boon, and with the exploding bulbs to usher it into our ken so dramatically, an exciting advance indeed.

For some time now our beloved Aunty Wese had been confined, on many days, to her bed. Her heart was tired out as Dr. Cook told us, and she seemed at times to have lost all will to live. She questioned her brother, Harry, why he tried to keep her here, for she now hopes every night to find herself in a better place, the next day. Everyone agreed that if anyone was ever ready and deserving of a heavenly reward, she was, though she was always a lover of this world, too. She died peacefully the night of March 26th, 1931.

A great number of friends and relatives attended a brief service at Riverbank followed by the funeral service of the Prayer book and no more, as insisted upon by Aunty Alice. The church was packed to overflowing.

## MISS LOUISA BARRETT

In 1877 a dearly beloved and revered lady began teaching in St. Paul's Sunday School and continued teaching all beginners with scarcely a Sunday missed for over 52 years.

No one ever forgot Miss Barrett and the sweet persuasion of her smile, nor did they forget her teachings. Half a century of continued and consistent Christian teaching most surely leaves a lasting mark upon children who receive it at their most impressionable age. It is felt by all who knew her, that here indeed was a saint walking and working among us. How we loved and looked up to her! And strong was her spirit upon us as we grew up and went away from home, strong in the knowledge that she and her sister, Mrs. Parke, would pay us a welcome and welcoming visit when we returned. These sisters were faithful and effective visitors to all Church and Sunday School members as well as to all newcomers. They meant a great deal to us all.

Besides teaching and visiting Miss Barrett was for many years President of the W. A. and a great worker in the Church, especially at Christmas season when miles of cedar rope were made for the adornment of the Church.

Miss Barrett in her gentleness seemed to epitomize all the beatitudes. She was not merely a teacher of spiritual things, however, but by her example showed us that practical Christianity could be one's daily life. We think that on the day she left us in 1930, God would have extended both hands in welcome and would be glad to have her in his higher service.

In 1875 a young deacon of the church by the name of Frederick Renaud was appointed to St. Paul's, accompanied by his mother, who was an ardent worker among young people. It was her influence which developed Mrs. Parke and Miss Barrett into the wonderful church visitors they became. It was during Rev. Mr. Renaud's four year stay in Port Dover that St. Paul's Sunday School room was built. Previous to its completion, Sunday School was held, first, in the Scofield residence above the present store owned by Mr. Thomas Caley. Later the classes were moved into the Church.

As noted in the chapter on Masonry, Mr. John S. Martin died about nine o'clock on the morning of Wednesday, May 13th, 1931

*Sketch of John S. Martin by Toby Barrett*     *Harry Wilmot Ansley*

after a long period of slow decline attributed to overwork more than anything else. He had sold off all his famous White Wyandotte poultry, known the world over as "The Bird of Curves."

Many Masons of the parish of St. Paul's were especially interested in attending a regular meeting of Erie Lodge No. 149, A.F. & A.M. on Monday evening, June 29th, 1931. Clayton Ansley, of Petersham, Mass. attended, specifically to view the Altar he had presented to the Lodge in memory of his Grandfather, Ozias Ansley and his Father, Harry Wilmot Ansley. He amused those present by pointing out that he had been born at almost the exact spot where the Inner Guard of the Lodge was now sitting, as the Ansley home was on the corner now occupied by the Masonic Temple.

On Sunday, August 2nd, there was a big turn-out of town folk to watch the Oxford Rifles parade, with great ceremony, to a special service in St. Paul's. In addition to their own Band, they marched to the music of a contingent of Highland Pipers and a Bugle Band. They were encamped for a week on the Fair Grounds, where the Composite School now stands, to drill and to experience life in the field.

On Friday August 28th, the town was saddened by the death of Crosbie Morgan. It was also the day of the picnic for the children of St. Paul's Sunday School, when Mr. Cornish and several parents of the congregation were pressed into service to drive the pupils to the St. Williams Re-forestry Farm. This was a favourite destination for such outings as picnic tables were set among the trees on the north side of the pond and there was ample room for games and competitions as well.

The funeral from St. Paul's, of Mr. Crosbie Morgan, on the afternoon of August 30th, was a very impressive ceremony as he was not only a prominent Mason, but a veteran, with W. H. Smith, of the Fenian Raids, of 1866. Many prominent and high ranking Masons took part in the impressive masonic service. Members of the Militia of Norfolk attended in their colourful dress uniforms, as well as a large party of Veterans, for a military service, including a firing party, who fired a parting salute at the grave-side.

A large number of Erie Lodge members, with their chaplain Reverend D.J. Cornish, attended a Masonic service in the Cheapside Anglican Church in Haldimand, on Sunday, September 13th, to honour their elderly country Doctor, Dr. Sherk, who was leaving the community he had served for so long. Mr. Cornish took the service. The old church there is of interest to members of St. Paul's as it was the parish of the grandfather and great-grandfather of our own John Strickler Martin. The ancestors of John Evans, whose blacksmith shop at the top of the Winding Hill was a favourite haunt of mine, were also parishioners of the Cheapside Anglican Church.

Although the great depression was being felt more than ever, as it continued to "depress," the citizens of Port Dover and Woodhouse, seemed to decide en masse, to ignore it. Everyone was in the same boat, so everyone came to the aid of any one member of the community who was in particular difficulty. We became even more close-knit, as the economic situation for so many worsened.

To pay for the installation of hydro, in Shand's School in the winter of 1931-32, a series of square dances, with Caller Jack McKenzie, were held in the larger homes in the section. Sponsored by the Marburg Women's Institute, participants brought food, Mr.

Harvey Shand and Mr John Evans, to the piano accompaniment of Hattie Barrett, sawed away on their fiddles until four and five o'clock in the morning, and the community shed their worries, at least for the moment, and thoroughly enjoyed themselves. Attitude toward our circumstances became of far more influence and importance than money, or the lack thereof. As Dad mused in his diary: "Everyone seems to be agreed that the Depression is really having a beneficial effect on us all. We are all so hard up that we have quit worrying about it, and as we have no money to spend on sprees away from home, we stay home and have far more fun amongst ourselves. After all, for innocent and unalloyed fun and merriment, a good big gathering of congenial friends and neighbours, with the shackles of propriety shaken by old time music and old-fashioned dances and unperturbed by the presence of strangers, dignified and grand, are the conditions most conducive. They will breed light hearts and happiness, in hard times or good."

"Mr. [Harvey] Shand last year had an attack of shingles brought on by financial worry. This year he is much harder up but has fiddled the blues away and looks and feels ten years younger. He takes considerable credit for this state of affairs, as it was his Golden Wedding party that opened the festive season, and his mellow old fiddle has been twanging merrily ever since."

Church members, too, enjoyed teas and card parties, with Reverend Mr. And Mrs. Cornish being often in the centre of it all. Dick Harding, our Welsh Herdsman, who for twenty years was responsible for our dairy herd of Milking Shorthorns, joined St. Paul's choir. Like most of his countrymen he loved to sing and was a real asset where the music of the church was concerned.

In the midst of all this the community was shocked and saddened by one terrible tragedy. On February, 2nd, 1932 Mr. Martin received a telegram that Mr. Cope, had been killed in a motor car accident in New York State. From the diary:

"The news was staggering and it seemed hard to believe that Cope; the incarnation of vivacity, humour and good fellowship, could be dead. As he was alone no one knows exactly what happened except that his car skidded and crashed into a pole. He must have been travelling at high speed and was killed instantly. Mrs. Cope, Mrs. Martin and Miss Cope were all in Florida. The funeral

*St. Paul's at Easter 1932*

was a Masonic one and of course a large one. As someone said in the Lodge-room, 'to have met Cope was to know him and to know him was to love him.' For him, it was no doubt better that he should go rollicking into the next world, in the same way he rollicked through this one. Sickness and suffering might have robbed him of his cheeriness and kindliness, so that, as was the case with poor John S. Martin, his loved one's memories of him would be darkened by the remembrance of a man, that was not their man at all."

The diary describes Sunday, February 28th, 1932 as "an Orgy of Church Going." Our whole family, with Jack Castles, who for over twenty years was shepherd of our Shropshire flocks, and Miss Campbell, attended the morning service of St. Paul's. "We all went down again in the evening to hear Mr. Boyle, at the Presbyterian Church. Following that service we went over to St. Paul's to attend what was called "A Sacred Musicale." At this the Choir, assisted by Miss Marie Mitchell with her violin and Mrs. McGaw MacDonald with her cello, entertained a packed church of enthusiasts."

On March 2nd, 1932 another stalwart of the parish of St. Paul's died in the person of Mr. Barwell. On Saturday, March 4th, "the Masons were out in force for the funeral of one of their most dedicated members, who was well liked, and will be sadly missed in the Lodge where his work was always precise and dignified. He was never critical, but kindly and friendly, to young and old alike among the members. He had been in poor health for a long time,

*Bishop Seager from portrait in Trinity Church, Simcoe*

so his passing brought a certain sense of relief to him and to the family."

March 27th, 1932 was Easter Sunday with large attendance by the faithful of St. Paul's. The evening service was particularly well attended, when the choir sang an Easter Cantata in place of the sermon. From the diary we learn that Dad had picked Aunty Alice up to take her to the service and as a result we sat with her in the front pew. His father sat further back in the church "to better appreciate the auditory effect from the cantata."

"Unless present plans are upset, I occupied for the last time the seat that has been regarded as the special property of the head of the family, I suppose since the church was built. Harry B. sat beside me. By next Sunday the Wardens propose to have new seats installed. It is foolish sentiment on my part but the removal of the old seats seems to me like sacrilege."

"My most vivid recollections of Fa [his grandfather, and founding member] are of him standing where I stood tonight repeating the creed, with one hand on his heart and the other grasping the walnut rail in front of him, in lieu of a sword hilt. No place on earth could be more hallowed to me, or to any of us, than the one where Aunty [Wese] offered her devotions from her earliest childhood."

"Even the caricatures and initials with which I desecrated the old seat in my early youth are more sanctified emblems of early attempts to straighten a bent twig, than disfiguring scratches. However, a sentimentalist cannot hope to stem the march of so-called progress. The old seats are uncomfortable, they say, and out of date, and must be discarded so that we may keep up with the Joneses."

The Early Years of Canon Cornish 357

*The Chancel Arch*

*Altar & East Window*

The Early Years of Canon Cornish 359

The Maytham Memorial

360  *The Parish of St. Paul's*

*The Francis Smith Memorial*

The Musselman Memorial

362  The Parish of St. Paul's

The Tibbetts Memorial

The Early Years of Canon Cornish 363

The Garner-Lowe Memorial

364  *The Parish of St. Paul's*

*The Ansley Memorial*

The Skey Memorial

366 *The Parish of St. Paul's*

*The John S. Martin Memorial*

The Early Years of Canon Cornish 367

The Alfred Buckwell Memorial

368  The Parish of St. Paul's

The Charles Barwell Memorial

The Early Years of Canon Cornish  369

The Choir Memorial Window

The T. B. Barrett Memorial

On March 29th, 1932, as we did not yet own a radio, we learn from the diary: "We drove over to Frank's to hear the Waterford [High School] Choir broadcast over the radio from C.K.G. W. Tim was singing with them and we were naturally pre-disposed to enjoy it, but it was the best thing I ever heard over the air. P. G. Marshall [school choir leader for the high schools of Norfolk] must be very proud of them. Marj. did not go as she had just had a half hour phone conversation with Mrs. Hammond and was tired from standing so long holding the receiver."

On Sunday, May 1st, 1932 we were on our way to church early as we knew there would be a capacity crowd. The newly elected Bishop of Huron, Bishop Seager, was coming for the first time as our Bishop, though he had visited Port Dover many times as a child. He told us that his grandparents lived in the house still located on the south-east corner of Nelson and St. Andrew's Street. He also told us that he had preached in St. Paul's years ago when he was first starting out in the Ministry.

Having confirmed a class of twenty-five candidates, the Bishop next proceeded to dedicate the beautiful memorial window, depicting King Solomon, to the memory of the Honourable John Strickler Martin, who as Grand Master of the Grand Lodge of Canada in the Province of Ontario, at the time of his death, represented King Solomon in Masonic ritual. The new seats were in place and dedicated as well as other furnishings and decorations, made possible by the Martin bequest. With the installation of the seats made by the McCall Furniture Company of St. Williams, the style, begun with the altar and choir seating by the Reverend Johnson, was continued into the body of the church.

My Grandfather and I found the new arrangement of seating in our regular front pew was almost impossible to use, as we had been accustomed. The comfortable old seat back in front of us, had been replaced with a high and distant straight panel. He asked me what we should do about it and I wasted no time in suggesting we move from the front pew to the second from the back pew on the other side of the aisle. To my surprise he agreed. I no longer felt I was under the critical eye of the whole congregation, but could now assume the role of critic myself. I could indulge now, quietly, in a long range project that had been quite impossible to carry out in the front pew of the church. During prayers I began to produce a pseudo-memorial to myself in the form of a tombstone, complete with appropriate lettering, carved labouriously with my thumbnail, into the hardwood back of the oak pew in front of me. It was a long-range project. My handiwork disappeared when the back seat, on either side of the church, was removed.

After the building of "Clonmel" my Grandfather layed out a Bowling Green on the property and soon a good many citizens of the area were enjoying regular bowling. Once lights were installed even more interest was shown, as local competitions were organised among groups and with bowlers from other centres as well. Reverend Mr. Cornish was one of the more avid bowlers and was very good at it. Wednesday afternoon games were popular during the summer and fall as local business men would take advantage of the Wednesday afternoon closing of most Port Dover businesses.

There was a very active group of bowlers in Cayuga and soon challenge matches were quite regular between Cayuga and the Port Dover members. After one such visit to Cayuga Reverend Mr. Cornish discovered, upon returning home, that he did not have his bowls with him. He immediately dropped a card in the mail to the Cayuga Club asking if, by chance, "they had found his bowls lying on their greens, after the Port Dover players had left." On returning from the post office he sat musing in his study and finally, in a non-committal way asked his wife;

"How do you spell bowls, Nell?"

She immediately exploded with: "Dave! You didn't put an 'e' in it, did you?" A messy thought to say the least.

There were other occasions when the good Canon did not seem to be quite with it. On giving out the notices one Sunday morning he requested that members of the congregation assist the Guild on Wednesday evening in providing for a Garden Party they were giving on the previous Tuesday.

I also remember, while sitting with my Grandfather, being intrigued by a sermon Canon Cornish gave involving the antarctic territories. He kept referring to the "artantic" and even though he realised, that there was something not quite right about his presentation, he could not correct it. We, of course found it highly amusing.

Another occasion that amused us to no end, though we had great sympathy for the recipient of our mirth, involved one of the Huron students, who on occasion would fill in when the Rector was absent. This would often be for evensong. On this particular evening we no sooner entered the church, than the almost unbearable stench of skunk assailed us. Everyone knew that a family of them lived under the building, but normally it was a friendly relationship that existed between us.

The poor student, whose name I do not remember, was very nervous to begin with and this unexpected turn of events seemed to increase his discomfort. We understood why when he mounted the pulpit to present his carefully prepared sermon. It was also apparent that he had no alternate sermon to fall back on for with a very red face he hesitantly announced his text to be: "And the fragrance of the ointment filled the house."

The St. Paul's A.Y.P.A. was very active during the 1930's and on Tuesday, December 2nd, 1932 they presented a play to an enthusiastic audience in the Parish Hall. Among those involved were Fern Evans, Eileen Garner, two of the Thompson girls, Bill Cornish, Jack Bayes, Jack Fulkrod, Oral Misner and Jack Fenton. They were all very good, but Oral Misner stole the show as he played the part of an old Sea Captain.

On January 22nd, 1933 it had been arranged with Mr. Cornish that Emily Barrett be christened but as it was pouring rain and foggy Mr. Cornish

A.Y.P.A. Play "Too Many Parents" in the Town Hall Dec. 2nd, 1932

was phoned and told the baby, who had a slight cold, would not appear. Seeing her parents in church, however, he announced the christening would take place right after the service. On leaving church Dr. Cook asked if the christening was off, to which Mr. Cornish replied: "Unless you can produce a baby."

Dr. Cook responded with: "I have already done my part in that department."

The following Sunday dawned with bright sunshine and so the christening took place after the morning service, with Emily taking it all in solemnly and without fuss. The town woke up that morning to learn that Ben Ivey's Dance Hall had burned to the ground during the night.

I was to start in the newly proposed boy's choir on Easter morning, but to my great relief had too severe a cold to go. Poor David Yerex, my cousin, who had promised to attend, only if I did, was the only culprit on hand. We did become regular members later but it was really after I went on the St. Paul's choir picnic with Granny, that I was formally invited to join the Junior Choir, being recruited by the new organist, Mr. George Raymond Martin. He had recently come to town, replacing Mr. Thorburn, as Manager of the Royal Bank. Other Junior Choir members were Charles Monroe, Hubert Jennings, David and Hilton Yerex, Austin and Charles Powell and if I remember correctly, on occasion, Max Monroe and Charles Haller. We all liked Mr. Martin, a short, jolly man, who expected us out for choir practice and took the teaching of us very seriously.

I had the feeling we were merely tolerated by the majority of the balance of the choir. This included John Walker, long-time choir leader, Andrew Lowe, Bruce Reid, Bill Adams, Mrs Arthur (Sadie) Thompson, Mrs. C. O. MacDonald, her daughter Peggy, Mrs. Susie Knowles, Eileen Garner, and others. To our general disgust Sadie Thompson began agitating to have some of the younger girls included in the junior choir as well, notably her daughter Helen. Soon others began to fill the front choir pew across from us in the persons of Barbara Jennings, Peggy Wamsley, Caroline Tibbetts and others. It was not the same.

In October we accompanied Mr. Cornish and the whole choir to the Anglican church in Dunnville in an exchange of the evening services. Charles, Hubert and I found this to be quite an adventure. We all enjoyed singing, and had a good understanding of what was required of us from the teaching of music in public school by Mr. A. W. Marshall. Charles Monroe and I attended Shand's School, S. S. #12, Woodhouse, which was said to be the first rural school in the Province of Ontario, to provide a music programme.

Parishioners, who obviously did not know us well, would often comment on our angelic appearance in our surplices sitting in the front row of the chancel. Mr. Cornish, realising our potential for restless misbehaviour, always dismissed us before the sermon. We invariably headed for Main Street and the ice cream parlour of Harry Moon's, known as the "Green Parrot." Here we could enjoy a cone for five cents while waiting for the church service to finish. Should one of us not have the required five cents, we were not averse to holding back the money supplied for collection, which the choir members collected in little red felt pouches. If we had no collection money on a particular Sunday, the pouches could always supply the nickel, essential to our enjoying an ice cream cone.

Practice for the choir boys was always held in the Sunday School after school on Fridays. Mr. Martin surprised us all one November day following practice by taking us out for supper, followed by a trip to the Picture Show. The following Friday we appeared for practice but Mr. Martin never showed up. It was learned later that he was so engrossed in preparing for a card party for the senior choir that he forgot all about us. He was strict but always a great deal of fun.

On many Sundays when we were growing up there were good arguments for turning out for church or perhaps not going. My Dad reveals his feelings on the subject thus: "My motives for hounding the kids out to church are probably not of the highest, but simply that I am conservative enough to believe, that as we had to go regularly when we were kids, we should bring them up in the same way, in the hopes that they will do the same with their progeny and so on. [I] regard it more, I am afraid, as a venerable custom, worthy to be perpetuated, than as a means whereby the spiritual life will be quickened, although, of course I should be happy, if by chance, it did bear fruit in that way."

As Christmas approached boughs of hemlock and a nicely proportioned tree had to be cut for decoration of the Church and Sunday School. This duty usually fell to Dad's lot, and with us in tow, it was promoted as a great adventure as we headed for an appropriate spot in the wood lot. On Monday, December 18th, 1933, the ladies were busy turning the hemlock limbs we had provided, into attractive wreaths for the church, while the men were busy preparing for a big night in the Masonic Lodge rooms.

Later their Lodge Installation Ceremonies were rudely interrupted by Lidney McQueen breaking in to report a fire in the fish shanties on the creek. It proved to be the shanty for the tug "Wilma." Many raced down to assist the firemen and managed to contain the fire though there was considerable damage to nets, reels and other fishing equipment.

Next day the flag pole in the park was draped with evergreens and coloured lights and a Christmas tree was put up on the corner of the Town Hall. Despite the depression, the festive season would be celebrated in an appropriate manner.

On January 11th, 1934 Dad responded to an urgent request from Mr. Penhall that he drop in to see him. His concern involved the affairs of St. Paul's and the fact that, in his mind, things were being very badly managed. He seemed to place much of the blame with Mr. Abram Hoover, one of the Wardens, and urged Dad in the strongest terms to allow his name to stand for Warden if nominated at the upcoming Vestry Meeting. As Dad left for a dinner at "Clonmel" with the Cornish's, the Morley Buck's, and Aunty Alice he felt he did not want "to become involved in their squabbles." He did sound out the dinner guests however, on the subject. The following evening he attended the meeting of the Select Vestry with the result that he and Art Thompson were rector's and people's wardens, respectively.

On Sunday, January 14th Dad undertook the first of his new duties as Warden by taking up collection with Morley Buck, as Art was suddenly called home. His father had suffered a severe heart attack. On January 19th he spent some time with Mr. Cornish who outlined the duties of rector's warden to him and also outlined plans he had for an extension to the Sunday School. As the income of the church was badly in arrears of expenses incurred, members of the congregation formed teams, on a volunteer basis to canvas the parishioners for help.

After a false start and dreading the exercise, Dad and Bill Wamsley spent an evening making their parochial calls in late February. They called on Mr. Orchard, Gordon Silverthorne and Mr. Stanley at his drug store and agreed that once they got at it, it was not such a bad job after all. They finished at 9:30 p.m. and went up to "Clonmel" where a group of the bowlers were enjoying their winter-time pastime of table bowls, on the billiard table. They broke up at mid-night. After church, on Sunday evening a week later, the wardens had a serious look at the church books at Art Thompson's home. They found them to be in a very precarious state, with the income barely meeting half of the current expenses.

Further bad news was received when Mr. G. R. Martin, St. Paul's popular organist received word that the bank was posting him to Aylmer. Mrs. Glen Ryerse was in hospital hovering between life and death from burns received when she attempted to coax her wood stove into better performance by throwing coal-oil into the fire pot. Orchardists learned that all Baldwin apple trees in the County had been killed by the severe winter just passed.

On Good Friday evening the family and many of the neighbours attended a special service in St. Paul's when the choir performed a cantata "Olivet to Calvary." It was very well received by a capacity congregation. Art Thompson slipped out in the midst of the production, to return with the news that the Detroit Red Wings were leading the Toronto Maple Leafs by one to zero at the end of the second period. The score remained the same throughout the third period and to the disappointment of many, their favoured Maple Leafs were eliminated.

On Saturday, April 7th the St' Paul's A.Y.P.A. hosted a weekend conference with many of the delegates being billeted in members homes. A pot luck banquet was held that evening in the Masonic Hall, which was very well received. Next morning the church congregation was swelled by the many delegates, as well as the Sunday School pupils who passed in their Lenten Mite Boxes.

Mr. Martin's replacement as bank manager was Mr. Theo MacMillan. He, his wife and daughter, Yvonne, were entertained at "Clonmel" on April 24th and found to be accomplished musicians. A very pleasant evening was enjoyed with the ladies at the organ and piano, while Theo proved to be an adept violinist. I went with Dad, Mother, Bruce Reid, Milford Evans and Eugene Smith to Waterford Anglican church on Thursday, May 10th, where our choir, combined with that of Waterford, to sing for a special Ascension Day service. Reverend Henderson of Hamilton preached.

On Friday, May 11th Dad and Art Thompson interviewed Mrs. MacMillan regarding her stipend, as she had accepted the position of organist for St. Paul's. The following day Mrs. MacMillan called Dad, as she wished to speak to the wardens again. Art was out of town. She was concerned about remarks that Art had made about Miss Battersby playing the organ gratis, and the fact she had been told they did not want to pay the same salary as Mr. Martin had received. It was explained to her that the church finances were in a bad state and for that reason only, they could not promise her as much. She was assured that they would do the best they could to maintain the previous salary and she reluctantly agreed to carry on and hope for better times in the future.

Attendance at St. Paul's on Sunday, May 13th was rather meagre as Frank Bond, Manager of the Culverhouse Canning Factory, had invited all our family and many others of the Parish as well as many of the Presbyterians to attend a special service in the United church. The occasion was the unveiling of the new memorial windows dedicated to the memory of his wife, Mrs. F. M. Bond and to his mother. Grace Church was packed with worshippers as a result.

The Synod met in London on May 15th, 1934 and Dad reports as follows: "Feeling my position as church warden made attendance at Synod a good excuse to enjoy a drive and get out of spraying the orchard, and as Marj. wanted new shoes, we hied ourselves to London taking Flossie [Shand] and Harvey and Mrs. Evans with us. It was a beautiful day and the countryside was at its best. We went by Aylmer but were too early to catch Mr. Martin at the Bank. I went over to Cronyn Hall where the sessions were in progress and the place pretty well filled with delegates and clergy. I found a seat beside my old friend, Reverend H. J. Johnson, who was glad to see me and all set to visit. We were in the back and I could not hear much of what was being said, nor was I greatly interested in what I did hear.

Mr. Cornish took me in tow at noon, having me sign the register, as neither of the official delegates showed up. We had lunch in a restaurant full of preachers, with the Bishop at Head Table. We got little to eat and had to wait about two hours for it. I did not go back to the sessions after but sat outside, where Mr. Johnson and I enjoyed cigars and a good visit. We then foregathered with the rest of our party, where Marj. had a chat with Mrs. Johnson in their hotel. The rest of us drove to the McCormick factory to buy biscuits and candy at cut rates. We had tea with the Sharpe's [friends of the Evans] after driving through the University grounds and sat around there until 9:00 p.m. We then came home - a well spent day."

On Thursday, May 17th, 1934 a tradition that had been dormant for about fifty years was revitalised when the Farmer's Market was opened again in the Market Square, or Powell Park. It had been gifted to the people of Port Dover for that very purpose by the town's founder, Israel Wood Powell in 1835. To the pleasant surprise of many towns folk there was a most enthusiastic reception of the idea, by both vendors and buyers. There was also a wide variety of produce and bedding plants available at good prices. It was destined to continue for a good many years.

*Powell Park, with the cannon & bandshell in the 1930's*

Friday, June 8th, 1934 "This has been the kind of a June day the poets sing about, if only we would get some rain, I believe, even the prosaic tillers of the soil, would break forth in song but to date there is no sign of it. Tonight Dick Harding, George Ryerse and I drove to Waterford to attend a Layman's Banquet. We heard the Bishop and Canon Crawford, from Africa, speak."

On Sunday, June 17th "Mr. Cornish prayed for rain at both matins and evensong, and on Monday we got it. If it was due to his intercession, he sure payed for himself to-day. It was the most welcome and the most needed rain we have had for years."

Sunday July 29th, was a bit different as Reverend Ralph Mason preached at Matins and evensong was cancelled in favour of a combined evening service that Reverend Mr. Cornish and the other Ministers in town had arranged. They proposed to continue this for the remainder of the summer. It was held in Powell Park, with some members of St. Paul's boycotting it to register their disapproval. The Reverend Ralph Mason would be heard from more often from now on as he planned to return to Port Dover to live. He had graduated as an Architect from the University of Toronto but never practised. He instead went into the ministry and for many years was the Anglican priest at the Don Jail in Toronto. He had turned his boyhood hobby of stamp collecting into a lucrative business. He being one of the first to issue a regular catalogue, prior to the turn of the century, of rare stamps for sale from his extensive collections.

This was brought home to me quite vividly, as an amateur collector, many years later when Miss Mason, his elderly daughter, smashed up the family car. Upon commiserating with her on her bad luck next Sunday in church she blithely passed it off with the comment; "Oh! Father will just sell a stamp and buy me a new one."

The following Sunday Dad had a call from his fellow warden, Art Thompson, to appear at the evening open air service in the park for the purpose of helping to take the collection. They attended much against their will as that style of service did not appeal to them. Two days later proved a "red letter day" for the family, however, when we all turned out for Tim's wedding to Dorothy

MacPherson of Waterford. My sister Norah stole the show as flower girl.

Sunday, October 21st, 1934 was the annual Children's Service with the Sunday School pupils attending. We boys in the Junior Choir came into our own when we proudly sang a piece we had been practising for some time, all by ourselves. The following Sunday an old, retired Baptist minister, the Reverend Mr. Mead, assisted Mr. Cornish, who had unfortunately broken his arm, with the service. At evensong a large congregation attended to hear Archdeacon Clark, from Brantford, give a soul-felt plea for the Missions.

Other highlights, as 1934 drew to a close, proved to be the family's annual trip to the Royal Winter Fair and my Grandfather's purchase of the champion Newfoundland puppy, King of Kingsley, as a birthday gift for my sister, Gay. Our show flock of Shropshire sheep shown ably by Fred Gurney, of Paris, won many ribbons at the major shows, as well.

Another was the broadcast of the Royal Wedding of Prince George and Lady Elizabeth Bowes-Lyon, heard in Port Dover starting at six o'clock on the morning of November 29th. We had no radio, so relied on reports from neighbours. Shand's School opened as usual for their morning singing lesson with A. W. Marshall that day, but Miss Muriel Brown, quite unwillingly, let everyone go home again due to the decree from Ottawa, supported by the trustees, that all schools close in celebration of the Royal Wedding.

That evening members of St. Paul's attended a Laymen's Banquet in the Sunday School. Four Oxford Groupers attended the affair from London and gave, more or less personal experience, talks. They proved

*Our Newfoundland dog, King of Kingsley*

to be very interesting. The Warden's were busy at this time canvassing the congregation for much needed funds, but with limited success. On Sunday, December 2nd, Mr. Cornish was assisted by Canon Ryerson, of Simcoe, who had recently retired from a career in the United States. Most were not impressed with his efforts. Canon Ryerson assisted the following Sunday and preached the sermon. Most felt that his time in the States had influenced his diction and grammar, which was not as pure as our parish was accustomed to.

Sunday mornings took on a new urgency in our household after February 1st, 1935 when my Mother was persuaded by Reverend Mr. Cornish to return to the Sunday School and take on the senior boys class. This meant getting chores done an hour earlier and all hands readied for the trip to town well before 10:00 a.m. It had been almost thirteen years since Mother had last taught a Sunday School class. Picking Aunty Alice up on the way in that first morning they found Aunty scornful of the whole idea and quite convinced my Mother could not do it.

Toward the end of the month the whole family attended a play in the Sunday School, put on by the young people of the A.Y.P.A. from St. Williams. It was entitled "The Arrival of Kitty" and those attending enjoyed it immensely. Happenings of note in March were the launch of the "Dyker Lass", Salter Watson's new fish tug, with its modern Mayer-form bow. "Crackling arguments" over municipal ownership of the skating rink, which Mr. Hoover was letting the town take over for less than the mortgage and a highly successful Carnival in the said rink.

My Mother was in her element if there was an excuse to dress up and the Carnival at the rink was just that excuse needed. She dressed Charlie Shand as a bride and Janet Monroe as her/his groom. I went complete with bow, quiver, green tunic and mask as Robin Hood and my sister, Gay, as a Spanish lady. There were some lavish costumes, both magnificent and hilarious. Charlie Bridgewater stole the show as Dr. Dafoe accompanied by his "quintuplets" in the persons of Cecil Yerex, Milton Woodger, Alex Spain, George Hallam and George Harbach. Mother was pressed into service as a judge, along with Mrs. Henry Sinclair and Tom

Caley. A special feature of the evening was an exhibition of figure skating by four members of the London Skating Club.

For Lent, Mr. Cornish had chosen to give "long rambling discourses" on the epistles of St. Paul's "as a lenten penance, and tonight I heard him say that some of them had been lost. I wished before he finished that they had lost the whole bunch of them." On April 3rd, 1935 a Vestry Meeting was held with considerable talk but little being done. The deficit was over $200.00 and no real prospect of holding it at that. The diary notes that; "A third of the congregation in church this morning was Barrett's and their connections."

On Tuesday, May 14th, 1935 Dad drove George Pelly, Willie Nixon and Moses Fisher, the town tailor, to London. George and Dad were alternate delegates to Synod. Willie went in search of his wife, a Doctor there, and Moses found a preacher friend who took him to Merlin for a visit with friends. The morning sessions failed to interest them. After lunch they registered and Mr. Cornish attempted, unsuccessfully, to convince them to stay over for the sessions of the following day. Later, as Baden-Powell was at the fairgrounds reviewing the country's Boy Scouts, George, with little trouble, persuaded Dad to drive them down to see him. They returned to Synod about four o'clock, where Willie Nixon met them and they returned home.

A week later Dad returned to London to the Masonic Hall for a meeting of the Chapter. He was accompanied by Willie Nixon, Bill Ferguson, Ernie Hinds and Dr. McGuire. The occasion was the conferring of an Honourary Degree of Past Principal as well as 3rd, 2nd, and 1st Principal on His Lordship, Bishop of Huron. There was a very large crowd in attendance and the banquet and other festivities meant it was 2:00 a.m. before they reached Port Dover again.

One evening in July the McMillan's invited the Wardens and their wives to hear Mr. McMillan Senior play his violin. As he was the winner for many years of the Gold Medal at the Exhibition in Toronto for old-time fiddling they enjoyed listening to his lively reels, hornpipes and jigs. Theo, his son, was a good violinist as well and often played sacred music in church to his wife's organ accompaniment.

About this time Miss Campbell, who stayed with us, decided to take her very elderly father, in his elderly touring car, to visit relatives in Hartford, close by the Six Nations Reserve. This elicits further comment in the diary; "The Hartfordites, as old Mr. Walker would say, 'are whimsical in their ways,' too. Their Church has split and the community is convulsed in seismic bitterness which appears to be characteristic of Baptist congregations. The revolting faction call themselves 'The Church of God' and resemble the Christian Scientists, in that they don't believe in Doctors and the Tunkards. They have a little diversion they indulge in, of washing each others feet, every now and again. Mabel tells me this in all seriousness and I have to exercise great restraint, to refrain from unholy mirth. 'Sech folks' as Mrs. Bagley would say."

My Mother entertained the ten boys in her Sunday School class at the farm where they had a whale of a time. As Dad did not return with the car until dark, the phone was ringing wildly as worried mothers called to see what had become of their boys. Dad eventually got them all delivered safely, however. A week later several of the congregation including the Cornish's, Dr. and Mrs. Cook, the Jennings, the Charlie Martins, Mrs. J. S .Martin, Mrs. Cope and Ethel and several of our family drove to Teeterville, to the camp ground and museum of Mr. Edgeworth. Here they enjoyed a great picnic, the museum and a relaxed afternoon.

The financial situation in the church was not improving and Mr. Cornish confided in his Wardens that, if they were not showing some improvement soon, the church would be forced to close. The following Sunday the organ motor refused to start which delayed the service for some time. Dad went in search of Joe Smith to fix it, but by the time they arrived back at the church, Art Thompson had it running. The regular Sunday School picnic was held on the lawn in front of the hotel at Fisher's Glen on August 28th. Everyone got a thrill from crossing the high rustic foot bridge, over the deep ravine there, to enjoy all the usual games and treats. A Vestry meeting was called to authorise Art Thompson to borrow from the Bank to pay Mr. Cornish his back salary.

On Saturday, September 28th, 1935 it seemed as if the whole town turned out for the wedding of a very popular couple, Eileen Garner to Andrew Lowe. The church was beautifully decorated, and overflowing with spectators and guests. Following the ceremony the guests returned to the Garner's for tea, cake and ice cream. The diary further reports that; "Bill [Garner] had some very smooth hard cider in the back shed, to the door of which there soon was a beaten path. Carl Colman had a few snifters and then spent the rest of the day trying to get Mr. Cornish to come round. He was finally successful, but Mr. Cornish thought a little hot Scotch would have been better. We were then invited in to kiss the bride and after the cider, everybody present looked pretty enough to kiss."

At Thanksgiving we all attended three services, two at St. Paul's and one at All Saint's, Vittoria. Professor Isherwood, from Wycliffe College preached at all three and, with a bit of humour added, was very well received. The choir was out in full force for all services. The next Wednesday, October 16th, a Vestry meeting was attended by the two Wardens, Bill Wamsley and Dr. Cook. They divided among them the names of those parishioners they felt were worth canvassing for additional funds.

On January 3rd, 1936 Art Thompson reported that the fund raising drive had netted $500.00 and the church books were in balance at last. On January 30th, Mr. Cornish convened a meeting in the Rectory of the Wardens, to confer with St. Paul's Club, Sunday School and A.Y.P.A. representatives on the question of remodelling the Sunday School. A lengthy discussion ensued. Two days later a further meeting confirmed that George Pelly would present some different sets of building plans and provide estimates of their costs. A further meeting in the Sunday School on

*Adah & George Pelly*

February 8th was convened to review several alternate plans as presented by George Pelly. A long discussion ensued, but as no firm costs were available as yet, no decision was made.

A meeting was called for 4:30 on February 24th, 1936 to make a final decision, however, on Sunday the 23rd, Mr. Cornish announced it from the pulpit as being in the evening. George Pelly confirmed this with Dad, as Rector's warden, Sunday night and then called at 4:15 Monday to say the meeting was in progress. The confusion over time of meeting put things in disarray and still, no firm decisions were made. The following August the Select Vestry met and decided, to decide something definite about the proposal, to build an addition to the Sunday School. By the end of the month another meeting discussed the pros and cons of the matter until almost midnight but was no further on in a definite commitment to build.

Finally on Thursday, September 24th, 1936 the excavation for the Sunday School addition was begun. On Sunday, October 4th, Sunday School classes were held in the Church as their quarters were filled with tools and construction materials. The footings were completed and forms in place for the basement walls. By the end of November, although there was rubble and old plaster everywhere, much to Art Thompson's chagrin, the new addition was ready for the final putty coat of plaster and eventual occupancy.

The year 1936 was an eventful one in the life of the Parish of St. Paul's. King George V died in January and on the 28th, at 4:30 a.m., I was up and routed out the family to hear the impressive description of the funeral service and procession from Westminster Cathedral. Then at 8:00 a.m. we heard the service from Windsor castle.

On Sunday, March 1st, 1936 a large congregation attended St. Paul's and as the diary reports; "Mr. Cornish had a radio in the pulpit and we heard the King's broadcast speech very clearly. He spoke feelingly and without attempts at histrionics of the deep appreciation he felt at the sympathy that had been evinced by his people, and people outside the Empire for himself, his mother and family. The simplicity of it was very touching and left the impression he meant every word he said."

The whole town was excited this spring, at the prospect of

four local boys, after winning a local amateur competition, competing for an amateur night at Shea's Theatre in Toronto. As Milford Evans, a neighbour, and Bruce Reid, a member of St. Paul's choir, with Knud Rasmussen and Harry Waddle made up the Quartette, Dad was pressed into service to drive them to Toronto on March 31st. They were jubilant over the audition results as it won them the right to compete at Shea's, a week later, and a contract to sing for a commercial for Kreushen Salts.

The commercial was to take place in a Toronto studio on April 8th, 1936, and again Dad drove them down. Bruce Reid asked permission to bring his "honey", Muriel MacDonald, and Dad agreed "as long as she didn't have to sit on his lap." To their consternation, on arrival, they found no one knew about them coming, or of their contract. It appeared that Mr. King, who hired them, had been inebriated at the time, had notified nobody, and had since gone to Chicago. They were told they would eventually get their $30.00 if the contract they had signed was located. To make the best of it they all went to see Laurel & Hardy in "The Bohemian Girl" and returned home. Eventually they went on to appear on the popular Major Bowle's Amateur Hour on radio.

George Pelly, Frank and Tobe Barrett represented St. Paul's at the Laymen's banquet at St. John's, Woodhouse on May 14th, where Dr. McLennan showed lantern slides of the North. On May 21st, the Ascension Day service in St. Paul's was outstanding as fifty-eight members of the choirs of the Deanery of Norfolk took part.

On July 11th, 1936 Mrs. Lawrence W. Skey died. I remember her fondly, from visiting with Aunty Alice, as a tiny, vivacious, old lady always dressed in black, with a cameo at her throat and clutching firmly a black bakelite ear trumpet in her right hand. She was ninety-four years of age. She lived in the brick house, on spacious grounds, on the north-west corner of Chapman and St. Andrew's Street, at 17 Chapman St. East. One of the prominent founding families of St. Paul's, her revered husband Lawrence had been Church Warden, Lay Reader and for many years, Sunday School Superintendent. Upon his death in 1911, the family placed a solid brass plaque in St. Paul's to his memory. The brass lectern we use today, was designed by Reverend Herbert J. Johnson, and

*Lawrence Skey, Long time Sunday School Superintendent & Lay Reader of St. Paul's*

*Rev. Lawrence Skey, son of Lawrence, as a young man*

given by friends, co-workers and pupils of the Sunday School in loving memory of his twenty-five year tenure, in the Sunday School.

The Skey family consisted of eight children, contemporaries of my Grandfather. Russell was a life-time friend of his, whose visits I looked forward to with great enthusiasm. He returned from a trip to California in the mid-30's with a beautiful model sailing vessel, which he had carved and fitted out, while travelling across the continent and back by train. He had named it "The Polly". This he presented to my Grandfather, saying with a wink at me, he knew who would end up owning it. We sailed it regularly on the pond and today it holds a place of honour on my desk at "Riverbank."

Russell admitted at this time that he had always hankered to attend University, and so, at age seventy-five, he had enrolled at the University of Toronto, in an Arts programme. On opening day the professor seeing him in his class, assumed he was a visiting dignitary and invited him to the front of the room. Russell assured him he was quite comfortable where he was as he was; "Just one of the boys, sir."

I also treasure a watercolour of the Port Dover harbour, painted for Russell Skey by his long-time friend, Clarence Barrett. Russell in turn gave it to Frank & Irene Barrett as a wedding present. Irene never liked it and years later she gave it to me. Russell's visits, with accounts of his latest escapades and reminiscences of his boyhood in town, buoyed our spirits immensely. I presented "The Polly" and Clarence's painting of the Harbour recently to the Port Dover Harbour Museum for all our citizens to enjoy.

A brother, Douglas Skey, often visited and invariably sat in front of us in church. He was the complete opposite to his brother Russell, sitting ram-rod straight, in an immaculate blue suit with not one strand of his long white hair out of place. He would look neither to the right or the left and I think was quite shy. Our whole family called him by the same name his mother always used, when referring to him: "Dear old Douglas," for it seemed to fit him perfectly.

A third brother, who returned and often preached in St. Paul's was Canon Lawrence E. Skey, of Toronto. St. Paul's basked in the reflected glory, as well, of a grandson of the original Lawrence Skey, Wing Commander Larry Skey, who was the first Canadian to win

*Lulu Skey, daughter of Lawrence & sister of the Rev. Lawrence Skey*

*Russell Skey, younger son of Lawrence Skey*

the Distinguished Flying Cross - D. F. C. - during W.W II. He went on to represent Trinity riding for the Conservatives for a four year term, in the Federal government.

There was a large congregation on July 19th, 1936 in part due to the many summer visitors in town. Five members of the Church Army were also present and took part in the morning service. The next Sunday before going to church we listened intently, over the radio, to the broadcast of the ceremonies at the Vimy Canadian War Memorial, which the King unveiled.

A special source of pride to our family this season was the success of our show flock of Shropshire sheep at local Fairs and across Canada, under the expert showmanship of Fred Gurney of Paris. This was of special importance to W. H. Barrett & Sons, as our sheep flocks were known, in the western provinces, and good Shropshire rams were in high demand for the breeding of commercial flocks in the Prairies.

On Wednesday, October 14th, we attended St. Paul's for the dedication of a bronze memorial plaque to Henry Morgan, his wife Margaret Benner Newell and their children. Mrs. Brent, Miss and Mr. Brodur, and our family were the only ones present. The parents were born in Ireland and were another of the founding families of St. Paul's Church. That afternoon many of the Women's Auxiliary attended a District W. A. tea held at St. John's, Woodhouse.

On Wednesday, November 4th, 1936, despite a heavy snowfall that continued all day Miss Watson and Aunty Alice came out to the farm for lunch. At four o'clock all hands attended a service at St. Paul's for the dedication of the newly installed Skey Memorial window by Bishop Seager. Ernie Skey and the Williams family from Buffalo were in attendance, along with the rest of the family. The American contingent received the sympathy of those present for having lost their vote the previous day, when Roosevelt swept the Country. The window was presented in loving memory of Lawernce W. Skey and his wife, Mary Frances Buckwell, by their children.

Following dinner at Clonmel with the Bishop and Mr. and Mrs. Cornish, everyone returned to the church, at 8:00 p.m. for a Confirmation service of three candidates. They were Mrs. Harry Ivey, Stanley Mills and Eugene Smith. Mrs. Willie Nixon, due to special circumstances, had been confirmed privately. Mr. Cornish was not quite himself, but for good reason, as their daughter, Betty, had been at death's door for the past week following an appendix operation. The Bishop preached an hour-long sermon to a very small congregation. He stayed overnight at Clonmel.

The diary reports what to many was an earth-shattering event with the announcement at 11:00 a.m. on Thursday, December 10th, 1936 that King Edward VIII had abdicated the throne.

"While there are various views on the subject, and feelings toward him, everyone feels blue over it. He was so well known, popular and had so many manly as well as kingly qualities, that I can't censure him for doing what every man does sometime or other, in greater or lesser degree, that is lose his head over a woman. Why he had to fall for a second hand old bat like Mrs. Simpson, when he had the whole world to pick from is a mystery. I can't help feeling, like a great many others, that there is something else behind it all that we do not know about."

"The Duke of York will be our next King and from all accounts he is a quiet, well behaved gentleman, with a charming family, who will do just as he is told and that seems to be what is needed."

The diary opens January 1st, 1937 on an optimistic note, thus: "The New Year bids to be as bright and prosperous as the weather, which though unseasonable was perfect. "Sun shining, creek running merrily, fields almost green and Jack [Castles] in his shirt sleeves planting a spruce hedge around the barnyard. According to all accounts the depression is over. More money was said to be spent all across the Country than ever before. Orchids and gardenias in Toronto were unobtainable at $10.00 a piece. A dance in Simcoe at the old time price of $2.50 a couple, wheat is worth well over a $1.00 a bushel and there isn't enough of it. More people are killed with cars than ever and we are hovering on the brink of another war. Of course there are still plenty of people on relief but that is easily brushed aside by quoting Scripture, 'The Poor Ye have always with You.' Taxes are higher but Guy Marston [County Road Engineer] has to live and Hepburn wants to balance his budget, so Cheerio!"

Later in the day Dad went into town and after running some errands met Art Thompson at the Sunday School to compare notes on the state of the Parish finances. Again quoting from the diary:

"Sympathised with Art Thompson and Jack Campbell in their altercations with Mr. Cornish. He has fanciful ideas and they have practical ones, so the new building is a series of compromises and is going to cost us plenty. Art has been out on a collecting spree and has gathered in better than $500.00, which will nearly pay our debts. He thinks he could have got more but did not want to pay the budget apportionment in full as Synod would only stick us for more money next year. Besides he wants to keep the congregation a little worried over the finances, if possible, so they will not rely entirely on Dad and Morley Buck and one or two others, eternally pulling them out of the hole."

On January 14th, 1937 Dad and Jack Castles picked up Frank Barrett, George Ryerse and Oscar Sutor and drove to St. John's church hall in the pouring rain to attend the Laymen's banquet. There was a good crowd in spite of the inclement weather and Reverend Mr. Dunlop, from Dunnville gave an especially rousing address. On January 18th there was a good crowd out for the Annual Vestry meeting, which was held in the new "church parlour." Art and Dad were returned as Wardens.

*Miss Edith Buckwell, wife of Peter Gamble*

*Miss Alice Buckwell*

The Parish was saddened by the death of Miss Alice Buckwell, who was buried from Bert Thompson's house, on January 28th, 1937. She was the last survivor of the children of Alfred and Louisa Waters Buckwell, who married in England and later emigrated to Canada. Edith married Peter H. Gamble, Francis married Lawrence Skey, and their son T. D. Buckwell was a Lieutenant in the Canadian Militia. Miss Alice Buckwell presented the font in St. Paul's in memory of her parents in 1920. She loved to cook and competed for prizes in the culinary arts at local Fairs for many years. The Buckwell family moved to Port Dover in 1844 from Brantford. A successful business man, Alfred Buckwell's home was located where the Erie Beach Hotel now stands. Among other enterprises he and his brother-in-law Thomas Waters operated a successful distillery in Port Dover. On Saturday, October 2nd, 1937 representatives of the older families of the Parish, including the Skeys, were present for the unveiling and dedication of the Memorial window to Alfred and Louisa Buckwell and their children.

On Friday, January 29th, the wardens and their wives and the McMillan's were invited to dinner at the Rectory. Following dinner they spent a hilarious evening playing "Buckaroo."

The whole community was shocked to learn of the loss to fire of the magnificent H. J. Falls Department store, in Simcoe, the night of February 13th, 1937. The Boston Bruins versus Toronto Maple Leaf hockey game had just finished when the glow of the fire, seen for miles around, started the rural phone lines buzzing. My parents and several neighbours braved the mud and rain to drive to the site. The diary reports: "We couldn't get out of our minds what a pitiful sight it was, that beautiful store in ruins. We had visions of poor old [Mr.] Falls with his stand-up collar and waxed moustache being gallant to his lady customers and the staid old elevator-man coaxing people into his elevator just for the pleasure of running the thing and telling them what was on the two upper floors."

On February 27th Dad attended a meeting at the Sunday School with Charlie Ivey and Sam Morris where Oscar Sutor tried to persuade them to form, a St. Paul's sponsored, Boy Scout Committee. The seed had been sown. On March 5th, Dad drove Charlie Ivey, and son Charles, Bruce Reid, Gordon Ivey and Oscar

Sutor to a District Boy Scout meeting in Delhi. On Sunday afternoon, March 7th, at 3:00 p.m., Oscar met with Dad and Charlie Ivey to discuss further the formation of a St. Paul's Scout Troop. By 5:00 p.m. they had a plan. A committee, consisting of Charlie Ivey, Dad, Harry Ivey, Bill Wamsley and Sam Morris was formed and Oscar Sutor was officially made the Troop leader. On March 26th I joined the new Troop, with several others, in the Sunday School.

By April we had a large group of boys enjoying hikes up the beach or to the Cedar Swamp for cook-outs, as well as weekly meetings for training in the Sunday School. I had ordered a complete regulation uniform. On Saturday, May 29th, 1937, my 15th birthday, our Troop attended a Scout Jamboree in Mohawk Park, Brantford. Those in attendance, including myself, were Oscar, Gordon and Bob Ivey, David and Hilton Yerex, Archie Morris, Hubert Jennings, Charles Haller, Morley Hagen, Dick Ryerse and Eugene Smith. There were all sorts of demonstrations, contests and humourous skits before a large crowd. Many other troops from far and wide took part. Hot Dogs and soft drinks were provided at six o'clock and everyone dispersed.

There were special programmes for the Church Services, on Sunday, May 9th, 1937, specially prepared for the celebration of the coming Coronation of King George VI and Queen Elizabeth. A large contingent of the local branch of the Royal Canadian Legion attended the evening service and Reverend T. B. Holland gave a description and meaning of the different features of the Coronation Ceremony. The diary reports that: "Mr. Cornish gave notice of Tuesday, instead of Wednesday, for the preparations for the Coronation, whereupon Rodney "Roddie" McKie, who was with the Veterans, corrected him in stentorian tones, much to the amusement of the congregation and Mr. Cornish too, I think. It didn't phase Mr. Cornish, of course, and he thanked Rodney for putting him right." Jacqueline [Yerex] also created a diversion by coming in, halfway through the service, to squeeze past Aaron Evans in the back seat, to settle herself between Hubert Jennings and Jimmy Sharman, very much unsettling them."

On Wednesday, May 12th, before 5:00 a.m. the procession was broadcast from London. The actual Coronation was broadcast later and in fact there was little else on the radio all day and into the night. "I heard the King speak at 2:00 p.m.– the highlight of the programme. He spoke very slowly and his voice seems much deeper than Edward's and his accent less noticeable to Canadian ears. We drove in to watch the school children, with their banners, march up Main Street to the School at 9:00 a.m. and hoist a new flag." Later our Scout Troop were driven to Tillsonburg, in the pouring rain, for celebrations and then we all gathered material for a huge mound of flammable stuff to be lit later that evening as a Beacon fire. The Women's Institute fed us all in the Town Hall.

On May 18th, 1937 George Pelly and Dad made their annual pilgrimage to Synod, but as full fledged delegates, not alternates. He reports a very impressive Bishop's Charge, followed by "a lot of twaddle" about the legality of delegates sitting in session if their Parish's had not paid the full Synod Assessment. They felt that, from Mr. Cornish's point of view, the only reason for registering for the sessions was to "give Mr. Cornish a good mark."

"Mr. Cornish insisted on taking us into the afternoon sessions where we listened to a seemingly useless and tiresome discussion on a motion by Archdeacon Andrews, making Select Vestry's compulsory in every Parish. Eventually Mr. Cornish, in common with many others, went to sleep. We seized this opportunity to quietly sneak out leaving him peacefully slumbering."

Sunday, June 27th, was a busy day, as the Odd-fellow's celebrated their annual Decoration Day at the cemetery and the Mason's had their annual pilgrimage to the grave of Most Worshipful Brother William Mercer Wilson at St. John's, Woodhouse. Mr. Cornish had caused consternation among the traditionalists of his congregation by reading the first lesson at both matins and evensong from Moffat's Translation. Aunty Alice was most displeased with him and told him so. This stirred Dad to do some research. "I read Quiller Couch's comparison of the authorised and revised versions, in which he says that though he regards the forty-seven translations of the authorised version as performing next thing to a miracle, he thinks at times they wrote pure nonsense, which is clarified by the revised version. All of this, of course, has nothing to do with Moffat's crudities."

I spent the night of July 5th with my friend Hubert Jennings, and nephew of Mr. Cornish. Mr. Cornish was leaving early the next morning, with us along, for a week's holiday at his cottage at Kettle Point on Lake Huron. Upon arrival our dream of swimming and lazing in the sun was soon shattered, when we were provided with scrapers to prepare the old cottage for a new coat of paint. We worked pretty hard, but also had a great time swimming and bringing up the round rocks which had, over eons of time, formed the "kettles" along the rocky shoreline and given the point its name. The cottage looked considerably better when we left for home.

There was quite a falling out between Art Thompson and Mr. Cornish on Sunday, July 18th, when Art, with out consulting anyone, cancelled the evening service. Mr. Cornish took umbrage at this, claiming Art had no legal right to do so. He held an "unofficial" service anyway. Aunty Alice attended, but reported only six other members of the Parish were in attendance.

There were several cases of infantile paralysis in town, which caused considerable concern. The start of school was delayed until September 13th, because of it. Dad drove Eileen Garner Lowe to Brantford in late August, where she joined some forty others, who were recovered victims of the disease, in donating blood for serum as an antidote against it.

The evening of Monday, November 22nd, 1937 saw the culmination of our confirmation classes when the Bishop confirmed me, David Yerex, Hubert & Barbara Jennings, Gordon Ivey, Ruth Ryerse, Patricia Blackhurst, a daughter of Tom Lowe, Byron Forrest, Mr. & Mrs. Theo. McMillan and Mr. & Mrs. W. F. Orchard, the Public School Principal. The St. Paul's Club organised a reception after the service in the Sunday School, where they served tea and sandwiches. The Bishop also handed out our Confirmation cards at that time, as well.

As the year end approached Mr. Cornish became more and more agitated about the state of the church finances. He took the Wardens to task for allowing the Select Vestry to see that all local debts were settled before paying the balance of the budget apportionment from Synod. It was obvious that the total requested would not be met. Mr. Cornish argued that the Diocesan Budget was a morale responsibility they could not ignore, but, the Wardens saw the local expenses as a legal, as well as moral, responsibility they were obligated to satisfy first.

Those of the family not afflicted with colds, namely Toods and Emily, attended the Christmas Morning service. Dad cynically made the point that "The Church decorations reflected the spirit of this tinsel-minded generation, with store-bought cellophane glister wreaths and bows and the size of the congregation was in keeping. Art being sick, I had to press Mr. McMillan into service to collect, a small plateful of quarters and a bill or two, for Mr. Cornish. On Monday, December 27th, 1937 to the surprise of many the day, for the first time ever, was proclaimed a Boxing Day holiday. Dad, finding the stores all closed, went around to Art Thompson's to discuss the sad state of the finances in St. Paul's.

On Saturday, January 15th, 1938 St. Paul's was gaily decorated for the wedding of Jack Fenton and the popular Peggy MacDonald, before a capacity crowd. It was a perfect day and everyone enjoyed themselves. The affairs of the church were still in a very precarious condition which seemed to finally be registering with the congregation. Art Thompson's year-end statement showed a large deficit, besides the budget apportionment being only half paid. There was a large turnout at the annual meeting of the Select Vestry, in part because of rumours flying that Art was so fed up, he planned to resign as Warden.

It was also being rumoured that if Art did not resign, Reverend Mr. Cornish would resign, in part because the rumour mill, working overtime, indicated this was all due to the Wardens plan to help financially, by reducing Mr. Cornish's stipend. The meeting proceeded with none of the expected unpleasantness, that some anticipated. Art Thompson was unanimously reappointed Warden. Mr. Cornish, obviously aware of other rumour and complaint among his parishioners that he did not visit enough, opined that if the ladies of the congregation did more visiting the attendance in church would be greatly improved.

Some of the ladies present, obviously, resented this inference and my Mother put Mr. Cornish on the spot by suggesting and then volunteering, to visit all the parishioners Mr. Cornish had visited, the week after he had made an initial visit. It was noted about a week after the meeting that Mr. Cornish had made quite a round of calls, so she had obviously touched a nerve, but he was also calling her bluff.

A further unpleasant duty was placed in Dad's lap to investigate a report that the Village Council had received bills from the hospital, where Margaret Cornish was very ill, inferring that she had been placed there as an indigent. He discovered that Mr. Cornish had misunderstood the situation, thinking that all patients were taken care of by Provincial or County funds, set aside in a special fund for the stamping out of Tuberculosis.

Thursday, January 27th, 1938 at 6:30 p.m. Dad dropped Marj. off at Mrs. Jennings for a party, before taking George Ryerse, Oscar Sutor and Andrew Lowe to St. John's Parish Hall for a Layman's Meeting and banquet. A good crowd was in attendance to hear Mr. Frank Newman, Superintendent of the Re-forestry Farm, speak on his work, illustrated by slides.

The threat to the Suspension Bridge at Niagara Falls, from a huge ice jam, had been in the news for some time. At 4:30 p.m. January 27th, it crashed into the gorge. While reporters and cameramen who had been awaiting its collapse for hours, were absent enjoying coffee and a break, Mr. Bill Kirkwood of Simcoe, an amateur photographer, was the only person present to record the collapse of the bridge, on film.

On February 7th, Dad was asked to pinch-hit for Mrs. James of Toronto who was unable to appear as speaker at the St. Paul's Club regular meeting, due to the illness of her father, Mr. W. H. Smith. He spoke on our recent trip to the British Isles, as he pointed out, "without being rotten-egged." Mr. MacMillan and Mr. Cornish were the only other males present.

The end of the same week a most successful Carnival was held in the rink with coloured ice, magnificently painted scenery, by Ted Harbach, and the London Figure Skaters, who were very good. A group from Toronto were even better, and brought with them four clowns, one of whom could jump over six barrels. His partner, in attempting to emulate him, invariably ended in the middle, scattering barrels in all directions, to the delight of all present. A one-legged skater astounded everyone with his antics. Miss Milne had her little girls do a drill which thrilled the locals and was well done. The diary adds that: "What was almost as enjoyable were the derisive jeers and rude comments of the bad little boys along the rails."

On February 15th, a poorly attended Vestry meeting was held. Discussion over the inability of the Sunday School drains to function properly was the main item of interest. It finished in time to allow Dad and Mr. Cornish to attend the 3rd period of the hotly contested Simcoe - Port Dover hockey match. Dover scored the winning goal just as the bell rang for a score over Simcoe of five to four.

Answering a complaint of unbearable gas fumes in the Sunday School, later in the month, Dad had the gas company send a repairman. After checking the furnace they found the chimney was plugged with bricks and mortar, an aftermath of its recent construction. That night a gas fume-less Choir party, attended by all members, their spouses and /or sweethearts, enjoyed playing cards until 10:00 p.m. They then had refreshments and danced until 1:00 a.m. Harry Moon, Cliff & Bert Reid and a variety of pianists provided the music.

The following Sunday Reverend Brett, of Jarvis, preached at evensong and Bruce Reid, Ellis Haun, Andrew Lowe and Jerry Hardicker, members of the A.Y.P.A. very capably read the service. On Saturday Mr. W. H. Smith, Port Dover's revered, long-time school Principal died. It seemed the whole village had turned out for the service from the United Church, on Monday, February 28th, 1938. In spite of his 91 years, he was still the great man of this locality. Both Dad and his father were students as were most of the residents of Port Dover and Woodhouse. Alan Law on the way to the cemetery recalled lovingly, the left-handed thrashings he had received from Mr. Smith. As he pointed out, all of them well deserved.

On Tuesday, March 1st, 1938 my parents in company with Mr. and Mrs. Smythe of Doan's Hollow enjoyed tea at Mrs. Parke's, my Aunty Alice. They then all attended an A.Y.P.A. dramatic contest at the Parish Hall. There were five one-act plays presented by St. John's, Simcoe, Port Rowan, Waterford and Port Dover. Our own young people won the cup, although the Trinity group of Simcoe, were a very close second. The rector, Reverend Mr. Caley, of St. John's, Port Rowan, was excellent in a comic role but the rest of their cast were pretty ordinary.

The diary reports a rather interesting service at evensong on March 27th when the A.Y.P.A. were officiating again. Bruce Reid read the first lesson from the "Gospel" according to Genesis. "No complaints, however, as he read very well. Mr. Cornish, at their request, undertook to explain the symbolic medallions painted on the walls as his sermon."

"He described the fouled anchor and admitted he did not know what that meant. The next, obviously a Swan plucking herself for the sake of her signets, he thought was a Phoenix, but as the light was bad he might be mistaken. The fact he had not made sure, during the last fifteen years, didn't apparently disturb him in the least. He announced next Sunday as Palm Sunday, in spite of Mrs. Cornish's vigorous head-shaking. On consulting Aunty Alice's book of 'Phrase and Fable' we learned that the bird is neither Swan nor Phoenix, but a Pelican, – emblem for charity, because it was supposed to revive its own brood with its own blood." [if this is so, the artist erred as well, as to me, it has always been a Swan.]

The night of April 2nd, Archie Milne's Sunera Mill burned, at the intersection of the railway tracks and Queen Street, just below the head of Main Street. It was completely destroyed.

On Good Friday, April 15th, 1938 our household all attended the morning service, where Reverend Mr. Todd, the United church minister from Simcoe preached the sermon. After the service Dad and Art Thompson measured the frontage of the Rectory and discovered, as they suspected, that they were paying taxes on the width of the road allowance between the Rectory and Buck's Park. It was announced that there would be a "bee" to tear the dead Boston Ivey off the walls of the church. The bee ended up being made up of Dad, his brother Frank and Mr. Cornish, but they got it done and the debris all burned.

Dad was not impressed with a Laymen's Banquet, he, George Ryerse and Mr. Cornish attended in Delhi on May 5th. They were the only ones from Dover and most of the evening was spent by L.E. Wedd and Reverend McMillan "chewing the rag over some fool committee." This was followed by a more or less stereotyped address by Canon Bice.

On May 10th, Frank Barrett drove, taking the two Wardens, George Ryerse and George Pelly to Synod in London. After registering they heard the Bishop's Charge which lasted until noon.

Synod did not reconvene until 3:00 p.m. owing to the funeral of Fred Betts, M. P., in the Cathedral. He had drowned while on a fishing expedition in Quebec. "We did not wait, but headed home, spearing the odd bottle of beer on the way."

Mr. Cornish exchanged pulpits with Reverend Mr. McMillan, on May 15th, who was making his visits as Rural Dean of Norfolk. This meant Mother had to take her old Sunday School class, which Mr. Cornish had been teaching. That evening regular evensong was suspended, but at eight o'clock, hoping to catch the congregations from the other churches, the Choir put on their annual musicale. It was very well attended. Next afternoon the Women's Auxiliary Deanery meeting was held in the Parish Hall.

On Sunday, June 12th, 1938 we all attended Sunday School, while Dad after delivering us, went down to Aunty Alice's as usual, to visit and bring her to church. It was a special day as Clayton Ansley and his sister, Mrs. Syers and their families were in attendance to unveil the memorial window to their parents, Harry Wilmot Ansley and his wife, Bessie Lees Ansley. Dad records that; "The window was placed in the corner where their old seat used to be. Rather decent of them, considering that Cousin Bessie was so bitter about her old pew being removed that she was only in church once afterwards, while she was alive. At 5:00 p.m. there was a special christening service, in place of evensong, of five babies including Michael Henry, son of Dorothy and Tim Barrett. Although at first frightened by the organ he was very well behaved, while the rest "howled lustily."

Mr. & Mrs. Harry Ansley, son Clayton and daughter, later becoming Mrs. Syers

It was about this time that Pat Yerex, having

attended evensong with his mother, came home to announce to Gramps that Mr. Cornish had prayed that everyone would feed the Snipe our supper or at least a part of it. This had everyone who heard it nonplussed. "Where did you get that idea?" asked Gramps. It was finally decided that as Mr. Cornish, at evensong, often replaced that part of the Lord's Prayer that states; "Give us this day our daily bread" with, it being evening, "Give us this night our daily bread." Pat being intrigued with his grandfather's recent discussion of Snipe shooting, had interpreted that sentence of the prayer as; "Give to the Snipe our daily bread," or supper.

On Thursday, June 16th Dad, Mother, Adah and George Pelly attended the last of the Laymen's banquets for the season, to which ladies were also invited, in St. William's. They were entertained after the banquet by the beautiful lantern slides of local flora and fauna presented by Monroe Landon of Simcoe. On Sunday evening, June 19th, the local Royal Canadian Legion Branch were in attendance at evensong to commemorate the signing of Magna Charta, in the hopes of counteracting some of the Communist and Fascist propaganda that was becoming so rampant across the Country.

By September of 1938, the threat of war in Europe was on everyone's mind, as Hitler was making ever more threatening gestures. British Prime Minister Neville Chamberlain flew to Germany to personally confront Hitler on the 14th, giving hope to many that he can make him see reason and avert further threat of invasion by Germany. On the 26th all radio stations carried a speech by Hitler, which he had ordered every man, woman and child in Germany to listen to. The diary reports that; "Not being able to understand it, and the comments in English being brief I did not stay long, but it sounded truly like 'A tale told by an idiot, full of sound and fury, —' Translated, it is a tirade and denunciation against the Czechoslovakian President Benes' cruelty to the Sudeten Germans, which coming from Hitler with his tyrannical oppression of the Jews, does not ring true. He made no mention of the plea for peace sent him from President Roosevelt.

As part of the Thanksgiving Day celebrations, on Sunday, October 9th, 1938 a Union service of the Port Dover congregations, was held in the United Church, to offer prayers and sincere thanks that war had been so narrowly averted in Europe. Padre Lambert of Toronto brought the message to a packed congregation. An already edgy population of both the U. S. A. and Canada were sent into a complete state of panic in some quarters by a radio broadcast, the evening of October 31st, 1938, which reported, in far too realistic terms for many, the Invasion of New York, by inhabitants of the Planet Mars. It was found to be a play produced by H. G. Wells. I remember it as being very scary and far too realistic for me, despite the fact we were all sceptical of it actually taking place.

The year wound down with the Bishop confirming ten girls and three boys on November 6th, with a full congregation in attendance. Fred Colman, popular butcher for many years, died the morning of November 16th. On December 1st, I attended a meeting of our Sunday School class at the Rectory to finalise a play we plan to put on for the Christmas Concert. Mr. Cornish was just leaving the church behind the wedding party of Betsy McLeod and Ross Thompson as we arrived.

On Saturday afternoon, December 17th while driving Mother into town, a strange shudder seemed to shake the whole car. We were quite baffled by it until we reached the down town, just as the fire truck raced by, to turn west on Nelson Street. We soon learned that Miss Dunbar had been badly injured when her house was demolished by a natural gas explosion, which had lifted it a foot off its foundations, and blown the front door right across the street. They report that it is doubtful if she will survive her injuries. Smelling gas she had gone to the basement and lighted a match to check the origin of the odour. She did not survive.

Our whole family were involved with the highly successful Sunday School Concert that played to an overflow audience on December 20th in the Sunday School. We put on Pyramus and Thisbe from "A Midsummer's Night Dream," under Mr. Cornish's direction, and were said to have carried it off very well. My sisters were all involved as well, with their classmates, and all hands received prizes. Everyone present professed to have thoroughly enjoyed themselves.

The diary for 1939 opens on a philosophical note with: "A beautiful, bright, sunny, snappy, cold New Year's morning, with a snow-covered landscape. Nature is doing her best to make this part of the World look and feel cheerful, and although business conditions are not all they might be, they might also be worse and we are not embroiled in war, which we might easily have been, so have a lot to be thankful for."

"Taxes are too high and farm prices are too much below other prices and there is too much unemployment. Consequently, there is a high cost of Relief – not because there isn't work to be done but because men won't work for what employers can afford to pay and very few seem to think that they should. I can not figure out why farmers should have to work for whatever they can get, and help to keep others who won't, on relief. Politicians and Labour men think otherwise, so I suppose we will have to endure it as part of the price of living in a free country."

Dr. Cook got the year off to a scary start for us kids by giving us all small pox vaccinations, as there were cases being reported in the Province as close as St. Thomas. The annual Select Vestry meeting was lightly attended and the Wardens re-appointed for another year. Mr. Cornish reported his keen disappointment in the inertia he found in the congregation and admitted that three years earlier he had applied to the Bishop for another parish. The Bishop had agreed, if Mr. Cornish could find another parish willing to make the exchange. If both were in favour, he would make it happen. The on-going years of the depression must have been dragging everyone down with it, and coupled with the ever present threat of war in Europe, it was no wonder that people became discouraged.

Quoting from the diary; "Mr. Cornish told us in his sad, whimsical manner that a delegation had come, heard him preach, and reported unfavourably, so the matter was dropped. His candour amused Dad [W. H. Barrett] immensely. George [Pelly] asked him if he did not like us here, and Dr. Blackhurst tried to extract a promise from him that he would make no more attempts to leave. Art [Thompson] said nothing. I told him he should not take the apathy of the congregation too much to heart as it is a situation common to church's everywhere. I also believe, though I did not say so, that Mr. Cornish should bestir himself more. He is not well and is not a go-getter and I don't think we would like him as well, if he were. I am not surprised at the dissatisfaction of the visiting delegation, whoever they were, as Mr. Cornish's charms are elsewhere than in his sermons, which are usually most tiresome. I don't mind them as I am generally asleep. He can preach very well, too, if he takes the trouble to prepare them."

On Sunday, April 2nd, 1939 the topic of conversation after church was the amazing, almost unbelievable report, of the ability of the new Trans-Canada Airline, to leave Toronto on a regular schedule at 10:30 p.m. one day and deliver passengers to Vancouver by lunch-time the next day. There was a fair congregation at 10:30, on Good Friday, when Mr. Cornish had the Baptist minister from Simcoe to preach and Mr. M'Haffy, of the United church, read the psalms.

Patriotic fervour was at a fever pitch across Canada on Wednesday, May 17th, 1939 as the radio reported the arrival of the King and Queen at Quebec City for a tour of the country. The King launched their tour with a speech from the Hotel Frontenac. Mrs. Bains, of Toronto, had invited Hubert Jennings and myself for a week-end visit, and to accompany her grand-daughters, to see their Majesties drive by the cheering throngs of well-wishers. We were driven in early Saturday morning to the Bain's home on Spadina Avenue, viewing all the bunting and flags along Yonge Street, especially the elaborate gold window dressing of both Eaton's and Simpson's down-town stores. Hubert and I had a grand time escorting the girls and found ourselves swept up in the general euphoria on Monday afternoon when the Royal Couple passed down Yonge St. graciously waving to all. The icing on the cake, for us, came when Uncle Dick's former partner, George McCullagh, won the King's Plate with his horse, "Archworth."

On Wednesday, June 7th, the whole town and most of Woodhouse was practically evacuated to Hamilton for a last chance to see the Royal Couple, before their return to Britain. Eleven Pullman cars were jammed with school children and town's people, the biggest load to leave town on the C. N. R. in many a day. The Veterans assembled at 5:00 a.m. at the Legion Hall to leave en masse for their allotted place on Main Street, Hamilton, where they met and acted as Honour Guard for the school children, when their train arrived. They had been allotted a shady spot right on the curb, and with lunches, settled in to wait. Finally, four or five hours later, a squad of motor-cycle policemen appeared and behind them the Royal Canadian Dragoons. The Dragoons surrounded the Royal car, which passed all too quickly, but we did get a fine view of them, smiling and waving to the thousands along their route.

A large contingent of choir boys from Waterloo descended on us, to be billeted for overnight, on Saturday afternoon, July 8th, 1939. They were a comical and lively bunch of city kids, who had a great time romping over the whole farm until dark. The Choirmaster and two of their fathers appeared to escort them to Sunday School next morning, which did not sit well with most of them. In fact they announced that; "They can't do that to us, we are on our holidays!" Do it they did, however, and they went off quietly, like the nice little fellows they were. They sang beautifully, and quite angelically, at matins later.

Through a whim of Mr. Cornish's, Sunday School was held in the church for the summer. I drove my sister Mary and Marjorie Gurr down on August 6th, as they were to take charge of the Primary class from that point on. It was a very hot morning and a large congregation, mostly summer people, were on hand for the morning service. There were no evening services. The following Sunday Reverend Chauncey Snowden, who was visiting from the U. S. with relatives in Nanticoke, took the service. Mr. Cornish was away supervising the newly established Huron Diocese Church Camp. He had been quite instrumental in its formation.

The threat of war grew in intensity throughout the summer, and Mr. Cornish now was including President Roosevelt of the United States, in his prayers for the Royal family. I suppose this was his attempt to contribute more toward British-American relations. The wardens approached Reverend Chauncey Snowden, holidaying from his duties in the States with his Nanticoke relatives, about taking services at St. Paul's during Reverend Cornish's holiday time. He refused them, however. As they had often done in the past, the Wardens called on Reverend Dunlop, of Dunnville, and he very obligingly agreed to fill in.

By September 1st, 1939 the radios were blaring the news that Hitler had annexed Danzig that morning and was conducting air raids over several Polish cities. War seemed inevitable. The news was confusing, however, and everyone had the sickening feeling that Chamberlain was going to give Hitler another chance to commit murder, and get away with it. Early Sunday morning, September 3rd, 1939 it was announced that Great Britain had declared war on Germany. France followed suit a few hours later. Australia and New Zealand had declared war immediately, as well. Canada, claiming it must wait until Parliament convened on Thursday, had not committed. Prime Minister McKenzie King, following a Cabinet meeting, announced that we will "co-operate" with Great Britain. The die is cast. Reverend Harrison Arrel, of Caledonia, took the service that morning in St. Paul's.

# Chapter Fifteen

# Canon Cornish – The War and Beyond

With the declaration of war by Great Britain on September 3rd, 1939, the repercussions began to hit home in our erstwhile quiet community and parish, almost at once. The report of the White Star liner "Athenia" having been torpedoed off the Irish coast was the shocking news to greet us the morning of September 4th. She was carrying a large number of Canadian passengers. Some one hundred and fifty had been killed by the exploding torpedo, but the remainder were thought to have been rescued from the life boats. Germany denied having any submarines in the area, but the Admiralty confirmed it was a torpedo attack. A mass flight of British aircraft flew over Germany at first light dropping leaflets, informing the German public of a good many plain truths that had hitherto been kept from them. No bombs were dropped.

Dad called on Murray Hamilton, at the Armouries in Simcoe, that morning to ask if there was any military service he could become involved in. He was told there had been no orders re recruiting as yet, but Murray would let him know as soon as any orders came through. They drove to Blight's in Jarvis for bran and oil-cake, saving $6.50 over the price in Port Dover, where, already the prices had gone up in anticipation of increases due to the war.

On September 6th, my mother attended a luncheon in the Women's Building of the Canadian National Exhibition, while Dad watched the judging of sheep in the livestock pavilion. Following the luncheon, mother was convinced by Premier G. Howard Ferguson and some of the ladies present, to organise a plan locally, to send fruit in the form of jam to destitute and displaced

*Canon David J. Cornish*

children in Britain. By the time Canada had formally declared war on September 9th, my mother was distributing copies of the Maple Leaf, to church groups and Women's Institute Branches throughout Norfolk, touting the banner headline; "Norfolk Jam for British Children." Uncle George Pelly was already on duty at the Doan's Hollow pumping station guarding our town water supply from possible sabotage by enemy aliens.

That Saturday I drove, while my mother visited all Presidents of the County Women's Institutes, to rally their members to the jam-making cause. On Sunday afternoon we visited the last of them in the western part of the County. Here we found some who were sceptical of the project, it would appear primarily because the idea came out of Dover though they did not actually say so.

Next morning my parents left for Toronto at 6:30 a.m. to visit Mr. Tomlinson who had promoted the making of jam for Britain in the first place. He assured them that if Norfolk women produced it, he would guarantee its delivery to needy British children and offered to write personal letters, to that effect, to all Church and Institute groups willing to participate. Soon Brantford and Toronto reporters were calling for particulars about the "Jam for Britain" project.

By September 15th the Port Dover Women's Institute had put up 111 quarts of jam, having scrounge the necessary sugar, which was very scarce, from some secret source. Mr. Ferguson, who was now officially chairman of the committee for the shipping of supplies to Britain for relief was delighted to hear from Port Dover of the positive steps being taken. The Sunday School kitchen of St. Paul's, in company with similar kitchens and other facilities throughout the County, was shifting into high gear for the production of jam. As the 16th was a Saturday I again drove my mother to the homes and halls of Norfolk, where an army of women were at work in their kitchens peeling, scalding and boiling down all kinds of aromatic preserves for the displaced children of Britain. The project had taken off like wildfire, as rural and urban women alike put their whole hearts into what they saw as a very practical, worthwhile answer to the threat of war.

Bruce Dell, of Dell's Bakery on the south-west corner of Main and Chapman Street called to offer, anonymously, a donation of one hundred pounds of almost unobtainable sugar to the jam project. Dad had to surreptitiously carry it out the back door of the bake shop and sneak it into the back door of Pat Patterson's Drug store to be hidden away. Pat then doled it out to worthy jam makers as they had need of it. Mother was in her element in all this, as her slogan had always been; "Better to put ten men to work, than to do the work of ten men."

On Monday, September 18th, the local jam committee met in Sam Morris's Maple leaf office to draft strategy and put out a flyer regarding it. Sam made his phone available for calls, regarding the progress of the jam-making groups around the County. Dad was collecting fruit, jars, sugar and other supplies for distribution to "jam-making cells" which also included two bushels of peaches from Charlie Stewart's orchard. The war hit home with a vengeance in Port Dover during their meeting with word that the British Aircraft Carrier, "H.M.S. Courageous" had been torpedoed. Miles Blackhurst, of Port Dover had been one of her crew and the town's first casualty.

The whole family were in shock on Thursday, September 21st, when news came that Aunt Win, who had been at Miss John's nursing home with her new baby, Andrew, had died. The funeral was held on Monday from "Clonmel." Dad, Dick, Frank, Tim, George Pelly and Karl Sovereign acted as pall bearers.

On Friday, September 29th disquieting news re the movement of the burgeoning supplies of jam came, with the suggestion that as the Red Cross were not co-operating, it might have to be distributed among those on relief here in Canada. This would prove doubly humiliating to all those who had worked so hard to produce it, as no-one locally had any sympathy with our relief recipients. Mr. Tomlinson called the next day to say he was personally coming to Dover to supervise the packing of the jam for shipment at once, via C. P. R., to Britain. He also invited mother to serve on the Dominion Board of Relief Workers.

A car load of Toronto people, of the Overseas Food Committee, accompanied Mr. and Mrs. Tomlinson, arriving in mid-morning for lunch at our place on Thursday, October 5th, 1939. Pat and Bess Patterson and Miss Minnie Misner joined them. Representatives of all Institutes and other jam makers came for the afternoon to hear directly from Mr. Tomlinson his plans for collecting and shipping the jam. They were here until late afternoon. The Scouts worked most of Saturday collecting boxes of jam to be stored for final packing at the Parish Hall.

On Wednesday, October 11th Dad, Mother, Art Thompson, Sam Morris, Mr. Mott, Mr. White and others packed over 160 cartons of jam, baling them up tight with Ivey's wire-baling machine, in the Sunday School. Jam kept coming in from all over the County, and being baled for overseas shipment, until there were about 320 cases in the Sunday School or in a vacant store in the McQueen block. They had collected five and a half tons of it and addresses to consignees in Britain had come from Toronto. Many who attended a St. Paul's Club tea on October 17th stayed to affix labels to the jam cartons, 5000 pounds to the Lord Provost of Glasgow, 5000 pounds to the Lord Mayor of a town in Lancashire.

The following morning a gang helped load it on two trucks, one from Harry Misner's and the other from the Norfolk Fish Company to be taken to a car on the Lake Erie & Northern Rwy. siding on Main Street. It now only had to survive attacks by Hitler's U-boats which had just carried out a daring attack on Scapa Flow, sinking "H.M.S. Royal Oak."

The Bishop confirmed a class of twelve including Bobby, Charles, Barbara Ivey and Hilton Yerex, on Sunday November 12th, 1939. There was no evensong as the Bishop and choir all took part in a service in Christ Church, Vittoria that afternoon.

Later in the month the Red Cross in Toronto suddenly took an interest in the remaining 1500 pounds of jam still in waiting in St. Paul's Sunday School and which their truck was to pick up.

*McGaw MacDonald & Tobe Barrett are accepted for Artillery training course*

Sam Morris, smelling a rat when Mr. Brooks of Simcoe sent a Crosby transport for it instead, refused to release it, as there was no guarantee it would go to Britain. They had worked too hard at getting it to that stage without the Port Dover Red Cross getting credit for its distribution. The last of it was shipped to their satisfaction before Christmas and everyone was elated when a telegram was received by Mother from the Lord Provost of Glasgow telling her 1500 households were enjoying their Norfolk jam. The few remaining jars were turned over to Mrs. Steele for distribution to needy families locally just before Christmas.

Meanwhile in mid-October Dad and McGaw MacDonald were examined and passed for acceptance in an Artillery instruction course that was to begin at once in the Simcoe Armouries. They with several others from the County were training and taking lectures in things military two or three nights a week in the Armouries. Men had been joining the militia in the 41st and 42nd Batteries and signing up for active service from throughout the County.

At the February 2nd, 1940 annual meeting of the Vestry the perennial deficit in the church finances were discussed by a small turnout of parishioners. Nobody had either the heart or the nerve to suggest a cut in Mr. Cornish's stipend but Art Thompson did suggest looking into joining with St. John's, Woodhouse instead of Christ Church, Vittoria. Mr. Cornish felt that was not a feasible plan.

On April 4th, Dad and I picked up Ellis Haun, Hubert Jennings, George Ryerse and young Clarence Mitchell as representatives of the Parish to a Laymen's banquet in the newly opened Parish Hall in Delhi. Mr. Finlay from London was the special speaker. A few days later the Wardens met with Mr. Cornish at the

Rectory to discuss taking their financial problems and possible solutions to the Bishop. Mr. Cornish wished further discussion with the men of the Parish, however. He also urged that a serious canvass of the congregation be made for special donations.

A glowing letter of praise for the past years jam making effort from Lady Reading of the British Women's Voluntary Services reinforced efforts to can even more in the coming year. No sooner were strawberries available than the Sunday School was a hive of activity with ladies hulling and preserving them. The Institutes and church groups across the County were also in full swing. The Jam Committee had negotiated with the Canadian Red Cross, over the winter, to supply five pound tin cans and crates for all jam made. Large batches were also put up by the Jam Factory in Simcoe through the local committee and Joe Jackson, their chemist, tested and approved all jam made as to quality and purity.

The local Red Cross were now organised into an efficient group, who met regularly in the Town Hall or St. Paul's Parish Hall. They were not only the link for the handling and shipping of "Jam for British Children" but also co-ordinated the knitting of socks, scarves and balaclavas as well as the regular shipments of cartons of cigarettes to the servicemen overseas.

On Saturday, April 27th, 1940 the diary reports "I spent the afternoon going to funerals. Pete Brock asked me to take his place at old Bill Rankins at 1:30 p.m. At 3:00 p.m. was the service, in the church, for poor old Russ Skey. In accordance with his own wishes he had been cremated and as none of us had ever buried ashes before it seemed like a queer performance. The service at the church was very short and rather informal, if that is the proper word. The burial at the cemetery was queerer still. Dad, Dick and I went up, with the men of the Skey family. Bert Thompson got the parcel containing Russ's ashes from the back of one of the cars. It was wrapped up in ordinary wrapping paper and tied with ordinary string and from its appearance might have been a box of chocolates, or, a pair of shoes. The "grave" was a hole, about eighteen inches square and two feet deep. Bert placed the parcel in it and Mr. Cornish went over part of the service. It all seemed a queer performance. We all went back to "Clonmel" from the cemetery and all the Skeys and Complins assembled there and had afternoon tea."

The following Tuesday, April 30th was a busy one, for Dad and Mother left at 7:30 a.m. for Toronto, where Mother appeared at Queen's Park to report to Miss Clark, Head of Women's Institutes and her committee of fruit growers, jam makers and Red Cross officials of the Province, on the operation of the "Norfolk Jam for British Children." She was quizzed on the making, collecting and shipping of it, and the net result of it all.

They picked up Dr. Blackhurst before leaving the city and were home in plenty of time to attend the Congregational Meeting in the Parish Hall that evening. There was a big turnout and Dr. Blackhurst, who had been agitating for a group to "do something," got his committee appointed with no trouble. On asking for suggestions for improving the services, Mr. Cornish was told by Art Thompson to keep sermons to under fifteen minutes and W. H. "Harry" Barrett suggested cutting out preliminary explanations of the psalms. Mr. Cornish took it all good humouredly. Dr. Williamson and his wife were there and he spoke in a way that brought it all to a very amicable conclusion.

On May 10th, Hitler invaded Holland and Belgium and Chamberlain resigned as Prime Minister of Britain. Winston Churchill took over at once, with a new coalition cabinet, to support the armies of the Netherlands and Belgium in holding their line with the aid of the British and French forces. The new airfield at Nanticoke is progressing rapidly and Air Force personnel and aircraft will soon begin to arrive on the site.

The church was filled with worshippers in response to the request of the King that Sunday, May 26th, 1940 should be a day of special intercession, throughout the Empire, for success for the Allied Arms. Chart Woolley, Reeve, also made a special request, through the Maple Leaf, that the King's wishes be observed by all citizens. All Port Dover churches were well filled and the Veterans turned out in force at an evening service in the Presbyterian church. Three days later Dr. Blackhurst's committee made a thorough inspection of the church from basement to belfry, to estimate what repairs might be needed and to estimate their cost.

Back-dated to June Dad, Bob Landon and McGaw MacDonald were among those granted commissions in the Royal Canadian Artillery. Many young men were joining the services for

*Camp at Niagara-on-the-Lake, August, 1940 - Fred Hoskins, Albert Bridgewater, Harry B. Barrett, George Bush, - seated - George Tennant & Jack Castles*

active duty, Richard Ryerse, Tom Ivey and others from the Parish of St. Paul's among them. My uncles, Frank, and Tim and I had joined the militia to attend drill one night a week, in the Armouries, in Simcoe. Others to join the militia from St. Paul's Parish, included Jack "Buck" Wamsley, Jack Castles, Clarence Strople, Bob Ferguson, George Bush and the three Buck boys, Bill, John Harris and Edward.

On Monday, August 26th, 1940 450 men from Norfolk County, including those listed above, left Simcoe for two weeks of army life and discipline at the camp at Niagara-on-the-Lake. We returned much more like soldiers on Saturday night, September 7th, and certainly in much better physical shape than when we left. Among others to attend camp from Dover were Walt Steele, Cracker Smith, Jock Noble, Cliff Reid, Royden Nunn, Jack Shand, Chris Green and Fred Hoskins.

On returning from drill at the Armouries on Friday, November 29th, as we turned east at the half-way house corner, a fiery glow lit the sky in front of us. We at once feared for our barns, but on nearing the head of Main Street realised that it was the old 1830's grist mill. By the time of our arrival it was completely consumed in flames. One of Port Dover's oldest buildings, in which

*The Port Dover flour & grist mill on site of the hamlet of Dover*

three generations of our family had played as children, was no more, it left a distinct lump in our throats. The radio reported that the crack Italian "Regiment of Death," sworn to die before surrender, are in full flight before a determined Greek force.

Hubert Jennings and I were in hot water with Art Thompson for being too exuberant in our ringing of the church bell the last Sunday of the year. As we hung on the rope, there was a tremendous crash and we were literally lifted off our feet by the bell rope. On Friday, January 3rd, of the new year I picked up Hubert and a ladder and we climbed into the belfry to see what we had done. The bell hung askew in its cradle, a bolt having worked loose over time and dropped one end free. We managed, with considerable effort, to get it back in place. at the same time realising that we had been falsely maligned for what had happened.

The annual 1941 vestry meeting drew very few parishioners and no fireworks. Art Thompson's attempts to interest the wardens of St. John's, Woodhouse, in promoting union had received a rather cold reception and as a result was not mentioned. The Wardens were returned for another term. The threat of reducing Mr. Cornish's stipend was still not carried out although the finances were still in a very precarious lack of balance.

The winter months passed slowly, with Mac MacKenzie's barber shop being central to the news of the town's gossip and activities. The war was the hottest topic of discussion and often brought out some interesting tales of earlier times, from the Police Chief, Dave McNeilly and others. A favourite concerned two very early settlers down the lake shore in the persons of Adrian Feury, who had served with Napoleon and William Corbett, who lost a leg while serving with Wellington, at Waterloo.

Dave recalled that they were both great old cronies, and got along well except when at logging or barn raising bees, when, on reaching a certain stage of intoxication, they had to be physically prevented from killing each other, when Corbett would accuse Faure of shooting his leg off. They both had vivid memories of lying all day on the field of battle, at Waterloo, shooting at each other.

Reverend Mr. Rickard, of St. John's, Port Rowan died suddenly in March and the wardens, thinking it an opportune time, went to see Mr. Cornish about approaching the Bishop to suggest joining with St. John's, Woodhouse. On April 3rd Dad and Art had their interview with the Bishop in London, but he was less than enthusiastic, suggesting only that he would be willing to send Canon Townsend down to give the congregation a pep talk. About this same time Peggy Wamsley and Alice Barrett joined the choir.

The wardens made their annual trip to Synod on May 13th though because the apportionment had not been paid, they hesitated to attend. Mr. Cornish had made a strong objection last year to their attending, when the parish owed the Synod, and had eventually paid it himself, he found it so embarrassing. As a result Dad informed Mr. Cornish that they would go. He was quite upset about it, but did announce in church the previous Sunday that as last year's dues were paid the wardens were entitled to attend, and Dad felt that to please Mr. Cornish they should attend the sessions. They arrived in time to hear the Bishop's charge, have lunch at the hotel and return to Cronyn Hall to register as delegates. After a visit with Mr. Cornish they headed for home leaving him with the impression they were staying for the afternoon's proceedings.

On Sunday, May 25th Miss Giles, one of the town's oldest merchants died in her 90's. The following day the British Battle Cruiser "H.M.S. Hood" was sunk near Greenland when the German Battleship "Bismark" dropped a shell in her magazines.

The ship exploded and sank with the loss of all hands. The militia was involved in several parades to promote the selling of Victory Bonds, the jam makers became active again as strawberries came on and the St. Paul's Sunday School kitchen and storage areas were pressed into service again. Art Thompson was very active in the selling of Victory Loans and reported that Port Dover and Woodhouse had reached their objective of $100,000.00 although the County were still short of theirs. Haldimand County, on the other hand, had made their objective in the first week of the campaign, being the first in Ontario to do so.

On Sunday, June 22nd, 1941 the Norfolk Militia again were mobilised for two weeks of intensive artillery training at camp in Niagara-on-the-Lake. On our return David Yerex and I began looking into going on active service, as most of our pals were doing the same. We favoured the Navy but they only wanted cooks and stewards. We did not bite on that one, but in early September we started an intensive radio training course at Westdale Collegiate under the Dominion-Provincial War Training Programme, leading to becoming Naval radar operators.

At a Congregational Meeting, called for July 15th, and attended by only eight including Mr. Cornish, the wardens very reluctantly informed him that they would be forced to cut his stipend. He did not raise too much objection but did think there should be a more representative meeting and more effort made to increase giving. In two weeks time Mr. Cornish would celebrate the 20th Anniversary of his coming to the Parish.

*Camp at Niagara-on-the-Lake, June 1941 - Jock Noble, John "Buck" Wamsley, seated - Clarence Strople. We were billeted in Bell Tents*

*Clayton Scofield & Harry B. Barrett, Room 1, Y.M.C.A., Hamilton, September, 1941*

In the first week of September the wardens had a much dreaded interview with Mr. Cornish, who had received no stipend for two months and they still had no money to pay him. As they reported he did not scold them, but did suggest a meeting of some of the men of the congregation at which a definite financial policy could be drawn up and put into place.

In August three tons of jam were shipped to Britain and women's groups were still producing it. Mother had arranged with the jam factory to put up large batches, if the ladies could provide it ready for processing in large barrels that they provided. A big push was on when Grant Fox turned over a large block of his peach orchard at Normandale on September 8th for picking. They had become too ripe for shipping, and would otherwise be lost. All our family, Mrs. Bess Patterson, her mother Mrs. Perry, Misses Knapp and Murchison, from the High School, Peggy Wamsley and other students had descended on the orchard to pick over fifty bushel hampers for jam. Other women from church and Institute groups were also busy all day. Hundreds of bushels were still likely to go to waste.

Mother then had to convince the jam factory to take this unexpected bonanza, as they had told her they could handle no more free jam for her. She finally got them to agree to process the peaches, if they were delivered peeled and cut into slices in the jam factory barrels. The farm truck was pressed into service to gather the hampers from the Fox orchard and then to pick up five barrels from the Jam factory in Simcoe and deliver them to St. Paul's Sunday School. Next morning Miss Murchison and Miss Knapp with all the girls from the High School, plus the regular ladies of

St. Paul's descended on the Parish Hall to peel, de-pit and section the fifty bushels of peaches before dumping them in the barrels. By late afternoon Dad and Jack Castles returned with the truck to deliver the finished product to the jam factory in Simcoe. They returned to collect the pits and peelings to be taken to the dump.

On Sunday, September 14th, 1941 all members of the militia were involved in a Re-Consecration Week provided for by a Government Proclamation. The Brigade paraded to the First Baptist Church, in Simcoe, where Harry Judd read the lesson, Sergeant Medley read prayers and a Reverend Hillyer, a missionary from Bolivia, preached a very good sermon.

The following Wednesday Dad received a card from Mr. Cornish reminding him that he had been elected a member of the Synod executive, and pointing out that it was a distinct honour and privilege to belong to such an august group. As there was a meeting called for September 18th, he further suggested that Dad bring L. E. Wedd, from Simcoe and R. K. Robinson, from Waterford with him. With all chance of overlooking the meeting gone, Dad complied with Mr. Cornish's suggestion and all three arrived in time for lunch at the Hotel London. The diary reports that; "We spent the afternoon at the meeting saying 'aye' to the various resolutions. I didn't find it very thrilling entertainment and am afraid I don't appreciate the honour. We left shortly before six, stopping in Ingersoll for a beer. Finding it a dry town, we made do with malted milks all round."

On December 3rd, 1941 Mr. Cornish, the wardens, Bill Wamsley and Frank Barrett were the only ones to attend a regular Vestry meeting. As Dad expected to be shipped out soon in the army he advised Mr. Cornish, who was very discouraged with the lack of interest generally, to look for a replacement warden. A highlight for St. Paul's, as the year wound down, was Dr. A. E. Williamson's recitation at evensong on December 21st, of "The Other Wise Men."

On December 7th, 1941 the U. S. A. were plunged into war with a vengeance by the bombing of Pearl Harbour, by the Japanese. They had caught the Americans completely off guard causing tremendous havoc in loss of life, planes and naval ships, while at the same time declaring war on both the U.S. and Britain. Further shocking news came on December 10th, with the sinking of the new Battleship "H.M.S. Prince of Wales" and the Battle Cruiser "H.M.S. Repulse" by Japanese suicide bombers, off Singapore. After Christmas Winston Churchill visited Washington to rally the Americans to the cause. Every Canadian to hear it, got a real lift from the report on radio of Churchill's speech to the Canadian Parliament in Ottawa, on December 30th, 1941.

The diary opens 1942 in a rather cynical tone with: "President Roosevelt, followed dutifully, as usual, by MacKenzie King, made a plea for a universal day of prayer today, but there was no evidence of it being observed hereabouts. After dancing the old year out and drinking the new year in, none of us were in the mood to pray, I suppose. Possibly they think the Almighty is going to see us through anyway, so why go to any extra trouble. Mr. Cornish had told us Sunday a United Prayer meeting would be arranged, and left town for the day and Mr. Mahaffy didn't bother. We fight for 'World Freedom,' but sometimes I think a darn good licking would do us all a lot of good."

*Alice Parke & nephew Tobe Barrett prior to his reporting to Camp Shilo, Manitoba for active service in the Royal Canadian Artillery*

Dad received orders from Colonel [Dr] Sandy English, of the Shilo Artillery Base near Brandon, to report for active duty in February. On the strength of this he told Mr. Cornish at the Annual Vestry Meeting that he could no longer serve as Warden. Dr. Andy Williamson was named in his place. Art Thompson returned as people's warden under protest, but would be lost without the challenge of balancing the budget and doing the day to day business of the church.

As the diary is no longer kept on a regular basis, with Dad in the Army, my chief source of information regarding the affairs of St. Paul's has also dried up. Do I hear a sigh of relief from my readers?

The community was shocked to learn of the passing of Edward Leigh Richardson "Dick" Tibbetts on Thursday, April 9th, 1942. Captain Tibbetts returned from overseas, in 1919, with his bride Martha "Molly" Stammers to assist his father in the Post Office. He also maintained a successful Insurance business and later assumed control of the Port Dover Fish Company, Ltd. and its subsidiary the Port Dover Box Factory. He was warden of St. Paul's for many years, a past master of Erie Lodge, active in the Royal Canadian Legion and Home Guard, a member of the Board of Education and Auditor for the Municipality. Last year he served as President of the local Canadian Red Cross Society. His presence among us will be sadly missed.

On Monday, June 29th, shock waves rippled through the community and far beyond, with news of the passing of my Grandfather W. H. "Harry" Barrett. Beautiful tributes were published in both the Globe and Mail and in The Maple Leaf. The funeral on Thursday, with the men from the farms as bearers, was impressive from its very simplicity, and richness of the Anglican service.

On July 12th, 1942 Frank Barrett formally gave up his long-time tenure as Secretary of the Sunday School and my sister Norah replaced him. She and my sisters had been serving as teachers and continued in that role. The attendance of both students and teachers had declined but it was hoped, that with the help of Mrs. Blanche Clark and prodding by my

*William Henry "Harry" Barrett, who died June 29th, 1942*

mother, that was about to be rectified. George Pelly, long-time Sunday School Superintendent, had also been lost to them as he was now working in Toronto.

The Jam making brigade for "Norfolk Jam for British Children" had been active again all season. In August Hodgson's Apiaries in Jarvis filled eleven cases of Red Cross cans with honey for the cause. Girls from the High School, with their teachers, were also pressed into service to aid the local W. A. and other ladies groups in putting up huge batches of preserves in St. Paul's Sunday School.

The Sunday School concert was held on the night of Wednesday, December 23rd, 1942 and as it was competing with the same celebration by Grace United was sparsely attended. The Christmas tree was a disappointment, being a last minute substitute scraggly cedar, from Mr. Cornish's hedge, despite the fact that Jack Castles had obtained a beautiful compact spruce from Mr. Ball of Lynn valley for the Sunday School's exclusive use. Jack's instructions were to leave it in Mr. Cornish's woodshed, which Jack thought he had done. As Mr. Cornish was in bed with laryngitis Jack did not disturb him, on making the delivery. Unfortunately Jack had left the tree in the Schubert's woodshed by mistake and Mrs. Schubert, not knowing where it had come from, gave it away.

Another last minute surprise to the organisers came when it came time to produce a Santa Claus. Mrs. Steele, who had always had a large part to play in previous concerts, had left St. Paul's congregation. What no one realised, however, was that she owned the Santa Claus suit that was always used, and had taken it with her. Not to be outdone, my sister, Gay, was dressed in her sister's red jacket, trimmed appropriately with wool in all the proper places, and played the part reasonably successfully.

The year 1943 brought another year of disruption and uncertainty due to the war. The jam committee was active again. The local Port Dover Branch of the Red Cross met regularly, to knit and send socks and cigarettes to local service men serving in camps at home and overseas. The W. A. of St. Paul's quilted endlessly as did the Women's Institutes of the County and beyond.

Alice "Gay" Barrett escaped rolling nickels and coppers from the Sunday School collection every week by visiting her father in

Shilo and being hired to drive the Anglican Sunday School van into remote areas of Brandon Diocese, in the province of Manitoba, for the Anglican church.

In October, after a year of convoy duty out of Newfoundland, I came home on leave to be married to Hellen Mary Bowlby Browne in St. John's, Woodhouse. By delaying the wedding to October 9th, Dad and Gay were able to attend from Brandon. Hubert Jennings was my best man and all three services were represented in the wedding party. Margaret Miller, serving in the Army in Ottawa, was Maid of Honour, while Hilton Yerex and Joe Cameron, of the Navy and Bill Browne, of the Air Force, with Ross Clapp, were ushers. Reverend William Creary, rector of St. John's married us and Clarence Mitchell was our soloist. The remainder of my leave was spent on Lake Kashagawigamog, near my mother's place of birth, the village of Haliburton.

*Hellen Mary Bowlby Browne & Harry B. - home on leave to marry*

On Sunday, January 2nd, 1944 Clarence Mitchell, who was serving as Treasurer of the Sunday School came to our place for lunch and to help in balancing the books for the year end. Later Hubert and Barbara Jennings came out as Hubert was home for the holidays and had been coerced into auditing the Sunday School accounts. Everyone had a very good time for the day, and Clarence and mother worked diligently on the accounts, I am told, though it never was clear whether the books were ever properly balanced or audited.

The following Sunday Mr. Cornish held a special Children's service in the church, instead of regular Sunday School. Lorraine McNeilly joined Gay in the choir for the first, having walked over from their home on the Scotch line to go in to church with her.

On January 18th, 1944 the Financial Statement was presented to an annual meeting of the Select Vestry by Alton E. Hoover and A. E. Williamson, Wardens, as audited by Theo. McMillan. Financially the church was finally thriving, having paid their apportionment, installed a stoker for $435.00, made repairs of $118.00 to the steeple, put up a sign board and had a bank balance of $1,158.32.

Some of their regular expenses included Insurance, $47., Heating of church, $184., S. S., $63., water rates - Rectory & Church $25., Taxes, $88.00. The annual stipend and salaries were: Rector, $1500., Organist, $300., Sexton, $140.00. The extra parochial expenses were; Budget and Jewish Missions - $540., Synod Assessment for 1943 - $36., Pollard Mem. Fund - $3.00.

The W. A. Report was made by Adeline Garner, Treas. The St. Paul's Club report by Frances J. Williamson, Treas. The Sunday School report by Clarence Mitchell, Secty-Treas. and the Church Choir report by Eileen Lowe, Secty-Treas. The report by Thos. Pope and Harry Lawrence, Wardens of Christ Church, Vittoria, showed a deficit of $39. on total disbursements of $410.75. Their synod assessment was $10. in arrears.

On Tuesday, February 22nd, a meeting was held in the Sunday School to attempt to revive the A.Y.P.A. There was a good attendance of interested young people and the revival seemed assured. Alice "Gay" Barrett was elected President at a later meeting and regular well attended meetings were held. The following day, the Ash Wednesday service, saw a choir of ten and a congregation of ten in attendance.

The long expected invasion on the second front was reported to be under way on June 6th, 1944. British, Canadian and American troops started landing in Normandy by both air and sea. The King spoke during the afternoon and Roosevelt in the evening and both urged people to prayer. On July 1st the girls from the A.Y.P.A. carried sheets in the Calithumpian Parade to collect for the Canadian Red Cross. Some of them sold tags for a War Charity in the afternoon, as did the Girl Guides. One of the training planes from the Jarvis School, blew up near the Dog's Nest, killing three airmen.

The Sunday School picnic, which had been postponed by bad

weather, was held at the farm on July 19th, with all those attending enjoying themselves. It was reported to-day that John Harris Buck had been badly wounded overseas. On August 1st the family received the sad news that my cousin Jack McGrath, was killed only twenty minutes after landing in Normandy in his Bren Gun Carrier. I spent a weekend with him in camp, in Aldershot, just over a year before, being the last of the family to see him. We had a marvellous time. The Royal Canadian Legion in Kinmount, Ontario, is named in his memory.

*I visit my cousin Jack McGrath in Aldershot, England*

By the end of August I had passed an examining board in Halifax, to be named a Commissioned Warrant and begin officer training in H.M.C.S. Cornwallis. In mid-September Dad was nominated as the Conservative candidate for the riding of Norfolk. On September 29th, Clarence Strople returned from overseas and another parishioner, Dick Ryerse was reported missing in action. On October 11th, 1944 Peggy Wamsley and Ralph Herring, an airman from Jarvis Training School, were married in a very pretty wedding from St. Paul's. A big reception followed in the Parish Hall for the happy couple. My sister Gay was a bridesmaid.

Church and Sunday School were held as usual on the morning of November 19th, 1944. During the afternoon a capacity crowd attended the one hundredth anniversary of the founding of Christ Church, Vittoria. The Bishop preached an impressive sermon relating to this special occasion.

Ten days later Charlie Martin received word that his son, John Martin, had his plane shot down over enemy territory. It was further reported that he had been seen to exit the crippled plane safely and that his chute had opened. The glimmer of hope that this bit of information gave was not long-lived, however. The whole community felt his family's intense sense of loss.

1945 opened with the thought on everyone's mind; "Will it bring Peace?" A year ago we were buoyed by the dis-allusion that the war would be over by Christmas, and the Germans could not possibly survive another winter of bombardment. We find instead that they are grand scrappers, these Nazis. We must give them credit for that. They evidently mean to make us pay dearly for every foot of German soil we gain from them.

This was the year of the record-breaking cold and snow blizzards for the first three months of the year. The Cockshutt and other roads were blocked to all traffic for weeks at a time. Yvonne McMillan, who had been sick for a long time, died on February 3rd. She was a very popular young woman and despite the difficulty of travel, there was a large crowd in St. Paul's on February 6th. Gay and her father walked into town and back home to the farm for her funeral.

The wartime activities of the community, by the W. A. of St. Paul's, the Red Cross and the Woman's Institutes carried on as intensely as before, if not more so. Jam, knitted socks, scarves and balaclavas and cartons of cigarettes were shipped in a never ending stream to all those who could use them. Telegrams of those reported missing in action came all too frequently and those wounded badly began to return.

Ben Ivey's dance hall had been a haven for the many, often homesick service personnel, training in the army bases locally and at the Jarvis Bombing and Gunnery School, whenever they were granted leave. Many spent a quiet hour in St. Paul's and the other churches of Norfolk when they were able and there was always a family willing to invite them

*I am granted commission in R.C.N.V.R*

home for a meal and an afternoon of fun and companionship. Throughout the war years, the Masons held regular dances in their Hall on Main Street which were well attended and enjoyed. Nichol's Hall was another source of dancing and at times roller skating.

News was received locally, about 9:30 a.m. on May 7th, 1945 that Germany had surrendered unconditionally to the Allies. Finally, on Tuesday, May 8th, Victory in Europe, V. E. Day, was declared. The church bells and the bell of the Town Hall began to ring wildly. Pat Yerex on hearing the bells started running up town. As he came opposite St. Paul's he could see Canon Cornish lustily pulling on the bell rope just inside the entrance. On seeing Pat, he beckoned to him and as he came closer, told him he would like him to continue to ring the church bell. As Pat took charge of the rope Canon Cornish looked him right in the eye and said; "Patrick! You must never forget this Day!"

Winston Churchill and Harry Truman broadcast to the world over radio at 9:00 a.m. and the King was heard at 3:00 p.m. The whole community was jubilant at the news. The choirs of all the churches joined for a mass service in Grace United Church that evening. The Legion turned out in full force and full regalia. The church was full to overflowing. Following the service a torch-light procession formed to march to the School grounds where a massive bonfire was lit and the revelry continued far into the night.

The war in the Pacific against the Japanese continued unabated and I had assumed that we would be transferred automatically, to that theatre. Ships were already being refitted for duty in the tropics. However all Canadian servicemen were given the option of volunteering for Pacific duty, and soon those who chose to, were granted sixty days of leave. I reasoned that I had volunteered for the duration. I was not about to volunteer a second time. Overnight I became one of two officers responsible for a skeleton crew and the refitting of our ship, or A & A's – alterations and additions – in Navy terminology, for Pacific service. By the time their sixty days of leave had expired the war with Japan was also over.

Soon Port Dover and Woodhouse boys were returning from overseas, and on the instigation of Sam Morris, Editor, of the

Maple Leaf, they were put through a welcoming ceremony on their arrival that few, if any, escaped. As most arrived by Radial car from Brantford, Cliff Long, the Conductor, would phone ahead from there, to Sam or Pat Patterson, that they were on their way. Someone would board the car at Main Street, to make sure they came all the way down to the Station. Half the town would be on the platform to receive them.

On Sunday, July 22nd, as St. Paul's matins ended, Johnnie Walker informed the congregation that Charles Misner, who had served on MTB's in the English Channel, was expected home at any moment on the Lake Erie and Northern Radial Car. Most went down to join the already burgeoning crowd of well wishers. As a bemused Charles descended from the car he was whisked across the platform to a waiting baggage truck, where all could get a good view of him, and willing volunteers started pulling it the length of the platform with an ecstatic Pat gleefully dancing ahead of them to clear the way.

Meanwhile Sam was directing traffic at the foot of Main Street and getting his entourage of flag-draped automobiles lined up for the parade. At this point there was a short delay as Charles had spotted his father's tug entering harbour, and had raced across to the pier to greet and be greeted, by Henry. He was soon returned to be loaded into Hattie Barrett's car, while the rest of those present followed them to the head of Main Street and back to his own home. Here it was necessary to introduce him to some of the younger members of his own family, who had been born or grown beyond recognition since he left home.

Some managed to escape this ordeal by hitch-hiking home or by some similar subterfuge. That same Sunday afternoon Dad joined Sam Morris, Fred Hoskins, Jack King, Pat Patterson and Harold Sherman, all in Sam's car to first call, and welcome home, Jerry Hardicker. They next drove out to Colin Ryerse's, as it had been learned that young Edmon had come in from Hamilton by auto with Ike Hewitt, fooling even his own family. He was not at home and Colin thought he had gone down the Lake shore with the Hammond's and Cruise's. They drove to Kitchen's Point where Mrs. Art Ryerse told them the boys had gone to Fisher's Glen, so the venture proved unsuccessful from Sam's point of view.

Colin told them Edmon had hardly been off the farm since he got home, picking up where he left off three or more years ago. The day he left he had been tinkering with an old engine, which he could not get to run. For the last couple of days he has been at the same old engine and so far has not got it going yet. Both Charles and Edmon, like so many other returning servicemen, brought British brides home with them from overseas. They both received instant acceptance into the parish of St. Paul's and are productively active, to this day, in Parish affairs.

That evening the Anglican church in St. Williams was celebrating its seventy-fifth anniversary, and the student, Mr. Lake, who had been there all summer, took charge of the service before a full congregation. The little frame church had just been given a new coat of white paint and looked very attractive, both inside and out. It was reported a week later that a small plane had crashed into the Empire State Building in New York, setting a fire in the building and killing nineteen people. They blamed a heavy fog for the mishap.

Peace, after almost six years of war, came at last officially on August 15th, 1945 – V. J. Day. That evening Sam Morris and Pat Patterson organised a parade to celebrate the occasion. Twenty-seven young ladies were seconded to carry one of the twenty-seven United Nation's flags each. They were in the lead of the procession to the park, where an open-air service of Thanksgiving was held. Reverend Mr. Cornish, Reverend Morley of Grace United, and Mr. Firman Smith took part. Reverend Mr. Hare of Knox Presbyterian was away. Father O'Rourke was listed on the programme as was Miss Williams of the church of the Nazarine, but neither of them were present. Ormy Backus substituted for Reeve Chart Woolley, who did not

*Home to civilian life again*

return from the Ex-wardens fishing trip, on the Bay, in time to participate.

Following the service in Powell Park, the Band, all the flag-bearers and the torch-bearers lead an enthusiastic parade of citizens to the School grounds where a huge bon-fire, topped with an effigy of the Mikado was fired. An enormous crowd remained to enjoy a colourful display of fireworks.

On November 2nd, Toby Barrett, M.P. was able to proudly report in the House of Commons, that Norfolk County, was the first County in all Ontario to reach their objective in the recent Victory Loan drive. The following day he learned that he had become a grandfather with the birth of Theobald Butler Barrett III. The sixth generation of the Barrett clan had joined the Parish of St. Paul's church, Port Dover. He was baptised on December 29th, 1945.

The family were very much involved on Sunday, November 11th, 1945 when Dad, David and Hilton Yerex and I, all as ex-servicemen at last, joined the Royal Canadian Legion parade to the Memorial Gates for the impressive Remembrance day ceremonies. We attended matins at St. Paul's immediately afterwards, where Archbishop Seager confirmed a class of some twenty-five candidates, some of whom were from Christ Church, Vittoria. The church was blessed with an overflow congregation, requiring extra chairs in the aisles.

The highlight for St. Paul's and our beloved Rector, the Reverend Mr. Cornish, in 1946, was his appointment by Archbishop Seager as Canon of St. Paul's Cathedral, London. This was in recognition, no doubt, of his many activities outside his normal duties as Rector, for the past forty-five years, of St. Paul's, Port Dover. Canon Cornish had represented the diocese, and was well respected, for many years on the General Board. He had been dedicated to the Huron Sunday School Association. Canon Cornish had served as deanery representative, secretary and chairman of the Diocesan Board of Religious Education over many years, as well..

As already mentioned Canon Cornish took a special interest in the religious welfare of the young people of the Parish and was instrumental in the establishment of the Huron Church Camp.

432   The Parish of St. Paul's

Locally he maintained a life-long interest in Erie Lodge, No. 149, A. F. & A. M., serving as Master and for many years as Lodge Chaplain. He took a keen interest in the Norfolk Historical Society, as well. Canon Cornish took a keen interest in the affairs of the local Library, serving for many years on that Board. He was a prime mover in the establishment of our present Centennial Library, giving it a hands-on boost by helping to clear the site of the historic, old, two-storey Brock home, which it replaced.

On February 26th, 1947 it was noted in the Register that the organist, Alex Clark had left St. Paul's for the position of organist in St. James Church, Ingersoll. Mr. Charles Skelcher, of Simcoe, replaced him on a temporary basis. He was soon accepted as our permanent organist, being replaced by Mrs. McMillan while holidaying in late June.

From January 30th, to May 1st, 1949 services were held in the Parish Hall while repairs were made to the Church arches, which were discovered to be deteriorating seriously. They had to undergo major rebuilding and redecorating, with heavy steel support beams

Baptism of Jennifer "Penny" at St. Paul's, 1947 - Mrs. Frank Barrett, Miss Erie Bowlby, Mrs. Tom "Phyllis" McGrath, Russell Milne Browne, Emily Barrett, Dorothy M. Barrett [in rear] Beverley Anderson, ? [hidden] Alice L. Barrett, ?, Frank Barrett, Culver Bowlby, Hellen Barrett, holding Penny, Toby III & father, Harry B., Canon David Cornish, Mrs. R. M. "Mabel" Browne, Mr. Rolph "Doc" Bowlby, Mr. Inder, Mrs. George "Adah" Pelly

being installed under the floor in the choir room and behind the organ. Other repairs were made and new wiring and lights installed, as well as walls being repainted.

While researching this period in our church history, on January 12th, 2005 I was surprised to note that Harry Gundry, whose death in his 109th year occurred last Sunday, January 9th, 2005, was baptised in St. Paul's with Walter Long, James Goodall and two other adult candidates, on Sunday, December 11th, 1949. Born in November, 1896, Harry was then 55 years of age.

*Steel support beam for west pillar of the arch in St. Paul's as seen from the Choir room*

Harry was a member of Christ Church, Vittoria. He lived his whole life, quietly, on his farm north-west of Port Ryerse, which had been the home originally of one of Norfolk's first school teachers and Judge, Judge Mitchell. A good farmer and dairyman, Harry continued to operate a tractor at age 105. He was described as a calm, gentle and dignified person, who I enjoyed visiting and found to be a wealth of information regarding early days in the Long Point Country.

On Friday, February 15th, 1952 two hundred attended a Memorial Service for King George VI in St. Paul's, Port Dover. Reverend Sleeman, represented the Anglicans with Canon Cornish, the incumbent, as well as Reverend George Morley, of Grace United and Reverend William Moorhead, of Knox Presbyterian Churches. The Legion Veterans, the Town Council and the School Board were all in attendance. Chairs had to be placed in the aisles to accommodate the overflow congregation.

About this time a flurry of historical rummaging by various members of the congregation was brought to fruition by Canon Cornish when he compiled his excellent booklet, "The First One

*Cast of A.Y.P.A members in "Fixing it for Father" a play put on in April, 1949 to help re-decorate St. Paul's. - Front row - Mrs. Ethel Steele, Muriel MacDonald Reid, Jack Bayes, Jimmy Davidson, Eileen Garner Lowe, Bruce Reid, Lorrayne McNeilly. Back row - William McNeilly, unknown, Blanche Snowden Clark, Jack Craig, Andrew Lowe, Mrs. Frank Bayes*

Hundred years." My mother, always interested in history of a local nature and active in Sunday School affairs, produced a summary of the activities in St. Paul's Sunday School written for the Centennial celebrations.

### The St. Paul's Sunday School

"The Sunday School room has for many, many years been a sort of Community Centre for the whole Village. To begin with; what man or woman who has lived in this neighbourhood more than forty years, did not attend St. Paul's S. S. or can not remember being in Miss Barrett's class.

And no matter what organisation of repute wished to hold a meeting, the door of the Parish Hall was never shut against them. The Red Cross must hold a clinic, the Lions a meeting place, the District Women's Institute a luncheon, St. Cecelia's Church a banquet, the Scouts and Guides a place to practice their rites. Where were they ever more welcome than in our Parish Hall?

Picnics, Sunday School feasts, Choir Socials, Quiltings, Sewing Bees, bazaars and Bake sales all have taken their place within its hospitable walls. Let us go back in imagination to 1903. At that time it was indeed the Sunday School room. Folding doors shut off what is now the parlour, just as it is today. The east door of that room led outdoors to where the patient horses stood in the drive shed waiting for the services to be over.

The expanding of the Women's Auxiliary, W.A., made more room necessary and the addition, known as the Primary Room, was built to permit quiltings. It only became the primary room when Miss Battersby built a W. A. room in her home.

When the Reverend Cyril Browne became Rector the tempo of the old building speeded up.

Mr. Browne was an evangelist and he loved boys. A tall, stooped, pale, delicate man, he was full of zeal. Soon the Sunday School Room was packed full of boys, many of whom as a rule went to their own church on Sundays, but met with Mr. Browne once a week for games and talks and picnics and swimming and hikes and stories of his adventures as a missionary.

On Sunday mornings we sang gospel hymns as we stood by our long benches. At Christmas he told us of the Indian Missions, and on an appointed evening a long table stretched the length of the room where each child came with a gift to place on that table. Parents and teachers came too, and all surrounded the laden table to explain and admire.

In 1910 the Reverend H. J. Johnson became our Rector. At that time there was a very musical group of young people belonging to the Church. It was not long until a lively Sunday School Orchestra was formed. They did most of their practising early Sunday morning before Sunday School classes started. With the music to interest them most of the boys and girls were there on time.

We sang with pleasure the hymns of the Church as the Orchestra accompanied us. Elva James or Roy Dell was the pianist. John Walker, Harry Moon, Murray Dillon and Percy Buck all played instruments.

We still sat on benches with the Teacher facing us on a chair and we were expected to memorise each week, the Collect for the day. Mr. Johnson stressed the Church seasons and the Church colours. On January 6th, the children met in the Sunday School for an Epiphany tea, followed by recitations and singing.

A group of Tuxis Boys was organised, affiliated with the Y.M.C.A. and weekly meetings were held by them.

In all these years the Sunday School Library was well patronised. The Librarian was kept busy exchanging books and keeping records. The Moving Picture was in its infancy and Radio was unknown, so books and papers filled a great need.

Superintendents' positions were filled by such people as Mr. Lawrence Skey and Miss Battersby. Later Col. Smith, Dr. Albert Cook, Mr. George Pelly, Mr. Charles Bridgewater and others."

by Mrs. T. B. Marjorie Barrett.

On September 28th, 1952 Canon David J. Cornish celebrated his last Communion as Rector of St. Paul's, having been the incumbent for over thirty-one years. To the delight of the Parish, but to no-one's surprise Canon and Mrs. Cornish elected to retire in Port Dover, moving into a comfortable brick house near the end of Grace Street, overlooking Lake Erie.

Here they both maintained an active and busy life. They had arrived in Port Dover with a growing family. In all they had five children. Their first-born, Stuart, died of Scarlet Fever, while very young. William, known to all as Bill, was next. His wife Florence, and daughter, Elizabeth, wife of John Blakemore, are well known residents, active in the Parish to this day. A daughter, Margaret, became Mrs. W. R. Shelley, of Deep River, and Betty married Mr. F. H. Seymour, of British Columbia. Their youngest, David Cornish, married Grace Kreuger. The Cornish children, attended school in Port Dover and grew to be young people of whom, over the years, any parent would be justifiably proud.

Upon Reverend Morley becoming seriously ill, Canon Cornish stepped in to take charge of services in Grace United. He was very well received by the United church congregation in their hour of need. Later the Presbyterians found themselves without a Minister, and Canon Cornish willingly stepped into the breach. On meeting a long-time friend on Main Street one morning, the conversation turned to the good Canon's services in the other churches.

His friend commented that "I suppose we will be hearing of you taking the Roman Catholic services, next." Canon Cornish hesitated briefly, but his modest reply was simply; "Well! If they should ask."

Continuing on in this vein, the friend commented that he could not really understand the Roman Catholic and Anglican Churches balking at union, which was being discussed in some quarters, at that time. Canon Cornish replied to this suggestion, in mock horror, with; "Oh! We are far to closely related to ever be wed!"

Canon Cornish had been working on his memoirs and though never published his comments; "On Becoming an Octogenarian" which Mrs. Burbidge also refers to, are of particular interest to me, now I am over three years into that exalted state. Here they are:

"A popular idea seem to be that, as one grows older, the desire to explore diminishes. I would like to correct this belief and kill the tendency where it exists. The land lies beyond that occupied by the Septuagenarian, and as the name has a richer, fuller sound, so the land of the 'Octos' is a richer, fuller land, a land of towering peaks, wider horizons, and landscapes flushed with beauties of colour and patterns undreamed of when a mere traveller, reluctantly plodding on through the seventies."

Upon reading this for the first time I was reminded of an oft repeated comment of my mother's when someone achieved the unexpected, which was;

"Now that's the Spirit that animated the great Lord Nelson."

Though Nelson never reached the ripe old age of eighty, let alone ninety years, I am beginning to realise what the comment can mean. By the seventies the grim reaper is beginning to show his cunning, and if you succumb to his blandishments, and give in to his arguments the end is near. If, however, you are blessed with the vision of the good Canon Cornish you can enjoy an even fuller appreciation for life, as you grow older, than you ever visualised before.

At other times I can appreciate the thinking that may have prompted my Grandfather to display the following tongue-in-cheek quote on a panel over his desk. It was as follows:

"Nelson is dead; Shakespeare is dead; and I don't feel so very well myself"

Canon Cornish often took a service in St. Paul's after his official retirement, as well as in other nearby churches or parishes. On his ninetieth birthday he preached the sermon in St. Paul's which incidentally, commemorated sixty years of service to the Anglican church since his ordination as a priest.

At ninety-five years of age Canon Cornish was still putting an optimistic, positive spin on things going on about him. As this quote attests, from an interview with the Canon, by the Maple leaf; "Never have the world's peoples been so aware of each other, their cultures, their desires, their faith. I don't see signs of failure; I see signs of success." Our world, to this day, could benefit from more people of Canon Cornish's calibre and positive outlook on life.

CHAPTER SIXTEEN

# *Reverend Herbert James Ernest Webb – 1952-1960*

Reverend Webb first officiated at a communion service on Sunday, October 5th, 1952 with a congregation of 124 in attendance, 73 of whom took communion. He was very well received. The following Wednesday he was officially inducted as Rector of St. Paul's, Port Dover, in an impressive ceremony. Nine Reverend gentlemen played a part in his Induction in the persons of Reverends D. J Cornish, Alan Gardiner, E. L. Vivian, L. W. Owen, J. M. Mills, C. D. Gemmell, J. W. McDonald, G. J. Pitts, and H. G. Humox.

Reverend Webb, who was born in London, England, in 1904, immigrated to Canada in 1926 to enrol in Wycliffe College, Toronto. As a student he spent the summers of 1927 and 1929 in the far north, around Sioux Lookout and Hudson Bay, serving on the railway to Churchill, Manitoba, in 1929. In the summer of 1928 he travelled throughout Ontario for the Canadian Bible Society.

He was ordained in June of 1930 in the diocese of Rupert's Land and while serving there he met his wife, Mary. He later served in the Peace River country, in the Diocese of Athabaska, on two separate charges with a period in between spent in the Diocese of Toronto. He held the charges of Beaton, Tottenham and Palgrave during that period of his ministry. Following his second stint in Athabasca he returned to Ontario to serve the parish of Bayfield, Middleton and Varna for two years before accepting the parish of St. Paul's which included Christ Church, Vittoria.

On December 8th, 1952 Mrs. H. R. Parke, my Aunty Alice,

died, in the house that she had been born in, over ninety-one years before. She had been active, to the very last, when felled by a stroke.

During one of the early vestry meeting, at which Reverend Webb presided, he made the suggestion that the name "Select Vestry" had outgrown its time and place, and he felt the Parish should modernise by calling their governing body a Board of Management. After a brief pause, while the import of this suggestion sank in, my father raised strong objections to the whole idea.

Reverend Webb, quite innocently added fuel, to the growing fire in my father's mind, by jokingly commenting that "I suppose you would like to see us return to the horse and buggy and meetings held by the full of the moon, too."

Dad replied that; "That is a ridiculous argument to use, automobiles have certainly improved our way of getting around, and carrying on business, although you have to agree, the horse has been proven to be a much safer means of transportation." He then pointed out that his objection stemmed from the fact it was a time-honoured, traditional name for the governing body of all Anglican Church's and as such, was in a small measure unique. He then com-

*Alison S. Kelland at the console of the organ in St. Paul's Church, Halifax, N.S. July, 1971. He was organist of St. Paul's, Port Dover from 1957 to 1962*

mented; "I suppose you will next want to make up your own prayers like the Methodists do." The subject was dropped for the moment.

On March 1st, 1953 a special fisherman's service took place at matins with prayers directed toward the opening of the fishing season. On April 15th, Kenneth Painter and Georgia Morris were married, with padre Lambert assisting, he and fellow veteran, Sam Morris, father of the bride, being both good friends and amputees. Again on September 19th, the church was full for the wedding of William Bowlby Browne and Alice L. "Gay" Barrett. On September 30th, 1953 Hubert Baldwin Barrett, the last of his generation, was buried. November 15th, was celebrated as Laymen's Sunday and eleven of the men of the congregation took part in the matins and evensong. On December 27th, Julia Alice, daughter of Hilton and Ruth Yerex, was baptised.

A great number of baptisms were performed throughout 1954. On May 9th, there were eight baptisms during the day. Reverend Clarence Mitchell had been ordained in Hamilton that morning and both he and Canon Cornish, assisted the rector at evensong in St. Paul's, that night.

On January 19th, 1958 Hugh Massy Barrett was baptised at 4:30 p.m. On the following Sunday, January 26th, 10 infants were baptised in St. Paul's, but no names are recorded. On July 6th, a Kelland baptism is noted. This would be Jeremy, son of Major Louis and Eleanor Sherk Kelland, of Camp Borden and the grandson of St. Paul's organist, Allison Kelland. Bishop George Huron confirmed 12 candidates at 3:00 p.m. on October 12th, 1958.

On March 1st, 1959 76 attended the annual Fishermen's Service. On Sunday, March 22nd, a special dedication service was held to dedicate the Burses and veils for the Cruets, or chalices, used in the communion service. During August Reverend Clarence Mitchell officiated for all services, during the Rector's holidays. [ Finally sympathy is shown for the beleaguered historian, as the names of those baptised, married or buried are recorded in full in the church register.]

During matins on Sunday, November 29th, 1959 with a congregation of 120, Mrs. W. H. "Hattie" Barrett was presented with a Dominion Life Membership in the Women's Auxiliary. The death and burial, on December 15th, of the beloved Chatelaine of the

Mrs. Harry "Hattie" Barrett, made Dominion Life Member of the W. A. in Nov. 1979

beautiful and historic old Ivey home by the 1806 dam site of Dover, Mrs. Charles Franklin "Imogen" Henry Ivey is recorded with great sadness by the parish.

On Monday, January 4th, 1960 the first service of three to celebrate the annual Week of Prayer was held in Knox Presbyterian church, and involved all three ministers. On Wednesday the second in the series was celebrated in Grace United church. The third and final service in the series was celebrated by Reverend Webb, in St. Paul's assisted by Reverend T. Boyd, of Knox and Reverend Gray Rivers of Grace United.

On February, 28th, Reverend L. A. Nelles officiated at matins as the Rector was in hospital, the evening service was cancelled. On Easter Sunday, April 17th, 1960, there were 63 communicants attended the 8:00 a.m. service, 221 attended matins and 46 evensong, with a total collection of $656.65 being recorded. Seven private communion services were performed.

The whole community was shocked to learn of the death of our very popular Dr. Andrew E. Williamson, from a massive heart attack, while attending a Medical Convention. His funeral from St. Paul's on April 22nd, was attended by over 200 mourners. On

Sunday, April 24th, 1960 the students of the Sunday School presented their Lenten boxes. Following the recording of 82 members of the parish in attendance at evensong, this final note appears: "This marks the end of 7 years, 7 months, as Rector of St. Paul's." Signed: H. J. E. Webb. The Webbs moved to London where he became Rector for the parish of St. Stephen's. In 1973 Mr. Webb retired. Reverend Webb died in London in 1980, having served faithfully as a priest of the Anglican communion for fifty years.

Over 32 years after Reverend Webb left St. Paul's, on November 17th, 1992 I was working on the finances of the Port Dover Harbour Museum Addition in our construction trailer, on site, when a young lady appeared, to introduce herself as Joyce Holwerda, of London. She had come to assess our use of the first part of our Government grant for the project. After an inspection of the building and our accounting, she joined William Gunn, Project Manager and me, for lunch and a friendly chat. Her opening comment was; "You have not met me before but you know my husband very well, I believe. He is George Webb, he talks of your family often, as he grew up here, while his father was Rector of St. Paul's Church."

CHAPTER SEVENTEEN

# The Reverend Alan Gardiner's Incumbency – 1960-1965

The Reverend Alan Gardiner's incumbency in St. Paul's officially began on May 1st, 1960. His induction as Rector of St. Paul's was carried out on Sunday, May 26th, by Archdeacon H. F. Appleyard, the Archdeacon of Brant, with the able assistance of Canon D. J. Cornish and the Reverends Larry W. Owen, David M. Miln, David G. Rees, and C. A. Wardner.

Like his predecessor, Reverend Webb, Reverend Mr. Gardiner was born in London, England. Coming to Canada, he graduated with a B. A. in 1923 from Bishop's, in Lennoxville, Quebec. The following year he obtained an M. A. from the same Institution. Enrolling in Trinity College, University of Toronto, he obtained an L. Th. in 1926, followed by a Bachelor of Divinity degree in 1928. Associated with the Diocese of Ottawa Mr. Gardiner was ordained first a Deacon and in 1926 a Priest of the Diocese, where he served until 1931.

In 1931 Reverend Gardiner moved to the Diocese of British Columbia to take charge as Rector of the Garrison Church, in Esquimalt. From 1936 until the outbreak of war in 1939 he served on the staff of Christ Church Cathedral, Victoria. With the declaration of war Reverend Gardiner volunteered for active service as a Chaplain, with the Canadian Army, serving overseas in that capacity for four years. At the end of hostilities he returned to Victoria, B. C. to join the staff of Brentwood College, in that city.

He eventually returned as the Parish Priest to the church in Cranbrook, B. C. In 1949 Reverend Gardiner came east to the Diocese of Huron, serving in the Parishes of Waterford and Mount

Pleasant and later in St. Stephen's in London. He, and his charming wife, came to St. Paul's in the spring of 1960 from St. Stephen's, London. The Wardens, as a welcoming gesture, had approved the expenditure of in excess of $10,000.00 for much needed renovations to the Rectory.

It was at this same time that I had given up active farming, and become a teacher of Agriculture in the Secondary School system. It was only a matter of time, therefore, before I was seconded to the Sunday School as a teacher of the senior boys, and a bit later I served as Superintendent under Reverend Gardiner's guidance.

I soon learned that "his bark was much worse than his bite," as they say. He could be quite abrupt, and did not suffer fools gladly, but once you broke through his apparent crusty exterior, he was a very warm, and sincere friend. His austere, military bearing, and bushy eyebrows seemed to frighten many of the students of the Sunday School, though that was furthest from his intention, but I know that my daughters were always in awe of him.

One Sunday morning as I was busy getting ready for opening exercises, Mr. Gardiner came in with a pained expression on his face, a noticeable, heavily bandaged finger, and an obvious desire

*Marriage of Emily Barrett - Rev. Alan Gardiner, Emily, Stephan Molewyk, Groom, Jacqueline Yerex, Rudy Godron*

for sympathy. I rose to the bait and asked, in a very concerned tone, what had happened to produce such an injury. He explained in some detail how he had been bitten, the night before, by a stray dog, running loose on the sidewalk. Maintaining my appearance of deep concern I exclaimed: "My Goodness! Is the dog all right?" If looks could kill I should have withered into oblivion, on the spot.

We shared an interest in ornithology. To my amazement, on being asked to step into the study one day, Mr. Gardiner set out before me two original volumes of Wilson's "Birds of America." I could not tear myself away from these rare and beautiful books, the first attempt by anyone to illustrate the birds of North America, beginning even before Audubon. Realising my interest and appreciation of Wilson's works, Mr. Gardiner tentatively offered to give them to me. Mrs. Gardiner vetoed this move, however, leading me to believe that she was the actual owner of them. I understand they are now a part of the collection of the Lawson Library at the University of Western Ontario, where, in truth, they belong.

On Sunday, July 2nd, 1961 a congregation of 110 witnessed the dedication of the oaken credence table a gift of Mrs. John S. Martin, in memory of her husband. Mrs. W. H. Barrett also gave the two brass alter candles, as a similar memorial to her husband. Repairs and re-bricking of the church tower was carried out that summer, as well as fencing of the Rectory grounds.

The Sunday School was bursting at its seams with 40 tiny tots in Blanche Clark's nursery school room, and 35 in the junior class, taught by Edna Winter. The dozen or more senior classes totalled an additional 200 students on the rolls. Harry Smith, one of the teachers, was also a qualified architectural designer, employed by Bud Smale's architectural firm in Simcoe.

Harry volunteered to design a layout of seven classrooms, with cement block walls and hallway in the unfinished basement, to provide badly needed space. Harry's plan was approved by the Vestry and stamped, as required by building control, at no charge by Bud Smale, Architect. Theo. "Jimmie" Rust was engaged to build the classrooms and he set to work. On checking the progress of the work, Bud found no workmen present, but he did find serious fault with the way it was being done. Without hesitation he grabbed a 2 by 4 and completely demolished an offending cement block wall.

Theo, on returning to the job next day, was livid over the way Bud had pointed out the error in construction. Realising where the error lay, however, he rebuilt the wall and completed the rest of the work properly, without further comment. As Harry commented, recently, Bud was a practical joker at heart, and he used that ploy to terminate an argument he could not seem to win with Johnnie Walker, the people's warden, and church representative overseeing the job. Harry's plan called for a landing and right-angle turn to the stair leading to the basement classrooms. Johnnie insisted it be one straight run. All attempts to prove to him that there was not sufficient room for this were to no avail. Bud finally threw up his hands, and appeared to give in.

Upon making his next inspection, Johnnie Walker's face lit up with pleasure, for he could see that the new stair was a straight run into the darkened recesses of the basement. Turning on the light, he walked down to the bottom, where to his chagrin he found the last step ended smack against the solid outer wall. There was no room whatsoever to get off it. Over-ruling contractor George Erinberg's objections, Bud had insisted the stair be built as Johnnie had ordered. With a very red face, Johnnie finally agreed to Harry's plan of a stair with a landing, as you will find it to-day. Bud had finally made his point. On October 22nd, the renovations to the Parish Hall were dedicated.

In 1962 the mortgage on the Parish Hall was burned with great fanfare. Long-time Choirmaster Johnnie Walker presented a Processional Cross to St. Paul's in memory of his wife, Charlotte "Lottie" Walker. It was dedicated on November 25th, in the presence of 138 parishioners. Reverend Stanley Sharples preached the sermon. A new furnace was also installed in the Church. About this time Archie Morris, who had been serving as Superintendent of the Sunday School, became ill. Harry Smith agreed to fill in for Archie on a temporary basis. Temporary in this instance was for the next six years, only terminated, in 1969, when Harry moved out of Port Dover to a new job in Woodstock.

In 1963 the Church and the Parish Hall were re-painted and the roof of the Church was re-shingled. In late July the parish-

Baptism of Stephanie Molewyk - Leonard Burfoot, ? , Stephan Molewyk, Emily Molewyk with Stephanie, Jo-Ann Watt, Canon David J. Cornish.

ioners were saddened by the death of W. A. "Bill" Cornish, the burial service being on July 28th, at 2:30 p.m. from St. Paul's, with Reverend Larry A. Owen, of Simcoe, assisting. Reverend Gardiner was on holiday for August and Canon Cornish and Reverend F. H. Allen shared the services. Canon Cornish officiated at the Forsythe - Parker wedding on August 3rd, and on August 17th, he officiated for the marriage of Harry Smith and Gwen Forrest.

A much sadder duty occurred on August 22nd, when Canon Cornish officiated at the burial of Hugh Andrew Yerex, killed tragically in an auto accident. There were 150 mourners present. In September the Board were informed that George Pelly, who had been a Superintendent and teacher in the Sunday School for many, many years was resigning from his Bible Class duties as he was moving back to his original home in British Columbia.

On September 22nd, an Altar Book, presented by Ken and Georgia Painter to the memory of Mrs. Ellen Elizabeth Slocomb was dedicated. Altar linen, and a Pulpit Lamp, donated by Mrs. G. A. Bell, were also dedicated in memory of G. A. Bell. On November 24th, 1963 a special memorial tribute was made at matins to the late President of the United States of America, John F. Kennedy.

On January 16th, 1964 the burial service took place of a long-time faithful choir member, Richard Adams. The beautiful Maytham Memorial window was installed and dedicated in 1964. At matins on April 12th, the oak memorial railings on the chancel steps, in memory of Andrew Yerex were dedicated. They were presented by Miss Florence John's, who raised Andrew at her Nursing Home on Main street, after the death of his mother, Winifred Barrett Yerex.

Although there is no explanation, Reverend Gardiner's name fails to appear in the register from May 4th, until July 5th, 1964. The services are taken by Canon Cornish or Reverend Kenneth Brueton, of Jarvis. On June 5th, Canon Cornish officiated at the burial of Theodore McMillan, whose wife served as organist for some time at St. Paul's. During the summer Johnnie Walker had the Sanctuary Chairs re-upholstered. On September 13th, Canon Cornish dedicated a Memorial window to Charles W. Barwell and his wife, Ollie J. Barwell, which was presented by their daughter Zeitha, Mrs. Alan M. Tibbetts.

Before the year was out the Choir of St. Paul's suffered yet another shock with the death on November 25th, 1964 of our organist, Charles John Cecil Skelcher. Once again our good Canon Cornish was called upon to performed the burial service. As noted in the Vestry minutes " his passing leaves a deep sense of loss in our hearts. His long service as Organist & Choirmaster of our Parish Church will long be remembered with sincere thanksgiving, by all who worked with him and worshipped at St. Paul's. He was a devout and self-sacrificing servant of the Master."

In those same minutes the Wardens, Ernie Ford & myself, reported on a long and pleasant visit we had with Mrs. Graydon "Joy" Field, who we had approached regarding becoming our permanent Choir Leader and Organist. She had already been filling in most satisfactorily during Mr. Skelcher's illness. She agreed to our request to serve for an indefinite period and it was my pleasure to make the motion that she be engaged for sixty dollars a month in that capacity. Thus began a long and happy relationship with all concerned.

Ending the year 1964 on a happy note, the Register records the Green - Clark wedding, the bride being Connie, daughter of

Blanche and Gerry Clark. The ceremony took place on the day after Christmas. Just five days later, Thomas Honey and Karen Gamble were happily married in St. Paul's. The Vestry had also received a letter from the Bishop agreeing to our request that St Paul's become a self-supporting Parish. This would come into in effect as of January 1st, 1965.

Flags were at half-mast in Powell Park, on the Post Office, at all Schools and throughout the town in honour of and respect for, Sir Winston Churchill, during the last week of January. A Memorial Service for the famous war hero and former British Prime Minister was held in St. Paul's Anglican church on Sunday, February 1st, 1965.

On January 28th, 1965 some 28 men of the fishing fleet, that were still actively fishing, had a set back in their plans, when, on returning to harbour they found the mouth of the creek completely blocked by mounds of ice. A storm had been building and there was some concern for their safety. Eventually all but the "Ciscoette," skippered by Artley Martin, with his son Jim, returned to the safety of the basin. The "Ciscoette" spent the night on the Lake, without incident.

Some of the men of St. Paul's, calling themselves "The Laymen's Group" had been meeting informally in the parish, since just after the war, in 1947. Their chief activity, as often recorded in Dad's diary, was to host a dinner in the parish, semi-annually. The Brotherhood of Anglican Churchmen, B.A.C., was first organised in Huron Diocese in 1951.

There is little in local records to indicate how long the Laymen's Group was still active beyond 1951. However, with the

*Joy Field, organist, Choir Leader and Historian of St. Paul's*

*B.A.C. members at work in the kitchen - Bob Ryerse & Jack Dennis*

blessing of the Reverend Alan Gardiner a meeting of the men of the Parish was called on April 13th, 1965. The St. Paul's chapter of the Brotherhood of Anglican Churchmen resulted from that initiative. The first President was Leonard Murrell. Hilton Yerex was named V. P., Charles Heaman, Secty. and Gerald Clark, Treasurer. A core group remains active, often sponsoring parish breakfasts, and raising money, as needed, for parish projects.

On Sunday, September 12th, 1965 Reverend Alan Gardiner officiated, and preached, at his last services as Rector of St. Paul's. A congregation of 106 attended matins and 127 were present for his final sermon at evensong. On the following Saturday, Reverend Gardiner officiated for the marriage of Peter Fowler Barrett to Karen Kolbe.

*St. Paul's chancel just prior to the fire, Nov. 20, 1962*

## Chapter Eighteen

# Reverend Donald Gray – 1965-1968

On Sunday, September 19th, 1965 the new Rector, Reverend Donald Gray, noted in the Church Register that "St. Paul's is changing men." A young man with a young family and it is hoped with young and fresh ideas, he was enthusiastically welcomed into the Parish. The following Sunday, Harvest Thanksgiving Service, was celebrated in a beautifully decorated church. Attendance is registered at 176 at matins, 46 at evensong and a Collection of $637.98.

Reverend Gray was officially inducted as Rector of St. Paul's on Wednesday evening, October 20th, 1965. Among those taking part in the solemn ceremony were Reverends G. Stanley Sharples, J. Donaldson, H. W. Harding, Stanley R. Smith, and F. Lymbaum. 133 parishioners were in attendance. At 4:00 p.m. the Gray's son, David Thomas Gray, was baptised. Evensong was cancelled on Sunday, October 31st, as parishioners were encouraged to attend a service at St. James United Church, Simcoe, where Bishop Luxton was preaching.

The St. Paul's Women's Auxiliary celebrated their 75th Anniversary with a service in St. Paul's on Wednesday, November 10th. Reverend Gray was assisted by Reverend Alan Gardiner and Reverend Herbert Webb in celebrating this important milestone in the history of our church, appropriately. 52 of a congregation of 60 celebrated communion. A highlight of the service was the presentation of a Dominion Life Membership in the W.A., to Mrs. D. J. Cornish and a Diocesan Life Membership to Mrs. Lowe.

Unexpected tragedy struck the venerable St. Paul's in the

form of an early afternoon fire on November 20th, 1965. Before it could be contained the pipe organ and men's choir room below it were completely destroyed. The heat melted the lead in the beautiful memorial east window, destroyed the flag and scorched the Bible on the lectern beyond repair. Smoke and water damage was extensive throughout the whole church. All the chancel furnishings were removed to the Parish Hall, where they were set up for use in services that would have to take place there, during the repair and redecoration of the church.

It was later learned that a ten year old juvenile youth had entered the choir rooms in the basement, either bent on mischief or looking for money. It was assumed that before leaving he had lighted the papers in a waste basket and the resultant flames had set some of the men's choir gowns alight. The fire had spread from there.

The burden, of restoring the damaged chancel, fell primarily to Reverend Gray and he tackled the onerous task with vigour and determination. The whole of the chancel walls and ceiling were

*Aftermath of the Fire on Nov. 20th, 1965*

stripped down to the lath and brick walls. The east window was damaged beyond repair and had to be removed. The angel choir surrounding its upper arch were lost for all time. When the building was ready for re-painting some changes and improvements were made. The windows were enclosed in a simulated heavy stone border, which replaced the previous narrow decorative and more intricate original window border. This same simulated ashlar treatment was carried over to the arch into the chancel. The chancel ceiling ornamentation was also altered from the original. Although the final result was outstanding, there was still something not quite right to many of us. It was the nostalgic memory of the loss of that heavenly host that no longer watched over all of us. For 31 years their absence gnawed at the edges of my consciousness.

In 2001 it became obvious that I was not alone in my feelings of loss from that disastrous fire. Olive Ryerse, among others over the years had missed them. Olive, however, did something about it, when she and her grandson Glenn Lindsay, commissioned Stacey Morrison, a local artist, to restore the angels, as a memorial to their daughter and mother respectively, Patricia Louise Lindsay, 1934 – 1999. Though the present representatives of the heavenly host are fewer in number than the original choir, they make up for it in their beauty, their flowing robes and their soft, glowing colours.

The life of the church, and death of parishioners, carried on as before. Hugh MacDonald was buried on December 20th, 1965, three days later Mrs. Harold "Katie" Smith was buried, with Canon Cornish assisting at the service. On January 6th, 1966 the burial service for Reverend Ralph Mason was conducted from Christ Church, Vittoria, with Reverend George Suell assisting. On a more pleasant note Reverend J. H. Vardy preached at matins on Sunday, January 30th, accompanied by his Grace United choir. On February 13th, in an exchange with the Presbyterians, Reverend John Callender officiated. A parade of the local Sea Scouts was a feature of matins on February 27th.

Finally, on March 27th, 1966 all the construction following the fire, culminated in the re-opening of the church for regular worship. Reverend K. C. Bolton preached at matins. Evensong was cancelled that the Rector and his Confirmation class might attend an "American Folk Mass," in Brantford.

Sunday, June 5th, 1966 was a red letter day in the life of St. Paul's when to celebrate his 90th birthday, Canon Cornish assisted at matins and preached the sermon. Two other facts are worthy of note; the day marked the 60th anniversary of his ordination and on August 7th, 1966 would mark 45 years, since he first arrived in St. Paul's to become our Rector.

Reverend K. Brueton officiated during the Rector's July holiday time. Reverend Gray performed the marriage, on July 16th, 1966 of James Vernon Kelly and Carol Joyce Howell. On July 30th Reverend Gray and Reverend Malcolm Muth officiated at the burial service for Mrs. Glenn Ryerse. Many of the parish were saddened to learn, on August 15th, of the death of Miss Clara Mason, daughter of Reverend Ralph Mason whose own death had been recorded less than eight months previously. Miss Mason was a good friend and a diligent worker in the church, though afflicted with an unfortunate ailment, that in earlier times would no doubt be referred to as "wry-neck." This caused Dad to once comment, quite uncharitably but very descriptively, that "Clara takes a hen's-eye view of everything." You had only to see an old hen searching a bit of barren barnyard for that last kernel of wheat, to grasp his meaning.

A new organ had been installed, considerable controversy followed, led by Stephan Molewyk, as to its having been located at the back of the church. The argument was that its distance from the choir in the chancel would be noticeably out of synchronisation with their singing. Though not an expert by any means, I can vouch for the fact that when sitting beneath it, when I do attend a service, I am convinced that my brother-in-law, Stephan, had a point. The organ was dedicated on September 11th, 1966 with an Organ Recital by Mr. Peter Coates.

Reverend Alan Gardiner preached the sermon for Harvest Thanksgiving on Oct 2nd, 1966. Two days later the burial service for Captain Oliver Cromwell was held with 125 mourners. On October 15th, 1966 Mrs. Mildred Robertson of the Central Diocesan Chancel Guild hosted a very successful one day Conference here. Mrs. Hilton "Ruth" Yerex was elected President of the Diocesan Chancel Guild and Mrs. Robert "Lois" Ryerse was elected Corresponding Secretary.

Mr. Arthur Thompson, for 14 years a warden of St. Paul's, was buried on November 10th, 1966 by Reverend Gray, assisted by Canon Cornish. The new Vestry and furnishings were used for the first time. It should be noted at this time that Johnnie Walker had presented the cupboards and sink-board in 1965, for the convenience and use of the Chancel Guild and Frank Barrett had presented a new double sink. It was also at that time that Mr. Walker had supplied the new chancel floor and carpet. The Bible Class of 1961 presented a new Church flag to replace the one lost to the fire.

On behalf of the Wardens and the Parish Reverend Donald Gray wrote to welcome the Reverend Ronald Hunt and offered to him the position of Honourary Assistant to the Parish. It was understood there would be no monetary advantage in the appointment. His assistance in the work of the Parish would be most welcome and appreciated, however.

Clarence Finch and Susan Gash were married on November 12th, 1966 with 100 guests in attendance. On November 27th a very successful youth service was held by Reverend Gray for the youth of both St. Paul's and Grace United. Over 300 attended and all found seating, a record. On December 9th a pretty wedding of Bernard Smuck and Gloria Champion saw a congregation of 100 celebrants. Two hundred mourners attended the funeral of Rita Parker on December 17th.

New Year's Day,

*The new window is installed & dedicated on Jan. 1st, 1967*

1967, was a day of celebration in St. Paul's when Bishop George Huron re-dedicated the beautifully renovated church. Reverend Donald Gray was determined to draw more young people to the church and its activities and his efforts were being seen to be paying off. The Sunday School was thriving and with the introduction of guitars and other musical instruments to the occasional service, he was proving to some that it was not the old and stuffy ritual many had imagined. Don was not averse to meeting the younger crowd in their natural haunts, in the taverns and bars of Port Dover, where he would join them occasionally in quaffing a beer or two.

This brought the odd glare or disapproving look, from some members of the congregation but they could not fault his serious manner in the conducting of the service and his sermons were topical, well presented and well researched. Soon some were hinting that he was too good a Rector to be left in Port Dover for very long. He was very attentive to his visiting duties, although again some thought he carried it a bit too far, when he would spend some of his holidays helping on the farms of parishioners. He joined right in, in seeding and harvest and in other farm chores, although he expected a fair wage for doing so. His wife, Pat, a Registered Nurse, worked at her profession during the whole of their stay in the parish. This was a first for a rector's wife, but the stipend was insufficient for a young and active family to survive on without the additional income these activities provided.

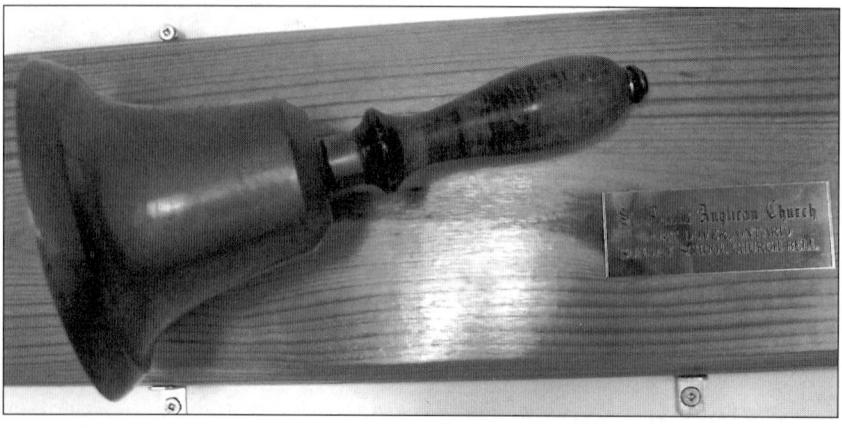

*The old Sunday School Bell, now mounted with plaque by Harry Smith*

Harry Smith, who as Superintendent of the Sunday School, worked closely with Reverend Gray, soon became a close friend. Many a knotty problem of the parish was discussed over a beer, often provided from Don's private stock, in Harry's living room. I am sure, unbeknown to most of the residents of Port Dover, let alone the parishioners of St. Paul's, Don Gray had established as a hobby, one of the most immaculate, and rigidly controlled wineries and micro- breweries in the area, in the Rectory basement. Here covered containers of fine wines, in the making, and carboys of amber chardonnays and rich dark red merlot's worked quietly toward perfection, to be bottled and aged at the appropriate time. In another corner a mini-vat of a rich, full-bodied beer or ale gave off the subtle aromas of fermentation. Reverend Gray would be fully justified if he boasted a bit of his prowess as an amateur vintner.

In the spring of 1967 a hot topic of discussion within the Anglican communion was Church Union. Our Vestry purchased 18 copies of the booklet for further study, before any contact was made with United Church officials. Reverend Gray and Reverend Vardy of the United Church voiced concerns over the programme of religious education in the local schools.

On May 9th, 1967 Canon Cornish assisted in the burial service for 86 year old Harry Hussey, famous for his work over many years, first as an architect, later as a trusted advisor to officials of Government in China. Born to Mr. & Mrs. George Hussey in 1882 Harry Hussey was a quiet, studious boy who from an early age worked with his father. His school chum

*Jonathon Ellis, owner of the Knitting Mill*

Norman Holden remembered him as a very honest, unselfish boy who had to quit school early and go to work in Jonathon Ellis's Knitting Mill for 75 cents a day. Through Continuation School he continued his education and when Mr. Ellis bought a Mill in Jamestown, New York Harry was sent down with Mr. Ellis's son to work there. When that business closed Harry was out of a job.

Rather than return home a perceived failure, Harry travelled in search of work, while studying architecture from books he obtained on the subject. After travelling as far afield as Mexico he finally landed a labourer's job in a Kentucky mine. He was 25 years old. Then the miners went on strike. An investigation was launched at which Harry Hussey was required to testify. His testimony was so lucid and logical that Harry gained the attention of the industrialist John D. Rockefeller, who had an interest in the mine.

Under Rockefeller's guidance Harry Hussey was soon touted as the architect of the new Y. M. C. A. building in Columbus, Ohio. He graduated from a Chicago Art Institute, while working in that city, and soon after was sent by the Rockefeller Foundation to design and build Medical buildings in China. Here he became friends of influential government leaders in both China and Japan. Soon this quiet, reserved Canadian was an important foreign advisor in the Chinese government service.

Harry Hussey during his 40 years in China could claim as personal friends such greats as Chaing Kai Shek, Sun Yet Sen, Yuan Shi Kai, Chang Tso-Lin, W. W. Yen, Wellington Koo and many others. In the late 1940's Harry wrote a biography of the Chinese Empress Tz'u Hsi entitled "Venerable Ancestor." Later he wrote a second book, entitled "Manchukuo."

Harry Hussey and his son Henry returned to Port Dover in 1927 for a visit, and in subsequent years as well. Henry was equally fluent in English & Chinese, returning to Canada in 1931 to enrol in Ridley College. Soon after arrival in China Harry began sending beautiful pieces of fine china and other rare artifacts of Chinese culture to his sister, Helen Hussey, who opened Port Dover's renowned "Oriental Shoppe" as a result. To this day, though no longer owned by the Hussey family, this is the place to shop for something a bit different, in Port Dover.

On July 5th, 1967 the burial of Charlie Bridgewater, cobbler and bandsman for many years in Port Dover, took place. The Ladies of the W. A. at this time, donated an impressive Funeral Pall for use by the Church. The marriage of John Blakemore and Elizabeth Cornish was celebrated on December 30th, 1967. Canon Cornish assisted, naturally, at the wedding of his grand-daughter.

The new East window was installed on February 5th, 1968 and on Sunday, February 11th, it was dedicated by Bishop H. F. Appleyard. February 17th, saw the end of an era, with the burial of the Grand-dame of Port Dover, in the person of Mrs. Morley Catherine Homer Buck, from her impressive frame mansion, once the centre of all that went on at the famous Buck's Orchard Beach Hotel. I remember how impressed I was as a boy with the beautiful grounds and porte cochere on the north side of the huge two storey home, when I would visit, in company with my Aunty Alice. Mrs. Buck sat regally as we entered, to be made welcome and offered tea, with a rich confectionary of some sort.

On Good Friday, April 12th, 1968 Reverend Gray conducted a three hour Service of Meditation. It commenced with a congregation of 80 parishioners, but by the end of the service only 10 participants remained. A private communion for five communicants,

*Home of Mr. and Mrs. Morley Buck, St. George Street*

followed by another informal service at the Johnson Nursing Home, on April 17th, 1968 as recorded in the church register, marks the last official entry of Reverend Donald Gray as Rector of St. Paul's, Port Dover.

My rather sad and lasting memory of the Gray family is of a half-ton battered, blue truck, pulling away from the Rectory with canvas-covered belongings piled higher than the cab itself, in the pick-up box. Tied tightly to the chassis, on top of this bulging cargo, was an upturned picnic table which had ensconced safely between its legs a slightly effervescent, 15 gallon carboy, of rich amber wine in the making.

Although Reverend Donald Gray now lives in Edmonton, Alberta, he regularly returns to Port Dover on holiday where he often spends some time camping on the grounds of his friends Bob and Barbara Ryerse down the lake shore. This past summer upon attended church one Sunday morning I was delighted to find Donald renewing acquaintances with friends he had made after becoming our rector forty years ago this year.

As a result of our brief visit in church I took a draft copy of this church history for Donald's perusal and we enjoyed a longer visit. On saying that he had some thoughts on the way the parish has developed over the intervening years I assured him I would welcome any thing he might wish to say and that I would be pleased to include anything he wished to put in writing for us.

Our conversation bore fruit in September when Barbara Ryerse kindly dropped off an e-mail from Donald intended for my use.

It begins with "Harry, Here are some thoughts." and ends with "Harry, Please do with this whatever you wish."

> I was 28 years old when I became a rector of St. Paul's Church, Port Dover in 1965. Bishop George Luxton, introducing me to the parish called it "the nicest small single-point parish in the diocese." It had a clearly "low church" worship style as was most common then within the diocese. Morning prayer was the principal service on Sunday three weeks out of four. Evening prayer was held every Sunday. Canon Cornish was very much alive and

active and of considerable support to me. His theology at that time was very liberal while I was much more orthodox. I remember him as saying to me at the end of the service "I wouldn't say that your sermon was all wet this morning but it was certainly very damp." I now find myself to be much more liberal and radical in my theological thinking than he ever was. How different is my thinking at age 68 than it was at age 28.

I was only in the parish for some few months when the fire occurred. I held fairly to the belief that churches should be open at all times for persons who wish quiet contemplative time with prayer. A twelve-year-old boy set fire to the place one Saturday afternoon. Much of my work for the next year and a half was in the rebuilding and redecorating of the church. We were greatly helped at that time by a friend of Bishop Luxton's whose name was Carl Dunker. He was the president of Dunker Construction Company of Kitchener. I believe it was due to his good influence and negotiation with the insurance company that we ended up with a replenished church.

The decorator that we hired (I think his name was McDougal) hired a local labourer as his assistant. We kept it very secret when I discovered after the hiring that the man was the father of the boy who set the fire. It reminded me of an old film of Charlie Chaplin where Charlie worked as a glazier who followed his son who went before him breaking windows. It was McDougal's idea to paint in what looked like stonework around the borders of the sanctuary. I believe the result is very attractive. I was (and am) concerned that the church was over decorated. The fire allowed for the opportunity to remove the angelic choir and the quotation around the entrance to the sanctuary. I was surprised to see them restored in recent years.

There were several things that distorted my understanding of my work in those years. The most significant was my own anxiety in supposing that I was not doing a good job for the parish. I was also plagued with financial difficulties. I simply could not make ends meet to supply the needs of my four children on the minimum stipend that I was making. So it was that during my summer holidays I went to work as a farm labourer near Brantford. I did not feel I had the right to complain because many workers at Ivey's or in fishing or farming were no better off than I was. Thus it was that I asked the Bishop to move me to an urban location. When my resignation was announced I was shocked by the dismay of many persons in the parish. It seems that I was appreciated much more than I had allowed myself to realize.

So it is that I left Port Dover feeling all the more guilty about letting down the parish and subsequently I have learned to not prejudge my circumstance by not consulting with those with whom I work.

The parish of Port Dover was very good for me and for my family and I consider it a great privilege to have been the appointed minister amongst you. I love to return during the summers and visit some of the persons I knew 38 years ago. Too many of them now reside in the cemetery to the north of town. I am grateful to have been part of your history and follow your progress with great interest.

Donald Gray.

Upon adding this to my wandering tale of our parish of St. Paul's I was left with the strong impression that the Reverend Donald Gray, our oldest living Rector, has never really left us, despite all that has transpired in the intervening years. In spirit at least he is still present and shares our trials and tribulations, as well as our jubilations, with us. May there continue to be a few staunch friends who have refused "to move north" and are here to provide a welcoming band of friends whenever he can manage a visit, for many years to come.

CHAPTER NINETEEN

# *Reverend Douglas Steele Henry – 1968-1983*

The Reverend Douglas Steele Henry first signed the St. Paul's church register as Rector on April 28th, 1968. His entries were very precise and neat. He only once noted the weather, however, during his fifteen years as rector. He brought quite a different style and approach to his ministry, as opposed to that of Reverend Donald Gray. No-one could wish for more gracious hosts than the Henry's when visiting them in the rectory. However Reverend Henry, until he felt he knew you well, seemed a very shy man, and an almost reluctant parish visitor.

He delighted in tinkering with mechanical devices and had an all consuming love for old clocks and vintage automobiles. The Rectory reverberated to the constant ticking of his extensive collection of antique time pieces. To be present in the rectory, on the hour, was to be enveloped in a cacophony of chimes, bells and unusual notes from the collection, as each seemed to vie with the others for your attention. The only such collection that I ever knew of, that outdid it, was that of "Toty" Smith, the jeweller, who was located in a small shop, next "The Fair", when I was growing up.

In November of 1968 the Vestry appointed Mr. Ernest Graff as Chairman of a Church Coordinator committee. It was hoped such a committee could help to make things run a little more smoothly than in the past and though he was not present that night Mr. Graff had agreed to accept the position if elected. Decisions were also made to accept as World Mission Projects, one in Venezuela over India. Support of a Teacher Training College in Koroguee, Africa was also agreed to, while support was given to a local project in Hornepayne and the East Parish of the Six nations Reserve. Harold Schilz agreed to look at the furnace which had been misbehaving.

The Orchestra Boys, who had been allowed to practice in the Sunday School, had drawn complaints from neighbours for perceived rowdyism. They were asked to use the basement until after Christmas. A request by them to hold a dance in the Parish Hall was declined. Bob Ryerse agreed to speak to them. Bruce Reid reported on the formation of a Glee Club and their desire to meet in the Parish Hall. This was approved.

In March of 1969 Clarence Finch agreed to take over the Treasurer's duties from Chuck Heaman. The position had been vacant for some time. The Board learned with regret that Harry Smith was moving from town and a new Sunday School Superintendent would be required. He had faithfully performed these duties for the past eleven years, and some form of formal recognition was recommended by the W.A.

Reverend Mr. Henry regularly attended the Sunday School classes and in his shy way endeared himself to the pupils, though many seemed a bit unsure of what to make of this rather eccentric man. They were all impressed with the long black cloak, with the crimson lining that he seemed to revel in wearing on cool autumn days. It must be admitted that he cut a distinguished figure as he strode from the rectory to the church, with the cloak flashing red as the breeze caught it. It is no wonder, too, that he soon acquired the name "Zorro" among many of the students of the Sunday School. He wore both the cloak and the name well.

Reverend Henry had suggested a Congregational Picnic in 1969 and a committee set to work arranging for such a celebration at the Potash School Conservation area on the last Sunday in June. A request was received from the family of the late T.B. Barrett to place a Memorial window in the Epistle side of the Chancel. This was approved, as was a request by the Howell family to place a plaque on the altar rail, which they had donated.

Soon after their arrival, Mr. Henry became frustrated by the very slow movement of wash water from the small ground-floor washroom. Carefully taking the trap and connecting drain apart, he found the cause of the blockage, to be a small red plastic model corvette, no doubt lost by one of Reverend Don Gray's youngsters.

Mr. Henry's next involvement with the sewage system serving the rectory developed into a much more involved operation. The whole system had become so sluggish that he decided to take drastic action. Everything on being tested, seemed in working condition inside the house. Therefore the problem must lie in the outside line leading to the town sewer itself. Having made this decision one warm summer day, and having located where the offending drain-pipe was, Reverend Douglas rolled up his sleeves and began to dig at the south-east corner of the house.

About mid-afternoon of the same day I was introducing Murray Grant to people I felt he should know as the new programme coordinator for Fanshawe College in Norfolk. We knocked on the rectory door but there was no response. As we turned to leave my eye caught the movement of something at the corner of the house. Closer investigation revealed a huge hole, over six feet in depth, and in the bottom the sweating, somewhat exasperated form of Douglas Henry, on the verge of heaving a shovelful of clay into our curious faces.

Upon recognising me a broad smile spread over his face as he fairly shouted "I thought you fellows would never come!" Pushing his shovel handle at me he added "Haul on this and get me out of this abominable hole." I complied and introductions having been made we were soon sitting comfortably in the study talking of educational matters, with cool gins and tonic all round. The offending tree roots, blocking the rectory sewer outlet, would be dealt with on another day.

On May 14th, 1970 Jack Dennis and Steve Molewyk attended a committee meeting instigated by Reverend Vardy of Grace United Church to discuss the drug problem among young people in the schools and the town. The position of Sunday School Superintendent was finally solved with the appointment of Mr. Jack Smith.

In 1971 the two back seats in the church were removed, to make more room for people wishing to reach the side aisles, and stored in the choir room. By September it was reported that Jack

Smith had resigned and R. Barker had agreed to assume the duties for the Church School.

February 29th, 1972 was a day of mourning by the whole community as Canon David John Cornish was buried from his beloved St. Paul's which he had served as Rector for so many years. He was in his 96th year. Assisting Reverend Henry with the service were Bishop Carman Queen, of Huron, Bishop Harold Appleyard and Reverend Larry Owen.

Honorary pallbearers were Hubert Jennings, Brian Varey, Frank Barrett, E. J. Cooper, E. M. Jacques, James Goodall, Ray Ivey, G. J. Clark and George Ryerse. The active pallbearers were Albert Blake, J. E. Maytham, Wm. F. Hagen, Carl Musselman, Bob Wagenaar and Bruce Greenslade.

As the St. Paul's Club had expressed interest in improved washrooms for the Parish Hall Frank Barrett presented plans for the same to be built on either side of the main entrance. George Powell's estimate for building, painting and wiring was $1,600.00, while plumbing and heating by Laird Mason was estimated to cost $700.00.

Each year at the annual Select Vestry meeting of the Parish, those present appointed delegates and alternates to Synod. At the 1976 Vestry meeting in January Blanche Clark and I were appointed as St. Paul's official delegates. We attended the one hundred and seventeenth session held in London on May 9th, 10th and 11th. This was a completely new experience for me, and I found the opening ceremonies in the Cathedral to be most impressive. George Syracuse, a Waterford delegate and member of the Executive Committee, took us under his wing as a guide, which we very much appreciated.

Later that summer I was appointed to the Executive Committee, where again George proved to be an invaluable mentor. The first meeting I attended was on September 24th, 1976. The highlight, however, of all those executive committee meetings was the one I attended on March 4th, 1977, when Canon Harvey Parker, of Trinity Church, Simcoe, drew me into discussions involving his original plan to deconsecrate Christ Church, Vittoria and have it sold. This is covered in more detail in the capsule history of Christ Church, Vittoria, found elsewhere in this volume.

On June 5th, 1977 a special service was held to celebrate the 125th Anniversary of the laying of the corner-stone of St. Paul's Church. The Rt. Reverend H. F. Appleyard, Reverend H. J. E. Webb and Reverend Donald Gray all attended to take part in the celebration of this milestone in the progress of our church.

On Sunday evening March 5th, 1978 the Right Reverend G. H. Parke-Taylor, Suffragan Bishop of Huron, was guest preacher for the Annual Fishermen's Service in St. Paul's. The stained glass windows were suitably decorated with fish nets, buoys and model fish tugs and schooners, the work of Ed. Forrest and Andrew Lowe. Refreshments were served later in the Parish Hall.

At 3:00 p.m. on June 24th, 1978 Reverend Henry married two young people who are active in our church today in the persons of James Charles Lomas and Constance Lydia Jean Hawke. Connie is a member of our choir and Jim serves as a Warden of St. Paul's. That same day the son of another busy worker and Warden of the church, Sylvia Bruley, was joined in Holy Matrimony.

At 4:00 p.m. William Scott Bruley was married to Marie Anne Lise Proulx. On December 24th as the year drew to a close a beautiful stained glass window was installed as a Choir Memorial Window, to the left of the altar and the organ console itself. This window was dedicated on Harvest Festival Sunday by Bishop David Huron.

The Annual Fishermen's Service and Blessing of the Nets took place in St. Paul's on March 4th, 1979. Reverend Malcolm Muth, son of the late Mr. & Mrs. James E. Muth and Minister of the Presbyterian Church of Caledonia, expressed his delight at being asked as guest preacher to take part in this special service in his home town, "especially during the town's centennial year." He then proceeded to give an inspiring sermon, relating to "the Lake which we all love and which is the economy of this town for over a century. It is God's good gift to His people."

Mr. James Nunn, of Brantford, formerly of Port Dover, as guest soloist sang "Brightly Beams our Father's Mercy." A combined choir led in the singing of the hymns. Sidesmen were brothers J. Henry Misner and Robert Misner. A social hour followed in the Parish Hall.

Mr. Henry had been waging a private war for some time with

*St. Paul's decorated for The Blessing of the Nets*

a family of skunks, who had taken up residence in the furnace room of the church. It would seem from past records that these odoriferous little creatures had been an unwanted part and parcel of St. Paul's, whether the congregation liked it or not, for many, many years. Mr. Henry, determined to change the pattern, had finally obtained and set a live trap in the hope of removing them from the church for all time.

To his delight, on checking the trap a couple of days later, he had not one, but two black and white prisoners in his trap. Gingerly spreading a dark cloth over the culprits Reverend Henry lifted the trap very gently and proceeded out of the furnace room toward the choir room stair. All was going very well until one of his prisoners moved to the opposite end of the trap, tipping it violently downward. The pressure of their bodies suddenly sprung the door open to catapult the bewildered skunks out onto the stairway. Reverend Henry froze in horror at this sudden turn of events, but to his great relief, after a brief squint from beady little eyes in his direction, they ambled amicably back down the steps to disappear into their lair behind the furnace again. Like others before him Mr. Henry, no doubt feeling himself fortunate to have survived the encounter unscented, abandoned any further attempts to dislodge them. A December 14th, 1979 entry in the register states; "Two skunks in the Choir room. Both odour and skunks remain on Sunday."

On February 24th, 1980 Reverend Henry invited Venerable Archdeacon Clarence Mitchell to be guest preacher for the annual fishermen's service. Two soloists also participated in the special service with Willard Challand singing "The Wonder of it All" and toward the close of the service the Reverend Miss Judy Archer, of Knox Presbyterian Church sang "Saviour Again to Thy Dear Name." Sidesmen were Jim Murphy and David Ryerse and Richard Molewyk was Crucifer.

Reverend Henry gave this prayer for the fisheries: "O Almighty God, who has made the sea and all that move therein; Bestow Thy blessing on the harvest of the waters, that it may be abundant in its season and on our sailors and fishermen, that they may be safe in every peril of the deep; so that we all with thankful hearts may acknowledge Thee, who art Lord of the sea and of the dry land; through Jesus Christ, our Lord."

At the conclusion of the service Mr. Bruce Reid, President of St. Paul's Choir, stepped forward to present an engraved plaque to a suitably surprised couple, - Eileen and Andrew Lowe. Bruce announced to all present that this couple has braved the elements almost every Sunday, both morning and evening for over half a century to sing in the Choir. It read;

> "To Eileen and Andrew Lowe. In grateful recognition of
> over fifty years of faithful and dedicated service to
> St. Paul's Church Choir, Port Dover.
> *May God Bless You Good and Faithful Servants.*
> Presented February 24th, 1980.

On Sunday, October 27th, 1980 a special children's day service was held in St. Paul's to commemorate the bi-centenary of the Sunday School movement. This was followed by refreshments in the Parish Hall with an open invitation to all to attend and help in celebrating the event.

We are told that on a Sunday in July of 1780 in Britain the editor of "The Gloucester Journal" collaborated with a local clergyman, Reverend Robert Raikes, in his attempt to educate wayward youngsters in the beliefs and tenets of the Christian faith. In this way he hoped to keep them off the streets where they were getting into all kinds of mischief, which in most cases led to them ending up in jail. His efforts began to bear fruit and the idea spread throughout Britain and eventually spread to the rest of the Christian world. The Reverend Robert Raikes is hailed today as the founding Father of the Sunday School Movement.

The first Sunday School to be established in Port Dover involved all denominations in existence here at the time. The children of all faiths met regularly for several years in the Methodist Church. Mr. George Hotchkiss provides more detail as to this effort when he writes that he began attending the Methodist Church and Sunday School on a regular basis. Mr. Webster, Customs officer for the Port, was the Superintendent of this multi-denominational school. As he was elderly and irregular in his own attendance Mr. Hotchkiss began to take on his duties,

*The Right Reverend Clarence Mitchell shares a joyful moment following the baptism of two Great Grandchildren of Canon & Mrs. David J. Cornish – namely, Mary Beth Blakemore & Joanna Cornish in St. Paul's Church, Port Dover*

and the following year was elected to that office. During his six or seven year tenure he noted that attendance grew from an initial 25 children to an average of 175 students. This co-operative arrangement came to an end when the Methodist Preacher of the time decreed that the School would from henceforth be a "Methodist Sunday School" only.

From that time onward the Anglican pupils were removed and it is thought that Mrs. Robert Riddell, who had arrived in Port Dover from Scotland in 1844 with her husband, established a Sunday School for St. Paul's church in rooms on the second floor of Scofield's store.

Of special interest to all his many friends in St. Paul's and indeed Norfolk County, was the election in Christ's Church Cathedral, Hamilton of Archdeacon Clarence Mitchell to the position of Suffragan Bishop of the Anglican Synod of Niagara, on April 20th, 1980. The son of Martha Schilz, long-time faithful member and choir member of St. Paul's, Clarence had been Rector of St. George's Church, Guelph since 1970, as well as Archdeacon of Wellington. At the request of Diocesan Bishop John C. Bothwell, Bishop-elect Mitchell was consecrated in the Cathedral on June 8th by Archbishop Lewis Garnsworthy of Toronto.

Rt. Reverend Clarence Mitchell was ordained a priest in 1954 and has served in parishes in Welland, Port Dalhousie, Burlington and Hamilton, where he was rector of the Church of the Ascension and honourary Canon of the Cathedral.

On May 25th, 1980 at morning service Reverend Douglas Henry dedicated a memorial window given by Eileen and Andrew Lowe, Sarah (Lowe) Cromwell and Olive (Lowe) Ryerse. The inscription and theme of the window is "I am the Light of the World" and it is given in loving memory of the donors parents, Mr. & Mrs. J. William Garner and Mr. & Mrs. Andrew J. Lowe.

In 1980 the following marriages are of interest to members of today's congregation. On March 22nd, David John Goodlet married Delinda Jane MacDonald. April 12th, Daniel James Jacobs married Jane Elizabeth Sullivan. August 9th, Chuck Gordon Townsend married Mary Margaret Burbidge. August 15th Bruce Alex Milner married Elizabeth Mary Clarke Barrett and on November 8th, James Bradley Mullin married Julia Alice Yerex.

On Christmas Day the register records; Matins - 10:00 a.m. No service! No Congregation!

The March, 1981 Annual Fishermen's Service and Blessing of the Nets saw a capacity congregation attend for special speaker, Port Dover's own, Bishop Clarence Mitchell. Willard Challand sang "How Great Thou Art" and choir members from other local churches joined St. Paul's choir in the singing of the hymns and special anthem. Highlight of the Service was the Blessing of the Nets by Rt. Reverend Clarence Mitchell. Decorations included the Ed. Forrest's model fishing tugs, anchors, fishing nets and life preservers, bearing the names of various vessels in the harbour. Refreshments followed in the Parish Hall of what else but tastefully baked fish prepared and served to those present by the St. Paul's Club.

In June 1981 Mrs. Florence Cornish & Mrs. Kathy Hammond, representing the Chancel Guild, presented a beautiful white quilted frontal as a memorial to departed members of St. Paul's Church. Reverend Douglas Henry dedicated it; "to the glory of God and sanctified it to the use of the services of this church." The frontal, of rich cloth with a sword in the centre motif, is a symbol of St. Paul the Apostle, as an upholder of the faith. It will be

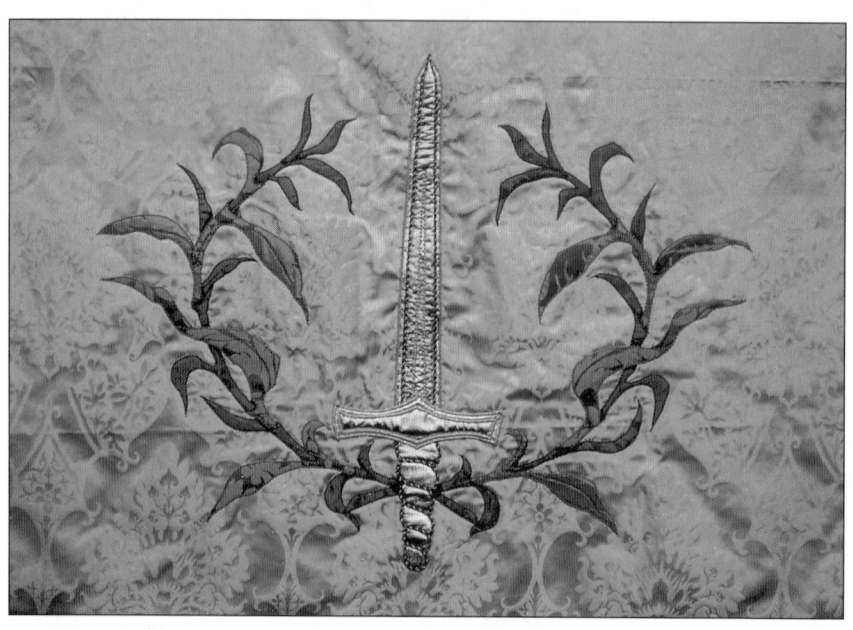

*The white quilted Frontal presented by the Chancel Guild*

used only for special religious holidays and for weddings if requested. Made in England it was brought back by Reverend and Mrs. Henry while on holiday in Britain. Ian Burbidge presented a saxophone solo during the service entitled "Bocherine Adagia."

On September 13th, 1981 I had the distinct pleasure of chairing a huge gathering of some 200 friends, students and staff of the Sunday School for my cousin Blanche Clark. We had assembled to pay tribute to Blanche's dedicated service as a Sunday School teacher of the primary classes for forty years, from 1940 to 1981. Everyone enjoyed refreshments, a large display of photographs documenting Blanche's life in the Parish and all were urged to sign the Guest Book. During the more formal part of the afternoon I was privileged to present a large framed scroll and a brooch, stylised from the emblem of a child's head from the International Year of the Child. I said in part that these were made as; "a thank you for sincere and selfless service..... for nearly forty years you have accepted our kids, and by precept and example, plus good common sense, moulded the character of our children..... these gifts are tangible proof of the love the children, parents and the parish have for you, Blanche."

*Tribute to Blanche Clark - Rev. Douglas S. Henry, Blanche Clark, Gerald Clark & Harry B.*

The plaque read as follows; "Presented to Blanche Clark by St. Paul's Anglican Church, Port Dover, Ontario in recognition of service to the children of St. Paul's. – 1940 - 1981.
> *Train up a child in the way he should go*
> *and when he is old he will not depart from it.*
Given this 13th day of September 1981."

On June 5th, 1982 the marriage of Gary Mark Furler to Roberta Lynn Misner is recorded. July 10th, Robert Colin Ryerse married Susan May Roberts. The year 1983 began on a low note with the funeral of my good friend Charles Landon Ivey. On January 23rd Lee Buffin changed the usual Sunday matins by narrating a film on "Anglicans in Missions."

Two particular weddings of interest to me and my family occurred in 1983. On February 12th, my son Theobald Butler "Toby" Barrett married Carolyn Louise Ewart and on May 28th, my daughter Jennifer Francis Bowlby Barrett married John David Wamsley. On June 26th, 1983 Bishop Morse Robinson was present in St. Paul's and Reverend Douglas Henry announced that he planned to retire on October 1st, 1983. On August 15th my uncle Hubert James Harold "Tim" Barrett, aged 70 years was buried.

On Reverend Douglas Henry's last service in St. Paul's a reception was held following matins to which the public were invited. The Henry's took holidays for the month of September after which they made their home in Galt, where their only daughter, Mrs. Cynthia Dobbie was living. Reverend H. Donaldson officiated at St. Paul's for the month of September.

From October 1st, 1983 until the arrival of Canon Kenneth Keith Brett on January 22nd, 1984 as our new Rector the following priests covered the regular services of St. Paul's Church. They were Reverends H. D. Herring, F. A. Cook, John Munro, Clifford W. Tomkins and A. Douglas Fuller.

## George H. Johnson Reminisces in 1981.

In June of 1981 George Johnson, son of Reverend H. J. Johnson, who served St. Paul's from 1911 to 1921, visited Reverend Douglas Henry after a long absence from Port Dover. He wrote to thank the Henry's for their warm welcome, and what to him was a home-coming after a sixty year lapse. His letter, which gives an often vivid insight into life in the rectory about ninety years ago, states, in part, as follows:

> "I arrived in Port Dover about February, 1911, at the tender age of three months. Since the former rectory had been sold, we lived for about three years in rented quarters. First in what Mother called "the green house", now white, that stands second south of Chapman, on the east side St. George.
> We moved from there to a large white frame house, [the Lawson house] on the north side of Market Street, across the railway tracks from the [Culverhouse] Canning factory. Early in 1914 my Father bought a Ford car which he kept in a barn behind the house. That summer we made a pioneering trip by car to Port Sydney, Muskoka, for our holidays. It was a four or five day trip over unpaved country roads, broken by visits to relatives and friends in Galt, Cookstown and Gravenhurst. I remember getting up at dawn to cover the last thirty miles over the old pioneer Muskoka road. We were there when the First War broke out.
> Curiously, I have no recollection of our move to the present rectory, in 1915 or 1916. From then on until we left about 1920, it was "home" to me as no other place could be, until Mary and I and our two boys settled here in Port Credit at the end of March, 1950. After some time in my Father's next Parish, I recall how heart-broken I was when Mother finally explained to me that we were never "going home" again.
> The past sixty years dropped away as though it had just been overnight, when Mr. Henry so kindly took me through those familiar rooms. During our years there my room was the one with the tall windows, over the front door. I was surprised to hear the evidence that entry to the large south bedroom had once been through "my" room, for the short dark hallway was always there in my memory. I cannot think the change was made in our

time, as such a major alteration is surely something I would remember. I do clearly recall a frame, three feet high, with vertical quarter inch iron bars, fastened outside the windows to keep the unwary from walking out and over the edge of the verandah roof. While at the front of the house one time a young friend asked why the bars were there. I gave a deadpan explanation that that was our jail. Mother appeared at the window a moment later, and he asked in some consternation why she was in jail.

Keeping warm in the winter months was a major problem. At times we lived almost exclusively in the two ground floor rooms on the north side of the hall. A kitchen range was in the north-east corner of the more central room, and a small gas heater in the other room. A certain minimum heat must have been maintained in the rest of the house, to keep the bathroom from freezing up.

At another time we lived entirely on the second floor. The only natural light coming into the bathroom was through a frosted glass window at shoulder height into the south bedroom, and I think also through frosted glass in the door at the head of the stairs. It was when we retreated to the second floor that this window was taken out and a door cut into the south bedroom in its place. With a gas range installed, the bathroom also served as a kitchen. In retrospect all this sounds like a most desperate expedient; but we were entirely dependent upon gas both for heating and lighting. In the depth of winter, the pressure would sink so low that there was hardly any flame at all in the stoves. We had at least one coal oil lamp that was pressed into service. Withall, I can't remember any time when we felt that the going was tough, however.

Mr. Henry, you mention the self-contained water supply which was based upon a tank or reservoir in the upstairs toilet. It was a large wooden, metal lined tank in the south wall, some four or five feet high and open at the top. Rain water was brought in from the roof, and in dry periods this was supplemented by a hand operated force pump beside the kitchen sink, which was under the south window. This drew water from the cistern under the floor at the north end of the woodshed. I can remember that my grandfather when he came to visit us would give the pump a hundred strokes as his morning constitutional.

The woodshed used to run back to within a few feet of the back fence. I recall a partition just about where the rear wall is now. The floor in the centre portion was cut away so that our car could be driven in on ground level, through large doors in the west wall. There was a privy in the north-west corner, reached by going up two or three steps and in the south-west corner was a hen house. My Father was an enthusiastic gardener. His main garden was to the south of the house, starting about ten feet from the building and going south to the hedge. It ran from the line of the verandah back to the rear fence. The front twenty or thirty feet was a flower garden, with the rest given over to vegetables. You mention fruit trees, which I did not immediately remember; now I recall a number of [I think] peach trees in a row, ten or fifteen feet from the house on the south side, running back almost to the back fence. Most westerly in this row was a large apple tree near the fence, in which I had a tree house.

There were several small red cherry trees along the back fence between the apple tree and the south-west corner. I did recall the large black cherry tree which was in the angle between the west wall of the house and the kitchen. My Father built a wooden floor in the shade of this tree, with access by the door which at that time opened at the end of the hall where you now have a ground floor washroom. This addition to our outdoor living facilities was not too successful, as the robins were wont to bombard it with partly eaten cherries.

In the front yard, south of the walk and midway between

the house and the street, there was a large mulberry tree that is no longer standing. I read in the Book of Knowledge that silkworms thrive on mulberry leaves, and was all for trying to raise some, but the scheme was aborted when we moved.

The cedar hedge used to run across the front of the property, along St. George Street. On summer weekends, visitors to the beach would park their cars up and down the street on our side. They were all touring cars and my young friends and I would go up and down the street testing the horns. It was always disappointing to find a car on which the horn did not operate with the ignition turned off.

None of the streets in the village were paved. Each spring a horse-drawn tank would come along and spread thick black oil on the roadway to keep down the dust. It also tended to make a fearful mess of small feet, to the dismay of all mothers. The only sidewalk was on the east side of the street, so our front walk was accordingly carried across the roadway by a rather hump-backed section of concrete. This rose four or five inches above the road level. It gave those in the back seats of passing cars a real hoist, especially if they were exceeding the speed limit of fifteen miles per hour. There were frequent squeals from young ladies who found themselves thus unceremoniously tossed into the air.

The house next to the Rectory on the north was built on what had been part of our property, I would say about 1919. I cannot recall our neighbours name, [Mr. & Mrs. Al. Schubert] but believe he was connected with the fisheries. This not only took away our large raspberry patch, but disrupted the sanitary arrangements, which had terminated in a primitive cesspool at the back of that property. It was replaced by the most modern of septic tanks, which was located somewhere near the southwest corner of the house, with weeping tile dug in, under our garden.

There was no electric power in Port Dover in our time.

The houses were all lit by gas fixtures, except our new neighbours, who had a wonderful Delco electric system of their own. There was a street lamp on a post at every corner, and they burned twenty four hours a day.

Our block along St. George Street has changed beyond all recognition since my childhood. The red brick house across the street is the same; it was occupied by Mr. and Mrs. Maneer. Between it and Market Street, at first, was the bowling green, fronted by an evergreen hedge along both streets. It also had a row of tall evergreens along the east side. A second red brick house, adjoining that of the Maneers to the north, was built within my memory and occupied by Mr. and Mrs. Janes. Mr. Janes was engineer on one of the three former harbour tug-boats that were based in Port Dover as fishery patrol vessels after the small cruiser "Vigilant" was retired. Mr. Janes was a particular friend of mine, and I spent many a happy hour in his engine room admiring the twin triple expansion steam engines with which the boat was equipped.

Mr. and Mrs. Morley Buck owned all the east side of the street south of the Maneers, except for one house on the corner. There was a large vacant lot just south of the Maneer house, then the Buck's large white frame house, surrounded by wide lawns. It was a beautiful house, with two full storeys, plus a useable attic. There was a large open porch at the front door, with a roof supported by round pillars in groups of three on either side. Toward the rear on the north side there was a port-cochere, balanced on the south side by a large screened porch, that the Bucks used as summer living room. A Promenade about four feet wide, with a broad railing supported by ornate pillars, ran from the port-cochere, around and across the front of the house, to a southern porch. On either side of the spacious front hall there were large living rooms. The dining room was on the north side opening onto the port-cochere. Mrs. Buck was a true southern belle from Alabama, who always spoke with a wonderful rich southern accent. The eldest son, Morley Junior, was a couple of years my senior. The second boy John Harris, was always my best friend. A third boy [Edward] was born about the time we left, and I never really knew him.

To the south of the Rectory property, the present street was nothing but a little-used lane. Buck's barn was standing, and between it and the lake there were just two summer cottages. West of them was an open space, where Mr. Buck pastured a horse. Buck's Orchard Beach Hotel lay to the south of the barn. It was a two storey, square structure, with a wide verandah across the front and a dining room and kitchen built onto the north side. To the south and west of the hotel, the level area was an apple orchard with picnic tables, that were frequently rented to parties who came either by car or via the Lake Erie & Northern railway. A large wooden pavilion was built along the hillside to the south of the hotel. Its ground floor could be used either for dances or picnic parties. Underneath it there was a bowling alley. Down on the flats by the lake Mr. Buck had a steam-driven merry-go-round. There was also a boat livery renting row-boats and canoes, and a long bathing house with cubicles which could be rented by those who wanted to change their clothes and go swimming.

Behind us at the end of the lane, there was a large, white frame house belonging to Captain Spain. In front of it was another lane leading to two or three cottages standing on the edge of the bluff, overlooking the lake. Another house stood directly behind the Rectory, and was either owned or rented by Mr. Zealand, from Hamilton. Next again to the north was Colonel Smith's home, overlooking the lake and with a long driveway leading to it from the street. Next was the fine, old brick house at the bend in Market Street, which then belonged to Dr. Jolley.

The 1952 history of St. Paul's mentions the very interesting old fence which once surrounded the church. A part of it was still there, leading up at least as far as the vestry door. Inside this door was the back of the organ, where the sexton, Mr. Evans, used to stand during services and pump the organ with a handle that came out a foot or more through the casing. There was a little lead weight on the end of a string attached to the bellows which had to be maintained within certain limits, or the beautiful music of the organ would die out in a series of painful wails.

One of the stories Dad liked to tell about Port Dover concerned Mrs. Skey, one of whose sons was Canon Skey of St. Anne's church, Toronto. When he was coming home on a visit one time, Mrs. Skey button-holed Dad after service to suggest that he ask the Canon to preach, saying "It would be a rest for you, and a treat for the Congregation!"

The artist who painted the mural over the east window spent some time in town working on it, and became enamoured of a young lady in St. Paul's choir. After the mural was in place, some of the ladies in the congregation wee scandalised to see her face translated to the heavenly choir.

In my extreme youth I tended to become restless while attending service with Mother, and while her attention was given to hymn or prayer I would drop down onto the floor, only to come up to look around some distance away. Just as I completed one of these forays during the reading of the lesson, Dad delivered the passage "This is my beloved son, in whom I am well pleased." His personal pleasure on seeing me was rather less than that of the Heavenly Father, and it is recorded that a red tinge moved upward from his collar.

I fear what started as a simple note of appreciation has expanded into a nostalgic binge. My apologies if all this bores you stiff. When I am next in Port Dover I shall knock again on the Rectory door; but this time with confidence that I have friends within.

      [signed] Sincerely, George H. Johnson

*Early photo of St. Paul's Church showing high fence and cedar shingles on steeple.*

## Chapter Twenty

# *Reverend Canon Keith Brett – 1984-1995*

Canon Keith K. Brett conducted his first service as Rector of St. Paul's on Sunday, January 22nd, 1984. The congregation were impressed. We had hosted he and his wife Van, for a meal, on their arrival in town and found them both very pleasant and friendly company. In managing the affairs of the Parish Canon Brett proved to be a firm but fair and very organised, diplomatic individual. Quiet and unassuming they proved to be very well liked by old and young alike.

Canon Brett's formal induction as Rector of St. Paul's took place at 4:00 p.m. on February 12th, 1984. The Service was conducted by Reverends K. J. Conyard, D. H. Woeller, R. McCulloch, Harvey L. Parker, C. A. Griffin, G. J. Darling and R. Hayne. A congregation of 250 of the parish were in attendance.

Canon Brett's home town was Markdale, Ontario. He obtained his degree in Theology from Huron College, University of Western Ontario, in 1959, becoming a Deacon the same year. He was named a priest in 1960, while becoming involved in a Diocesan Training Programme. He also obtained a Diploma in Management Development from Mohawk College.

Reverend Keith Brett served as Regional Dean of Oxford from 1967 to 1970. From 1974 to 1978 he served as Regional Dean of Brant. During his career he served for eight years on the Diocesan Executive Committee as well as long service on the Programme Council and the Moral Values Committee. In recognition of his outstanding service to his parishes and the diocese he was appointed at the 1980 Synod, a Canon of the Cathedral of St. Paul's, in

*Canon Kenneth Keith Brett at his desk*

London. On coming to St. Paul's, Port Dover, Canon Brett was named Regional or Rural Dean of Norfolk from 1985 to 1987 and again for 1989.

Canon Brett took a keen interest in the communities he served through the Canadian Red Cross, and in keeping with his interest in the welfare of the youth of his parishes he served for eight years on the Brant Board of Education. On his appointment to St. Paul's Canon Brett was approached regarding his allowing his name to stand for the Norfolk Board of Education. He announced this to the St. Paul's Board of Management, telling them if there ware no objections forthcoming, he would allow his name to stand for nomination. He subsequently served on the Norfolk Board of Education for a further two and a half years. While in Port Dover Canon Brett served with distinction as Padre of the Hugh Allan Branch #158, Royal Canadian Legion.

Canon Brett had an innate ability to gain the confidence and respect of the young people of the Parish. He wasted no time in developing a dedicated and loyal troupe of servers to assist him with the altar duties, during each service. His influence in the affairs of the Sunday School were also soon evident. At matins, on February 24th, 1985 Canon Brett organised a special young people's service complete with a church parade of the participants from the Parish Hall. There were 188 in attendance for this special service, featuring our youth.

May 26th, 1985 marked 25 years since the ordination of Canon Keith Brett in 1960. Speaker at the 7:00 p.m. service to celebrate with the good Canon and his wife, were over 200 parishioners and friends. Bishop Brown, of Toronto, was guest speaker and the reception in the Parish Hall later taxed the facilities to the utmost. Canon Brett was presented with a purse and a portable communion. The St. Paul's Club presented him with a refurbished church window which amused him greatly at the time.

The Parish was shocked to learn on July 16th, 1985 of the sudden death of Craig Field, son of Graydon and our faithful organist, Joy Field. An overflow congregation of over three hundred mourners attended his funeral service on July 18th. I had considered Craig a special friend since having him as a student during my first year of teaching in 1959, in the Hagersville High School. I presented the line drawing of St. Paul's, by my daughter Elizabeth, that hangs in the narthex of St. Paul's, to Craig's memory.

Graydon Field reported to the September 1986 Board of Management that the Port Dover and District Horticultural Society had requested permission to hold their regular monthly meetings, which were always on a Wednesday evening, in the Parish hall. It was agreed that the request be granted as long as

*Royal Canadian Legion Padre K. K. Brett, to Hugh Allan Branch 158, Port Dover, addresses the Remembrance Day gathering. - Colour Guard Marion McNeilly, Lois Phillips, Maurice Long, Trumpeter & Don Doyle, Master of Ceremonies*

*Canon Brett celebrates 25th Anniversary since ordination on May 26th, 1985*

there was no conflict with other organisations already using the hall. They still continue to meet in the Parish Hall and there is always a large and enthusiastic turn out for their annual flower show in the Parish Hall. It was also announced that the Youth Group would be starting the year's activities at once in September.

In December the Board were informed that Don Doyle would be leaving in January for a five month visit to Uganda in Africa. It was suggested a report would be of great interest to all on his return. Alan Baldock, who had recently returned from an extended visit to Jamaica, reported on his work while in that country.

In November of 1987 a presentation to the Board, from Geofrey and Sandra Manuel, regarding scouting in Port Dover sparked lively discussion. They are seeking sponsors and meeting places for the Sea Scouts as many young people are showing an interest in belonging if accommodation can be found. Further information would be forthcoming. A later Board Meeting was informed that the Scouting programme was under control and permission had been granted for them to meet in the Parish Hall basement.

For thirty-five years I served as a director of the Norfolk Farmer's Mutual Fire Insurance Company. Our parent body the

Ontario Mutual Insurance Association, held an annual convention each March, in Toronto. On the one hundredth anniversary of the founding of the Norfolk Company, Bert Abbott, a past President of the Norfolk Mutual and director of the Ontario Mutual Insurance Association was named the President of the Ontario Mutual Insurance Association. For his year in office he asked me to serve as his Chaplain. Each of the several hundred members attending the Convention received a complimentary copy of the history of the past one hundred years of the "Norfolk Mutual Fire Insurance Company", which I had written earlier.

Honoured to be asked to undertake this important duty for the convention, I agreed, but then had concerns about carrying out my new duties satisfactorily. The most onerous were providing opening prayers for the morning and afternoon sessions during the three day convention and having an appropriate grace to offer at the beginning of breakfast, luncheon and dinner each day, with a special expected for the final Annual Awards Banquet. My predecessors had often been staunch older farmers of the Baptist or Methodist persuasion, who took their Chaplaincy in a very serious and long-winded fashion.

Hoping not to fall into that trap, I went to see Canon Brett and explained my predicament. He smiled in a somewhat condescending way, as much as to say this should be no

*Memorial to Craig Field given by Harry B. Barrett and drawn by Elizabeth Barrett, in 1979*

problem for a good Anglican, and informed me that everything I needed was to be found in the Book of Common Prayer. His further inference being, I felt, that I should have known that to begin with and I suppose I should have. On following his advice I was greatly surprised to find an appropriate prayer, or guidance to it, for every situation I was required to respond to at the Toronto meetings.

Once the Convention was nearing a close I was even more surprised at the comments and compliments I received from all quarters at the tone and sincerity expressed in my offerings followed by requests by many to know where they too, might find such guidance. The Anglican Book of Common Prayer is truly a remarkable volume, the evolution of which, has provided an answer for I suspect every situation a person might find themselves exposed to in life. In comparison, the Book of Alternate Services does not even come close, in my opinion.

On Sunday, July 12th, 1992 at 2:00 p.m. the whole community, in a state of shock, mourned the tragic death of Barbara Baldock as many attended her funeral in St. Paul's. Assisting Canon Brett in the funeral service were Rt. Reverend Clarence Mitchell, Canon Harvey L Parker and Reverend B. Burry. On Sunday, May 2nd, 1993 the Baldock Memorial was dedicated by Canon Brett.

Toward the end of January, 1994, Canon Brett was taken ill and from January 30th through to April 27th, 1994 Rt. Reverend Clarence Mitchell took charge of the services and responsibilities of the Parish. From Sunday, May 1st through to Sunday May 29th, Reverend H. D. Herring officiated, at which time Canon Brett was well enough to resume his duties. On September 26th, 1994 the St. Paul's Club celebrated the 65th Anniversary of their founding.

My sister Emily Molewyk sent the following story to the Huron Church News as being noteworthy, and they obviously agreed with her by printing it with a picture in the October 1995 issue. I quote: "On the eighth Sunday after Trinity this year, three young men assisted Canon K. K Brett at the eleven o'clock Communion Service in St. Paul's Church, Port Dover. They were servers Will Hourigan and Cody Parker and server-in-training Murray McKnight.

What makes this unique is that the three are second cousins, all descendants of T. B. Barrett, who was a founding member of St. Paul's and a Warden and Lay Reader in the mid-1800's, making them the sixth generation of the Barrett family to worship at St. Paul's."

As T. B. Barrett's parents left their 1830's farm near Sorel, in the Lower Province in the mid-1850's, to purchase a farm overlooking the Walsingham marsh west of Port Royal, Norfolk County, I am quite sure that they too had occasion to worship in St. Paul's as well.

Canon Brett officially retired toward the end of the year 1995. On Sunday afternoon, August 27th, 1995 Canon Brett and his wife of 36 years, Evangeline, affectionately known to all as Van, met with over 125 parishioners for an open house retirement party in the Parish Hall. Canon Brett announced to the assembled throng that: "This is home, we have bought a house in Dover. We have had such a marvellous time here. This being the last official stop, it is the ideal place with the ideal climate." They are the parents of three children. Reporting their status in 1995 we find Janice and her husband David Martin, with the Armed Forces. He was recently posted to Ottawa. Karen and her husband David Peters, with their children Michelle and Timothy, live in Port Dover. They both are teachers in Norfolk. Son Wayne is an internal auditor for IKO of Brampton and lives in Brantford.

The official Retirement Party in Honour of the Reverend Canon K. Keith Brett was held in the Port Dover Community Centre on September 17th, 1995. The Programme's outer cover held line drawings of the various churches in which Canon Brett had served during his 36 years as a parish priest. It was my extreme pleasure and honour to be the Master of Ceremonies for this prestigious event.

Following Grace by Right Reverend Clarence Mitchell a sumptuous repast was enjoyed by over 200 guests. The Head Table guests were introduced to everyone. Next a somewhat mysterious Trio, "The G. G's" [the Geritol Geishas] performed, with apologies to Gilbert & Sullivan.

The following list of: **"Roasters and Greetings"** gives an indication of the range of Canon Brett's activities and interests.

Bishop Clarence Mitchell.
The Venerable Terry Dance, Archdeacon of Norfolk & Oxford.
Reverend Stephen Hendry, Regional Dean, Norfolk
Reverend Brian Elder, Grace United Church, Port Dover.
Barbara MacDonald, President, Royal Canadian Legion, Hugh Allan Branch.
Kathy Hoover, President, Legion Ladies Auxiliary.
Toby Barrett, MPP. Province of Ontario.
Rita Kalmbach, Mayor, City of Nanticoke.
Walt. Long, Trustee, Norfolk Board of Education.
Jake Beerepoot, President, Port Dover Lions Club.

**A Retiring "Volley".**

**MUSIC**

Violin Duet: Rebecca & Victoria Zimmer.

**Benediction**

All join in / Tune Edelweiss

May the Lord, Almighty God Bless and Keep you forever.
Grant you peace, perfect peace, Courage in every endeavour.
Lift up your eyes and see His face and His grace forever.
May the Lord, Almighty God Bless and Keep you forever.

***************************

George Daley, son of Mr. And Mrs. Don Daley, tells us an amazing story of how his life was turned around by Canon Brett. George had rebelled against the discipline of School and strayed into a life he described himself as one of a wild out-of-control life style of drugs and despair. Inevitably George wound up in court and was sentenced to a good many hours of Community Service. This led to his serving those hours cleaning pews, sweeping floors and washing the stained glass windows of St. Paul's Church, Port Dover, under the supervision of Canon Brett. Canon Brett realising where George was heading slowly but surely gained his confidence and began to influence his thinking toward a better way of life.

George would be the first to tell you that through Canon Brett's help he suddenly found Jesus Christ and then he asked

God's forgiveness for all the wrong things his corrupt life-style had led him to do. He returned to school and graduated from Grade 13. He moved on to training in the Church Army and from there to obtaining a B. A. Degree from King's College, Halifax. On July 7th, 1990 Donald George Daley was married to Stacie Diane Montfort who he met while doing summer internship ministry in northern New Brunswick. They were married in St. Michael and All Angels Anglican Church, in Newcastle Bridge, New Brunswick. The marriage was solemnised by the bride's father, the Reverend John Paul Wadlin. The happy couple returned to Halifax that George might finish his degree.

From there he studied and obtained a Master in Divinity from Wycliffe College of the University of Toronto, in 1997. During this time George was able to serve as an assistant minister in St. Paul's. On October 17th, 1999 George Daley was ordained a Deacon in the Cathedral Church of St. Alban the Martyr, in Prince Albert, by Bishop Anthony Burton. George proudly wore a stole given him by the wife of his mentor, Van Brett. He began his ministry in the Diocese of Saskatchewan.

George Daley was ordained as a priest on June 24th, in Hudson Bay Saskatchewan. Several parishioners from St. Paul's attended and made a presentation to him on behalf of the Parish of St. Paul's, Port Dover. In a letter of March 12th, 2000 George writes to his friends in St. Paul's on behalf of Stacie, their son Jackson and himself. He is enthusiastic about his work in the north and ends with this invitation: "God Bless, and if you are ever in Hudson Bay come to St. Patrick's where, of course, we use the book of Common Prayer.

*George Daley in St. Paul's, Port Dover*

CHAPTER TWENTYONE

# Reverend Robert Doerr – 1996-2003

On Wednesday morning, January 3rd, 1996, at 10:00 a.m. the Reverend Robert "Rob" Doerr officiated at his first service as Rector of St. Paul's. I had first met Rob several years earlier when my grandchildren, Jane and Sally Wamsley, were baptised in St. John's Church, Port Rowan, he being the rector at that time. It was there, as well, that I first experienced his practice of sitting on the chancel steps, while the junior Sunday School members gathered around him, prior to the regular sermon, to hear a story appropriate to their studies in Sunday School or to that particular time in our church year.

Rob had grown up as a Lutheran and his first venture into the world of work was as an accountant. However as he sought answers to theological questions, he found the most satisfying explanations in the Anglican faith. This in turn lead him to enroll in Huron College of the University of Western Ontario, where he obtained a Bachelor of Arts and Philosophy degree. He then enrolled in 1983 in a Master of Divinity programme in Huron College. Being ordained at St. Paul's Cathedral, London in that same year, he later became a priest at the Church of the Ascension in Windsor.

Since that appointment Rob has served in St. Andrew's Church, LaSalle, St. John's, Port Rowan, the Church of the God Shepherd, Woodstock and in Christ Church, Huntington. Rob and his wife Carol Honsberger, came to the Parish of St. Paul's as newly-weds, he having met and married Carol in Woodstock. Carol holds a Bachelor of Music Education, and a Master of Education degree from the University of Western Ontario. They

*Rev. Rob Doerr & his wife Carol*

both love music and both were a boon to our church choir. Carol conducted a junior choir very effectively within the senior group.

Rob became very active in the Ministerial Association of Port Dover and encouraged ecumenical activities like the annual Advent Walk which has involved the Roman Catholic, Presbyterian, United and his own Anglican churches. On Canon Brett's retirement, Rob assumed the position of Padre of the Hugh Allan Branch, #158, Royal Canadian Legion in his place.

It had always been obvious that some kilns of brick for the building of our church were of inferior quality, being lighter in colour and soft in texture. Rob was concerned about the undue weathering of the softer brick, and as a result a fund was established for the major repair work of these faulty brick in both the Church and the Rectory. The bricks were thought to have been made along the banks of Patterson Creek, where the Ivey greenhouses were later built in 1910. This was known at that time as the William S. Petit brickyard. Fund raising was begun for this both extensive and expensive project and by the summer of 1998 the whole of the tower at the entrance to St. Paul's was surrounded by scaffolding. The work was carried out by the Everest Restoration Company.

On Friday, May 15th, 1998 the Brickwork Committee sponsored a programme at Lighthouse Festival Theatre advertised widely as a "Brick Fixing Fund Raiser." They pointed out in the programme flyer for the evening that "St. Paul's Anglican Church has taken on the task of replacing and repairing the aging brickwork on the Church proper, the Parish Hall and the Rectory, at 223 St.

George St. The Church has served the Port Dover community well for nearly 150 years and the current congregation accepts the responsibility of maintaining the buildings for future generations. This is a restoration, not a renovation project and our goal is to have a completed project that appears to have been untouched."

The evening was kicked off by "David Sutherland's Magic" followed by the very professional "Simcoe Barbershoppers." A 20 minute intermission allowed the purchase of refreshments at the Theatre bar. This was followed by "JABOP" – Just a bunch of people – Next the patrons were entertained by "Stewart Smith's Fiddlers". The evening was brought to a close by another gig from "JABOP". When the effort was assessed the next day it was found to have generated a profit $1,600.00.

Another brilliant plan for raising funds for the brick restoration was devised by John and Kay Rundle, and enthusiastically put into operation by the brick committee. The Rectory which had been neglected over the years was badly in need of rejuvenation and redecorating. Under the guise of a "Rectory Revival" more than ten interior decorators were invited to demonstrate their craft on different rooms in the rectory. They set to work in January at considerable inconvenience to Rob Doerr and his wife, but the promised improvement was the carrot that convinced even a sceptical Rob to put up with the unsettling time he could visualise coming his way. By July of 1999 all was finished and the tours by the public could begin. As Rob said at the official opening; "This has not been done by magic. A lot of work and worry has gone into the project with spectacular results."

At the opening ceremony several former residents joined Reverend Rob Doerr in turning the key to the front door. Among them were the late Reverend Henry's wife Marjorie, Barbara Copeman and her brother Hubert Jennings, nephews of Canon Cornish, who spent many happy hours, visiting in the rectory while growing up in town. Florence Cornish, whose husband Bill lived there with his parents as a boy. Van Brett who had lived there for the term of Canon Brett's incumbency at St. Paul's. All were loud in their praise of the tasteful way in which the house had been coordinated and improved. Tours of the house were to continue from 1:00 to 7:00 Tuesday through Sunday until July 25th, 1999.

On March 1st, 1996 St. Paul's lost a long-time supporter and choir member in the person of Muriel Smith Misner, wife of Robert Misner, who as a life-long fisherman, for years quietly attended to the decoration of the church for the annual Fishermen's Service and Blessing of the Nets. On May 7th, another stalwart choir member, Eileen Garner Lowe, was buried from St. Paul's.

During the Rector's holidays in July, 1997 Canon Brett and Rt. Reverend Clarence Mitchell took charge of the services. On September 28th, 1997 an evening Memorial Service of "The Battle of Britain" during World War II was celebrated with Canon Brett and Don Doyle, Lay Reader assisting. On November 9th, 1997 a Church Parade of the Royal Canadian Legion, Hugh Allan Branch, # 158 of Port Dover, attended St. Paul's, where a congregation of over 150 heard an inspiring sermon by their Padre, Canon Keith Brett.

On May 24th, 1998 Rt. Reverend Clarence Mitchell took charge of the Confirmation Service for the Bishop of Huron before a congregation of two hundred. On June 7th, some 150 parishioners attended the Parish Picnic.

On June 11th, 1998 the congregation of St. Paul's were shocked to learn of the death of their beloved Rector of twelve years, Canon Kenneth Keith Brett, who had so recently retired to become a resident of our town. The sympathy of the entire town went out to his wife Van, and the whole family. The funeral on Saturday, June 13th, at 11:00 a.m. from St. Paul's was conducted by Rt. Reverend Percy O'Driscoll and Rt. Reverend Clarence Mitchell before a congregation of over 250 mourners, 175 of whom celebrated Holy Communion. Also taking part in the service were the incumbent Rob Doerr and the Reverend Brian Elder, of Grace United Church, as Reader.

On October 25th, 1998 at 4:00 p.m. a re-dedication of the St. Paul's church building was celebrated by Rt. Reverend Clarence Mitchell and Reverend George Daley, with 91 parishioners present. On November 9th, a Remembrance day church parade was held by the Hugh Allan Branch of the Royal Canadian Legion.

On March 7th, 1999 a congregation of 165 attended an Annual Fishermen's Service in an appropriately decorated St. Paul's, at evensong. George Daley assisted. On Saturday, March

*Choir Leader, Joy Field & Graydon on their anniversary*

27th, at 8:00 a.m. a Communion Service was held for 24 members of the Prayer Book Society. They were taking part in a retreat at Crabapple Creek farm hosted by fellow member Dorothy Burfoot.

A Memorial Service to "The Battle of the Atlantic" was celebrated on May 23rd, 1999. On September 12th George Daley, who credits his whole life being turned around by the interest and guidance of Cannon Keith Brett, was present and assisted with matins. The congregation, in turn, wished George success and "God Speed" in his new duties that he is about to assume in Western Canada, in the Diocese of Saskatchewan.

On January 30th, 2000 there was a retirement celebration for Joy Field who was retiring as Organist ot St. Paul's after 35 years of dedicated service. In that time she estimated she had played for nearly 200 weddings, many funerals and more than 1,500 Sunday Services. Joy confessed to a love of music since the age of four. Her mother was an accomplished musician and her father played well too. At age 12 she began playing at Parkview United church in Stratford. It was a pump organ that taught her early both patience and endurance, Joy confessed. During her last service in St. Paul's as organist Joy's grand daughters, both accomplished violinists, played for the congregation.

On February 19th, 2000 a party was held in the Erie beach hotel for Joy Field, hosted by 95 members of St. Paul's congregation and friends, to celebrate her service to St. Paul's Choir. A photograph and scroll was presented from St. Paul's, flowers from the Port Dover Lion's Club and special good wishes were extended from the Lakeshore Women's Institute and the St. Paul's Club.

To celebrate the millenium St. Paul's commissioned Elizabeth Barrett Milner to paint a picture for St. Paul's, in accordance with the church's 2000 years of faith. Liz suggested depicting local landmarks, such as the lighthouse, a fish tug at the mouth of the river, the old Town Hall, now Lighthouse Festival Theatre and in one corner St. Paul's with its distinctive steeple, while the other corner displays a dove flying above it all. All this to be shown under the banner of "Spiritus Gladius" overlying the background of a sword, in reference to St. Paul, defender of the faith. This was unveiled at coffee hour following matins on January 9th. This now hangs in the Parish Hall and it also graced the front cover of the Church Bulletins for the year 2000.

*Bulletin Cover for St. Paul's to celebrate 2000 years of Faith. By Liz Barrett-Milner*

By 2001 St. Paul's was once again graced by angels in flowing robes on either side of the east window above the altar. They were re-instated at the request of Olive Ryerse as a memorial to her daughter, Patricia. Rob explains that they are painted in "a blurry fashion, a bit unfocused. It should be fuzzy, because they are other worldly."

On March 4th, 2001 the traditional Fishermen's Service was held to celebrate our major industry, Fishing, in what at one time was touted as the largest fresh-water fishery in the world. The church, lighted by candles, was decorated with nets, model fishing tugs and other articles associated with the craft. Taking part with our rector Rob Doerr, Reverend James Douglas of Knox Presbyterian Church preached the sermon. Reverend Brian Elder of Grace United Church led the congregation in the Prayers for the People. Father Ed Bellefeuille, of St. Cecilia's Roman Catholic Church pronounced the Blessing of the Nets. The two Pats, Patrick Yerex and Patrick Murphy had outdone themselves in preparing their specialty, smoked fish. Other tasty delicacies were also provided for a reception in the Parish Hall after the service.

*Quilt to commemorate the 150th anneversary of St. Paul's Church, Port Dover*

Rt. Reverend Clarence Mitchell officiated in July during Rob's holiday time. On September 16th, 2001 the Hugh Allan Branch, Royal Canadian Legion paraded for the Festival of Harvest Thanksgiving. On December 2nd St. Paul's sponsored the Advent Walk with 265 participants.

Beginning in February 2002 scaffolding was erected in the body of the church for the removal of the tile and remains of the old covering of the ceiling. This exposed the rich tongue and groove original wood ceiling which was repaired, cleaned and varnished by volunteers from the congregation. Services were held in the Parish Hall while all this was in progress. The original lettering "Enter Into His Gates With Thanksgiving" was restored to the Arch leading into the Chancel. At Matins on February 10th, 2002 the lettering was dedicated with Rt. Reverend Clarence Mitchell assisting.

All the planning for the 150th Anniversary of the Laying & Dedication of the Cornerstone of St. Paul's in 1852 culminated in the Year 2002. On Saturday, June 22nd Bishop Howe officiated at Confirmation with almost 200 in the congregation.

The next day, Sunday, June 23rd, 2002 the Church was packed to the doors as Bishop Howe performed further dedication services in relation to the 150th anniversary, including a granite plaque that was inset to the left of the main entrance to St. Paul's. It read as follows:

St. Paul's Anglican — 150 Years — Established 1852.
This stone Rededicated by the Rt. Rev. Bruce Howe
June 23, 2002 — The Rev. Rob Doerr, Rector.

Following the morning service lunch was served in the Parish Hall. The celebrations continued in the Parish Hall, when many of the congregation plus several friends from out of town, who had a connection with the Parish in the past gather to reminisce. As Chairman of the often hilarious event I thoroughly enjoyed myself, and I believe everyone present found the afternoon equally gratifying and enjoyable. Pictures and a tape were produced of it. Rob Doerr announced that he had some letters and a scroll to present. He then read a message of congratulations from Mayor Kalmbach

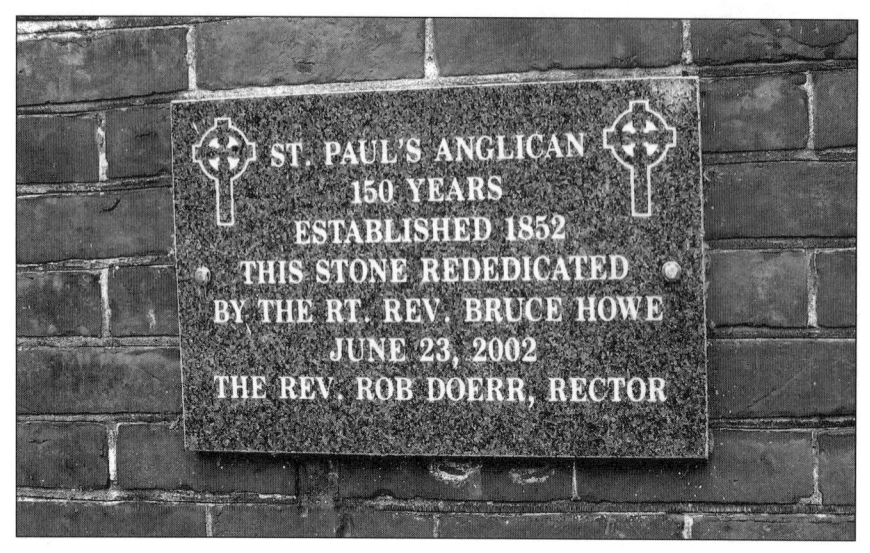

*Granite Plaque*

and a framed certificate, signed by her on behalf of the county of Norfolk. He next joked as he asked me to present the next presenter. It was Toby who was present to bring personal greetings as our Member of the Provincial Legislature as well as present the Parish with a scroll from the People of the Province signed by Premier Ernie Eves. Rob also read a letter from David Cornish, who though unable to attend enclosed a cheque of $1,000.00, in honour of his parents Canon David J. and Mrs. Cornish.

I next read a nostalgic letter from Al Baldock which began with "So the congregation is 150 years old! Some of you don't look it." Then several of those present came forward to recount, in most cases, a funny story or experience they remembered from earlier days. Some of those who entertained us were Alan Tibbetts, from Fort Francis, George Webb from London, Helen Thompson, Barbara Jennings Copeman, Peggy Wicker, Elizabeth Cornish Blakemore, Bridget Blackhurst Brown, Connie Clark Green, Katie Buck Brooks, Don Doyle, Harry Smith, Pat Yerex and others. Rev. Rob Doerr and Rt. Rev. Clarence Mitchell, who you would expect to bring a bit of dignity to the occasion, did not disappoint us. Their stories were as hilarious as any told if not more so.

Helen Thompson brought to life days before the time or memory of many present. She remembered the primary room she attended at the back of the Sunday School with Miss Barrett as their teacher. Later she recalled sewing for the Junior Women's Auxiliary as a member. When a bit older she joined the A. Y. P. A. and recalled the many good times they all had. She particularly remembered performing in a play they put on entitled "Let's Get Married" which was directed by Harry Moon. They later performed it for the general public in the Town Hall Theatre, as well as presenting it in other communities in the County.

On October 27th, 2002 Reverend Rob Doerr took charge of his last morning service as Rector of St. Paul's. Entered in the remarks column of the Church Register is the one comment, "Farewell." The following Wednesday at 10:00 a.m. he officiated at his final service. From that point onward until May 25th, 2003 the Reverend Allen Cook took the regular services in St. Paul's.

## Reverend Brian Wearne – 2003-2005

On June 1st, 2003 the Reverend Brian Wearne officiated at his first service as Rector of St. Paul's Church, Port Dover. On the evening of June 22nd, 2003 Bishop Peter Townsend assisted by Reverend David Wearne officially inducted Reverend Wearne as our Rector. From July 2nd to July 27th, 2003 Rt. Reverend Clarence Mitchell took charge of the services for the month during Brian & Mrs. Wearne's holidays. As his wife was a teacher her timetable governed their holiday time.

The congregation soon realised that Reverend Brian Wearne was of a quite different temperament to his predecessor. He also had very fixed ideas as to his duties as a parish priest and rarely hesitated to voice them. I enjoyed his somewhat quirky sense of humour, I suppose because it closely matched my own. Those who attended his mid-week study sessions found him more relaxed and very knowledgeable of his subject. He seemed more suited in many parishioners minds to a role as a serious teacher of theology.

In November 2004 the congregation were delighted to hear that the work of a long-time parishioner was finally to be recognised. Rev. Brian Wearne announced that Archie Morris, a Warden and past Sunday School Superintendent, was to be honoured as a recipient of one of the Bishop's Awards for Excellence in Ministry. On November 7th, 2004 Archie was presented with the

*Archie & Georgina Morris*

award in the Cathedral in London. I would suggest that his wife Georgina should share in some of the honours, and I am sure Archie would agree, for few have been more faithful as a choir member over many, many years. We congratulate you both.

As the year 2004 drew to a close the joys of the Christmas season were muted for many of us with the death and funeral on December 20th, of my cousin and one of my closest friends, David Hubert Couke Yerex. I am left with a wealth of great memories of our growing up together between the wars however. On the last day of the year the funeral was held for Norma Parkinson, 99 years of age.

As time went on it became more obvious that Brian lacked some of the essential people skills that go to make a successful parish priest. In July of 2005, to the surprise of many in the congregation Reverend Brian Wearne tendered his resignation as the Rector of St. Paul's Church, Port Dover.

As always Rt. Reverend Clarence Mitchell immediately filled the void by taking charge of the services, etc. of the Church for the month of August, 2005. The Wardens with his help have arranged for the months of September and October. This rambling history of St. Paul's is also drawing to a close, as in late September it is going to the Printers to be organised, pictures added, and in due course will appear as a "fete acompli" on my part.

A further task that I had hoped to accomplish before the February 10th, 2006 Anniversary of the holding of the first service of worship in the new St. Paul's Church, on February 10th, 1856, was to have a plaque in place in loving memory of my paternal Grandparents. On speaking to Brian Wearne some months ago about doing this he informed me that the Bishop frowned on this practice and he was not sure that I could have it done. I asked immediately for the Bishop's address as I intended to write to him directly on the matter.

Brian suggested I let him look into it. I later asked to come before the Board of Management with my request. On doing so, after some questions, I obtained their permission to proceed.

I also informed them of my efforts since the year 2000 in producing a history of "The Parish of St. Paul's" and if I were successful in getting it into printed form I intended to present a complimentary copy to each family who at that time were members of St. Paul's Parish.

Brian wished me well and I left the Vestry Meeting with the impression that all was well. After negotiations with Robert Judd, of Vision in Design, in Scotland, Ontario the W. H. Barrett plaque was ordered and designed. It arrived in mid-July and on Thursday, July 28th, 2005 it was installed on the east wall of the church, opposite the seat my Grandfather Harry Barrett and I occupied, following the installation of the new pews donated by his friend and neighbour, John S. Martin.

Upon informing Rt. Reverend Clarence Mitchell of the plaque being in place, and as both he and temporary organist Peter

*The Author's family - Barbara Hourigan, Toby, Elizabeth Barrett-Milner, Harry B., Hugh Massy and Jennifer "Penny" Wamsley*

*Memorial Plaque to W. H. Barrett*

Barrett were completing their allotted services for the summer the following Sunday, July 31st, 2005, it was agreed that he would dedicate it at once. As Peter's Grandmother was named on the plaque, as well as mine, it seemed most appropriate that it be officially accepted into St. Paul's on that particular Sunday.

The text of the Plaque, complete with the Barrett Crest, is as follows :

TO THE GLORY OF GOD
And
IN LOVING MEMORY OF
William Henry "Harry" BARRETT. D. V. M.
1864 —— 1942
Rebecca Julia "Winonah" Pelly BARRETT
1876 —— 1898
Hattie Mabel "Enah" James BARRETT
1883 —— 1970

St. Paul's, Port Dover

St. Paul's awaits a Rector
as the year 2005 ends

ST PAUL'S ANGLICAN CHURCH (1852)
Port Dover, Ontario

*St. Paul's by Rickard, used on Newsletter cover*

APPENDIX ONE

# St. Paul's Church Memorials

The following gifts and memorials made to the Glory of God and in Loving Memory of loved ones by members of the congregation are recorded in a Book of Remembrance kept in the Chancel of the Church.

1859 – A gift of a small marble or alabaster Font, made in Ireland, and originally used in the Hamilton Cathedral. Presented by Mrs. Grace O'reilly.

1894 – Two brass Altar Vases, to the memory of Arthur Lawrence Newell - August 13th, 1890 to March 16th, 1894. [son of the Rector.]

1895 – Two silver Collection Plates, gift of Mrs. Crosbie Morgan.

1903 – A brass Book Rest, to the memory of Ras Williams.

1904 – The East Window, in memory of John Palmer Battersby, 1874 - 1896 & Edith Beatrice Battersby, 1878 - 1900. Presented by the Family. Also in memory of Hilton Hathaway Lynch, 1878 - 1898 & Georgiana Augusta Lynch, 1857 - 1899. Presented by the Family. Also in memory of Maria Jane Battersby, June 22nd, 1895 - July 22nd, 1905.

1904 – An Alms Basin, presented by Mrs. C. E. Tibbetts in memory of her parents.

1911 – A Lectern, in memory of Lawrence Skey, Lay Reader and Sunday School Superintendent. Presented by his friends, fellow workers and former pupils.

1911 – The Pulpit, in memory of The Right Reverend Maurice Scollard Baldwin. Rector of St. Paul's - 1862 - 1865 — Bishop of Huron - 1883 - 1904.

1911 – A Prayer Desk, in memory of Theobald Butler Barrett, November 17th, 1817 to December 27th, 1910. Presented by the Family.

1920 – A Baptismal Font, in memory of Alfred & Louisa Buckwell and their family. Presented by Alice Buckwell.

1920 – The Communion Table, in memory of the men of St. Paul's who gave their lives in the Great War.

1923 – The Organ, in memory of Clare M. Langs by J. H. Herring, New Bedford, Mass.

1929 – A Lectern Bible, in memory of Theobald Butler Barrett. Presented by his Family.

1930 – A Window in the Nave, in memory of William Francis & Charlotte Emily Tibbetts.

1930 – A Brass Plaque, in memory of Thomas Waters & Georgianna Spence Stevens, his wife. Presented by their children.

1930 – A Brass Plaque, in memory of Lawrence Skey, 1835 – 1911. Presented by wife & children

1931 – A Portrait of Archbishop Williams. Presented by the Williams Family.

1932 – A brass Altar Cross, in memory of & appreciation to the Lawrence E. Wedd Family.

1932 – Two brass Altar Vases, in memory of the Newell & Morgan Families, by Mrs. J. W. Brent.

1932 – A Window in the Nave, in memory of John Strickler Martin. Presented by Mrs. Martin.

1932 – A Lantern for the Church Entrance. Presented by The St. Paul's Club.

1932 – A Prayer Desk, in appreciation to Lilian E. Martin for the gift.

1936 – A Plaque, in memory of Margaret Benner Newell, Henry Morgan & their children, members of the original St. Paul's Congregation. Presented by Miss Jemima Morgan.

1936 – A Window in the Nave, in memory of Lawrence Skey & Mary Frances Buckwell, his wife. Presented by their children.

1937 – A Window in the Nave, in memory of Alfred & Louisa Buckwell and their children.

1938 – A Window in the Nave, in memory of Harry Wilmot Ansley & Bessie Lees Ansley. Presented by Ozias Clayton Ansley and Beatrice Ansley Syer.

1942 – A Union Jack, Staff & Stand presented to St. Paul's by Mrs. John S. Martin.

1943 – A Window in the Nave, in memory of Alice Amelia Decoe, beloved wife of Francis C. Smith. Presented by Francis C. Smith.

1950 – A Window in the Nave, a gift to St. Paul's by Minerva Musselman.

1951 – Two brass Altar Vases, in memory of her family. Presented by H. Minnie B. Maytham.

1958 – Seasonally Coloured Bookmarks, in memory of Martha Stammers Tibbetts, Mary Sabra Martin & Clara Mabel Campbell. Presented by Mary, Norah & Emily Barrett.

1961 – Two brass Altar Candlesticks, in memory of William Henry Barrett. Presented by his wife.

1961 – The Credence Table, a gift to St. Paul's by Mrs. John S. Martin.

1962 – The Processional Cross, in memory of Lottie Walker. Presented by her husband, John Walker.

1963 – A set of Altar Linens presented to St. Paul's by The Women's Auxiliary.

1963 – A Pulpit Light, in memory of Graham Arther Bell.

1963 – The Missal, in memory of Francis Waterford Slocomb & Ellen Elizabeth, his wife. Presented by Kenneth & Georgia Painter.

1964 – A Window in the Nave, in memory of My Husband & Family, by Minnie B. Maytham.

1964 – A Font Roll, a gift to St. Paul's by Mrs. Douglas Richardson.

1964 – A Window in the Nave, in memory of Charles W. Barwell & Ollie J. Barwell. Presented by Mrs. Allan M. Tibbetts.

1966 – Several Trees on the Church Grounds, a gift of Mrs. John (Barra Lowe) Gots.

1966 – This Memorial Book, in memory of Robert Charles Bloye, died April 19th, 1966, aged 33 years. Presented by his wife Barbara and children, Kerry & Susan.

1966 – New Vestry Furnishings, in memory of Emily Louisa Barrett. by Mrs. W. H. Barrett. "She lived so near to Heaven that the transition was not very great."

## St. Paul's Church Memorials 511

1966 – The Altar Rail, in memory of Keith Frederick Diver Howell, December 25th, 1932 – November 16th, 1965. Presented by the Howell Family.

1966 – A Copy of the New testament to St. Paul's, as a gift from Scotty Lariviere.

1967 – On January 1st Rt. Rev. G. N. Luxton, Bishop of Huron, dedicated the new organ installed after the fire of November 20th, 1965. The balance of indebtedness was a gift of the St. Paul's Club. Organ built & installed by Keates Organ limited, of Acton, Ontario. The new Organ, 1966, continues the Memorial to Clare M. Langs, donated by J. H. Herring.

1967 – A Chalice, in memory of Miss Clara Mason. Presented by he Altar Guild.

1967 – A paten, in memory of Andrew Yerex. Presented by the Yerex Family.

1967 – The Chancel Step's Railing, in memory of Andrew Yerex. Presented by Florence Johns, who raised him after his Mother's death.

1967 – A Funeral Pall, hand-stitched by members of the Women's Auxiliary, and presented to St. Paul's Altar Guild by The Women's Auxiliary.

1968 – Donation towards the new East Window, in memory of Mrs. Lilian C. Martin. Presented by the Cope Family.

1968 – On Sunday, February 11th, Rt. Rev. H. F. Appleyard, Bishop of Georgian Bay, dedicated the Memorial Window over the Altar following the fire of November 20th, 1965. The balance of the indebtedness was finally fully paid by The St. Paul's Club, April 1971. Rev. Donald Gray was Rector. Window designed and made by G. Maile Studios, Canterbury, Kent, England.

1969 – A New Lectern Bible, in memory of Theobald Butler Barrett, to replace the original one, damaged by fire. Presented by his Family.

1969 – A Memorial, in memory of James Garnet Colman, a life-long member of St. Paul's Church and an outstanding citizen of this community. Presented by Mr. & Mrs. Andrew C. (Garner) Lowe, on behalf of her father, a friend for many years.

1973 – In memory of the following devout members of St. Paul's who have made generous bequests to the Church. Mrs. Hattie M. Barrett, formerly organist of the Church. Percy L. Kindree, served on the Board of Management. John Walker, over 30 years Choir Leader, and a number of years, Church Warden.

1973 – A Donation in memory of Muriel (Monroe) McKnight, July 9th, 1973, by M. H. Barrett.

1974 – A Plaque, in memory of Canon David J. Cornish, 1876 – 1972. Rector of St Paul's, 1921 – 1952, & Helen Stuart Cornish, his wife, 1881 – 1973. Presented by St. Paul's congregation.

1975 – A Window in the Chancel (Epistle Side), in memory of Theobald Butler Barrett, 1895 – 1969 & Marjorie Hazel Clarke, 1892 – 1974, his wife. Presented by their Family.

1975 – A Candle Lighter, in memory of Dora Carter. Presented by David, Thomas, Judy, John & Elsie Finch.

1975 – A Silver Tray, in memory of Herbert K. Champion, for use of St. Paul's Organisations. Presented by Mary Champion, his wife.

1978 – The Chain-link Fence across the back and one side of the Parish Hall, in memory of Kenneth Thompson. Presented by Fern Thompson, his wife.

1979 – A Window in the Chancel (Gospel Side) in memory of All Past Organists & Choir Members of St. Paul's. Presented by St. Paul's Church Choir in its Centennial Year.

1979 – The Warden's Wands, presented to Robert Powell & Stephan Molewyk, Wardens of St. Paul's, on the 50th Anniversary of The St. Paul's Club, by The St. Paul's Club members.

1980 – A Window in the Nave, in memory of Adeline Musselman Garner, J. William Garner, Sarah Macdonald Lowe & Andrew J. Lowe. Presented by Eileen Garner Lowe, Sarah Lowe Cromwell, Andrew C. Lowe & Olive Lowe Ryerse.

1981 – The White Altar Frontal, a gift to St. Paul's Church, by The Chancel Guild.

1984 – An Office Candlestick, in memory of Clarence & Maude Finch and Martha & William I. Carter. Presented by John & Elsie Finch.

1984 – Gifts of several Prayer Books, presented by: Mr. & Mrs. Allan Wicker. Mr. & Mrs. Fred Smythe. Mr. & Mrs. William Barker.

1984 – A Gift of Prayer Books, in memory of Herbert K Champion. A further gift of Prayer Books, in memory of Mary C. Champion. Presented by Frederick & Caroline Diver.

1985 – A gift of Prayer Books, in memory of Steve Molnar. Presented by his Grand Daughter, Marie Brown.

1985 – A Gift of Prayer Books made on the occasion of George Daley's Confirmation on October October 6th, 1985. Presentation by The Daley Family.

1985 – A Contribution for Books, in memory of Viola Evans, Mabel Campbell, Mrs. C. O. MacDonald & George Pelly. Presented by One of Their Sunday School Pupils.

1985 – A Contribution toward Repair of the Church Spire, in memory of T. B. & M. H. Barrett. Presentation made by Alice L. Browne, Dorothy M. Burfoot, Sister Nonah, S. S. J. D., Emily Molewyk & Harry B. Barrett.

1986 – Five Server's Crosses, in Remembrance of Terry's Confirmation, by The Ralston Family.

1986 – A Framed Pen & Ink Drawing of St. Paul's Church, by Elizabeth Barrett, to be hung in the Narthex, in memory of David Craig Field. Presented by Harry B. Barrett.

1987 – A Ginkgo Tree, planted north of the Parish Hall, in honour of Andrew Lowe on his 80th Birthday. Presented by St. Paul's Choir & Congregation.

1987 – The Sanctuary Lamp, in memory of The Reverend Canon David John Cornish, Helen Agnes Cornish, Edith Anne Cornish, Ethel Elizabeth Jennings, William Gordon Cornish, Helen Elizabeth (Betty) Seymour, Margaret (Cornish) Skelly & David Colin Cornish. Presented by the Cornish Family.

1987 – A Union Jack, Staff & Stand to replace the one destroyed by the 1965 fire, which was donated by Mrs. John S. Martin. Given by Eileen & Andrew Lowe.

1989 – A Baptismal Ewer, Brass Candle Sticks & Flower Pot, in memory of John & Phila Vokes and Thomas Vokes. Presented by Ina Vokes and Ruth Scratch & Family.

1989 – The Nave Table, designed & made by Jack Dennis, and stained and finished by Jack Dennis and Graydon Field. Presented by St. Paul's Club Members in Honour of 60 years of Service to the Parish and Community by the Club.

1990 – Large Print Hymn & Service Books. Presented by the Ralston Family in Remembrance of Leigh-Anne's Confirmation.

1990 – The Lower Parish Hall Lights, a special gift from the Marion Stewart Estate.

1992 – Books of Common Prayer, in memory of Elsie Batten, Stella Brock, Sarah Cromwell, Minnie Quanbury and Dagmar Thompson. Presented by St. Paul's Women's Auxiliary.

1992 – A Memorial Display Cabinet, in memory of Barbara E. Baldock. Presented by Mr. & Mrs. A. W. Jordan.

## St. Paul's Church Memorials 513

1993 – Twelve Pew Hymn Books & Kneelers at the Communion Rail and in the Sanctuary, in memory of Captain George Arthur Turner. Presented by Marcia Turner & Family.

1992 – A Brass Font Liner, in memory of Barbara Baldock. Presented by St. Paul's Sunday School.

1993 – Six Hymn Books, in celebration of the 85th Birthday of Frederick M. Mann. Presented by Malcolm & Sharon Mann and Family.

1993 – One large Print Prayer Book, in memory of Martha Schilz. Presented by St. Paul's Women's Auxiliary.

1996 – One Large Print Hymn Book, in memory of Hilda Henson, by The Women's Auxiliary. – One Large Print Hymn Book, in memory of Eileen Lowe, by The Women's Auxiliary.

1996 – The Computer System, St. Paul's Church, in memory of George Moyse Smythe, Susanna Mary (Smythe) Brown & Frederick Joseph Smythe. Presented by Robert Smythe.

1997 – The Ambry, in memory of Byron Forrest. Presented by Doris Forrest, his wife.

1998 – Donation to The Brick Restoration Fund, in memory of Aaron W. Evans – Caretaker at St. Paul's from 1921 to 1941. ** Isabelle Evans – W. A. Member and Dorcas Secretary ** Viola Evans – Choir Member and Sunday School Teacher ** By Fern Evans Thompson.

1998 – Donation to The Brick Restoration Fund, in memory of Rev. Herbert J. Webb, Rector of this Parish – 1952 – 1960. & Mary Windross Webb, beloved wife and helpmate. Presented by Katie Buck & Jim Murphy.

1998 – One Large Print Book of Common Prayer, in memory of Jean Porritt, by St. Paul's W. A.

1999 – Combination Prayer & Hymn Books, in memory of Derek Skeldon. Presented by Malcolm, Sharon, Chris & Kathleen Mann.

2000 – Special Year 2000 Bulletin Covers [Painting by Elizabeth Barrett-Milner.] in memory of the Clergy who have served this Parish faithfully for the past 148 years, by Robert Smythe.

2000 – A Brass Plaque to the memory of Canon K. Keith Brett, Rector of St. Paul's, – 1984 – 1995. Presented by his Family and the Parishioners of St. Paul's.

2000 – Altar Candle Sockets and Joiners, in memory of Dr. Helen McClennon Nixon & Mary Nixon Kilby. Presented by Dorothy Mary Burfoot.

2000 – Altar Candle Followers, in memory of Jonathon A. Finch. Presented by Grandparents John & Elsie Finch.

2000 – A Large Print Hymn Book, in memory of Jean Porritt. Presented by her Family.

2000 – A Fair Linen & a Credence Cloth, in memory of Past Members of St. Paul's Church Chancel Guild. Presented by The Chancel Guild.

2000 – A missal, in memory of Derek Skeldon. Presented by he Skeldon Family.

2000 – A Combination Hymn & Prayer Book for the Servers, in memory of Derek Skeldon. Presented by the Mann Family.

2005 – A Plaque to The Glory of God & In Loving Memory of William Henry "Harry" Barrett, 1864 – 1942, D. V. M. and his wife, Rebecca Julia "Winonah" Pelly Barrett, 1876 – 1898. And his wife, Hattie Mabel "Enah" James Barrett, 1883 – 1970. Presented by Grandson, Harry B. Barrett on July 31st, 2005, who spoke of their lives prior to Dedication by Rt. Rev. Clarence Mitchell. Hattie Barrett's Grandson, Peter Barrett was also present, serving as Organist.

APPENDIX TWO

# St. Paul's Church Register

July 21st, 1889 - December 31st, 1911

| Date | Attend. | Coll. | Comments |
|---|---|---|---|
| Aug 11 | 180/203 | $10.90 | Mr. Mason of Hamilton preached |
| Nov 3 | 81/113 | 4.80 | M. F. Tibbetts baby baptised |

1890 – Incumbent Reverend J. R. Newell

| Date | Attend. | Coll. | Comments |
|---|---|---|---|
| Jan 19 | no record | | Incumbent ill. Skey officiated. |
| Feb 13 | 300/85 | 16.07 | Bishop Maurice (Scollard Baldwin) Huron confirmed 17 candidates |
| Apr 4 | 0/87 | 7.50 | [for the Jews] Good Friday evening service. |
| Apr 6 | 85/97 | 6.80 | Easter Sunday, Communicants - 48 |
| Jun 1 | 27/52 | 1.55 | Thos R. D., celebrant, Rev's W. Davis, Rich, W. Johnstone assist. |
| July 6 | 95/80 | 4.71 | Rev. Merton Shore officiated. H. D. Edwards baby baptised by J. R. N |
| Oct 5 | 65/70 | 4.42 | Communicants 46. S. G. Gamble baby baptised in evening |
| Oct 12 | 35/80 | 11.33 | To Algoma missions. Organist overslept herself no music. |
| Nov 30 | 95/99 | 13.40 | Ann. Mission mtg. D. J. Caswell officiated at matins. |
| Dec 25 | 130/0 | 27.88 | Communicants 55. Beautiful Christmas decorations |

1891 – Incumbent Reverend J. R. Newell

| Date | Attend. | Coll. | Comments |
|---|---|---|---|
| Apr 26 | 75/81 | 5.17 | Rev. Eernest M. Gates officiated at evensong |
| Jun 21 | ? /81 | 4.11 | Incumbent at St. John's, Theobald B. Barrett, Lay Reader officiated |
| July 5 | 130/121 | 8.14 | Rev. Lawrence E. Skey read prayers |
| July 7 | 0/270 | 0.00 | Maurice S. Huron confirmed 16. Vittoria, 8.30 p.m. confirmed 12 |
| Jul 26 | no record | 14.30 | Mr. L. Skey officiated |
| Aug 9 | 170/135 | 9.09 | Mr. Woodruff read prayers |
| Aug 30 | 153/140 | 9.02 | Mr. G. N. English officiated at evensong |
| Oct 4 | 70/0 | 1.95 | L. Skey, L. R. officiated for Oct. 4th & 11th while incumbent in Detroit |
| Oct 11 | 50/0 | 1.55 | for vacation and repair. |
| Oct 25 | 69/73 | 13.31 | Collection to missions in Algoma |
| Nov 12 | 0/95 | 5.00 | Collection to Huron College. Thanksgiving. |
| Nov 29 | 65/81 | 3.66 | Communicants 36. Mr. Skey read prayers for both services. |
| Dec 25 | 119/ | 27.85 | Communicants 36. Wet, foggy and muddy. |

1892 – Incumbent, Reverend J. R. Newell

| | | | |
|---|---|---|---|
| Jan 3 | 67/91 | $4.15 | Organist sick, no music for services. |
| Feb 14 | 87/57 | 10.35 | Collection to W. & O.   J. Frederick Renaud officiated. Very wet. |
| Feb 28 | 92/97 | 15.00 | Missionary meeting. Collection to missions |
| Mar 2 | 30/ | 1.06 | Ash Wednesday service |
| Apr 15 | /73 | 25.35 | Good Friday, collection for the Jews. |
| Jun 19 | | | 300 attend funeral of Reverend Williams |
| Jul 10 | 125/141 | 13.32 | Coll. To Widows & Orphans. Rev. E. Chilcott B. A. read prayers |
| Aug 7 | 230/235 | 43.00 | Coll. For St.John's, Newfoundland |
| Aug 21 | 215/225 | 27.40 | Coll. For furnace. Mr. Warren Hastings officiated |
| Sept 4 | 100/180 | 9.14 | Communicants 53. Rev. R. Hicks officiated |
| Sept 18 | 75/70 | 4.86 | Miss Battersby returns from six months vacation |
| Oct 2 | 60/0 | 2.32 | Mr. L. Skey officiated while incumbent on vacation for October. |
| Oct 9 | 140/250 | 6.93 | Cloudy |
| Nov 10 | 0/115 | 5.00 | Coll. For Huron College. Celebrate Nat. Thanksgiving Thurs. evening |
| Dec 11 | 60/75 | 8.57 | Coll. To Sunday School |
| Dec 25 | 95/ | 19.75 | Communicants 44. |

1893 — Incumbent Reverend J. R. Newell

| | | | |
|---|---|---|---|
| Jan 1 | 51/141 | 2.85 | 137 fair weather church people to-day. (?) |
| Mar 5 | 60/ 0 | 2.37 | Mr. L. Skey officiated. Fine. |
| Mar 19 | 75/120 | 6.28 | Rev Richard Johnstone officiated |
| Mar 31 | /76 | 13.20 | Good Friday, collection for the Jews |
| Apr 30 | 290/39 | 8.77 | Masons present at matins [Erie Lodge # 149. A.F. & A. M.] |
| Jul 30 | 211/260 | 11.94 | Reverend Lawrence E. Skey officiated |
| Aug 20 | 300/320 | 18.80 | Rev. J. C. Farthing & vested choir, St. Paul's, Woodstock present. |
| Sep 17 | 70/90 | 5.43 | Rev, Alfred Garden officiated |
| Sep 28 | | | 281 attend funeral of Mary J. Shaver at 2.00 p.m. |
| Oct 15 | 45/0 | 1.52 | Incumbent in Chicago. Mr. Skey took Oct15 & 22 services, no sermon |
| Nov 19 | 83/63 | 4.01 | Furnace used for first time. Bishop's letter read. |
| Nov 23 | 0/310 | 9.50 | National Thanksgiving, $5.00 to Huron. Petit gave two coronet solos |
| Dec 17 | 40/0 | 1.55 | Incumbent ill. Mr. L. Skey, L. R. officiated |
| Dec 25 | 103/ | 19.85 | Communicants 41 |
| Dec 31 | ?/? | 4.32 | Incumbent ill. Mr. L. Skey officiated. Snow storm |

1894 — Incumbent Reverend J. R. Newell

| | | | |
|---|---|---|---|
| Jan 20 | | | 125 attend the funeral of Mr. Arthur Battersby |
| Feb 4 | 73/92 | 4.45 | Communicants 31. Mrs. Dillon's last service as Church organist |
| Mar 2 | 200/ | 18.57 | Coll. To Bishop Richard(Young) of Athabaska, who spoke. (Friday) |
| Mar 11 | 63/60 | 7.92 | Rev. Newell's child very ill. Mr. Skey held evensong |
| Mar 17 | 220 | | Rev'ds R. Hicks, R. Gardner, A. Garden assist, funeral at 2.30 for Rev. J.R. Newell's son, Arthur Lawrence Newell |
| Apr 1 | 100/125 | 5.26 | Three baptisms. $11.13 to Sunday school |
| May 2 | 300 | 4.20 | Bishop Maurice S. Huron confirmed 18 candidates |
| May 4 | 250 | | Funeral of Captain Thomas Bayley at 10.30 a.m. |
| May 15 | 150 | | Funeral of Anne Colman Wells at 2.00 p.m. on Tuesday |
| May 20 | 85/76 | 3.37 | 260 attend Masonic service of Erie Lodge at 3.00 p.m. Coll. $4.32 |
| Jun 10 | 96/100 | 9.86 | Coll. To Missionary fund. One baptism |
| July 1 | 315/110 | 7.60 | 13th Battery, Norfolk Militia under Capt. Ross march to service. |

| | | | |
|---|---|---|---|
| July 8 | 150/121 | $11.38 | Coll. To Widows & Orphans |
| July 22 | 200/275 | 12.10 | No choir. L. Skey read prayers. Two baptisms. |
| July 29 | 275/0 | 8.05 | Rev J. C. Farthing & vested choir, new St. Paul's, Woodstock sing |
| Sep 27 | 40 | | Funeral of Elizabeth Richardson at 10.30 a.m. |
| Dec 2 | 72.97 | 4.52 | Communicants 36. Church is lighted by electricity for the first time. |
| Dec 23 | 79/93 | 4.08 | 275 attend funeral of Elizabeth L. Gamble at 2.00 p.m. |
| Dec 25 | 130 | 19.62 | Communicants 61 |

1895 — Incumbent Reverend J. R. Newell

| | | | |
|---|---|---|---|
| Jan 8 | | | 200 attend wedding of Jasper F. Lynch & Tinita Millman. L. Skey assist |
| Feb 24 | 110/200 | 12.68 | Ann. Missionary mtg. Rev. A. H. Wright officiated |
| Feb 26 | /275 | 11.88 | A. H. Wright gave missionary lecture for Saskatchewan Diocese |
| Feb 27 | 27/ | 1.01 | A. H. Wright read prayers for Ash Wednesday service |
| Mar 17 | | | 300 attend funeral for James W. Scott. Service at 2.00 p.m. |
| Apr 7 | 290/ | 16.60 | Coll. To Mr. Sayeki. Signed in Chinese. Joseph Smythe's son baptised |
| May 8 | /275 | 5.26 | Bishop Maurice Huron confirmed 9 candidates |
| May 12 | 27/68/115 | 4.65 | Eucharist at 9.00 a.m. for 27 celebrants |
| May 19 | /5/6/ | 4.03 | Choir on strike ! |
| May 29 | | | Marriage of W. F. Dunkin & Maud Farrar at 5.00 p.m. |
| June 9 | 120/90 | 7.50 | Child of Christian Quanbury baptised |
| June 16 | 6/120/100 | 6.83 | Eucharist to 6. New Choir to the fore! |
| June 23 | 330/115 1 | 3.64 | Forresters present for matins. |
| June 30 | 350/130 | 11.30 | 13th battery attend matins under Capt. Ross |
| July 28 | 300/290 | 15.20 | Rev. J. C. Farthing officiates for matins |
| Aug 4 | 290/200 | 11.38 | Communicants 85. Rev. Alfred Brown officiated |
| Aug 11 | | 8.21 | Rev. Arthur Murphy officiated, attendance not recorded. |
| Sept 23 | | 1.95 | Rev. R. Gardiner held 8.00 a.m. service |
| Sept 28 | 60/ | 1.70 | Incumbent away. L. Skey officiated at matins |
| Nov 18 | /60 | 3.05 | Monday evening address by Rev. Henry E. Benoit, collection to him |
| Nov 21 | 54/ | 4.30 | Thursday morning address by Rev. A. H. Wright. Thanksgiving day |
| Nov 24 | 81/125 | 11.58 | Evening missionary mtg. Rev. A. H. Wright took meeting & Collection |
| Dec 10 | /75 | 1.70 | Rev. Henry Benoit gave Tuesday evening lecture on the Church |
| Dec 25 | 120/ | 19.43 | Communicants 52 |
| Dec 29 | 110/125 | 5.87 | Rev. A. H. Wright officiated for evensong |

1896 — Incumbent Reverend J. R. Newell

| | | | |
|---|---|---|---|
| Feb 23 | 61/110 | 26.15 | Morning collection of $23.50 for Armenia relief |
| Apr 5 | 130/125 | 8.28 | Easter Sunday, Comm. 70. Good Friday Coll. $16.02 for the Jews |
| Apr 12 | 125/150 | 5.73 | Rev. F. Ryan officiated |
| May 17 | 115/110 | 11.52 | Crew of "Petrel" march to matins |
| June 28 | 120/125 | 5.70 | Bishop Maurice Huron attends matins |
| Aug 2 | 250/275 | 10.62 | Rev. May read prayers at matins. Rev. Chas. E. Whitcombe, Rector of St. Mathews, Hamilton took evensong. |
| Aug 9 | 175/200 | 7.08 | Rev. J. L. Wright officiated. Rev. E. Chilcott, of Norwich read prayers |
| Aug 16 | 225/250 | 9.91 | Rev. C. A. Seager, Curate, St. Thomas, Toronto took evensong |
| Aug 23 | 200/280 | 10.80 | Rev. Lawrence E. Skey, Rector of Merriton took evensong |
| Aug 30 | 120/115 | 6.25 | Mr. Mason read prayers |
| Sept 10 | /60 | | Thursday evening baptism of 18 candidates. |
| Sept 13 | 71/109 | 5.32 | Sent 32 cents to M. F. [Missionary Fund] |
| Nov 8 | 85/67 | 6.13 | Sent $1.13 to M. F. |

| Dec 13 | 95/100 | $8.07 | $3.07 for Missionary meeting |
| Dec 25 | 96/ | 13.58 | Communicants 50. |

1897 — Incumbent Reverend J. R. Newell

| Jan 3 | 85/112 | 1.80 | Comm. 29. Collection envelopes used for the first time |
| Jan 17 | 60/97 | 8.30 | Collection to the Sunday School |
| Feb 21 | 109/100 | 20.56 | Collection to India |
| Mar 17 | /76 | 1.26 | Wed. lenten service. Lecture on St. Patrick's Day |
| Apr 25 | ?/? | 1.12 | Rev. C. Walter MacWilliams officiated. No attendance recorded |
| May 9 | 98/120 | 3.12 | Rev. J. C. Farthing officiated at evensong |
| May 27 | 20/0 | 0.00 | Incumbent [had] kink in throat. L. Skey took service |
| Jun 20 | 93/300 | 5.62 | Evensong held at 4.21 p.m. [no explanation] |
| July 25 | 175/235 | 8.90 | Rev. J. E. Haud had matins. Rev. Lawrence E. Skey had evensong |
| Aug 29 | ?/? | 2.28 | Rev. F. C. Piper in charge. PROHIBITION: Woolley roaring at Pavilion. |
| Sept 12 | 101/120 | 4.24 | Rev. M. J. Goodheart took evensong. 1 baptism at matins. |
| Dec 25 | 110/ | 19.60 | Communicants 41. Christmas Day. |

1898 — Incumbent Reverend J. R. Newell

| Feb 9 | /98 | 7.71 | Rev. J. J. Renaud officiated for Annual Missionary Meeting |
| Feb 13 | 110/100 | 5.19 | Collection to Widows and Orphans |
| Feb 23 | 31/ | 0.00 | Rev. Newell held Ash Wednesday service, no address or collection. |
| Mar 2 | /40 | 1.15 | Rev. F. C. Piper officiated for this and 5 other Wednesday services. |
| June 19 | 95/110 | 4.28 | F.W. Denton child baptised, the mother stood alone |
| July 24 | 100/112 | 5.37 | Oh! So Hot! |
| Aug 14 | 180/200 | 11.04 | Rev. Newell on holiday. Rev'ds W. A. Young, Horace E. Bray, Richard Hicks and Fred C. Piper officiated on consecutive Sundays |
| Sept 29 | /275 | 6.92 | Harvest Home, Rev. Edward A. Irving, Dundas assisted by Rev. E.H. Maloney, Nanticoke & Arthur Francis, Cayugah. Beautiful decorations |
| Oct 30 | 102/300 | 6.38 | Rev. J.R. Newell's last service as Rector. Rev. T. A. Fawcett assisted. |
| Nov 6 | 85/100 | 4.31 | Rev. M. M. Goldberg first officiated as rector of St. Paul's. |
| Dec 11 | 111/95 | 3.93 | Children's Service |
| Dec 25 | 105/ | 28.28 | Christmas day. Communicants 63 |

1899 — Incumbent, Reverend M. M. Goldberg

| Feb 12 | 36/56 | 4.47 | Collection to Widows and Orphans. Too cold to preach. |
| Mar 5 | 74/79 | 2.93 | Communicants 47. High winds, bad roads. |
| Mar 12 | 73/96 | 5.67 | Rev. Fred C. Piper officiated. Collection to Mission Fund |
| June 18 | 155/140 | 7.93 | I.O.O.F. attend Matins. Rev. D. Waters officiated at evensong |
| July 16 | 110/115 | 5.86 | Rev. J.R. Newell officiated at matins |
| Aug 13 | 180/300 | 10.33 | Woodstock supplied choir. Rev. Lawrence Skey officiated at evensong |
| Sept 24 | 70/60 | 2.15 | Rev. W. M. Hinds officiated. Very stormy |
| Oct 22 | 50/60 | 11.38 | Harvest Home Service. Dark & wet |
| Nov 8 | /24 | 0.00 | Wednesday evening service in Sunday School room |
| Dec 17 | 75/120 | 3.71 | Exchange with Rev. P. L. Spencer |
| Dec 25 | 120/ | 23.39 | Christmas Day. Communicants 37 |

1900 — Incumbent to April 29, Reverend M. M. Goldberg

| Jan 14 | 60/260 | 4.74 | War in South Africa. Snow |
| Jan 28 | 55/50 | 7.31 | Collection for Sunday School Prises [sic] |
| Feb 11 | 80/130 | 17.71 | Collection to Patriotic Fund |

| | | | |
|---|---|---|---|
| Mar 21 | /16 | $2.10 | Rev. R. L. Spenser in charge of Wed. evening Missionary Meeting |
| Apr 15 | 110/120 | 5.73 | Easter. Archdeacon McKay took evensong |
| Apr 17 | /25 | 1.40 | W. A. M. S. Mtg. for Indian Mission of Saskatchewan |
| Apr 29 | 70/120 | 3.84 | Rev. M. M. Goldberg's last Sunday as Rector of St. Paul's, Port Dover |
| May 6 | 50/0 | 1.40 | Lay Services were held through May & June, shared by Rev. J. Spencer & C. S. M. [Canon Cornish noted in 1937 that C. S. M. was Charles S. Mason of Brantford, a founder & resident of Brant Hill. He was father of Rev. Ralph Mason, who we will hear more of later] |
| July 1 | 325/130 | 9.47 | Rev. R. Herbert held first service as new Rector. "D" Co. of 13th Regiment of Militia attend matins. |
| July 29 | 350/48 | 28.25 | Coll. To Famine Fund. Woodstock Choir boys attend matins. Wet. |
| Sept 2 | 90/110 | 5.98 | Communicants 43. Oh ! So Hot ! |
| Sept 20 | /150 | 14.97 | Rev. Richard Hicks in charge. Counter attraction at Methodist church |
| Sept 30 | 72/150 | 3.76 | Rev. T. A. Fawcett, of Wycliffe College took evensong |
| Oct 18 | /52 | 1.90 | Mtg. for Huron College. Norfolk County Fair, Simcoe, drew many away |
| Oct 25 | 75 | | Funeral of Mrs. [Crosbie] Morgan |
| Nov 3 | 200 | | Funeral of Miss Edith Battersby. Rev. R. Hicks assists |
| Dec 2 | 80/125 | 3.27 | Communicants 43. Rev. H. Softly officiated. Fine & mild |
| Dec 23 | 50/130 | 3.22 | Rev. F. Fawcett read prayers. 100 attend funeral for Miss Lawrie- 2:00pm |
| Dec 25 | 85/ | 34.45 | Communicants 40. Beautiful & mild |

1901 — Incumbent Reverend R. Herbert

| | | | |
|---|---|---|---|
| Jan 20 | 30/ | 1.10 | Rev. Herbert ill. L. Skey took matins |
| Feb 2 | | | Saturday, 10.00 a.m. 100 attend Memorial Service for Queen Victoria |
| Mar | | | Most of page missing |
| Apr 10 | /400? | 4.79 | Maurice S. Huron confirmed 25. Coll. To Missionary Fund |
| Jun 30 | 180/190 | 5.84 | Mr. Mason read prayers. Coll. To Sunday school |
| July 4 | /75 | 4.00 | Rev. G. M. Kelty, Jarvis, assisted by Revd's. Spenser, Jarvis & H. Calton, Nanticoke took Thurs. evening, Rev'd W. Cotton & Woodruff took rest July |
| Aug 11 | 290/235 | 15.19 | Expected call for Choir boys, but did not happen. C. S. Mason took first two Sunday services in September |
| Oct 6 | 70/110 | 2.85 | Furnace not going, church cold |
| Nov 3 | 110/ ? | 1.97 | Bible Society Mtg at 7.30 p.m. No Service |
| Nov 28 | ? | 1.80 | National Thanksgiving. Coll. To Huron College |
| Dec 11 | 00/175 | 4.31 | Rev. Lawrence Skey of Niagara officiated both services. Beautiful Day |
| Dec 25 | 80/ | 37.32 | Communicants 53. Fine |

1902 — Incumbent Reverend R. Herbert

| | | | |
|---|---|---|---|
| Jan 5 | 50/0 | 0.85 | Mr. L. Skey, L. R. took matins, no evensong |
| June 1 | 75/190 | 2.60 | Solo by Miss Bochmar Howell at matins |
| Jun 15 | 52/150 | 3.21 | Reference made to 50th Anniversary of Laying of Cornerstone of St. Paul's |
| July 27 | 250/325 | 7.85 | Rev. J. C. Farthing read prayers. Choir boys of Woodstock attend |
| Aug 9 | | | Saturday, 10.30 - 96 attend short address & Coronation Service. |
| Aug 17 | 170/200 | 6.65 | Rev. J. R. Newell returns to officiate for two Sundays. |
| Sept 28 | 100/160 | 5.79 | Rev. L. B. Branghall officiated. Coll. to Rectory account |
| Oct 19 | 60/80 | 2.26 | Thomas H. Fawcett, Divinity Student, officiated |
| Oct 26 | 55/ | 1.03 | Rev. Lawrence Skey, Rector of Warwick, officiated for Oct. services assisted by Rev. J. R. Newell. [very shaky signature] |
| Nov 9 | 90/150 | 4.27 | Rev. J. R. Newell, of Markdale read the lessons |
| Dec 25 | 90/ | 44.00 | Christmas Day. Communicants 42 |

1903 — Incumbent Reverend R. Herbert

| Mar 11 | /70 | $2.01 | Coll. to M. S. C. C. Wed. at 7.00 p.m. ten are baptised |
|---|---|---|---|
| Apr 7 | /300 | 3.94 | Bishop Maurice S. Huron confirmed 12 candidates. Coll. to Diocese M.F. |
| Apr 26 | 90/120 | 2.50 | Rev. L. H. Cotton officiated |
| Jun 21 | 90/0 | 2.80 | Mr. L. Skey, Lay Reader, officiated |
| July 12 | 275/350 | 12.27 | Rev. J. C. Farthing of Woodstock officiated |
| Aug 16 | 190/215 | 8.96 | Rev Mr. Howeth of Hamilton, officiated |
| Sept 27 | 75/80 | 3.11 | Services in Sunday school, church closed for repairs. Lay services held Oct 4th & 11th in S. S. in the mornings |
| Nov 8 | 80/100 | 2.45 | Total cost of repair - $579.45.Income, envelopes, 350.30 Plate 82.81 Former Parishioners 150.00. For a total of $583.11. |
| Dec 20 | 60/175 | 3.56 | L. Skey officiated in a.m. Bishop Maurice S. Huron at evensong |
| Dec 25 | 84/ | 47.61 | Communicants 40. |

1904 — Incumbent, Reverend R. Herbert

| Feb 14 | 52/0 | 1.90 | No sermon. Coll to Diocesan Missions |
|---|---|---|---|
| May 22 | 100/95 | 2.33 | Rev. F. W. Hovey officiated |
| June 19 | 225/85 | 10.12 | Foresters present |
| July 31 | 125/100 | 6.71 | Rev. Richard Hicks officiated |
| Aug 28 | 115/90 | 47.26 | Rev D. Walter Collins officiated. Coll. for Repair Fund |
| Oct 9 | 84/75 | 6.87 | Coll. to Diocesan Missions. Rev. Herbert on holiday. Matins only. No rec. |
| Oct 30 | 100/100 | 3.42 | Rev Wm. Murton Shore officiated for Memorial Service for the late Bishop Maurice Scollard Baldwin. |
| Nov 20 | 80/110 | 2.81 | Celebrate 10th Anniversary of re-opening of the Church. |
| Dec 25 | 120/150 | 53.02 | Christmas Day. 60 communicants. No sermon. |

1905 — Incumbent, Reverend R. Herbert.

| Jan 8 | 130/175 | 4.21 | Rev. J. Frederick Renaud of Montreal officiated |
|---|---|---|---|
| Mar 12 | 250/ | 3.47 | Bishop David (Williams) Huron confirmed 8 candidates |
| Mar 19 | 80/64 | 2.05 | Whole confirmation class in attendance |
| May 21 | 84/225 | 3.71 | Rev. L. Norman Meeker officiated at evensong |
| July 16 | 115/90 | 4.01 | Rev. T. Fawcett officiated at evensong |
| July 23 | 100/98 | 7.04 | Coll. to Sunday School. Rev. W. H. Snelgrove officiated at matins |
| Aug 20 | 100/90 | 5.60 | C. S. Mason officiated. Also for next two Sunday services |
| Dec 10 | 60/150 | 3.31 | Rev. Lawrence E. Skey officiated |
| Dec 25 | 22/92 | 57.00 | Christmas Day. Communicants 22 & 41 |

1906 — Incumbent, Reverend R. Herbert

| Jan 14 | 70/85 | 49.81 | Collection to Foreign Missions. Raining slightly |
|---|---|---|---|
| Feb 25 | 40/80 | 5.07 | Collection for General Synod expense. Slightly damp |
| Mar 14 | /55 | .75 | Rev. Spenser of Jarvis took Wednesday Lenten Service |
| May 27 | ?/? | 7.92 | Rev. Henry M. Shore officiated. Rector in the Old Country. From now to Aug. 26th, Rev. Henry Shore officiated for 14 services, Rev. W. Harvey Moore for 2, Rev. Horace E. Brey for 2, Mr. C. S. Mason for 4, Rev. P.L. Spencer for 2,Rev. J. L. Godden for 1, Rev. Robert H. Ferguson for 2. |
| Sept 2 | 91/65 | 5.00 | Rev. R. Herbert officiated. Communicants 41 |
| Oct 14 | 75/80 | 3.60 | Harvest Thanksgiving. Rev. Richard Hicks officiated |
| Oct 28 | 60/70 | 12.33 | Diocesan Jubilee |
| Dec 25 | 121/100 | 44.00 | Christmas Day. Communicants 21 & 42 |

1907 — Incumbents, Reverend R. Herbert / Reverend Cyril G. D. Browne

| | | | |
|---|---|---|---|
| Jan 27 | 115/123 | $4.78 | This was the last Sunday Rev. R. Herbert officiated as Rector. |
| Feb 3 | 65/78 | 2.70 | Rev. S. S. Hardy officiated, then Rev. T. J. Hamilton, Rev. Henry M. Shore, Rev. W. B. Hawkins, & Mar 3rd to 31st Rev. W. R. Westly. |
| Apr 7 | 95/67 | 3.65 | Rev. T. H. Cotton officiated, then Rev. W. B. Hawkins, Rev. Chas. F. Washburn and Rev. G. Benson Cox. |
| May 5 | 105/85 | 2.75 | Rev. Cyril G. D. Browne officiated for first time as Rector of St. Paul's |
| May 19 | 100/90 | 3.70 | Rev. W. J. Perry & Rev J. Ward officiated. Communicants 46 |

Throughout his tenure Rev. Cyril Browne commented on the weather in some detail each Sunday. "Lovely Day", "Very hot", "Fine Day", "Wet", "Fine - snow", "Stormy - very wet", "Snowing hard", "Fine and cold" " Damp, dull & raining" , "Threatening rain".

| | | | |
|---|---|---|---|
| May 26 | 95/80 | 21.37 | Coll. for M. S. C. C. Rained early, severe thunderstorm |
| July 28 | 143/120 | 63.05 | Special appeal for heat, light & repairs to S. S. & rectory |
| Sept 8 | 75/45 | 3.31 | Rev. T. A. Fawcett officiated, no sermon at evensong |
| Sept 15 | 94/97 | 15.50 | Jubilee Collection. Lovely Day |
| Oct 27 | 65/90 | 3.88 | Rev. lawrence Skey officiated. Wet day |
| Dec 15 | 102/104 | 3.10 | Good deal of snow, fine day with sleighing |
| Dec 25 | 28/99/0 | 73.10 | Communicants 25 & 30. Fine |
| Dec 31 | /75 | 0.00 | Watch Night Service at 11.15 p.m. Fine night |

1908 — Incumbent, Reverend Cyril G. D. Browne

| | | | |
|---|---|---|---|
| Feb 3 | no record | 4.45 | Bishop David (Williams) Huron confirmed a class of 23 |
| Mar 18 | /72 | 0.87 | Rev. J. Frederick Renaud took Wednesday evening service |
| Apr 17 | /105 | 13.78 | Good Friday, offertory for the Jews |
| Apr 19 | 38/151/147 | 12.92 | Easter. Communicants 36 & 50 |
| May 17 | 118/110 | 17.00 | Matins by Rev. R.J. Parker, Evensong Rev. T.G. Wallace. |
| Aug 16 | 74/100 | 10.23 | Collection for Widows & Orphans. Wet, then fine |
| Aug 30 | 87/51 | 5.14 | Mr. C.S. Mason officiated |
| Sept 20 | 135/145 | 19.50 | Harvest Thanksgiving. Offertory to Diocesan Missions |
| Nov 8 | 87/96 | 7.40 | Offertory to Huron College |
| Dec 25 | 37/82/- | 65.75 | Communicants 35 & 34 |
| Dec 31 | /41 | 0.00 | Watch Night Service at 11.15 |

1909 — Incumbent, Reverend Cyril G.D. Browne

| | | | |
|---|---|---|---|
| Jan 3 | 95/86 | 3.66 | Rev. H. J. Leaske officiated. Communicants 43. Dull |
| Jan 17 | 48/89 | 101.70 | Collection to Foreign Missions |
| Mar 21 | 88/107 | 4.50 | Rev. Richard Hicks officiated. Fine  very. |
| Apr 25 | 73/261 | 10.87 | Oddfellows attend evensong. Wet in a.m., then fine |
| May 23 | 100/96 | 16.92 | Matins, Rev. S. Gould. Evensong, Rev Chas. H. P. Owen. Offertory to M.S.C.C. - Palestine & the Blackfoot Indians. |
| June 24 | ? | | Rev. F. E. Howell conducts special Deanery Mtg. W. A. meet |
| July 18 | 130/100 | 8.27 | Rev T. F. Wallace, Rector in Woodstock, officiated. Cooler |
| Sept 12 | 93/93 | 5.40 | Rev. John Ransford in charge. Also for Sept. 26th & Nov. 7th, 1909 |
| Oct 17 | 68/135 | 27.33 | Children's Day. Collection to Sunday School |
| Dec 25 | 26/90/- | 43.85 | Christmas Day. Communicants 26 & 40. Snowing |
| Dec 31 | /40 | 0.00 | Watchnight Service. Fine night |

1910 — Incumbent, Reverend Cyril G. D. Browne

| Feb 6 | 79/60 | $1.57 | Communicants 30. Very cold, 0 degrees (F) |
| Feb 27 | 65/0 | 0.00 | Matins suspended, no evensong. [no explanation. Rev. Browne ill?] |
| Mar 6 | 100/67 | 3.05 | Frank O. Vain, a student, officiated at most services, Mar 6th to Aug 14th. |

[Canon Cornish notes in 1938 that Rev. Frank Vain is now Rector of the Church of the Ascension, Windsor. Others assisting or officiating during this period are Reverends Cyril Browne, Richard Hicks, Bain Howard, George Fournet, H. G. Leaske, Cameron Waller, E. Frank Salmon, Horace E. Brey, Lawrence E. Skey, W. C. Roberts, G. M. Cox, A. Stanley Brey, ( ? ) and Percy N. Harding.

| Aug 21 | 115/105 | 7.50 | Rev. Cyril Browne is in charge again, but often needs help. |
| Nov 27 | 80/119 | 4.10 | Rev. Cyril Browne signed the Register for the last time as Rector of St. Paul's. He reported a fine day. |
| Dec 4 | 61/68 | 7.27 | Rev. W. C. Roberts officiated and again on Dec. 11th & Dec. 18th. |
| Dec 25 | 86/53/0 | 31.95 | Rev. G. M. Cox officiated. Communicants 62 |
| Dec 31 | /12 | 0.00 | Rev. W.C. Roberts officiated for a New Year's Eve service. |

1911 — Incumbent, Reverend H. J. Johnson

| Jan 1 | 68/67 | 4.40 | Rev. W. C. Roberts officiated as well as on Feb. 5th. Rev. A. Stanley Bree officiated for all services in January. |
| Feb 12 | 67/76 | 2.15 | Rev. Percy N. Harding officiated |
| Feb 19 | 101/88 | 3.50 | Rev. H. J. Johnson officiated this Sunday for the first time as Rector. |
| Apr 9 | 71/74 | 2.35 | Recorded Income: Sunday Sch. Altar books - $2.65. Repairs - $17.40. Guild for carpet - $32.99. Total cost = $53.04. |
| Apr 16 | 32/110/88 | ? | Easter Sunday. Communicants 32 & 36 |
| Apr 23 | 78/174 | 7.97 | I.O.O.F parade to Morning service. |
| May 14 | 79/78 | 11.56 | Collection to the Chinese Famine Fund |
| July 30 | 139/97 | 30.03 | Rev. E. G. Dimond officiated. Collection raised to go for new roof. |
| Sept 24 | 50/50 | 1.40 | Services held in Sunday School during repairs to roof etc. |
| Nov 5 | 102/60/140 | 34.40 | Archdeacon W. A. Young officiated to 1. Re-open the church. 2. Dedicate Memorials. 3. Induct Rev. H. J. Johnson as Rector of St. Pauls |
| Dec 3 | 128/58 | 3.85 | Bishop David (Williams) Huron confirmed 11 candidates. |
| Dec 17 | 56/0 | 0.55 | Mr. W. Tibbetts, Lay Reader, took Matins & Evensong. Also Dec 24th |
| Dec 25 | 27/66/- | 37.01 | Christmas Day. Communicants 27. |

1912 - Incumbent Reverend H.J. Johnson.

| Jan 21 | 53/51 | 17.01 | Collection to the Foreign Missions. M.S.C.C. Cold. |
| Feb 21 | 12/14 | 1.90 | Ash Wed. severe storms. Feb 25th collection $7.35 to local S. S. |
| Apr 1 | | | Monday of Holy Week. Agnes Dei Reed assisted all week. |
| Apr 5 | 67 | 7.30 | Good Friday. Conversion of the Jews. Apr 14th George Johnson assisted. On May19th David. M. Rose & A.A.Bice officiated. |
| May 29 | 78/59 | 3.10 | Wednesday services, Rural Dean Armstrong & J. Birmingham. |
| Aug 11 | 60/73 | 4.67 | Mr. Morton Brown, Lay reader, in charge. |
| Aug 25 | 63/50 | 4.40 | Worst electric storm known for many years at 9:00 a.m. The following Sunday at 3:00p.m. 3 houses struck in severe storm. |
| Sept 15 | 98/70 | ? | S. S. Boyle, Trinity College officiated. R. H. Brett on Sept. 22nd. |
| Nov 24 | 76/53 | 1.78 | J. H. Summerhill officiated at evensong. |
| Dec 2 | /120 | 5.47 | Bishop David (Williams) Huron confirmed 12 candidates on Mon. |
| Dec 25 | 22/67/- | 46.60 | Christmas. Communicants 22 & 34 respectively. |

522 The Parish of St. Paul's

1913 - Incumbent Reverend H. J. Johnson.

| | | | |
|---|---|---|---|
| Jan 26 | 47/75 | $1.19 | Rev. J. H. Summerhill officiated at evensong. |
| Apr 6 | 51/62 | 1.72 | Rev. George Johnson officiated. Communicants 29. |
| Apr 27 | 40/154 | 6.92 | Rev. R. Herbert assisted with both services. |
| May 18 | 64/75 | 3.72 | Rev. H. A. Wright officiated. |
| June 15 | 85/83 | 6.30 | Rev. Lawrence E. Skey officiated. |

On June 29th Rev. F. V. Vair, the incumbent in Otterville officiated, July 6th Mr. A. C. Barclay, Lay Reader, July 20th Rev. K. Alexander preached to 150 at the evening service. On Aug 3rd 94 heard Rev. R. Herbert at evensong. On September 7th Rev. L. J. Charlton officiated. On September 28th Rev. J. H. Summerhill officiated at evensong and October 5th Rev. T. L. Armstrong. D. D. officiated at both services. November 9th first snow, a deluge!!! is recorded.

| | | | |
|---|---|---|---|
| Oct 19 | 92/42 | 3.24 | Children's Day. Special envelopes were used. |
| Dec 25 | 37/71 | 58.60 | Christmas. Communicants 37 & 31. |

1914 - Incumbent Reverend H. J. Johnson.

| | | | |
|---|---|---|---|
| Apr 12 | 29/129/95 | 11.47 | Easter. Communicants 29 & 45. 1 baptism. |
| May 3 | 80/175 | 2.65 | Rev. Charles Leo Abbott officiated. May 10th Rev. H. H. Tancock . |
| Aug 9 | 98/60 | 7.55 | W. F. D. Smith, a Huron College student officiated. |
| Aug 16 | 99/70 | 6.81 | Rev. Edwin Lee officiated. Miss M. Cayugas preached. |
| Sept 26 | 92/97 | 2.30 | Rev. J. A. Bloodsworth officiated. Communicants 25. |
| Nov 13 | | | Rev. Culp & Rev. Robertson assist in Friday service of Intercession. |
| Dec 6 | 72/161 | 4.96 | Bishop David Huron confirmed 7 candidates. Communicants 37. |
| Dec 25 | 27/60/- | 38.20 | Christmas. Communicants 27 & 40 respectively. |

1915 - Incumbent Reverend H. J. Johnson

| | | | |
|---|---|---|---|
| Jan 3 | 65/75 | 0 | Rev. A. C. Barclay officiated. |
| Mar14 | 75/83 | 0 | Services held in the Sunday School. On Mar. 21st W. F. Tibbetts took the 11:00 a.m. service. On Wednesday, March 25th, 28 attend a Union Service. |
| Apr 25 | 93/100 | 2.15 | Rev. A. B. Farny officiated at evensong. On May 2nd Rev J.H. Summerhill took evensong & May 9th Mr W. F. Tibbetts took matins & Rev. J. D. Christie evensong. |
| Jun 20 | 5/80/55 | 5.35 | Rev. G. W. Latmeir spoke on the Dominion Alliance. Comm. 5. |
| July18 | 6/105/50 | 6.92 | Rev. James Ward, Rector St. Johns. Woodhouse took evensong. |
| Aug 1 | 110/100 | 3.15 | Captain Pegenat spoke on War and A. Y. P. A work. Monday August 2nd he held four services. (Representing the Salvation Army ?) |
| Aug 15 | 7/120/55 | 7.40 | Rev. Edwin Lee assisted. Miss G. Cayugas also present. |
| Oct 3 | 8/120/110 | 8.75 | Harvest Thanksgiving. Rev. H. F. D. Woodcock assisted. Comm 8-61 |
| Dec 6 | | | Bishop David Huron confirmed 6 candidates at 1:45 p.m. |
| Dec 25 | 10/31/ | 62.72 | Christmas. Surpliced Choir in attendance. |

1916 - Incumbent Reverend H. J. Johnson.

| | | | |
|---|---|---|---|
| Feb 6 | 77/73 | 4.55 | Rev. A. T. Lowe officiated. Snowing. Feb 13th no evening service. |
| June 25 | 116/55 | 5.42 | Rev. J. Fredrick Renaud officiated. On July16th no sermon preached due to the heat. July 23rd no evensong. July 30th James Loard in p.m. |
| Aug 28 | 86/56 | 4.84 | Voice failed, no sermon in the evening service. On Sept 3rd W.F. Tibbetts officiated, and on 10th Morton Brown, both Lay Readers. |
| Oct 3 | | | Rev. James Ward, Rural Dean holds deanery mtg. Communicants 6. |

| | | | |
|---|---|---|---|
| Dec 24 | 65/ | $0.95 | Christmas Eve service held in Vittoria. |
| Dec 25 | 20/59/- | 74.00 | Christmas. Communicants 20 & 37 respectively. |

1917 - Incumbent H. J. Johnson.

| | | | |
|---|---|---|---|
| Jan 14 | ?/ | 0.85 | Very cold, short service, no sermon. Three more such entries in Jan & Feb. one service in S. S. due to cold. Apr 1st no service due to sickness |
| May 27 | 79/86 | 0 | Rev. C. Brown officiated. Communicants 42. August 12th to Sept. 9 Rev. C. Brown officiated at all services. |
| Nov 4 | 78/0 | 1.30 | No evensong to allow attend. at Trinity to hear Bishop of Kootenay |
| Nov 25 | ? / | | Mr. Tibbetts found gas pressure so low he cancelled services. Cold. |
| Dec 2 | | | Bishop David (Williams) Huron confirmed 22 candidates. |
| Dec 16 | ?/? | | Rev. A. B. Farny read Bishop's pastoral & gave a patriotic address. |
| Dec 25 | 24/60/ | 67.05 | Christmas. Communicants 24 & 47 respectively. |
| Dec 30 | ?/ 0 | | Very cold. Litany read in the Sunday School. No evensong. |

1918 - Incumbent H. J. Johnson.

| | | | |
|---|---|---|---|
| Jan 6 | 76/68 | 0 | Records are very erratic, no offertory recorded. Services in S.S. in Jan. |
| May 19 | | | Frank W Trevitt of Huron signed register, nothing further. |
| July 21 | 110/37 | 7.41 | Rev. C. Ward Butcher officiated. Also for July 28th & August 4th. |
| Sept 8 | 60/40 | 2.66 | J. Louis Barber officiated for all September. Communicants 44. From |
| Oct. 21st to Nov 4th | | | Church & S. S. closed by reason of epidemic of Spanish Influenza. |
| Nov 21 | /200 | 0 | Thanksgiving service (Thursday) A. B. Farney & E. Appleyard officiated |
| Dec 25 | 7/ ? / | 58.30 | Christmas. |

1919 - Incumbent Reverend H. J. Johnson.

Records are very sketchy and incomplete. No offertory is recorded for the whole year. On May 6th the Rector officiated at a Memorial service to dedicate the Alter. Captain J. E Jenkins preached the sermon. On May 25th L. Read took the evening service at which Girl Guides, Forward W.(?) and the Y. M. C. A. participated. In August the rector was suffering from sciatica and matins only were read. R. Mason took some evening services. In September Mr. Brand, Mr Brown and Mr. Andrews took the first three Sundays. On October 12th Rev. G. K. Wexford celebrated Harvest Thanksgiving with 190 & 106 attending matins & evensong respectively.

| | | | |
|---|---|---|---|
| Dec 21 | 86/ | | 3 adults were baptised. Christmas service at Vittoria in the evening. |
| Dec 22 | /175 | 113.16 | Bishop of Huron (David Williams) confirmed 16 candidates at 7:30 p.m. |
| Dec 25 | 25/120/ | | Christmas. Communicants 25 & 48. |

1920 - Incumbent Reverend H. J. Johnson.

| | | | |
|---|---|---|---|
| Jan 11 | 130/76 | 0 | A.G.M.W.F. Cockshutt speaker. |
| Feb 8 | 250 | | Rector ill. John S. Martin, W. F. Tibbetts & Mr. Bose held Union Service. Speaking on A. L. M. Feb 15th Rector confined by sciatica. Feb 22nd W. Brown & James Ward officiated. |
| Apr 4 | 26/96/76 | | Easter. Communicants 26 & 58. Apr. 11th Mr. Marnum assisted. |
| Apr 25 | 78/275 | 18.97 | A. B. Farney assisted. I.O.O.F. attended evening service. |
| May 23 | 150/ ? | 8.88 | Dedicated a new Font. Baptised 5. |
| Aug 8 | ?/? | ? | Rev. S. A. Macdonnell officiated for Sept. assisted by H. W. Zealand. |
| Sept 26 | 125/95 | 7.42 | Thanksgiving. Rev. A. B. Farney officiated, Rev. J. Ward preached. |
| Dec 19 | ?/? | ? | Bishop David (Williams) Huron confirmed 8 candidates. |
| Dec 25 | 26/60/70 | 66.10 | Christmas. Communicants 26 & 48. |

1921 - Incumbent Reverend H. J. Johnson / Reverend David J. Cornish.

| | | | |
|---|---|---|---|
| Jan 30 | ?/? | $3.50 | Sermon on sex appeal. |
| Feb 13 | ?/? | 9.65 | Rector's 10th Anniversary. ( in the parish) |
| Apr 10 | | | Rev. W. J. Doherty officiated. No other entry to April 24th, when Mr. Doherty was in charge, and again May 1st. Attendance 112 to 120 at matins and evensong with offertory over $4:00 both Sundays. In May Frank Anderson, J. Edmonds, R.W. Butcher(?), James Ward and A. B. Forney were in charge of the services. Mr. Johnson must have left the parish. In June R. C. Capper took two services and Frank Anderson five. On July 3rd J. Edmonds was in charge and Frank Anderson took the six remaining services in July. |
| Aug 7 | 196/117 | 21.81 | Rev. David J. Cornish held his first services at St. Pauls, Pt. Dover. Comm. 70. Monday he returned to Forest for his family. |
| Oct 23 | 172/260 | 28.18 | Erie 149, A.F. & A.M. Masonic evening service. 1 baptism. |
| Nov 6 | 162/95 | 12.40 | Comm. 61. Veterans Service. M. Dillon gave violin solo. |
| Nov 11 | 35/ | | Armistice Day. Devotional only. |
| Dec 18 | 40/189 | 5.71 | Bishop David Huron confirmed 10 candidates. 12 were unable to attend, mostly from Vittoria due to great snow storm in a. m. |
| Dec 25 | 124/ | | Christmas day. |

1922 - Incumbent Reverend David J. Cornish.

| | | | |
|---|---|---|---|
| Jan 1 | 89/ | $4.65 | Wm. F. Tibbetts, Lay Reader officiated. Rector ill with Rheumatic Fever. Jan 8th J. D. Christie (Huron) officiated as Rector still ill. |
| Feb 26 | 110/102 | 7.55 | Church cold, Bishop Abrahams assisted. Mission service. |
| Mar 12 | 102/125 | 5.65 | Rev. F. A. Robinson assisted. |
| Apr 2 | 128/107 | 5.95 | Communicants 63. Ice Storm, no lights. |
| Apr 4 | | | Miss Langs funeral at the church. Covel "Gint" Rankin drowned. |
| Apr 14 | 100/ | $19.31 | Good Friday, for the Jews. Rev. H. Dillon, Methodist assisted. |
| June 11 | 74/82 | 2.86 | H. Rickey Parsons took evensong. |
| June 18 | 86/ ? | 3.90 | F. A. Rickard assisted. |
| July 2 | 168/102 | 17.47 | Communicants 84. Tuxis of Tillsonburg present. |
| July 16 | 18/ ?/? | 10.33 | Communicants 18 (8:00 a.m.) S. School envelopes presented also. |
| Sept 10 | 103/75 | 8.06 | Henry Smith officiated. |
| Oct 8 | 85/73 | 6.30 | C.V. Foreman officiated. |
| Oct 15 | 3/101/100 | 9.30 | Communicants 3. Last celebration of early communion until Xmas. |
| Nov 5 | 149/148 | 1.65 | John Morris held Thanksgiving Service. Communicants 72. |
| Nov 12 | 111/105 | 8.46 | Canon Ryerson officiated. He has retired from U. S. A. to Simcoe. |
| Dec 10 | | | Five services were held in the Town Hall pending completion of repairs and installation of the new organ. |
| Dec 25 | 110/ | 70.00 | Christmas Service held in the Presbyterian Church. December 31 two services held in the Town Hall. |

1923 - Incumbent David J. Cornish.

| | | | |
|---|---|---|---|
| Jan 14 | 132/167 | 11.48 | Church was re-opened. 11" fall of snow. |
| Jan 21 | 211/203 | 20.46 | Bishop David Williams (Huron) officiated for the dedication of the new organ presented by J. Henry Herring of New Bedford, Mass. in memory of Clare Langs |
| Feb 14 | | | Funeral for Captain Leslie Battersby. The Lenten services have been cancelled due to extreme cold. |
| Apr 20 | | | 6 attend branch mtg of W. A. Friday afternoon. Rain. |
| May 20 | 5/88/180 | 10.91 | Dr. Robinson officiated at evensong. Comm. 5 & 42. Heavy rain. |

| | | | |
|---|---|---|---|
| May 31 | | | Rev. H. J. Johnson baptised David Yerex & Clayton Scofield. |
| June 1 | | | Wedding of Sam H. Morris and Frances Slocombe. |
| June 24 | 91/ ? | $3.75 | Corporate Communion of W. A. Mrs. Smith & Miss Vyse leaving. |
| July 13 | | | Baptism of John William Harnick. |
| July 29 | 156/67 | 16.41 | James Ward assists. War & Peace Sunday. |
| Sept 16 | 84/ ? | 5.80 | J. A. Bloodsworth officiated. C. Cameron Wallen for Sept. 23rd and J. A. Bloodsworth for Sept30th. |
| Oct 14 | 106/149 | 38.25 | C.K. Masters assisted for Thanksgiving Services. Rain in a.m. Mud in p.m. |
| Nov 11 | 165/122 | 17.02 | Armistice day. |
| Dec 7 | | | Alex Spain baptised. |
| Dec 16 | 190/111 | 0 | Bishop David (Williams) Huron confirmed 14 candidates. |
| Dec 25 | 33/64/0 | 0 | Communicants 33 & 44. Dec 31 baptism; Virginia Jane Silverthorne. |

1924 - Incumbent Reverend David J. Cornish

| | | | |
|---|---|---|---|
| Jan 6 | 60/25 | 2.10 | Communicants 34. Blizzard, church so cold evensong held in the S.S. |
| Feb 24 | 89/87 | 5.15 | Baptised Chas. Bridgewater's two children. |
| Mar 2 | 77/156 | 17.25 | Masons of Erie Lodge attend evensong. |
| Apr 6 | 106/135 | 6.45 | Communicants 51. Alfred J. Vale officiated at evensong. Pictures of Hay River shown in the Sunday School. |
| Apr 26 | | | Saturday baptisms of three adults and 4 infants. |
| Apr 27 | 119/91 | 5.90 | Oddfellows service at Methodist Church, "Valley of the Dry Bone." |
| May 11 | 150/99 | 9.69 | Mother's Choir in the morning service. |
| May 27 | | 73.55 | 75 attend Rogation Tuesday. 25th Anniversary of the W. A. |
| June 29 | | 0.75 | 19 attend Ascension day service with F. G. Rickard & John Robertson |
| July 6 | 171/164 | 14.05 | J. Franks assisted. Rosa Tuck sang at both matins & evensong. |
| July 27 | 148/0 | 12.91 | Rev. C. K. Masters officiated. July 21 Art Thompson baptised. |
| Aug 14 | /53 | 3.36 | Doris Marie Kitchen baptised. Presbyterian 75th Anniversary. |
| Aug 24 | 142/66 | 16.15 | Rev. H. Newton Smith, Rector of York, officiated at evensong |
| Sept 14 | 82/90 | 3.50 | Mr. C. J. Franks, a student at Trinity College, officiated. |
| Oct 26 | 125/119 | 18.26 | Harvest Thanksgiving. Rev. W. L. Snelgrove took evensong. |
| Nov 16 | 75/48 | 1.66 | Cold. Masons attend Methodist church. |
| Dec 2 | /150 | 0.00 | Bishop David (Williams) Huron confirmed 9 on Tuesday evening |
| Dec 25 | 25/76/ | 0.00 | Alms at 10.30. Communicants 25 & 39 respectively |

1925 — Incumbent, Reverend David J. Cornish

| | | | |
|---|---|---|---|
| Jan 11 | 100/51 | 1.60 | Rev. F. A. Robinson officiated |
| Feb 15 | 68/102 | 8.53 | Pages & Dates confused. The Minor Prophets discussed. |
| Mar 8 | 90/71 | 3.15 | Opening of the Methodist organ. Thursday lenten services held |
| Apr 19 | 100/68 | 2.70 | Children's Lenten boxes presented |
| June 1 | | | Baptism of Sam H. Morris on 2nd ann. of marriage & H. Misner's 2 boys |
| June 27 | | | Wedding of Alan Tibbetts & Zeitha Barwell |
| July 5 | 70/56 | 19.04 | Baptism of Svenson, communicants 70. July 20th baptise 8 Cassidy children. July 24th baptise Clifford Husted's 5 children & his sister-in-law & one child of Lorne Husted. July 26th, baptise Dorothy M. Barrett. |
| Aug 23 | ?/84 | 6.75 | Rev. Shoemaker Jr. baptised Gregory, Ross & Cassidy. [children ?] |
| Sept 27 | 74/55 | 3.27 | Rev. C. J. franks officiated. [Incumbent on holiday ?] |
| Oct 4 | 71/42 | 2.68 | Rev J. F. Myers officiated |
| Oct 11 | 63/54 | 3.10 | Rev. Mark Turnbull, superannuated, officiated. Radios are becoming popular & common; once a day attendance also becoming popular. |
| Oct 18 | 116/106 | 9.27 | Archdeacon W.J. Doherty officiated for Thanksgiving service |

| | | | |
|---|---|---|---|
| Oct 29 | | | Funeral service at 2.00 p.m. for Mrs. James |
| Nov 1 | 75/56 | $2.86 | Rev. R. Herbert, Preston, officiated. Nov. 8th baptise H. Yerex, 2 Jennings |
| Nov 11 | | | Armistice Service, 32 attend. |
| Nov 18 | | | Rev. Edwin Lee holds Deanery Meeting in Sunday Sch. Coll. $3.55 |
| Dec 25 | 23/91/ | 109.30 | Christmas Day. Communicants 23 & 52 |

1926 — Incumbent, Reverend David J. Cornish

| | | | |
|---|---|---|---|
| Jan 17 | 81/96 | 4.30 | Regular services. Jan. 18th, funeral of A. M. Thompson |
| Jan 24 | 58/66 | 3.25 | Great storm beginning Saturday, stormy week, one of the worst. |
| Mar 31 | | | Men's service cancelled, no lights, highways & phones out too. No W.A. |
| Apr 2 | 77/ | 12.01 | Good Friday. Apr 4th Cantata at United Ch. drew a lot of people. |
| May 9 | 96/95 | 5.32 | Mother's Day. |
| July 11 | 115/68 | 12.57 | Rev. H. A. Mowat assisted. As a Scouter he was called back when a Scout War canoe capsized and many drowned, near Lindsay. |
| Aug 1 | 94/50 | 7.91 | Mrs. Buck & Mrs. Pearson, of Port Rowan, sang |
| " 29 | 118/127 | 12.56 | Rev. T. Atkinson, of Granton, took evensong, also Sept 26th service |
| Oct 10 | 124/127 | 12.15 | Rev. H.M. Lang-Ford took evensong. Rev. Frank Leigh officiated Oct 17 |
| Nov 14 | 74/0 | 1.90 | Rector ill, evensong cancelled. 15 attend Nov11th service. |
| Nov 30 | | | Baptism of 5 adults and one youth. |
| Dec 5 | 138/41 | 8.80 | Bishop David Huron confirmed 25 candidates |
| Dec 25 | 42/85/ | 0.00 | Christmas services. Communicants 42 & 80 |

1927 — Incumbent Reverend David J. Cornish

| | | | |
|---|---|---|---|
| Jan 6 | | 3.25 | Thurs. eve. United Service with Rev. Wray Davidson, for Missions |
| Jan 21 | | | Mr. Millman of Japan brought a message re missions. |
| Feb 27 | 50/67 | 5.55 | Community Night at the rink. |
| Apr 10 | 95/98 | 6.41 | Rector taken ill, Roy Scott finished the service. |
| Apr 24 | 102/73 | 9.28 | Children's Sunday. Frank Barrett & George Ryerse assisted |
| June 18 | | | Marriage of Joseph A. Kitchen & Annabelle Harnick |
| June 22 | | | 60 of congregation attend Norfolk Deanery Meeting |
| July 10 | 120/65 | 11.70 | Rev. Henry Smith officiated, also for July 17 services |
| Aug 7 | 120/50 | 3.80 | Baptise Keith Victor Cornish, son of cousin of Rev. Cornish. [Keith was killed in action during the Korean War.] |
| Aug 21 | 124/88 | 11.29 | Rev. Lantz K. Gardner officiated. Rev. George W Pitker assited |
| Aug 27 | | | Marriage of Rushton Yates & Frances Henry |
| Sept 25 | 89/45 | 4.50 | Rev. F. G. Richard officiated |
| Oct 9 | 114/56 | 4.40 | Rev. Horace W. Snell, of Stratford, officiated |
| Nov 27 | 112/ ? | 7.20 | Bishop David (Williams) Huron confirmed 15 candidates |
| Nov 30 | /15 | | St. Andrew's Day. W. A pledges $3.40. |
| Dec 25 | | | Christmas Day. Communicants 27 [8.00 a.m.] 86 [10.30 a.m.] |

1928 — Incumbent, David J. Cornish

| | | | |
|---|---|---|---|
| Jan 8 | 72/63 | 6.10 | 40 attend Week of Prayer, Rev. L. C. Secrett officiated |
| Mar 11 | 75/82 | 6.44 | Rev. L. C. Secrett officiated |
| Mar 21 | | | Lantern Slides in the Parish Hall, 60 attend |
| Mar 28 | | | Funeral at 2.00p.m. of Mrs. W. J. Thompson |
| Apr 15 | 80/76 | 8.25 | Baptise Barbara Joan Bays – a Leap Year baby |
| May 25 | | | Marriage of Frank Barrett & Irene Pickford |
| June 3 | 64/38 | 4.80 | Rev. R. J. W. Perry officiated |
| June17 | 62/39 | 5.90 | Rev. W. J. Comox officiated |

| | | | |
|---|---|---|---|
| July 1 | 114/68 | 10.33 | Mrs. Gibbons sang for both services. 60 communicants. |
| July 8 | 137/32 | 9.75 | Rev. P. H. Streeter officiated at matins, baptised six children |
| July 22 | 73/55 | 10.55 | Rev. Mark Turnbull officiated. Rev. C. D. Warren gave the sermon. |
| Aug 5 | 125/42 | 13.67 | Rev. Griffin Thompson officiated. Exceedingly hot. |
| Aug 12 | 110/43 | 13.50 | Rev. Arthur Eyre & Rev. Frank North officiated. Aug. 19th Rev. F.G. Lambe officiated. |
| Sept 9 | 56/51 | 3.93 | Rev. H. E. Webb took matins. Bible Society met. |
| Oct 20 | 75/54 | 6.60 | Baptism of Norah Marjorie Barrett |
| Nov 5, 6, 7. | | | Sisters Brooks & Boardman, Captains Rogers, Gearing & Pollock of the Salvation Army hold services. |
| Nov 11 | 91/276 | 29.76 | Veterans, the Port Dover Band & large crowd attend evensong. The baptism and churching of M. I. Sullivan. L. G. Skey assisted. |
| Dec 2 | 87/0 | 3.85 | Baptise 3 Dalton children. Archbishop David Huron in Vittoria. No evens. |
| Dec 25 | 38/65 | | Communicants 38 & 50 |
| Dec 30 | 88/54 | 7.70 | Rev. F. A. Symington officiated. |

1929 — Incumbent, Reverend David J. Cornish.

| | | | |
|---|---|---|---|
| Jan 23 | | | Bishop Edwin F. Athabaska spoke on Wednesday evening in Parish Hall |
| Jan 27 | 64/43 | 4.70 | Rev. C. W. Vernon in attendance |
| May 19 | 75/40 | 3.75 | Rev. J. W. Ward, St. Stephens, Toronto attended May 23rd. |
| June 23 | 73/39 | 6.15 | Rev. M. A. Garland officiated |
| Aug 4 | 9/107/42 | 15.75 | Rev. Lawrence E. Skey officiated |
| Sept 6 | | | Funeral for Mr. Lawrence Skey. Rev. H. J. Johnson assisted. Funeral for Mr. Battersby, of Toronto, Aged 99 years. |
| Sept 15 | 84/46 | 6.80 | Rev. R. E. David officiated |
| Sept 22 | 67/56 | 5.70 | Rev. Horace bray officiated, and for the following Sunday |
| Oct 6 | 59/55 | 3.98 | Rev. Edwin Lerr.[ ? ] officiated |
| Oct 13 | 106/104 | 16.55 | Rev. H. L. G. Clarke officiated |
| Oct 27 | 117/77 | 9.12 | Rev. W. J. Bradbury officiated. Baptised Knowles & Campbell babies. |
| Nov 2 | | | There were eight baptisms. Nov. 11 38 attend Armistice Day service. |
| Dec 15 | 94/34 | 3.90 | Sleet storms for a week. No evensong Dec. 22nd due to storms |
| Dec 25 | 26/86/70 | 50.20 | Christmas Day. Communicants 26 & 56 respectively. |

1930 — Incumbent, Reverend David J. Cornish

| | | | |
|---|---|---|---|
| Feb 2 | 90/57 | 5.80 | M. A. Hunt, Past Master, Jarvis A. F. & A. M took evensong |
| Feb 9 | 121/73 | 13.55 | Rev. R. Herbert & Rev. W. J. Andrews officiated. Mr Edward F. Jones present & at opening of St. Paul's on Feb. 10th, 1855. 75th Anniversary. |
| Feb 16 | 197/53 | 12.60 | Archbishop David Huron confirmed 15 candidates. |
| Apr 6 | 78/69 | 5.95 | Funeral for George Thompson at 2.30 p.m, 250 mourners. |
| Apr. 8, 9, 10, 11 | | | Rev. P. H. Streeter, Rector of Norwich, held services each day. |
| May 4 | 97/187 | 20.40 | Rev. T. Bird Holland officiated for evensong |
| Jun 1 | 71/51 | 3.60 | Thos. F. Morgan, L. R. took matins, Rev. T. B. Holland took evensong |
| July 27 | 6/100/27 | 8.60 | Thomas F. Morgan, Lay reader, officiated |
| Aug 24 | 3/123/53 | 16.95 | Rev. A. Grassett Smith officiated |
| Sept 21 | 78/45 | 4.85 | Rev. E. Llewelyn Roberts officiated |
| Sept 28 | 135/39 | 13.05 | The Tibbetts window is unveiled and dedicated |
| Oct 2 | | | Marriage of Wilfred Gilbert & Olive Ward |
| Nov 9 | 84/55 | 6.45 | Rev. Lawrence E. Skey officiated. Baptise Rose Ryerse & children of Richard & Rose Harding. |
| Nov 11 | | | Armistice Day Service. 30 attend. Dr. McCorkindale assisted |
| Dec 25 | 83/102 | 6.10 | Christmas Day. Communicants 37 & 60 respectively |

1931 — Incumbent, Reverend David J. Cornish

| | | | |
|---|---|---|---|
| Jan 18 | 75/56 | 5.60 | Rev. W. Gibson officiated |
| Feb 8 | 79/151 | 5.10 | Baptism of Carol Joyce Howell |
| Apr 12 | 133/103 | 11.00 | Laymen's service. Mr. Harrison Arrell, K. C. & J. C. Coles officiated |
| May 16 | | | Funeral of The Honourable John Strickler Martin. Dr. Cody preached the sermon. Archbishops Williams, Fotheringham, Andrews & six additional clergy in robes, plus the Provincial Cabinet & Masonic Dignitaries attend. |
| June 7 | 77/178 | 16.10 | Memorial Service for Hon. John S. Martin |
| July 26 | 109/149 | 24.00 | Rev. A. L. G. Clarke officiated. Choir of Grace United Church our guests |
| Aug 2 | 15/250/36 | 23.60 | Oxford Rifles parade to morning service |
| Aug 23 | 148/39 | 13.55 | Rev. F. B. Leazon, of the Island of Bermuda, officiated |
| Aug 30 | 5/81/39 | 7.55 | Funeral for Crosbie Morgan at 2.00 p.m. |
| Sept 20 | 13/79/40 | 7.90 | W. Gibson, matins. C. H. P. Owen, even. Corp. Comm. 13 A. Y. P. A. |
| Oct 4 | 91/59 | 8.55 | Rector on holiday. Rev. C.J. Lamb officiated. On Sept 27th Rev. M.A. Hunt, Oct 11th & 18th Rev. H. B. Ashley officiated. |
| Oct 25 | 96/61 | 3.65 | Laymen's Service. Rev. C. G. Dunlop, Rector of Streetsville officiated |
| Nov 11 | | | Legion Service. Boy Scouts, Band & Girl Guides attend |
| Dec 25 | 32/96 | | Christmas day. Communicants 32 & 59 respectively |

1932 — Incumbent, Reverend David J. Cornish

| | | | |
|---|---|---|---|
| Jan 7 | | | United Day of Prayer, led by Rev. R. Boyle. 94 in attendance |
| Feb 6 | | | Funeral for J. Arthur Cope, at 2.00 p.m. 200 mourners. |
| Feb 28 | 82/138 | 2.60 | A Sacred Musicale celebrated at 8.30 p.m. |
| Mar 5 | | | Funeral for Charles W. Barwell. 150 mourners. |
| Mar 14 | | | Funeral for Gladys Law. 100 mourners. |
| Apr 3 | 121/80 | 10.80 | New seats are now in use. Reception mixed. |
| Apr 17 | 113/111 | 10.50 | Rev. Horace W. Snell officiated. Apr 27 Baptised 9, 5 were adults. |
| May 1 | 350 | 28.60 | Bishop Charles [Seager] Huron confirmed 22 candidates |
| May 8 | 127/63 | 11.46 | Mother's Day. John S. Martin Window unveiled, it & seats dedicated. |
| June 12 | 117/58 | 9.45 | Rev. J. A. Davis, matins. Alfred J. Vale, Prin. Chapleau School, evensong |
| June 19 | 11/93/192 | | Rev. P. H. Streeter, matins. Bishop Charles Huron, Masonic service in p.m |
| July 31 | 8/123/31 | 14.30 | John Morris took matins. Records incomplete for October. |
| Nov 6 | 82/164 | 1.64 | Canadian Legion & Girl Guides attend service |
| Nov 11 | | | 25 attend Armistice service. Jacqueline Yerex baptised Nov 13th. |
| Nov 30 | | | St. Andrews day. W. A. invite Presbyterian & United Societies to Par. Hall |
| Dec 18 | 71/76 | 3.90 | T. Morgan & C. K. Masters assist. A perfect rainbow appears on Christmas Eve. No snow, no frost. |
| Dec 25 | 31/140 | | Christmas Day. Communicants 31 & 80 respectively. |

1933 — Incumbent, Reverend David J. Cornish

| | | | |
|---|---|---|---|
| Jan 3 | | | Prayer Week. 53 attend. Rev. Ferguson, Presbyterian of Simcoe, officiated |
| Jan 29 | 73/76 | ? | Baptism of Emily Barrett. |
| Feb 7 | | | Funeral of Edith H. Adams. Mar 6th, Funeral of James B. Leaney |
| Mar 9 | | | Mission Meeting for Children of Rupert's Land. 50 attend |
| May 14 | 97/0 | ? | Thomas F. Morgan, Lay Reader, officiated. Matins only. |
| May 28 | 101/99 | 69.95 | Thanksgiving. Rev. W. A. Henderson officiated |
| May 31 | | | Deanery Meeting of the Women's Auxiliary, |
| Apr 19 | 119/ | ? | Good Friday. Rev. A. R. Ferguson officiated. Apr 16 Dunneville Choir. |
| May 5 | 101/ | 2.90 | Jubilee Service. 4.00 p.m. baptised Madeline L. Parkinson, Robert J. & William J. Castles, Paul D, Thompson, Anna M. Howarth, Chas. A. Dring |

St. Paul's Church Register 529

June 9  6/67/36       ?       Rev. H. Newton Smith took evensong
June 16 7/66/24      1.70    Rev. S. G. Pimrock officiated.
June 23 96/152       11.95   Bishop Charles [Seager] Huron confirmed 13 candidates
July 27                       Bishop Charles Huron confirmed Mrs. Charlton Woolley privately
Aug 25  3/149        6.70    Rev. Chauncey Snowden assisted

From Sept 8th to October 27th the following Reverend gentlemen officiated.: C. G. Dunlop, Canon Ryerson, Harrison Arrell, K. C., Macklem Brett, E. L. Vivian, T. W. Sherwood, T. H. Innes, S. G. Limrock, and C. E. S. Windus. Christmas Communicants were 28 & 58.

1936 — Incumbent, David J. Cornish

Jan 7   72/          2.90    Rev. J. A. Mahaffy, Grace United, presided over Week of Prayer
Jan 28                        Memorial Service for late King George V. 119 attend.
Mar 22  70/39        3.80    Baptise 5 children at 4.45 p.m. On Ascension Day Rev. Edgar W. McWegnly, Sarnia, Rev. W. E. V. McMullin, Simcoe, Rev. A. H. Harrison Delhi, and Rev. T. H. Inns, Waterford combine to conduct the service in St. Paul's, Port Dover.
June 18                       Marriage of Fredrick Smith & Innes Colman. Full Church.
July 13                       Funeral of Mrs. Lawrence W. Skey, aged 94 years.
July 19  9/114       ?       A. L. Morrell, C. A. officiated. July 20th, Rogation Service held in view of the prolonged drought.
Aug 2   ?/126/       ?       Chauncey E. Snowden, of Philadelphia officiated. Visiting in Nanticoke
Sept 6  4/89/23      ?       Additions & Alterations begun in Sunday School. Several officiate to Nov
Oct 14 - Wednesday            Plaque to Henry Morgan dedicated. Present Mrs. Brent, Miss & Mr. Badur, Mrs. Jordan and the Barretts.
Nov 4                         Bishop Seager dedicated the Lawrence W. Skey Window at 4.15 p.m.

1937 — Incumbent, Reverend David J. Cornish

Jan 3   68/28        ?       Rev. A.W. K. Herdman officiated. No offertory is recorded in the Register for the whole year, save June 6th, $6.35.
Jan 7                         Week of Prayer. Rev. F. W. Mahaffy & Rev. Cornish officiated.
Jan 17                        Opening of new Sunday School.
Feb 21  97/28                 Rev. W. S. McMillen officiated for matins
Mar 28  18/19/229             Easter Day. Easter Cantata in the evening.
May 9   89/86                 Royal Canadian Legion attend evensong. Rev. T. B. Holland preached
June 13 87/24                 R. S. Mason officiated at evensong
July 18 32/121/87             Rev. Chauncey E. Snowden, officiated
Aug 15  5/97                  Mary Georgette Nixon baptised at 5.00 p.m.
Sept 5  99/0                  Rev. W. E. N. McMillen, Simcoe, officiated. On September 12th & 19th G. S. Dunlop & Harrison Arrell officiated respectively.
Sept 26 66/17                 Baptism at 2.00 p.m. of Patricia Marie Rasmusson
Oct 10  93/68                 Rev. S. H. Brownlee officiated
Oct 17  73/58                 Baptism at 2.30 p.m. of Edna Marie McMillan
Nov 11                        Remembrance Day Service. 34 attend
Nov 28  98/0                  Rev. H. J. Coil of Paris officiated. No hydro, no evensong.
Dec 22                        Bishop Charles [Seager] Huron confirmed 123 candidates.
Dec 25  26/80                 No further record in register.
Dec 30                        Funeral of Mrs. Harry W. Ansley.

1938 - Incumbent, Reverend D. J Cornish.

Jan 2   63/53                 Communicants 38

| | | | |
|---|---|---|---|
| Jan 17 | | | Marriage of John Fenton & Margaret MacDonald |
| Jan 30 | 46/49 | 1.95 | A. Y. P. A. service at evensong. |
| Feb 1 | | | Funeral at 2.00 p.m. of Mrs. Dr. Lemon |
| Feb 27 | 72/42 | 2.70 | Rev. M. Brett of Jarvis officiated at A.Y.P.A. evensong. |
| Apr 15 | 61 | | Good Friday Service. Rev. T. R. Todd, United Ch., Simcoe preacher. |
| Apr 24 | 149/42 | 4.50 | Children's service in a.m. AYPA in p.m. IOOF at Knox church. |
| May 2 | 89 | | Choir Musicale – 8.00 p.m. |
| May 8 | 94/34 | 5.50 | Baptism ; Joseph Ross Clark May 15 - W.W. McMillen preacher. |
| May 25 | 60 | 69.10 | Deanery meeting of the W. A. W. W. McMillen officiated. |
| June 11 | | | Funeral at 1.00 p.m. of Mr. E. Skey |
| June 12 | 12/82/0 | 5.80 | Unveiling of Ansley Memorial window by Harry Syers, accepted by T.B. Barrett, Warden. Col. Syers preached. Present were Mr. & Mrs. Clayton Ansley, a son & Mrs. H. Syers, a daughter of the Ansleys. Baptismal Service – 5 baptised. |
| June 19 | 108/82 | 6.30 | Royal Canadian Legion attend morning service. |
| June 21 | | | Marriage of B. Hawke & Lydia McQueen at 4.00 p.m. |
| July 31 | 11/106/ | 5.85 | Baptism; a McArthur, 2 Misners, Glen Ryerse. |
| Aug 7 | 9/98/72 | 9.55 | Baptism; 2 Simpsons, 2 Gilberts, Ken Thompson, Byron Forrest, a Knowles. - a hot, hot day. |

August 28th the Rector went on holidays after taking the 8.00a.m. communion service, Chauncey E. Snowden preached on August 21st . Rev. J. G. White officiated for matins on the 28th, J. Farrell on September 4th, Chas. G. Dunlop on the 11th, H. W. Snell on the 18th and John H. Mills officiated for both Thanksgiving services. On September 29th, the incumbent D. J. Cornish, was in charge of the funeral of Mrs. Harry Moon at 2.30 p.m. on September 29th. There were 150 in attendance. On October 9th, a Civic Thanksgiving Service was held in the United Church [to celebrate Prime Minister] Chamberlain's Peace Pact. Oct. 16th baptism at 4.45 p.m. of Marilyn Louise Wicker.

| | | | |
|---|---|---|---|
| Nov 6 | 207/34 | 8.75 | Bishop Charles [Seager] Huron confirmed 11 candidates. |
| Nov 20 | 84/118 | 11.45 | Erie Lodge, AF & AM members attend matins. |
| Dec 1 | | | Marriage of Ross Thompson & Betsy McLeod. at 7.00 p.m. |
| Dec 3 | | | Marriage of Combe & Silverthorne at 5.30 p.m. |
| Dec 25 | 31/82/12 | | Communicants - 8.00 a.m. -31, 11.00 a.m. - 57, 5.00 p.m. - 12. |

1939 – Incumbent, D. J. Cornish. Wardens : T. B. Barrett & A. B. Thompson.

| | | | |
|---|---|---|---|
| Jan 11 | 60 | | Week of Prayer, D. H. Currie preacher, Rev. M'Haffey, United Church present. Incumbents hold one service in each Church each year. |
| Jan 22 | 12/52/9 | | Corporate Communion, AYPA at 8.00a.m., Evensong cancelled due to ice and cold, but 9 came so an informal service was held. |
| Mar 3 | | | Marriage of Carl Trumper & L. Vernon Cook |
| Mar 5 | 44/36 | 1.20 | Communicants - 37. W. W. McMillen officiated at evensong. |
| Mar 22 | | | Funeral of Vida Evans at 2.30 p.m. |
| Apr 2 | 77/35 | 2.70 | Palm Sunday. Holy Baptism : Margot Donald Howell at 12.30 p.m. |
| Apr 16 | 77/26 | 3.20 | Annual Sunday Sch. service at 10.00 a.m. Sunday after Easter. Lenten offering to support Indian Boy. |
| May 7 | 18/73/29 | | Corporate Comm. AYPA, breakfast in Parish Hall at 9.00 a.m. |
| May 18 | 9 | | Ascension Day. Deanery Service at 10.30 a.m. The first in many years. |
| July 2 | 7/89/0 | 0.35 | Evening services discontinued for July & August. Prayers for rain in July. Rector on holiday in September. Rev. Charles G Dunlop & J. Farrell take some services, others not recorded. One signature illegible. The Choir sang in Vittoria on afternoon of Sept. 24th. Wed. Sept. 27th the marriage of Genery to Mead is recorded. |

| | | | |
|---|---|---|---|
| Oct 15 | 129/63 | | Harvest Thanksgiving. W. W. McMullin, matins. Philip H Sawyer, even |
| Oct 29 | 81/74 | 5.00 | W. J. Bradbury preached at evensong. Rev. T. B. Holland & Rev Brown of Jarvis in attendance as well. Nov. 5th - 5 baptised. |
| Nov 11 | | | Private baptism of Robert C. Ryerse on Saturday at 4.00 p.m. of necessity in preparation for confirmation. |
| Nov 12 | 143/ | | Bishop Charles Huron confirmed 12 candidates. |
| Nov 19 | 25/93/34 | 4.85 | Corporate Communion of AYPA & breakfast. Entertained several new communicants. |
| Nov 19 | 25/93/34 | 4.00 | Holy Baptism at 5.00p.m., 2 Jensen, 1 Rowbottom & Thomas H. Low. |
| Dec 25 | 43/64 | | Communion, 43 at 8.00 a.m., 47 at 10.30 a.m. |

1940 – Incumbent D. J. Cornish. - Wardens: T. B. Barrett & A. B. Thompson.

| | | | |
|---|---|---|---|
| Jan 13 | | | Marriage of Alvin Hewer & Margaret Hoover at 6.30 p.m. |
| Jan 18 | | | Burial of the Dead - Thursday 11 a.m, Miss Watson, interred Stratford |
| Mar 22 | 53 | 4.90 | Good Friday   D. H. Currie officiated at 10.30 a.m. service. |
| Apr 21 | 84/32 | 4.55 | Baptism at 4.30 p.m. - McArthur and Beatrice Ivey. |
| Apr 27 | | | Funeral of Russell Skey at 3.00 p.m. April 28th - IOOF attend evensong |
| May 5 | 91/37 | 4.25 | Ralph L. Latimer preacher. May 12th - Male Choir, Simcoe, evensong |
| May 23 | 77/21 | 4.90 | Baptism at 12.20 a Hewson, Brantford. 2.00 p.m. Les Murphy. |
| July 14 | 8/157 | | Baptism of Arlene Norma Parkinson. |
| July 20 | | | Marriage of Dr. William Robert Scully & Margaret Winnifred Cornish |
| July 21 | 117/ | | Children's Service in place of Sunday School - Instruction in Worship. |
| Aug 11 | 142/ | | C E Snowden preacher. |
| Aug 17 | | | Marriage of F.(?) Forrest & Helen Harbach. Mon. funeral of – Kilduff |
| Aug 18 | 71/ | | Baptism of Eric Rasmussen. To this date Baptisms in Vittoria Records. |
| Sept 14 | | | Funeral of Mrs. J. H. Golding Sept. 22nd, Chas. G. Dunlop officiated, Sept 29th, J. Harrell, Oct 13th , Ashlyn A Trumper, St Matthews, London |
| Nov 11 | | | Baptism of Ross & Edith Franklin & Nov 16th Margaret MacDonald |
| Nov 17 | 149 | | Bishop Charles Huron in attendance. |
| Dec 15 | | | Baptism at 4.45 p.m. of James Allan & William Follington. |
| Dec 25 | 24/81 | | Communicants - 8.00 a.m. - 24; 10.30 a.m. - 56. |

1941 – Incumbent - D. J. Cornish.

| | | | |
|---|---|---|---|
| Jan 9 | 52/ | | Prayer Week - D. H. Currie officiated at 8.00 a.m. service. |
| Jan 19 | 71/77 | | Boy Scouts & Cubs attend 7.00 p.m. service at evensong. |
| Jan 24 | | | Funeral on Friday at 2.30 p.m. for Mrs. Quanbury. |
| Mar 2 | 75/45 | | R.S. Mason officiated. 42 communicants. |
| Mar 9 | 76/ | | Warden A.E. Williamson officiated, no evensong, Rector sick. |
| Mar16 | 74/18 | | R.S. Mason officiated, and again preached March 30th. |
| Apr 11 | 55/ | | Good Friday; W.J. Holley preached at 10.30 a.m. |
| Apr 13 | 30/171/37 | | Communicants - 30 & 89. Baptism of Constance Kay Clarke, 4:30 p.m. |
| Jun 15 | 73/76 | | Loyal Orange Lodge attend service at 3.00 p.m. |
| July22 | | | Funeral at 2.30 p.m. for Laura Falloon. Marriage of ? Gunton & ? ? |
| Aug 5 | | | Baptism of Brenda Aylis, dau. of Robert John Murphy, R.A.F. |
| Aug 10 | 215/ | | 42nd Battery parade to service. |
| Aug 17 | 87/ | | R.S. Mason preached. Note: Rev. Ralph Mason is converting the old Skey house to a duplex, spending the odd Sunday in town. |
| Aug 23 | | | Marriage of Roy William Phibbs & Fern Williams |
| Aug 31 | 87/ | | Baptism of Barbara Jean Booth at 12.15. |
| Sept 11 | | | Marriage of Bruce Reid & Muriel MacDonald at 11.00 a.m. |

| Sept 27 | | Marriage of Clarence Strople & Betty Ivey, on Saturday, 3.00 p.m. |
| Sept 28 | 109/ | A. E. Williamson, Warden, officiated. Rector in Waterloo |
| Oct 12 | 135/ | Maurice H. H. Jan(?) of Tillsonburg officiated. Merlyn Mae, dau. of John Arthur Bouser, N. S. - R.A.F. baptised at 4.30 p.m. |
| Nov 9 | 55/20 | R.S. Mason preached. Nov. 11th, Donna Reid & Druscilla Ryerse were baptised. |
| Nov 14 | | Marriage of ? Robb & ? Martin. |
| Nov 16 | 167/ | Bishop Charles Huron attended for Confirmation. No record of number. |

1942 – Incumbent, D.J. Cornish.

| Jan 7 | 40/ | 2.71 | Week of Prayer - Rev. R.W. Currie & Rev. W. J. M'Haffy assist. |
| Feb 29 | 101/35 | 5.90 | Rev. Victor C. Spenser preacher. |
| Apr 13 | | | Funeral at 2.30 p.m. of L. R. Tibbetts |
| Apr 26 | 91/21 | 4.30 | Dedication of Flag presented by Mrs. John S. Martin. |
| May 24 | 93/28 | 1.10 | Baptism at 4.45 p.m. of Barry MacKenzie Wicker. |
| June 7 | 68/24 | 4.00 | Communicants 55. W. W. McMullin officiated at evensong. |
| June 12 | | | Funeral at 2.00 p.m. of Mrs. Frank Smith. |
| June 14 | 53/77 | 8.30 | Erie lodge, AF & AM attend evensong in a body. |
| June 27 | | | Marriage of Dillon McCarthy, Preston to Yemin Long, Stoney Creek. |
| July 4 | | | Marriage of Lieutenant Stokes to ? Lowe, both of St Thomas, Tillsonburg. July 20th - baptism of Francis Wray Fisher, child of Ralph Fisher |
| July 2 | | | Funeral of William Henry (Harry) Barrett. |
| July 26 | 87/128 | 5.20 | Loyal Orange lodge attend evensong. |
| Aug 3 | | | Marriage of Arthur Moyer, R.C.A. & Jessie Cunningham, of Waterloo. |
| Aug 14 | | | Marriage of Ottwell Parker & Vernice S. Wigart. Cement sidewalk almost completely renewed in front of the church on July 21st. |
| Aug 27 | | | Marriage of Winnett Benson Ivey & Isabel Marie Hopkins. |
| Aug 29 | | | Marriage of Carl Kennedy & Marie Rutherford, both of Tillsonburg. |
| Sept 5 | 123/ | 6.90 | Prayer Services at the King's request - Great Britain Day of Prayer. |
| Sept 27 | 55/ | 2.20 | Baptism of 2 Bingleman boys, Alton Hoover's son & Margaret Hoover's son. On Oct 11th the Couvalier, Harnick & Weimier babies were baptised. Rev. T. Bird Holland officiated for the Sept 13th & 20th services. |
| Oct 18 | 149/49 | 21.44 | Rev. J. H. Geoghegan, Strathroy officiated. Baptised Pierson baby & Fred McMillan's son. |
| Oct 25 | 78/ ? | 9.70 | Baptised Fredric Robert Smith, son of Allan Smith & Air Force daughter (?) of Mr. & Mrs Howell. |
| Nov 15 | 71/31 | 7.87 | Rev. W. A. Townshend officiated at matins. |
| Dec 20 | 56/20 | 4.45 | Baptise John Ivey's baby girl. |

1943 – Incumbent, Reverend D. J. Cornish.

| Jan 5 | /70 | | Tues., 8.00 p.m. United Services of Prayer. Rev. Morley, United church read the psalms, Rev. D. J. Currie, Presbyterian, preached. |
| Feb 14 | 41/7 | 31.21 | Stormy night. 6 degrees below zero, fahrenheit |
| Mar 7 | 39/21 | 28.05 | Baptism of Penny Lee Evans. |
| Apr 23 | 110/ | 17.57 | Good Friday: Rev. Currie, Presbyterian, F. W. Morley, United assist. |
| May 2 | 76/98 | 51.43 | Norfolk Lodge, IOOF & Rebecca's. |
| July 18 | | | Baptism; Adam Brown's dau. Judith Ann Marie. July 23rd, baptism; John Henry Howarth's dau. Shirley Anne. July 28th, baptism; Linda Bonnie, dau. of Neil Ransom Postill & Bonnie Bethea Thomas, his wife. |
| Aug 3 | | | Baptism; of Iris Arlene, dau. of Arline Thompson Hastings. I baptised the mother, confirmed & married her. |

*St. Paul's Church Register* 533

| Aug 8 | 77/ | 60.11 | Warden A. E. Williamson officiated. Rector at summer camp. |
| Sept 5 | 58/ | 70.60 | Warden A. E. Williamson officiated. Sept. 12th, Rev. Robert Brett officiated. |
| | | | Sept. 26th - Baptism; Garth David Crossett, of Tillsonburg, father in the Army, & John Richardson Blakemore, of Port Dover. |
| Oct 10 | 89/20 | 49.44 | Baptism at 12.15 of Barbara Dianne Forrest. (Mother Helen Harbach) |
| Oct 16 | | | Baptism of child (Cathie) of Ross Thompson. |
| Oct 24 | 106/94 | 247.78 | Rev. E.F. Bishop, Waterloo at matins. H. Snell, Brantford, at evensong |
| Nov 7 | 79/19 | 44.25 | Baptism of Imogen Knister. Nov. 13th - baptism of Nan McKay. |
| Nov 14- | 130/ | 56.80 | Confirmation by Bishop Seager at 3.00 p.m. |
| Nov 23 | 22/ | | Baptism of Barra Louise, dau. of Ilene (Garner) & Andrew Lowe Jr. |
| Nov 28 | 71/27 | 90.72 | Baptism of Peter Grieves (?) Highst |

1944 – Incumbent, D. J. Cornish.

| Feb 27 | 76/43 | 48.86 | Baptism of David Hopkins Ivey |
| May 7 | 65/ ? | 34.65 | Baptism of Wayne Gordon Longe. |
| May 21 | 80/12 | 31.90 | Baptism of David Williamson & Barbara Anne Goodall. |
| June 24 | | | Marriage of Michael Barabash & Leota May Adams. |
| July 23 | 85/ | 49.95 | Baptism of Gary Batten at 12.30 a.m. |
| Aug 13 | | | Baptism of adopted child of Arthur Douglas Thompson, RCAF. |
| Aug 19 | | | Baptism of James Alexander Barrett, son of H.J.H. Barrett, at 3:00 p.m |
| Sept 10 | 68/ | 26.22 | Rev. W. H. Brett officiated, and again on Sept. 17th. Coll. $59.35. |
| Oct 15 | 103/87 | 46.36 | Rev. Curson in a.m. & Rev. C. W. Mixer in p.m. |
| Oct 22 | 59/33 | 65.45 | Stephen L. Gilbert, student from Port Rowan officiated. |
| Nov 19 | 58/- | 33.40 | Christ Church Vittoria's 100th Anniversary |
| Dec 24 | 102/- | 14.95 | Carol Service & Communion - 57 communicants. |

1945 – Incumbent, D. J. Cornish

| Jan 9 | 57/ | 4.75 | Wednesday service of the Week of Prayer, Rev. A. W. Hare, Presb. |
| Jan 21 | 45/90 | 67.50 | Oddfellow's & Rebecca's visit for evensong in a body. |
| Feb 21 | 12 | | Wednesday lenten service, Rev. A. W. Hare, Presbyterian, officiated. |
| June 24 | ?/? | ? | Baptism of Elizabeth Cornish & 2 daughters of Colin Ryerse. Only the Choir was present for evensong, short service, no offertory. |
| July 8 | 70/ | 64.08 | Rev. Ernest L. Lake officiated. |
| July 29 | ? | ? | Rev. A. C. Calder preached. |
| Aug 5 | 98/ | 47.70 | Rev. T. Bird Holland officiated. Communicants  65. |
| Aug 17 | | | A marriage recorded, but no particulars. |
| Aug 18 | 3/127/ | 77.34 | Communicants - 3. Dr. Chauncey Snowden preached sermon. |
| Aug 26 | 106/ | 77.80 | Baptisms; Gwendoline Gail Fletcher, born1/10/45 & Janet Elizabeth Butts, born 10/2/41. Rev. R. H. Brett officiated for September. |
| Oct 7 | 86/97 | 65.37 | IOOF & Rebecca's attend evensong in a body. |
| Oct 14 | 123/76 | 265.78 | Thanksgiving service, Rev. Fred H. Wase, Dunnville officiated. At 4:45 p.m. baptism of Ralph & Jaquelin Fisher (difficult to interpret) Rev. D. J. Cerzai (?) oficiated at evensong. |
| Oct 21 | 85/16 | 76.76 | E. Lloyd Lake officiated. |
| Nov 9 | | | Holy Baptism: Betty St. Louis, Peggy Powell, Robert Cromwell, Sylvia Lawrence. |
| Nov 25 | 54/87 | 55.48 | T. B. Holland assists at baptism of George Michael Field at 4.30 p.m. Archdeacon McIntosh preached at evensong. |
| Dec 8 | | | Marriage of William Roy Barker & Dorothy Richardson. |
| Dec 23 | 125/ | 87.40 | First appearance of a Junior Choir - 24 present. |

534  The Parish of St. Paul's

| Dec 24 | 81 | | Evening Prayer, 11:15 p.m. Communicants - 60. Offering to Rector. |
|---|---|---|---|
| Dec 25 | 43/ | 16.00 | Morning Prayer at 10:30 a.m. Communicants - 23. Offering to Rector. Holy Baptism : by Rev. Hare, Presbyterian Minister, of his grandchild, Service conducted by the Rector. |
| Dec 29 | | | Baptism of Theobald (incorrectly registered as Tobias)Butler Barrett, son of Harry Bemister Barrett. |
| Dec 30 | 71/46 | 90.67 | Carol Service at evening service by the Junior Choir. |

1946 – Incumbent D. J. Cornish.

| Jan 6 | 89/109 | 206.60 | Rector makes entry that $2.00 of offertory be credited to 1945 year. |
|---|---|---|---|
| Jan 11 | | 6.19 | United Day of Prayer, Rev. A. Hare & Rev. George Morley assist Rector. $2.15 of offertory given to Jewish Association. |
| Jan 19 | | | Marriage of Walter Long & Barbara Ryerse. |
| Mar 10 | 105/59 | 51.52 | Col. Taylor preached at evening service re A. A. A |
| Mar 31 | 87/51 | 40.61 | Rev. Chester C. Mixer, Simcoe, officiated at evensong. |
| Apr 3 | /35 | 2.50 | Wednesday service, Rev. J. M. Cameron preached . Slides after. |
| Apr 19 | 80/ | 23.55 | Rev. John M. Smith of Old Windham. Offering to Jewish Mission. |
| Apr 28 | 102/50 | 150.01 | Baptism of Byron Forrest's dau. Gwendolyn |
| May 11 | | | Marriage of George Petito & Margaret MacDonald. |
| June 16 | 80/24 | 55.50 | Presentation to Rector D .J. Cornish, on 40th Ann. of Ordination |
| June 23 | 87/16 | 41.65 | Ralph Blight, student, Huron College, officiated. |
| July 26 | | | Marriage of ? Hancock & ? McAvoy, both of Waterloo, Ontario |
| Aug 3 | | | Marriage of Alfred Long & Trumen. Baptise Janet Heather Dugit. |
| Aug 11 | 139/ | 85.14 | C. E. Snowden, St. Paul's Memorial, Philadelphia officiated. |
| Aug 24 | | | Baptism at 4.00 p.m. of Stephen George Cruise. |
| Sept 1 | 84/ | 44.53 | Baptism of Wendy June Hallam & Cheryl Louise Parker. |
| Sept 8 | 67/ | 28.30 | Rev. T. B. Holland officiated & again on Sept. 15th. A. E. Williamson officiated at matins, Sept. 22nd. |
| Oct 13 | 92/ | 54.81 | Baptism of Gordon Arnold Filmon & daughter, Mrs. Edith Mae Follington, & daughter of Harry Howarth. |
| Oct 27 | 162/108 | 305.30 | Thanksgiving service, J.C. Coles preached. At 4.30 p.m. baptised Jacqueline Marjorie, daughter of John Spain. Rev. C. J. Draper preached at evensong. |
| Nov 10 | 51/81 | 42.15 | Royal Canadian Legion, Br. 158, 14 attend evensong. |
| Nov 17 | 66/64 | 153.90 | Baptism at 4.30 p.m. of 2 children of Ross Thompson, son of Jack Fenton, 2 children of Grant Hawke, 2nd child of Win Ivey, and Carl Trumper. Oddfellows & Rebecca's attend evensong. |
| Dec 24 | /100 | | Communicants - 60. Carols, the Hallelujah Chorus, no sermon. |
| Dec 28 | 20/ | 0.00 | Severe ice storm. Congregation - 7; Choir - 13. No collection. |

1947 – Incumbent D. J. Cornish.

| Jan 5 | 49/ | | Holy Communion. Evening service cancelled. |
|---|---|---|---|
| Jan 12 | 70/21 | 43.12 | Choral evensong, Alex Clark of Brantford, organist. |
| Feb 9 | 47/44 | 29.19 | Baptism of 2 youngest children of Elmer Misner, & Gordon Loryes (?) youngest. |
| Feb 23 | 52/70 | 35.16 | Rev. C. C. W. Mixer officiated at evensong. On Feb. 26 informed that organist Alex Clark left for St. James, Ingersoll. |
| Mar 2 | 63/40 | 35.05 | Mr. Ch. Skelcher, of Simcoe, organist pro tem. Communicants - 48. |
| Mar 23 | -72/27 | 47.30 | Blizzard lasting two days, many roads blocked. |
| Apr 4 | ?/ | 24.68 | Good Friday service at 10.30 a.m. Major East, United church, Jarvis, in charge. Offertory to Jewish Missions. |

| | | | |
|---|---|---|---|
| Apr 12 | | | Baptism of sons of Lorne Johnstone & Bruce Ward. [James] |
| Apr 27 | | | Baptism of John Roland, son of Horace Gibbons. 16 in attendance. |
| May 11 | 97/43 | 49.10 | Les Jenkins assisted the Rector. Special young people's service. |
| May 25 | 5/47/28 | 38.05 | Baptism of William Ray, son of Bruce Greenslade at 4.30 p.m. |
| June 22 | | 65.65 | Canon F. J. Hardy, Sarnia preached. Baptised Robert James Goodall & Linda Diane Russell. June 29 - Mrs. McMillan played organ as Mr. Skelcher on holiday. |
| June 30 | | | Marriage of Kenneth Meade & Lucy Spain. |
| July 2 | | | Baptism of Lynda Lee Petito & Margaret MacDonald's baby. |
| Aug 3 | 132/ | 30.50 | Rev. Chancey Snowden officiated. |
| Aug 10 | 98/ | 44.55 | Baptism of Sherrill Anne, dau. of B. O. Barker, Toronto, relative of Mrs. Duncan McKen. |
| Aug 17 | 84/ | | Baptism of Jennifer Frances Bowlby Barrett, dau of Harry B. Barrett & John Harris Buck II, son of John Harris Buck. |
| Aug 24 | 2/91/ | 37.45 | Rev. E. A. Olley, preacher. Very hot & muggy. |
| Aug 31 | 64/ | 43.40 | Baptism of Terry Williams, son of Theo William Adams, Toronto &Margaret Jackson and Edith Marie Fennell (?) wards of Charlotte & William Adams. |
| Sept 14 | 50/ | 23.25 | Rev. T. B. Holland officiated and also for Sept. 21st & 28th. |
| Oct 19 | 196/ | 221.71 | Harvest Thanksgiving, Rev. A. H. O'Neil preached the sermon. |
| Oct 26 | 74/ | 38.80 | Rev. Ralph Porritt assisted. Andrew MacDonald baptised at 4.30. |
| Nov 2 | 82/28 | 112.00 | Baptism of Warren Cunningham & Nancy Leitch. |
| Nov 7 | 156/ | 84.55 | Confirmation by Archbishop Seager of 8 adults & 24 youths & maidens. |
| Nov 9 | 55/ | | Baptism of Charles Landon Ivey, Raymond Hadley Ivey & Ralph Clayton Herring. First cold day this autumn. |
| Dec 24 | /68 | ? | Carol service, 11.15 p.m. Communicants - 60. No sermon. |

1948 – Incumbent D. J. Cornish.

| | | | |
|---|---|---|---|
| Jan 4 | 55/ | 40.35 | Communicants - 35 |
| Feb 12 | ? | 4.95 | Ash Wednesday -Lenten addresses, a study of St. Paul. |
| Mar 13 | | | Marriage of James Olley & Betty Crosbie. |
| Mar 14 | ?/? | 34.98 | Ralph E. Porritt officiated at evensong. |
| Mar 26 | 61/ | 22.18 | Good Friday. Rev. George Morley, United ch. Preached sermon. |
| Apr 3 | | | Marriage of Douglas Crosbie & Irene |
| Apr 10 | 40/23 | 27.66 | Baptism of Ann May, grand-daughter of Moses fisher. |
| May 2 | 79/23 | 77.32 | Communicants, 50 matins, Rev. E .L.Vivian officiated at evensong. May 6 - 10/0 Communicants, 5. First 8.00 a.m. Ascension service in years. |
| May 30 | 97/19 | ? | Last evening service by motion of Select Vestry. |
| June 3 | | | Marriage of Hamilton To Patricia Blackhurst at 3p.m. |
| June 4 | | | Meeting of Deanery W. A. : Rev. H. A. C. Mixer, Archbishop Townsend & Canon Cook, Indian Director, spoke in the morning. |
| June 11 | | | Marriage of Willis Homisgo & Fuschia Dagleish. Ladies of St. Paul's Club catered to 125 people. |
| June 13 | | | Baptism of Vicki Ruth Ryerse, Peter Scott Ryerse, Sheryl Lynn Laurie, Clayton Scofield. |
| June 20 | | | Baptism of child of Robert Misner, Joyce Baguley, Ross Hallam & Roland Waddle. |
| June 27 | | | Baptism of 2 children of J. J. Jarrett, one of Earl Stamp. |
| Aug 15 | 10/69/ | 40.10 | Baptism of 2 boys of Golda Thompson & Robert Gordon Speck . |
| Aug 20 | | | Marriage of Duineau (?) Groves & Pearl Oxford. |
| Aug 22 | | | Baptism of Robert William Groves, parents only present. |
| Sept 1 | | | Family 25th Thanksgiving & Communion of summering in Port Dover, of (local) Whitesides & Whitsides of Windsor. |

536 The Parish of St. Paul's

| Sept 5 | 62/ 0 | 32.95 | Rev. J. M. Crarey officiated. 40 communicants. Sept 12th & 19th Rev. Ralph Porritt officiated. Sept 26th Rev. R. H. Brett officiated. |
| Oct 10 | 150/ | 267.31 | Rev. H. L. Jennings, St. Paul's, Brantford officiated. Baptism of Taylor, Ryerse & Mackay by D.J.Cornish at 4:30 p.m. Evensong by Chester Mixer. |
| Oct 17 | 78/36 | 77.32 | Lambeth Conference message was read. Baptism of Richard Montyn Watkinson & Joyce Louise Porritt. |
| Oct 12 | | | Funeral for Moses Fisher, - Aged 95 years, 11 months at 2:30 p.m. |
| Oct 31 | 90/ ? | 64.80 | Rev. E. L. Vivian officiated at evensong. |
| Nov 7 | 90/23 | 90.92 | Communicants, 60. Six baptisms at 4:30 p.m. |
| Nov 11 | | | Remembrance Day Service resumed after 6 year interval during war |
| Dec 12 | 68/61 | 71.66 | Rev. S. W. Semple assisted at evensong. |
| Dec 24 | 112 | | Christmas Eve service at 11.30. Communicants 92. Christmas day services at 8.00 a. m. & at 10.00 a.m. |

1949 – Incumbent D. J. Cornish.

| Jan 7 | 54/ | 3.55 | Universal Prayer Week. Fri. 8.00 p.m., Rev. M Edworthy, United Church minister, Simcoe, officiated. |
| Jan 23 | 122/28 | 188.77 | Baptism of a Laycock, Pierson & John Ivey. |
| Jan 30 | | | From January 30th to May 1st, 1949 services were held in the Sunday School while the Church arches were rebuilt & redecorated. New beams installed under the floor of the Choir room, behind the organ. Furnished & stairs built. |
| Mar 27 | 94/40 | 33.23 | Baptism of Greenslade's baby girl. |
| Apr 3 | 82/8 | 51.85 | Baptism of 2nd son of Dr. Boyce Sherk of St. Catherines. Rev. Mr. Hare, presbyterian minister & Grandfather, assisted. |
| Apr 15 | 60/ | 11.91 | Good Friday - Rev. Cecil T. Brenn, Old Windham United, preached. |
| Apr 24 | 60/85 | 64.55 | Oddfellows & Rebecca's attend evensong. |
| May 22 | 114/50 | 72.95 | Rev. J. N. H. Mills officiated at both services. |
| May 29 | 203/164 | 154.76 | Special service: Prof. M. Parker, Huron College. Ven. Archdeacon F. W. Wallace, Hamilton assisted. |
| June 19 | 72/? | 54.11 | Baptism of Robert. David Skelly, grandson of D. J. Cornish, son of Douglas Aphir & Daughter of Betty Olley. |
| Jul 17 | 32/0 | 34.30 | Last entry in 1938 to 1949 Church Register or Vestry Book. |

July 24th, 1949 to December 29th, 1957.

| Date | Attend. | Coll. | Comments |
| July 24 | 8/112/0 | 80.33 | Bapt., 4.30. Douglas Malyn Penhall, & son, Michael Richmond P. |
| July 31 | 108/0 | ? | Bapt., 4.30. Robert Davidson Dugit, son of John & Margaret. |
| Aug 14 | 11/122 | 81.12 | Dr. C(hauncey) E. Snowden preached. |
| Aug 31 | | | Marriage, Albert Chesto, Jew & Joan Marline Peckham, both of Wingham, with orchestra of Summer Gardens for the season. |
| Sept 1 | | | Marriage, Bruce Doherty, embalmer & Lawreen Knowles |
| Sept 9 | | | Bapt., Lawrence David, son of John & Jennie Blakemore. |
| Oct 23 | 197/95 | 592.85 | Rev. McRitchie, Aylmer in a.m. Mr. Geo. McElheran in p.m. |
| Oct 30 | 78/0 | 58.77 | Bapt., Cheryl Lynne Mead, dau. of Ken & Lucy Spain Mead. |
| Nov 9 | | | Marriage, Charles Franklin Kitchen & Jane Carol Dines. |
| Dec 11 | 85/0 | $70.80 | Bapt., Norman Tarr, 1909. Walter Charles Long, 1927.Muriel Cath. Stuckey-Parker, 1927. Harry Gundry, 1896. James Goodall, 1911. |
| Dec 18 | 193/78 | 223.31 | Confirmation. |

St. Paul's Church Register 537

Dec 25   22/90/0           22 communicants at 8.00 & 50 at 10.30 service.

1950 – David J. Cornish, incumbent.

| | | | |
|---|---|---|---|
| Jan 1 | 5/68/11 | 48.20 | Communicants - 5 at 8.00, 46 at matins. |
| Apr 23 | 55/22b. | 40.08 | Bapt., Wendy Anne, dau of Wm. Jas. & Joyce Townend Walker. |
| Apr 26 | | | Marriage, Geo. James Burcham & Margaret Powell in parents home |
| June 4 | 8/102/0 | 51.40 | Evensong discontinued, early service started for season. |
| June 11 | 8/138/0 | 78.35 | Bapt., Raye Ellen, dau. of Charles & Verna Fritzley Watkinson and David Geo. Stuart, son of Wm. & Florence Mason Cornish & Jane Isobelle, dau of David & Grace Krueger Cornish. |
| June 18 | 8/86/0 | 45.20 | Bapt., Thos. Alexander, son of Alex. & Dorinne Chattington Pow. |
| June 25 | 5/75/0 | 36.00 | Bapt., Patrick Michael, son of David & Doris Caley Yerex and Barbara Russell, dau of Harry B. & Hellen Mary Browne Barrett. |
| July 9 | 5/83 | 58.85 | Rev. Crarey [St. Johns] officiated at 8.00, Mr. Inder at matins. |
| July 23 | 12/133 | 67.80 | Bapt., Margaret Rosalie, dau of John & Margaret Davidson Dugit. |
| Aug 6 | 4/95 | 82.56 | Ralph E. Porritt preached. |
| Sept 2 | | | Marriage, Harold Stuart Schilz & Martha Richardson Mitchell. |
| Sept 9 | | | Marriage, Lyman Brooks Lowe & Evelyn Jean Reid |
| Sept 10 | 47/0 | 32.05 | Mr. Chas. Inder officiated for 3 weeks, rector on holiday. |
| Oct 15 | 156/75 | 349.98 | Rev. L. A. Nelles officiated at matins, Rev. Alan Gardiner evensong |
| Oct 20 | | | Bapt., Conrad, son of John Harris & Annie H. Claire Tait Buck. |
| Oct 28 | | | Marriage, Wm. Alexander Spain & Eva Louise Ottley. |
| Nov 5 | 72/?/0 | 46.62 | Bapt, Bonnie Lee Petito, Niagara Falls, N. Y. at 4.30 p.m. |
| Nov 19 | 84/112 | 115.21 | Bapt., Mary Jane, dau. of Wm. J. & Bernice Manilla Ivey Wamsley |
| Dec 25 | 90/ | $16.00 | Christmas service at 10.30 a.m. - Communicants 77. |

1951 – David J. Cornish, incumbent.

| | | | |
|---|---|---|---|
| Feb 17 | | | Marriage, Morris Lawson Caffell & Jean Vivian Chapin, Baptists. |
| Mar 4 | 95/67 | $129.21 | Huron Crusade: Chas. F. Wilkins & O. J. Whithead officiated. |
| Mar 22 | 80 | | Thur. 8.30 p.m. Simcoe Choir sang St. Mark's Passion. |
| Apr 8 | 105/26 | 7.15 | ? Bapt., Gordon Arnold, son of G. A. & Annabel Follington Gilmore. Sharon Marie, dau. of Thomas & Lucille Cooper Evans. Frances and James Rich. Children of James & Irene Simmons Follington. |
| Apr 15 | 104/24 | 95.53 | Rev. C. E. Ladds officiated for evensong. |
| June 24 | 8/89/0 | 63.33 | Bapt., John R. and Gary E. sons of Robt. R & Muriel Smith Misner. |
| July 22 | 4/85 | 63.29 | Bapt., Mary Eliz. dau. of Neil A. & Norma Gregory Burns [RCAF] |
| July 28 | | | Marriage, John Albert Reid & June Myrtle Leitch |
| July 31 | -Tues.- | | Bapt., Dennis, son of Wm.& Roxie Yaghjian Mooradiau,Brantford. |
| Aug 5 | 8/80 | 99.94 | Rev. C. E. Snowden, Overbrook, Philadelphia preached. |
| Aug 19 | 4/82 | 70.00 | Bapt., Margaret Ann, dau. of Wm. G & Florence E Mason Cornish. |
| Sept 2 | ? | 53.54 | Mr. Clarence Mitchell officiated. Sept. 9; Dr. A. E. Williamson & Sept 16 A.W. Richardson took the service. Rector on holiday. |
| Sept 30 | 80/0 | 95.42 | Bapt., Ronald D. and Larry M. sons of Cameron M. & Phyllis Alma McKinney Fletcher. And Kenneth E., son of James Martin & Joyce Ella McKinney Martin. Phyllis & Joyce are sisters. |
| Oct 27 | - | | Sat.- - Marriage, Stewart H. Brown & Bridget Blackhurst |

November Note : Princess Elizabeth & Duke of Edinburgh - travel across Canada and back to Montreal. Friday Nov. 2nd .Nov. 4th attend church in St. Agathe

| | | | |
|---|---|---|---|
| Nov 18 | 6/63 | 78.68 | Rev. Fred J. Hills, Delhi officiated for matins. Nov 4. Heavy snow. |
| Dec 9 | 3/84/27 | 122.03 | Bapt., Max Raymond, son of Herbert & Georgie A Saville Stickney Also Harold Stuart Schilz b. 1897 to James Nicholas & Annie Stuart Schilz.[pre confirmation] |
| Dec 11 | 102 | 42.65 | Confirmation of 4 men, 3 women, 6 boys & 4 girls. |
| Dec 23 | 11/72/? | $93.69 | Bapt., Hilton Gregory, son of Hilton Barrett & Ruth G. Carter Yerex |
| Dec 23 | 102 | 67.00 | 11.15 p.m., 85 Communion. Clarence Mitchell, soloist & server |
| Dec 29 | | | Marriage, Arthur F. George, Estevan, Sask. & Agnes Jean Thornton |
| Dec 31 | | | Marriage, James Hugh Seymour & Helen Elizabeth Cornish |

**1952 - Incumbent, David J. Cornish**

| | | | |
|---|---|---|---|
| Feb 15 | 200 | | Memorial Service for King George VI. Rev. Sleeman, Anglican, Rev. Geo. Morley, United, Rev. Wm. Moorhead, Presb. – Council, Veterans, School Bd etc. in attendance - chairs in isles (sic) |
| Feb 17 | 85/197 | 144.53 | Evening Service taken by Girl Gides (sic) & Boy Scouts. |
| Mar 2 | | | Marriage, Samuel Hallam Ross & Joyce Marjorie Phipps |
| Mar 5 | 23 | 24.05 | 1st Lenten Wednesday, L. W. Owen took 7.45 service. |
| Mar 8 | | | Marriage, Robert Collin Ryerse & Lois Kathryn Gibbons |
| Mar 23 | | | Baptism, Beverly Ann, dau of Michael Snukuts (escaped Latvia) & Joan Hawes. Sponsors; A Olachnowicz, P. Salis & Florence Tucker |
| Apr 20 | 8/102 | 70.24 | Easter Service, Rector ill, Mr. Charles Inder officiated. |
| Apr 27 | 88/88 | 78.63 | E. Ford took matins, Bruce Reid & Andrew Lowe took evensong. |
| May 18 | 8/86 | 60.57 | Baptism, Elizabeth Ann, dau. of James D. & Mary Smythe Struthers |
| May 25 | ?/49 | 60.73 | Baptised, Donald Joe, Stella Lilly, David Geo., Martin M. Irene H. Marie Lillie, children of Wm. Henry & Lillie Lenvary Jacobs. Also Clarence T., Shirley J., Douglas W., children of Eric & Thelma Misner Baguley. |
| Jun 1 | 41/72 | 86.99 | 41 communicants, 8.30. Clarence Mitchell assists for 3 Sundays. |
| Jun 21 | | | Marriage, Garbut John Goodall & Cora Lazella Steinhoff |
| Jun 22 | 252/147 | 250.94 | Rev. E. A. Slemin & R. B. Brown, matins; Rev. J. Frank, Tor. Even. |
| Jul 6 | 18/86 | 60.43 | 3 pm Funeral, Mrs. Theo. McMillan, organist for many years. A sad, sad loss to the church & village. Church full & people outside. |
| Jul 19 | | | Marriage, Donald J.Ritchie, Port Arthur & Norah Virginia Blackhurst |
| Jul 27 | 18/78 | ? | Pray for rain. Baptise Margaret Susan, dau of David Colin & Grace Krueger Cornish. |
| Aug 8 | | | Marriage, Fredrick Geo. Sullivan & Doris Ann McLeod |
| Aug 10 | | | Baptism, Robert David and Terry Douglas, sons of Charles & Videt Espden Monroe. Father was also baptised. A tobacco farmer. |
| Aug 24 | 3/85 | 84.30 | Baptism, Michael Charles, son of Charles F. & J Carol Dines Kitchen |
| Aug 31 | 5/65/56 | 73.55 | Baptism, Samuel A. and George A. S. sons of F. G. Archie & Georgina Madgett Morris, alsoWm. Robert son of W. R. Grant & Lydia J. L. McQueen Hawke, also Victoria Ann dau. of Frank D. Grice & Anna Elizabeth Longfield. Also Eleaonor M. and John G. Arthur, children of Edmon A. & Isobel E. Groat Ryerse. |
| Sep 1 | | | Marriage, John J. Waters & Evelyn May Leitch. |
| Sep 7 | | | Baptism, Patti Lane, dau of Francis A & Bernice M. Abel Sullivan. |
| Sept 20 | | | Marriage, Thomas E. H. Copeman & Barbara Elizabeth Jennings. |
| Sep 21 | 6/100 | 70.97 | Baptism, Dianne C. dau. of Wm. Ezra & Velma Parker Stone. |
| Sep 28 | 7/196 | 188.20 | Cannon D. J. Cornish last communion as Rector of St. Pauls. 31 yrs. |
| Oct 4 | | | Marriage, John E Matthews & Ruth E. Lowe. D. J. Cornish & H. Webb officiate. |

| | | | |
|---|---|---|---|
| Oct 5 | 124/ | 98.41 | H. J. Webb officiated, 73 communicants. |
| Oct 8 | | | 7:30 pm - Induction of H. J. Webb - participating were Alan Gardiner, J.M. Mills, C. D. Gemmell, J. W. McDonald, G. J. Pitts, H. G. Humox, L.W. Owen, E. L. Vivian, D. J. Cornish. |
| Oct 16 | | | Burial, Mrs. James Franklin Parish Gates, age 80. |
| Oct 26 | 117/35 | 70.15 | Presentation of Sunday School prizes and awards. |
| Nov 3 | | | Burial of Thomas Henry Ward., age 72. |
| Nov 22 | | | Marriage, 2.00 pm - Douglas H. Calvert & Jane F. Feargue 3:00 pm - James F. Ewing & Shirley Marie Pierson. |
| Nov 30 | 25/115/28 | 112.27 | Baptisms, Cynthia L. dau. of Victor C. & Donna L. Whitnum Ryerse. Thomas E. son of Thomas Ernest & Elsie Lunn Greenall also Linda D. and Wayne D. child. of Donald S. & Barbara A. Peachey Wright. |
| Dec 1 | | | Burial, Mrs. Margaret Anne Evans Ross, age 91. |
| Dec 6 | | | Marriage, Bernard Anthony Doherty & Margaret Ilene Chambers. |
| Dec 10 | | | Burial, Mrs. Alice Butler Barrett Parke, age 91. |
| Dec 25 | 14/70 | | Communicants - 14/37. Shortened matins and talk to the children |
| Dec 28 | 72/60 | 22.85 | Evening Carol Service. |

1953 — Incumbent, H.J.E. Webb.

| | | | |
|---|---|---|---|
| Mar 1 | 86/42 | 97.85 | Special Prayers for Opening of the Fishing Season. |
| Mar 22 | 105/51 | 94.63 | Rev. L. W. Owen, Trinity, Simcoe in charge at evensong. |
| Apr 1 | | | Burial, - Hinatsu |
| Apr 5 | 53/249/48 | 427.56 | Baptism, Albert Garrett Reid, adult, son of Henry Percy & Alice Reid |
| Apr 6 | | | Burial, — Innes. |
| Apr 12 | 290/27 | 149.51 | Confirmation; 35 candidates. William Hallam, Asst. Bishop, Huron. |
| Apr 15 | | | Marriage, Kenneth Painter & Georgia Morris. Padre S. Lambert assts |
| Apr 26 | 111/30 | 73.54 | Baptisms, 4.30 - 65 present. Douglas R. son of Walter C. D. & Barb. Ryerse Long.- Pamela A. L. dau. of Robert C. & Lois G. Ryerse. – Linda A. dau. of George J. & Margaret Powell Burcham. – Wendy D. dau. of Jonathon & Eileen Saunders Bartlett. – Gloria J. dau. of Thomas Chester & Sylvia A. Pritchard Grice. – Delinda Jane dau. of Andrew G & Delinda Firmi MacDonald. – Christine Anne dau. of John A. & June M. Leitch Reid. – Ruth M. dau of Emma Steiss. |
| May 10 | | | Baptism, Michael Guy son of Charles E. & Betty E Gould Wilson. |
| May 16 | | | Marriage, – Comer & — Thornton |
| May 31 | 122/57 | 100.53 | Baptism, Judy E. dau. of Gordon E & Eileen M.. Terrio Longe. Special services of Preparation held for Coronation. |
| Jun 14 | 6/105/27 | 92.98 | Baptism, Roland Kyle son of Wm.C. & Alice L. Ryerse McNeilly. |
| Jun 29 | | | "Churching" – Monday. |
| Jul 5 | 18/88/13 | 66.22 | Baptism, Robert Ewing son of Samuel A. & Edna Naylor McMeekin |
| Jul 25 | | | Marriage, – Stratford & – Ryerse. |
| Jul 26 | 13/100/19 | 95.65 | Baptism, David Stanley son of Stanley Albert & Florence A. Bayes Bunker. – Wm. Morris son of Wm. M. & Drusilla Ryerse Bryant. |
| Aug 30 | 18/85/21 | 69.14 | Baptism, Wm. A. G. son of Albert G & Vernice Appleton Reid. |
| Sep 13 | 7/96/17 | 97.45 | Baptism, James Douglas son of James F. & Shirley Pierson Ewing. |
| Sep 19 | [full] | | Marriage, Wm. Bowlby Browne & Alice Louise Barrett |
| Sep 29 | 2:30pm | | Marriage, ——- Carter & ——— Robinson |
| Sep 30 | | | Burial, Wed. 2.00 p.m. Hubert Baldwin Barrett. |
| Oct 4 | 84/24 | 101.65 | Baptism, Michael Derald son of Michael & Joan Hawes Snukuts. |
| Oct 25 | 96/29 | 108.03 | Baptism, Leonard James son of Gordon A. & A.Follington Gilmore |

Nov 15  7/151/58  148.21  Layman's Sunday – A. E. Williamson M. D., D. J. Dickson, J. Goodall, W. Adams, W. McNeilly, J. Walker took part in morning service. B. Reid, S. Morris, A. Hoover, A. Lowe, E. Ford took part in evensong.
Nov 29  16/103/32  102.52  Baptism, Ruth Elizabeth dau. of Thos Douglas & Margaret Thibideau Richardson.
Dec 27  90/47  137.31  Baptism, Julia Alice dau. of Hilton B. & Ruth G. Carter Yerex. There were 5 private Communions in Christmas week - 16 comm.

1954 – Incumbent, H. J. E. Webb.

Jan 10  93/ 36  306.72  Baptism, Geo. Arthur son of Fred. G. & Doris A. McLeod, also Linda J. & David A. & Ruth E. children of Arthur H. & Hazel J. Sinden Sullivan, also Mary Margaret & Fredrick Joseph children of Percy & Sarah May Lomath Lavers
Jan 24  96/38  101.23  Baptism, Peter D. son of Douglas Abram & Irene Simmons Crosbie.
Feb 20  Marriage, — Cromwell - Reid
Mar 14  118/35  118.96  Baptisms, 2.00 p.m. Adults, Olive E. Wannamaker & Thelma Lavers 4:00 p.m. - Susan A. & Gail A. children of John R. & Olive E. Whitehead Wannamaker, also Janet Irene dau. of James M. & Joyce E McKinney Miller, also Douglas E. & Thelma D. children of Cameron M & Phyllis A. McKinney Fletcher, also Patricia M. dau. of Harold O. & Marg. E. DeLottinville Fletcher, also Lonnie K. son of Paul F. & Lonna M. Cable Fletcher. [9 souls]
Mar 20  Marriage, ———
Mar 21  12/78/40  58.08  Baptism, Susan J. dau. of Gordon R. & Maxine Y. Walker Scott.
Mar 24  Conditional baptism, Leo Joseph Barry.
Mar 28  199/90  154.39  Confirmation, George Huron. Evensong - Rev. H. M. Dawes with illustrations. - Sermon "In His Steps" - Kodachromes of Palestine.
Mar 29  Burial, Ward.
Apr 25  96/28  76.02  Cannon D. J. Cornish officiated. 5 private Communions, Easter week
May 2  98/38  127.22  Baptisms, Richard A., Dorothy B., Thomas R., William R. children of William Roy & Dorothy Agnes Richardson Barker.
May 9  90/157  243.25  Baptisms, Edward A. son of Alan M. & Golda E. Field Matthews. At 2:00 pm Janet L. wife of Earl L Brown. At 4.45 pm Terrence D. son of Earl L. & Janet L. Brown, also Mary M., & Robert R. children of Robert R. & Matilda Laemers Ford, also Danny G. & Judith L. child of Bruce C. & Leota Fidelia Hare Husted, also Carla Delaine dau. of John James & Evelyn May Leitch Waters. Cannon D. J. Cornish & Clarence Mitchell assisted at evensong. [Reverend Clarence Mitchell having been ordained a priest that morning in Hamilton.]
May 27  96  20.06  Ascension Day evening service for Deanery Chapter. Assisting Alan Gardiner, D. J. Cornish, F. Lightbourn, L. W. Owen.
Jul 11  17/117/21  118.62  Baptisms, 3.00 pm - Alan Terrence Sumio, son of Thomas Yosaburo & Nao J. Ujiye Hinatsu, also Pamela Y. dau. of Douglas Haney & Jane F. Feargue Calvert, also Barbara Dianne dau of George James & Margaret Anne Powell Burcham.
Aug 1 to Aug 29  R. E. Armstrong took morning and evening services - 5 Sundays.
Sept 5  10/66/22  112.45  Baptisms, infant Ivey & Strople at 3.00 p.m.
Oct 3  142/77  304.16  Harvest Festival – T. E. Jones assists – a very wet day
Oct 16  Holy matrimony – Shortt - Butler.

| | | | |
|---|---|---|---|
| Oct 24 | 119/45 | 188.17 | Layman's Sunday - W. Z. Nixon preached and B. Reid, A. Wicker & C. Strople, assisted in a.m. W. J. Adams preached and H. B. Barrett, H. J. H. Barrett & E. Ford assisted in p.m. |
| Oct 30 | | | Holy Matrimony – Watters [sic] – Ryerse. |
| Nov 14 | 153/23 | 145.90 | Reginald Athabasca preached. |
| Dec 24 | | | Holy Matrimony, Christmas Eve – Follington - Knight. There were 7 private communions performed Christmas week – 1 communicants. |

1955 — Incumbent – H. J. E. Webb.

| | | | |
|---|---|---|---|
| Feb 6 | 126/23 | 192.76 | Theological Education week - Rev. Clarence Mitchell preached. $5.00 each sent to Huron and Wycliffe colleges. |
| Feb 13 | 61/99 | 98.61 | Confirmation by Bishop George Huron. D.J.Cornish, C. Ladds assisted. |
| Feb 27 | 62/255 | 74.92 | Infant baptism - Dickson, — Scouts, Guides,Cubs, Brownies parade |
| Mar 6 | 81/55 | 88.50 | Fishermen's Service. |
| Mar 13 | | | Baptism - infant Lindsay. |
| Apr 16 | | | Baptism - 2 infants – Rowling twins. |
| Apr 17 | 122/26 | 92.30 | Easter. Infant baptism – Dennis. Apr. 18 – Coll. - Parish Hall $138.35. |
| Apr. 24 | 98/94 | 95.42 | Parade of I.O.O.F. and Rebeccas |
| May 2 | 5 | | [Monday] Deanery Chapter – Communion |
| May 7 | | | Holy Matrimony – Shand – Evans. |
| May 8 | | | Infant baptisms – Sullivan, Jollimore ? |
| May — June | | | Building Fund collected — $342.95. |
| June 12 | 126/36 | 118.25 | Infant baptism – Waxers. |
| June 18 | | | Holy Matrimony – Misner-Loewen June 19th - infant baptism - Howell. |
| July 3rd to July 24th | | | Reverend Clarence Mitchell took services for the month. Rev. H.M. Dawe preached on July 31st, Rev Webb had returned from vacation. |
| Aug 14 | 108/30 | 177.90 | Chauncey E Snowden preached at morning prayer service. |
| July — Aug | | | Building Fund collected —- $450.09 |
| Sept 5 & Sept 9 | | | Holy Matrimony - Webster – Winn / Jackson – Ivey respectively. |
| Oct 1 | | | Holy Matrimony - Collins - Gilbert. |
| Oct 2 | 132/53 | 414.50 | Harvest Festival — Rev. Victor K Blake was preacher. |
| Oct 8 | | | Holy Matrimony, Canon Cornish & H. Webb in chge. - Long – Brown. |
| Oct 16 | 127/40 | 85.17 | Family, children & Youths Service. |
| Oct 23 | 116/23 | 136.63 | Laymen's Service. G. Saracuse, [sic] Waterford, preached. B. Reid, H.J. H. Barrett, A. Morris, W. McNeilly and E. Ford assisted. |
| Oct 30 | | | Infant baptisms - MacDonald & McNeilly. |
| Sept — Oct. | | | Building Fund collected — $698.50. |
| Nov 6 | 90/128 | 151.70 | Parade of Royal Arch Masons. Bishop Walter Niagara, and Rev. Clarence Mitchell attend. |
| Dec 24 | 110 | 23.30 | Christmas Eve - 11.30 communion service. |
| Dec 25 | 19/96/48 | 75.70 | At 7:00 p.m. 48 attended a Carol Service. 5 Private Services held. |
| Nov — Dec | | | Building Fund collected — $376.05. |

1956 — Incumbent - H. J. E. Webb.

| | | | |
|---|---|---|---|
| Jan 7 | | | Holy Matrimony – Bruce - Mossing. |
| Jan 10th & 14th | | | Burials of the Dead - Mrs. Orval Shortt & James E. Ryerse. |
| Jan 15 | 122/35 | 107.45 | Two infant baptisms – Dumond. - Jan 21, Burial – Misner ? |
| Jan 22 | 101/31 | 119.95 | Infant baptism — Cromwell. |
| Feb 5 | 113/43 | 127.14 | Celebrate Centenary of First Service. (Feb 10th, 1856) W. W. Files pres. |
| Feb 12 | 101/38 | 112.55 | Celebrate Centenary – H. F. Appleyard gave the sermon. |

| | | | |
|---|---|---|---|
| Feb 26 | 185/41 | 144.60 | Bishop William Townshend confirmed 21 candidates. 2 adult baptisms. |
| Feb 27 | | | Burial of Dr. Williamson. |
| Jan — Feb | | | Building Fund collected — $581.55. |
| Mar 4 | | | Memorial Service - Rev. Webb & S/L Rev. E.W.S. Gilbert for Paul H. Crosbie, who died overseas with the R. C. A. F. |
| Mar 17 | | | Holy Matrimony – Nesbitt - McKen. |
| Apr 1 | 269/30 | 308.40 | Easter – Communicants - 53 at 8.00 a.m. & 116 at 11.00 a.m. |
| Mar — Apr | | | Building Fund collected — $512.30 |
| May 4 | | | Holy Matrimony – Chambers - Gilbert. |
| May 13 | | | Infant baptism - Walker - Sullivan. |
| May 27 | 112/23 | 88.20 | Infant baptism - Strople. May 29th - Burial - Cornish. |
| June 2 | | | Holy Matrimony - Matthews - Misner & McQuillan - St. Louis |
| June 10 | 125/15 | 117.00 | Six infant baptisms. |
| June 17 | 101/22 | 99.90 | Infant baptism at 4.30 p.m. - Fletcher. |
| May — June | | | Building Fund collected — $463.30. |
| July 15 | 126/17 | 119.65 | Infant baptisms - 3.30 p.m. -Barry. - 8.15 p.m. - Van Schalkwyk. |
| July 22 | 113/16 | 134.32 | Infant baptisms - the Richardson twins. |
| July 29th to Aug 21st | | | Vacation - Canon Cornish covered I Sunday's three services and two burials - Emerson Porritt on Thursday Aug. 16th & Davidson on Aug. 21. G. Stanley Sharples, Rector in Delhi covered 9 services. |
| July — Aug. | | | Building Fund collected — $270.85 |
| Sept 16 | 101/21 | 102.60 | Infant baptism - Hopwarth, - Kyle. |
| Sept 23 | 105/18 | 121.00 | Infant baptism - Rechnitzer. |
| Sept 29 | | | Holy matrimony - McNeilly - Reid. Sept 30 - infant baptism [unnamed] |
| Oct 10th | | | Holy matrimony - Mitchell - Morris. |
| Oct 21 | 165/20 | 151.76 | Family Service. An infant baptism - Burcham. |
| Oct 28 | 126/0 | 178.35 | Laymen's Sunday. Assisting - E. Ford, H. Yerex, A. Wicker, B. Forrest, H.J.H. Barrett. Rev. M. McKay, layman of St. Jude's, Brantford - preached the sermon. The evensong was cancelled for a Deanery Laymen's service which was to have been held in Simcoe. |
| Sept — Oct | | | Building Fund collected — $738.55. |
| Nov 4 | | | Infant baptisms - Reid, Calvert. |
| Nov 18 | 268/0 | 252.86 | Confirmation by Bishop George Huron assisted by Canon Cornish & Rev. Webb at 11.00 morning prayer. At 3.00 p.m. approximately 275 attended the Dedication of the Parish hall by the Bishop assisted by Rev. Webb, Canon Cornish and R. Coupland. |
| Dec 2 | 102/66 | 136.41 | Members of Erie Lodge, A.F. & A.M. attended evensong. Canon Cornish gave the sermon. |
| Dec 23 | 145/27 | 177.99 | Infant baptism - Barker. |
| Dec 30 | 95/42 | 104.05 | Rev. G. Stanley Sharples took matins and the sermon. Carol service at 7:00 p.m. |
| Nov — Dec | | | Building Fund collected — $1655.35. |

1957 — Incumbent – H. J. E. Webb.

| | | | |
|---|---|---|---|
| Jan 6th & 13th | | | Last two entries for Building Fund collections are made. $194.55. |
| Jan 20 | 120/23 | 146.18 | Celebrated "Loyalty Sunday." T. B.B. [Barrett] & A. E. W. [Williamson] initial the register as Wardens. |
| Feb 3 | 97/18 | 212.34 | Infant baptisms at 4.30 p.m. [David & Kerry] Wamsley. Though not recorded the children of Ralph & Peggy Wamsley Herring were baptised. |
| Feb 4 | -Monday - | | Deanery Chapter service, 6 communicants. |

| | | | |
|---|---|---|---|
| Feb 23 -Saturday - | | | Holy Matrimony - Whitehead - [Helen] Thompson. — March 2nd marriage of Bloye - Finch. |
| Mar 3 | 62/41 | 63.95 | Annual Fishermen's Service. Friday, March 8th, Woman's World Day of Prayer at 3.00 p.m. |
| Mar 13, 20, 27, & April 3, 10. | | | On Wednesday evenings at 8.00 p.m. Cottage Meetings were held in various homes of the Parish. Rev. Webb notes on occasion "Evening Prayer & Litany (revised) or Holy Communion (revised). |
| Apr 28 | 86/70 | 115.22 | Parade of I. O. O. F. and Rebeccas to Evensong. |
| May 13 - Monday - | | | Burial of the Dead – J. Harnick. May 19 - Baptism of infant Johnson. |
| June 1 | | | Holy Matrimony – Belbeck – Arbour. |
| June 9 | 114/0 | 278.72 | Diocesan Centennial Service. No evening service on account of Diocesan Pilgrimage to the Mohawk Chapel [Brantford] |
| June 15 | | | Holy Matrimony - at 2.00 p.m. [Les] Murphy - [Rosemary] Howell. - at 3.00 p.m. [John] White - [Beatrice] Ivey. |
| July 7 | | | Adult baptism – Morden. July 14 - Infant baptisms, Winters, Watters, [sic] Douglas. |
| Aug 3 | | | Holy Matrimony – Carr – Staley. Aug 31 – Furler – Winter. |
| Sept 10 | | | Holy Matrimony – Luton - Jamieson Sept. 21 – Verheyen - Leece. |
| Sept 29 | 197/35 | 366.37 | Rev. David M. Milne in charge of Matins for Harvest Thanksgiving. |
| Oct 2 | | | Holy Matrimony – Lees - Keffer. |
| Oct 18 | | | No services held due to insufficient attendance |
| Sept 20 | 148/0 | 119.50 | Children's Service & Infant baptism – Jarvis. |
| Oct 27 | 160/28 | 183.50 | Bishop William Townshend confirmed 10 candidates. |
| Nov 17 | 126/20 | 154.53 | Infant baptism – Finch. |
| Nov 30 23- | | | St. Andrew's Day - W. A. Corporate service. Self Denial Fund - $22.80. |
| Dec 8 | 97/30 | 116.30 | Infant baptism – Kitchen. |
| Dec 24 | 107 | 3 env. | Christmas Eve - 11.30 communion. Open offering to the Rector. |
| Dec 25 | 29/79 | ? | Christmas day - 8.00 a.m. communion - 29. 10.30 a.m. 38 communicants, Children's Christmas Message and Blessing. |
| Dec 29 | 130/79 | 268.65 | At 12.30 a special communion service for 30 communicants was held to celebrate the 50th Wedding Anniversary of Canon and Mrs. D. J. Cornish. At 7.00 p.m. a Carol service was held. Four private communion services were held for 7 parishioners. |

\*\* Taken from Vestry Book entries from July 24th, 1949 to December 29th, 1957. \*\*

January 1st, 1958 to March 20th, 1966.

1958 – Incumbent - H. J. E. Webb.

| | | | |
|---|---|---|---|
| Jan 19 | 121/15 | 111.33 | Dedication of Bookmarks. 4.30 - Infant baptism - [Hugh] Barrett. |
| Jan 26 | 105/20 | 114.10 | Baptism of 10 infants at 4.30 p.m. – no names recorded. |
| Feb 2 | 97/36 | 184.84 | Commissioning of Canvasses. |
| Mar 2 | 94/50 | 169.84 | Fishermen's Service. March 3rd - 13 communicants attend Deanery Ch. |
| Mar 16 | 135/19 | 125.46 | Two infant baptisms – Matthews and Ross. |
| Mar 28 | | | Burial — Mrs. S. Turner. |
| Apr 4 | 65 | 32.45 | Good Friday – Collection for Church Mission to the Jews. Five private communions to 9 communicants during Easter week. |
| Apr 23 | | | Burial — Lowe. May 7th, Burial — Hinatsu. |
| Jun 4 | | | Wednesday Communion - 72 attend - Chapter and W. A. share - 13.40. |
| Jun 15 | 155/16 | 141.86 | Infant baptism — Miller. |

## 544 The Parish of St. Paul's

| | | | |
|---|---|---|---|
| July 6 | 106/29 | 107.24 | Rev. Clarence M. Mitchell gave sermon. Infant baptism - Kelland. |
| July 13 | 146/12 | 111.76 | Infant baptism — Ames. |
| July 26 | | | Holy Matrimony — Backus - O'Neill. |
| Aug 3 to Aug 24 | | | Rev. G. Stanley Sharples officiated for Aug 3rd, followed by Rev. D. Rees [during Rev. Webb's holiday time.] |
| Aug 31 | 0/90/0 | 138.05 | No 8.00 a.m. communion service as no communicants. At 4:00 p.m. an infant baptism for Dines and for Pelito. |
| Sept 14 | 103/0 | 93.65 | Infant baptism Ryerse. Evening service withdrawn. Co-operating in Bible Society Service at Presbyterian Church. |
| Sept 28 | 180/47 | 681.59 | Harvest Festival. Rev C. J. Queen preached. |
| Oct 5 | 84/16 | 176.37 | Adult baptisms at 5.00 p.m. – Long & Dennis. |
| Oct 12 | 98/132 | 231.19 | [Bishop] George Huron confirmed 12 candidates at 3.00 p.m. |
| Oct 26 | 189/31 | 161.32 | Family Day Service and Infant Baptism – Murphy. |
| Nov 2 | 90/17 | 150.89 | Instead of sermon at evensong - a presentation of Beaumont's 20th Century Folk Mass. Mine disaster is noted. |
| Nov 9 | 101/0 | 138.39 | Infant baptism - Bartlett. Evening service withdrawn in favour of a Community Memorial Service in Presbyterian Church. |
| Dec 2 | 22 | 55.65 | St. Andrew's Day (transferred) W. A. Corporate communion. |
| Dec 27 | | | Holy Matrimony – McVey - [ ] Jean Milner. |
| | | | Five private communion services in Christmas season, 12 communicants |

1959 — Incumbent - H. J. E. Webb.

| | | | |
|---|---|---|---|
| Jan 6 | | | Epihpany - 10.30 a.m. No congregation for celebration. Very cold. |
| Jan 8 | | | Burial of the Dead – Mrs. Johnson. |
| Jan 18 | 76/14 | 124.13 | Bishop's Letter read [at Matins] |
| Mar 1 | 76/37 | 101.75 | Annual Fishermen's Service. March 2nd, 5 attend Deanery Chapter. Service held every Wednesday in Lent in the Parish Hall. |
| Mar 22 | 87/23 | 95.00 | Dedication of Burses & Veils for Cruets. |
| Apr 5 | 78/15 | 92.11 | Easter Service. 5 private communion services held. 10 communicants. |
| Apr 26 | 83/23 | 97.07 | Infant baptism – Richardson. |
| May 10 | 109/25 | 163.67 | Rev'd David M. Miln officiated for communion service at evensong. |
| June 1 | | | Memorial service for Mrs. Constance C. Benson. Rev'd R. A. Hunt & Dr. W. J. Mumford assisted. |
| June 4 | | | Burial of the dead - Mrs Beatrice [Ansley] Sayer, H. Southcott assisted. |
| June 13 | | | Holy Matrimony - Smith - Butler. |
| June 14 | 86/50 | 89.69 | Erie lodge masons parade to evensong. |
| June 20 | | | Holy Matrimony — Winters - Steiss. |
| June 27 | | | Holy Matrimony — Bemner - Gilbert. |
| Aug 2nd to 30th | | | Rev'd Clarence M. Mitchell officiates for St. Paul's while Rev'd Webb was on vacation. Aug. 5th, Burial of Fred Weir. Aug 8th Marriage of Kenneth Smith and Joan Forrest. Aug 23rd, Baptism of Scott Warren Taylor. [at last someone has sympathy for the beleaguered historian and writes the candidates full name. The incumbent occasionally omits it completely.] |
| Sept 12 | | | Holy Matrimony — Stone - Pow. |
| Oct 9 | | | Burial of the Dead — Mrs. C. Ansley. |
| Oct 18 | 113/15 | 114.78 | Infant baptism - Simpson. |
| Nov 8 | 72/0 | 98.15 | Infant baptisms – Watkinson, Wamsley, Ames. Evening Service cancelled for Annual Community Memorial Service at U[nited] Ch. |
| Nov 29 | 119/18 | 128.75 | Presentation of Dominion Life Membership in Woman's Auxiliary to Mrs. W. H. Barrett. |

| | | | |
|---|---|---|---|
| Dec 1 | - 20 attend | | St. Andrew's Day communion(transferred) W. A. self denial fund 23.70 |
| Dec 4 | | | Burial of the Dead – Mrs. C. H. Page. |
| Dec 13 | 87/16 | 241.45 | Infant baptism – Howell. |
| Dec 15 | | | Burial of the Dead – Mrs. Charles Franklin [Imogen] Ivey. |
| Dec 20 | 93/14 | 274.56 | Infant baptism at 4:30 p.m. – Long. |
| | | | During Christmas Season – 6 private celebrations - 12 communicants. |

1960 — Incumbent – H. J. E. Webb, to end of April.

| | | | |
|---|---|---|---|
| Jan 8 | | | Friday, Week of Prayer, celebrated with Rev. T Boyd & Gray Rivers (United Church) the third and last of a series held jointly. Monday in Knox Presbyterian and Wednesday in Grace United. |
| Jan 6 | -Saturday - | | Holy Matrimony – Heaman - Howell. |
| Feb 28 | 92/0 | ? | Rev. L. A. Nelles officiated at matins. No evening service, as the Rector was in Hospital. |
| Apr 17 | 63/221/46 | | Easter. Evensong & Infant baptism – ? -, Collection - 656.65. 7 private communion services, 13 communicants. |
| Apr 22 | | | Burial of the dead – Dr. A. E. Williamson, over 200 [mourners] |
| Apr 24 | 110/82 | 138.63 | Presentation of Lenten Boxes at 10.00 a.m. in S. S. Infant baptisms at 5.00 p.m. – Miller, Finch, and Winters. Note by Rector: "This marks the end of 7 years, 7 months as Rector of St. Paul's. Signed : H.J.E. Webb." |

1960 —— Incumbent, from May 1st, — Alan Gardiner.

| | | | |
|---|---|---|---|
| May 26 | 128 | 50.58 | Induction Service for Reverend Alan Gardner. H. F. Appleyard, Archdeacon of Brant, assisted by Rev'd L. W. Owen, Rev'd David M. Miln, Rev'd David G. Rees, Rev'd C. A. Wardner ? and Canon D. J. Cornish. |
| May 30 | | | Burial at 2.30 p.m. 40 mourners - Miss Tooth. At 3.00 p.m. 30 mourners - Mr. Bush. May 31st was a day of Prayer for South Africa. |
| Jun 26 | 111/16 | 135.07 | Baptism – Evans. |
| July 28 | | | Burial - Patrick Wamsley. |
| July 31 | 157/11 | 158.43 | Church Parade at 11.00 a.m. Rev'd James Donaldson preached. |
| Aug 28 | 10/99 | 107.65 | C. M. Mitchell officiated for 8.00 a.m. W. S. Morris for matins. |
| Sep 5 | 17/65 | 91.75 | Rev. W. L. Marr ? officiated. |
| Sept 25 | 191/47 | 656.84 | Harvest Thanksgiving. A baptism at 3.00 p.m. [no name given] |
| Oct 1 | | | Holy Matrimony & Communion – [Stephan] Molewyk - [Emily] Barrett. |
| Oct 5 | | | Private communion - 3 parishioners - Batten. |
| Oct 25 | | | Burial - Rogers. |
| Nov 6 | 122/16 | 187.81 | At 3.00 p.m. Remembrance Day Service, assisting Canon D.J. Cornish, Mr. Boyd & Mr. Rivers. |
| Nov 8 | | | Burial – Mabel Kaar. |
| Nov 15 | 144/21 | 173.35 | Used new prayer book for first time at Vittoria. |
| Nov 20 | 205/12 | 220.47 | Visitation Sunday. Baptisms - Johnson & Boptuan ? |
| Nov 27 | 156/43 | 237.81 | Rev. L. A. Nelles officiated for 2 morning services, Masons of Erie Lodge visited. David Miln officiated for evensong. |
| Dec 11 | 114/25 | 194.46 | Baptism of Susan Chambers, 11:00 a.m., of Mr. Parke & children, 7 p.m. |
| Dec 18 | 101/60 | 315.48 | Snow storm. Carol Service + 9 lessons at 7.00 p.m. Private communion services for Eager, Ward, Garner & Evans. |

Reverend Gardiner provided a Summary of the year.
| | |
|---|---|
| No. of Sunday services | 145. |
| No. of weekly services | 22. |
| No. of services of Holy Communion | 53. |
| Average attendance at 8.00 a.m. | 14. |
| Average attendance at 11.00 a.m. | 68. |
| Average attendance - 11.00a.m. Sunday | 143. |
| No. of weekly services of Holy Communion | 15. |
| No. of Baptismal Services | 21. |
| Marriages | 3. |
| Burials | 11. |
| No of Communicants - Easter | 187. |
| No. of Private Communions | 16. |

1961 — Incumbent Alan Gardiner.

| | | | |
|---|---|---|---|
| Jan 4 | | | Prayer Service - Canadian Council of Churches - Rev. T. H. Boyd. |
| Feb 2 - 14 - | | | Baptism - Gail Stephens. |
| Feb 7 - 30 - | | | Burial - Lawrence Skey. Feb. 11th, 125 mourners - Mrs. Garner. |
| Feb 13 - 165 - | | | Burial - Mrs. Landon Ivey. Feb 14th, 115 mourners - Mrs. Ward. |
| Feb 15 - 105 - | | | Burial - Dr. Slocombe. Feb 22nd, 35 mourners - ? Innes. |
| Mar 14 - 78 - | | | Burial - Linley [Lidney] McQueen. |
| Mar 31 | 87/63 | 32.92 | Good Friday services. 10:00 a.m. Children 11:00 a.m. Missions. |
| May 6 | | | Holy Matrimony – Canon Cornish officiated, 51 present. Milne - Ewing. |
| May 13 | | | Burial - 76 mourners - Mrs. Fletcher. |
| May 15 | | | Baptisms 11 present – C. M. Grace & S. M. Gash. |
| May 21 | 178/12 | 181.89 | Rev. David Brown assisted. 52 attend Men's breakfast. |
| May 28 | 287/15 | 295.69 | Archdeacon Wm. Townshend for confirmation service. Canon Cornish. |
| May 31 | | | Private communion for [Miss] Musselman, [Geo. & Adah] Pelly. |
| June 11 | 124/20 | 170.10 | Baptism - Buck, Powell. |
| July 1 | 35 present | | Holy Matrimony – Innes - Matteram. |
| July 2 | 110/15 | 176.46 | Dedication of Credence Table, Canon Cornish assists. |
| July 7 | | | Private communion – Miss Evans. |
| July 27 | | | " " – Mrs. Wardel[l]. |
| Aug 19 | | | Holy Matrimony – [Ch.] Ivey – [C] Grace. |
| Aug 20 | 107/12 | 145.80 | Choral Evensong - Dull & dank day. |
| Aug 26 | | | Holy Matrimony - 3:00 p.m. Richards - Hawke. |
| Aug 27 | 91/7 | 131.25 | Baptism by Canon D. J. Cornish - Gerald Thomas Smallcombe. His father in R. C. N., Halifax. Rev. Gardiner on holiday, Rev. W. L. Morris & Canon Cornish officiate until September 24th. |
| Sept 24 | 161/45 | 562.90 | Harvest Festival. G. J Vite, Christ Ch. Kitchener assists. At 4.00 p.m. Canon Cornish baptised William Hambleton Cameron Parkinson. |
| Sept 29 | | | Burial - Alton Hoover - 125 mourners. |
| Oct 8 | 113/14 | 323.10 | Baptism – Catherine D. Talbot. Oct 10th, baptise - Lampman. |
| Oct 16 | | | Holy Matrimony - Rm ? - Talbot. |
| Oct 20 | | | Burial – Michals, 25 mourners. |
| Oct 22 | 125/14 | 182.09 | Dedication of Hall. |
| Oct 28 | | | Holy Matrimony - Lampman - Knight. 45 present. |
| Nov 16 | | | Burial - Mrs. Gutcher - 40 mourners. |
| Dec 10 | 104/16 | 20.90 | 9.45 White Gifts, baptism - 12.30 - 8 present - Sheila Chambers. |
| Dec 22 | | | Burial service - Myrtle Leitch. 175 mourners. |

## St. Paul's Church Register 547

Dec 25  67         19.40    Christmas service at 10.00 a.m. Canon Cornish assisted.
                            Private Communion services for Mason, Wardel[l], Barber, Eagers,
                            Bridgewater and at the Nursing Home.

### Summary

| | |
|---|---|
| No. of Sunday services | 166. |
| No. of Weekly services | 58. |
| Holy Communion Services, Sunday | 67. |
| Average attendance - 8.00 a.m. | 17. |
| Average attendance - 11.00 a.m. | 93. |
| No. of week-day services of H. Communion | 49. |
| Baptisms - 19, Marriages - 7, Burials | 18. |
| Private Communions | 19. |
| Average Sunday attendance | 156. |

1962 — Incumbent – Rev. Alan Gardiner.

Jan 4    36         8.53    Thur. 7.30 p.m. Community Prayer Service. A. Gardiner, G.A.,
                            B. Moore, T. H. Boyd, took part.
Jan 14   113/17     244.16  Installation of W. A. Officers.
Feb 8                       Burial – ?
Feb 25   100/11     202.15  Rector ill from Feb 21st to Feb 26th, Canon Cornish officiated. Rev. A.
                            B. Moore, Grace United exchanged on Feb 25th.
Mar 24                      Holy Matrimony – Helfer - Sauenweld.
Apr 14                      Baptism - Shelley Ann Stewart. Apr 24 – Burial – Steele.
Apr 28                      Holy Matrimony – Misner - Mason.
Apr 29   91/12      276.70  Easter service. 9:45 a.m. Children's Thank Offering - 125 present.
                            3:00 p.m. Baptism - Katherine Janet ? - 17 present.
May 31                      Ascension Day. David Noel, Waterford officiated. 14 present.
June 8                      Baptism - Donna Jean G-.
June 10  93/153     62.65   Confirmation service by Wm. Townshend.
June 24  109/15     205.65  Baptism - 11.00 a.m. - Barrett. 3.00 p.m. - Philips.
June 30                     Baptism - Matteram, - Murphy. July 3rd, - baptisms - Jamieson, Field.
Aug 1                       Rector on vacation until Sept 2nd, - Canon Cornish officiated on most
                            Sundays. A wedding is recorded for Aug. 3rd, no details. Rev. J. M. Donaldson
                            in charge Aug. 4th, Rev. T. H. Payne in charge Mon. Aug. 5th.
Aug 4                       Holy Matrimony - Waddle - Kilpatrick. Aug 11th, - Cathcart – Nixon and
                            at 4:00 p.m. - Nigh - Wicker.
Aug 26                      Baptism at 4:00 p.m. - Brooks, Rev. Webb officiating. 16 present.
Sept 12                     Baptism – Ruby Irene Clapp.
Sept 22                     Holy Matrimony – Jones – Ryerse.
Sep 30   186/30     833.43  Harvest Thanksgiving. Rev. C. M. Mitchell preached in a.m. and
                            Rev. D.E. Mel ? at 7:00 p.m.
Oct 6                       Holy Matrimony – Harrison – Crabb.
Oct 10                      Wednesday at 4:30 a Little Helper's Party was held. 50 present. $10.90.
Oct 14   103/20     166.16  Baptism at 3.00 p.m. – Terisa Gail Dring.
Nov 10                      Burial – no details or name.
Nov 11   126/21     172.01  Remembrance Day Service.
Nov 25   138/15     376.14  G. Stanley Sharples preached at 11.00. Dedication of Processional Am.
Dec 2                       Baptism of Cynthia Louise Bartlett. Dec 16 baptism, no name recorded.
Dec 21                      Holy Matrimony – Kilby - [Mary] Nixon.

548  The Parish of St. Paul's

Dec 30   85/10     338.30    Rev. Carman J. Queen officiated at 11.00 & Rev. Donaldson at 7.00 p.m.

SUMMARY
| | |
|---|---|
| No of Sunday Services | 168 |
| No of Weekday Services | 67 |
| Average attendance    - 8.00 a.m. - 14 - 11.00 a.m. - 74 | |
| No weekday Communion Services | 48 |
| Baptismal Services | 26 |
| Marriage Services | 10 |
| Burials | 13 |
| Private Communion Services | 14 |
| Average Sunday Attendance | 134 |

1963 —— Incumbent – Reverend Alan Gardiner.

| | | | |
|---|---|---|---|
| Jan 8 | | | Installation of Officers of the Women's Auxiliary. |
| Jan 10 | 47 | 13.95 | World Day of Prayer - guests Rev. G. A. B .Moore & Rev. T. H. Boyd. |
| Feb 27 | | | Ash Wednesday Children's Service at 9.45 a.m. |
| Mar 1 | | | Burial - Mr G. Clark. |
| Apr 21 | 120/17 | 150.40 | Easter Day. At 10.00 a.m. 162 attended a Youth Service of Thanks. |
| May 11 | | | Holy Matrimony – Hayward – Thompson. May 12th, Baptism, no name. |
| May 19 | 109/8 | 339.07 | Baptism - Judy Anne –?— |
| May 30 | | | Joint Meeting of W. A. and the Deanery. Stanley Sharples assisted. |
| June 12 | 110 | 50.02 | Confirmation by George Huron at 8.00 p.m. - a Wednesday. |
| June 28 | | | Burial of Thomas Basil Knowles. 75 mourners. |
| July 3 | 120/23 | 154.05 | Baptism by Canon D. J. Cornish of Herbert Jay Smallcombe of Halifax. |
| July 21 | 124/21 | 321.03 | Baptism of Catherine May Follington. |
| July 28 | | | Burial of W. A. Cornish at 2.30 p.m. Rev. L. A. Owen assisted. |
| Aug 3 | | | Holy Matrimony – Forsythe – Parker. Canon Cornish officiated. |
| Aug 4 | | | Rector on vacation to Sept 1st. Rev. F. H Allen & Canon Cornish shared the services. On August 17th Canon Cornish officiated at the marriage of Harry Smith and Gwen Forrest. On August 22nd he officiated at the burial of Andrew Yerex, killed in an auto accident. 150 mourners. |
| Sept 8 | 105/10 | 19740 | Baptism of Francis Elizabeth Painter at 3.00 p.m. 26 in attendance. |
| Sept 18 | | | Baptism of Richard Hugh Molewyk. |
| Sept 22 | 132/40 | 226.41 | Dedication of Altar Book, Altar Linen and Pulpit Light. |
| Oct 6 | 103/15 | 122.60 | Jack Cooke, Lay Reader officiated at evensong. |
| Oct 27 | 124/55 | 200.24 | Members of Erie Lodge, A.F. & A.M. attend evensong. |
| Nov 1 | | | Burial service for Thomas Richardson. 200 mourners. |
| Nov 4 | 109/16 | 183.07 | Baptism at evensong of Frank William Cuthbert. |
| Nov 9 | | | Baptism of Heaman child at 3.30 p.m. Nov 14th - of Michael Robt Laver. |
| Nov 24 | 131/12 | 170.59 | Memorial tribute at matins to the late President John F. Kennedy. |
| Nov 29 | | | Burial of G. H. Hallam at 2.30 p.m. |
| Dec 18 | | | Marriage of Thompson – Belbeck |
| Dec 23 | | | Burial of Roland Waddle. |
| Dec 29 | 101/12 | 563.42 | Rev Kenneth Brueton of Jarvis officiated. |

## St. Paul's Church Register 549

### SUMMARY – 1963

| | |
|---|---|
| No of Sunday Services | 157 |
| No of Weekday Services | 62 |
| Communion services | Sundays – 64. Weekdays – 51 |
| Average Sunday attendance | - 8.00 a.m. - 16. 11.00 a.m. - 89 |
| No. of Baptismal Services | 18 |
| No. of Marriages | 6 |
| No. of Burial Services | 9 |
| No. of Private Communion Services | 14 |

1964 —— Incumbent – Rev. Alan Gardiner.

| | | | |
|---|---|---|---|
| Jan 12 | 86/8 | 318.51 | Rev. W. T. Salmond officiated for matins and evensong. |
| Jan 16 | | | Burial of Richard Adams. |
| Feb 16 | 118/12 | 163.10 | Baptism at 12.30 of Thomas Andrew Ivey. On March 1st baptism of the Ryerse children. |
| Mar 8 | 125/11 | 287.23 | Baptism at 12.30 – no name given. |
| Apr 12 | 153/14 | 427.66 | Dedication of Memorial Railings presented by Miss Johns in memory of Andrew Yerex, who she cared for after his mother's death |
| Apr 14 | | | Baptism of John Scott MacDonald, Misner. |
| Apr 19 | 129/21 | 195.51 | Baptism of Beverly Anne Barker. |
| Apr 22 | 7/110 | 37.60 | Confirmation of 11 candidates by Bishop William Townshend at 8:00 p.m. Assisted by A. Gardiner, K. Brueton, D. J. Cornish. |
| Apr 28 | | | Burial of Robert Eager. |
| May 3 | | | The Register gives no explanation but Rev. Alan Gardiner takes no further services until July 5th. Rev. K. N. Brueton takes charge with some services taken by Canon Cornish. On May 30th the marriage of Faulkner - St. Louis is recorded. May 31st Rev. E Bartram assists at morning communion. June 5th, Canon Cornish officiates at the burial of Theodore McMillan. |
| July 11 | 104/12 | 162.05 | Baptism of Susan Lee Moorschan [?] by Rev. A. Gardner. |
| Aug 15 | | | Marriage of Ashbaugh - Lavers at 2.00 p.m. |
| Sept 3 | | | Private communion for Mrs. John S. Martin. |
| Sept 13 | 120/10 | 213.17 | Canon Cornish dedicated the Barwell Memorial Window. A baptism is recorded but no name is given. |
| Sept 21 | | | Burial of Edward Payne. |
| Sept 26 | | | Marriage of Williamson – Holmes. 85 attend the ceremony. |
| Oct 18 | 120/19 | 198.35 | Baptism of Jan Misner. Nov 6th, baptism of Noreen Eule [?] |
| Nov 28 | | | Burial of Charles John Skelcher. |
| Dec 5 | | | Marriage of Rhundlander – Thompson. |
| Dec 26 | | | Marriage of Green – [Connie]Clark. |
| Dec 31 | | | Marriage of [Thomas] Honey – [Karen] Gamble. |

550  The Parish of St. Paul's

SUMMARY – 1964.
No. of Sunday Services                                  162.
No of Weekday Services                                   64.
No of Sunday Communion Services                          64.
No of Weekday Communion Services                         54.
Average Sunday attendance         - 8.00 – 14. 11.00 – 79.
No. of Baptismal services                                19.
No. of Marriages                                          9.
No. of Burials                                           15.
No. of Private Communion services                        14.
Average Sunday attendance                               147.

1965 —— Incumbent — Reverend Alan Gardiner.

| | | | |
|---|---|---|---|
| Jan 3 | 90/16 | 156.60 | Rev. K. N. Brueton officiated at all three services. Initial offering - 14.00 Huron Church News offering - 14.05. Rev. Gardiner made private communion visits to Bartlett, Mason, the hospital, Clarence E. Strople, and Richardson in the month of January. |
| Feb 21 | 238/12 | 112.09 | Scouts and Girl Guides attended matins. |
| Mar 14 | 110/25 | 145.90 | Baptism of Sherrie Lynn Field at evensong. |
| Mar 21 | 103/20 | 130.13 | Baptism of Lisa Marie C. W - C. K. [?] |
| Mar 25 | | | Burial of Irene Bartlett. |
| May 5 | | | Baptism of David O. Brian. [?] |
| May 22 | | | Marriage of Kamilakahan – Hinatsu. |
| May 23 | 216/9 | 234.98 | Confirmation by Bishop William Townshend and Can. Council Service. |
| June 9 | | | Bishop Luxton officiated at a Deanery Meeting. 12 attend. |
| June 26 | | | Marriage of Givens – Ivey. |
| June 27 | 139/11 | 291.30 | Baptism of Lampman and Follington. |
| July 4 | 117/11 | 163.10 | Rev. K. N. Brueton officiated at all services until Aug 1st as Rector on vacation. July 11 Baptism of Karen Lee Mooradian. |
| Aug 14 | | | Interment of Ashes of Myrtle Randle. |
| Sept 12 | 106/127 | 360.85 | Reverend Gardiner notes that he preached his last sermon as Rector of St. Paul's Church at Evensong, September 12th, 1965. |
| Sept 18th | | | Marriage of [Peter] Barrett – [Karen] Kolbe by Reverend Gardiner. |

Reverend Donald Gray takes charge and notes on September 19th that St. Pauls is changing men.

| | | | |
|---|---|---|---|
| Sept 24 | | | Burial of Mrs. Gladys Follington. |
| Sept 26 | 176/46 | 637.98 | Harvest Thanksgiving Service. Bishop's Pastoral letter is read on Church Union. |
| Sept 30 | | | Burial of Frank Blake at 2.00 p.m. |
| Oct 20 | 6 /133 | -?- | Induction of Rev. Donald Gray as Rector of the Parish. Assisting G. Stanley Sharples, J. Donaldson, H. W. Harding, Stanley R. Smith, F. Lymbaum[?] and W. S??? Baptism at 4:00 p.m. of David Thomas Gray. |
| Oct 30 | | | Marriage of Arthur Robert Cross to Kristi Margaret Rasmussen. |
| Oct 31 | 133/0 | 153.08 | Evensong cancelled as Bishop Luxton at St. James United, Simcoe. |
| Nov 10 | 60 | 48.75 | Rev. Webb & Rev Gardiner assist. The 75th Anniversary of the W. A. 52 took communion. Dominion Life Membership to Mrs. D J. Cornish and Diocesan Life Membership presented to Mrs. Lowe. |
| Nov 16 | | | Burial of Mr. William Smith. |
| Nov 19 | | | Burial of Keith Howell. Rev. Alan Gardiner assisted. |

*St. Paul's Church Register 551*

| | | | |
|---|---|---|---|
| Nov 20 | | | Fire at about 2.30 p.m. Organ and Men's choir room completely destroyed. Smoke and water damage throughout the church. Flag destroyed. Lead in the East window melted. Bible on the Lectern scorched. All chancel furnishings moved to Parish Hall and set up for services. Replacement and complete redecoration required. |
| Nov 24 | | | 12 present for communion at 10:00 a.m. Burial of William Paul. Canon Cornish officiated. |
| Dec 1 | | | 20 attend 10:00 a.m. communion. W. A. St. Andrew's Day Service. Marriage of John Murchison and Fern Meyers - held in Knox Church. |
| Dec 11 | | | Funeral of Kenneth Thompson. Funeral home full. |
| Dec 12 | 5/98 | 110.25 | Rev. K. Brueton officiated as Rector sick with the flu. |
| Dec 20 | | | Burial of Hugh McDonald. |
| Dec 23 | | | Burial of Mrs. Harold Smith. Canon Cornish assisted. |
| Dec 26 | 118/2 | 289.11 | Family Service- Lessons and Carols. Birthday of D. Gray. |

1966 —— Incumbent — Rev. Donald Gray.

| | | | |
|---|---|---|---|
| Jan 6 | | | Burial of Rev. Ralph Mason at 2.30 p.m., in Christ church, Vittoria. Geo. C. Suell assisted. |
| Jan 30 | 114/4 | 199.15 | Joined at 11.00 by J. H. Vardy, who preached and United Church choir. |
| Feb 13 | 86/6 | 84.45 | Rev John Callender preached at matins, exchange with Presbyterians. |
| Feb 27 | 149/17 | 237.85 | Parade of Sea Scouts at matins. |
| Mar 20 | 117/12 | 340.40 | Last entry in this Register. 3rd Sunday in Lent. |

March 27th, 1966 to February 26th, 1975.

| | | | |
|---|---|---|---|
| Mar 27 | 200/0 | 322.85 | Reopening of the Church following the fire on November 20th,1965. Rev. K. C. Bolton preached. Evening service cancelled in orrder that the Rector and Confirmation class could attend "American Folk Mass" in Brantford. |
| Apr 6 | | | Burial of Mrs. Sadie Thompson, choir member for 60 years. 85 attend. |
| Apr 22 | | | Burial of Bob Bloye. L. Owen assisted. 150 mourners. |
| Apr 26 | | | Burial of Melvin Fletcher. 120 mourners. |
| May 1 | | | Baptism - ? May 4th Installation of new members of Chancel Guild. |
| May 14 | | | Marriage of Wanda Powell & Peter Bell. 150 attend. |
| May 17 | | | Burial of William Powell – suicide. 130 mourners. |
| May 22 | 135/10 | 170.98 | Baptism of Lynda Diane Kilpatrick. Rev Gardiner assisted. 15 attend. |
| May 25 | | | Wednesday service cancelled – Deanery Service in Delhi. |
| May 29 | 228/15 | 222.75 | Confirmation by George Huron. Interment of earlier cremations. Eleanor Mae Phipps and Mrs. Silverthorne. |
| June 5 | 198/6 | 676.90 | Canon Cornish assisted & preached on occasion of his 60th Anniversary of his ordination and on his 90th birthday. |
| June 19 | 124/14 | 115.25 | Baptism at 3.00 p.m. of Kelly Louise Longe. 8 attend. |
| July 3rd to Aug 3rd | | | Rev. K. Brueton officiates for most services while Rector on vacation. On July 16 Rev. Gray performs marriage of James Vernon Kelly and Carol Joyce Howell. He also takes the 8.00 a.m. communions on July10, 17th, 24th, & 31st. On July 30th Rev. D Gray & Rev. Malcolm Muth officiated at the burial of Mrs. Glen Ryerse. |
| Aug 7 | 77/9 | 112.70 | Canon D. J. Cornish assisted as well as taking the Aug 10th Wed. service. |
| Aug 14 | 102/4 | 373.85 | Rev. E. H. Miles officiated at matins. |
| Aug 17 | | | Burial of Miss Clara Mason. 40 mourners. |
| Aug 20 | | | Marriage of Lee Buffin & Barbara Goodall. 150 attend. |

| Aug 28 | 134/5 | 108.33 | Baptism of Scott Lariviere. Sept 7th Canon Cornish took Wed. service |
| Sept 11 | 197/12 | 308.40 | Dedication of the new organ. Organ recital with Mr. Peter Coates. |
| Sept 18 | 108/45 | 179.43 | Meeting of the Canadian Bible Society at matins, Rev W. H. Moore gave a 45 minute sermon. Sept. 25 Burial at 2.00 p.m. of Lili Spain, at Thompson Funeral Home. 79 mourners. |
| Oct 2 | 157/35 | 557.25 | Harvest Thanksgiving. Rev. Alan Gardiner preached the sermon. |
| Oct 4 | | | Burial of Captain Oliver Cromwell. 125 mourners. |
| Oct 15 | | | Host to a day Conference - Mrs. Mildred Robertson - of the Central Area Diocesan Chancel Guild. |
| Oct 22 | | | Marriage of Carol Baker & Larry Hopper. 125 attend. |
| Nov 10 | | | Burial of Art Thompson, who served for 14 years as Warden of St. Pauls. Canon D. J. Cornish assisted. First use of new Vestry & Furnishings. |
| Nov 12 | | | Marriage of Clarence Finch & Susan Gash. 100 attend. |
| Nov 20 | 137/9 | 228.70 | Rev. Herb Heming officiated at matins& evensong. |
| Nov 27 | 112/300 | 123.75 | A Youth Service was held by Rev. Gray for the youth of St. Paul's & Grace United. No Collection received. Over 300 in the Congregation. It was thought to be a record number, with all seated and none turned away. |
| Dec 9 | | | Marriage of Gloria Champion & Bernard Smuck. 100 attend. |
| Dec 17 | | | Burial of Rita Parker. 200 mourners. |
| Dec 18 | 120/0 | 316.28 | Service held in Johnson Nursing Home at 2.00 p.m. Baptism at 4:00 p.m. no name given. Carol service in Grace United at 7.00 p.m. |

1967 —— Incumbent Reverend Donald Grey.

| Jan 1 | 97/10 | 289.10 | New Years Day. Bishop George Huron held Re-dedication Service. |
| Feb | 19 238/6 | 175.47 | Youth Service. Scouts, Guides, Brownies & Rangers attend. |
| Mar 13 | | | Burial of Mrs. John S. Lilian Martin. |
| Apr 6 | | | Burial of infant daughter of Mr. & Mrs. Wayne Talbot. |
| Apr 9 | ? | 0.0 | Adult baptism of William Marsh, Eric Watson, Ted Rowlings & Mrs. Mabel Ford. |
| Apr 10 | | | Burial of William Ivey at Thompson Funeral Home. |
| Apr 14 | | | Burial of Mrs. Victoria Richardson. 225 mourners. |
| Apr 15 | | | Baptism at 9:00 a.m. of James Maytham. Marriage at 2:00 p.m. of Musselman & Garrett by Canon D.J. Cornish. |
| Apr 16 | 258/10 | 281.97 | Confirmation Service by H. F. Appleyard, Bishop of Georgian Bay. |
| Apr 30 | 129/140 | 330.50 | Ladies Choir of St John's Church, Kitchener at evensong. Also the I.O.O.F Lodge & Rebeccas. |
| May 6 | | | Marriage of Alan Misner & Ruth Sullivan. 125 attend. |
| May 9 | | | Burial of Harry Hussie [sic] [Hussey]. Canon Cornish assists. |
| May 13 | | | Marriage of Ronald McIsaac & Brenda Harnick |
| June 1 | | | Burial of Tom Stedman. 95 mourners. |
| June 11 | 87/9 | 164.65 | Bruce Reid gave the sermon at 11.00 a.m. Rev H. D. Herring off. At 7.00 |
| June 23 | | | Marriage of Douglas Howden & Barbara Bloye in Vittoria. |
| June 30 | | | Marriage of Gerry Rauckman & Lynda ? |
| July 5 | | | Burial of Charles Bridgewater. |
| July 7 | | | Burial of Miss Lydia Lundy. Interment in Vanessa. 45 mourners. |
| July 19 | | | Burial of Mrs. Lydia MacLaughten. |
| July 22 | 131/7 | 229.70 | Marriage of George Field & Carman Tejada at 12.00 p.m. |
| Aug 2nd to Aug 30th | | | Vacation for the Rector. Rev. K. Brueton officiated at most services, assisted by Rev. J. Donaldson, Rev K. J. Caudwell & Canon Cornish. There was one baptism noted, no name, and Banns noted - Aug 13th. |

St. Paul's Church Register 553

| | | | |
|---|---|---|---|
| Oct 1 | 106/0 | 654.30 | Service of Harvest Thanksgiving. Oct 8th National Thanksgiving service. |
| Oct 27 | | | Burial of Mrs. Nellie Nall. Interment in Simcoe. |
| Oct 29 | 165/10 | 269.87 | Baptism, no name. Rev. Ray K Turrell preached. Canon Cornish assisted. |
| Nov 19 | | | Layman's Sunday. [No other entry as to attendance or collection.] |
| Nov 26 | 150/11 | 682.90 | Rev. Bill Straw officiated. |
| Dec 3 | | | Baptism of adult - Miss Betty Wales. |
| Dec 30 | | | Marriage of John Blakemore & Elizabeth Cornish. Canon Cornish assists. |

1968 —— Incumbent – Reverend Donald Gray.

| | | | |
|---|---|---|---|
| Jan 3 | | | No Wednesday Service – no explanation. |
| Jan 19 | | | Burial of Albert Hopkins. |
| Feb 5 | | | Marriage of McLutee [?]   also a note - Window installed. |
| Feb 9 | | | Burial of William Jordan. |
| Feb 11 | 168/11 | 436.91 | Dedication of new East Window by Bishop H. F. Appleyard. |
| Feb 21 | | | Private Communion at Mrs. W. H. Barrett's for 4 communicants. |
| Feb 24 | | | Marriage of Clarence Teeple & Betty Wales |
| Feb 22 | | | Interment of Mrs. Nancy Forney Skey by Canon Cornish. |
| Feb 17 | | | Interment of Mrs. Morley Catherine Homer Buck by Canon Cornish. |
| Mar17 | 137/10 | 203.12 | Adult Baptism of 3 young men. |
| Apr 1 | 130 | 59.17 | Confirmation by Bishop George Huron at 7.30 p.m. - a Monday. |
| Apr 7 | 170/? | 207.41 | At 7.30 a Cantata - Olivet to Calvary -J.H. Mander, United Church Choir |
| Apr 5 | | | Marriage of Bernard Dawtry & Wendy Walker. |
| Apr 12 | Good Friday - | | 3 hour Meditation: 80 began – 10 at the end. |
| Apr 17 | | | This marks the last entry by Rev. Donald Gray, with a private communion for 5 and at the Johnson Nursing Home. |
| Apr 20 | | | Marriage of Wayne & Susan Teeple at 2.30 by Rev. J. Donaldson - full. |
| Apr 21 | 12/77 | 0.0 | Rev. L. A. Nelles officiated for 8.00 a.m. & 11.00 a.m. services. |

1968 — April 28th — Reverend Douglas S. Henry first signs as officiant for St. Pauls.

| | | | |
|---|---|---|---|
| Apr 28 | 109/8 | 217.95 | The entries are very neat and precise and more legible. In the remarks column H[arold] G. Schilz & S[tewart] K. Long sign as Wardens? |
| May 18 | | | Marriage of Robert John Fuller & Columba Bianca Chimisso. |
| May 22 | | | Adult baptism of Robert Earl Awde. |
| June 1 | | | Marriage of Thomas Robert White & Carol Elizabeth Ford. |
| June 22 | | | Marriage of Terry Pemberton Parkinson & Shirley Anne Oakes. |
| June 23 | 86/7 | 194.50 | Baptism of Jennifer Anne, dau. of John Ronald Beamer & Sheila, his wife Born in Simcoe on April 11th, 1968. |
| July 19 | | | Marriage of John David Lloyd & Gloria Jean Taylor. |
| July 20 | | | Marriage of David Arthur Sullivan & Linda Faye Wingrove |
| Aug 4 | 110/9 | 262.09 | Canon D. J. Cornish assisted and signed the Preacher column. |
| Aug 17 | | | Marriage of John David Waind & Wendy June Hallam. |
| Aug 19 | | | Marriage of Howard Leo Deming & Evelyn Ilene Franks in Vittoria. |
| Aug 25 | 59/5 | 103.82 | Baptism of Stephen Michael, son of Robert Leroy Field & Eleanor Mayo. |
| Sept 15 | 92/10 | 182.40 | Baptism of Peter Allan, born Feb.17,1965, & Laura Lynn, born Apr. 8th, 1968,children of David John Nigh & Marilyn L. Wicker, his wife. |
| Sept 29 | 87/8 | 141.23 | Baptism of Kelly Michelle, born Sept. 11, 1968, dau. of Eric Bernard Dawtry & Wendy Anne Walker, his wife. |
| Oct 5 | | | Marriage of Bruce Bockus [sic] & Judith Anne Jordan. |
| Oct 6 | 94/5 | 242.16 | Baptism of Maureen Angela, born Aug. 18, 1968. Dau of Clarence Angelo Finch & Susan Margaret Gash, his wife. |

554 The Parish of St. Paul's

| | | | |
|---|---|---|---|
| Oct 19 | | | Baptism of Jackline Jean, born sept. 16, 1966, Cowansville, P. Q. dau. of Henry Giroux & Helen Margaret Bevand, his wife, at 4.00 p.m. Marriage of William John Ralston & Patricia Gail Stephens. |
| Nov 2 | | | Marriage of William Edward Marsy & Christine Elizabeth Dennis. |
| Nov 3 | 89/4 | 404.20 | Baptism of Mark Donald, born Aug. 9, 1968, son of Donald Edward Ford & Mabel Irene Fehrman. |
| Nov 8 | | | Canon D. J. Cornish officiated at Wednesday morning service. |
| Nov 10 | 84/6 | 895.70 | Rev Clarence W Foreman preached the sermon. |
| Nov 16 | | | Baptism of Roy Henry, born Oct 14, 1943 in East Angus, P. Q. to Lucien Oscar Giroux & Gertrude Dougherty, his wife. |
| Nov 18 | | | Adult baptism. Linda May Smith, born Mar.2nd, 1950. |
| Dec 1 | 154/3 | 169.07 | Canon Cornish assisted at matins & made donation to Huron Coll. 50.00. |
| Dec 7 | | | Baptism of Tia Marie, born June 21, 1968 & Marie Margaret Nault, adult. |
| Dec 24 | 147 | | Christmas Eve communion, 11.00 p.m. Canon Cornish assisted. |
| Dec 29th | | | All services cancelled. No heat or light due to Dec. 28th ice storm. |

1968 — STATISTICS

| | | | |
|---|---|---|---|
| Average Sunday Attendance | 114. | Confirmed | 14. |
| Public Communions | 103. | Private | 21. |
| Baptisms | 21. | Marriages | 15. |
| Burials | 6. | | |

1969 —— Incumbent – Reverend Douglas S. Henry.

| | | | |
|---|---|---|---|
| Jan 10 | | | Marriage of Daniel Fletcher & Linda May Smith. |
| Jan 26 | 73/? | 185.95 | Evensong withdrawn for "Prayer for Unity" at Grace United. Anglican - Henry; Presbyterian, McDonald; United, Vardy; R. Catholic, Lochach. |
| Feb 23 | 113/7 | 257.94 | Baptism of Paul James, born Apr. 19, 1967, & Mary Lisa Michelle, born May 19, 1968. Children of Frances Mary Follington, at 1.00 p.m. and of Michael John, born Jan 15, 1969, Simcoe, son of John Charles Kilpatrick & Ruth Ann Waddle, his wife. |
| Mar 16 to Mar 29 | | | Rev. K. Brueton officiated at five services & Canon Cornish at one. |
| Mar 29 | | | Burial Service for Theobald Butler Barrett. Rev. A. Gardiner assisted. |
| Apr 5 | | | Burial of James Garnet Colman, aged sixty-nine years. |
| Apr 6 | 211/10 | 600.91 | Easter Day. Canon D. J. Cornish assisted. |
| Apr 7 | | | Burial of Hilda Ada Van Dort, aged seventy-two years. |
| May 11 | 102/19 | 252.26 | Baptism of Sharon Dianne, born Apr. 11, 1968 in Renfrew. Daughter of Gerald Charles Swarts & Carol Leota Dianne Hawke, his wife. |
| June 1 | 71/6 | 197.10 | Canon Cornish preached at matins. At 3.00 p.m. Bishop George Huron conducted a Confirmation Service. |
| June 12 | | | Burial of Ruby Irene Jago, aged 67. Bishop H. F. Appleyard assisted |
| June 28 | | | Marriage of Ronald Hume, age 23, & Martha Anne Murray, age 19. |
| June 29 | 160/2 | 294.80 | Children's Service & Parish Picnic. |
| July 20 | 18/61 | 141.75 | Baptism of Lorraine Caroline, born June 30,1962, & Katherine Frances, born Feb 8, 1964, dau. of Albert Byron Collins & Sandra Caroline Gilbert, his wife. At 1.00 p.m. the baptism of Frederick John, born Dec 13, 1964 & Earnest William, born Oct. 18, 1963. Children of Shirley Ann Howarth. |
| July 27 | 16/44/0 | 165.50 | Baptism of Jaqueline Grace, born May 11, 1969, dau. of John Charles Smith & Eleanor Gaurin, his wife. |
| Aug 10 | 13/580 | 238.03 | Baptism of James Nicholas Alcide, born Mar. 12,1969 in Toronto. Son of Morley Gordon Maracle & Margaret Rose Hood, his wife. |

## St. Paul's Church Register 555

| | | | |
|---|---|---|---|
| Aug 30 | | | Baptism of Kimberley Anne, born July 20, 1969 in Brampton. Daughter of Bernard Leroy Smuck & Gloria Jane Champion, his wife. |
| Sept 26 | | | Marriage of Robert William Powell & Barbara Elizabeth Walker. |
| Nov 1 | | | Marriage of John Brent MacDonald & Linda Anne Burcham. |
| Nov 16 | 6/35/5 | 520.10 | Baptism at 2.00 p.m. of Keith William, son of James Wm. Mummery & Rhea Maribelle Robinson, his wife. Baptism at 7.00 p.m. of Ricki Marie, dau. of Victor Herbert Powell & Lottie Marie Robinson. |
| Nov 30 | 13/48/6 | 166.20 | Baptism of Charles Roy, son of Charles James Meade & Elizabeth Ann Teeple, his wife. Also Lisa Jane, dau. of Clarence Gordon Teeple & Betty Jean Wales, his wife. |
| Dec 7 | 8/76/4 | 195.00 | Baptism of Darlene Louise, dau of Stanley Robert McMillan & Evelyn Marie Ewing, his wife. |
| Dec 24 | 81 | | Christmas Eve service at 11.30 p.m. Canon Cornish assisted as he does periodically throughout the year. He assisted again on Dec. 30th. |

### 1969 — STATISTICS

| | | | | |
|---|---|---|---|---|
| Average Sunday attendance | 96 | | Baptisms | 15. |
| Average Sunday Communicants | | | Confirmed | 8. |
| Main Service | | 65 | Marriages | 4. |
| Early Service | | 12 | Burials | 8. |
| No. of Public Communions | | 120. | Private Communions | 14. |
| Average Evensong attendance | 5. | | | |

1970 — Incumbent Reverend Douglas S. Henry.

A Vestry Meeting was held on Wednesday January 28th, *.00 p.m. preceded by a pot luck supper at 6.00 p.m. On Jan. 6th the Executive of the St. Paul's W. A. was installed.

| | | | |
|---|---|---|---|
| Jan 25 | 11/46/0 | 262.65 | No evensong. Ecuminical service at Grace United Church at 7:00 p.m. |
| Feb 4 | | | Adult baptisms - Shirley Lynn Teeple & Gary William Talbot. |
| Feb 7 | | | Marriage of Gary William Talbot & Shirley Lynn Teeple. |
| Feb 8 | 13/57/5 | 208.20 | Baptism at 1:00 p.m. of Leslie Anne, dau. of Wayne Teeple & Susan Olner, his wife. At 2:00 p.m. of Michael John, dau. [sic] of Leonard Smith & Noreen Ottley. At 3:00 p.m. of Scott Allan, son, & Kathryn Ilene, dau., of Bernard Doherty & Margaret Chambers, his wife. |
| Feb 23 | | | Norfolk Deanery Clericus. |
| Mar 15 | 9/66/6 | 195.74 | At 7.00 Primate's world Relief & Development Fund – 415.50. |
| Mar 16 | | | Burial of Douglas MacDonald. Rev. D. Gray assisted. |
| Mar 22 | 17/85/4 | 247.61 | Baptism at 3:30 p.m. of Murray Alan, son of Alan Edmond Jamieson & Dora Florence Williams, his wife. At 4:00 p.m. of Sarah Elizabeth, dau. of Clarence Angelo Finch & Susan Margaret Gash, his wife. |
| Apr 12 | 22/82/24 | 290.36 | Baptism at 1.00 p.m. of Deborah Pearl Guiler, born Feb. 3, 1956 to Ronald E. Guiler & Lilah Jean Porritt, his wife. At 3.30 p.m. An adult baptism of John Edward, son of John E. Maytham & Sally Connery. At evensong the Royal Arch Masonic Lodge paraded. |
| Apr 19 | 14/60/158 | 312.16 | At evensong Bishop of Georgian Bay, H. F. Appleyard conducted the Confirmation of 15 candidates. |
| Apr 26 | 20/64/43 | 178.56 | Baptism of Deborah Lynn dau. of James Thomas Field & Mary Catherine Jamieson. At 7:00 p.m. the Church parade of I.O.O.F. and Rebecca's. |
| May 10 | 21/53/7 | 350.70 | Baptism of Willa Helen & Wilma Cecile, daughters of Wilfred Carrier & Jean Giroux, his wife. |

556  The Parish of St. Paul's

| | | | |
|---|---|---|---|
| June 9 | | | Burial of John Walker, in his 95th year. (Oct 21st, 1875). |
| June 21 | 18/71/0 | 177.45 | Baptism of Kavila Dawn, born Nov 25, 1069, Woodstock. Daughter of Harry Joseph Smith & Gwendolyn Helen Forrest, his wife. |
| June 27 | | | Baptism of Donald Ernest, son of Roger James Simpson & Marjorie Lillian Phillips, his wife. |
| July 3 | | | Infant Baptism of Ian Duncan, son of John Brent MacDonald & Linda Ann Burcham, his wife. |
| Aug 16 | 11/59 | 229.05 | Baptism at 3:00 p.m. of Paul Carlyle, son of Oscar George Carlyle Howden & Elizabeth Ann Crozier, his wife. Also Raymond David Keith, son of Rolph Frederick Champion & Ingrid Eleonore Krolbe. |
| Sept 4 | | | Burial of John Pemberton Blakemore, aged 67 years. |
| Sept 9 | | | Adult baptism of Bonnie Louise Greenslade. |
| Sept 25 | | | Marriage of Victor Robert Lamouroux & Kerry Joan Wamsley. |
| Oct 3 | | | Marriage of Roger Gordon Meade & Catherine Ann Victoria Glover. Reverend G. A. Brooke assisted. |
| Oct 7 | | | Baptism of Bonnie Marie, dau. & George Steven Hardley, son of George Porter Farrow & Edna Doris Gamble. |
| Oct 17 | | | Marriage of Murray Scott Dobbie & Cynthia Marianne Henry. |
| Oct 24 | | | Marriage of Frederick Edward Harris & Bonnie Louise Greenslade. |
| Nov 3 | | | Burial of William Harold Smith, aged 74 years. |
| Nov 20 | | | Burial of Hattie [James] Barrett, widow of W. H. Barrett, aged 88 years |
| Nov 30 | | | Burial of Major Rupert Simpson, of Toronto, aged 89 years. |
| Dec 4 | | | Burial of Jane L. Kindree, nee Dunbar, aged 84 years. |
| Dec 19 | | | Baptism of Laura Lee Lynn, dau. of Ronald Daniel Fletcher & Linda May Smith, his wife. |
| Dec 23 | | | Blue Choir carpet installed as gift of Harold Schilz. |
| Dec 24 | 134 | 124.00 | Christmas Communion Service at 11.30 p.m. Canon Cornish assisted. |

STATISTICS — 1970

| | | | |
|---|---|---|---|
| Average Sunday Attendance | 82 | Baptised | 23. |
| No. of Easter Communicants | 164 | Confirmed | 15. |
| No. of Marriages | 5 | Buried | 14. |

1971 — Incumbent – Reverend Douglas S. Henry.

| | | | |
|---|---|---|---|
| Jan 10 | 9/71 | 212.25 | Baptism of Dawn Marie, dau. of Bryant Frederick Bidgood & Marlene Ruth Phillips, his wife. |
| Jan 27 | | | Pot luck supper at 6:00 p.m. followed by Vestry Meeting. 19 present. |
| Feb 7 | 5/42 | 157.85 | Canon D. J. Cornish assisted & again on March 7th. |
| Mar 13 | | | Marriage of Allan Stewart Kirk & Judy Eileen Longe. |
| Mar 16 | | | Baptism of Robert James Hume. |
| Mar 21 | 13/59 | 206.70 | Baptism of Daniel Byron, son of Albert B. Collins & Sandra C. Gilbert. |
| Apr 3 | | | Marriage of Arthur Edward Evans & Linda Jean Sullivan. |
| Apr 17 | | | Burial of George William Manuel, aged 69 years. |
| Apr 28 | 7/58 | | Induction at 7:30 p.m. Rev. D. W Ain ??, Rev. H.L. Parker, Rev. D. Donaldson, Rev. A. H. Jaud, Canon D. J. Cornish and D. S. Henry. |
| May 1 | | | Marriage of Ronald Douglas Sheppard & Sandra Louise Greenslade. Marriage at 4.30 of Brian Stephan McColland & Jane Isobel Cornish by Canon D. J. Cornish, assisted by Rev. Douglas S. Henry, Rector. |

## St. Paul's Church Register 557

| | | | |
|---|---|---|---|
| May 15 | | | Marriage of Francis John Ivey & Linda Dianne Wright at 10.00 a.m. Marriage of Paul Richard Stacey & Catherine Margaret Robinson. Rev. Ronald H. Hunt officiated. |
| May 24 | | | Marriage of Alan Leigh Finch & Dorothy Barbara Barker. Rev C. M. Neiubull [?] assisted. At 2:30 p.m. the marriage of Gerald Paul Sirois & Deborah Marlene Simmons. The Rector officiated. |
| Jun 1st to July 9th | | | Rector on vacation. K. N. Brueton officiated for most services, assisted by Rev. F. Tomkinson, Canon Cornish and Rev. D. F. Bousfield. |
| June 5 | | | Marriage of Bruce Alan Milner & Wendy Lou Walton by Rev Brueton. At 8.00 p.m. a Holy Communion service to celebrate Canon Cornish's 95th birthday & 65 years since his ordination. |
| July 9 | | | Marriage of Michael Stephan Greg Mayr & Patricia Jean Moyer, Canon D.J. Cornish assisted. |
| July 12 | | | Baptism of Linda Louise Oakes. |
| July 17 | | | Marriage of James Connery Maytham & Debra Lyn Arn. Canon Cornish assisted. |
| July 18 | 8/48 | 214.60 | Baptism of Stephanie Lynne Meade. |
| July 24 | | | Marriage of John Richard Cassidy & Linda Louise Oakes. |
| July 31 | | | Marriage of Gerald Carl Uimonen & Lillian Dianne Wilkinson. |
| Aug 14 | | | Marriage of Douglas Arthur Backham & Marianne Theresa Butler. |
| Sept 18 | | | Baptism by Canon D. J. Cornish of John William, son of John Richard Blakemore & Elizabeth Helen Cornish, his wife. |
| Sept 21 | | | Burial of Henry Albert Batten, aged 71 years. |
| Oct 10 | 18/81 | 448.90 | Baptism of Jason David, son of David Glen Faulkner & Dianne Marie St. Louis, his wife. |
| Oct 16 | | | Marriage of Leonard Robert Toombs & Pamela Anne Lillian Ryerse. Rev. Donald Gray assisted. |
| Oct 17 | 12/50/0 | 234.85 | Baptism of Mark Christopher, son of Roger Bobo & Karon Clement, |
| Oct 23 | | | Marriage of Harvey Joseph Roszlein & Stella Lily Jacobs. |
| Nov 1 | | | Burial of Ethel Elizabeth Jennings, nee Cornish, aged 79 years. |
| Nov 7 | 9/60/0 | 176.35 | Baptism of Scott William, son of Donald Edward Ford & Mabel Irene Ferhman, his wife. |
| Nov 28 | | | Baptism of Cathy Jo-Anne dau. of Donald Harold Lefler & Joanne Elizabeth Buckle, his wife. |
| Dec 18 | | | Marriage of Atilio Crotta & Thelma Darlene Fletcher. |
| Dec 31 | | | Marriage of Allan James Harvey Muth & Christine Gloria Rice. |

STATISTICS ——— 1971

| | | | |
|---|---|---|---|
| Average Sunday Attendance | 94 | Baptisms | 13 |
| No. of Easter Communicants | 210 | Confirmed | 10 |
| Marriages performed | 20 | Burials | 11. |

1972 — Incumbent – Reverend Douglas S. Henry.

| | | | |
|---|---|---|---|
| Feb 14 | | | Burial of Florence Ball, mother of Mrs. Henry Misner. |
| Feb 29 | | | Burial of Canon David John Cornish, in his 96th year. Taking part in the service and assisting Rev. Douglas Henry were Bishop Carman Huron, Bishop Harold Appleyard, Rev. Larry Owen. |
| Mar 12 | 10/80/0 | 379.86 | Baptism of Shelley Ann, dau. of Maynard Youngston Montgomery & Pauline Catherine Nadeau, his wife. |
| Mar 19 | 7/69/0 | 307.35 | Baptism of Michelle Jannetta, dau. of Leonard John Smith & Noreen E. Ottley, his wife. |

| | | | |
|---|---|---|---|
| Mar 26 | 10/88 | 237.20 | Baptism of Julie Ann, dau. of Robert William Powell & Barbara Elizabeth Walker his wife. |
| Apr 8 | | | Baptism of Cheryl Denise, dau. of Lyman Brooks Lowe & Evelyn Jean Reid, his wife. |
| Apr 9 | 10/186 | 471.35 | Confirmation by Rev. A. Henry O'Neil, ABP. |
| May 7 | 11/77 | 207.50 | Baptism of Eric Von, son of Bernard Dawtry & Wendy Ann Walker, h.w |
| June 24 | | | Marriage of Ronald Terrence Desbois & Thelma Elsie Ryerse. |
| July 2 | 13/62 | 298.55 | Baptism of Tracy Lin, dau. of Arthur Edward Evans & Linda Jean Sullivan. |
| July 22 | | | Marriage of Lawrence David Blakemore & Daphne Irene Miller. Rev. Clarence M. Mitchell assisted. |
| Aug 6 | | | Baptism of Cheryl Lynn, dau. of Stanlet Robert McMillan & Evelyn Marie Ewing. |
| Aug 9 | | | Baptism of Andrew Blair, son of Adrian Grenon & Sharon Sutton, his w. |
| Aug 18 | | | Marriage of David Leonard Bush & Kerry Lynn Knowles. |
| Aug 19 | | | Marriage at 1:30 of Barry Francis Smout & Elizabeth Anne Strople. Marriage at 3:30 of Renault Marier & Elizabeth Ann Struthers. Marrlage at 5:00 of Vincent William Joseph Cunningham & Janet Elizabeth Graff. |
| Aug 26 | | | Marriage of Robert Lee Seip & Raye Ellen Watkinson. |
| Sept 3 | 11/42 | 208.95 | The Rector started vacation following this service and Rev K . Brueton Rev. Jim Powell, & Rev L. A. Nelles, officiated for the month. Rev. R. S. Rokeby, on Sept. 24th, conducted a baptismal service, but no name was noted in the Register. |
| Oct 12 | | | Burial of Luella Jane Rosa Hallam, aged 78 years. |
| Oct 19 | | | Burial of Cecil Couke Yerex, aged 82 years. |
| Oct 28 | | | Marriage of Gary Wayne Green & Carole Marie Chabot |
| Oct 29 | 14/58 | 269.34 | Baptism at 11.00 a.m. of Jason Wayne, son of Wayne Gordon Longe & Elizabeth Louise Quinn, his wife. At 1.30 p.m. the baptism of Heather Jane, dau of Ian Barnard Poole & Patricia Maureen Bicknell, his wife. |
| Nov 18 | | | Marriage of Robert Michael Wamsley & Nancy Olive Hurst. |
| Nov 19 | 8/60 | 157.50 | Baptism of Cheryl lynn, dau. of Joseph Arthur Webster & Mary Sevina Winn. |
| Dec 3 | 12/57 | 120.25 | Baptism of Karen Lynn, dau. of Clarence Gordon Teeple & Betty Jean Wales, his wife. |
| Dec 8 | | | Marriage of Dennis Wayne Randall & Nancy Ellen Powell. |
| Dec 20 | | | Adult baptism of Cheryl Lynn Spiece |
| Dec 26 | | | Marriage of Robert Michael Chanda & Cheryl Lynn Spiece. |
| Dec 27 | | | Burial of Miss Edna Elizabeth Sheridan, aged 87 years. |

STATISTICS — 1972.

| | | | | |
|---|---|---|---|---|
| Average Sunday Attendance | 77. | Baptisms | 15. |
| No, of Easter Communicants | 149. | Confirmed | 14. |
| Marriages | | 12. | Burials | 14. |

1973 — Incumbent – Reverend Douglas S. Henry.

| | |
|---|---|
| Jan 23 | Vestry Meeting held in Parish Hall, with 26 present for Pot Luck supper by St. Paul's Club. 23 attend meeting at 8.00 p.m. concluded at 9.00 p.m |
| Mar 27 | Burial of Helen A. Cornish, nee Stuart, aged 92 years. Bishop Harold F. Appleyard, Rev. L. A. Nelles, Rev. Larry W. Owen assisted. |

St. Paul's Church Register  559

| | | | |
|---|---|---|---|
| Apr 4 | | | Holy Communion at 10.00 & Retreat at 3.00 p.m. Rev. R. Douglas Perry, of Jarvis assisted. |
| May 19 | | | Marriage of Kenneth Ronald Gray & Laureen Barbara Templeman. |
| June 7 | | | Burial of James A. Powell, died June 5th, [also] Stephen Alexander Powell, aged 86 years. |
| June 10 | 16/57 | 262.09 | Baptism of James Frederick, son of Frederick Edward Harris & Bonnie Louise Greenslade, his wife. |
| June 16 | | | Marriage of James Richard Follington & Barbara Laura Broughton. |
| June 17 | 11/52 | 372.89 | Baptism of Kristal Roxanne, dau. of Allen Misner &Ruth Ellen Sullivan, his wife. At 2.00 p.m. the Baptism of Christopher Arron, son of Gerald Charles Swarts & Carol Leota Hawke, his wife. |
| June 22 | | | Marriage of Frederick John Schoenhals & Sandra Joan Wesley. |
| July 15 | 8/38 | 149.35 | Baptism of Tracy Lee, dau. of Thomas Ronald Barker & Susan Lee Waddle, his wife. |
| July 29 | 15/61 | 270.95 | Baptism of Eric Patrick Clinton, son of Douglas R. Long & Brenda Rose Havens, his wife. |
| Aug 12 | 16/44 | 187.80 | Baptism of Donald John Thomas, son of Francis John Ivey & Linda Dianne Wright, his wife. |
| Sept 8 | | | Marriage of Richard Lorne Myers & Cheryl Denise Lowe. |
| Sept 22 | | | Baptism of Judy Marie Cooper, dau of George Cooper & Ellen Slade, his wife, at 6.30 p.m. followed by the Marriage at 7:00 p.m. of Robert Wallace Near & Judy Marie Cooper. |
| Oct 7 | 10/48 | 135.50 | Baptism of Dale Wallace, son of James William Mummery & Rhea Maribelle Robinson, his wife. |
| Oct 8th to Nov 3rd | | | Rector on vacation. Rev. L. A. Nelles, Rev. D. G Bousefield & Rev K. Brueton officiate for that period. |
| Oct 28 | | | Baptism by Rev. R, S. Rokeby of child of ?? |
| Dec 12 | | | Baptism of Sharlene Melissa Anne, dau of William Edward Marsh & Christine Elizabeth Dennis, his wife. |
| Dec 21 | | | Marriage of George Walter Smith & Jantze (Jennie) DuPon. |
| Dec 28 | | | Marriage of Stanley Gordon Bannister & Elizabeth Anna Worthing. |
| Dec 29 | | | Marriage of Norman Peter Andrew Huner & Suzanne Maria LaPrairie. |

STATISTICS — 1973.

| | | | | |
|---|---|---|---|---|
| Average Sunday Attendance | 68 | Baptisms | 12. |
| No. of Easter Communicants | 152. | Confirmed | 1. |
| Marriages | 8. | Burials | 17. |

1974 — Incumbent  – Reverend Douglas S. Henry.

| | | | |
|---|---|---|---|
| Jan 13 | 4/56 | 211.15 | Baptism of Gordon Frederick Alexander, son of Wayne Longe & Elizabeth Quinn, his wife. |
| Jan 27 | | | Vestry Meeting in the Parish Hall. 39 present. |
| Mar 19 | | | Deanery Clericus. |
| Mar 29 | | | Burial of Marjorie Hazel [Clarke] Barrett, aged 81 years, widow of T.B. (Tobe) Barrett & Mother of the author of this work. |
| Apr 12 | | | Burial of Edith Edna Lenora McIntosh, nee MacInnes, in her 101st year. |
| Apr 18 | | | Burial of Eva Isobel Eastaffe McBride, nee MacInnes, in her 101st year. |
| Apr 27 | | | Marriage of George Michael Malott & Robin Elizabeth Ransome. |
| May 5 | 14/38 | 177.40 | Baptism of Jason Christopher, son of Dennis Wayne Randall & Nancy Ellen Powell, his wife. |

560   The Parish of St. Paul's

| May 16 | | | Burial of William G. H. Adams, aged 67 years. |
| May 25 | | | Marriage of David Craig Field & Janice Lorraine Cook. |
| June 2 | 17/57 | 408.30 | Evensong at 3.00 p.m. & Dedication of the Cornish Memorial Plaque. |
| June 9 | 7/52 | 285.77 | Baptism of Michael Stephen, son of Atilio Crotta & Thelma Fletcher, h.w Baptism of Walter Robert Cameron, son of Ronald Fletcher & Linda May Smith, his wife. |
| June 27 | | | No Communion service due to Election of Suffragan Bishop, in St Paul's Cathedral, in London at 10.00 a.m. |
| June 29 | | | Baptism of Richard James Robert, son of James Richard Misner & Jean Sharon Haygart, his wife. |
| July 28 | 10/40 | 211.40 | Baptism of Terrence Douglas, son of Douglas Wayne Ralston & Judith Anne Kiemela, his wife. |
| Aug 29 | | | Burial of William Edward Butler, of Toronto, aged 72 years. |
| Sept 14 | | | Burial of Herbert Kendall Champion, aged 70 years. |
| Sept 19 | | | Marriage of Cornelius Simpson Vaughan & Ethel Jean Tuck. |
| Oct 3 | | | Burial of Margaret Ethel Misner, spinster, aged 62 years. |
| Oct 4 | | | Marriage of David Alfred Murdoch Geddes & Vicki Leith Ryerse. |
| Oct 5 | | | Baptism of Mary Katherine, dau. of Clarence Angelo Finch & Susan Margaret Gash, his wife. |
| Oct 6 | 11/174 | 535.12 | Confirmation by Bishop Morse Robinson. |
| Oct 10th to Nov 6th | | | The Rector was on vacation. On Oct 12th Rev. Robert Bennett officiated for a marriage, but only entry was "the church was full". Rev L. A Nelles & Rev. Roy Dungey officiated for the first two Sundays and. D.F. Bousfield for the rest. On Oct 26th, Rev. Larry Owen married Gunter Wolfgang Malich & Wendy Joan Fort. |
| Dec 4 | | | Burial of Herman Ross Hallam, aged59 years. Rev. Karl A Hansen assists |
| Dec 7 | | | Marriage of Murray Joseph Pursley & Adriana Cornelia Rosalie VanVliet |
| Dec 10 | | | Rev. K. Donaldson officiated. Deanery of Norfolk Clericus. |

STATISTICS — 1974

| Average Sunday Attendance | 73 | Baptisms | 7 |
| No. of Easter Communicants | 128 | Confirmed | 16. |
| Marriages | 7 | Burials | 20, 7 in church. |

1975 — Incumbent – Reverend Douglas S. Henry.

| Jan 5 | 7/63 | 215.93 | Adult baptism of Kathy Eileen Hutchinson, Port Dover and Kenneth Lee Balcombe, Brantford. |
| Jan 11 | | | Marriage of Michael Joseph Hourigan & Barbara Russell Barrett. |
| Jan 26 | 4/72 | 259.20 | Shortened matins, followed by Vestry Meeting in the Parish Hall, at 12:10 p.m. Thirty-nine present. |
| Feb 1 | | | Marriage of Hugh Clarence Zimmer & Kathryn Louise Field at 4:00 p.m. Marriage of Kenneth Lee Balcomb, 21 & Kathy Eileen Hutchinson, 18. |
| Feb 12 | | | Burial of Sam A. Morris, aged 25 years. |
| Feb 22 | | | Marriage of David William Berta & Catherine Louise MacDonald. |

End of Registry book pages.

St. Paul's Church Register 561

FEBRUARY 1975 - 2005

June 20　Funeral of Samuel Henry Morris, aged 83 years.
Oct 12　Dedication of Memorial window in Chancel, Gospel side, to Mr. & Mrs. T.B. Barrett
Nov 23　Confirmation of 6 candidates by Bishop Harold Appleyard
1975 statistics - Baptisms, 11, Confirmation, 6, Marriages, 11, Burials, 14, [3 from church]
Average attendance - 49.

1976 — Incumbent, Reverend Douglas S. Henry

Jan 25　Vestry Meeting held after shortened matins in Parish Hall. 39 present.
May 16　Blanche Clark & Harry B. Barrett made Synod report at matins - 53 in congregation.
May 19　Wednesday, Funeral of Janet Misner, aged 67 years.
June 6　7:00 p.m. Bishop Morse Robinson confirmed 14. Congregation 155.
June 27　Parish Picnic at Backhouse Mill.
Sept　Reverend Donaldson officiated for the month, Rector on holiday.
Nov 9　Norfolk Deanery Clericus held at St. Paul's.
Dec 1　Corporate Communion for the Women's Auxiliary.
1976 statistics - Baptisms, 17, Confirmation, 14, Marriages, 7, Burials, 8, [2 from church]
Average attendance, 126.

1977 — Incumbent, Reverend Douglas S. Henry.

Feb 6　Annual Vestry meeting postponed from Jan 30th due to severe storm.
　　　A light lunch provided after shortened matins, in Parish Hall.
Apr 8　7.30 p.m. - Cantata - Grace United & St. Paul's choirs. Choir 19, Congregation 97.
Apr 12　Wednesday. Funeral of Ray Hartley Ivey, aged 69 years.
May 22　Blanche Clark made Synod report at matins.
June 5　Celebrate 125 Anniversary of Laying of Cornerstone. Rt. Reverend H. F. Appleyard, Reverends Donald Gray, and H. J. E. Webb assist.
July 16　Funeral of Helen Olmstead Morris Fort, aged 55 years. Reverend Donald Gray assists.
Aug 28　Baptism of William Barrett Hourigan
Dec 30　Marriage of Samuel Anthony Moore to Muriel Catherine Parker.
1977 statistics - Baptisms, 13, Confirmation, 0, Marriages, 11, Burials, 14, [1 from church]
Average attendance, 62.

1978 — Incumbent, Reverend Douglas S. Henry.

Jan 29　Annual Vestry meeting held in the church after shortened matins.
May 6　Marriage of Richard Albert Durwyn and Katherine Mary Dennis.
June 11　Sunday School picnic. Baptisms of William David Cornish, Christopher David & Lawrence Bernard Blakemore.
June 24　3:00 p.m. Marriage of James Charles Lomas and Constance Lydia Jean Hawke.
　　　4:00 p.m. Marriage of William Scott Bruley and Marie Anne Lise Proulx.
Oct 1　Confirmation of 18 candidates by Bishop Morse Robinson. 152 in congregation.
Dec 10　2:00 p.m. Baptism of George Adam Graydon, son of Hugh & Kathryn Field Zimmer.
Dec 24　Installation of Choir Memorial window.
1978 statistics. Baptisms,13, Confirmations, 19, Marriages, 8, Burials, 7 [2 from the church]
Average attendance 78.

1979 — Incumbent, Reverend Douglas S. Henry.

Apr 14　Saturday. Funeral of Imogen Elizabeth Henry Ivey, aged 78 years.
Apr 17　Tuesday. Funeral of Maud Lois Pickford, aged 71 years, [sister of Mrs. Frank Barrett.]

Sept 22    Marriage of Michael William Murray Saunders and Deborah Christie Copeman.
Oct 21     Harvest Festival. Bishop David Huron dedicated the Choir Memorial window.
Dec 14     Two skunks in the choir room. Both odour and skunks remain on Sunday.
Dec 24     Carol Service. Congregation 110, 89 take communion. Only weather entry: RAIN!
1979 statistics. Baptisms, 10, Confirmations, 0, Marriages, 3, Burials, 7, [3 from church] Average attendance, 77.

1980 — Incumbent, Reverend Douglas S. Henry.

Jan 27     Annual Vestry meeting following shortened matins, in the Parish Hall.
Feb 12     Funeral of Mrs. Samuel 'Francis' Morris, aged 81 years.
Feb 13     8:00 p.m. Baptism of Abbie Lynn & Jennifer Lynn, twin daughters of Donald Keith Howell and Katherine Anita Ward.
Feb 24     7:00 p.m. Fishermen's Service. Sermon: Reverend Clarence Mitchell. Congregation.172.
Mar 22     Marriage of David John Goodlet and Delinda Jane MacDonald.
Apr 12     Marriage of Daniel James Jacobs and Jane Elizabeth Sullivan.
May 15     2:30 p.m. Funeral of Mrs. Alma Schofield, cremated in California. Reverend H. A. Montgomery officiated.
May 28     Funeral of George Simmons, aged 71 years, died in Leamington.
June 15    Baptism of Kristofer David Field son of David Craig Field and Janice Lorraine Cook.
Aug 9      Marriage of Dwick Gordon Townsend and Mary Margaret Burbidge.
Aug 15     Marriage of Bruce Alex Milner and Elizabeth Mary Clarke Barrett.
Sept 13    Baptism of Murray Russell Daly, son of Michael and Barbara Russell Barrett Hourigan.
Oct 26     Celebrate anniversary of Sunday School at matins, Reverend Donaldson officiated.
Nov 8      Marriage of James Bradley Mullin and Julia Alice Yerex.
Nov 16     Confirmation by Bishop Geoffrey Parke-Taylor. 4 candidates.
Dec 25     Matins - 10:00 a.m. No Service! No Congregation!
1980 statistics. Baptisms, 19, Confirmation, 19, Marriages, 15, Burials, 8, [5 from the church] Average attendance, 83.

1981 — Incumbent, Reverend Douglas S. Henry.

Jan 28     Annual Vestry meeting in the Parish Hall. Pot Luck supper at 6.30 p.m.
Jan 21     Funeral of Susan Marie Knowles, aged 77 years.
Mar 1      7:00 p.m. Fishermen's Memorial Service. Reverend Clarence Mitchell assists. 200 in attendance.
Mar 7      Funeral of Richard Pelly Barrett, aged 84 years.
May 2      Marriage of Ross Edward Keegan and Karen Ann Howell.
June 21    Graydon Field gave Synod report at matins.
Aug 1      Marriage of Michael MacDonald and Lilian Augiakian. Reverend Keghan Zakarian off.

1982 — Incumbent, Reverend Douglas S. Henry.

Jan 10     Baptism of Jesse Thomson, son of James Connery and Pamela Thomson Maytham.
Feb 20     Baptism of Leigh Allan, dau. of Bruce and Elizabeth Barrett Milner.
Mar 7      7:00p.m. Fishermen's Service. Sermon by Reverend Clarence Mitchell.
May 16     2:00 p.m. Baptism of Amanda Leigh, dau. of James Lomas and Constance Hawke.
June 5     Marriage of Gary Mark Furler and Roberta Lynn Misner.
June 27    Baptism of Joanna Katherine Elizabeth, dau. of David George Stewart Cornish and Susan Katherine Oswell. And of Mary Elizabeth Anne, dau. of John Richardson Blakemore and Elizabeth Helen Cornish. Reverend Clarence Mitchell officiated.
July 10    Marriage of Robert Colin Ryerse and Susan May Roberts.
July 18    Ecuminical Fishermen's Service held at 11:00 a.m. in Powell Park.

*St. Paul's Church Register* 563

Aug 3   Funeral of Kenneth Leroy Dunbar, aged 26 years, at Long Point.
Aug 28  Marriage of Alain St. Jacques and Wendy Jill Wilson.
Sept 14 Funeral of "Peggy" Vernice Sarah Reid, wife of Bert Reid, aged 58 years.
Sept 19 Baptism of Jordan Lea, son of Gary L. and Janet Lea Greenslade Hepburn.
Oct 6   Funeral of Olive Frances Ward Gilbert, aged 83 years.
Nov 28  Baptism of Allison Lee, dau. of Brad Mullin and Julia Yerex Mullin.
Statistics. 1982. Baptisms, 22, Confirmation, 5, Marriages, 7. Burials, 10. Ave. Att. 77.

1983 — Incumbent, Douglas S. Henry.

Jan 8    Funeral of Charles Landon Ivey, aged 45 years.
Jan 16   Baptism of Rebecca Kathryn Zimmer.
Jan 23   Film shown at matins - Anglicans in Missions - narrated by Lee Buffin.
Feb 12   7:00 p.m. Marriage of Theobald Butler Barrett and Carolyn Louise Clapp Ewart.
Feb 26   Marriage of John Leslie Misner and Eleanor Isobel MacDonald.
Mar 12   Baptism of Christopher John & Jennifer Louise, children of Peter F. & Karen R. Barrett
Mar 13   Baptism of Emily Elizabeth daughter of Ross Edward and Karen Ann Howell Keegan.
May 28   Marriage of John David Wamsley and Jennifer Frances Bowlby Barrett.
June 19  Shortened matins for Sunday School picnic at Hay Creek Conservation Area.
June 26  Bishop Morse Robinson in attendance, Reverend Henry announces retirement, Oct 1/83.
July 5   Funeral, cremation, of Dorothy Mary Blackhurst, aged 92 years.
July 24  Fishermen's Service in Powell Park. Matins cancelled.
Aug 15   Funeral of Hubert James Harold Barrett, aged 70 years.
Sept     Rector's holidays. H. Donaldson officiated for the month.
Oct 1 to Jan 22, 1984. The following took services - Reverends H. D. Herring, F. A. Cook, John Munro, Clifford W. Tomkins, A. Douglas Fuller and J -?- Reverend D. Fuller officiated for funeral of Arthur Leitch, December 9th, 1983 and for Grace Federow, December 14th, 1983.
Statistics. 1983 - Baptisms, 14, Confirmation, 0, Marriages, 10, Burials, 7.
Average attendance, 80. Families registered - 260.

1984 — Incumbent, Canon Keith K. Brett.

Jan 22   Canon K. K. Brett officiated for his first service in St. Paul's church as Rector.
Feb 12   4:00 p.m. Induction of Canon Keith Brett by Reverends K. J. Conyard, D. H. Woeller, R. McCulloch, Harvey L. Parker, C. A Griffin, G. J. Darling and R. Hayne. 250 attend.
Mar 4    7:00 p.m. Fishermen's Service. 150 attend. Collection $253.90.
June 25  Funeral of Alberta Parker, aged 82 years.
June 29  Funeral of Daryl Richard Clement, aged 28 years.
Sept 8   Marriage of Lyle McKnight and Stephanie Molewyk.
Nov 25   Baptism of Brett Butler Harry Barrett.

1985 — Incumbent, Canon Keith K. Brett.

Feb 24   11:00 a.m. Young People's Church Parade and Service. 188 attend.
July 2   Funeral of Katie Powell, aged 95 years
July 18  Funeral of Craig Field, aged 40 years. Congregation of 300 parishioners.
Dec 22   Funeral of Millis Colman, aged 83 years.

1986 — Incumbent, Canon Keith K. Brett.

May 20   Funeral of June Hallam Patrick, aged 66 years.
May 28   Funeral of Arthur Follington, aged 53 years.
Sept 15  Funeral of Leonard Burfoot, aged 66 years. 102 mourners.

1987 — Incumbent, Canon Keith K. Brett.

| Mar 1 | Fishermen's Service. Congregation 147. Bishop Derwyn Huron present. |
| --- | --- |
| Apr 23 | Funeral of Hugh Templeman. |
| May 10 | Music of the Church Year. Choir of All Saints, Peterborough in attendance. |
| June 24 | Funeral of Charles Burcham, aged 88 years. |
| July 25 | Funeral of Andrew C. Lowe, aged 80 years. |
| Aug 21 | Funeral of Frank Barrett, aged 88 years. |
| Sept 7 | Funeral of Stephan Molewyk, aged 68 yrs. Reverends D. S. Henry, John Munro & J.W. Hofland assist. |
| Oct. | Rector on holiday for month. Reverends John Munro & J. W. Hofland officiate. |
| Nov 4 | Funeral of Colin Ryerse, aged 88 years. |

1988 — Incumbent, Canon Keith K. Brett.

| Feb 6 | Funeral of Gerald Clark, aged 76 years. |
| --- | --- |
| Mar 6 | Fishermen's Service. Reverend R. E. Doerr assists. |
| July 13 | Funeral of Kathleen Manuel, aged 82 yers. |
| Aug 26 | Marriage of Stacey Wark and Margaret Molewyk. |
| Sept 25 | Confirmation by Bishop Percy R. O'Driscoll. 144 in attendance. |
| Oct 15 | Funeral of Stella Mitchell, aged 89 years. |
| Dec 17 | Marriage of David Peters and Karen Brett. |
| Dec 23 | Funeral of Marjorie Mummery, aged 68 years. |

1989 — Incumbent, Canon Keith K. Brett.

| Apr 21 | Conference at St. Paul's of the Brotherhood of Anglican Churchmen. 95 in attendance. |
| --- | --- |
| Apr ? | Funeral of Roy Forrest, aged 69 years. Burial of ashes as Roy died in Florida. |
| June 28 | Funeral of Harold Stuart Schilz, aged 92 years. |
| July 17 | Funeral of William "Bill" Smith, aged 78 years. |
| Oct 10 | Funeral of Angela Jones, aged 43 years. |
| Oct 19 | Funeral of Barbara Templeman, aged 66 years. |
| Nov 11 | Funeral of Jason Lamouroux, aged 18 years. |
| Nov 18 | Funeral of Carl Matthews, aged 61 years. |
| Nov 27 | Funeral of Sarah Cromwell, aged 84 years. |
| Nov 30 | Funeral of Miriam Cline, aged 50 years. |
| Dec 22 | Funeral of Stanley Lorriman, aged 76 years. |

1990 — Incumbent, Canon Keith K. Brett.

| Jan 4 | Funeral of Harry McGhie, aged 69 years. |
| --- | --- |
| Jan 17 | Funeral of Carl Musselman, aged 85 years. |
| Feb 1 | Funeral of Byron Edward Forrest, aged 78 years. |
| Feb 6 | Funeral of Elizabeth Ford, aged 90 years. |
| Feb 9 | Funeral of Stella Brock, aged 94 years. |
| Feb 23 | Funeral of Mary Imogene Dines, aged 80 years. |
| July 11 | Funeral of Bruce Reid, aged 76 years. |
| Oct 18 | Funeral of William C. McNeilly, aged 77 years. |
| Oct 30 | Funeral of Helen Nixon, aged 92 years. |

1991 — Incumbent, Canon Keith K. Brett.

| Mar 14 | Funeral of Wilmer Berton "Bert" Thompson, aged 103 years. |
| --- | --- |
| June 12 | Funeral of Hattie Asseltine, aged 98 years. |

St. Paul's Church Register 565

June 24   Funeral of George Tennant, aged 82 years.
Aug 22nd to Sept 4th, 1991 - Rector on holiday. The Rt. Reverend Clarence Mitchell officiated.
Nov 9     Funeral of Louis William Kolbe, aged 96 years.
Nov 22    Funeral of Mrs. R. P. Alice Roberts Barrett, aged 81 years.
Dec 5     Funeral of Minnie Quanbury, aged 101 years.
Dec 23    Funeral of John Thomas Adams, aged 69 years.

1992 — Incumbent, Canon Keith K. Brett.

Jan 14    Funeral of Thelma Anna Thompson Hardicker, aged 87 years.
Mar 2     Funeral of Eileen Longe, aged 70 years.
Mar 14    Funeral of Frederick Sullivan, aged 70 years.
May 3     Easter. Confirmation of 11 candidates by Bishop of St. Clair, Jack P. Peck. 198 present. Collection $2,470:00.
May 7     Funeral of Mrs. Alan Dora Jamieson, aged 83 years.
May 23    Funeral of Susan Teeple, aged 42 years.
June 6    Funeral of Leo James Barry, aged 79 years.
Jun 22    Funeral of Verna Gamble, aged 78 years.
July 12   2:00 p.m. Funeral of Barbara Baldock. Rt Reverend C. M. Mitchell, Reverend Harvey Parker and Reverend B. Burry assist.
July 14   Funeral of Archie Edward Clement, aged 70 years.
July 28   Funeral of Jonathon Alexander Finch aged 8 years.
Aug 6th, to Aug 18th Rt. Reverend Clarence Mitchell officiated.
Aug 15    Funeral of Blanche Clark, aged 81 years.
Aug 27    Funeral of John Landon "Buck" Wamsley, aged 71 years.
Sept 12   Funeral of Ivy May Parker, aged 80 years.
Sept 17   Funeral of Evelyn Annie Reid, aged 80 years.
Nov 21    Funeral of Charles Thomas Ryerse, aged 92 years.

1993 —— Incumbent, Canon Keith K. Brett.

Jan 6     Funeral of Nancy Elizabeth Holloway, aged 98 years.
Feb 5     Funeral of Frederick Joseph Smythe, aged 89 years.
Mar 7     Fishermen's Service and Blessing of the Nets. Sermon by Rt Reverend C. M. Mitchell.
Apr 1     Funeral of William "Bill" Parker, aged 62 years.
Apr 27    Funeral of Thomas Charles Dring, aged 86 years.
May 2     Dedication of the Baldock Memorial.
May 22    Funeral of Martha Agnes Richardson Mitchell Schilz, aged 90 years.
June 22   Memorial Service at 3:00 p.m. for Hellen Mary Bowlby Browne Barrett, aged 70 years.
Aug 27    Funeral of Harold W. Smith, aged 72 years.
Oct 4     Funeral of William John Bruley, aged 64 years.
Nov 18    Funeral of Gordon Misner, aged 56 years.
Dec 18    1:30 p.m. Funeral of Dorothea Wilhamina Ivey, aged 82 years.. 60 attend.

1994 — Incumbent, Canon Keith K. Brett.

Jan 26    Canon Keith K. Brett officiated at services until January 26th, after which he became ill.
Jan 30th to Wednesday, April 27th, 1994 Rt. Reverend Clarence Mitchell officiated during the illness of Canon Keith Brett.
Feb 23    Funeral of Ethel Burcham, aged 86 years.
Feb 26    Funeral of Ivey Forsythe, aged 88 years.
Apr 5     Funeral of Jennie Victoria Blakemore, aged 82 years.
Sunday May, to Sunday, May 29th, Reverend H. D. Harding officiated during Canon Brett's continuing illness.

| | |
|---|---|
| June 13 | Memorial Service conducted for Barbara Anne Buffin, aged 51 years. |
| June 19 | Confirmation Service by Jack P. Peck, Bishop of St. Clair. |
| June 29 | Marriage of Harry B. Barrett and Joan Carolyn Sherk Wamsley. Rt. Reverend Clarence Mitchell and Canon Keith Brett officiating. |
| Aug 13 | Funeral of Eileen Evelyn Osmond, aged 77 years. |
| Aug 24 | Funeral of Donald Francis Ross, aged 76 years. |
| Sept 6 | Funeral of Lloyd Jerome Stegmire, aged 80 years. |
| Sept 12 | Funeral of Mildred Florence Misner, aged 85 years. |
| Sept 26 | Celebrate the 65th Anniversary of the founding of St. Paul's Club. |
| Oct 18 | Funeral of Raye Ellen Watkinson, aged 44 years. |
| Nov 28 | Funeral of Hilton Barrett Yerex, aged 69 years. |
| Dec 23 | Funeral of Emerson Pierson, aged 60 years. |

1995 — Incumbent, Canon K. Keith Brett.

| | |
|---|---|
| Jan 24 | Funeral of Charles Watkinson, aged 74 years. |
| Mar 15 | Funeral of Minnie Aleta McBride Leitch, aged 87 years. |
| Mar 23 | Meeting at 6.30 and dinner of the Deanery Brotherhood of Anglican Churchmen. |
| Apr 1 | Funeral of Effie Dring, aged 86 years. |
| Apr 10 | Funeral of Arthur Henry Sullivan, aged 74 years. |
| Apr 15 | Funeral of Myrtle Gamble Knister Grace, aged 93 years. |
| Apr 26 | Funeral of Alan Wicker, aged 88 years. |
| May 11 | Funeral of Nellie Hannah Hurling, aged 89 years. |
| May 27 | Funeral of James Coffer, aged 69 years. |
| June 9 | Memorial service for Walter Durling, aged 82 years. |
| July 15 | Funeral of Edward Albert Smith, aged 81 years. |
| Aug 19 | Funeral of Florence Wilkinson, aged 80 years. |
| Aug 24 | Funeral of Grace Leaney, aged 80 years. |
| Aug 26 | Church crawl sponsored by the Prayer Book Society. |
| Sept 6 | Funeral of Robert Wilkinson, aged 83 years. |
| Oct 15 | Services taken by the Reverend R. Birtch. |
| Oct 21 | Funeral of Gwendolyn Durling, aged 70 years. |
| Oct 22 | Reverend A. E. Hawes celebrated the 8:00 a.m. Communion service, again on Oct. 29. |
| Nov 29 | Funeral of Lydia McQueen Hawke, aged 81 years. |

1996 — Incumbent, Reverend Robert Doerr.

| | |
|---|---|
| Jan 3 | Reverend Rob Doerr officiated at his first service, Communion Wednesday, 10:00 a.m. |
| Feb 10 | Marriage of Joukes and Hisaw |
| Feb 24 | Marriage of Hanson and Barber. |
| Mar 1 | Funeral of Muriel Misner, aged 70 years. 237 mourners. |
| Apr 1 | 11:00 a.m. Funeral of Aleck Straighton, aged 77 years. |
| Apr 1 | 2:30 p.m. Funeral of Hilda Henson, aged 93 years. |
| May 1 | Funeral of Edith Adams, aged 63 years. |
| May 3 | Funeral of Eva Marguerite Tees, Aged 87 years. |
| May 7 | Funeral of Eileen Louise Garner Lowe, aged 86 years. |
| June 8 | Funeral of Betty Gash, aged 81 years. |
| June 11 | Funeral of Robert Cromwell, aged 64 years. |
| June 14 | Funeral of Douglas Martyn Penhall, aged 90 years. |
| July 8 | Funeral of Lloyd Pierson, aged 93 years. |
| July 27 | Funeral of Victor Carl Ryerse, aged 80 years. |
| July 28 | Don Doyle officiated at matins. |

St. Paul's Church Register 567

Aug 10    Graveside service for Norma Lucille Penhall, aged 89 years.
Oct 5     Funeral of Almeida Rosalie "Babe" Varey, aged 80 years.150 mourners.
Nov 5     Funeral of Florence Alice Watson, aged 90 years.
Nov 12    Funeral of Winn B. Ivey, aged 86 years. 85 mourners.
Nov 25    Funeral of Winifred May Howell, aged 87 years.100 mourners.
Dec 18    Funeral of Leslie "Ross" Oakes, aged 88 years.

1997 — Incumbent, Reverend Rob Doerr.

Jan 3     Funeral of Kathleen "Ruth" Eastbury, aged 78 years.
Feb 5     Funeral of Reverend Ralph Porritt, agrd 81 years, at Funeral Chapel. Rt. Reverend Clarence Mitchell assists.
Feb 23    Church parade of Port Dover Sea Scouts and Girl Guides.
Mar 19    Memorial service for Robert Clifford Scofield, aged 77 years.
Apr 4     Funeral of Margaret Richardson, aged 63 years. Rt. Reverend Clarence Mitchell assists.
Apr 13    Canon George Ferris officiated at Matins. Amy Barker inducted as Server. 138 attend.
May 25    7:00 p.m. Dedication of organ update.53 in congregation.
June 8    Parish Picnic.
July2 – July30 Services by Canon K. Keith Brett & Rt. Reverend Clarence Mitchell.
July 19   Funeral of Pansy Ryerse, aged 100 years.
Aug 12    11:00 a.m. Graveside service for Mary Caroline Champion, aged 87 years. 1.30 p.m. Memorial Service. Rt. Reverend Clarence Mitchell assisted.
Aug 21    Funeral of Ina Luenda Vokes, aged 90 years.
Aug 22    Funeral of Robert Gordon Miller, aged 74 years. 100 mourners.
Aug 25    Funeral of George "Gerry" Hardicker, aged 75 years. 75 mourners.
Aug 28    Interment of the ashes of A. James Skey, of London, England, aged 81 years.
Sept 28   7:00 p.m. Memorial service of the Battle of Britain. Canon Brett & Don Doyle assist.
Nov 1     Funeral of Alan Edmon Jamieson, aged 96 years.
Nov 9     11:00 a.m. Church Parade of Hugh Allan Branch, Royal Canadian Legion. 152 in congregation. Padre Canon Keith Brett preached the sermon.
Nov 22    Funeral of Anna Neilson, aged 55 years. Rt. Reverend Clarence Mitchell assisted.
Dec 1     Funeral of Merle Cunningham, aged 77 years. Canon Keith Brett assisted.

1998 — Incumbent Reverend Rob Doerr.

Jan 27    Funeral of Charles Belisle, aged 72 years. 50 mourners.
Feb 17    Funeral of Margaret Druscilla Ryerse, aged 98 years. 150 mourners.
Feb 19    Funeral of George Smith, aged 90 years, of Mississauga. 50 mourners.
Feb 26    11:00a.m. Funeral of Annie "Jean" Porritt, aged 94 years. 55 mourners.
          1:30 p.m. Funeral of Muriel Lavona MacDonald Reid, aged 81 years. 60 mourners.
Mar 17    Funeral of Gordon Emerson Longe, aged 78 years. 60 mourners.
Apr 15    Funeral of Michael Albert Ackland, aged 64 years. 79 mourners. Bayview Cemetery.
May 24    Confirmation by Rt. Reverend Clarence Mitchell, for the Bishop of Huron. Cong.198.
May 29    Funeral of Ethel Eileen Ford, aged 87 years.
June 7    Parish Picnic. 147 attend.
June 13   Funeral of Reverend Canon Kenneth Keith Brett, aged 67 years. Rector of St. Paul's for12 years, Saturday at 11:00 a.m. Service conducted by Rt. Reverend Percy O'Driscoll & Rt. Reverend Clarence Mitchell. 253 mourners, 174 Communicants.
July 9th to Aug 2nd Rector's holiday. Rt. Reverend Clarence Mitchell officiated.
July 12   Matins by Reverend Mike Payne and George Daley. 79 in congregation.
July 31   2:00p.m. Funeral of Dalton Long, aged 89 years, by Reverend Rob Doerr. 40 mourners.
Sept 5    Marriage of Ryerse and Brown

568  The Parish of St. Paul's

| | |
|---|---|
| Sept 7 | Funeral of Sarah "Sally" Finch, aged 83 years. by Rt. Reverend Clarence Mitchell. |
| Sept 23 | Funeral of Susan Joan Wood, aged 37 years. 30 mourners. |
| Sept 25 | Funeral of Janet E. Monroe Hall, aged 80 years. 60 mourners. Buried Woodhouse United |
| Oct 25 | 4:00 p.m. Re-dedication of Church Building by Rt. Reverend Clarence Mitchell and George Daley. 91 in congregation. |
| Nov 8 | Remembrance Day Church Parade by Hugh Allan Branch, Royal Canadian Legion. |
| Nov 14 | Funeral of Dorothy Mary Muers, of Kitchener, aged 91 years. |

1999 — Incumbent, Reverend Rob Doerr.

| | |
|---|---|
| Mar 7 | 7.30 p.m. Annual Fishermen's Service, George Daley assisted. 164 in congregation. |
| Mar 27 | Saturday 8:00 a.m. Communion for 24 members of the Prayer Book Society involved in a week-end Retreat at Crabapple Creek Farm, R. R. 2, Port Dover. |
| May 7 | Marriage of Robert Swanson and Joyce Kelly. |
| May 13 | Funeral of Beatrice Daisy Leaney, aged 93 years. |
| May 14 | Funeral of Terence Albert Green, aged 68 years. |
| May 18 | Funeral of Aileen Marjorie Pope, aged 93 years, burial in Woodhouse United cemetery. |
| May 23 | Memorial Service to the Battle of the Atlantic. 41 in congregation. |
| June 6 | Funeral of Edward Colman Buck, aged 78 years, of Tucson, Arizona. |
| June 16 | Funeral of Robert "Ross" Furler, aged 67 years, of Trenton, Ontario. |
| July 4th to July 31st Rt. Reverend Clarence Mitchell officiated for Rector's holiday time. | |
| July 11 | George Daley officiated for matins. |
| July 19 | Funeral of James Pettit Biggar, aged 85 years. |
| July 31 | Funeral of Derek William Skeldon, aged 55 years. |
| July 31 | Funeral of Helen Catherine Lorraine Doyle, aged 70 years. Reverend John Dowds, & Rt. Reverend Clarence Mitchell assisted. |
| Aug 27 | Funeral of James Gillespie, aged 76, by Rt. Reverend C. Mitchell, Bayview, Pt. Rowan. |
| Sept 12 | George Daley assisted at matins and was wished "God Speed" in his new duties in the West, by the congregation. |
| Oct 9 | Funeral of Verna Barnett, aged 76 years. Graveside service. |
| Oct 27 | Marriage of Ryerse Forrest. |
| Dec 18 | Funeral of Alice Lorraine McNeilly, aged 83 years. |
| Dec 21 | Funeral of Ronald Gash, aged 83 years, in Bayside cemetery, Port Rowan. |

2000 — Incumbent, Reverend Rob Doerr.

| | |
|---|---|
| Jan 3 | Funeral of Ronald Hinatsu, aged 63 years. |
| Jan 30 | Retirement celebration for Joy Field, organist. |
| Feb 1 | Funeral of Dorris Caley Yerex, aged 77years. 75 mourners. |
| Feb 5 | Funeral of Margaret Mary Elizabeth Meade, aged ? years. 200 mourners. |
| Feb 17 | Funeral of Ivan Glen Reid, aged 91 years. 75 mourners. |
| Feb 26 | Funeral of Robert Thomas Sillery, aged 68 years. 50 mourners. |
| Mar 5 | Dedication of brass plaque in memory of Canon Kenneth Keith Brett, assisted by Rt. Reverend Clarence Mitchell. |
| Apr 9 | Mayor Rita Kalmbach speaker at matins. |
| Apr 11 | Funeral of Helen Isobelle Ivey Lorriman, aged 87 years. 50 mourners. |
| May 14 | Matins. Visit from All Saints Peterborough Choir. |
| May 20 | Funeral of Lily Jacobs, aged 92 years. 36 mourners. |
| June 3 | Funeral of George Leslie "Les" Murphy, aged 64 years. 400 mourners. |
| June 12 | Funeral of Lorna Jeanette Kendall, aged 74 years. 85 mourners. |
| June 13 | Confirmation by Bishop Robert Green, 16 candidates. 179 congregation. |
| June 21 | Funeral of Hilda Florence Brown. 79 mourners. |

July 2 to July 30 Rector's holidays. Rt. Reverend Clarence Mitchell officiated.
July 14    Funeral of Charles Edward Misner, aged 81 years. 240 mourners. Assisted by Rt. Reverend Clarence Mitchell & Reverend Malcolm Muth.
July 15    Funeral of Patricia Ryerse Gamble, aged 66 years. Rt. Reverend Clarence Mitchell assisted. Eulogy by Patrick Yerex.
July 29    Funeral of Margaret Doris Forrest, aged 87 years. 87 mourners. Rt. Rev. C. Mitchell asst.
Aug 4      Funeral of Ruth Frayer of Pembroke, aged 90 years.
Aug 14     Funeral of Allan Misner, aged 53 years. 400 mourners.
Aug 16     Funerals of John "Jack", aged 79, & Audrey Florence Sproat, aged 60. 25 mourners.
Oct 12     Funeral of David Cains, aged 87 years.
Oct 30     Funeral of Anna May Goodall, aged 87 years.
Nov 2      Funeral of James Fraanklin Lewis, aged 72 years.
Nov 5      Remembrance Service at matins. Parade of Hugh Allan Branch, Royal Canadian Legion.
Nov 29     Funeral of Dorothy Douglas, of Barrie, aged 87 years.
Dec 3      Advent Walk with 216 participants.
Dec 27     Funeral of Bruce Lydney McQueen, aged 62 years,. Bayview Cemetery, Port Rowan.

2001 — Incumbent, Reverend Rob Doerr.

Jan 31     Funeral of John Leroy Pos, aged 75 years.
Mar 4      7:30 p.m. Fishermen's Service, congregation of 89. Reverend James Douglas assisted.
Mar 8      Funeral of Thomas Ardmore, aged 40 years.
Mar 21     Funeral of Marjorie Sarah Willamina Diver, aged 95 years.
Apr 12     Funeral of James Goodall,  80 mourners.
Apr 19     Funeral of Elizabeth Grace "Betty" Ivey Strople, aged 84 years.
Apr 22     Funeral of Sharon Powell,
May 14     Funeral of Maudie "Mick" Colven McFarlane.100 mourners.
May 29     Funeral of Mary VanLoon, aged 65 years. 65 mourners. Rt. Reverend Clarence Mitchell assisted.
June 5     Funeral of Kenneth Leroy Meade, aged 80 years. 60 mourners.
June 17    Special Youth Service. Congregation 89.
July 1st to July 25th Rector on holiday. Rt. Reverend Clarence Mitchell officiated.
Aug 3      Funeral of Loreen Augusta Hammond, aged 80 years.
Sept 16    Festival of Harvest Thanksgiving. Parade of Hugh Allan Branch, Royal Canadian Legion
Dec 2      Advent Walk sponsored by St. Paul's. 264 participants.
Dec 26     Funeral of Samuel Anthony Moore, aged 89 years.

2002 — Incumbent, Reverend Rob Doerr.

Jan 26     Marriage of John William Manuel and Sarah Ann VanNess
Feb 3      Services held in the Parish Hall due to ceiling renovations in the Church.
Feb 10     Dedication of Lettering over the arch "Enter Into His Gates With Thanksgiving." at matins. Congregation 152. Rt. Reverend Clarence Mitchell assisted in service.
Feb 15     Funeral of Robert List Wright, aged 82 years.100 mourners.
Mar 3      Blessing of the nets at evensong.
Mar 24     Funeral of Velma Constance Stone, aged 79 years. 160 mourners.
Apr 4      Funeral of Mabel Ethel Howarth, aged 81 years.
May 7      Funeral of William "Bill" Parkinson, aged 94 years.
May 22     Funeral of Velma Ruby Evans, aged 87 years.
June 8     Funeral of Marion Lee Maude Michener, aged 76 years.
June 21    Funeral of Nancy Penelope Drewniak, aged 81 years.
June 22    Confirmation at 7.30 p.m. by Bishop Bruce Huron. 192 in congregation.

570 The Parish of St. Paul's

June 23 Dedication of H. E. by Bishop Bruce Huron. 150th Anniversary of St. Paul's, Port Dover. 225 in congregation.
July 3rd to July 28th Rector on holiday. Rt. Reverend Clarence Mitchell officiated for all services.
July 5 Funeral of Barbara Ivey Fisher, aged 76 years. Graveside sevice. 15 mourners
July 15 Funeral of Katherine Collins, 43 mourners.
July 19 Funeral of Lloyd Melvin Meade, aged 91 years.
Aug 8 Funeral of Alan John Presland, aged 71 years.
Aug 16 Funeral of Kathleen Luttrell Pugh, aged 92 years.
Aug 28 Funeral of Patricia McDonald, aged 67 years.
Oct 5 Funeral of William Frederick Pratt, aged 88 years.
Oct 27 Reverend Rob Doerr officiated at his last matins in St. Paul's as Rector. "Farewell."
Oct 30 Last service taken by Reverend Rob Doerr is this Wednesday morning.
Nov 3 Service by Reverend Gordon ?
November 10th, 2002 to May 25th, 2003.
The services are taken during this period by Reverend Allen Cook.
Nov 8 Funeral of Jane Naoko Hinatsu, aged 88 years.
Nov 14 Funeral of Rose Pierson, aged 99 years. Over 100 mourners.

2003. Reverend Allen Cook taking services to May 31st.
Feb 7 Memorial service for Robert Stephen Powell, taken by Rt. Reverend Clarence Mitchell.
Mar 11 Funeral of Hazel Irene Barry, aged 86 years. Service by Rt. Reverend Clarence Mitchell.
Mar 27 Funeral of Ellen May Hawes, aged 88 years. Service by Rt. Reverend Clarence Mitchell.
Apr 26 Funeral of Dorothy Dell Barrett, aged 86 years. By Rt. Reverend Clarence Mitchell.
May 17 Funeral of Jean Penfold by Rt. Reverend Clarence Mitchell.
June 1 Reverend Brian Wearne officiated for first service as new Rector of St. Paul's.
June 12 Funeral of Elmore McDonald Misner, aged 91 years.
June 22 Induction at 7:00 p.m. of Reverend Brian Wearne by Bishop Peter Townsend & Reverend David Wearne
July 2nd to July 27th, Rt. Reverend Clarence Mitchell officiated during Rector's holiday.
July 18 Funeral of John Jefferson "Jack" Finch, 112 mourners.
July 19 Funeral of Betsy Marion Thompson, aged 80 years.
Oct 1 Funeral of Harold French

2004 — Incumbent Reverend Brian Wearne.

May 28 Funeral of Deane Henry,
July 11th to July 24th, 2004 Rector on holiday, Services taken by Rt. Reverend Clarence Mitchell.
July 15 Funeral of James Oakes, 113 mourners.
July 20 Funeral of John Cyril Meade, 109 mourners.
July 21 Funeral of Stewart Thomas Cline, 14 mourners.
Aug 19 Funeral of Gladys Dove, by Rt. Reverend C. Mitchell. 125 mourners.
Sept 24 Funeral of damien ? By Rt. Reverend C. Mitchell. 21 mourners.
Dec 20 Funeral of David Hubert Couke Yerex, aged 80 years. 117 mourners.
Dec 31 Funeral of Norma Parkinson, aged 99 years.

2005 —— Incumbent Reverend Brian Wearne.

Jan 23 Annual Vestry Meeting.
Feb 6 Evensong, Rt. Reverend Clarence Mitchell officiated.
Feb 28 Funeral of Peggy Parker. Rt. Rev. C. Mitchell assisted. 102 mourners.
Mar 6 Fishermen's Service & Blessing of the Nets at Evensong.
Mar 10 Funeral of Roberta Misner Furler. 182 mourners.

| | |
|---|---|
| Mar 21 | Funeral of Phyllis Irene Nugent, Rt. Rev. C. Mitchell assisted. 40 mourners. |
| Mar 26 | Funeral of Douglas Finch, Rt. Rev. Clarence Mitchell assisted. 226 mourners. |
| Apr 30 | Funeral of Raymond Butchart [BAS] 200 mourners. |
| May 7 | Saturday, Prayer Book Society Retreat, Crabapple Creek. Host Mary Burfoot. |
| May 8 | Men of the Parish provide a Mother's Day Breakfast. |
| June 5 | Confirmation Service at 11:00 a.m. 112 in congregation. Total offering $2,196.50. Evensong – Last Service as Rector by Reverend Brian Wearne. |
| June 12 | Rt. Reverend Clarence Mitchell takes charge for the summer months. |
| June 19 | Holy Communion - Reverend B. E. Robertson. Father's Day Breakfast in Parish Hall. |
| July 17 | Baptism of Henry William Currie. Offering $1,969:00. |
| July 23 | Memorial Service for Carol (Howell) Kelly. 77 mourners. |
| July 31 | Dedication of Memorial Plaque to W. H. Barrett, Rebecca Julia Pelly & Hattie James. |

APPENDIX THREE

# Wardens of St. Paul's Church – 1856-2005

**WARDENS**

| | | |
|---|---|---|
| 1856 | | |
| 1859 | William Inman | |
| 1863 | Edmund Matthews | Ozias Ansley |
| 1871 | A. Battersby | B. Powell |
| 1880 | A. Battersby | H. Ansley |
| 1884 | Richard Stephens | A. Battersby |
| | C. Morgan | A. H. Cook |
| 1897-98 | Lawrence Skey | W. F. Tibbetts |
| 1899-00 | Chas. H. Corton | John R. Davis |
| 1901 | | |
| 1928-29 | W. J. Wamsley | A. B. Hoover |
| 1930-33 | A. B. Thompson | A. B. Hoover |
| 1934-40 | T. B. Barrett | A. B. Thompson |
| 1941-42 | Dr. A. E. Williamson | A. B. Thompson |
| 1943-47 | Alton E. Hoover | Dr. A. E. Williamson |
| 1948 | John Walker | Dr. A. E. Williamson |
| 1949-56 | John Walker | Frank Barrett |
| 1957 | Dr. A. E. Williamson | F. R. Weir |
| 1958 | Byron Forrest | F. R. Weir |
| 1959-61 | Ernest S. Ford | J. Henry Misner |
| 1962 | Ernest S. Ford | C. E. Strople |
| 1963-64 | Ernest S. Ford | Harry B. Barrett |
| 1965-66 | Harold Schilz | Charles Watkinson |
| 1967-69 | Gerald J. Clark | Robert Ryerse |

# WARDENS

| | | |
|---|---|---|
| 1970-73 | Stephan Molewyk | Bruce E. Reid |
| 1974 | | |
| 1978-80 | Stephan Molewyk | Robert Powell |
| 1981-83 | Murray Jamieson | Lee Buffin |
| 1984-87 | Stephan Molewyk | Bruce Reid |
| 1988 | Allan Baldock | Bruce Reid |
| 1989-90 | Don Doyle | Jack Misner |
| 1991-92 | Don Doyle | Harry Pos |
| 1993-94 | David Wood | Harry Pos |
| 1995-97 | Archie Morris | Herb Rogers |
| 1999-00 | Archie Morris | Ron Barker |
| 2004-05 | Don Walker | Jim Lomas |

APPENDIX FOUR

# Some Miscellaneous Accounts Relating to St. Paul's

Entries that may be of interest to parishioners in the year 2005.

1863.
April 6.  Wine for church, purchased & Paid for by O. Ansley, Church Warden.
April 7.  To Pd. Rev'd. M. S. Baldwin in full of his stipend   —   $245.00.
June 5.  Pd. T. B. Barrett expenses to Simcoe on 7th & 11th April to engage Minister. - $2.00.
Apr 26.  & May  Church Collections entered. 96 cents to $1.35. Total =   $7.29.
Jun 15.  To Mrs. Bishoprick for attending to Church 3 weeks @ .50 cents. – $1.50.
Jun 23.  Cash on a/c from G. F. Allan for Timber taken off Glebe land – $8.00.
Jun 25.  Pew Rent in full to Easter from Dr. Marr - $8.00. Also Pew Rent payments by F. W. Ellis - $3.00. N. [elson] Langs - $7.00. R. Stephens - $1.25. J. C. P, O. McCoy - $!.75. Mrs. Dixon - $3.50. Mrs.Dobbs - $1.75. Thos. Waters - $5.00. Mrs. Howard - .63. John Becker - $1.25. Ansley & Barrett - $3.50. Wm. Dixon - $1.50.
Jul 31.  E. Gilman - $3.50. N. O.Walker - $3.50. R. Lloyd - .75. George Husted - $7.63. Dr. Seagar - $8.00. N. Langs - $1.50.
Aug 1.  Revd Mr. Harris on a/c of 1st Quarter's salary. - $30.00.
Aug 7.  Remittance to Church Society ( J. W. March) collection for church missions - $10.63. Pew Rent payments for balance of year from Saml. Gamble, D. Buckwell, F. Jones, Mrs. Clyde, E. Matthews, Mrs. Culver, Mrs. Drope, Mrs. Dixon. Wm. Dixon (Butcher) H. H. Higman. Mrs. Sheppard, Mrs. Mcneilledge, G. M. Buck, Mrs. Capt. Hall.
Nov.21  Account of George Husted for keeping Rev. Harris's horse for 20 Sundays. - $2.50.
Dec 23.  1/4 cord of wood & cutting & taking into church - $1.00. ? cord. - $1.00. Cut & put .56.
Dec 29  To Hussey & attendant for plastering church. - $6.00. To Mrs. Bishoprick to clean up after plasterers. $1.25.
Dec 30.  Pd. T. Waters in full of Loan of $125.00. - $13.02.

1864.
Jan 4.  Rent of Glebe land by J. Stuart, cash - $6.13. F. Jones due bill pd [for Glebe] $21.87.
Jan 11.  To D. Buckwell - 1 Bottle of Wine. - $1.25. 14th, 1 Bottle of Wine $1.00.
Jan 18.  To 2 dozen Hymn Books. $3.00. Pew Rent pmts. begin to come in for 1864.
Jan 27.  Sale of Hymn Books at Sabbath School. - $1.70.
Mar 12.  Donation from Mrs. Dobbs for Widows & Orphans Fund. - $6.00.
June. 23 Freight, box of Wine, - .75 cents. Pd. Rev. Mr. Baldwin for Communion Wine. - $6.00.
Sept 25, Oct 2. & 9. — No Service. No Collection. Mrs. Bishoprick 5 weeks to Oct 30. - $3.75.

Nov. 21  Balance to O. Ansley for Rent of Glebe Land for 1863 by J Stewart [Stuart?] - $30.00.
Dec 25   Christmas Offertory. - $10.95. Evening collection. - $0.72.

1867.
June 27  Pd. to Mr. Bishoprick in full to 30 inst. Wages. $7.50. Glebe Rent rec'd. - $22.50.
July     5 Pd. to {Rev.} Mr. Irwin Stipend to June 30th, - $100.00. Postage to London. - .05 cents.
Aug 24   Pd Insurance. $9.90. Assessment of Bishop's expenses for Secretaries letter. - $4.00
Oct 18   Pd. Rev'd W. Tibbetts on a/c - Stipend. - $71.00.
Oct 21   Pd John Salt for taking down doors and hanging them outside. - $1.25.

1868.
Jan 20   Remitted to Rev'd J. W. Marsh, Secty. Church Society.
         P. O. Order $7.84, Discount - .38 cents, Fee & Postage. - .11 cents = $8.33.
Feb 1    G. Fowler - Rent of Glebe to December 27th, 1867. - $20.00. W. Leaney - Wine, $ 2.50
Apr 8    Pew Rents collected to date - $81.91.
Apr 27.  Pd. Dr. Tibbetts Stipend to June, 30th, 1868. - $100.00.
Mar 11   Sold 21 trees to G. F. Thompson. - $21.00. 7 trees to J. S. Allan. @ $1.25. – $8.75.
Aug 16   Pew Rents this quarter. - $67.75. Dec. 30 Pew Rents this quarter. - $71.75.
Aug 23   Pd. McCarty - Wood. - $6.25. Pd. Kelly - cutting wood. $1.88. W. Leaney, Wine - $4.00.
Dec 1.   Pd. Varey's account. - $20.00.   Pd. Wm. Bagley for load of wood. - $2.00.

1869.
Jan 1    Pd. Dr. Tibbett's Stipend to Jan. 1st, 1869. - $100.00
Mar 28   Pd. Cas[t]leton - Planting 11 trees in ground. $1.80. Pd. - Shade for Pulpit Lamp, $3.00.
Mar 29   Pd Mrs. Bishoprick in full 52 weeks. - $39.00. Also 3 days work scrubbing. - $2.25.
Mar 29   Pew rents to Easter 1869. - $65.50. Rent of Glebe [lands]. - $20.00.
Mar 30   Pd. Rev'd Dr. Tibbett's Stipend to date. - $100.00.   Pd. Blacking for Stoves. - .25 cents.
June 2   Pd. E. G. Hart for 200 Blank Receipts. - $1.50. Pd. Caselton for trees - $2.85.
June 12  From Mr. G. Carpenter, Rent of Glebe [land] due Apr. 1st. - $22.50.
Aug 7    Pd. S. Gamble for new Insurance Policy. - $1.50.  Pd. Ins. Premium, 1868/69. $3.69.
Aug 17   Pd. Wm. Turner for Holder for Pulpit Lamp. - .50 cents.
Aug 18   Received from B. Powell for trees sold off Glebe during his term of office to
         G. Eagles - $4.00. Pd. William Leaney for Communion Wine. - $1.00.
Oct 27   Pd. Nobert McKittrick for fencing the trees at the Church. - $1.75.
Dec 17   From L. Skey - Nett proceeds of Concert. - $52.82.
Dec 31   To Pew Rents collected since Sept 30th, as per separate account. - $66.00

1870.
Feb 13   Collected this morning for Church Society. - $11.04, in evening. - $7.47.
Feb 14   Paid to Rev'd. W. Logan - $11.04, to Rev'd. W. Bartlett - $7.47.
Feb 16   Remitted above to Rev'd I.. W. March by P. O. order - $18.48. Fee & Postage. - .13.
         Total = $1851. Pd for 2 cord of fire wood. - $5.75.
Mar 2    Pd. Dr. Tibbetts a/c Stipend. - $50.00. Mar 31 Mrs. Bishoprick for quarter. -  $13.00.
Apr 2    Rec'd to Rent of Glebe by O. Sharpe. - $22.50. Pew Rents, last quarter. $67.00.
Apr 11   Pd. B. Powell's a/c. $8.41. Repairs to Roof. - $1.70. Communion Wine. - .50.
May 2    To R. McKitterick, repairs to Church. - $7.00. To Dr. Tibbetts, Stipemd. $50.00.
Jun 27   To W. Hall for shingles. - $3.37. Repair by C. L Thomas. - $2.00.
Jul 18   To Dr. Tibbetts expenses attending Synod. - June 1869 - $10.00. June 1870 - $10.00.
Jul 22   To Robert Wood for Lumber. - $7.52. New fence & repair of it. - $5.75
Aug 3    To Rev. Dr. Tibbetts stipend. - $50.00.  To L. Skey for Wine. - $1.00.

Sep 30  Pew Rents collected to date. $32.80. Church collection this quarter. - $32.80.
Nov 7   Pd. B. Vary [sic] for repair of outside of Church. - $6.50. Bolt for door. - .25 cents.
Nov 29  Collected by Mr. L. Skey in aid of church funds, as per list. - $45.50.
Dec 31  Pd Dr. Tibbetts a/c Stipend. - $50.00. Dec 23. Found in church decorations by
        Dr. Tibbetts. - .25 cents. Pew Rent collections. - $66.50.
Dec. 6th, 1879 – Captain Shaw's estimate for work on Spire: Lumber - $3.35, Iron Straps etc. - $2.30, Spikes - $0.65, Work Hire of Screws etc - $18.00. Total = $24.30.
April 12th, 1880 - Agreed with Captain Shaw to go to work at once, according to Specification, for the above price. ALS.


Port Dover, a/c June, 1880.
    Received from A. Battersby the sum of Seventy-five ($75.)
    Dollars a/c my stipend in full to 30th, Instant.
                             Signed Wm. B. Evans.


St. Paul's Church in a/c with Lawrence Skey.
| | |
|---|---|
| Dr. June 1880 - To attend Meeting of Synod as Lay Delegate. | $3.00. |
| Nov. 30. - To Paid Insurance on S [unday] S. [chool] House Insured for $400.00 @ .60 [cents] | $2.40 |
| Total | $6.40 |

Received payment in full, 19th, March. 1881 – Signed Lawrence Skey.


Port Dover, October 1st, 1880.

I hereby agree to sweep and dust St. Paul's Church at least once a week and at other times if necessary , to light the stoves and to attend to them so as to have the church comfortable during service on Sundays or any other day when used. To light a [nd] clean the lamps when necessary. To blow the organ at morning and evening service also on practice evenings. To cut the wood for the vestry stove. To keep the stove clean. To keep the church grounds clean and the walks clear of snow during the winter.

All this I agree to attend to properly on receipt of $2.50 per month from May 1st to November 1st and $3.00 per month from November 1st to May 1st.
                       Signed – William Leaney.
                       Witness – L. Skey.


Port Dover, October 25th, 1880.
    St. Paul's Church, Dr. to Wm. Collier, 2 & 1350/2000 tons [of coal] @ $6.50.
    Nov. 4th, 1880 — Rec. Payment. Signed H. Morgan

Port Dover, February 14th, 1881.
    Received eight dollars thirty-five cents collected in Church yesterday for Sunday School purposes. $8.34.                    Signed.  Lawrence Skey.

Port Dover, March 29th, 1881.
St. Paul's Church. In account with J. McBride, Dispensing Chemist, Dealer in Drugs, Chemicals, Stationary, Wallpaper, Fancy goods, etc. — Pure wines and liquors for medicinal purposes.
Between October 2nd 1880 & April 4th 1881 Coal Oil in the amount of 2 or 3 gallons a time @ 20 cents a gallon, had been ordered 24 times. 3 wicks @ 5 cents and 2 lamp chimneys @ 10 cents had also been purchased for a total of $8.59. Paid April 4th, 1881.
Recd. Payment. Signed J. McBride, per Taylor.


Port Dover, Ont. November 5th, 1883
Received of Rich. Stephens, Warden of St. Paul's Church, $3.50 in full of caretaking of church to the 30th, Sept. — and $5.00 in full of caretaking of church - and cleaning stove pipes - and replacing outside windows - to the 31st of October.
Signed : Sydney Hodge.


June 5th, 1884.
At a Meeting of the Congregation of St. paul's Church called by the Wardens, on Monday evening of the 12th inst. : It was resolved.
That certain necessary repairs to the Church and fence round the church grounds should be made, and a subscription list circulated for voluntary contributions to meet necessary expenses in carrying out the above resolution.

| A. Battersby - Paid | $10.00 | Mrs. A. C. Wells - Paid | $10.00 |
|---|---|---|---|
| Lawrence Skey - Paid | $ 3.00 | Wm. F. Tibbetts - Paid | $ 2.00 |
| N. B. Scofield - Paid | $ 2.00 | T. B. Barrett - Paid | $ 2.00 |
| Mrs. Fawcett - Paid | $ 2.00 | Mr. [Dr.] A. H. Cooke - Paid | $ 2.00 |
| Crosbie Morgan - Paid | $ 2.00 | J. F. Battye | $ 2.00 |
| L. G. Morgan - Paid | $ 2.00 | | |
| Total collected = $39.50. | | Less Battye $2.00. = $37.50. | |

Dr. To H. Fairchild   —   6 Cedar Posts at 15 cents each - 90 cents. Repairs on fence - 75 cents. July 10th, 1884   —   Received Payment of $1.65.   Signed; H. Fairchild.


Port Dover, June 20th, 1884.
St. Paul's Church in a/c with Lawrence Skey.
Dr. To Paid Myers for iron gate catch for School house fence   — .40 [cents]
To Paid Myers for iron gate catch for Church fence   — .50 [cents]
Received payment in full of $0.90.   Signed; Lawrence Skey.


Port Dover, June 24th, 1884.
Received from W. F. Tibbetts, sum of five dollars and fifty cents for labor done on Church & Sunday School Fence.
Signed; Matthew Hodge.

578  The Parish of St. Paul's

| June 26th, 1884. | Wardens of St. Paul's Church. To Ansley & Tibbetts. | |
| --- | --- | --- |
| June 26th, | To 25 lbs. of Pure Lead - $2.00. 1 Gal. oil, .85. 50 lbs Lead $4.00 | $6.85 |
| June 26th, | To 25 lbs. y.[ellow] ochre - $1.50. 1/4 lbs. L[amp] Black - $0.10 | $1.60 |
| June 26th, | To 2 lbs. Putty -$0.12. 3 Gals. Oil - $2.55. Sandpaper - $0.02 | $2.69 |
| June 30th, | To 3 3/4 lbs. Putty - $0.22. (July 2nd,) Varnish - $0.50 | $ .72 |
| July 3rd, | To 25 lbs Lead - $2.00. 1 Gal. Oil - $0.85 | $2.85 |
| July 7th, | To 25 lbs. Lead - $2.00. 25 lbs. Y. Ochre - $1.50 | $3.50 |
| July 8th, | To 25 lbs. Lead - $2.00. 1 lb. Putty - ,06. 5/8 Gal Oil - .53 | $2.59 |
|  |  | $20.80 |
| July 8th, | By 13 lbs of Y. Ochre returned - | $0.78 |
| September 1st, 1884 | – Received payment, Ansley & Tibbetts. | |

Port Dover, August 9th, 1884   – Warerooms, North Market Street. –
                    To L. Hoffmann, Dr.
        – Dealer in Parlor & Bedroom Suites, House Furnishings, etc.
        Picture Framing Done on Short Notice.   Undertaking a Specialty.
Mr. M. M. Dillon.

| Aug. 7th, | To Casket & Shell | $35.00 | |
| --- | --- | --- | --- |
|  | To Bottle Egy Balm | $ 1.00 | |
|  | To Plate - $3.00.  Hire of Hearse - $2.00 | $ 5.00 | |
|  | To Badges, Pillows and Straps | $ 1.00 | $42.00. |
| Aug 29th, | Received Payment in full, with thanks. | | |
|  | Signed L. Hoffmann / HH. | | |

We the undersigned hereby agree to pay the sums opposite our respective names for the purpose of defraying the funeral expenses of the late Reverend M. M. Dillon.

| Ladies Fund Surplus | $10.75 | Mrs. Wells | $10.00 |
| --- | --- | --- | --- |
| C. Low | $ 5.00 | H. B. Barrett | $ 2.00 |
| L. Skey | $ 3.00 | O. Ansley | $ 2.00 |
| Ansley & Tibbetts | $ 2.00 | Dr. Battersby | $ 1.00 |
| L. G. Morgan | $ 1.00 | Wm Low | $ 1.00 |
| A. Battersby | $ 4.25 | | |

Total collected = $42.00
August 29th, 1884.  By Paid Hoffmann bill per Voucher = $42.00.

1901.
    In the Church Archives, collected & catalogued by Mrs. Graydon Field, are a dozen printed Post Cards from "The Incorporated Synod of the Diocese of Huron" on which the Secretary-Treasurer, J. M. McWhinney, B. A. recorded monthly receipts sent by C. H. Corton, Warden of St. Paul's, Pt. Dover, for both Port Dover & Vittoria.
    The cards have designated columns where each months receipts are to be credited, and they are entered there as received. Diocesan Mission Fund gets March, June, September & November receipts. Widows & Orphans get July & February receipts. Under Foreign is Epiphany, January & Good Friday- Jews. Under Domestic is Ascension & Algoma, October. There are columns for Thanksgiving Day - Huron College. Sunday School Lenten offerings & Synod Assessment.

Some Miscellaneous Accounts Relating to St. Paul's Church 579

Scofield Account

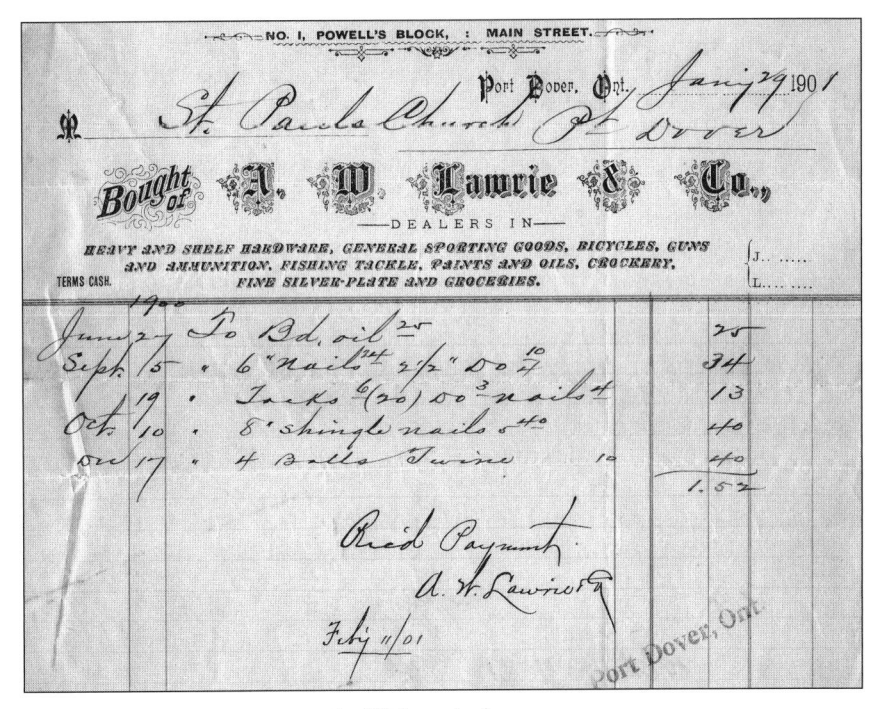

A. W. Lawrie Account

| | |
|---|---|
| Apr 6 | To Church Lighting to Easter 1901, in a/c with Pt. Dover E. Light Synd. - $25.00. |
| Apr 15 | To [Rev] R. Herbert. - Stipend [for the] week of April 15th, 1901 - $8.00. |
| May 3 | To Middleton Thompson, Sexton - Caretaking for April - $4.25 from C. H Corton. |
| June 1 | To Wm. Tibbetts Ry. fare to London. - $3.70. Hotel. - $2.00. Telephone. - .40 = $6.10. |
| July 8 | Received from C. H. Corton, Warden the sum of #4.00 being offertory on occasion of the Women's Auxiliary Service in St. Paul's on July 4th, 1901. [Signed] E. P. Battersby. |
| July 17 | To W. C. Smith, - House, Sign & Carriage Painter. Paper Hanging etc. - Painting with Graining. - $7.00. Hanging 45 Rolls. - $5.50. Painting room. - $2.50, Floor. - $2.75. |
| July 26 | To C. H. Calton - Synod of Huron Expository. 6 Hymnal Companion. - $3.90. 6 Hymnal Chant books. - $3.00. = $6.90. Regret to say, but we did not order Psalters. J. McWhinney |
| July 24 | To Andrew Innes, Furniture, Undertaking & Embalming. - 80 feet of moulding. - $2.40. 2 Screen Doors. - 2.25. R Screen Windows. - $1.00. = $5.65. |
| Aug 5 | To Thos. E Ryan, Hardware. Glass & Glazing, .40. Twine, .40. 2 lamp chimneys, .30 |
| Aug 16 | To Pt. Dover Coal Co'y for 11,400 [lbs] Egg Coal @ $5.75. - $32.78. |
| Aug 26 | To [Rev.] R. Herbert (leave of absense [sic]) 3 weeks ending Sept. 9th, - $24.00. |
| Sept & Oct. | To John Waddle, Pt. D. Planning Mills - Door frames & matched lumber. - $7.92. |
| Oct 8 | To Scofield & Co. - April: 4 gal Oil - $1.00. May: Pitcher - .10. Castor oil - .10. June: 1 gal Oil - .25 July: 1 gal. Communion Wine including Demijohn. - $1.75. Express on above-.35. 2 gal Oil - .50. 28 rolls wall paper - $2.80. 46 ? yards of Border - $2.76. 10 rolls wallpaper - .80. 6 rolls ceiling paper - .26. To Rectory $6.92. Church - $4.26. |
| Oct 9 | To George Hussey for repair of Furnace room at Rectory. 3 ? bus lime - .871/2 cents. 3 3/10 days - T. James - $8.25. 3 3/10 days - R. Austin - $4.12. C. Greenbury 2 loads sand - .30. 15 loads of dirt - 1.50. Lime - .10. C. Brock sand & water. - .30. Total - $15.44. |
| Oct 10 | To R. M. Taylor, Druggist for Wine - .70 cents. |
| Oct 11 | To St. Paul's Warden - Taxes on Block 4D, Lots 22 & 24 - $3.80. Collector M. Hodge. |
| Oct 11 | To Rev. R. Herbert - Taxes on Block31, Lots 10 & 11. Assessed at $1500. - $28.50. |
| Oct 16 | To Jesse Thompson - for trimming trees around the Church & cartage of brush. - $1.65. |
| Oct 24 | To F. A. Perkins for cleaning well. - $1.50 from Mr. Corton. |
| Nov 12 | To John C. Belbeck - 1400 soft brick. - $6.30. |
| Nov 13 | To M. Martin - Platform around Pump, Cistern & Kitchen Door. Also repairs to Rectory - Bed Room, Front Room & Basement. - $4.00. |
| Dec 11 | To Campbell Bros. Simcoe - 1 Floral Wreath. - $3.00. Telegram - .25. Contributions of .25 cents each by the Members of the St. Paul's Church Choir to purchase of Wreathas follows : Mr. Lawrie  Mrs. Lawrie  Ethel Waddle  Jesse Innes  Miss Harris  Miss Hewes  Miss Kennedy  Miss Battersby  Mr. Martin  Mr. Durkee  Miss Mabel Goodwin also; Gertie Reeves - .10 cents. Listed but no amount shown are Miss Ansley  Miss[es] Lori & Venna Dixon  Miss[es] Erie & Bertha Blaikie. - $2.85. |
| Dec 21 | Received from Mr. Corton. - $1.00. For washing surplices four times. |
| Dec 16 | To Canadian Church Magazine for 40 copies Can. Ch. Journal @ .08 cents. - $3.20. |
| Dec 31 | To Upper Canada Tract Society for 15 Children's Friend. - $3.00. 25 Children's Own Magazine. - $2.50. Sent to Mr. L. Skey. |

Some Miscellaneous Accounts Relating to St. Paul's Church  581

L. G. Morgan Account

McQueen Account

Appendix Five

# Warden's 1863 Report

A Report of the Church Wardens of St. Paul's Church, Port Dover, to the existing Committee of the Church Society of the Diocese of Huron.

The Church Wardens of St. Paul's beg respectfully to report that the Mission Fund for the present year, [1863], is $38.86. The amount is less than they would desire to have it, is yet greater than that of any previous year. There is therefore good reason for congratulations.

The Wardens feel it also incumbent upon them to report, that many causes have combined to limit the ability of the congregation to extend greater aid to the Missionary Fund.

During the past year contributions have been solicited for lighting the Church, for the liquidation of old debts, for aid to other funds in connection with the Church Society, for relief of suffering operatives of Great Britain and other objects, and all of these have been responded to in a spirit of liberality by the congregation, and added to these circumstances this is the first year that a resident Minister has been appointed solely to this place — — the congregation of Vittoria having been previously united with this in furnishing the salary of the Minister. The Church Wardens therefore cannot but congratulate the congregation on the increased amount, small as it is, to the Mission Fund.

This congregation is as yet in its nonage, having been able only the last ten years to attempt to walk alone, and its steps which were at first tottering, now begin to assume a firm and steady pace, showing that it is approaching the end of its minority, and the stamina exhibited in youth, gives promise of a strong and ingenious full age.

The Wardens beg to submit to the Committee and the Congregation the following accounts and disbursements during the year ending Easter 1863.

| | | |
|---|---|---|
| Erection of Church Fence | $ 55.00 | L. S. S. |
| Paid for extra lamps, etc | $ 25.00 | |
| Collections at Offertory | $ 80.00 | |
| Mission and other Funds to date | $ 25.00 | |
| Suff's operatives of Great Britain | $ 71.00 | |
| Sabbath School Library Stove, etc, etc. abt. | $ 25.00 | |
| Collected by the Ladies for the Church Society, for the present year | $ 38.84 | |
| | | |
| Total | $ 319.84 | |
| Collection at the Committee meeting | $ 6.61 | $ 326.45 |

This shows a total of $ 326.45 raised by the Congregation independent of the Incumbent's Salary. All of which is respectfully submitted by;
    [signed by]         Edward Matthews.
    Port Dover,         Osias Ansley.
    January 23rd, 1863.

APPENDIX SIX

# Families Recorded as Members of St. Paul's Church in 1878

* - Indicates those on original pew rent list of 1856 to 1859.

| | |
|---|---|
| *Ansley, | Ozias & Clara Hortense [Langs] |
| Ansley, | Harry W. & Elizabeth,- Ozias Clayton, age 2. |
| Battersby, | J. P. & Eleanor, - Eleanor [Irish] |
| Battersby, | Arthur & Susan. |
| Battersby, | Charles & Maria, - John Palmer, Henry C. P., Edith Beatrice. |
| *Buckwell, | Alfred & Louisa, - Edith, Alice. |
| *Barrett, | Theobald Butler & Emily [Langs], - Emily Louisa, Alice Butler, William Henry, Hubert Baldwin, Arthur Clarence. |
| Bishoprick, | Adam & Catherine, - Sarah Elizabeth. |
| Brock, | Mrs. William. |
| Coleman, | Alex & — , - Arthur, Frederick, Anne. |
| Cook, | Arthur |
| Chrystter, | G. |
| Churchill, | James & Anne, - Ruth, 19, Ellen, 15, James, 10, George Henry, 7, Frances Alberta, 3. |
| Fletcher, | |
| Faulkner, | |
| Griffeth, | Mrs. Ellen. |
| *Gamble, | William, |
| Harris, | E. |
| Hyllier, | R. |
| Hammond, | Edward & Prescilla [sic] - Anne Elizabeth, 19, Francis Edward, 16, George John, 13, William Henry, 11, Frederick Laurence, 4. |
| *Husted, | George & Mrs. – . |
| *Harvey, | Mrs. Jeffrey [Catherine]. |
| Hodge, | Matthew & Jane. |
| *Lees, | Mrs. — . |
| * Lees, | Mrs. Andrew, - Clifford. |
| Lawrie, | Mrs. — . - Arthur. |
| Leaney, | Mrs. Alexina, - William H., 17, James B., 13, Charlotte, 12, Robert Thomas, 10. |
| Lawson, | Alexander & Mrs. — , |
| *Morgan, | Henry & Mrs. — , - Lewellen, Crosby, Florence, Newell. |
| *Mudford, | Charles & Anne, - Hannah, Sarah, Ellen, Robert. |

| | |
|---|---|
| Martin, | - ?- & Mrs. — , - Annie. |
| Moore, | John & -?- , - Agnes. |
| Moore, | David & -?- , - Mary. |
| Mason, | Charles & Eliza, - Henry George, 2, Mary A. |
| Mencke, | Frederick & Mrs. — , Alice Amelia, 16, Frederick. |
| *McCoy, | John Prince of Orange & Maria. |
| *McNeilledge | Mrs. Mary Anne, - Elizabeth, Rapelje, Rapelje Matilda. |
| Mcneilledge | Colin & Mrs. — . |
| McBride, | John. |
| Powell, | Mrs. Berkley, - William Beverly, 13, Margaret Christina, 11, Charles Stanley, 10, Jane Marion, 8. |
| Powell, | Edward & Mrs. P. |
| Phipps, | Spencer J. B. & Mary Helen, - Eleanor M. Annette, 8, Catherine Barre, 6, Arthur Robert Spencer, 4, Ethel Susan Frances. |
| Payne, | John & Ellen, - Mary, 14, John, 12, Ellen, 11, William Henry, 7, Frederick, 5, Frank, 3, Margaret Elizabeth, 1, Susan. |
| Routh, | William & Mary Anne. |
| Reed, | –?— |
| *Skey, | Lawrence & Mary Frances, - Kate Anne, `6, William Russell, 14, Louisa Caroline, 12, Lawrence Edward, 11, Earnest Wilton, 9, Arthur Herbert, 7, Duglas [sic] Weston, 2, John Frederick Harvey. |
| Scofield, | Norman. |
| *Stephens, | Richard "Dickie." |
| Smith, | James & Susan. |
| Steel, | –?– . |
| Walker, | Dr. Nathaniel O. & Mary, - Mary Elizabeth, 18, George, 16, Alice Victoria, 14, Frederick Ernest, 12, Philip Drayton, 10, Paul Higman, 5, Emily Annie Gertrude, 2. |
| Wells, | –?— . |
| *Williams | Mrs. Chas? - Benjamin. |
| Waldick, | –?— . |

APPENDIX SEVEN

# The Women's Auxiliary of St. Paul's Church

This vital organisation to the well-being of our church, has existed in Port Dover since December of 1890. By the time this rambling account appears in print [if it ever does] that will be in the order of 115 years. Tracing their record of achievement I am finding is a nebulous, often wraith-like exercise. They seem to have been, since the beginning, far better at doing what is required at the moment for the well-being of the parish and her missions, than of keeping an accurate record of what they were doing, or, who was responsible for doing it.

In 2001 Hilda Butler, gave an excellent report on the W. A's. activities over the years, to the Diocese of Huron. I am more than happy to use that report, as Mrs. Burbidge has already done, as a basis for their activities over the years. Since it was Hilda Butler who plunged me into this historical [some are saying hysterical] effort in the first place, I would be less than diplomatic, if I ignored her excellent summary of the W. A's activities, over the years. Here, then, is the Report to the Diocese of Huron, as written by their own historian, Hilda Butler.

*The St. Paul's Port Dover Branch of the Women's Auxiliary to the Missionary Society of the Church of England in Canada received their charter on December 10th, 1890. They were the second parish in the Diocese of Huron to do so.*

*Up until then, women did not have an active post in the church, but when Roberta Tilton from Quebec Diocese persuaded her Bishop to let women show they were capable and wanted to share the mission of* the church, the women of this parish were glad to organise a W. A. They soon found there was work to do. The mission parishes in Canada needed help.

Bales of clothing and one quilt were sent each year to a mission parish in Alberta. Later we were given another parish closer to home. W. A. meetings always included study – about missions. The members always attended the annual Deanery meeting and sent delegates to the Diocesan Annual Meeting.

On November 10th, 1965, we celebrated our 75th anniversary with a Communion Service followed by lunch in the Parish hall for about ninety people – members and guests, among whom were three former Rectors, who assisted at the service. Entertainment in the afternoon was a skit, "A Backward Look," portraying the history of the branch told by members chatting around a quilt – a perennial project of the branch.

On July 29th, 1987, we held a tea and bake sale on the rectory lawn to celebrate the 135th anniversary of our church. The members were all in centennial costume, including hats and gloves. This event, though now held in the parish hall, became an annual event to help raise the money to mail our bales, which still go out twice a year. We also include a display of interesting items from the past.

To celebrate our 100th anniversary, on November 14th, 1990, we hosted a Deanery Tea with a display of quilts and historical documents. Each branch in the Deanery contributed to the programme by sharing memories of the women's work in the parish down through the years.

We have 16 members in our present group ranging in age from 65 to 92. We meet every week. Once a month is our business meeting with study. For the rest, we still make quilts to send in bales and do quilting for others to raise money for postage and for support of several missionary projects.

"Mission is our Motto."

We know that when the St. Paul's W. A. was granted their charter in 1890, that the Rector's wife Mrs. J. R. Newell was named their first President and that she held that office until the Newell's left the parish, in 1898. For the next 28 years very little remains of their records, due primarily to a fire in 1922, which destroyed Miss E. P. Battersby's house and with it the minute books and correspondence of the W. A. It is thought that the presidency during this period from 1898 to 1926 was carried by two ladies, Miss E. P. Battersby and Miss E. L. Barrett.

In 1926 Miss Barrett was forced to resign the presidency due to failing health and the Rector's wife, Mrs. D. J. Cornish, was named to replace her. Mrs. Cornish held the title for the next 25 years. In 1953, Mrs. W. H. "Hattie" Barrett became the president, to be followed in 1956 by Mrs. H. J. "Mary" Webb. In 1957 and 1958 the post was held by Mrs. Harold "Martha" Schilz and Mrs H. Batten, respectively. From 1958 to the present it is uncertain who the officers were for any one year. The ladies seem to have little interest in sorting it all out either. They do agree that over that roughly 47 year period the presidency was shared by Mrs. T. E. "Hilda" Butler, Mrs. Harold "Martha" Schilz, Mrs. Glen "Olive" Ryerse and Mrs. Len "Dorothy Mary" Burfoot.

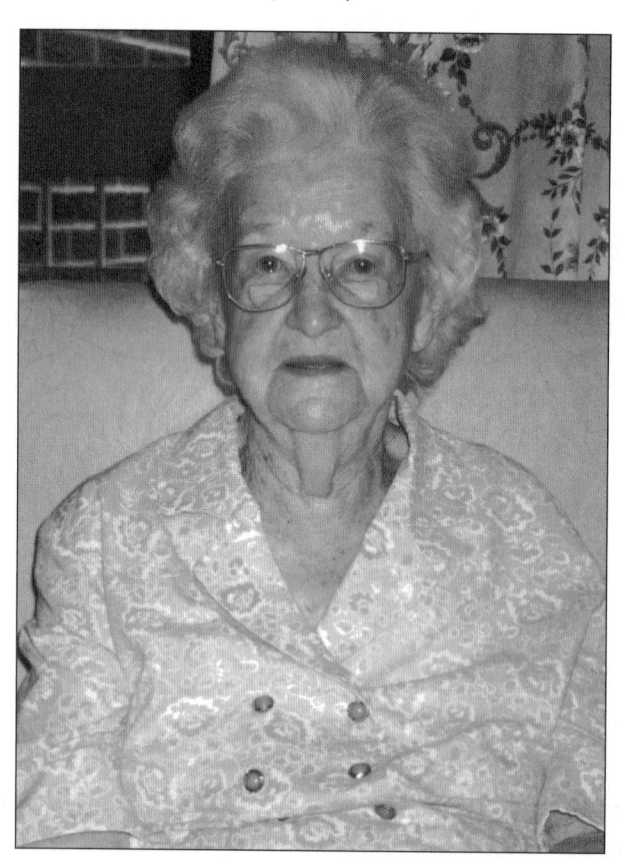

*Hilda Butler*

APPENDIX EIGHT

# Quilts

Quilts were an important part of the life of every household in Port Dover and the Parish of St. Paul's, from the very beginning. Most of the ladies prided themselves on their quilting abilities and the patterns and stitches were as diverse as the imaginations of their makers.

Quilting bees provided an opportunity to socialise and keep abreast of the news of the day, while providing an essential piece of very necessary bedding for the household. The ladies of St. Paul's also found a quilt was an excellent source of funds, if raffled on completion, for church purposes, as well. Many of them over the years were sent to the Indian missions where they were very much appreciated.

In 1914 "The Willing Workers" of St. Paul's hit on a novel idea to raise funds for the purchase of the first choir gowns of St. Paul's. For a donation of ten cents they would stitch in red the name of the donor, or, anyone they designated, into a square of their proposed quilt. In most cases eight names were stitched in each square. The finished quilt which was recently framed and mounted in the Parish Hall behind plexiglass, by Harry Pos, is made up of forty-eight squares.

Many of the donors were non-Anglican and our attempts to identify them to-day has been a frustrating exercise. Many "victims" of the quilter's fund raising were obviously Privates in the local 133rd Battery, referred to as "Norfolk's Own." The names follow, grouped by square, with an attempt to identify them with the help of Georgia Painter. We both ran out of time to cover every name. I am beholden to Carol Pos for transcribing the 298 names from the original quilt, no mean task in itself, I can assure you.

**Square 1** – an embroidered maple leaf

**Square 2**
Mr. George Slocomb - brother of Frank. A farmer
Mr. F[rank] Slocomb - built the base of the Grandstand and early sidewalks of Port Dover & Jarvis, charging 10 cents per square foot.
Mrs. H[arry] Moon - a sister of Henry Misner Sr.
Miss Erie Law
R[oland] Waddle - served on the Vigilant.
Hazen Waddle - son of David (Dave) Waddle. Worked for some time in the mines, in the north.
Sam Morris - WW I veteran, later Publisher and Editor of the Maple Leaf.
Archie Morris - Sam's brother, killed in action. Archie Morris Memorial Prize in the Sunday Sch.

**Square 3**
Bob Moore
Mabel Simmons
Emily Spain
Margaret Fuller
William McCaffrey
J. T. Webster
Ethel Pickett
Edward Balna

**Square 4**
Miss Erie Law - a repeat.
Miss L. Faulkner
C[harles] W. Barwell - Port Dover businessman and entrepreneur. Owned Dominion Hotel, Globe Park. Involved with early gas wells in Pt. Dover with Murray Dillon.
W. J. Thompson
W. C. Buchner - would this be Will Boughner ?
Captain Robinson - Commander of the Fisheries Patrol vessel "Vigilant"on the Great Lakes.
Mr. J[ohn] Walker - Choir Leader of St. Paul's. Agent for Nash autos and owner of Gem Theatre.
Mrs. J. [Lottie] Walker - wife of above. The Processional Cross of St. Paul's is in her memory.

**Square 5**
Arthur B. Thompson - Insurance agent, Warden for many years. Wife Sade Davis choir member.
Liang [Laing]& Son - Owned feed store, now vacant lot, east of M. Hagen's dentist's office.
Mrs. W. J. Thompson
Phyillis [Phyllis] Brock
A. Ross Smith
Mrs. B. F. Jaques
Thelma Jacques

**Square 6**
Mrs. C. A. Austin
Mr. C. A. Austin
Mrs. Alice Rose
Mr. J. C. Creelling
Mrs. J. C. Creelling
Mrs. W. J. Williams
Miss Nina Duncan
Mr. Austin [?]

**Square 7**
Mrs. H. M. Johnson
Mr. H. M. Johnson
Mrs. H. J. Johnson
Rev. H. J. Johnson - incumbent of St. Paul's from 1911 to 1921.

**Square 8**
Willing Workers. They made the quilt.

**Square 9**
Jean Vautrim
Minnie Hill
Lily Fowler
Gladys Shirton
Emerson J. Hambleton
Mary J. Cox
Nellie O'Neill
Mrs. W. Mc Donagh
Jean H. Edie
Phoebe Hambleton

**Square 10**
Agnes Exelby - a school teacher. Lived on Maiden Lane, off Queen st. at the Head of Main Street.

May Perry - sister of Mrs. J. G. "Pat" Patterson, whose husband "Pat" was the Rexall Druggist.
Mrs. Williams
Miss Williams
Mrs. S. Jacques
Mrs. F. W. Stringer - wife of the school Principal, and local historian. Lived in Bara Lowe house.
Gladys Moore
Lulie Moore

**Square 11**
G. H. Johnson
L. H. Barrett
Mrs. C. Martin
Zeitha Barwell - daughter of Mr. & Mrs. Charles Barwell, who married Alan Tibbetts. Soloist.
Mrs. C. W. Barwell
Mrs. R. A. W. Hobbes - wife of Manager of the Royal Bank, both being very active in St. Paul's.
William Barwell - son of Charles W. Barwell.
Mrs. John Addison

**Square 12**
Maggie Ross - her husband was a Veterinary.
Katherine Lowe
B. Graham
Jane Matthews
Fred Tuck - – Rosa Tuck
Mrs. I. Jackson
Wm. Stamp
Mrs. H[ugh] McQueen - Hugh McQueen owned the Norfolk Hotel.

**Square 13**
Pte. Allan Tibbetts
Ethel Trusdale - The Trusdale's, with Mr. Bond owned "The Fair."
Roy Cieberton
T. [Toty] Smith - clock sales & repair, store next "The Fair", which was replaced by Royal Bank.
Quintin Barrett - son of Hubert, ran Barrett & Tibbetts bath houses after return from serving inSiberia in W.W.I, married Gladys Farrar and had hunting camp, near Ft Francis.

Lenora Deal - Clare Deal owned service station at Halfway House.
Pte Ernest Williamson
Sylvia Grassett

**Square 14**
Miss Edith McBride
Miss Evelyn McBride
Miss Lola McBride
Mr. John McCoy - son of James P. of O. McCoy
Miss Maria McCoy - last McCoy owner of the McCoy farm, later owned by Albert McBride
Miss Venna Dixon - married Truman Walker, farmed s-east half Lot 13, Con. 3. Woodhouse
Miss Helen Thompson - daughter of Bert Thompson, funeral director. Owned Furniture store.
Master Ross Thompson - son of Bert who became undertaker with his father.
Mr. George Dixon
Mrs. George Dixon
Miss Lulu Dixon
Mr. Herbert Cook
Mrs. Herbert Cook
Mrs. A. Duncan

**Square 15**— in 3rd row of the quilt. Contains stitch outline of St. Paul's church, Port Dover. 1914.

**Square 16**
Mrs. J[oan] Howell - wife of Jack Howell.
Mrs. H. R. Revere
Mrs. E. ["Ted"] Nicholls - Ted owned garage and dance hall, Market St., now Carpet One.
Miss [Clara M. ] Campbell - taught at Shand's, S. S. No. 12, Woodhouse and in St. Paul's S. S.
Art Anderson - Arthur Anderson owned the Hardware store under the clock tower. Lived on N-E corner of Clinton & St. Andrews, later built house on S-E corner of Market & St. Patrick St., demolished by Legion. Art of tug "Al [Schubert] Mid [Thompson] Art."
Isobel Butler
S[ilas] L. Butler - operated a dry goods store.
Mr. John Allen - Sailing Schooner Captain.

**Square 17** - this square is blank.

**Square 18**
Pte. R. Bleusft [?]
Pte. J[im] E. Muth - came to Port Dover as crew in "Vigilant", married – Macdonald
Pte. Joe Alele
Pte. F. Follington

**Square 19**
Pte. J. W. Spain
Pte. H. Moore
Pte. L. Husted
Pte. J. H. Morris - Jim Morris came to Dover as crew of Vigilant. Later owned the Barber shop.

**Squares 20** - this square is blank.

**Square 21**
E[veret] R. Strople - worked at the upper plant of Ivey's Roses. Father of Clarence.
Jack Anderson - son of Arthur Anderson. Worked for James N. Allan, Dunnville. Legion member.
Thos. McGeachie
Sarah McGeachie
C. A Lyons - father of Mrs. Bill "Madge" Hagen.
H. F. Henry - "Huck" Henry, brother of Mrs. Charlie "Imogene" Ivey. Their father a gas driller.
John Allison
Pte. A. Morris - Archie Morris, killed in W. W. I.

**Square 22**
Miss M. Hudson
Miss E. Hudson
Miss J. Kearney
Mrs Dillon
Mrs. Skey - wife of Lawrence Skey
Miss Newell
Mrs. P. Kindrey
Mrs. J. Ladd
Mrs. J. Kindrey
Mrs. S. Martin

**Square 23**
W. C. Murray
W. S. Strode
C. E. Gamble

Sam Zuen
John C. Kearney
George W. Reynolds
N. S. Silverthorne
W. M. Davis

**Square 24**
Pte. R. W. Barr
Pte. A. J. Barr
Pte. H. Blake
Pte. R. Barr

**Squares 25 & 26** – each display a maple leaf.

**Square 27**
Pte. Peter Shand - awarded D.S.M. in W.W.I.
Pte. John Watts
Pte. W. Paton
Pte. A. Kennedy

**Square 28**
Mrs. John Ivey
Miss Phylis Ivey
Mrs. Bruce Dell
Mr. Bruce Dell - popular Baker on south-west corner of Main & Chapman streets.
Mrs. Alex Millar
Mr. W[illiam] Laing
Enid Walker - sister of Truman
Mr. Truman Walker - absent-minded farmer of 50 acres Lot 13. Con. 3. Woodhouse.

**Square 29**
Mrs. C. Lowes
Lou Howey
Sadie Collison
Marie Howey

**Square 30** - is a blank square.

**Square 30**
W. H. Smith- 1846 - 1938. Only son of Samuel Smith, who came to farm a mile east of Pt. Dover with his parents, as a small boy in 1823. Principal of Public School for 50 years.
H.[ubert] B[aldwin] Barrett - owned clothing store in Powell Block, later Customs officer.
[Miss] M. E. Giles - kept dry goods store on Main Street into her 90's.

W. F. Tibbetts 1852 - 1930. Businessman Postmaster 45 years, appointed 1886. Reeve in 1880.
Geo. D. Smith
Mrs. Geo. D. Smith
G. E. Ross Smith
Ralph Smith

**Square 31**
Pte. R. O. Hickman
Pte Milton E. Cruise - from farm at Marburg, killed in W. W. I
Pte W. Lowe
Pte. E. Brock -

**Square 32 & 33** have embroidered Maple Leaves.

**Square 34**
Pte John Hube
Pte. Geo. Haun
Pte J. King
Pte. H. W. Brooks

**Square 35**
Beatrice Kains
Miss Kains
Mrs. Kains
Mrs. Laurie
Hubert Laurie
Bessie Laurie
Edith Laurie
Mrs. Bell

**Square 36**
Mrs. Byron Brock
Miss E. Hudson
Miss M. Hudson
Miss F. Kearney – school teacher
Mrs. Skey – Mrs. Lawrence Skey
Mrs. Dillon – organist, St. Paul's church.
Miss Newell
Mrs. J. Kindree
Mr. S. Martin
Mrs. T. Ladd
Margaret Oakes

**Square 37**
H. P. Battersby
Mr. D[ave] Waddle - born 1861, farmer, mar-

ried Kate Slocomb. Owned Commercial for 20 years
S[ilas] L. Butler - a repeat.
Alexander Cummings
Chas. R. Innes
Mrs. James V. Barber
E. R. Strople - a repeat.
Winnifred A. Barrett - daughter of Hubert Barrett, married Cecil Yerex.

**Square 38** - is a blank square

**Square 39**
Pte. Henry Cable
Pte. S. Stasa
Pte. J. C. Hargraves
Pte S[am] H. Morris - amputee, returned to publish Maple Leaf, father of Archie, a S. S. Super.

**Square 40**
Pte. Fred George
Pte. Sam George
Pte. Ed. George
Pte. W. F. George

**Square 41** – is a blank square

**Square 42**
Mrs. C.[lare] Deal - Clare owned the service station at the Halfway House
Mrs. Marshall
Leota Marshall
Archie Edmundson - drowned with "Gint" Rankin. Lived in Brant hill house overlooking harbour.
Ethel Trusdale - a repeat.
Pearl Crossett
Mr. J. E. Bush
Mrs. Bush
Norman Bush
Mrs. E. Porritt
Miss Porritt
Harold Porritt

**Square 43**
G[eorge] Bemister - H. Barrett's great uncle. Staunch Anglican of Haliburton, Ont.
Marjorie Clarke - born Haliburton, taught in Pt. Dover, lived with Bagleys, married T. B. Barrett.

Gladys Law - lived 325 St. George St.
Dorothy Clarke - Post Mistress, Haliburton. Sister of Marjorie. Father Harry Hawkins Clarke.
E. G. Bain - sister of Janet who lived in Haliburton, Ontario.
Essie Bagley - taught music, piano. Father Ed. Bagley, lived n-east corner St. George - Nelson. J[anet] L. Bain - kept house for Harry H. Clarke and raised Marjorie, Dorothy & Phylis on death of my grandmother, Fannie Bemister Clarke, in Haliburton.
Mrs. Ed. Bagley - was Mary Mandeville, wife of Edward Baguley, who operated Baguley & Miller General store on Main street.
T. B. Barrett - eldest son of W. H. "Harry" Barrett, born Spallumcheen, B. C. in 1895. Father of the author. Port Dover Band member and farmer. M.P. Norfolk 1945/49.
H. H. Clarke - son of lightkeeper, Long Point. Store keeper for Mrs. J. Anderson, Haliburton.
E. P. Bagley - storekeeper, Port Dover, Town treasurer. Member of Port Dover Brass band.
A. Roy Dell - Baker, Port Dover.

## Square 44
Edna Jeffries
Mabel Hambleton
Mary Dobbin
Garnette Copeland
Gladys Walker
Mirrna McMaster
Gladys Blake
Bessie Hambleton
Jean Hill
Hollie Burns
Square 45
Nellie Moore
Violet Boyce
James Scott - wholesale dry goods merchant. Married Carrie Barrett, eldest daughter of T. B. B.
Effie Grundell
Liana Grundell
Ethel Leaney
Mrs. A. Reid
Mrs. Boyce

## Square 46
W. H. Caley
Hugh McQueen - owner of Norfolk House. Good boxer.
G N. Kaufman
Isobel Symington
Charlie Long
Emma Bloxom
J. G. Patterson - "Pat", genial owner of Rexall Drug Store, & telephone exchange, in the Tibbetts block. Now Eaton's Computer Services.
Walker Evans - long-time sexton of St. Paul's Church.

## Square 47
L. M. Ryerse
F. Oakden
Capt. Robert Herbert
Capt. Ewart MacKay
Norman Bush
Mrs. G. Buckley
Eileen Cook — daughter of Dr. Albert Cook. Home demolished when Dover Dairy Bar was built.
Herman Cook - son of Dr. Albert Cook.

## Square 48
Mrs. Thomas Murray
Miss Jennie Kearney
Miss Innes Coleman - dau. of Carl Colman, married William Smith, plumber.
Mrs. Fred Coleman - related to William "Bill" Wamsley, Head Rose-grower for T. A. Ivey Ltd.
Mr. Sidney Stass [or Stasa]
Mrs. Dickerson
Mr. Carl Coleman - butcher, son of Fred. Port Dover Band member.
Mr. Middleton Thompson - born Nanticoke, son of Jesse & Matilda Jackson Thompson. A Port Dover Band member, died Dec. 20, 1947.

## Square 49
Arthur Wilson
Clifford Lown
Joseph Kitchen
Leslie Powell - married Kate Spain, farmed east of Port Dover.

Lloyd Ryerse - Marburg farmer, married Adah Donald.
Frank Barrett - youngest son of W. H. Barrett. Married Irene Pickford.
Allan Law - lived at the Dog's Nest. Thresher man and maker of superb pear wine - "Peary"
Bert Monroe -
Pte. Cecil Powell - Rtd Dec 10, 1915 - This is embroidered in centre of this square.

**Square 50**
Mrs. Moon
Emma Bloxom
Mrs. G. Steele
Mrs. Slocomb - wife of Frank Slocomb
Myrtle Greenbury
Francis Slocom[b]- married Sam H. Morris.
Miss Irkshaw ?
Leslie Horne
Mrs. Horne
Evelyn Horne
Mr. G. Thompson - farmer of Nanticoke, married Margaret Hambleton in 1854. Bought furniture business of Joe Horsley in 1904. Sons James Hambleton & Wilmer Berton. Died 1930 aged 76.
Ethel Leighton

**Square 51**
Miss S[adie] McQueen - beloved school teacher, in Port Dover Public School.
Laurel Misner - sister of Henry H. Misner. Nursing Sister throughout World War I.
Mr. H[enry] Sinclair
Mrs. Henry Sinclair - active municipal councillor.

**Square 52**
Miss M. L. Maine
Miss A. J. Gillies
Miss Lenora Allen
Miss Mame Dorman
Master K[enneth] Thompson - married Fern Evans.
Miss Thelma Thompson - married Gerry Hardicker
Miss Norma Thompson - married Wm. "Bill" Parkinson, owned White Rose station, hd. of Main.

**Square 53**
Charles Misner
Mrs. John Misner
Margaret Misner - daughter of Henry H. Misner Sr.
Elmore Misner - son of Henry H. Misner Sr.

**Square 54**
Stuart Ryerse
Silas Nichols
Robert Beecraft
Lorne Husted
Mrs. Hugh Moore
Garnet Coleman - butcher, younger son of Fred Coleman.
Mr. Clifford Lees
Mr. F[red] Coleman - Fred owned Coleman's Butcher Shop. Punter-guide for Long Pt. Co.

**Square 55**
Mrs. L. R. Tibbetts
Mr. James Ellis
Mrs. James Ellis
Miss Josephine Dixon
Mrs. Grover Murdock
Dr. G[rover] Murdock

**Square 56**
Mrs. Alf[red] Ryerse
Mrs G. Downs
Lola Storey
Pearl Downs
Luella Kitchen
Mrs. J. Pickford - wife of Jack Pickford a Yorkshireman, farmed lot 13, Con 2, Woodhouse.
Bea Monteith
Charity Monteith

APPENDIX NINE

# Membership List of 1922

A small 6 1/2 by 5 1/2 brown-covered booklet lists the members, by heads of households, for St. Paul's Church as at January 1st, 1922. A page is devoted to each letter of the alphabet.

| | | |
|---|---|---|
| Andrews, Mrs. D. H. | Colman, Mr. F. B. | Ivey, Mr. L. B. |
| Ansley, Mrs. Bessie | Colman, Mr. Garnet | Innes, Mr. Chas. |
| Barrett, Mr. T. B. | Colman, Mr. Carl | Jacques, Miss Freda |
| Barrett, Mr. Frank | Cook, Dr. A. H. | James, Mr. J. G. |
| Barrett, Miss E. L. | Cornish, Rev. D. J. | Jackson, Miss M. |
| Barrett, Mr. H. B. | Carter, Mr. Fred | Joliffe, Mr. L. V. |
| Barrett, Mr. W. H. | Cook, Mr. Herb. | Jamieson, Mr. Edmund |
| Barwell, Mr. C. W. | Davidson, Mrs. J. B. | Kindree, Mr. Percy L |
| Barwell, Mr. C. W. Jr. | Dyer, Mrs. Harry | Kennedy, Mr. W. H. |
| Ballard, Mr. J. | Dixon, Mr. C. W. | Kurz, Mr. Clarence |
| Butler, Mrs. E. | Dyer, Miss Dessa | Long, Mr. Archie |
| Battersby, Miss E. P. | Dunbar, Mr. Wm. | Leaney, Mr. J. B. |
| Best, Mrs. J. H. | Dixon, Mrs, George | Long, Mrs. G. W. |
| Battersby, Mr. L. C. | Evans, Mr. A. W. | Low, Mrs. David |
| Buck, Mr. W. Morley | Evans, Mr. Walker | Laings, Miss C. M. |
| Buck, Mr. J. H. | Evans, Mr. Floyd | Lowe, Mr. W. D. |
| Buckwell, Miss A. | Faulkner, Mr. Frank | Lowe, Mr. Andrew |
| Bush, Mrs. J. E. | Fawcett, Mr. Henry | Law, Mrs. |
| Boyce, Mr. Thos. | Fisher, Mr. M. | Lawson, Mrs. L. A. |
| Bowley, Mr. E. E. | Freeman, Mr. C. P. | Leaney, Mr. Robert |
| Bayes, Mr. Frank | Falloon, Mrs. W. E. | Lemmon, Dr. W. W. |
| Bowlby, Mr. Bradford | Fields, Mr. David | Lown, John |
| Bayley, Mrs. | Gamble, Mrs. C. E. | Lown, Clifford |
| Butler, Mr. T. H.   r. r. 1 | Greenbury, Mr. James | Martin, Mrs. Geo. |
| Bailey, Capt. | Garner, Mr. J. W. | Martin, Mr. John S. |
| Bush, Mrs. Isaac | Gibbons, Mr. J. C. | McNeaney, Mr. Barney |
| Battersby, Mr. Harry C. | Harding, Misses | Mills, Mr. Wm. |
| Battersby, Mrs. Arthur | Hallam, Mr. George | Morris, Mr. James H. |
| 69 Charles St. Toronto | Hoover, Mr. A. B. | McMillan, Mr. Robt. |
| 12 Kendal Ave. Toronto | Holden, Mrs. W. R. | Marsh, Mr. Reuben |
| Crysler, Mr. Frank | Husted, Mr. Wm. | Moore, Mr. Sam |

Manuel, Mr. Douglas
Moore, Mr. Hugh
Martin, Mr. Omar
Misner, Miss E.
Misner, Mr. H. H.
McLaughlin, Mrs. A.
Morgan, Miss
Morgan, Mr. Crosbie
Moon, Mr. Harry
Mann, Mr. J. E.
Morris, Sam H.
Nicolls, Mr. E. L.
Newell, Miss
Quanbury, Mrs. J. C.
Reynolds, Mr. J. W.
Ross, Mrs. Chas.
Ryerse, Mr. W. A.
Ross, Mr. Sam
Robinson, Capt. P. C.
Robinson, Mr. Geo. O.

Schram, Mrs. G. S.
Sovereign, Miss Adah
Skey, Mrs. L.
Spain, Mr. J. W.
Smith, Mr. T. W.
Slocomb, Mr. F. W.
Silverthorne, Mr. Roy
Smith, Mr. W. Harold
Stringer, Mr. F. W.
Spain, Mr. Alex
Smith, Col. D. T.
Steele, Mrs. George
Steele, Mr. Ed.
Tibbetts, Mr. W. F.
Tibbetts, Mr. L. R.
Thompson, Mr. J. J.
Thompson, Mr. Geo.
Thompson, Mr. Mid.
Thompson, Mr. W. J.
Thompson, Mr. W. J.

Thompson, Mr. J. H.
Thompson, Mr. W. Bert
Thompson, Mr. Jesse
Tisdale, Mrs. Jos.
Thompson, Mr. Airlie
Thompson, Mr. Art.
Vokes, Mr. James
Vyse, Mrs. F.
Wicker, Mr. Wm. E.
Wamsley, Mr. Wm.
Wheeler, Miss
Walker, Mr. John
Whiteside, Mr. W. F.
Waddle, Mr. Dave
Waddle, Mr. Hazen
Waddle, Mr. Roland
Ward, Mr. D. J.
Wadham, Mr. Albert
Yerex, Mr. Cecil
Zealand, Mr. H. W.

APPENDIX TEN

# An Agreement to Pay

Explanation : Although no date appears on this document, one supposes it was drawn up by the Wardens of St. Paul's, perhaps in the 1880's. Many names listed in two columns, have no amount entered opposite them. A few who have pledged an amount have a zero entered opposite inferring that their pledge was not honoured.

We, whose names are hereto subscribed, agree to pay weekly, "or in the event of our absence," as soon after our return as possible, the amount opposite our names, for the maintenance of St. Paul's Church, Port Dover.

| | | | | |
|---|---|---|---|---|
| C. Morgan | 20 | | Mr. Martin | 10 |
| Mrs. C. Morgan | 23 | | S. J. Gamble | 20 |
| C. H. Lees | 20 | | H. Hall | 25 |
| Dr. Jolley | 20 | | Mr. Heath | 10 |
| T. W. Smith | 20 | | W. F. Tibbitts [sic] | 20 |
| L. Battersby | 2.00 | | O. Ansley | 20 |
| J. P. Battersby | 25 | | Alex Colman | 15 |
| Mr. Harding | 00 | | J. Leaney | 10 |
| Dr. Hamilton | P. 2  2.00 | | L. G. Morgan | 06 |
| Mrs. Phipps | P. 2  1.00 | | Mrs. Scofield | — |
| Miss E. P. Battersby | 15 | | F. W. Denton | 15 |
| J. R. Davis | 10 | | A. W. Laurie | 25 |
| W. J. Thompson - corrected – 15 | | | Douglas Skey | 05 |
| A. Innes | 10 | | R. M. Mead | — |
| Tim Stone | 00 | | H. W. Ansley | 50 |
| Wm. Corton | 10 | | Dr. Walker | 00 |
| Col. Thompson | 00 | | Mrs. Bishopric | — |
| Mrs S. Battersby | 06 | | E. Harris | — |
| Miss Battersby | 15 | | Mrs. Buckwell | 12 |
| Mrs. Morgan | 06 | | Miss Buckwell | 00 |

An Agreement to Pay 599

| | | | |
|---|---|---|---|
| Fred Colman | 15 | Morley Buck | — |
| Mrs. Misner | 05 | E. J. Low | 37 |
| T. B. Barrett | 50 | C. R. Low | 15 |
| Mrs. P. Lawson | — | Mrs. J. Waddel [sic] | 10 |
| H. Fawcett | 10 | R. Blakie | — |
| Mr. Hodge | 15 | Mrs. Quanbury | 00 |
| Dr. Battersby | — | Miss Quanbury | 00 |
| Mr. Petty | 00 | Miss Anderson | 00 |
| Mr. Brocklebank | 20 | Gerty Re[e]ves | 00 |
| L. Skey | 50 | Miss Newell | 06 |
| Mrs. Butter | — | Thomas Fawcett | 10 |
| C. Quanbury | 10 | John Quanbury | 00 |
| H. Mallett | 05 | Miss A. Wilson | — |
| James Goodwin | 00 | Wayne Hamilton | 00 |
| David Hicks | 25 | Mrs. J. Horne | — |
| Mrs. A. Warren | 10 | George R. Mead | 05 |
| Mrs. Hamilton | 10 | J. F. Smythe | 18 |
| Miss Barrett | 00 | Miss A. Colman | 10 |

Mrs. C. Williams & Mrs. J. G. Waddle are entered on the list but their names are crossed out with ink. All those entered with "00" are entered in pencil, as if they were perhaps never contacted. Those with "—" have no mark whatsoever.

APPENDIX ELEVEN

# Members of St. Paul's A.Y.P.A from pre-1930 to 1938

The following names have been gleaned from attendance records and payment of fee lists found among records of minutes etc. of the organisation. Many listed were active for the whole period. Some names may have been visitors only.

| | | |
|---|---|---|
| Golda Thompson | Arlene Thompson | Helen Thompson |
| Innes Colman | Bill Cornish | Jack Fulkrod |
| Gordon Evans | Miss Mason | Johnny Jarrett |
| Gilman Scofield | Ross Thompson | John Ivey |
| George Jackson | Margaret Cornish | Bill Barwell |
| Oral Misner | Beverley Schram | M. Silverthorne |
| Howard Nunn | Ralph Porritt | Hubert "Tim"Barrett |
| Nancy Dyer | Fern Evans | Eileen Garner |
| Oscar Sutor | William Adams | George Ryerse |
| Rev. D. J. Cornish | Thelma Thompson | Viola Evans |
| Bruce Reid | Ross Hallam | Kenneth Thompson |
| Jack Leaney | Lawrence Wedd | Margaret Davidson |
| Elijah Palmer | Andrew Lowe | Margaret McDonald |
| Roy Bolt | Ruth Campbell | Lydia McQueen |
| Grant Hawks | Peter Wedd | Robert Fulkrod |
| Bruce Ward | Harry Howarth | Jack Bayes |
| Ernie Quanbury | Milford Evans | Norma Harback |
| Jack Maytham | Gertrude Silverthorne | Alex Wood |
| Rose Downey | Jack Fenton | Marjorie Spain |
| Coral Charlton | Bill Furlong | Francis Gamble |
| Reginald Pike | Ethel Lowe | Kay Lowe |
| Sada Falloon | Grace Scott | Betsy McLeod |
| Jerry Hardicker | Alfred Moxon | Midleton Thompson |
| Anna Howarth | Vance Hazelbrook | Clarence Abbey |
| Kenneth Laurie | Spud Leaney | Phyllis Pendley |
| Stan McK | Irene N | Betty Cornish |
| S. McInery | G. M. Martin | Joe Given |

H. Howard
John Sterling
Pat Hoskins
Lorne H
Vera King
Dick Ryerse
Mary Holland
Grace Townsend
Robert Ferguson
Charles Bridgwater
Isla Nunn
Elmer Lewis
Harry Waddle
David Yerex
Hilton Yerex
Peggy Wamsley
Bruce Greenslade
Joan Blackhurst
Ellis Haun
Tobe Snowden

Jack Hind
Jack Quanbury
Gordon Ivey
Kay Lowe
Dorothy Best
Helen Caley
Helene Chadwick
Gertrude Stinson
Vernon Dixon
Sidney Phillips
Elsie Hoskins
Eugene Smith
J. Rasmussen
Harold Smith
Harry B. Barrett
Colin Campbell
Charles Haller
Dot Courtnage
Patricia Blackhurst

E. Fergue
Charles Blackhurst
Alice Miller
Mabel Long
Helena Thompson
Leslie Quanbury
Cyril House
Sid Townsend
Hubert Jennings
Muriel MacDonald
Yvonne McMillan
Knud Rasmussen
David Cornish
William Muth
Ruth Ryerse
Marion Parker
Alma MacDonald
Jimmie Sharman
Lola McNeilly

APPENDIX TWELVE

# Membership List –
# St. Paul's Parish – 1976

Mr. W. G. H. Adams
Dr. & Mrs. I. P. Asselstine
Mr. & Mrs. T. B. Barrett
Mr. & Mrs. Harry B. Barrett
Mr. & Mrs. Harry Batten
Mr. & Mrs. John Blakemore
Mr. & Mrs. Richard Briseau
Mrs. Marie Brown
Mr. Mrs. George Burcham
Mr. & Mrs. T. E. Butler
Mr. & Mrs. Grant Chambers
Mrs. F. W. Clark
Mr. & Mrs. Garnet Colman
Mrs. Ruth Cooper
Mr. & Mrs. Thos. Copeman
Miss Pat Coe
Mr. & Mrs. Jack Dennis
Mr. & Mrs. Ed. Dyster
Miss Evans
Mr. & Mrs. Frank Farr
Mr. & Mrs. James Field
Mr. & Mrs. John Finch
Mr. & Mrs. Walter Fletcher
Mr. & Mrs. A. Follington
Miss Dorothy Ford
Mrs. Robert Ford
Mr. & Mrs. Ron Gash
Mrs. M. E. Gilbert
Mr. & Mrs. Gregg
Mr. & Mrs. Robt. Griffen
Mr. & Mrs. Ross Hallam
Mrs. Jean Harris
Mr. & Mrs. Ronald Hayne
Mrs. Thos. Hinatsu

Mr & Mrs. Blake Adams
Mr. & Mrs. George Barker
Mr. & Mrs. Frank Barrett
Mr. & Mrs. Ronald Barry
Mrs. Jessie Bell
Mrs. Barbara Bloye
Mr. & Mrs. Don Brooks
Mr. & Mrs. Lowell Brown
Mr. Mrs. Chas. Burcham
Mrs. Theresa Butler
Mr. & Mrs. Ivan Chambers
Mr. & Mrs. Albert Collins
Mrs. E. B. Cope
Canon & Mrs. D. J. Cornish
Mr. & Mrs. J. Robt. Cromwell
Mr. Thos. Dawson
Mrs. R. Desbats
Mrs. Shirley Dutka
Mrs. Wm. Falloon
Mr. & Mrs. Gus Federow
Mr. & Mrs. - Field
Mr. & Mrs. Ray Finch
Mr. & Mrs. C. Fletcher
Mr. & Mrs. Art Follington
Mr. & Mrs. Donald Ford
Mr. & Mrs. Byron Forrest
Mr. Peter George
Miss Lillian Gill
Mr. & Mrs. B. Greenslade
Mrs. Margaret Guiler
Mrs. George Hallam
Mr. & Mrs. Howard Harris
Mr. & Mrs. Chas. Heaman
Mr. Ronald Hinatsu

Mr. & Mrs. Donald Ames
Mrs. W. H. Barrett
Mr. & Mrs. H. J. H. Barrett
Mr. John Bartlett
Mr. Mrs. Albert Blake
Mr. & Mrs. Ch. Bridgewater
Miss Stella Brock
Mr. & Mrs. Wm. G. Bruley
Mr. & Mrs. Wm Butler
Mr. & Mrs. Cardiff
Mr. & Mrs. Gerald Clark
Mr. Carl Colman
Mr. & Mrs. Ed. Cooper
Mrs. Florence Cornish
Mrs. Oliver Cromwell
Mrs. Robert Davis
Mr. & Mrs. Thos. Dring
Mrs. Ellen Eager
Mrs. B. Farley
Mr. & Mrs. Edward Field
Mr. & Mrs. Graydon Field
Mr. & Mrs. Clarence Finch
Mr. & Mrs. James Follington
Mr. & Mrs. E. S. Ford
Mr. & Mrs. Allie Ford
Mrs. Helen Fort
Mr. & Mrs. George Gibbons
Mr. & Mrs. James Goodall
Mr. & Mrs. Jas. Greenslade
Mrs. Jesse Guy
Mr. & Mrs. John Harnick
Mr. & Mrs. Grant Hawke
Mrs. G. Hewitt
Mrs. A. B. Hoover

Mrs. Marnie Hoover
Mrs. Elizabeth Howell
Mr. & Mrs. A. Husted
Mrs. Harry Ivey
Mr. & Mrs. John Ivey
Mrs. W. H. Jacobs
Mr. & Mrs. Alan Jamieson
Miss Florence Johns
Mrs. H. Kennington
Mr. & Mrs. Charles Kitchen
Mr. & Mrs. John Knister
Mrs. C. Kyle
Mr. Jim Law
Mr. & Mrs. Gerald Logger
Mr. & Mrs. Gordon Longe
Mr. & Mrs. Andrew Lowe
Mr. & Mrs. Robert Luton
Mrs. Sydney Marsh
Mr. & Mrs. Bert Matthews
Mr. & Mrs. Jack Maytham
Mr. & Mrs. Jack Milner
Miss Margaret Misner
Mr. & Mrs. Henry R. Misner
Mr. & Mrs. Stephan Molewyk
Mr. & Mrs. Sam Morris
Mr. & Mrs. Len Murrell
Mrs. Ella Murphy
Mr. William Mummery
Mrs. Barbara MacDonald
Mrs. Edith McIntosh
Mr. & Mrs. Wm. McNeilly
Mr. & Mrs. Arthur Nall
Mrs. E. L. O'Neill
Mr. & Mrs. Douglas Parker
Mr. & Mrs. Wm. Parkinson
Mr. & Mrs. Wm. Phillips
Mrs. Marjorie Pope
Mr. & Mrs. Alex Powell
Mr. & Mrs. Albert Reid
Mrs. J. Richardson
Mr. & Mrs. Donald Ross
Mr. & Mrs. Edward Rowlings
Mr. & Mrs. Victor Ryerse
Mr. & Mrs. Colin Ryerse
Miss Carrie Louise Scott
Mr. & Mrs. Roger Simpson
Mr. & Mrs. George Smith
Mr. & Mrs. Harry Smith
Mr. & Mrs. Bernard Smuck

Mr. & Mrs. J. H. Howarth
Mr. & Mrs. Earl Hume
Mr. & Mrs. Wm. Hutchinson
Mr. & Mrs. Ray Ivey
Mr. & Mrs. Charles L. Ivey
Mr. & Mrs. Thomas Jacobs
Mrs. Ethel Jennings
Mr. & Mrs. James Kelly
Mr. & Mrs. John Kilpatrick
Mr. & Mrs. J. W. Kitchen
Mr. & Mrs. David Knowles
Mr. & Mrs. Roy Lacey
Mr. Arthur Leitch
Mr. & Mrs. Walter Long
Miss Betty Longe
Mrs. A. J. Lowe
Mr. & Mrs. George Manuel
Mrs. J. S. Martin [deceased]
Mr. & Mrs. Alan Matthews
Mrs. J. Maytham Sr.
Mr. & Mrs. J. Henry Misner
Mr. & Mrs. Robert Misner
Mr. & Mrs. Donald Misner
Mrs. L. E. Monck
Mr. & Mrs. Archie Morris
Mr. & Mrs. Les Murphy
Mrs. James Murphy
Mrs. Jack Mossing
Mr & Mrs Maynard MacDonald
Mr. & Mrs. Fred MacMillan
Mr. & Mrs. Bruce McQueen
Mr. & Mrs. William Nixon
Mr. & Mrs. Reg Parker
Mr. & Mrs. Jack Parker [St. G.]
Mr. & Mrs. Kenneth Painter
Mr. & Mrs. Lloyd Pierson[Ln Pk]
Miss Jane Pope
Mrs. Art Powell
Mr. & Mrs. Bruce Reid
Mrs. Tommy Richardson
Mr. & Mrs. James Routledge
Mr. & Mrs. David Ryerse
Mr. & Mrs. Robert Ryerse
Mr. & mrs. Clinton Ryerse
Mrs. Dorothy Scott
Mr. & Mrs. Wm. Sinden
Mr. George Smith, Jr.
Mrs. Florence Smith
Mr. & Mrs. Alex Spain

Mrs. Winnifred Howell
Mrs. Jean Hurst
Mr. & Mrs. Charles Ivey
Mr. Gordon Ivey
Mr. Jay Ivey
Mr. & Mrs. Leonard Jago
Mr. & Mrs. Gordon Johnson
Mr. & Mrs. Roy Kennedy
Mrs. Jane Kindree
Mrs. Howard Knight
Mrs. Susan Knowles
Mr & Mrs. Everett Lampman
Mr. & Mrs. Jack Lockyer
Mr. & Mrs. S. K. Long
Mr. & Mrs. John Lowshaw
Mr. & Mrs. Lyman Lowe
Mr. & Mrs. L. H. Maracle
Mrs. R. S. Mason
Mr. & Mrs. Jack Matthews
Mr. & Mrs. Ken Meade
Mr. & Mrs. Elmore Misner
Mr. & Mrs Charles Misner
Mr. & Mrs. Gordon Misner
Mr. B. Morris
Mr. William Morris
Mrs. Florence Murphy
Mr. & Mrs. J. Mummery
Mr. & Mrs. A. MacDonald
Mrs. Eva McBride
Mr. & Mrs. Stan MacMillan
Mr. & Mrs. Wm. McQuillan
Mr. & Mrs. James Oakes
Mr & Mrs Jack Parker [St.P]
Mr. & Mrs. Wm. Parker
Mr. & Mrs. Don Pentz
Mr. & Mrs. L. Pierson [St. G]
Mrs. Jean Porritt
Miss Minnie Quanbury
Mr. & Mrs. Doug Richardson
Mr. & Mrs. George Ross
Mrs. M. Rowden
Mr. & Mrs. Leo Ryerse
Mrs. Olive Ryerse
Mr. & Mrs. Harold Schilz
Mr. & Mrs. George Simmons
Mrs. Innes Smith
Mr. & Mrs. Wm. J. Smith
Mr. & Mrs. Harold Smith
Mr. & Mrs. William Spain

| | | |
|---|---|---|
| Mr. & Mrs. Alan Spence | Mr. & Mrs. Thomas Stedman | Mrs. Stedman Sr. |
| Mrs. Edward Steele | Mrs. Rose Steiss | Mr. & Mrs. Cobie Stephens |
| Mr. & Mrs. Howard Stewart | Mrs. Marion Stewart | Mr. & Mrs. William Stone |
| Mr. & Mrs. Robert Stonewall | Mrs. Betty Strople | Mrs. Douglas Struthers |
| Mr. & Mrs. Arthur Sullivan | Mr. & Mrs. Fred Sullivan | Mr. & Mrs. Frank Sullivan |
| Mr. & Mrs. Gerald Swartz | Mr. & Mrs. W. E. Taylor | Mrs. J. J. Thompson |
| Miss Helen Thompson | Mr. & Mrs. W. B. Thompson | Mrs. Fern Thompson |
| Mr. & Mrs. Ross Thompson | Mr. & Mrs. J. H. Thompson | Mr. & Mrs. Carl Trumper |
| Mr. & Mrs. Peter Turk | Mr. & Mrs. Albert VanLoon | Mr. & Mrs. Brian Varey |
| Mrs. John Vokes | Mrs. Roland Waddle | Mr. John Walker |
| Mr. & Mrs. William Walker | Mr. & Mrs. Charles Watkinson | Mr. & Mrs. Eric Watson |
| Mr. & Mrs. William Wamsley | Mr. & Mrs. Jack Wamsley | Mr. & Mrs. Robert Wamsley |
| Mr. & Mrs. Bert West | Mr. & Mrs. Gordon White | Mr. & Mrs. Allan Wicker |
| Mr. & Mrs. Barry Wicker | Mrs. Theresa Wicker | Mrs. Jean Williamson |
| Mr. & Mrs. Wilfred Winter | Mr. & Mrs. A. L. Winter | Mr. & Mrs. Gerald Wright |
| Mr. & Mrs. Donald Wright | Mr. & Mrs. Hilton Yerex | Miss Annette Zealand |

APPENDIX THIRTEEN

# St. Paul's Club Presidents & Chancel Guild Presidents

**PRESIDENTS OF THE ST. PAUL'S CLUB**

| | | | |
|---|---|---|---|
| 1929 - 1942 | Helen Cornish | 1974 | Blanche Clark |
| 1943 - 1945 | Olive Gilbert | 1975 | Betty Lockyer |
| 1946 - 1947 | Francis Williamson | 1976 | Joy Field |
| 1948 | Blanche Clark | 1977 | Lydia Hawke |
| 1949 | Kate McMillan | 1978 | Barbara Copeman |
| 1950 | Dorothy Ivey | 1979 | Lois Ryerse |
| 1951 | Marnie Hoover | 1980 | Judi Ralston |
| 1952 | Mila Thornton | 1981 | Susan Gordon |
| 1953 | Imogine Dines | 1982 | Dianne Ivey |
| 1954 | Anna Goodall | 1983 | Valerie Skeldon |
| 1955 | Minnie Maytham | 1984 | Julie Dennis |
| 1956 | Betsy Thompson | 1985 | Joy Field |
| 1957 | Muriel Moore | 1986 | Mary Fralick |
| 1958 | Dorothy Blake | 1987 | Judi Ralston |
| 1959 | Helen Smith | 1988 | Stephanie McKnight |
| 1960 | Donna Ivey | 1989 | Janice Hamilton |
| 1961 | Doris Forrest | 1990 | Valerie Skeldon |
| 1962 | Rena Richardson | 1991 | Barbara Copeman |
| 1963 | Theresa Butler | 1992 | Frances Parker |
| 1964 | Doris Forrest | 1993 - 1994 | Cheryl Copeman |
| 1965 | Margaret Richardson | 1995 | Kim Rose |
| 1966 | Betty Johnson | 1996 - 1997 | Bernice Pos |
| 1967 | Doris Forrest | 1998 - 1999 | Dorothea Wiley |
| 1968 - 1969 | Eva Spain | 2000 | Barbara Copeman |
| 1970 | Golda Matthews | 2000 - 2001 | Julie Smith |
| 1971 - 1972 | Margaret Richardson | 2002 | Louise Walker |

## CHANCEL GUILD PRESIDENTS

| | | | |
|---|---|---|---|
| 1955 - 1956 | Eleanor Long | 1970 - 1972 | Stella Knight |
| 1957 | Anne Dennis | 1973 | Shirley Gibbons |
| 1958 - 1959 | Marie Brown | 1974 - 1975 | Martha Taylor |
| 1960 - 1961 | Joyce Walker | 1976 - 1977 | Sandy Collins |
| 1962 - 1963 | Ruth Yerex | 1978 - 1996 | Florence Cornish |
| 1964 - 1965 | Lois Ryerse | 1997 - 2001 | Elsie Finch |
| 1966 - 1967 | Anne Dennis | | |
| 1968 - 1969 | Hilda Brown | | |

## CHANCEL GUILD MEMBERS

In general the following ladies served in the time periods listed. Some for only a brief time, others over a long period of years.

| | | | |
|---|---|---|---|
| 1955 - 59. | Hellen Barrett | Marie Brown | Anne Dennis |
| | Eleanor Long | Clara Mason | Babe Varey |
| | Mrs. Webb (H) | Mary Barrett | Ruth Yerex |
| | Lois Ryerse | Emily Barrett | Joyce Walker |
| | Edna Winter | Hilda Butler | Ena Shallwick |
| | Eleanor Powell. | | |
| 1960 - 70 | Beth Drennan | Mrs. Gardiner (H) | Win Patterson |
| | Helen Fort | Ann Stonewall | Dean Thompson |
| | Dorothy Barker | Ann Dennis | Eleanor Long |
| | Clara Mason | Emily Molewyk | Lois Ryerse |
| | Joyce Walker | Edna Winter | Ruth Yerex |
| | Marie Brown | Shirley Gibbons | Joan Wamsley [Tres. 1965 - 73] |
| | Hilda Brown | Sandra Collins | Dean Lampman |
| | Eleanor Long | Frances Butler | Marie MacMillan |
| | Mrs. Henry (H) | Barb. Howden | Stella Knight |
| 1971 - 80 | Martha Taylor | Florence Cornish | Catherine Hammond |
| | Bridget Brown | Diane Ivey | Elsie Finch |
| 1981 - 90 | Jean Wood | June Miller | Miriam Painter Woods |
| 1991 - 00 | Georgina Morris | Julie Smith | Jackie Smith |
| | Bertha Mianer | | |
| 2001 - 05 | Helen McMurray | Elsie Finch | Catherine Hammond |
| | June Miller | Julie Smith | Georgina Morris |
| | Emily Molewyk | Mary Cromwell | Florence Cornish |
| | Ann Dennis. | | |

APPENDIX FOURTEEN

# 2002 Quilt of St. Paul's

This 2002 quilt was stitched to represent bricks, upon which the names of parishioners were stitched.
\*\* following a name indicates they are deceased.

Brick 1. Lorne & Mildred Butler
Kevin & Cheryl - Diane - Kim
Rick & Vickie Guaglins
Lorne - Vanessa - Sam

Brick 2. Cameron & Betty Buttram
John Kerry
Amber - Scott - Cameron - Erin

Brick 3. Gord & Betty Johnson
Richard - Susan - Tammy - Joey

Brick 4. Clare & Julia Dennis
Graham - Gregory - Angela - Phillip

Brick 5. Hilda Henson - Jim & Pat Henson - Lynn - Joan - Diane - Jill - Jesse - Adrian - Kirk - Paige.

Brick 6. Chuck & Margot Heaman
Jane Woolcott & Jeffrey Heaman

Brick 7. Ed & Susan Gordon. Jennifer Michael - Don & Lorraine Doyle

Brick 8. Ernest\*\* & Ethel Ford
Dorothy - Donald.

Brick 9. Barbara MacDonald
Jay MacDonald

Brick 10. Peter & Helen MacMurray
David - Kim - Melanie - Caitlyn - Daniel - Rachel

Brick 11. Bill & Norma Parkinson
Bill - Mardella - Arlene.
Lily Jacobs and family

Brick 12. Jerry\*\* & Thelma\*\* Hardiker
Wayne & Gladys Linde.

Brick 13. Desmond & Florence Lawrance
Linda Gauthier. Jane Halliday
Susan Smith. Natasha - Brandon
Adria - Sarah & Ashton

Brick 14. An embroidered fish.
Brick 15. Bernie & Gloria Smuck
Martin & Kimberley Tafertahafer
Connor & Mihayle

608 The Parish of St. Paul's

Brick 16. Billie Farmer
Agnes Chapelle

Brick 17. John 1914 - 1991 & Elizabeth R. Dorner
Elizabeth H. - Robert Wilson

Brick 18. A Fish
Brick 20. Tom** & Eva** Tees
Betty J. (Liles) Tees. Deborah - Brenda
Daryl - Bryan - Ian** Liles.

Brick 19. Joanne & Ralph Watt
Sandra - Bruce - Peggy
Court Elliott. Keith Schmucker.

Brick 21. Albert** & Dorothy Blake
Stanley** & Helen Lorriman

Brick 22. Kathy & Gary Copeland, Morgan
Andrew - Jim** & Murial Lewis.

Brick 23. Shirley & Alan Presland
Nadine Chubaty & Ian. James
Tony - Jamie - Rose - Ethran

Brick 24. Rolph & Ingrid Champion
Raymond & Ryan

Brick 25. Michael & Eileen Champion
Alison & Rob Gennoe
Rebecca Champion

Brick 26. Minnie Bell Maytham**
Jack & Sally Maytham
John - James

Brick 27. Stewart** & Eleanor Long
Janice - Michael

Brick 28. Harold & Marjorie Schneider
Pat & Bill**. Bruce. Gay & Louie. Bruce.

Brick 29. Tony & Betty Schneider
Tony Jr. Branson. Andrew. Pam
Kylie Sharys Abigale

Brick 30. Beverley & Brad Snow
Matthew - Michael - Marcus
Brick 31. A stitched fish

Brick 32. Rev. Canon William F. Whyte**
Margery Alice Whyte**
Brick 34. A stitched fish

Brick 33. Jim** & Anna** Goodall
Barbara** Goodall Buffin
Brick 35. A stitched fish

Brick 36. Allison & Kay Burbidge
Mary. Ian. Douglas

Brick 37. John & Joan Murphy
Iain. Marjorie Topher Mary

Brick 38. Les & Rosemary Murphy
Kevin Michael Patrick

Brick 39. Don & Louise Walker
Stella Mitchell - 1898 – 1988

Brick 40. Helen Vokes

Brick 41. Ivan & Alice Chambers - Susan Sheila.
Sharon LaBonte Jaques. Jim Jacques.
Michelle & Staphen LaBonte

Brick 42. Shelley & Jamie Cable
Sarah & Billy. Eliza & Troy.

Brick 43. Bill** & Margerie** Mockett
Jim** Mockett

Brick 44. Moses** & Lilly** Fischer
Gladys** Pansy** Ralph**

Brick 45. Clinton** & Pansy** Ryerse
Richard** Ruth ** Barbara.

Brick 46. Walter & Barbara Long
Douglas Connie Bradley

Brick 47. Mrs. C. O. MacDonald
Jack** & Peggy** Fenton

Brick 48. Tom & Hilda Butler
Bill & Frances.
Carl   Kim   Jeffery

Brick 49. Michael** & Margaret Ackland
Lynne Michelle Ackland - Metcalfe
Darcy   Melissa   Holly

Brick 50. Helen & Ernie Mathews
Ann   Ray   Delores Kough
Pat Sorbara.   Maggie & Marty

Brick 51. Thomas** & Rena** Richardson
T. Douglas & Margaret** Richardson

Brick 52. John & Kay   Jamie Lee Rundle
Brick 54. Francis Caroline** Ward
Olive** & Gilly** Gilbert
Hazel** Knowles Marsh
Jeanne Nyberg   David & Donna Knowles
Kerry   Jeanne   David   Sandra

Brick 53. Molly Allen.   Sandra   Susan   Michael
Brick 55. Jack & Annie Dennis
Christine & Bill Marsh
Michael   Sharlene
Katheryn & Richard Duayn
Regan   Ryan   Robin

Brick 56. Brian & Jean Wood   Stephen
Debbie   Susan   Pamela   Mark

Brick 57. Alan & Jeanette Jones
Sidney & Eileen Jones

Brick 58. Ted & Sandy Aphoven
Kim & Mike Ciavarelli
Kourtenay & Mike Jr.
John & Lorraine Ophoven

Brick 59. Frank C.** & Alice Amelia** Smith
Nellie**   Katie**

Brick 60. Mary Richardson.   Tom & Gail Richardson.   Terry   Danielle
Cathy & Chris VanTrigt.   Scott   &   Michael

Brick 61 Ethel Jennings**
Edith Cornish**

Brick 62. Cecil + & Dorothea Wiley
Maurice & Shirley Plastow.   Holly Plastow

Brick 63. Robert & Muriel** Misner
Rick   Gary   Roberta & Gary Furler

Brick 64. Donna** & Benny Bezzo
Jarri   Jeff.

Brick 65. Valerie & Grant Chambers
Rick   Ron   Tricia
Richard** & Lorna Kendall

Brick 66. Alex & Jean Patrick
Terry & Martha Taylor

Brick 67. Lowell & Hilda Brown
John & Kay.   Jaime   Lee Rundle

Brick 68. Bill** & Lorrayne** McNeilly
Bill   Deanna   Lanny   Kyle   Jeanette.

Brick 69. James E.** & Katie** Ryerse
Rosa** Ryerse
Margaret Ryerse Watters

Brick 70. Harold** & Martha** Schilz
Bishop Clarence & Joyce Mitchell
David   Peter**   Catherine Longpre.

Brick 71. Rev. Francis Evans 1828 - 1858
Rev. J. Vicars   1858 - 1860
Rev. M. S. Baldwin 1860

Brick 72. Rev. Samuel Harris 1863
Rev. John Irwin 1866
Rev. W. Tibbitts 1867 - 1875.

Brick 73. Wm. Francis** & Charlotte** Tibbetts.   Hugh**   Dick** & Martha**
Alan** & Zeitha**   ——   Caroline & Bill Carlson.

610 The Parish of St. Paul's

Brick 74. Albert & Sandy Collins
Lorraine  Catherine  Dan

Brick 75. Margaret & Charles** Meade  Claire &
Catherine Hammond.  Joe & Elaine Huxley
Kent & Janet Knechtel  Randy Hammond

Brick 76. James Pettit Biggar
Martha Biggar Rogers  Herb Rogers.

Brick 77. Les** & Florence Murphy
Les  Jim  Mary Ellen  John.

Brick 78. Mary Ellen DuPon
Melanie  Colleen  Ashley  Hailea

Brick 79. Melanie DuPon & Ty Harrell
Leighton  Kieren

Brick 80. The Daley Family
George  Stacie Jackson
Rev. M. M. Dillon – 1881 - 1884

Brick 81. Rev. J. F. Renaud — 1875 - 1877
Rev. Wm. Evans – 1880

Brick 82. Rev. J. R. Newell – 1884 - 1898
Rev. Mordicai Goldberg – 1898 - 1900
Rev. Robert Herbert – 1900 - 1907

Brick 83. A stitched fish.
Brick 84. Tamra Mann  Robinson Mann
Nicholas Gamble Knechtel

Brick 85. Warren** & Jean** Jackson
Muriel MacDonald

Brick 86. The Kendall Family.
Robert & Joan Kendall  Bruce & Kathy Buffett
Erin  Lindsay  Christopher  James  Jaclyn.

Brick 87. Jack & Janie Hamilton
Sean & Michelle  Derek
Peter & Elizabeth Bell**

Brick 88. Derek & Val Skeldon
Debbie  Andrew
Joanne & Andrew Coats.

Brick 89. Bill** & Florence Cornish
Elizabeth & John Blakemore  Ann
David & Susan Cornish
John Wm.  William
David  Joanna  Marybeth
Helen Cornish
Rev. D. S. Henry – 1968 - 1983.

Brick 90. Rev. Cyril Brown – 1907 - 1910
Rev. Herbert Johnson  – 1911 - 1921
Rev. Canon D. J. Cornish – 1921 - 1952
Brick 91. Rev. H. J. E. Webb – 1952 - 1960
Rev. Alan Gardiner – 1960 - 1965
Rev. Donald Gray – 1965 - 1968

In the centre of the quilt is an embroidered outline of St. Paul's Church with the dates 1852 – 2002 beneath it. The bricks with the incumbent ministers for those years are on either side of the depiction of the Church in the quilts centre.

Brick 92. Mary Webb
Frances  George

Brick 93. Julie & Terry Smith & family
Andy & Jackie Smith  Chris  Nikki  Lauren

Brick 94. John W.** Smith  Hilda M. Smith
Baby Connor Smith**
Joan E. Richardson**

Brick 95. The Watson Family
Harry** & Winifred**
Don**  Harry Jr.**  Jim**

Brick 96. Doug & Judi Ralston
Terry  Leigh Anne
Capt. George A. + & Marcia Turner

Brick 97. Rick & Kathy Cosby
Christine  Rebecca  Jessica

Brick 98. Canon Ab. & Ellen Hawes

Brick 99. The Brett Family
Canon Keith & Van   Janis   Martin
Karen Peters   Wayne Brett.

Brick 100. Rev. Rob Doerr & Carol Honsberger
Milford Doerr** & Elsie Doerr
Frank & Lois Granger   Matt   Ethan.

Brick 101. Michael Payne
Murray Cunningham

Brick 102. Mary Champion
Marjorie Diver   Wynn Howell**

Brick 103. The Leitch Family.
Arthur** & Myrtle** Leitch.   Jack &
June Reid   Jack** & Evelyne Waters
Bill & Nancy Hornischferger.

Brick 104. David & Miriam Woods
Michelle.

Brick 105. Fred Abel**
Bernice Sullivan

Brick 106. Allan** & Peggy Wicker & Family
Marilyn   Barry

Brick 107. Kathleen Thompson & Family
Barbara   Judy   Patricia

Brick 108. Lily Gibbons   George A. & Shirley
Gibbons   Christine & Dean   Vallis   Adam

Brick 109. The Cast & Crew of The Last
Resort - theatre masks in corners of brick.

Brick 111. Donald & Bertha Misner
Paul & Nancy   Peter & Lynda
Ellen & Ken Nicholls
Jodi   Leigh   Sarah

Brick 110. Bob Ryerse - Barbara A. Ryerse
Pamela & John Beresford - Jeff Wilson
Joanne Laeken - Jamie   Jeremy
Jeffrey & James Toomes - Joshua

Brick 112. Merle McKen Nesbitt
Kathryne & Rodney Linn   Lauren

Brick 113. Jim & Connie Lomas
Nicholas   James   Amanda   Leigh
Lydia Hawke**
Shannon Swarts**

Brick 114 Graydon & Joy Field
Craig 1945-1985 & Janice Field, Kerry Christopher
Katherine & Hugh Zimmer
Adam   Rebecca   Victoria

Brick 115. Barbara Copeman
Elizabeth   Virginia   Richard
Alexis   Lee
Michael & Debbie Saunders
Meagan   Haley   Michael

Brick 116. Charles & Thelma Misner
Allan   Marcia

Brick 117. Karen & Glen Wallace   Matthew   Jason
Tyler George J. & Nancy Gibbons Quintin Graham

Brick 118. Elizabeth Ryerse, Holly Balcomb
Katherine & Alf Wilkinson   Alex   Ryan
Katie   Laura Mitchell   Rob & Sue Ryerse
Margaret & Gerry Brown   Matthew
Sean   Joe   Tim

Brick 119. Brad & Melanie Wilson
Bobby   Reily   Abby
Joel & Pat Wilson   Jerilyn   Katy
Joey   Kassidy

Brick 120. Mae Haggerty   Carol Hoffman
Doris Forrest & Barney** Forrest

Brick 121. Liz Hisaw & Family
Jimmie Ann   Angela   Steve   Mary Ann

Brick 122. R. Hubert & Mary Jennings
The Rev. Paul & Elizabeth Jennings
Magdalena   Cecilia   Bruno

Brick 123. Malcolm & Sharon Mann
Kathleen   Chris

Brick 124. Norman & Marjorie Brown
Brent D.　Allen R.　Tom C.　Sonya
Mark　——　Kevin Jackson
Jonathon　　Matthew
Charles**　Barbara　Beatrice
Brick 126. Patricia Hayward
Ruth Best Knox
Dan & Judy Overbaugh
Walter & Barbara Long

Brick 129. The Bruleys
Bill** & Sylvia　Scott & Lise　Aimee
Steve & Pat　　Troy　Tyler
Jeff & Brenda　Zachary & Jennifer

Brick 131. Fred** & Berneice Smythe
Mary　Robert
Helen A. M. Thompson

Brick 133. W. Ross & Betsy Thompson
Catherine J. Thompson
Robert D. Thompson

Brick 135. Gerald** & Blanche** Clark
Joe　Connie

Brick 137. Harry B. & Joan Barrett
John L. Walmsley – 1921 - 1992　 [there should be no first l in Wamsley]
Hellen M. Barrett – 1922 - 1993
Hugh Massey Barrett
Michael & Barbara Hourigan　William　Russell

Brick 139. David & Dorris Yerex
Pat & Elaine Yerex

Brick 141. Ron & Susan Barker
Tracy　Eric　Bill　Amy
Becky Lynn MacKie　Melissa Matthew Ryerse

Brick 143. Glenn** & Olive Ryerse
Patricia Lindsay Gamble　Glen
Lindsay　Adrianne　Donald　Zachary

Brick 145. Bill** & Adeline** Garner
Andrew** & Eileen** Lowe　Barra Gotts

Brick147. David & Jennifer Walmsley
Jane　Sally　Bruce & Elizabeth Milner
Leigh　　Sandfield

Brick 125. Mr. & Mrs. Aaron Evans**
Viola**　Kenneth** & Fern Thompson
Paul Thompson

Brick 127. Charles** & Imogene** Ivey

Brick 128. Joan Forrest Smith
Gwen Forrest Smith

Brick 130. John & Bernice Pos　　Jo-Anne
Harry & Carol Pos　Kimberlee　Kathryn

Brick 132. George** & Margaret Thompson
W. Bert** & Dagmar** Thompson

Brick 134. Frank** & Beulah Saville
Bruce** & Muriel** Reid

Brick 136. Theobald Butler** & Emily** Barrett
　　　　　1817 - 1910　　　　1827 - 1902
Theobald Butler**　&　Marjorie Barrett**
　　　1895 - 1969　　　　　 1892 - 1974
Brick 138. Theobald Butler & Caolyn Barrett
Shawn　Brett　Brittany

Brick 140. Jan Reid

Brick 142 .Douglas & Carla Ryerse
Linda　David　Paul　Becky

Brick 144. David & Jean Ryerse
Nina　Eric　Lorie　　Jason Ray
Olivia Johnston　Channing　Carlas Ryerse

Brick 146. Minerva** Musselman

Brick 148. Patrick Walmsley**
Kerry Walmsley Jager
Jason**　Jeremy　Jonathan

Brick 149. Ethel Vandercroft
Brad & Julie Mullin   Allison   Margo
Brick 151. Archie & Georgina Morris
Samuel A.**   David

Brick 150. Hilton** & Ruth Yerex

Gregory & Rose Yerex   Nicholas   Sean

Brick 152. George & Donna Morris
Samuel G.   Isaac   Joel & Heather
Morris   Blake   Trevor   Alicia

Brick 153. Jean Porritt**       Art** & Mary
Follington    Leonard Bartlett   Bill & Cathy
Campbell   Lyndsay   Jacob   Kassandra

Brick 154. Robert Miller**
June Miller and Family

Brick 155. A. O. B.** & Dorothy Blackhurst
Joan**   Tucker**   Patricia
Virginia   Bridget   Miles

Brick 156. W. H.** & Hattie** Barrett
Frank** & Irene** Barrett
Tim** & Dorothy Barrett
Michael   Peter   Jimmie

Brick 157. Bill & Alice Browne
Charlotte   Norah
Norah – Sister Nonah, S. S. J. D. – Barrett

Brick 158. Leonard 1920-1986 & Mary
Burfoot.   Kim & Frances Parker
Cody   Leigh   Samantha   Eric
Philip & Mary Burfoot   Brian   Katie

Brick 159. Hubert Baldwin Barrett 1867 - 1663
Maude Scofield Barrett**   Winifred Barrett
Yerex**   Jacqueline Yerex Clark

Brick 160. William Henry Barrett 1864- 1942
Rebecca Julia Pelley 1876 - 1898
Hattie Mabel James 1883 - 1970

Brick 161. Bill & Edna Pratt

Brick 163. A stitched fish

Brick 162. Jack & Elsie Finch   David
Thomas   Judy   Jonathon 1983 - 1992

Brick 164. Andrew J** & Mima** Lowe
Oliver** & Sarah** Cromwell   Robert** & Mary

Bricks 165 & 167. Are stitched fish

Brick 168. Lyle & Stephanie McKnight
Murray   Amanda   Norah

Brick 166. Bruce & Anna Greenslade
Janet & Gary Hepburn   Geordi   Jonathon

Brick 169. Stephan 1919 - 1927 & Emily Molewyk
Margaret & Stacey Wark   Quintten**   Aiden

Brick 170. Richard Molewyk & Violet Bussey.
Emily   Brianne   Kyle.

Christopher   Justin   Stephan